Goa

written and researched by

David Abram

ROUGH
GUIDES

NEW YORK • LONDON • DELHI

www.roughguides.com

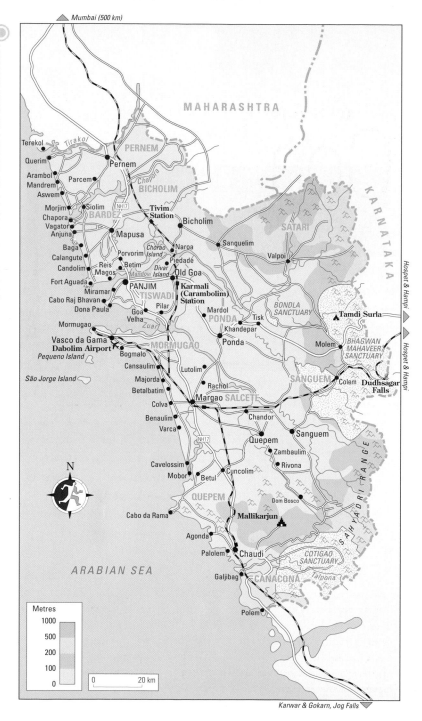

Mumbai (500 km)

MAHARASHTRA

KARNATAKA

PERNEM

Tirakol

Terekol
Querim
Arambol
Mandrem
Parcem
Aswem
Pernem
Chapora
BICHOLIM
Morjim
Siolim
Tivim
Station
Chapora
NH17
Vagator
BARDEZ
Mapusa
Bicholim
Anjuna
Baga
Chorao
Island
Naroa
Sanquelim
SATARI
Porvorim
Piedadé
Calangute
Candolim
Reis
Betim
Divar
Valpoi
Magos
Island
Fort Aguada
Mandovi Island
Old Goa
Miramar
PANJIM
Karmali
(Carambolim)
Station
Cabo Raj Bhavan
TISWADI
Dona Paula
Pilar
Mardol
BONDLA
SANCTUARY
Tamdi Surla
Goa
Velha
Tisk
Mormugao
Zuari
PONDA
Khandepar
BHAGWAN
MAHAVEER
SANCTUARY
Vasco da Gama
MORMUGAO
Ponda
Molem
Dabolim Airport
Bogmalo
Pequeno Island
Cansaulim
Lutolim
Colem
Dudhsagar
Falls
São Jorge Island
Majorda
SANGUEM
Betalbatim
Rachol
Colva
Margao
SALCETE
Benaulim
Chandor
Varca
Quepem
Sanguem
Zambaulim
NH17
Rivona
Cavelossim
Cuncolim
Mobor
Betul
Dom Bosco
QUEPEM
Cabo da Rama
Mallikarjun
SAHYADRI RANGE
Agonda
Palolem
Chaudi
COTIGAO
SANCTUARY
ARABIAN SEA
Galjibag
CANACONA
Talpona

N

Polem

Hospet & Hampi

Metres
1000
500
200
100
0

0   20 km

Karwar & Gokarn, Jog Falls

ii

Introduction to

Goa

If any word could be said to encapsulate the essence of Goa, it would have to be the Portuguese *sossegarde*, meaning "carefree". For Goan expatriates, the term conjures up memories of long, lazy evenings on pillared verandahs, surrounded by tropical vegetation and the heady scent of cashew and frangipani flowers, with the crash of surf drifting through a curtain of coconut palms. The pace of life in this former colonial enclave, midway down India's southwest coast, has picked up over the past twenty years, but in spite of the increasing chaos of its capital, beach resorts and market towns, Goa has retained the laid-back feel that has

traditionally set it apart from the rest of the country. While most of the subcontinent was colonized by the stiff-upper-lipped British, Goa's European overlords were the rather more dissolute Portuguese.

Goa was Portugal's first toehold in Asia and served as the linchpin for a vast trade empire for over 450 years. However, when the Portuguese colonial mission began to flounder in the seventeenth century, so too did the fortunes of its capital. Cut off from the rest of India by a wall of mountains and hundreds of miles of unnavigable alluvial plain, it remained resolutely aloof from the wider subcontinent. Not until 1961, after an exasperated Indian prime minister, Jawaharlal Nehru, gave up trying to negotiate with the Portuguese dictator Salazar and sent in the army, was Goa finally absorbed into India. A

Fact file

- Edged by 105km of coastline, Goa is 65km wide at its broadest point and covers a total surface area of 3700 square kilometres; you can drive from one extremity to the other in three and a half hours. Mumbai, the nearest large city, lies just under 500km north in neighbouring Maharashtra; bordering the state in the south and west is Karnataka.

- In March 2001 (the date of the last census) the population of Goa stood at 1,344,000, of whom 65 percent were Hindu, 29 percent Christian (Roman Catholics) and 5 percent Muslim. Around 10,000 immigrants arrive in the state annually.

- The literacy rate is currently 82.3 percent – relatively high for an Indian state. The net domestic product hovers around Rs25,000 (£335) per head of population.

- Konkani, granted official status only in 1987, is the mother tongue of most Goans, while Portuguese, the language of government until the end of the colonial era in 1961, is understood only by a tiny elite. English is most people's second language, spoken by nearly everyone in the towns and coastal resorts.

decade or so later the **hippy trail** wriggled its way south down the Konkan Coast, ensuring that this hitherto remote enclave of Latin-influenced culture would never be quite the same again.

Since the 1970s, the state has largely shaken off its reputation as a dropout zone, but hundreds of thousands of foreign visitors still flock here each winter, the vast majority of them to relax on Goa's beautiful **beaches**. The Goan coast, however, is only a part of the picture. A short foray **inland** will take you into the state's real heart – a lush patchwork of paddy fields, coconut and areca plantations, and gently meandering rivers. Further east, the jungle-covered hills of the **Western Ghats** separate Goa from the drier Deccan plateau, scattered with tiny thatch-roofed settlements and isolated communities of forest-dwelling farmers.

Outside the Christian heartland, the temples, rituals and exuberant festivals of **Hinduism**, the religion of more than two-thirds of the state's population, mingle easily with more recently implanted traditions. Unlike many parts of India, religious intolerance is a thing of the past here; faced by the threat of merger with

neighbouring states, Goans have always put regional cohesion before communal differences, and some of the state's principal religious festivals – notably Christmas, Carnival and Diwali – are celebrated by adherents of both faiths.

> **Exploring the less touristy areas inland is likely to yield some of the most memorable moments of your trip**

If you've never travelled in Asia before, Goa may come as something of a shock. Its beaches certainly conform to the glossy holiday brochure image, but once outside the tourist spots many first-time visitors are surprised to find themselves in workaday India, where migrant labourers live in shanty encampments on the outskirts of market towns, rice is planted by hand, and the majority of villagers subsist on an average annual wage that is far lower than the cost of a flight from Europe. Don't, however, let this deter you from venturing outside the resorts. Exploring the less touristy areas inland is likely to yield some of the most memorable moments of your trip, combining beautiful scenery with the chance to encounter a way of life that is worlds away from the headlong commercialism of the coastal strip.

Where to go

Which **beach** you opt for when you arrive largely depends on what sort of holiday you have in mind. More developed resorts such as **Candolim**, **Calangute** and **Baga**, in the north, and **Benaulim**, in the south, offer plenty of accommodation, shopping and tourist facilities. Even if you don't fancy crowded beaches and purpose-built hotels, it can be worth heading for these centres at first, as finding places to stay in less commercialized corners is often difficult. **Anjuna**, **Vagator** and **Chapora**, where accommodation is generally more basic and harder to come by, are the beaches to aim for if you've come to Goa for the techno scene. To get a

taste of what most of the state must have been like ten or fifteen years ago, however, you'll have to travel further afield – to **Arambol**, a sleepy fishing village and hippy hang-out in the far north; or to **Agonda** and **Palolem**, near the Karnatakan border in the far south.

Foremost among the attractions away from the coast are the ruins of the Portuguese capital at **Old Goa**, 9km from Panjim – a sprawl of Catholic cathedrals, convents and churches that draws crowds of Christian pilgrims from all over India. Another popular day excursion is to Anjuna's Wednesday **flea market**, a sociable place to shop for souvenirs and the latest rave gear. Further inland, the thickly wooded countryside around **Ponda** harbours numerous temples, where you can experience Goa's peculiar brand of Hindu architecture. The *taluka* (district) of Salcete, and its main market town, **Margao**, is littered with wonderful Portuguese mansions, churches and seminaries. In addition, wildlife enthusiasts may be tempted into the interior to visit the nature reserves at **Molem**, in the far east of Central Goa, and **Cotigao** in the south, which both support fragile populations of rare animals.

With so many tempting beaches, markets, monuments and nature reserves within the state, it's no surprise that few visitors venture across the Goan border into neighbouring Karnataka. But beyond the shelter of the Western Ghats, amid the plateau lands of the Deccan Trap, lie the remnants of several ancient capitals. Among these is one of the most spectacular archeological sites in South India, the ghost city of **Hampi**. Today, weed-choked palaces, temples and discarded statues are virtually all that remains of this once opulent metropolis, capital of the Vijayanagar dynasty, but a visit here will give you a vivid insight into the extravagant art and culture of pre-colonial Hindu India, while the day-long train journey to the site can be an adventure in itself.

For this reason, we've included a detailed account of Hampi in Chapter

Goan coconuts

If you're lucky, the first sound you'll hear on your first morning in Goa will be the rustle of palm fronds. The ubiquity of the **coconut tree** (cocos nucifera) may be an essential part of the state's appeal as a holiday destination, but for the locals, it represents wealth, health and – most of all – hard graft. Goans consume something like 40 million coconuts per year (one per family every day), and the business of harvesting and looking after the trees comprises a way of life for one-sixth of the population.

A vital source of mineral-rich, clean drinking water, coconuts find their way into virtually every Goan dish – from fiery fish curry to sticky sweet bebinca and dodol. The meat – or copra – yields a wonderfully rich oil for cooking, soap and cosmetics, while the sea-water-resistant husk – coir – is spun to make nautical rope (you'll see it stitching wooden planks together on the sides of Goan outriggers). The trunks also provide building timber, and the leaves are plaited to make brooms and panels for shacks and hut roofs. The most characteristically Goan use of the coconut tree, however, is as a source of sap, which is distilled to make feni – a strong local liquor. Between six and eight thousand 'toddy tappers' climb their trees two or three times daily to extract the juice. Most are poor by Goan standards and many suffer from alcohol problems, which explains why falling out of coconut trees is one of the most common violent deaths in Goa.

For visitors, falling nuts are more of a worry. Keep an ear out for the tell-tale whack of a machete that precedes the crash to earth of harvested coconuts, and never fall asleep under a palm tree, no matter how cool it might feel.

4, **Around Goa**, which also features the highlights along the **Konkan coast**, the lush strip running south from Goa in the shadow of the Sahyadri Hills. Chapter 5 covers **Mumbai** (**Bombay**), a hot, congested, upbeat city that is the arrival point for most international flights. Mumbai gets a pretty bad press, and most people pass straight through, but those who stay find themselves witness to the reality of modern-day India, from the deprivations of the city's slum-dwellings to the glitz and glamour of Bollywood movies – a stark contrast with Goa.

When to go

The best **time to go** to Goa is during the dry, relatively cool winter months between mid-November and early April, when daytime temperatures are perfect for lazing on the beach and the sea is blissfully warm. From the end of April onwards the heat and humidity begin to build, culminating in June, when a giant wall of black cloud marches landwards from the Arabian Sea. When the **monsoon** finally breaks, violent storms wrack the coast for days on end, and over the coming months some two and a half metres of rain fall. Not until October do the skies start to clear, and even then you can expect spells of intense humidity, grey skies, haze and occasional rain storms, alternating with bursts of strong sun.

For the past five years or so, the monsoons have spilled into November, shortening the tourist season. This has put the peak period, from mid-December to the end of January, under increased pressure. Finding a room or a house to rent at that time – particularly over the Christmas and New Year fortnight when the tariffs double, or triple – can be a real hassle in some resorts, notably Anjuna, which is inundated with party-goers. So if you're travelling without pre-booked accommodation, it may be worthwhile reserving a room by phone before you leave.

Average daily temperatures and monthly rainfall

	Jan	Feb	Mar	Apr	May	June	July	Aug	Sept	Oct	Nov	Dec
max (°C)	31.9	31.9	32.3	32.7	33.2	29.0	28.7	29.0	29.5	31.0	32.0	32.0
rainfall (mm)	0	0	2	4	65	402	1331	376	211	169	10	2

things not to miss

It's not possible to see everything that Goa has to offer in one trip – and we don't suggest you try. What follows is a selective taste of the region's highlights: idyllic beaches, outstanding monuments, spectacular festivals and great places to stay. They're arranged in five colour-coded categories, which you can browse through to find the very best things to see and experience. All highlights have a page reference to take you straight into the guide, where you can find out more.

01 Goan breakfast Page **42** • Steel yourself for a day on the beach with a traditional worker's breakfast of spicy pea curry and bread rolls.

02

Christmas in Goa Page **49** • The perfect escape from Santa and shopping malls: cribs under the palm trees, candle-lit Mass in Konkani and Christmas dinner at a beach shack.

03

Arambol beach Page **164** • Hangout for Goa's long-stay hippy contingent, complete with holistic therapies and wholefood bakery.

04

Portuguese palacios Page **185** • Goa is littered with elegant colonial-era mansions dating from the seventeenth and eighteenth centuries.

05 **Full-moon parties** Page **154** • Fluorescent-painted palm trees, phosphorescent waves and a tropical full moon form the backdrop to Goa's legendary Christmas–New Year's revelry.

06 **Turtles** Page **160** • Dedicated wardens protect the Olive Ridley marine turtle hatchlings which crawl into the surf on two Goan beaches each winter– a heartwarming sight.

07 **Mapusa market** Page **122** • The liveliest and most authentic street market in the state, held every Friday morning.

08 **Cashew nuts** Page **80** • The cream of Goa's export crop, on sale at select shops.

09

Karmali Ghat Page **205** • In the far south, the Western Ghats creep close to the coast, creating a wonderfully scenic route to Palolem.

10

Traditional fishing boats, Benaulim Page **198** • Handsome wooden outriggers provide a living for locals and welcome shade for tourists

11 Anjuna Flea market Page 148 • Riotously colourful beachside bazaar (Wednesday only) showcasing tourist souvenirs from across India, at negotiable prices.

12 Colonial architecture, Margao Page 178 • Dilapidated eighteenth-century palacios and Baroque churches form the heritage highlight of South Goa's main market town.

13 Panjim Inn Page 73 • A pair of impeccably restored colonial town-houses, filled with period furniture and old Portuguese atmosphere.

14 Usgalimal carvings Page 190 • Hunting scenes and weird geometric shapes gouged into a river bend over 20,000 years ago.

15 Hampi Page **224** • Monkeys scurrying over ruined temples, a sacred river and magnificent boulder landscapes, only an eight-hour train ride inland.

16 Fontainhas Page **76** • Sample the old-time ambience of Panjim's colonial enclave from the verandah of an atmospheric hotel.

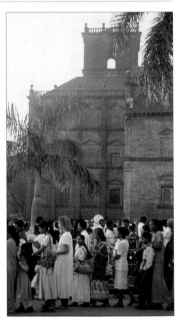

17 Old Goa Page **87** • Grand vestiges of the once-vast Portuguese capital include a campus of giant churches and the glass-sided tomb of St Francis Xavier.

21
Patnem-Rajbag beach
Page **211** • A dodgy undertow ensures this fine beach south of Palolem sees relatively few visitors, but it's ideal for a long amble.

22
Backwater boat rides
Page **133** • Crocodile-spotting trips from the northern resorts take you into the little visited world of Goa's mangroves and backwaters.

23
Terekol Fort
Page **166** • In the remote north, this old fort has been converted into a romantic heritage hotel, with stylish decor and sweeping sea views.

Contents

Using the Rough Guide

We've tried to make this Rough Guide a good read and easy to use. The book is divided into six main sections, and you should be able to find whatever you want in one of them.

Colour section

The front colour section offers a quick tour of Goa. The **introduction** aims to give you a feel for the region, with suggestions on where to go. We also tell you what the weather is like and include a basic fact file. Next, our author rounds up his favourite aspects of Goa in the **things not to miss** section – whether it's amazing beaches, great food or a special place to stay. Right after this comes a full **contents** list.

Basics

The Basics section covers all the **pre-departure** nitty-gritty to help you plan your trip. This is where to find out which airlines fly to your destination, what paperwork you'll need, what to do about money and insurance, about Internet access, food, public transport, car rental – in fact just about every piece of **general practical information** you might need.

Guide

This is the heart of the Rough Guide, divided into user-friendly chapters, each of which covers a specific area. Every chapter starts with a list of **highlights** and an **introduction** that helps you to decide where to go, depending on your time and budget. Likewise, introductions to the various towns, resorts and regions within each chapter should help you plan your itinerary. We start most town accounts

with information on arrival and accommodation, followed by a tour of the sights, and finally reviews of places to eat and drink, and details of nightlife. Longer accounts also have a directory of practical listings. Each chapter concludes with **public transport details** for that region.

Contexts

Read Contexts to get a deeper understanding of what makes Goa tick. We include a brief **history** of the region, articles about **religion**, **environmental issues**, **natural history** and **Goan music and dance**, and a detailed further reading section that reviews dozens of **books**.

Language

The **language** section gives useful guidance for speaking Konkani, the mother tongue of most Goans, and pulls together all the vocabulary you might need on your trip, including a comprehensive **menu reader**. Here you'll also find a **glossary** of terms.

Index + small print

Apart from a **full index**, which includes maps as well as places, this section covers publishing information, credits and acknowledgements, and also has our contact details in case you want to send in updates and corrections to the book – or suggestions as to how we might improve it.

Map and chapter list

- Colour section
- Contents
- **B** Basics
- **1** Panjim and Central Goa

- **2** North Goa
- **3** South Goa
- **4** Around Goa
- **5** Mumbai

- **G** Contexts
- **L** Language
- **I** Index

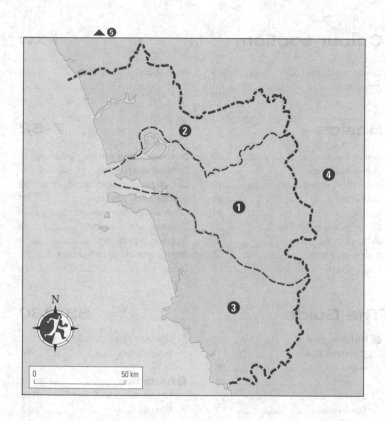

Contents

Colour section i–xvi

Basics 7–62

The Guide 63–280

Contexts 282–335

Language 337–345

Index and small print   347–354

Map symbols

maps are listed in the full index using coloured text

▭50▭	Highway	🏊	Waterfall
═══	Main road	🌴	Palm grove
▬▬▬	Railway	🚩	Lighthouse
- - - -	Footpath	⌃⌃	Mountain range
▥▥▥	Steps	▲	Mountain peak
▄▄▄	Wall	⫽	Mountain pass
───	Waterway	∴	Ruins
— —	Ferry route	⊙	Statue
– – –	Chapter division boundary	🏛	Stately home
▬▪▬▪	State border	⛽	Petrol station
▬▬ ▪▪	District boundary	@	Internet access
✈	Airport	⊞	Hospital
★	Taxi, rickshaw, bus	⬭	Stadium
ⓘ	Information office	▬	Building
✉	Post office	▬	Church
🛕	Hindu temple	⊞	Christian cemetery
🕌	Mosque	▦	National park
▣	Restaurant/bar	▦	Park
⚘	Viewpoint	⠿	Beach
⚘	Swamp	⁊	Rocks
🚢	Ferry Symbol	⊓	Muslim cemetery
♦	Point of Interest	◉	Crater

Basics

Basics

Getting there

There are no direct scheduled services to Goa from anywhere outside India, but you can fly direct by charter from the UK. Otherwise, the best alternative is to catch a flight to Mumbai with a scheduled airline and pick up an onward service from there, either by plane or rail (the 500-kilometre bus journey is for die-hards only). Travelling to Mumbai from North America involves at least one or two changes of plane. From New Zealand or Australia, the quickest route is via Southeast Asia.

Airfares worldwide always depend on the **season**, with the highest being roughly November to March, when the weather in India is best; fares drop during the shoulder seasons – April to May and August to early October – and you'll get the cheapest prices during the low season, June and July, when Goa's beaches are wracked by monsoon gales and the weather is relentlessly wet and stormy. The most expensive fares of all are those coinciding with Diwali in November and over Christmas and New Year.

Considerable savings can be made by going through a **specialist flight agent** – either a consolidator, who buys up blocks of tickets from the airlines and sells them at a discount, or a **discount agent**, who in addition to dealing with discounted flights may also offer special student and youth fares and a range of other travel-related services such as travel insurance or tours. Some agents specialize in **charter flights**, which may be cheaper than anything available on a scheduled service. You may even find it cheaper to pick up a bargain **package deal** from one of the tour operators listed on p.12, p.15 or p.16, and then find your own accommodation when you get there.

If India is only one stop on a longer journey, you might want to consider buying a **Round-the-World** (RTW) ticket. Some travel agents can sell you an "off-the-shelf" RTW ticket that will have you touching down in about half a dozen cities (Mumbai is on many itineraries); others will have to assemble one for you, which can be tailored to your needs but is apt to be more expensive. Figure on £950/$1400–£1500/$2360 for a RTW ticket including India, open for one year.

Booking flights online

Many airlines and discount travel websites offer you the opportunity to book your tickets **online**, cutting out the costs of agents and middlemen. Good deals can often be found through discount or auction sites, as well as through the airlines' own websites.

When hunting online for a **charter flight** ticket, the trick is to search for "holidays" rather than "flights". Indian aviation law prevents package companies who wish to sell off unused seats from advertising them as "flight onlys", which means the cheapest deals nearly always masquerade as packages, bundled with "dummy" or "bunkhouse" accommodation.

Online booking agents and general travel sites

ⓦ**travel.yahoo.com** Incorporates a lot of Rough Guide material in its coverage of destination countries and cities across the world, with information about places to eat, sleep, etc.

ⓦ **www.bargainholidays.com** Cheap flights from the UK only, and a good first stop for flight-only deals to Goa.

ⓦ **www.cheapflights.com** Bookings from the UK and Ireland only; for the US, visit ⓦ www.cheapflight .com; for Canada, ⓦ www.cheapflights.ca; for Australia, ⓦ www.cheapflights.com.au. All the sites offer flight deals, details of travel agents, and links to other travel sites.

ⓦ **www.cheaptickets.com** Discount flight specialists (US only).

ⓦ **www.etn.nl/discount.htm** A hub of consolidator and discount agent Web links, maintained by the nonprofit European Travel Network.

ⓦ **www.expedia.com** Discount airfares, all-airline search engine and daily deals (US only; for the UK

@www.expedia.co.uk; for Canada @www.expedia.ca).

@**www.flyaow.com** Air travel info and ticket reservations.

@**www.geocities.com/thavery2000** Has an extensive list of airline toll-free numbers (from the US) and websites.

@**www.hotwire.com** Bookings from the US only. Last-minute savings of up to forty percent on regular published fares. Travellers must be at least 18 and there are no refunds, transfers or changes allowed. Log-in required.

@**www.lastminute.com** Offers good last-minute holiday package and flight-only deals (UK only; for Australia @www.lastminute.com.au).

@**www.priceline.com** Name-your-own-price website that has deals at around forty percent off standard fares. You cannot specify flight times (although you do specify dates) and the tickets are non-refundable, non-transferable and non-changeable (US only; for the UK, @www.priceline.co.uk).

@**www.skyauction.com** Bookings from the US only. Auctions tickets and travel packages using a "second bid" scheme. The best strategy is to bid the maximum you're willing to pay, since if you win you'll pay just enough to beat the runner-up regardless of your maximum bid.

@**www.smilinjack.com/airlines.htm** Lists an up-to-date compilation of airline website addresses.

@**www.travelocity.com** Destination guides, hot Web fares and best deals for car rental, accommodation and lodging as well as fares. Provides access to the travel agent system SABRE, the most comprehensive central reservations system in the US.

@**www.travelshop.com.au** Australian website offering discounted flights, packages and insurance.

Package holidays

The advent of direct charter flights and the comparatively low cost of food and accommodation in Goa have made it among the most affordable winter **package holiday** destinations in the world – for sun-starved northern Europeans, if not North Americans and Australasians. Depending on the kind of hotel you choose, a fortnight's break will set you back anywhere between £425 and £2500. Prices also vary according to the time of year, soaring from mid-December to mid-January, and bottoming out from late March to mid-April when the charters stop. However, even during the peak Christmas–New Year period, last-minute bargains regularly appear in travel agents'

windows and on websites, as tour operators scramble to sell off unbooked holidays.

In addition to standard accommodation and half-board deals, most companies offer optional extras, ranging from **excursions** around the state to longer trips elsewhere in India, including Mumbai, Kerala, Agra (to see the Taj Mahal) and Rajasthan. Several UK-based operators – and nearly all those including Goa on **tours from North America, Australia and New Zealand** – offer Goa as part of a more extensive tour of South India, while others use the state as a venue for **special interest holidays**. Among the more popular of these are bird-watching, windsurfing and scuba diving; a couple of companies will even organize your wedding, complete with bullock-cart carriage and a locally tailored dress.

Holidays may be booked directly from the tour companies or through travel agents. As few retailers deal with all the different operators, it's a good idea to phone around for a range of quotes, check out what's available online and look through the travel pages of daily newspapers and weekend supplements. Another good tip is to avoid half-board or all-inclusive holidays: in Goa it's much cheaper, and more enjoyable, to eat out than stay in your hotel.

Flights from the UK and Ireland

BA and Air India fly direct **scheduled services** every day from London Heathrow to Mumbai, with Singapore Airlines covering the route twice weekly. A range of other airlines, including Alitalia, Gulf, Emirates and KLM, fly with brief stopovers in their hub cities (KLM flies from regional airports to Mumbai via Amsterdam for no additional cost). Flying time is around ten and a half hours, and return fares are quoted at around £600/700 in low/high season, although you can usually find cheaper deals as low as £400, or less.

For the onward leg **from Mumbai to Goa**, most people book their internal ticket at the same time as they buy their international one. In the UK and Ireland, you can obtain tickets for three of the four domestic carriers which fly the route (Indian Airlines, Air India and Jet Airways, but not Sahara). The fare – quoted at a higher dollar rate for non-Indian nationals – should cost exactly the same as it would if you bought it in India, although it's always worth checking (the airlines' published fares are listed on their Web sites) as some unscrupulous agents will try to slap on mark-ups. For further details of onward travel from Mumbai see p.82.

At present, two **charter** airlines operate flights to Goa from the UK. Some stop in the Gulf for an hour en route to refuel; others go non-stop. **From Gatwick**, you can fly out Thursdays or Saturdays with Britannia or Monarch, who also offer departures from **Manchester** (Thursdays and Saturdays). In addition, Monarch flies out of **Birmingham** on Saturdays. The flight time from Gatwick, including refuelling, is around eleven and a half hours; add on around 45 minutes for departures from Manchester. Note too that schedules can vary according to demand.

CAA regulations prohibit the sale of **flight-only tickets** to Goa from outside India, but there's nothing to stop you from purchasing an all-in package holiday and ditching the accommodation part of the deal once you've arrived. This can still work out much cheaper than a scheduled flight via Mumbai, especially if you manage to pick up a last-minute bargain.

Note that the Indian government does not as a rule allow **Indian nationals** (ie holders of Indian passports) to travel on charter flights to Goa.

One-way tickets are also occasionally available for marginally less than the cost of the round trip, and you can usually buy the return leg from Goa at the travel agents Davidair in Candolim (see p.134), for £150–300, depending on the season. Note that **single flights from Goa to the UK** are in great demand towards the beginning of April, when most of the long-stayers return home, and that you should book well in advance if you plan to travel at that time.

There are no direct flights to either Goa or Mumbai **from Ireland**. However, BA flies direct to Mumbai from London, and several carriers, including Alitalia, Lufthansa and Royal Jordanian, fly there from Dublin, Cork or Shannon via their home capitals. Discounted fares hover around €635. The best way to find the cheapest deals is through an agent. Alternatively, book from London, or through the Web sites listed below.

Airlines in the UK

Aeroflot ☎ 020/7355 2233, ⊛ www.aeroflot.co.uk.
Air France ☎ 0845/359 1000; ⊛ www.airfrance.co.uk.
Air India ☎ 020/8560 9996 or 8745 1000, ⊛ www.airindia.com.
Alitalia ☎ 0870/544 8259, ⊛ www.alitalia.co.uk. Mid-price option to Mumbai routed through Milan. Note that stopover durations can vary considerably.
Biman Bangladesh Airlines ☎ 020/7629 0252.
British Airways ☎ 0870/850 9850, ⊛ www.ba.com.
Egyptair ☎ 020/7734 2343 or 7734 2395, ⊛ www.egyptair.com.eg.
Emirates Airlines ☎ 0870/243 2222, ⊛ www.emirates.com.
Gulf Air ☎ 0870/777 1717, ⊛ www.gulfairco.com.
KLM Royal Dutch Airlines ☎ 08705/074 074, ⊛ www.klm.com.
Lufthansa ☎ 0845/7737 747, ⊛ www.lufthansa.co.uk.
Pakistan International Airlines ☎ 020/7499 5500, ⊛ www.fly-pia.com.
Royal Jordanian ☎ 020/7878 6300, ⊛ www.rja.com.jo.
SriLankan Airlines ☎ 020/8538 2000, ⊛ www.srilankan.lk. A good and reasonably priced airline offering flights to South India. Change at Colombo for services to Chennai, Tiruchirapalli and Thiruvananthapuram (Trivandrum).
Thai Airways International ☎ 0870/606 0911, ⊛ www.thaiair.com.

Airlines in Ireland

Air France ☎ 01/605 0383, ⊛ www.airfrance.com/ie.
Alitalia ☎ 01/677 5171, ⊛ www.alitalia.co.uk.
British Airways ☎ 1800/626 747, ⊛ www.ba.com.
Lufthansa ☎ 01/844 5544, ⊛ www.lufthansa.co.uk.
Royal Jordanian ☎ 061/712 8741, ⊛ www.rja.com.jo.

Domestic airlines in India

Air India ⊛ www.airindia.com.
Indian Airlines ⊛ www.indian-airlines.net.in.
Jet Airways ⊛ www.jetairways.com.

BASICS | Getting there

Flight and travel agents in the UK

Arrowguide Ltd ☎020/7629 9516, 🖳www
.arrowguide.co.uk. Long-established, polite and
throughly reliable consolidator that specializes in
cheap flights to India.
Bridge the World ☎0870/444 7474, 🖳www
.bridgetheworld.com. Specializing in Round-the-
World tickets, with good deals aimed at the
backpacker market.
Co-op Travel Care ☎0870/112 0099, 🖳www
.travelcareonline.com. Flights and holidays around
the world.
Destination Group ☎020/7400 7045, 🖳www
.destination-group.com. Good discount airfares.
Flightbookers ☎0870/010 7000, 🖳www
.ebookers.com. Low fares on an extensive selection
of scheduled flights.
North South Travel ☎ & ☎01245/608 291,
🖳www.northsouthtravel.co.uk. Friendly, competitive
travel agency, offering discounted fares worldwide –
profits are used to support projects in the developing
world, especially the promotion of sustainable tourism.
Premier Travel Northern Ireland ☎028/7126
3333, 🖳www.premiertravel.uk.com. Discount flight
specialists.
Quest Travel ☎0870/442 3542, 🖳www
.questtravel.com. Specialists in Round-the-World
and Australasian discount fares.
Rosetta Travel Northern Ireland ☎028/9064 4996,
🖳www.rosettatravel.com. Flight and holiday agent.
STA Travel ☎0870/1600 599, 🖳www.statravel
.co.uk. Worldwide specialists in low-cost flights and
tours for students and under-26s, though other
customers welcome.
Top Deck ☎020/7244 8000, 🖳www
.topdecktravel.co.uk. Long-established agent
dealing in discount flights.
Trailfinders ☎020/7628 7628, 🖳www
.trailfinders.co.uk. One of the best-informed and
most efficient agents for independent travellers; they
produce a very useful quarterly magazine worth
scrutinizing for round-the-world routes.
Travel Cuts ☎020/7255 2082 or 7255 1944,
🖳www.travelcuts.co.uk. Canadian company
specializing in budget, student and youth travel and
Round-the-World tickets.
usit NOW Northern Ireland t028/9032 7111,
🖳www.usitnow.ie. Student and youth specialists for
flights and trains.

Flight and travel agents in Ireland

Apex Travel ☎01/241 8000, 🖳www
.apextravel.ie. Specialists in flights to Australia,
Africa, Far East, USA, Canada.

Aran Travel International ☎091/562 595,
whomepages.iol.ie/~arantvl/aranmain.htm. Good-
value flights to all parts of the world.
Joe Walsh Tours ☎01/676 0991, 🖳www
.joewalshtours.ie. General budget fares agent.
Lee Travel ☎021/277 111, 🖳www.leetravel.ie.
Flights and holidays worldwide.
McCarthy's Travel ☎021/427 0127, 🖳www
.mccarthystravel.ie. General flight agent.
Trailfinders ☎01/677 7888, 🖳www
.trailfinders.ie. One of the best-informed and most
efficient agents for independent travellers; they
produce a very useful quarterly magazine worth
scrutinizing for round-the-world routes.
usit NOW ☎01/602 1600, 🖳www.usitnow.ie.
Student and youth specialists for flights and trains.

Specialist tour operators and package holiday companies

Abercrombie and Kent ☎0845/070 0615,
🖳www.abercrombiekent.co.uk. Upmarket
sightseeing tours for small groups or individuals in
chauffeur-driven air-conditioned cars.
Cosmos ☎0161/476 5678, 🖳www
.cosmos-holidays.co.uk. Beach breaks in two- to
five-star resort hotels, with optional extensions to the
Delhi-Agra-Jaipur "Golden Triangle".
Cox and Kings ☎020/7873 5000,
🖳www.coxandkings.co.uk. Resolutely upmarket
tailor-made tours to India, offering seven- and
fourteen-night stays in the *Fort Aguada Beach Resort*.
First Choice ☎0870/750 0465, 🖳www.firstchoice
.co.uk. Standard resort packages, at a range of prices.
SD Enterprises ☎020/8903 3411, 🖳www.inrail
.co.uk. Competitively priced charter fares, with
disposable "bunk-house" budget accommodation or
stays in star-rated hotels. This outfit is also the UK's
leading domestic transport specialist, and can help
devise itineraries around other regions of the country
from Goa.
Highlife Holidays ☎020/8452 3388, 🖳www
.highlifeholidays.co.uk. Top-end beach holidays in
luxury hotels.
Imaginative Traveller ☎0800/316 1404,
🖳www.imaginative-traveller.com. Three days in
Goa tacked onto the end of a 22-day trip around the
highlights of Kerala and Karnataka.
Jewel in the Crown Holidays ☎01293/533
338, 🖳www.jewelholidays.com. Self-catering and
hotel holidays at choice locations across the state,
with optional extensions to Delhi and Agra. They also
do escorted tours, "Blazing Trails", on Enfield
motorbikes.
JMC ☎0870/758 0203, 🖳www.holidays.jmc.com.
Owned by Thomas Cook and affiliated to the airline

of the same name, this is one of the UK's largest operators, offering an exhaustive range of package holidays to Goa at competitive prices.

Kuoni ☎ 01306/742 000, 🖰 www.kuoni.co.uk. Standard resort-based packages, or longer tours of India.

Lazy Days in Goa ☎ 01643/862 159, 🖰 www .lazydays.co.uk. Quality accommodation in north and south Goa, ranging from one-bed apartments to country houses on private estates.

Pettits India ☎ 01892/515 966, 🖰 www .pettits.co.uk. Five-star holidays in the *Fort Aguada Beach Resort* and other luxury resorts.

Somak Holidays ☎ 020/8423 3000, 🖰 www .somak.co.uk. Top-end packages in select hotels such as the *Taj Exotica* and *Goa Marriott*, plus optional excursions to Mumbai and Kerala.

Thomson Worldwide ☎ 020/7387 9321, 🖰 www.thomson-holidays.com. Fourteen-night deals, mostly in swish resorts.

Western & Oriental Travel ☎ 020/7313 6611, 🖰 www.westernoriental.com. Bespoke tours, incorporating North Goa's most exclusive hotels.

Flights from the US and Canada

Goa is on the other side of the planet from the **US** and **Canada**. If you live on the East Coast it's somewhat shorter to travel via Europe, while from the West Coast it's quicker via the Pacific, but either way it's a long haul, involving one or more intermediate stops, and you'll arrive fresher and less jet-lagged if you can manage to fit in a few days' layover somewhere en route.

From the East Coast, you'll stop over somewhere in Europe (most often London), the Gulf, or both. Figure on at least eighteen hours' total travel time. Air India and PIA discount their tickets heavily through a few specialist, understaffed New York consolidators. Marked-down tickets on European carriers – notably British Airways, Air France, KLM/Northwest and Lufthansa – are frequently sold by other discount agents. Other airlines flying between the eastern US and India include Aeroflot, Gulf Air and Egypt Air. Alternatively, you can simply hop on any of the dozens of airlines that fly to London (see p.13–14) and pick up a flight to India from there.

Prices are most competitive **out of New York**, where the cheapest low-season consolidated fares to Mumbai hover around

$1400 in low season and rise to $1750 in high season. From Washington or Miami, figure on $1600 in low season and $1850 in high season; from Chicago $1600 to $2000; and from Dallas/Fort Worth $1800 to $3000.

From the West Coast, it takes about as long to fly east or west – a minimum of 22 hours' total travel time – and if you're booking through a consolidator there may not be much difference in price. Thai Airways, Cathay Pacific, Northwest, Malaysia Airlines and Singapore Airlines are the main carriers flying over the Pacific to India, via their respective hubs. Air India doesn't do the trans-Pacific route, but can book passengers on Northwest to any of several Asian capitals and then fly them the rest of the way.

From Los Angeles or San Francisco, you're looking at a minimum of $1250 to fly to Mumbai in low season, and up to $1750 in high season.

The only direct flight **from Canada** to India is Vancouver–Delhi on Air Canada (via London, and taking around 20 hours). All other routings involve a plane change and more layover time. Air Canada flies during shoulder and high season from all major Canadian cities to London, where passengers can join the Vancouver–Delhi flight; the rest of the year they fly through Zurich. Other airlines offering services to India, via their capitals, include British Airways, Air France, Lufthansa, KLM and Aeroflot. This list doesn't convey the full range of possibilities, however. A discount agent will probably break the journey into two, using one of dozens of carriers for the transatlantic (or trans-Pacific) leg. Typical discounted low and high season fares to Delhi or Mumbai from Montréal, Toronto and Vancouver are CDN$2000/ $2600.

For **domestic connections** booked in North America, add roughly US$100/ CDN$140 for Mumbai–Goa.

Airlines in North America

Aeroflot US ☎ 1-888/340-6400, Canada ☎ 416/642-1653, 🖰 www.aeroflot.com.
Air Canada US/Canada ☎ 1-888/247-2262, 🖰 www.aircanada.ca.
Air France US ☎ 1-800/237-2747, 🖰 www.airfrance.com; Canada ☎ 1-800/667-2747, 🖰 www.airfrance.ca.

Air India ☎1-800/223-2250 or 212/751-6200, ⊛www.airindia.com.
Alitalia US ☎1-800/223-5730, Canada ☎1-800/361-8336, ⊛www.alitalia.com.
All Nippon Airways US ☎1-800/235-9262, ⊛svc.ana.co.jp/eng/index.html.
Asiana Airlines ☎1-800/227-4262, ⊛www.flyasiana.com.
Biman Bangladesh Airlines ☎1-888/702-4626 or 212/808-4477, ⊛www.bimanair.com.
British Airways ☎1-800/247-9297, ⊛www.british-airways.com.
Cathay Pacific ☎1-800/233-2742, ⊛www.cathay-usa.com.
Czech Airlines US ☎1-877/359-6629 or 212/765-6022, Canada ☎416/363-3174, ⊛www.czechairlines.com.
Delta Air Lines domestic ☎1-800/221-1212, international ☎1-800/241-4141, ⊛www.delta.com.
EgyptAir US ☎1-800/334-6787 or 212/315-0900, Canada ☎416/960-0009, ⊛www.egyptair.com.eg.
Emirates Air ☎1-800/777-3999, ⊛www.emirates.com.
Gulf Air ☎1-800/FLY-GULF, ⊛www.gulfairco.com.
Kuwait Airways ☎212/659-4200, ⊛www.kuwait-airways.com.
Lufthansa US ☎1-800/645-3880, Canada ☎1-800/563-5954, ⊛www.lufthansa-usa.com.
Malaysia Airlines ☎1-800/552-9264, ⊛www.mas.com.my.
Northwest/KLM domestic ☎1-800/225-2525, international ☎1-800/447-4747, ⊛www.nwa.com, ⊛www.klm.com.
Pakistan International Airlines ☎1-800/221-2552 or 212/760-8484, ⊛www.piac.com.pk.
Polynesian Airlines ☎1-800/264-0823, ⊛www.polynesianairlines.com.
Qantas Airways ☎1-800/227-4500, ⊛www.qantas.com.
Royal Jordanian Airlines ☎1-800/223-0470 or 212/949-0050, ⊛www.rja.com.jo.
Royal Nepal Airlines ☎1-800/266-3725, ⊛www.royalnepal.com.
Singapore Airlines ☎1-800/742-3333, ⊛www.singaporeair.com.
SriLankan Airlines ☎1-877/915-2652, ⊛www.srilankan.lk.
Swiss ☎1-877/359-7947, ⊛www.swiss.com.
Tarom Romanian Air ☎212/560-0840, ⊛tarom.digiro.net/index_en.html.
Thai Airways International US ☎1-800/426-5204, Canada ☎1-800/668-8103, ⊛www.thaiairways.com.
TWA domestic ☎1-800/221-2000, international ☎1-800/892-4141, ⊛www.twa.com.

United Airlines domestic ☎1-800/241-6522, international ☎1-800/538-2929, ⊛www.ual.com.
Virgin Atlantic Airways ☎1-800/862-8621, ⊛www.virgin-atlantic.com.

Travel agents, consolidators and travel clubs in the US and Canada

Air Brokers International ☎1-800/883-3273, ⊛www.airbrokers.com. Consolidator and specialist in Round-the-World and Circle Pacific tickets.
Airtech ☎212/219-7000, ⊛www.airtech.com. Standby seat broker; also deals in consolidator fares and courier flights.
Airtreks.com ☎1-877-AIRTREKS or 415/912-5600, ⊛www.airtreks.com. Round-the-World and Circle Pacific tickets. The website features an interactive database that lets you build and price your own round-the-world itinerary.
Council Travel ☎1-800/2COUNCIL, ⊛www.counciltravel.com. Nationwide organization that mostly specializes in student/budget travel. Flights from the US only.
Educational Travel Center ☎1-800/747-5551 or 608/256-5551, ⊛www.edtrav.com. Student/youth discount agent.
SkyLink US ☎1-800/AIR-ONLY or 212/573-8980, Canada ☎1-800/SKY-LINK, ⊛www.skylinkus.com. Consolidator.
STA Travel US ☎1-800/781-4040, Canada 1-888/427-5639, ⊛www.sta-travel.com. Worldwide specialists in independent travel; also student IDs, travel insurance, car rental, rail passes etc.
Student Flights ☎1-800/255-8000 or 480/951-1177, ⊛www.isecard.com. Student/youth fares, student IDs.
TFI Tours ☎1-800/745-8000 or 212/736-1140, ⊛www.lowestairprice.com. Consolidator.
Travac ☎1-800/TRAV-800, ⊛www.thetravelsite.com. Consolidator and charter broker with offices in New York City and Orlando.
Travel Avenue ☎1-800/333-3335, ⊛www.travelavenue.com. Full-service travel agent that offers discounts in the form of rebates.
Travel Cuts Canada ☎1-800/667-2887, US ☎1-866/246-9762, ⊛www.travelcuts.com. Canadian student-travel organization.
Travelers Advantage ☎1-877/259-2691, ⊛www.travelersadvantage.com. Discount travel club; annual membership fee required (currently $1 for 3 months' trial).
Worldtek Travel ☎1-800/243-1723, ⊛www.worldtek.com. Discount travel agency for worldwide travel.

Specialist tour operators

Absolute Asia ☎212/627-1950,
ⓦwww.absoluteasia.com. Two of their deluxe,
custom-designed itineraries wind up in Goa, after
extensive regional highlights.
Adventure Center ☎1-800/227-8747,
ⓦwww.adventurecenter.com. Offers "Goa and the
Deep South", a 23-day camping trip including Goa,
Mumbai and Chennai. Their "Treasures of Central
India" is a fifteen-day hotel-accommodated tour that
also includes Goa in its itinerary.
Cox & Kings ☎1-800/999-1758, ⓦwww
.coxandkings.com. One of the world's longest
established upmarket operators. They don't offer Goa
as a standard brochure option, but will tailor-make
tours.
Greaves India ☎1-800/318-7801, ⓦwww
.greavesindia.com. Three-day tailor-made
extensions to Goa can be tacked on to any of their
top-end tours.
Himalayan Travel ☎1-800/225-2380, ⓦwww
.himalayantravelinc.com. Offers a nineteen-day
escorted "Images of the Deep South" tour, which
includes six days in Goa. They also arrange
independent tours to Goa.
Myths and Mountains ☎775/832-5454,
ⓦwww.mythsandmountains.com. Imaginatively
put-together tours across the subcontinent. The
South India option includes Goa, with an emphasis
on cuisine and architecture.
Worldwide Quest Adventures ☎1-800/387-
1483, ⓦwww.worldwidequest.com. Specialists in
trekking and cycling holidays to Asia. Although it
doesn't figure in their fixed tours, they will customize
a package to Goa.

Flights from Australia and New Zealand

There are no nonstop flights to India from
either **Australia** or **New Zealand**; you have
to make at least one change of plane in a
Southeast Asian hub city (usually Kuala
Lumpur, Singapore or Bangkok). The choice
of routes and airlines is bewildering, and
most agents will offer you a combination of
two or more carriers to get the best price.

The best-value tickets from Australia are
on departures from the west coast. Flying
from Perth to Mumbai in **low/shoulder season** (Feb 1–Nov 21) costs A$1100–1400
with Singapore Airlines, SriLankan Airlines,
Malaysia, Ansett or Air India, and from
around A$1700 during **high season** (Nov

22–Jan 31). Qantas/British Airways also
offers a competitive low-season fare from
the west coast to Mumbai of around
A$1300, and there are daily departures con-
necting with these flights from most
Australian cities, with less frequent departures from Cairns and Darwin (2–3 times a
week). Coming from the east coast –
Sydney, Melbourne or Brisbane – typically
costs A$50–100 more.

Flying **from New Zealand**, the cheapest
fares to India are generally with Singapore
Airlines, Thai Airways, Air New Zealand and
Air India (or more probably a combination of
all four). Tickets range from just under
NZ$2000 to around NZ$2250 if you leave
from Auckland; add on approximately
NZ$150 for flights from Wellington or
Christchurch.

Round-the-World fares from Australia
and New Zealand using the above airlines
can take in India; for example, Thai Airways,
Air New Zealand, Qantas and Malaysia
Airlines can route you through Mumbai as
part of a RTW deal from around A$2200/
NZ$2600.

Airlines in Australia and New Zealand

Air France Australia ☎02/9244 2100, New
Zealand ☎09/308 3352, ⓦwww.airfrance.com.
Air India Australia ☎02/9299 2022, New Zealand
☎09/303 1301, ⓦwww.airindia.com.
Air New Zealand Australia ☎13 24 76, New
Zealand ☎0800 737 000,
ⓦwww.airnewzealand.com.
Ansett Australia Australia ☎13 14 14 or
02/9352 6707, New Zealand ☎09/336 2364,
ⓦwww.ansett.com.au.
Ansett New Zealand Australia ☎1800 022 146,
New Zealand ☎09/526 8300, ⓦwww.ansett.com
.au.
British Airways Australia ☎02/8904 8800, New
Zealand ☎09/356 8690, ⓦwww.british-airways
.com.
Cathay Pacific Australia ☎13 17 47, New Zealand
☎09/379 0861, ⓦwww.cathaypacific.com.
KLM Australia ☎1300 303 747, New Zealand
☎09/302 1452, ⓦwww.klm.com.
Lufthansa Australia ☎1300 655 727, New
Zealand ☎09/303 1529 or 008/945 220, ⓦwww
.lufthansa.com.
Malaysia Airlines Australia ☎13 26 27, New
Zealand ☎09/373 2741 or 008/657 472,
ⓦwww.malaysiaairlines.com.

Qantas Australia ☎13 13 13, New Zealand ☎09/357 8900 or 0800 808 767, ⓦwww .qantas.com.
Royal Jordanian Airlines Australia ☎02/9244 2701, New Zealand ☎03/365 3910, ⓦwww .rja.com.jo.
Singapore Airlines Australia ☎13 10 11 or 02/9350 0262, New Zealand ☎09/379 3209 or 0800 808 909, ⓦwww.singaporean.com.
SriLankan Airlines Australia ☎02/9244 2234, New Zealand ☎09/308 3353, ⓦwww.srilankan.lk.
Swiss Australia ☎1300 724 666, ⓦwww .swiss.com.
Thai Airways Australia ☎1300 651 960, New Zealand ☎09/377 3886, ⓦwww.thaiair.com.

Travel agents in Australia and New Zealand

Flight Centre Australia ☎13 31 33 or 02/9235 3522, ⓦwww.flightcentre.com.au; New Zealand ☎0800 243 544 or 09/358 4310, ⓦwww.flightcentre.co.nz.
Holiday Shoppe New Zealand ☎0800 808 480, ⓦwww.holidayshoppe.co.nz.
Northern Gateway Australia ☎1800 174 800, ⓦwww.norgate.com.au.
STA Travel Australia ☎1300 733 035, ⓦwww.statravel.com.au; New Zealand ☎0508/782 872, ⓦwww.statravel.co.nz.

Student Uni Travel Australia ☎02/9232 8444, ⓦwww.sut.com.au; New Zealand ☎09/379 4224, ⓦwww.sut.co.nz.
Trailfinders Australia ☎02/9247 7666, ⓦwww.trailfinders.com.au.

Specialist tour operators

Abercrombie and Kent Australia ☎03/9536 1800 or 1300 851 800, New Zealand ☎0800 441 638, ⓦwww.abercrombiekent.com.au. Specialist in individual mid- to upmarket holidays.
Adventure World Australia ☎1800 221 931 or 02/9956 7766, New Zealand ☎09/524 5118. Bespoke air and accommodation packages and regional tours. NZ agents for Peregrine.
Classic Oriental Tours Australia ☎02/9266 3988, ⓦwww.classicoriental.com.au. Goa features on their 18-day "North to South" tour, but they also put together tailor-made packages for individuals and small groups.
San Michele Travel Australia ☎1800 222 244 or 02/9299 1111, ⓦwww.asiatravel.com.au. Budget and upmarket air and accommodation packages and tailor-made excursions for groups or individual travellers.
Travel.com.au Australia ☎1800 000 447, ⓦwww.travel.com.au. Agent for a broad range of tour operators. You can select set itineraries or tailor-make your own packages on their website.

Visas and red tape

Gone are the days when foreign nationals could arrive visa-less in India and stay as long as they pleased: nowadays everybody (except Nepalis and Bhutanis) needs a visa, including children.

Multiple-entry **tourist visas** are valid for **six months** from the date of issue (not of departure from your home country or entry into India), and cost £30/US$60/Can$62/A$55/NZ$55.

The best place to apply for one is in your country of residence, from the **embassies and high commissions** listed below. In the **UK, application forms** may be obtained in advance by post, downloaded from the Internet (ⓦwww.hcilondon.org), or picked up on the day. You'll need an original passport

valid for a minimum of six months and two passport-type photographs, in addition to the fee. In London, the Indian High Commission issues queue numbers Mon–Fri 8.30am–noon; a wait of around 45 minutes to one hour is par for the course. Before you leave the building, carefully check all the details listed on your visa (particularly the dates), and make sure the document has been signed, as mistakes can cause serious inconvenience if discovered in India. US passport holders should note that an addi-

Lost passports

Losing your passport in India can be a stressful experience, not least because without it you are technically not allowed to change money, or leave the country. Thankfully, for UK nationals at least, help is at hand in the Goan capital, Panjim, where the **British Consulate of Mumbai** have a **Tourist Assistance Office**. As well as offering advice and help in the event of a serious accident or death, its chief, Ms Shilpa Caldeira, can issue temporary passports to replace lost ones. This can be done in two working days provided you know your passport and visa numbers; if you don't, expect a longer wait of up to a week or more. The office – over near the Kadamba bus stand at 13/14 Dempo Towers, Patto Plaza (⊤0832/243 8897, Ⓕ0832/564 1297, ⓦwww.ukinindia.com) – charges £50 for this invaluable service. In case of emergencies only, Ms Caldeira may be reached on ⊤9822/102 428.

In theory, other foreigners who lose their passports have to travel to their country's nearest consulate or embassy in Mumbai to obtain replacement travel documents. However, it is usually possible to arrange for the relevant forms and fees to be exchanged by post, saving you the hassle of a long and expensive journey north. Whatever kind of passport you hold, be sure to **photocopy** its main pages, including the one bearing your visa, which will speed up the replacement process if it's lost or stolen.

---

tional charge of £15 is made for Indian visas issued in the UK.

Applying for an Indian visa **in the US**, you can download application forms from the embassy website; **in Australia** the equivalent visa application can be found at ⓦwww .ourweb.com.au/indconsul/index.html.

Finally, bear in mind that Indian high commissions and consulates around the world observe **Indian holidays**, which can be frustratingly long and frequent. Give them a ring, or check out their websites, well in advance to ensure they are open on the day you intend to make your application, which should be well in advance of your departure date. This is especially important over Diwali (October/early November), when the offices may be closed for one week or more.

Tourist visas are also available **by post**. Allow a minimum of twenty working days in the UK, and check in advance the cost of the postage and packaging. In the US this takes around fifteen days if you mail your application, accompanied by two passport photos.

An alternative, if you're short of time or live a long way from the embassy, is to pay a **visa agency** to obtain the visa on your behalf, which in the UK costs from around £25 plus the price of the visa. In Britain, try The Visa Service, 2 Northdown St, Kings Cross, London N1 (⊤0990/343 638, ⓦwww .visaservice.co.uk), which offers a 48-hour service; you could also try Visa Express, 31

Corsham St, London N1 (⊤020/7251 4822, Ⓔvisaexpress@cwcom.net). In the US, try Express Visa Service, 2150 Wisconsin Ave, Suite 20, Washington DC (⊤202/337-2442, ⓦwww.expressvisa.com) which charges $45 for a six-day service or $120 for a next-day service.

Contrary to what you might hear on the travellers' grapevine, it is no longer possible to **extend tourist visas** in India (unless you have a very good reason to do so, such as illness). If you want to stay for longer than six months, you have to leave the country and apply for a new visa; most people do this in Colombo, capital of neighbouring Sri Lanka. In Nepal, reapplication is less straightforward. At the time of writing, the website of the Indian High Commission in Kathmandu stated that no reapplications would be entertained.

Another peculiarity worth being aware of is that foreign passport holders who enter India by charter and take a scheduled flight to another country during their stay in India aren't allowed to leave India by charter afterwards. In other words, hop up to Nepal, or down to Sri Lanka, after arriving in Goa by charter, and you'll be forced by emigration to purchase a brand new scheduled ticket.

For details of **other visas** – foreigners of Indian origin, business travellers and even students of yoga can get five-year visas – contact your nearest Indian embassy.

Indian diplomatic representatives abroad

Australia High Commission: 3–5 Moonah Place, Yarralumla, Canberra, ACT 2600 ☎02/6273 3999, ✉hicanb@ozemail.com.au. Consulates: Level 27, 25 Bligh St, Level 27, Sydney, NSW 2000 ☎02/9223 9500, ✉indianc@enternet.com.au; 15 Munro St, Coburg, Melbourne, Vic 3058 ☎03/9384 0141, ☏9384 1609. Honorary Consulates: Level 1, Terrace Hotel, 195 Adelaide Terrace, East Perth WA 6004 (mailing address: PO Box 6118 East Perth WA 6892) ☎08/9221 1485, ✉india@vianet.net.au; Brisbane ☎07/3260 2825, ☏3260 2826.

Bangladesh High Commission: House 120, Rd 2, Dhanmondi Residential Area, Dhaka ☎02/865373, ☏863662, ⌨www.hcidhaka.org. Consulate: 1253–1256 Nizam Rd, Mehdi Bagh, Chittagong ☎031/654201, ☏654147.

Bhutan Embassy of India, India House Estate, Thimphu, ☎09752/22162, ☏23195, ⌨www.eoithimpu.org.

Burma (Myanmar) Embassy: Oriental Assurance Building, 545–547 Merchant St (PO Box 751), Yangon (Rangoon) ☎01/82550, ☏89562.

Canada High Commission: 10 Springfield Rd, Ottawa, ON K1M 1C9 ☎613/744 3751, ☏744 0913, ⌨www.hciottawa.ca. Consulates: 2 Bloor St W, #500, Toronto, ON M4W 3E2 ☎416/960 0751, ⌨www.cgitoronto.ca; 325 Howe St, 2nd floor, Vancouver, BC V6C 1Z7 ☎604/662 8811, ⌨www.cgivancouver.com.

Japan Embassy: 2–11, Kudan Minami 2-Chome, Chiyoda-ku, Tokyo 102 ☎03/3262 2391, ☏3234 4866, ⌨www.embassy-avenue.jp/india.

Malaysia High Commission: 2 Jalan Taman Dlita (off Jalan Duta), PO Box 10059, 50704 Kuala Lumpur ☎03/253 3504, ☏253 3054, ⌨www.hcikl.org.my.

Nepal Embassy: Lainchaur (off Lazimpath), PO Box 92, Kathmandu ☎01/410900, ⌨www.south-asia.com/Embassy-India. Allow a week – plus extra fee – to fax Delhi; British nationals and some Europeans need letters of recommendation. Mon–Fri 9.30–11am.

The Netherlands Embassy: Buitenrustweg-2, 2517 KD, The Hague, ☎070/346 9771, ☏361 7072, ⌨www.indianembassy.nl.

New Zealand High Commission: 180 Molesworth St (PO Box 4005), Wellington ☎04/473 6390, ☏499 0665, ⌨www.hicomind.org.nz.

Pakistan High Commission: G-5, Diplomatic enclave, Islamabad ☎051/814371, ☏820742; Consulate: India House, 3 Fatima Jinnah Rd (PO Box 8542), Karachi ☎021/522275, ☏568 0929.

Singapore Embassy: India House, 31 Grange Rd (PO Box 9123), Singapore 0923 ☎737 6777, ☏732 6909, ⌨www.embassyofindia.com.

Sri Lanka High Comission: 36–38 Galle Rd, Colombo 3 ☎01/421605, ⌨www.indiahcsl.org; Consulate: 31 Rajapihilla Mawatha, PO Box 47, Kandy ☎08/24563.

Thailand Embassy: 46 Soi 23 (Prasarn Mitr), Sukhumvit Rd, Bangkok 10110 ☎02/258 0300, ☏258 4627, ⌨www.indiaemb.or.th; Consulate: 113 Bumruangrat Rd, Chiang Mai 50000 ☎053/243066, ☏247879, Visas take five working days to issue.

UK High Commission: India House, Aldwych, London WC2B 4NA ☎020/7836 8484, ⌨www.hcilondon.org. Consulates: 20 Augusta St, Jewellery Quarter, Hockley, Birmingham B18 6GL ☎0121/212 2782; 17 Rutland Square, Edinburgh EH1 2BB ☎0131/229 2144. All open Mon–Fri 8.30am–noon.

USA Embassy of India (Consular Services): 2107 Massachusetts Ave NW, Washington DC 20008 ☎202/939-7000, ☏939-7027. Consulates: 3 East 64th St, New York, NY 10021 ☎212/774-0600, ⌨www.indiacgny.org; 540 Arguello Blvd, San Francisco, CA 94118 ☎415/668-0683, ☏668-9764, ⌨www.indianconsulate-sf.org; 455 North Cityfront Plaza Drive, Suite 850, Chicago Il 60611 ☎312/595 0405 (ext 22 for visas), ⌨http://chicago.indianconsulate.com/; 201 St Charles Ave, New Orleans, LA 70170 ☎504/582-8106; 2051 Young St, Honolulu, HI 96826 ☎808/947-2618.

Vietnam Embassy of India, 58–60 Tran, Hung Dao, Hanoi ☎04/8244990, ☏8244998; Consulate General of India, 49 Tran Quoc Thao Street, 3rd District, Ho Chi Minh City ☎08/231539, ☏294495.

Foreign embassies, consulates and high commissions in India

Australia 16th Floor, Maker Tower, E Block, Cuffe Parade, Colaba, Mumbai ☎022/2218 1071 or 2204 2044.

Canada 4th Floor, Maker Chambers VI, J Bajaj Marg, Nariman Point, Mumbai ☎022/2287 6027.

France 2nd Floor, Datta Prasad Building, 10 NG Cross Rd, Cumballa Hill, Mumbai ☎022/2495 0948.

Germany Honorary Consul, 10th Floor, Hoechst House, Nariman Point ☎022/2283 2422.

Ireland Royal Bombay Yacht Club Chambers, Apollo Bunder ☎022/2202 4607.

Netherlands Forbes Bldg, Chiranjit Rai Marg, Fort ☎022/2201 6750.

New Zealand 50-N Nyaya Marg, Chanakyapuri, New Delhi ☎011/688 3170, ℰ687 2317.
South Africa Gandhi Mansion, 20 Altamount Rd ☎022/2389 3725.

UK 13/14 Dempo Towers, Patto Plaza, Panjim ☎0832/243 8897.
USA Lincoln House, 78 Bhulabhai Desai Rd, Cumballa Hill, Mumbai ☎022/2363 3611 or 2811 3611.

Information, websites and maps

The Indian government maintains a number of tourist offices abroad, where you can pick up a range of pamphlets on Goa. Their main purpose is to promote government-run hotels and festivals rather than inform, but they can be extremely helpful and knowledgeable. You'll find the government's tourism website at www.tourismofindia.com.

Other sources of information include travel agents and the larger package tour companies operating in Goa. These are in business for themselves, of course, so their advice may not always be totally unbiased.

In Goa itself, both the national and state government run **tourist information offices**, providing general travel advice and handing out an array of printed material, from handy state maps to glossy leaflets on specific destinations. Government tourist offices are open Monday to Friday 9.30am–5pm and Saturday 9.30am–1pm; the main branch of the Indian government's tourist office is on Church Square in Panjim (see p.72). This place operates independently of the information counters and bureaux run by the state tourism department, Goa Tourism, and local tourism-development corporation, GTDC, who collectively offer a wide range of travel facilities, including guided tours, car rental and their own hotels.

Indian government tourist offices abroad

Australia Level 2, Piccadilly, 210 Pitt St, Sydney NSW ☎02/9264 4855, ℰsydney@tourismindia.com; Level 1, 17 Castle Reagh, Sydney, NSW 2000 ☎02/9232 1600, ℰ9223 3003, ℰsydney@tourismindia.com.
Canada 60 Bloor St (West), #1003, Toronto, Ontario M4W 3B8 ☎416/962-3787, ℰtoronto@tourismindia.com.
Netherlands Rokin 9–15, 1022 KK, Amsterdam

☎020/620 8991, ℰamsterdam@tourismindia.com.
Singapore 20 Karamat Lane, 01–01A United House, Singapore 0922 ☎065/235 3800, ℰsingapore@tourismindia.com.
Thailand Singapore Airlines Bldg, 3rd Floor, 62/5 Thaniya Rd (Silom), Bangkok ☎02/235 2585 or 235 6670, ℰ236 8411.
UK 7 Cork St, London W1 2LN ☎020/7437 3677, ℰlondon@tourismindia.com.
USA 3550 Wilshire Blvd, Suite #204, Los Angeles, CA 90010 ☎213/380-8855, ℰla@tourismindia.com; Suite 1808, 1270 Ave of Americas, New York NY 10020 ☎212/586 4901, ℰny@tourismindia.com.

Online resources

Carry out a search for "Goa" on the Internet and your search engine will return a list of hits ranging from sites for Goa Trance aficionados to hippy nonsense homepages in Danish and Dutch. Most are of limited interest to the average tourist, but the following are worth a browse before you travel:
Goa Art ☸www.goa-art.com. Showcase for the work of six young Goan artists.
Goa News ☸www.goanews.com. Roundups of current news and recent archive material, plus links to all the state's regional media sites. They also offer a selection of articles filed under subject headings for easy browsing.
Goa Research Net ☸www.geocities.com/Athens/Forum/1503. A selection of in-depth articles on contemporary Goa, with book reviews and links.
Goacom ☸www.goacom.com. A commercial portal, so its hotel and restaurant reviews are far

from impartial, although the travel information can be helpful, and it hosts a bewildering array of links to other Goa-related sites.

Goa World ⓦ www.goa-world.net. An ever expanding range of Goa info – most of it geared for locals and Goan expats – beefed up with a better-than-average choice of Konkani music and a selection of photos which you can email as E-cards (ⓦ www.goa-world.net/fotofolio). This site also hosts a hotlink to the online edition of the regional news magazine, *Goa Today*.

India Express ⓦ www.indiaexpress.com. Check out the latest articles, and archive material dating back a couple of years, from the regional issue of India's largest newspaper. Special features on Goa, from the *Herald*, appear at ⓦ www.indiaexpress.com .goa/gomantak.

Iyengar Yoga School ⓦ www.maggiehughes.com. Site dedicated to Goa's foremost Iyengar yoga school, based in the north of the state, with details of courses and bio-data on its staff. For more Goa yoga sites, see p.151.

Maps

The first, and only, truly **accurate map** of Goa is John Callanan's excellent *Goa and Its Beaches* (1:200,000; published by Roger Lascelles). Combining detailed coverage of the state's road network with scale plans of all the towns and resorts, it is indispensable if you're planning to travel any distance by rented motorcycle or car. As yet, few shops in Goa stock it, so get hold of one before you leave from the outlets listed below and opposite, or via John's own website ⓦ www .johnthemap.co.uk.

Visitors who stick to the resorts, however, generally manage well enough with the ubiquitous government-published *Tourist Map* (Rs10), available at most information offices and counters, and perfectly adequate for jaunts along the coast. It features all the major roads, byways and sights, although the information can be vexingly inaccurate at times, particularly if you venture off the beaten track.

In addition, there are a number of other state maps on the market that include insets of city and town plans. However, as these tend to be far from reliable, we recommend you use the more carefully researched street plans contained in this book.

Getting good **maps of India** in India itself can be difficult; the government forbids the

sale of detailed maps of border areas, which include the entire coastline. So if you're planning to venture into Karnataka or Maharashtra, or are travelling to Goa from Mumbai, it makes sense to bring one with you. The most detailed map of the country available throughout Europe, the US and Australia is Nelles Verlag's 1:1,500,000 *Map of South India*, which features colour contours and is a handy route-planning aid. Bartholomew's 1:4,000,000 *Map of South Asia* is the international bestseller for the subcontinent; Lascelle's version, on the same scale, is also worth considering.

Map outlets

UK and Ireland

Blackwell's Map and Travel Shop 50 Broad St, Oxford ☎01865/793 550, ⓦ maps.blackwell.co.uk.
Easons Bookshop 40 O'Connell St, Dublin ☎01/ 858 3881, ⓦ www.eason.ie.
Heffers Map and Travel 20 Trinity St, Cambridge ☎01865/333 536, ⓦ www.heffers.co.uk.
Hodges Figgis Bookshop 56–58 Dawson St, Dublin ☎01/677 4754.
The Map Shop 30a Belvoir St, Leicester ☎0116/ 247 1400, ⓦ www.mapshopleicester.co.uk.
National Map Centre 22–24 Caxton St, London SW1 ☎020/7222 2466, ⓦ www.mapsnmc.co.uk, ⓔ info@mapsnmc.co.uk.
Newcastle Map Centre 55 Grey St, Newcastle upon Tyne ☎0191/261 5622.
Ordnance Survey Ireland Phoenix Park, Dublin ☎01/802 5300, ⓦ www.osi.ie.
Ordnance Survey of Northern Ireland Colby House, Stranmillis Ct, Belfast ☎028/9025 5755, ⓦ www.osni.gov.uk.
Stanfords 12–14 Long Acre, London WC2 ☎020/7836 1321, ⓦ www.stanfords.co.uk.
The Travel Bookshop 13–15 Blenheim Crescent, London W11 ☎020/7229 5260, ⓦ www .thetravelbookshop.co.uk.

US and Canada

Adventurous Traveler.com US ☎1-800/282-3963, ⓦ adventuroustraveler.com.
Book Passage 51 Tamal Vista Blvd, Corte Madera, CA 94925 ☎1-800/999-7909, ⓦ www .bookpassage.com.
Distant Lands 56 S Raymond Ave, Pasadena, CA 91105 ☎1-800/310-3220, ⓦ www.distantlands .com.

Elliot Bay Book Company 101 S Main St, Seattle, WA 98104 ☎1-800/962-5311, ⓦ www.elliotbaybook.com.

Globe Corner Bookstore 28 Church St, Cambridge, MA 02138 ☎1-800/358-6013, ⓦ www.globercorner.com.

Map Link 30 S La Patera Lane, Unit 5, Santa Barbara, CA 93117 ☎1-800/962-1394, ⓦ www.maplink.com.

Rand McNally US ☎1-800/333-0136, ⓦ www.randmcnally.com. Around thirty stores across the US; dial ext 2111 or check the website for the nearest location.

The Travel Bug Bookstore 2667 W Broadway, Vancouver V6K 2G2 ☎604/737-1122, ⓦ www.swifty.com/tbug.

World of Maps 1235 Wellington St, Ottawa, Ontario K1Y 3A3 ☎1-800/214-8524, ⓦ www.worldofmaps.com.

Australia and New Zealand

The Map Shop 6–10 Peel St, Adelaide, SA 5000 ☎08/8231 2033, ⓦ www.mapshop.net.au.

Specialty Maps 46 Albert St, Auckland 1001 ☎09/307 2217, ⓦ www.specialtymaps.co.nz.

MapWorld 173 Gloucester St, Christchurch ☎0800/627 967 or 03/374 5399, ⓦ www.mapworld.co.nz.

Mapland 372 Little Bourke St, Melbourne, Victoria 3000 ☎03/9670 4383, ⓦ www.mapland.com.au.

Perth Map Centre 900 Hay St, Perth, WA 6000 ☎08/9322 5733, ⓦ www.perthmap.com.au.

Insurance

With the potential health risks involved in a trip to Goa – see pp.22–29 – travel insurance covering medical expenses and emergency flights is well worth it. You can also insure your money and belongings against loss or theft. Before paying for a new policy, however, it's worth checking whether you are already covered: some all-risks home insurance policies may cover your possessions when overseas, and many private medical schemes include cover when abroad. In Canada, provincial health plans usually provide partial medical cover for mishaps overseas, while holders of official student/teacher/youth cards in Canada and the US are entitled to meagre accident coverage and hospital in-patient benefits. Students will often find that their student health coverage extends during the vacations and for one term beyond the date of last enrolment.

After exhausting the possibilities above, you might want to contact a specialist **travel insurance company**, or consider the travel insurance deal we offer (see box). A typical travel insurance policy usually provides cover for the loss of baggage, tickets and – up to a certain limit – cash or cheques, as well as cancellation or curtailment of your journey. Most of them exclude so-called dangerous sports unless an extra premium is paid: in Goa this can mean scuba diving and windsurfing, though probably not jeep safaris. Many policies can be chopped and changed to exclude coverage you don't need – for example, sickness and accident benefits can often be excluded or included at will. If you do take medical coverage, ascertain whether benefits will be paid as treatment proceeds or only after return home, and whether there is a 24-hour medical emergency number. When securing baggage cover, make sure that the per-article limit – typically under £500 – will cover your most valuable possession. If you need to make a claim, you should keep receipts for medicines and medical treatment, and in the event you have anything stolen, you must obtain an official statement from the police.

Rough Guides travel insurance

Rough Guides offers its own travel insurance, customized for our readers by a leading UK broker and backed by a Lloyd's underwriter. It's available for anyone, of any nationality and any age, travelling anywhere in the world.

There are two main Rough Guide insurance plans: **Essential**, for basic, no-frills cover; and **Premier** – with more generous and extensive benefits. Alternatively, you can take out **annual multi-trip insurance**, which covers you for any number of trips throughout the year (with a maximum of 60 days for any one trip). Unlike many policies, the Rough Guides schemes are calculated by the day, so if you're travelling for 27 days rather than a month, that's all you pay for. If you intend to be away for the whole year, the Adventurer policy will cover you for 365 days. Each plan can be supplemented with a "Hazardous Activities Premium" if you plan to indulge in sports considered dangerous, such as skiing, scuba diving or trekking.

For a **policy quote**, call the Rough Guide Insurance Line on UK freefone ☏0800/ 015 0906; US toll-free ☏1-866/220 5588, or, if you're calling from elsewhere ☏+44 1243/621 046. Alternatively, get a quote or buy online at: ⓦwww.roughguidesinsurance.com.

Health

Goa is arguably the most salubrious state in India, and very few travellers fall seriously ill while they are there. However, it can be all too easy during lengthy, healthy spells on the beach to forget that you are still in South Asia, and that normally innocuous things such as a salad, a rare steak or a drink mixed with untreated water can pose very real health risks.

Precautions

Although standards of sanitation in Goa are generally high – particularly in international-style resort hotels – a few common-sense **precautions** are in order, bearing in mind that things such as bacteria multiply far more quickly in a tropical climate, and that you will have little immunity to Indian germs.

When it comes to **food**, remember that Western dishes are every bit as, if not more, likely to cause you grief as local meals. Be particularly wary of prepared dishes that have to be reheated – ask yourself how long they've been on display in the heat. Anything boiled, fried or grilled (and thus sterilized) in your presence is usually all right, though meat can sometimes be suspect; anything that has been left out for any length of time is best avoided. Raw unpeeled fruit and vegetables should always be viewed with suspi-

cion, and you should steer clear of salads unless you know they have been washed in purified water. Fruit-sellers on the beaches sometimes handle peeled food with their left hands (see p.49), so make sure you douse your slice of pineapple or melon with safe water before eating it.

Be vigilant about **personal hygiene**. Wash your hands often, especially before eating, keep all cuts clean, treat them with iodine or antiseptic, and cover them to prevent infection. Be fussier about sharing things like drinks and cigarettes than you might be at home; never share a razor or toothbrush. It is also inadvisable to go around barefoot and best to wear flip-flop sandals even in the shower.

Among items you might wish to carry with you – though all are available in Goa itself, at a fraction of what you might pay at home –

are antiseptic cream, plasters, lints and sealed bandages, a course of Flagyl antibiotics and a box of Imodium (Lomotil) for emergency diarrhoea treatment, rehydration sachets, insect repellent, antihistamine cream for bites, and paracetamol or aspirin.

Advice on avoiding **mosquitoes** is offered under "Malaria" on p.26. If you do get bites or itches try not to scratch them: it's hard, but infection and tropical ulcers can result if you do. Tiger balm and even dried soap may relieve the itching.

Intestinal troubles

Diarrhoea is the most common bane of travellers. When mild and not accompanied by other major symptoms, it may just be your stomach reacting to unfamiliar food.

Some of the illnesses and parasites you can pick up in India may not show themselves immediately. If you become ill within a year of returning home, tell whoever treats you where you have been.

Accompanied by cramps and vomiting, it could well be food poisoning. In either case, it will probably pass of its own accord in 24–48 hours without treatment. In the meantime, it is essential to replace the fluids and salts you're losing, so take lots of water with **oral rehydration salts** (commonly referred to as ORS, or called Electrolyte in Goa). If you can't get them, use half a teaspoon of salt and three of sugar in a litre of water. It's a good idea to avoid greasy food, heavy

What about the water?

One of the chief concerns of many prospective visitors to Goa is whether the water is safe to drink. To put it simply, it's not, though your unfamiliarity with Indian micro-organisms is generally more of a problem rather than any great virulence in the water itself.

As a rule, it is not a good idea to drink **tap water**, although in towns such as Panjim and Margao it is usually chlorinated. However, you'll find it almost impossible to avoid untreated tap water completely: it is used to make ice, which may appear in drinks without being asked for, to wash utensils and so on.

Bottled water, available in all but the most remote places these days, may seem like the simplest and most cost-effective solution, but it has some major drawbacks. The first is that the water itself might not always be as safe as it seems. Independent tests carried out in 2003 on major Indian brands revealed levels of **pesticide** concentration up to 104 times higher than EU norms. Top sellers Kinley, Bisleri and Aquaplus were named as the worst offenders.

The second downside of bottled water is the **plastic pollution** it causes. The average tourist in Goa gets through between two and three bottles of mineral water per day, which makes 28–42 over a typical fortnight's holiday. Multiply this by 250,000 – the approximate number of foreign tourists who come to Goa each year – and you end up with a colossal plastic bottle mountain.

For Goans, the **bottle build-up** has become a nightmare. With no refuse collection, it falls to the guesthouse owners, hoteliers and restaurateurs to dispose of the empties. Most do this by throwing them in a huge pile behind their house, which they then burn at the end of the season, creating clouds of poisonous brown smoke. A considerable number also end up on the beaches or floating in the sea.

The best solution from the point of view of your health and the environment is to purify your own water. **Chemical sterilization** using tablets is the cheapest method. **Iodine** isn't recommended for long trips, but **chlorine** is completely effective, fast and inexpensive, and you can remove the nasty taste it leaves with neutralizing tablets or lemon juice.

Alternatively, invest in a **purifying filter**. An ever increasing range of compact, lightweight products are available these days through outdoor shops and large pharmacies, but anyone who's pregnant or suffers from thyroid problems should check that iodine isn't used as the chemical sterilizer.

spices, caffeine and most fruit and dairy products; but some say bananas and pawpaws are good, as is coconut milk, while curd or a soup made from Marmite or Vegemite (if you happen to have some with you) are forms of protein that can be easily absorbed by your body when you have the runs. Drugs like Lomotil or Imodium simply plug you up, undermining the body's efforts to rid itself of infection, but they can be a temporary stopgap if you have to travel. If symptoms persist more than a few days, a course of antibiotics may be necessary; this should be seen as a last resort, following medical advice.

It's a good idea to look at what comes out when you go to the toilet. If your diarrhoea contains blood or mucus, the cause may be dysentery or giardia. With a fever, it could well be caused by **bacillic dysentery**, and may clear up without treatment. If you're sure you need it, a course of antibiotics such as tetracycline should sort you out, but they also destroy "gut flora" in your intestines (which help protect you), and if you start a course, be sure to finish it, even after the symptoms have gone. Similar symptoms without fever indicate **amoebic dysentery**, which is much more serious, and can damage your gut if untreated. The usual cure is a course of metronidazole (Flagyl), an antibiotic which may itself make you feel ill, and should not be taken with alcohol. Similar symptoms, plus rotten-egg belches and farts, indicate **giardia**, for which the treatment is again metronidazole. If you suspect that you have any of these, seek medical help, and only start on the metronidazole if there is definitely blood in your diarrhoea and it's impossible to see a doctor.

Finally, bear in mind that **oral drugs**, such as malaria pills and contraceptive pills, are likely to be largely ineffective if taken while suffering from diarrhoea.

Bites and stings

In addition to a range of tropical wasps and bees that can pack a hefty punch, while in Goa you should keep an eye open for **snakes**, particularly while crossing rice paddies – the traditional habitat of the Indian cobra. Descriptions of the four deadliest of the eight species of venomous vipers pres-

ent in Goa appear in "Contexts" (see p.322). The best way to **avoid them** is to make plenty of noise while walking along country footpaths and across paddy ditches, and never poke around in holes or crevices in the ground. During the late evening and after dark, it is also a good idea to carry a long stick in case you encounter one, always use a flashlight and wear sturdy shoes (rather than flip-flops or sandals) if you go out at night. It's rare for people to be **bitten**, but if you are, the first thing you should try to do is identify the snake; this will make it easier for the doctors to decide which serum to inject you with when you arrive at the hospital, where you should go immediately.

Common **symptoms** of snake bites are swelling, bruising and pain, nausea and vomiting. In extreme cases, numbness, nerve pain, tingling in the neck or face, muscle spasms, and haemorrhaging may also develop. If they do, tie a tourniquet around the affected limb, releasing it for a minute and a half every quarter of an hour. Remember at all times (and reassure the person who's been bitten) that it is extremely rare to die from snake bites. The same applies to **scorpion** and **centipede** stings, and to **spider** bites; however, you should always try to identify whatever has bitten you.

Jellyfish won't kill you either, but you're more likely to be stung by one than by anything else. Tell-tale signs that they are lurking in the sea are if you come across dead ones on the beach, dumped by hand-net fishers. The larger specimens often have long dangling tentacles that will give a nasty shock if they get wrapped around you. The best thing to do after being stung is to bathe the wound in very hot water; the toxin that causes the pain breaks up at high temperatures. Get the staff at the nearest beach shack to help you. Antihistamine tablets (available at just about every pharmacy in Goa) also relieve the symptoms, as do anti-inflammatory painkillers such as Ibuprofen. In severe cases, jellyfish stings will leave slight scars that may last for up to nine months.

Heat trouble

The sun and the heat can cause a few unexpected problems. Many people get a bout of prickly heat rash before they've acclimatized. It's an infection of the sweat ducts caused by excessive perspiration that doesn't dry off. A cool shower, zinc oxide (aka "prickly heat") powder and loose cotton clothes should help (avoid nylon and other synthetic fabrics that won't absorb sweat). **Dehydration** is another possible problem, so make sure you're drinking enough liquid, and drink rehydration salts when hot and/or tired. The main danger sign is irregular urination (only once a day, for instance), but dark urine also probably means you should drink more.

It's vital not to underestimate the burning power of the Goan **sun**, which will fry any exposed skin not protected with a high-factor block. Take particular care during your first week or two, and on days when there is a lot of high cloud around, which can make the sun seem deceptively benign. Many people also fall asleep on the beach and awake to find themselves in the full glare of the sun with their skin burnt to a cinder. In addition, a light hat is a good idea, especially if you're doing a lot of walking.

Finally, be aware that overheating can cause **heatstroke**, which is potentially fatal. Signs are a very high body temperature without a feeling of fever, but accompanied by headaches and disorientation. Lowering the body temperature (with a tepid shower, for example) is the first step in treatment. If symptoms persist, seek medical advice.

HIV and AIDS

AIDS is still a relatively unknown quantity in India, and often regarded as a foreign problem, but indications are that HIV levels are already high among prostitutes, and the same presumably applies to intravenous drug users. You are also, of course, at risk from your fellow travellers. It is therefore extremely unwise to contemplate casual sex without a condom. Take some with you (Indian ones may be less reliable; also, be aware that heat affects the durability of condoms), and insist on using them.

Should you need an injection or a transfusion in Goa, make sure that new, sterile equipment is used; any blood you receive should be from voluntary rather than commercial donor banks. If you have a shave

from a barber, make sure he uses a clean blade, and don't submit to processes such as ear-piercing, acupuncture or tattooing unless you can be sure that the equipment is sterile.

Vaccinations

No inoculations are legally required for entry into India, but meningitis, typhoid and hepatitis A jabs are recommended, and it's worth ensuring that you are up to date with tetanus, polio and other boosters.

Hepatitis A is not the worst disease you can catch in Goa, but the frequency with which it strikes travellers makes a strong case for immunization. Transmitted through contaminated food and water, or through saliva, it can lay a victim low for several months with exhaustion, fever and diarrhoea. The new Havrix vaccine has been shown to be very effective and lasts for up to ten years – unlike gamma globulin, the traditional serum against hepatitis, which offers little protection and wears off after three months.

Symptoms by which you can recognize hepatitis include yellowing of the whites of the eyes, general malaise, orange urine (though dehydration could also cause that) and light-coloured stools. If you think you have it, steer clear of alcohol, try to avoid passing it on, and get lots of rest. More serious is **hepatitis B**, passed on like AIDS through blood or sexual contact. There is a vaccine, but it is only recommended for those planning to work in a medical environment. Otherwise, your chances of getting hepatitis B are low.

Typhoid is also spread through contaminated food or water, but is rare in Goa. It produces a persistent high fever with malaise, headaches and abdominal pains, followed by diarrhoea. Vaccination is by injection (the single-shot variety, with one inoculation for a booster), giving three years' cover.

Cholera, spread the same way as hepatitis A and typhoid, causes sudden attacks of watery diarrhoea with cramps and debilitation. Again, this disease rarely occurs in Goa, breaking out in isolated epidemics. If you get it, take copious amounts of water with rehydration salts and seek medical treatment; there is a vaccination but it offers very little protection. Most medical authorities now recommend vaccination against **meningitis** too. Spread by airborne bacteria (through coughs and sneezes for example), it is a very unpleasant disease that attacks the lining of the brain and can be fatal.

You should have a **tetanus** (or lockjaw) booster every ten years whether you travel or not. It is picked up through contaminated open wounds – if you cut yourself on something dirty and are not covered, get a booster as soon as you can. Assuming that you were vaccinated against **polio** in childhood, only one (oral) booster is needed during your adult life. Immunizations against mumps, measles, TB and rubella are a good idea for anyone who wasn't vaccinated as a child and hasn't had the diseases.

Rabies is widespread in Goa, and the best advice is to give dogs and monkeys a wide berth, indeed not play with animals at all, no matter how cute they might look. A bite, a scratch or even a lick from an infected animal could spread the disease; immediately wash any wound gently with soap or detergent, and apply alcohol or iodine if possible. Find out what you can about the animal and swap addresses with the owner (if there is one) just in case. If the animal might be infected, act immediately to get treatment – rabies is invariably fatal once symptoms appear. There is a vaccine, but it is expensive, serves only to shorten the course of treatment you need anyway, and is only effective for a maximum of three months.

Malaria

Malaria, caused by a parasite transmitted in the saliva of female Anopheles **mosquitoes**, is currently the number one killer in the developing world. Compared with the rest of India, its incidence in Goa is relatively small (15,000 cases and 17 deaths were reported in the year ending June 2000), but it is still advisable to take precautions, especially if you plan to visit in the period towards the end of, or immediately after, the monsoon (Aug–Oct), when outbreaks are fairly common. Partly as a result of increased immigration from more heavily malarial regions of the country, and partly because of the sudden growth in the number of construction sites (where mosquitoes breed in stagnant pools and feed off labourers already infected), the disease has become endemic in more populated areas, notably (in order of the number of cases reported): **Calangute**, **Panjim**, **Margao** and **Colva**. In these four places, moreover, there have been almost as many cases of the potentially fatal **Falciparum** strain of malaria as the less serious **Virex** form. As a result, doctors recommend all visitors to Goa take **preventative tablets** (prophylactics) according to a strict routine, cov-

Dogs

Stray dogs hang around everywhere in Goa, especially on the beaches and outside café-shacks, where they scavenge for scraps. Stay in a village for any time and one is bound to latch on to you, but it's a good idea to avoid stroking them, no matter how in need of love they look. Quite apart from the rabies risk, most carry a plethora of parasites and skin diseases. Leaving your temporary pet, whose ribs will have disappeared after weeks of being well fed, can also be a wrench.

If you really want to improve the lot of Goa's stray dogs, get in touch with **International Animal Rescue**, whose volunteers and full-time vets care for dogs rescued from around Goa at their centre near Anjuna. Their work is entirely dependent on **donations** and sponsorship, most of which comes from tourists. For Rs450 (£7.50) you can sponsor an individual dog; Rs3000 (£50) buys a whole kennel. Look out for their collection boxes around Baga and Calangute hotels, or call in person at the International Animal Rescue headquarters, **Animal Tracks**, at Assagao. Alternatively, visit their website at ⓦwww.iar.org.uk; background on the Goa centre and its work appears at ⓦwww.iar.org.uk/Pages/indnews.html.

If you see a dog, or any other animal, urgently in need of veterinary care, you can contact IAR on ☎0832/255328, or take the animal direct to the centre by rickshaw or taxi.

ering the period before and after your trip (malaria has a variable incubation period of a few days to several weeks, so you can become ill long after being bitten).

The basic drug used is chloroquine (trade names include Nivaquin, Avloclor and Resochin), usually two tablets weekly, but Goa has chloroquine-resistant strains, and you'll need to supplement it with daily proguanil (Paludrine) or weekly Maloprim. A weekly drug, mefloquine (Lariam), was supposed to replace all these, but during its first year on the market many travellers complained of serious side effects, notably acute depression, and few doctors these days recommend it. Australian authorities now prescribe the antibiotic tetracycline instead.

Chloroquine and quinine are safe during pregnancy, but Maloprim, Fansidar, mefloquine and tetracycline should be avoided. **Side effects** of anti-malaria drugs may include itching, rashes, hair loss and even sight problems, which is why many visitors choose to rely on less sophisticated methods of prevention.

The best way to avoid catching malaria, of course, is to make sure you don't get bitten. If there are mozzies around, sleep under a net – one which can hang from a single point is best (you can usually find a way to tie a string across your room to hang it from) – burn mosquito coils (available in most general stores) or use DEET-based repellent (an Indian brand called Odomos is widely available and effective). Mosquito "buzzers" are useless. Though active from dusk till dawn, female Anopheles mosquitoes prefer to bite in the evening, so be especially careful at that time. Wear long sleeves, skirts and trousers, avoid dark colours, which attract mosquitoes, and put repellent on all exposed skin.

If you go down with malaria, you'll soon know about it. The fever, shivering and headaches are like severe flu and come in waves, usually beginning in the early evening. Malaria is not infectious, but can be dangerous and sometimes even fatal if not treated quickly, so at the first sign of serious symptoms, see a doctor and insist on a blood test if your temperature fluctuates.

Another reason to avoid getting bitten is that mosquitoes spread **Japanese**

encephalitis. There have been several outbreaks of this fatal disease in Goa in recent years, all of them during or shortly after the monsoons (Aug–Oct). Symptoms are similar to malaria.

Medical resources for travellers

For up-to-the-minute information, make an appointment at a **travel clinic**. These clinics also sell travel accessories, including mosquito nets and first-aid kits. Information about specific diseases and conditions, drugs and herbal remedies is provided by the websites below; you could also consult the *Rough Guide to Travel Health* by Dr Nick Jones.

Health-related websites

⊛ **health.yahoo.com** Information on specific diseases and conditions, drugs and herbal remedies, as well as advice from health experts.
⊛ **www.fitfortravel.scot.nhs.uk** UK NHS website carrying information about travel-related diseases and how to avoid them.
⊛ **www.istm.org** The website of the International Society for Travel Medicine, with a full list of clinics worldwide specializing in travel health.
⊛ **www.tmvc.com.au** Contains a list of all Travellers' Medical and Vaccination Centres throughout Australia, New Zealand and Southeast Asia, plus general information on travel health.
⊛ **www.tripprep.com** Travel Health Online provides an online-only comprehensive database of necessary vaccinations for most countries, as well as destination and medical service provider information.

Travel clinics

UK and Ireland

British Airways Travel Clinics 156 Regent St, London W1 (Mon–Fri 9.30am–5.15pm, Sat 10am–4pm, no appointment necessary; ☏020/ 7439 9584); 101 Cheapside, London EC2 (hours as above, appointment required; ☏020/7606 2977); ⊛www.britishairways.com/travel/healthclinintro. Vaccinations, tailored advice from an online database and a complete range of travel healthcare products.
Communicable Diseases Unit Brownlee Centre, Glasgow G12 0YN ☏0141/211 1062. Vaccinations, including yellow fever.
Dun Laoghaire Medical Centre 5 Northumberland Ave, Dun Laoghaire, County

Dublin ☎01/280 4996, ✆01/280 5603. Advice on medical matters abroad.

Hospital for Tropical Diseases Travel Clinic 2nd Floor, Mortimer Market Centre, off Capper St, London WC1 (Mon–Fri 9am–5pm by appointment only; ☎020/7388 9600. A consultation costs £15 which is waived if you have your injections here. A recorded Health Line (☎0906/133 7733; 50p per min) gives tips on hygiene and illness prevention as well as listing appropriate immunizations.

Liverpool School of Tropical Medicine Pembroke Place, Liverpool L3 5QA ☎0151/708 9393. Walk-in clinic (Mon–Fri 1–4pm); appointment required for yellow fever, but not for other jabs.

MASTA (Medical Advisory Service for Travellers Abroad) Forty regional clinics – call ☎0870/606 2782 for the nearest; ⊛www.masta .org. Also operates a 24-hour Travellers' Health Line (UK ☎0906/822 4100, 60p per min), providing written information tailored to your journey by return of post.

Nomad Pharmacy 40 Bernard St, London, WC1; 3–4 Wellington Terrace, Turnpike Lane, London N8; Mon–Fri 9.30am–6pm, ☎020/7833 4114 to book vaccination appointment. Advice tailored to your travel needs is free if you go in person; their telephone helpline (☎0906/863 3414) costs 60p per minute.

Trailfinders Immunization clinics (no appointments necessary) at 194 Kensington High St, London W8; Mon–Fri 9am–5pm except Thurs to 6pm, Sat 9.30am–4pm; ☎020/7938 3999.

Travel Health Centre Department of International Health and Tropical Medicine, Royal College of Surgeons in Ireland, Mercers Medical Centre, Stephen's St Lower, Dublin 2 ☎01/402 2337. Expert pre-trip advice and inoculations.

Travel Medicine Services PO Box 254, 16 College St, Belfast BT1 ☎028/9031 5220. Offers pre-trip medical advice and help afterwards in the event of a tropical disease.

Tropical Medical Bureau Grafton Buildings, 34 Grafton St, Dublin 2 ☎01/671 9200, ⊛tmb.exodus.ie.

US and Canada

Canadian Society for International Health 1 Nicholas St, Suite 1105, Ottawa, ON K1N 7B7 ☎613/241-5785, ⊛www.csih.org. Distributes a free pamphlet, *Health Information for Canadian Travellers*, containing an extensive list of travel health centres in Canada.

Centers for Disease Control 1600 Clifton Rd NE, Atlanta, GA 30333 ☎1-800/311-3435 or 404/639-3534, ⊛www.cdc.gov. Publishes outbreak warnings, suggested inoculations, precautions and other background information for travellers. There's also an International Travelers Hotline on ☎1-877/ FYI-TRIP.

International Association for Medical Assistance to Travellers (IAMAT) 417 Center St, Lewiston, NY 14092 ☎16/754-4883; 40 Regal Rd, Guelph, ON N1K 1B5 ☎519/836-0102; ⊛www.iamat.org. A non-profit organization supported by donations which can provide a list of English-speaking doctors in India, climate charts and leaflets on various diseases and inoculations.

International SOS Assistance Eight Neshaminy Interplex Suite 207, Trevose, USA 19053-6956 ☎1-800/523-8930, ⊛www.intsos.com. Members receive pre-trip medical referral info, as well as overseas emergency services designed to complement travel insurance coverage.

MEDJET Assistance ☎1-800/9MEDJET, ⊛www.medjetassistance.com. Annual membership program for travelers ($175 for individuals, $275 for families) that, in the event of illness or injury, will fly members home or to the hospital of their choice in a medically equipped and staffed jet.

Travel Medicine ☎1-800/TRAVMED, ⊛www.travmed.com. Sells first-aid kits, mosquito netting, water filters, reference books and other health-related travel products.

Travelers Medical Center 31 Washington Square West, New York, NY 10011 ☎212/982-1600. Consultation service on immunizations and treatment of diseases for people travelling to developing countries.

Australia and New Zealand

Travellers' Medical and Vaccination Centres ⊛www.tmvc.com.au; 27–29 Gilbert Place, Adelaide, SA 5000 ☎08/8212 7522, ✉adelaide @traveldoctor.com.au; 1/170 Queen St, Auckland ☎09/373 3531, ✉auckland@traveldoctor.co.nz; 5/247 Adelaide St, Brisbane, Qld 4000 ☎07/3221 9066, ✉brisbane@traveldoctor.com.au; 5/8–10 Hobart Place, Canberra, ACT 2600 ☎02/6257 7156, ✉canberra@traveldoctor.com.au; Moorhouse Medical Centre, 9 Washington Way, Christchurch ☎03/379 4000, ✉christchurch@traveldoctor.co.nz; 270 Sandy Bay Rd, Sandy Bay, Hobart 7005 ☎03/6223 7577, ✉hobart@traveldoctor.com.au; 2/393 Little Bourke St, Melbourne, Vic 3000 ☎03/9602 5788, ✉melbourne@traveldoctor.com.au; Level 7, Dymocks Bldg, 428 George St, Sydney, NSW 2000 ☎02/9221 7133, ✉sydney@traveldoctor.com.au; Shop 15, Grand Arcade, 14–16 Willis St, Wellington ☎04/473 0991, ✉wellington@traveldoctor.co.nz.

Getting medical help

Pharmacies can usually advise on minor medical problems, and most doctors in Goa speak English. Basic medicaments are made to Indian Pharmacopoeia (IP) standards, and most medicines are available without prescription (always check the sell-by date). **Hospitals** vary in standard. The GMC (Goa Medical College) in Panjim is nominally the best equipped, but hopelessly over-stretched and altogether a stressful experience for anyone accustomed to Western standards of efficiency and hygiene. Everyone who can afford it opts for treatment in one of Goa's many **private clinics**. These tend to be cleaner and more comfortable than state-run ones, but may not have the same facilities. Both private and state medical centres may require patients to buy necessities such as plaster casts and vaccines, and to pay for X-rays, before procedures are carried out. However, charges are usually so low that for minor treatment the expense may well be lower than the initial "excess" on your insurance.

Accidents and emergencies

Goa has witnessed a disturbing spate of fatal, or near-fatal, **accidents** involving tourists over the past few years, most of them connected with motorcycles. It is therefore essential when travelling by rented transport to know where to go if either you, or someone you are with, gets badly injured, as few hospitals in the state have the sophisticated equipment or specialist doctors needed to speedily diagnose serious injuries. Making straight for the right clinic instead of the wrong casualty department can save your life.

In **north Goa**, the Vrindavan Hospital in Mapusa is the only place in the area with a CT scan unit (essential for dealing with head injuries). The Goa Medical College (GMC) in **Panjim** (℡0832/222 3026 or 222 6288) also has one, but is appallingly unhygienic and in a chronic state of disrepair; if you're in **south Goa**, make your way to the Salgaonkar Medical Research Centre near Vasco da Gama (℡0832/251 2524). For orthopedic injuries such as suspected broken bones, Dr Bale's 24-hour surgery in Porvorim (℡0832/221 7709 or 221 7053), 4km north of Panjim on the main Mapusa road (NH17), is another safe bet.

Emergency telephone numbers for **ambulances** and local hospitals are given in the "Listings" sections where available. In the majority of cases, however, you'll get to hospital a lot quicker by flagging down a car or finding a taxi to take you.

Costs, money and banks

India is, unquestionably, one of the least expensive countries for travellers in the world, and although the cost of living, and prices, in Goa are far higher than most other parts of the country, a little foreign currency still goes a long way.

With provisions for tourists ranging from luxury five-star resorts to palm-leaf shacks, **what you spend** depends entirely on you. On a budget of as little as £7/$10 per day, you'll manage if you stick to the cheapest of everything and don't move about too much; double that, and you can permit yourself the odd splurge meal, the occasional mid-range hotel, and a few souvenirs. If you're happy spending £20–30/$30–40 per day, however, you can really pamper yourself; to spend much more than that, you'd have to be staying in the best hotels and eating in top restaurants.

Accommodation ranges from £2/$3 per night upwards, while a mid-range seafood meal in an ordinary beach café is unlikely to cost even that much. How you **travel around** makes a big difference: public transport costs pennies, but a day on a rented motorcycle or a long-distance taxi ride can set you back what you might expect to spend on a couple of days' accommodation. Costs also vary considerably between resorts: basically, the more touristy the area, the higher the prices. A snack in or around Fort Aguada and Candolim, for example, could come to the same as a slap-up South Indian meal in Panjim or Margao, while the price of a pineapple in Mapusa market inflates ten-fold between there and Calangute beach. Note also, that since the end of 2000, **admission prices** to major archeological sites such as Hampi have rocketed.

Some independent travellers tend to indulge in pernickety penny-pinching, which Goans find rather pathetic – they know how much an air ticket costs, and have a fair idea of what you can earn at home. Bargain where appropriate, but don't begrudge a few rupees to someone who's worked hard for them: consider what their services would cost at home, and how much more valuable the money is to them than it is to you. Even if you get "ripped off" on every rickshaw journey you make, it will only add at most one percent to the overall cost of your trip. Remember too, that any pound or dollar you spend in Goa goes that much further, and luxuries you can't afford at home become possible here: sometimes it's worth spending more simply because you get more for it. At the same time, don't pay well over the odds for something if you know what the going rate is. Thoughtless extravagance can, particularly in remote areas, contribute to inflation, putting even basic goods and services beyond the reach of local people at certain times of year.

Indian money

India's unit of currency is the **rupee**, usually abbreviated "Rs" and divided into a hundred paise. Almost all money is paper, with notes

of 1, 2, 5, 10, 20, 50, 100 and 500 rupees. **Coins** start at 1 paisa, then range up through 5, 10, 20, 25 and 50 paise, and 1, 2 and 5 rupees. The exchange rate at the time of publication is around Rs70/Rs45 to £1/$1.

Banknotes, especially lower denominations, can get into a terrible state, but don't accept torn ones; nobody else will be prepared to take them, so you'll be stuck with the things. You can change them at large branches of big banks such as the State Bank of India, or slip them into the middle of a wad when paying for something (which is probably how they'll have been passed to you).

Large denominations can also be a problem, as **change** is often in short supply, particularly in small towns and villages. Many Indian people cannot afford to keep much lying around, and you shouldn't necessarily expect shopkeepers or rickshaw *wallahs* to have it (and they may try to hold on to it if they do). Paying for your groceries with a Rs100 bill will probably entail waiting for the grocer's errand boy to go off on a quest around town trying to change it. Keeping a wad of Rs5 or Rs10 notes handy isn't a bad idea (you can get bundles of fifty stapled together in banks; holes from the staples don't count as rips, as long as they don't reach the edge of the note).

Traveller's cheques and credit cards

Take along a mixture of cash and traveller's cheques to cover all eventualities, and keep a few small denominations for the odd foreign-currency purchase. US dollars and pounds sterling are the easiest **currencies** to convert. Major hard currencies such as Australian dollars, euros and Japanese yen can all be changed easily in tourist areas. If you enter the country with US$10,000 or the equivalent, you are supposed to fill in a currency-declaration form.

Traveller's cheques aren't as liquid as cash, but they are obviously more secure. Not all banks and foreign-exchange desks, however, accept them, and those that do can be quirky about exactly which ones they will change – well-known brands such as Thomas Cook (who have an office in

Panjim), American Express or Visa are your best bets.

A **credit card** is a handy back-up, as an increasing number of hotels, restaurants, large shops and airlines now take plastic. The Bank of Baroda issues rupees against a Visa card at many of its branches. Their exchange rates tend to be good, but they charge commission of one percent on the transaction and a Rs100 fee for the card authorization call (which has to be relayed to Singapore). Remember that all cash advances are treated as loans, with interest accruing daily from the date of withdrawal; there may be a transaction fee on top of this.

Several banks now have **ATM machines**, but only in the larger towns and resorts, and not all ATMs will accept foreign cards even if they sport Visa and American Express signs; you are best advised to enquire first before sticking your card into the slot. Details of where to find ATMs and what cards they accept are given throughout the Guide chapters of this book.

A compromise between traveller's cheques and plastic is **Visa TravelMoney**, a disposable pre-paid debit card with a PIN which works in all ATMs that take Visa cards. You load up your account with funds before leaving home, and when they run out, you simply throw the card away. Up to nine cards can be purchased to access the same funds – useful for couples or families travelling together – and it's a good idea to buy at least one extra as a back-up in case of loss or theft. The card is available in most countries from branches of Thomas Cook and Citicorp. For more information, check the Visa TravelMoney website at ⓦwww.usa .visa.com/personal/cards/visa_travel_money .html.

Changing money

Changing money in Goan banks tends to be a time-consuming business, involving lots of form-filling and queuing at different counters, so change substantial amounts at any one time. Main branches in towns and major resorts are the most efficient.

Outside **banking hours** (Mon–Fri 10am–2pm, Sat 10am–noon), large hotels change money for residents (albeit at a lower rate), and there's a small State Bank of India

counter at Dabolim airport that opens at flight times. However, the best all-round places to change foreign notes and traveller's cheques are the branches of **private exchange companies** that have recently sprung up in Panjim and the main coastal resorts. These tend to be fast and efficient, and change at bank rates. Otherwise, a number of reputable **travel agents** are licensed to change money. Failing that, there's always the **black market**: most taxi drivers will change large banknotes, although you'll have to haggle over the rate.

Wherever you change money, hold on to **exchange receipts**, or "encashment certificates"; they will be required if you want to change back any excess rupees when you leave the country, or buy things like air tickets with rupees, and if you need a tax clearance form. Note that the State Bank of India now charges for these.

It is illegal to carry rupees into or out of India, and you won't get them at a particularly good rate in the West anyway (though you might in Thailand, Malaysia or Singapore). The janitors in Dabolim airport have cottoned on to this, and devised a lucrative sideline by offering large-denomination foreign coins, given to them by tourists as tips, in exchange for your excess rupees. Several readers have written to us complaining about the exorbitant (unpublished) rates given by the money-changing counters in the departure hall for changing rupees back into foreign currency.

Other travellers have complained they've been cheated **on arrival in Goa** by the state Bank of India desk beyond passport control, in the departure lounge; check your encashment certificate and exchange rate carefully against your cash before you leave the building.

Wiring money

If for any reason you need to have money sent from your home country to Goa in a hurry, it is reassuring to know that these days this can be done quickly and easily. The catch is that **international money transfers** are expensive, with hefty commissions of between fourteen and twenty percent slapped on top of the amount sent, plus other annoying hidden charges.

While it is theoretically possible to have money wired through an Indian bank, you're much more likely to receive it on time with the help of an international agent, such as **Thomas Cook**, who offer money transfers from their office in Panjim (near the Indian Airlines office, at 8 Alcon Chambers, Devanand Bandodkar Rd ☎0832/222 1312, ℱ222 1313). The actual transfer is carried out by MoneyGram, an American company. All you have to do is get a friend or relative back home to pay in the cash you need at their nearest agent – a list of which appears on their website ⓦwww.moneygram.com – plus the commission (which at the time of writing was roughly £14/$21 on top of the first £100/$150 sent, with larger sums charged according to a sliding scale). The payee is then given a transfer reference number, which they have to relay to you by phone, fax or email; when you turn up at the Thomas Cook office in Panjim, you'll need to be able to quote this, and provide ID. At your end, no extra charges have to be paid. However, MoneyGram insists on converting the original sum into US dollars before reconverting it into rupees, often at an unfavourable exchange rate, with the result that the amount you eventually receive may be considerably less than that originally paid in.

Another US company, Western Union, offers a similar service. It's marginally more expensive than **MoneyGram**, but they have a huge number of agents worldwide (a full list of which can be found on their website, ⓦwww.westernunion.com), of which three are in Goa: Transcorp Int. Ltd, Shiv Krupa Building, opposite Dom Bosco School, St Inez, Panjim (Mon–Sat 9.30am–6pm; ☎0832/222 4304); Sita World Travels, 1st Floor, 101 Rizvi Chambers Building, Caetano Albuquerque Rd, Panjim (Mon–Fri 9am–6pm, Sat 9.30am–1.30pm; ☎0832 /222 1418); and Weizmann Ltd, 650 Costa Dias Building, National Highway 17, Margao (Mon–Sat 10am–6pm; ☎0834/233 1679).

Baksheesh

The most common form of *baksheesh* – basically slipping someone money on the quiet in exchange for some kind of service – is **tipping**: this can encompass anything from help finding a room or carrying your luggage, to cracking open a coconut on the beach. Large amounts are not expected – ten rupees should satisfy all the aforementioned. Taxi drivers and staff at cheaper hotels and restaurants do not necessarily expect tips but always appreciate them, of course, and they can keep people sweet for the next time you call. Some may take liberties in demanding *baksheesh*, but it's often better just to acquiesce rather than spoil your mood and cause offence over trifling sums.

More expensive than plain tipping is paying people to **bend the rules**, many of which seem to have been invented for precisely that purpose. The prime culprits here are the police, who invariably take bribes rather than arrest or officially fine people for petty offences (such as driving without an international licence). Being caught with drugs is more serious. For some pointers on how to deal with the rapacious Goan cops, see "Crime and personal security" on p.56.

The last kind of *baksheesh* is **alms giving**. In a country without social security, this is an important custom. People with disabilities are the traditional recipients, and it seems right to join locals in giving small change to them, especially when visiting temples. Kids demanding money, pens or the like are a different case, pressing their demands only on tourists. In return for a service it is fair enough, but to yield to any request encourages them to go and pester others. Think twice before you do so.

Getting around

Before Independence, the many rivers that drain Goa's coastal plain made getting around a stop-and-start affair. Nowadays, however, bridges have largely superseded the old estuary ferries, and the state is covered with surfaced roads. Served by streams of clapped-out buses, these connect all the major settlements and resorts on the coast with the three towns of the interior. To get away from your fellow tourists, though, you'll want to get off the main roads and spend some time exploring rural Goa. The best way to do this is to rent some form of transport, although a train line does run from Vasco da Gama into the interior, allowing you to penetrate the dense jungle-covered terrain of the Western Ghats. The main public transport **routes** and **timings** are listed at the end of each chapter in "Travel details".

Buses

Cheap, frequent and running just about everywhere accessible by road, **buses** are by far the most popular mode of transport in Goa, and you're bound at some point to catch one, if only to get into town or to the next resort. Visitors not yet initiated into the joys of Indian public transport are unlikely to forget the experience.

If you're lucky or catch the bus near the beginning of its route, you might get a seat. Otherwise, be prepared for an uncomfortable crush as more and more passengers squeeze themselves and bags of shopping (some of it still alive) up the centre aisle. **Private buses** are particularly notorious for overloading. Conductors dangle out of the side doors chanting their destination with the rapidity of horse-racing commentators.

One consolation for the crush is that **fares** are so low as to be virtually free by Western standards. The fifty-minute journey from Panjim to Margao, for example, costs less than Rs20 (around 30p/50c). Travelling by bus is also a great way to experience the Goans' Goa. Bumping along at often breakneck speeds with distorted Konkani pop music blaring through the sound system, you could find yourself sitting next to a neatly dressed office *wallah* on his way home from work, or a Kunbi fisherwoman with her basket of fish fresh off the family boat. And if the scary driving starts to get to you, have faith in the protective deities that always sit in shrines near the driver's seat, decked with

garlands of flowers: multicoloured Hindu gods or radiant Madonnas, depending on the religion of the bus owner.

Tickets are generally sold by conductors on the bus itself – keep some small change handy for this – although the state transport company, **Kadamba**, sells them from hatches in the main bus stands. Bus **information** for specific destinations is given in the relevant account in the Guide section of this book.

Motorbikes, mopeds and cycles

It is hard to overstate the sense of freedom that breezing around the open roads of Goa on a **motorcycle** can bring. On a rented bike you can reach the state's remote beaches and cover long distances with relative ease. The downside, of course, is that two-wheelers can be perilous. On average, 220 people die on Goa's roads each year. Before driving away, therefore, ensure the lights and brakes are in good shape, and be especially vigilant at night: many roads are poor and unlit, and stray cows and bullock carts can appear from nowhere.

Motorcycles are available at most of the coastal resorts. Officially, you need an inter-

> It is essential if you rent a motorcycle in Goa to know where the best **accident and emergency units** are located. Details of these appear in "Health" on p.29.

national driver's licence to rent and ride anything. Owners and rental companies rarely enforce this, but some local police use the rule to extract exorbitant *baksheesh* from tourists. If you don't have a licence with you, the only way around the problem is to avoid big towns such as Panjim, Margao and Mapusa (or Anjuna on Wednesday – market day), and to carry only small sums of money when driving. If you are stopped for not having the right papers, it's no big deal, though police officers may try to convince you otherwise; keep cool, and be prepared to negotiate. It is also a good idea to get some evidence that the bike is rented and insured before heading off.

Rates vary according to both season and vehicle; most owners also insist on a hefty deposit and/or passport as security. The cheapest bike, a Honda Kinetic 100cc, which has automatic gears, costs Rs100–150 per day. These are reliable and fine for buzzing to the beach and back, but to travel further you need a bit more power.

Other options include the stylish Enfield Bullet 350cc that is, nevertheless, heavy, unwieldy and – at upwards of Rs250 per day – the most expensive bike to rent. For all-round performance and manoeuvrability, though, you can't beat the fast and light Yamaha RD100cc, which is economical on fuel and generally well suited to the windy Goan roads. These go for Rs125–200, depending on what kind of shape the vehicle is in. Finally, the bikes to avoid, at all costs, are the notoriously unreliable Indian-made Rajdoot, and old Baja-Vespas, whose gears and brakes are invariably substandard.

Two-stroke **fuel** is sold at service stations (known locally as "petrol pumps") in Panjim, Mapusa, Calangute and Margao, Chaudi, and at Arambol in the far north. In smaller settlements, including a number of resorts such as Anjuna and Colva, you can only buy fuel by the Bisleri bottle in general stores or through backstreet suppliers. Details of these are given throughout the Guide, but you should avoid them whenever possible

as some bulk out their petrol with low-grade kerosene or industrial solvent, which makes two-stroke engines misfire and smoke badly. Most villages also have a **motorcycle-repair** specialist (aka a "puncture *wallah*"), although in theory the person you rented your machine from should foot the bill for routine maintenance (including punctures, blown bulbs and any mechanical failures). Damage to the bike incurred during a road traffic accident, of course, has to be paid for by you. It is important you agree on such details with the owner before driving away.

Cycling

Indian-made "sit-up-and-beg" Hero **bicycles** – ideal for a gentle jaunt along the hard sand but fiendishly hard work over longer distances – may be rented in most towns and resorts. The going rate is Rs30–50 per day, and you could be asked to leave a deposit, or even your passport, as **security**. In Panjim, they are rented out at standard Indian (ie non-tourist) rates of Rs2–3 per hour; you may, however, find the capital's anarchic traffic a little too nerve-wracking for comfort. Before peddling off, try the cycle out for size, and make sure the back wheel lock works.

Bringing a bike from abroad requires no special paperwork, and most airlines allow you to take cycles at no extra cost. However, spare parts and accessories are invariably of different sizes and standards in Goa, and you may have to improvise. Bring basic spares and tools, and a pump. Panniers are the obvious thing for carrying your gear, but inconvenient when not attached to your bike, and you might consider sacrificing ideal load-bearing and streamlining technology for a backpack you can lash down on the rear carrier.

Taxis and car rental

It's much more usual for tourists in Goa to be driven than to drive: car rental firms generally operate on the basis of supplying chauffeur-driven vehicles, while taxis are available at cheap daily rates.

Japanese six-seater Maruti mini-vans are the most common type of **taxi** nowadays, but you'll also come across plenty of Hindustan Ambassadors – the classic Indian

automobile based on the old British Morris Oxford. In larger towns, taxis queue at ranks; elsewhere, they tend to hang around outside the upmarket hotels. **Rates**, even for short journeys, are always negotiable (there are no metered taxis in Goa), so ask a member of staff in your hotel reception what the correct fare should be before setting off.

For longer sightseeing trips, you can either engage a taxi *wallah* yourself, or arrange a car in advance through your hotel. **Self-drive** is also now available in Goa, though the service seems to be intended more for middle-class Indians out to impress their friends and relatives than tourists. You will, in any case, be a lot safer if you leave the driving to someone more at home with the state's racetrack rules of the road. If you're willing to risk it, try one of the following, who all have desks at Dabolim airport (see p.173): Hertz ☎0832/222 3998; Sai Service ☎0832/251 4817; and Wheels ☎0832/222 4304. Rates for 24hr/150km range from around \$55 for a no-frills non-a/c Ambassador or Maruti to double that for an air-conditioned Ford. Remember that you need a valid international driver's licence to drive in Goa.

Motorcycle taxis and auto-rickshaws

Goa's unique pillion-passenger **motorcycle taxis**, often referred to as "pilots", are ideal for nipping between beaches or into town from the resorts. Bona fide operators ride black bikes (usually Enfields) with yellow mudguards and white number plates. Fares should be settled in advance, and rarely amount to more than Rs40 for about a twenty-minute trip. Apart from buses, this is the cheapest form of public transport in Goa.

That most Indian of vehicles, the **auto-rickshaw** is the front half of a motor scooter with a couple of seats mounted on the back. Cheaper than taxis, better at zipping in and out of traffic, and usually metered (though you'll have to insist), auto-rickshaws are a little unstable and their drivers often rather reckless, but that's all part of the fun.

In Goa, auto-rickshaws are painted black and yellow, and licensed rickshaw *wallahs* are obliged to wear a regulation-issue khaki-coloured jacket. However, the fares are far from uniform, and you'll have to haggle before you arrive at a reasonable rate. As a rule of thumb, Rs25 should take you just about anywhere in Panjim, Margao and Mapusa. For longer rides, motorcycle taxis are much quicker and better value.

Ferries

If auto-rickshaws are the quintessentially Indian mode of transport, flat-bottomed **ferries** are their Goan equivalent. Crammed with cars, buses, commuters on scooters, fisherwomen and clumps of bewildered tourists, these rusting blue-painted hulks provide an essential service, crossing the coastal backwaters where bridges have not yet been built. They're also incredibly cheap (a couple of pence/cents one-way), and run from the crack of dawn to late in the evening.

Among the most frequented river crossings in Goa are: Panjim to Betim, across the Mandovi (every 15min); Old Goa to Divar Island (every 15min); Divar to Naroa (every 20–30min); Querim to Terekol, over the Tiracol River (every 30min); and Cavelossim in southern Salcete to Assolna (every 20–30min), for Cape Rama and Quepem. A **launch** also chugs across Mormugao Bay between Vasco da Gama's harbour and Dona Paula (four daily). However, this and most other services are frequently disrupted during the monsoons, between August and October, when the rivers flood.

Trains

Many travellers arriving in Goa from Mumbai or South India do so by **train**, but if you fly direct and do not venture outside the state you may well never need to catch one.

The **Konkan Railway** line runs daily express trains from Goa to Mumbai (as well as south into Karnataka and Kerala). **Fares** for the twelve-hour journey to the Maharashtran capital start at Rs275 for standard sleeper class, rising to Rs1225 for II class a/c or Rs2310 for luxurious I class a/c. However, these services are not always available at short notice from the booking halls at Margao station and the Kadamba bus stand in Panjim. If you're certain of your travel dates in advance, consider **booking**

online (at ⊕www.konkanrailway.com). There are downsides with this – you're only entitled to relatively expensive three-tier a/c fares (Rs1250 one-way) and must make your booking between two and seven days before your date of departure – but all in all, online reservation is much the most convenient way to secure a seat.

In addition to the coastal line, a recently upgraded broad-gauge track runs east from Mormugao harbour, near Vasco da Gama, towards the interior, via Margao, linking up with the main Mumbai–Bangalore network on the far side of the Western Ghat mountains. The main reason you might wish to use it would be to visit **Hampi**, in Karnataka; more details of this service appear on p.221.

Tours and cruises

GTDC operates guided bus **tours** out of Panjim and major coastal resorts to sights around the state. The itineraries, however, cover too much ground in too little time, and are somewhat rushed for most people. Those offered as **optional excursions** by package tour companies and large hotels, on the other hand, tend to be conducted at a more civilized pace, although they're very expensive by Goan standards. Details of tour options from different towns and resorts appear throughout the Guide section.

Backwater **cruises** along the Mandovi River from Panjim are a kind of aquatic equivalent of GTDC's bus tours. Once again, these tend to be more popular among domestic than foreign tourists, although the only "sights" to speak of, given that most take place after dark, are the troupes of dancers and musicians who accompany the cruises with Konkani folk tunes and hits from Hindi films. A more detailed rundown of launch trips from Panjim features on p.73.

Boat trips from the coastal resorts are popular among foreign tourists. Billed as "dolphin-spotting" or "crocodile-watching" cruises, they usually last all day and the price includes meals, drinks and transport to and from your hotel or designated pick-up point. Competition among the operators is stiff, but the fares (invariably advertised in pounds sterling to make them seem better value than they actually are) put these tours well beyond the reach of most Indian pockets. However, some will think it well worth shelling out for a luxury cruise on the British-built catamaran Viva-Fiesta, or its sister ship, Precious Dragon, a genuine Chinese junk imported from Hong Kong, which run daily trips along the north Goan coast. For more details, see p.133.

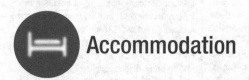

Accommodation

There are a vast number of beds for tourists in Goa, and most of the year you can rely on turning up pretty much anywhere and finding a room – if not in a hotel, then in a more modest guesthouse. Only in December and January, the state's high season, are you likely to experience problems. At this time, it is worth arriving at each new place early in the day, and taking whatever is available in the hope that you will be able to exchange it for something better later on.

Costs vary enormously, depending on the level of comfort offered, but also the time of year and resort. Outside peak season it always pays to haggle a little over the tariff, especially if you intend to stay for more than a week. Rent a room or house for upwards of a month, with an advance cash payment, and a thirty to fifty percent reduction on the quoted daily rate shouldn't be out of the question.

Inexpensive rooms

Budget accommodation in Goa, catering mainly for backpacking tourists, ranges from

Accommodation price codes

All **accommodation prices** in this book are coded using the symbols below. The codes refer to the **cheapest double room** in **high season** (Nov to mid-Dec & mid-Jan to March), but not the peak period around Christmas, when hoteliers charge what they think they can get away with. Where hotels have a range of room options available this is shown by a spread of codes. Local taxes have been included in each case, unless specifically stated otherwise.

❶ up to Rs150. Very basic rooms in family houses.

❷ Rs150–300. Bottom of the attached bathroom bracket, usually with a small verandah or balcony.

❸ Rs300–500. Modest but comfortable guesthouse accommodation.

❹ Rs500–700. Swish by Indian standards, with bathroom en suite, verandah and a quiet fan.

❺ Rs700–1000. Upper mid-range hotel accommodation, with room service and a fridge.

❻ Rs1000–1500. Immaculate Western-style hotel room, satellite TV, fridge and air conditioning. Some four-star hotels fall into this bracket.

❼ Rs1500–2000. Luxurious centrally air-conditioned rooms that come with most mod cons, including access to a pool.

❽ Rs2000–3000. Grander than the previous category, but with essentially the same levels of comfort

❾ Rs3000 and upwards. Top-notch five-star style: ritzy rooms, a choice of restaurants, coffee shop, sports facilities, pool, lawns, shopping and in-house travel agent.

grim concrete cells to large rooms in cosy family-run guesthouses. Naturally, the further off the beaten track you get, the cheaper the accommodation; it's most expensive in Panjim, where prices are typically between 25 and 50 percent higher than elsewhere. In the more popular resorts such as Calangute and Baga, room rates may double in peak season. At other times, however, Rs200–300 should buy you a decent double room with a fan, window and attached shower-toilet. Cold taps and "bucket baths" are the order of the day – not really a problem in the Goan climate – and it's always wise to check the state of the bathroom and toilet before parting with any money.

In more remote villages, accommodation usually consists of bare rooms in modest family houses. Washing water generally comes from the well, and **toilets** are small outhouses that the local pigs keep clean by eating human waste products, alleviating the need for sewers. Conditions like these may be more rudimentary than what you're used to, but they are usual for most Goans, and, more importantly, place a much lighter burden on the fragile coastal ecology than do water-intensive Western-style hotels.

Local opposition to construction in villages such as Palolem in the south and Arambol in the north has created an accommodation shortage which some entrepreneurial villagers have got around by building Thai-style **palm-leaf** and **bamboo huts**, sometimes referred to as "tents". These are erected in November and taken down again before the onset of the monsoons. While some offer nothing more than scant shelter, others are equipped with comfortable wooden beds, fans, electric light and mosquito nets; the latter variety cost as much as, if not more than, equivalent-sized rooms during high season, but tend to be crammed far too close together, providing little privacy. Washing and toilet facilities in "tent camps" may also be far more basic than you'd expect for the price; if this is likely to bother you, check out the toilets (and their ratio to the number of huts) before you agree to stay.

Mid-range hotels

Mid-range hotels in the Western mould, with reception areas, room service and a restaurant, nowadays account for the bulk of Goa's accommodation. Rooms in such places are frequently booked up en bloc by European package companies, forcing up their tariffs. However, a large number still rely mainly on walk-in customers, and have kept their prices competitive. A spacious room, freshly made bed, fan, your own spotless (usually "sit-down") toilet, balcony and hot and cold running water can cost as little as Rs450 (around £6/$10). Extras that bump up the price include satellite TV, fridges and, above all, **air conditioning**. Abbreviated in this book (and in Goa itself) as a/c, air conditioning is not necessarily the advantage you might expect – in some hotels you can find yourself paying double for a system that is so dust-choked, wheezy and noisy as to preclude any possibility of sleep – but providing it is what seems to entitle some hotels to consider themselves mid-range.

Upmarket hotels

Most of Goa's upmarket hotels fall into one of two categories: slick modern establishments pitched at business travellers and wealthy Westerners, or luxury international-style resort complexes catering for package tourists and rich Indians from Mumbai and Bangalore. While the former are confined to the state capital, Panjim, the latter crop up in all but the most remote coastal villages.

Inevitably, the star resorts are nearly always situated on or within easy walking distance of a beach, usually amid well-watered lawns and with their own restaurants, coffee shops and sports facilities. If you haven't booked your room through a package firm, though, you'll pay through the nose for it. **Rates** for walk-in customers, though very reasonable compared with similar places in Europe, the States and Australia, are staggeringly expensive by Indian standards, starting at around Rs2500. Note that prices are often quoted in, and you are expected to pay in, US dollars.

Long-term rentals

Houses are often rented by the month, or season. If you can get two or three people to share costs, and want to put down roots in a village or coastal resort, this is an option worth considering. However, the best places in settlements such as Anjuna, Chapora and Arambol – the established hangouts of long-staying travellers – tend to be snapped up well in advance of the season by visitors who return to the same house year after year. Seasonal lets also tend to be unfurnished, and you'll probably have to shell out on mattresses, locks and cooking equipment; these can be resold before you leave.

To arrange rental, find a village where you want to stay and ask around. Rents vary from village to village, but you can usually pick something up in October or November for Rs5000–9000 per month. Obviously, the more money you can pay up front and the longer you intend to stay, the less the house should cost.

Eating and drinking

In keeping with the Konkani proverb *"prodham bhookt, magi mookt"* ("you can't think until you've eaten well"), food and drink are taken very seriously in Goa. They are also prepared and consumed at a typically laid-back pace, and you can expect to spend at least a couple of hours each day lounging at a table, whether in a sand-blown beach bar or on a palm-shaded restaurant terrace. Indeed, meal times may well provide some of the most memorable moments of your trip: there can be few better ways to savour those legendary sunsets, for example, than over a freshly grilled sharkfish steak, washed down with a bottle of ice-cool beer or a long *feni*.

Nor are such gastronomic delights likely to dent your budget. The overwhelming majority of eateries in Goa are simple palm-thatch **beach shacks**, where a slap-up fish supper will set you back around Rs150 (£2.50/$4). While more established resorts like Calangute, Candolim and Colva boast a clutch of swanky shacks – complete with tablecloths, candles and expensive sound systems – the majority are small, family-run places built at the beginning of each season with palm leaves and bamboo. Service in these more modest outfits can be unbelievably slow and fixtures rudimentary, but the food is usually fresh and tasty, and the staff sociable.

Aware that the shacks deservedly do a much brisker trade than their restaurants, some hotel owners have gone out of their way to make life difficult for owners of popular beach cafés. At the very least, the staff in your hotel will probably try to dissuade you from eating on the beach, telling you the shacks are unhygienic.

Bowing to pressure from the influential hoteliers' lobby, the local government has

> For a glossary of Goan and Indian food see Language, p.341.

done little to alleviate the shack owners' problems. On the contrary, quick to spot a lucrative source of *baksheesh*, it recently introduced a **lottery system** for beach shacks whereby anyone wishing to run one has to make an application, which is put into a hat. A set number of forms are then drawn, and the applicants invited to pay a large sum (Rs20,000–35,000) to the government for one season's licence. The trouble is, as anyone can apply, regardless of their fitness to run a beach bar-restaurant, hundreds of people who have absolutely no intention of doing so put in applications. If their form is drawn, they pay for a permit and resell it for ten times or more what they paid. Quite apart from depriving low-income families who've run beach shacks for years of their livelihood, the lottery system has also lowered standards, as shack owners seek to recoup ever greater licence fees or pay-offs by reducing the size of portions or cutting back on staff.

Most **upmarket restaurants** tend to be air-conditioned, marble-lined halls or poolside terraces in four- or five-star hotels; expect to pay in excess of Rs350 (£5/$8) for an attentively served three-course meal. Standards and choice in this bracket have increased considerably over the past couple of years with the arrival of expatriate European chefs and restaurateurs in many of the busier resorts. As a result, you can enjoy gourmet French, Italian and German food at a fraction of what comparable meals would cost back home. The only catch is that foreigners rarely seem to last more than three or four seasons in Goa, handing their restaurants on to successors who often fail to live up to expectations.

Many eating places state whether they are **vegetarian** or non-vegetarian either on signs outside or at the top of the menu. The terms used in India are **"veg"** and **"non-veg"**, and we have adopted these throughout our eating reviews. You'll also see **"pure veg"**, which means that the food is appropriate for higher-caste Hindus (strictly no eggs, fish or alcohol are served).

Goan food

If you come across a group of locals eating in a village café or roadside *dhaba* (food stall), chances are they'll be tucking into a pile of **fish curry and rice**. Goa's staple dish, eaten twice each day by most of its population, consists of a runny red-chilli sauce flavoured with dried fish or prawns, and served with a heap of fluffy white rice, a couple of small fried sardines and a blob of hot pickle. Cheap and filling, this is mixed into a manageable mush and shovelled down with your fingers, a technique that generally takes Westerners some time (and several messy faces) to master.

Outside the state, Goa is known primarily for its distinctive **meat** specialities. Derived from the region's hybrid Hindu, Muslim and Latin-Catholic heritage, these tend to be flavoured with the same stock ingredients of coconut oil and milk, blended with onions and a long list of spices, including Kashmiri red chillies. The most famous of all Goan dishes, though, has to be **pork vindaloo**, whose very name epitomizes the way Konkani culture has, over time, absorbed

and adapted the customs of its colonial overlords. The dish, misleadingly synonymous in Western countries with any "ultra-hot curry", evolved from a Portuguese pork stew that was originally seasoned with wine (*vinho*) vinegar and garlic (*alho*). To this *vinhdalho* sauce, the Goans added palm sap (*toddi*) vinegar and their characteristic sprinkling of spices. Pork was prohibited by the Muslims, but made a comeback under the Portuguese and now forms an integral part of the Goan diet, particularly on festive occasions such as Christmas, when Christian families prepare **sorpatel**: a rich stew made from the shoulders, neck, kidneys and ears of the pig. Another Portuguese-inspired pork speciality is **leitao**, or suckling pig, which is roasted and stuffed with chopped heart, liver, green chillies and parsley.

Goa is also one of the few places in India where beef is regularly eaten (as steak or minced and baked in pastry "patties"), although you're more likely to be offered chicken simmered in **xacuti** (pronounced "sha-*koo*-tee") sauce. This eye-wateringly hot preparation, traditionally made to revive weary rice planters during the monsoon, was originally vegetarian (in Konkani, *sha* means "vegetable", and *kootee* "cut into small pieces"), but is nowadays more often used to spice up meat of various kinds.

Not surprisingly, **seafood** features prominently in coastal areas. Among the varieties of **fish** you'll encounter are shark, kingfish, *pomfret* (a kind of flounder), mackerel, sardines and various kinds of snapper. These are lightly grilled over wood fires, fried, or baked in clay ovens (*tandoors*), often with a red-hot paste smeared into slits on their sides. The same sauce, known as **rechad**, is sometimes used to cook squid. Shrimps, however, are more traditionally baked in pies with rice-flour crusts (*apas de camarao*), while crab and **lobster** are steamed or boiled and served whole. Another, more affordable, local delicacy which seafood lovers shouldn't miss are **tiger prawns**, which are as tasty and succulent in Goa as anywhere in the world. The same is true of squid (*kalamari*), although it has to be said that Goans tend to overcook it until it is rubbery and tasteless.

Finding **authentic Goan food** can be surprisingly difficult as it is essentially home

Feni

Distilling was first introduced to Goa more than four hundred years ago by Catholic missionaries. While the priests stewed up grape skins to make Portuguese firewater (*aguardente*), however, the locals improvised with more readily available substances such as coconut sap and cashew-fruit juice. The result, refined over the years to a rocket fuel concoction known as **feni** (from the Konkani verb root *fen*, meaning "to froth"), has become the common man's tipple: a crystal-clear spirit that is, according to one aficionado, "to the Goan life what the sky is to a bird: a medium of limitless wonder and potential".

The most common variety of *feni* is made from coconut sap, or **toddi**. Three times each day, the *toddi* tapper shimmies up his individually numbered trees, which he normally rents from the local landlord on a share-crop basis, to release plastic seals bound around new shoots at the heart of the palm. The *toddi* then dribbles into a terracotta pot. At this stage it is slightly sweet, but by the end of the day the liquid becomes cloudy as it starts to ferment. **Urrack**, produced by boiling up the freshly fermented *toddi* and straining it through cotton, is rarely drunk. More often, it is distilled a second time, sometimes with cumin or ginger added as flavouring.

The juice used to make the stronger and more expensive **cashew feni** is squeezed from the yellow fruit of the *caja* tree, brought to Goa from Brazil three hundred years ago by the Portuguese and now the source of the state's principal cash crop, **cashew nuts**. The extraction work was traditionally done by treading the pulp in large wooden barrels; nowadays, though, mechanical presses are more common. Once extracted, the juice is distilled in exactly the same way as its coconut cousin. However, cashew *feni* has a distinctly different taste, sometimes compared to Mexican tequila.

Both types of *feni* may be drunk neat, but you'll find them a lot more palatable diluted with water, soda or a soft drink (Limca and a twist of lemon works wonders with coconut *feni*). A couple of tourist bars in the major resorts also offer pleasant *feni* cocktails (one hotel even advertises cashew *feni* "slammer" nights). If you over-indulge, though, brace yourself for the Mother of All Hangovers the following morning: Goa's trademark drink, whatever you disguise it with, is rough stuff.

cooking: few tourist restaurants can hope to match the attention to detail lavished on special feast-day dishes by Goan house-wives, who routinely spend hours grinding fresh spices and coconut together on huge stones in the back garden. Among few places you can be assured of tasting local cuisine at its very freshest and best is *Martins Restaurant* in Betalbatim (see p.197).

For seafood, which has become beyond the reach of most Goans' pockets as the tourist industry has forced up prices, the state's ubiquitous palm-thatch beach cafés offer unbeatable value. Meals in these rough-and-ready places cost a fraction of what you'll pay in a hotel restaurant, and they are invariably fresh and safe, in spite of the signs posted outside many of the star resorts advising residents to steer clear of

them – more because they poach custom than poison punters.

Rice and breads

In tourist restaurants, meat and seafood are generally served with chips and salad, but locally grown short-grain "red" **rice** is the main staple in the villages. In addition, the Portuguese introduced soft wheat-flour **bread rolls**, still made early each morning in local bakeries and delivered by cyclists, who announce their arrival with old-fashioned rubber honkers – one of the quintessential sounds of village Goa. Restaurateurs mis-takenly assume foreign visitors prefer Western-style spongy square loaves, so if you want to try the infinitely tastier indige-nous variety, make a point of asking for **pao** (or *poee* in Konkani).

Another delicious Goan bread to look out for is *sanna*, made from a batter of coconut milk and finely ground rice flour that is leavened with fermenting palm sap (*toddi*). These crumpet-like rolls are steamed and served with pork and other meat dishes because they are great for soaking up spicy Goan gravies.

Desserts and breakfasts

No serious splurge is considered complete without a slice of the state's favourite dessert, **bebinca**. A festive speciality prepared for Christmas, this ten-layered cake, made with a rich mixture of coconut milk, sugar and egg yolks, is crammed with cholesterol, but an absolute must for fans of solid old-fashioned puddings. The same is true of **batica**, another sweet and stodgy coconut cake that is particularly mouthwatering when served straight out of the oven with a dollop of ice cream. If you find yourself in a traditional Goan village over Christmas or during one of the many religious festivals, you may also be lucky enough to taste **dodol**, the most prized of all local sweets. The reason you don't come across this gelatinous delicacy very often is that it requires a phenomenal quantity of fresh coconut milk and time to make. Typically, a team of three women will get through thirty or forty nuts, whose milk is mixed and boiled in a huge pot with slabs of sugar cane for up to six hours without stopping. The goo has to be kept moving so that it congeals evenly, but the result is heavenly. It is traditional for Goans to send *dodol* made from family trees to absent relatives working abroad.

Breakfast is a far more unsophisticated affair, usually consisting of oily omelettes, but you could ask for an **alebele**, a pancake stuffed with fresh coconut and syrup. A healthy tropical fruit salad, steeped in coconut milk and homemade set yoghurt (*curd*), is another great way to start the day. Alternatively, look out for a South Indian canteen, where you can order a crepe-like *masala dosa*, filled with spicy potato and nut, or lighter *idly* (steamed rice cake) with *wada* (doughnut-shaped, deep-fried lentil cake) dipped in fiery *sambar* sauce and

subje (white coconut chutney). The majority of Goans, however, habitually start the day with **baji-pao**, a small plate of vegetables stewed in a spicy, coconut-based sauce, into which is dunked a fresh bread roll, washed down with filter coffee. At breakfast time, *baji-pao* joints also invariably offer hot samosas, triangles of deep-fried maize flour stuffed with spicy potato and peas, and *batata-wada*, balls of potato masala rolled in light batter and fried. You'd be hard pushed to spend Rs20 on a Goan breakfast like this.

Indian food

For those who get fed up with Goan-style fish and chips, **Indian** food is the next best option. Don't, however, expect the same kind of cooking you find in English-Indian curry houses. Curry is actually something of a misnomer. The word, which in India is used to describe one particular aromatic herb (the *corri* leaf), denotes a wide range of dishes, each made with its own characteristic blend of spices, or *masala*.

As in most parts of the world, different regions of the subcontinent have produced their own distinctive cuisines, and mid-range and upmarket restaurants in Goa invariably serve a representative cross-section of these. In the town, you'll also come across a scattering of cheaper, smaller **South Indian**-style snack bars. Vegetarians, in particular, will find these **udipi** or "**tiffin**" **restaurants** a welcome sight, as the food they prepare is always "pure veg". The quintessential South Indian snack is the *masala dosa*, a large crispy pancake made with rice flour and stuffed with a spicy potato concoction. It is usually dished up on large tin trays, together with a small splodge of *chatni* (ground coconut and yoghurt flavoured with mustard seeds and tamarind) and *sambar* (a spicy, watery gravy). The same side dishes also accompany other popular South Indian snacks, such as *uttapams*, thick, soft pancakes made from partially fermented rice flour, and *parotta*, wheat-flour dough rolled into spirals, flattened and then fried in hot oil. At breakfast time, tiffin canteens serve piping hot *idlys*, or steamed rice cakes, while in the afternoon you can usually order a range of deep-fried snacks such as *pakoras*, *samosas* or potato cakes called *boonda* (aka *batata-wada*).

Served between 11.30am and 2.30pm, the main meal of the day, however, is called a **thali**, after the large stainless steel tray on which it is brought to your table. *Thalis* comprise a large pile of rice, four to six different vegetable preparations served in small round cups, a couple of runny sauces or lentil-based *dals*, *chapatis* (unleavened wheat-flour bread cooked on a hot griddle), papadam and *raita* or yoghurt. In the majority of tiffin restaurants, this filling meal will set you back around Rs30–50 (70p/$1).

To sample **North Indian** food at its best, you'll have to head for the upscale hotels, or restaurants such as *Delhi Durbar* in Panjim (see p.78), where the menus are dominated by **Mughlai cooking**. Introduced to the subcontinent by the Persians, refined in the courts of the mighty Moghul emperor and now imitated in Indian restaurants all over the world, northern cuisine is known for its rich cream-based sauces, kebabs, *naan* breads and *pilau* rice dishes delicately flavoured with cloves, almonds, sultanas, cardamom and saffron.

The other popular northern style, elevated to an art form by the notoriously sybaritic Punjabis, is **tandoori**. The name refers to the deep clay oven (*tandoor*) in which the food is cooked. *Tandoori* chicken is marinated in yoghurt, herbs and spices before cooking. Boneless pieces of meat or seafood, marinated and cooked in the same way, are known as *tikka*, and may be served in a medium-strength *masala*, or in a thick butter sauce. They are generally accompanied by *rotis* or *naan* breads, also baked in the *tandoor*.

Non-Indian food

Chinese food is served in most multi-cuisine restaurants, although it tends to be cooked by local chefs and is not what you might call authentic. Still, rice and noodle dishes make a pleasant change, and are easier on the digestive system if you're having stomach problems. The same is true of **Tibetan** food, which you'll find in a couple of established restaurants in Calangute and Candolim, where families of Tibetan refugees have settled.

Western food is also widely available in the resorts. Expensive international-standard hotels often lay on buffets and fussy à la carte menus prepared by foreign-trained chefs. However, a growing number of restaurants in the resorts (chiefly Baga) also rustle up quality pizzas, pasta, lasagne, stroganoff, German bread and cakes, and even full English breakfasts, using imaginatively adapted local ingredients.

Fruit

Lovers of tropical **fruit** will find plenty to get their teeth into in Goa. Lying on the beach, you'll be approached at regular intervals by fruit *wallahs* carrying baskets of bananas, watermelons, oranges, pineapples and, from late March onwards, succulent mangoes. Once you've fixed a price, the fruit is peeled and sliced with a machete. It's safe to eat, but you may want to sluice it over with sterilized water to be doubly sure, especially if the vendor has touched it with his or her left hand (see p.49).

Fresh **coconuts** are the healthiest fruit of all. Their milk and meat are chock-full of vitamins, and a fair-sized nut will tide you over between breakfast and supper time if you're marooned on the beach. Itinerant vendors usually carry a couple, but in more off-track areas you're better off asking a *toddi* tapper to cut you one straight from the tree. Goans prefer to eat young green nuts, whose flesh is softer and milk sweeter. The top is hacked off and two holes punctured with the tip of a machete: you can drink the milk through these or with a straw. Afterwards, the fruit *wallah* or *toddi* tapper will crack the nut open so you can scoop out the meat.

Among the less familiar fruit, the *chickoo*, which looks like a kiwi and tastes a bit like a pear, is worth a mention, as is the watermelon-sized jackfruit, whose green exterior encloses sweet, slightly rubbery segments, each containing a seed. Papayas are also sold at most markets, and green custard apples crop up in fruit sellers' baskets, although you'll probably need to be shown how to peel away their knobbly skins to expose the sweet yellow fruit inside.

Drinks

BASICS | Eating and drinking

With bottled water, tea and coffee widely available, you may have no need of **soft drinks**. These have long been surprisingly controversial in India. Coca Cola and Pepsi have recently made comebacks, after being banned from the country for seventeen years – a policy originally instigated to prevent the expatriation of profits by foreign companies. Since the return of the cola giants, militant Hindu groups have made them the focus of a new boycott campaign against multinational consumer goods. The absence of Coke and Pepsi also spawned a host of Indian copies such as Campa (innocuous), Thumbs Up (almost undrinkable), Gold Spot (sickly sweet fizzy orange), and Limca (rumoured to have connections with Italian companies, and to include additives banned there). All contain a lot of sugar, but little else: adverts for Indian soft drinks have been known to boast "Absolutely no natural ingredients!".

You may choose to quench your thirst with straight **water** (treated, boiled or bottled; see also p.23), or brands of sweetened **fruit juice**: Frooti is debatably the best of these. If the carton looks at all mangled, though, it is best not to touch it as it may have been recycled. Duke's mango drink, which comes in a clear glass bottle like Coca Cola, is also worth a try, and is most refreshing when mixed with soda.

Goa's greatest cold drink, however, has to be **lassi** – a mixture of curd and water that is drunk with sugar, salted or mixed with fruit. It varies widely from smooth and delicious to insipid and watery, and is sold at virtually every café, restaurant and canteen in the state. In addition, freshly made **milkshakes** are commonly available at establishments with blenders. They'll also sell you what they call a **fruit juice**, but which is usually fruit, water and sugar (or salt) liquidized and strained. With all such drinks, as appetizing as they may seem, you should exercise great caution before deciding to drink them: try to find out where the water came from first.

Alcohol

Drinking **alcohol** is not the shameful activity it is in most other parts of India. Indeed, the easy availability and low cost/tax-free status of beers and spirits in Goa contribute in no small part to the state's popularity with domestic tourists: busloads of bar crawlers from neighbouring Karnataka and Maharashtra pour in on Saturdays and Sundays to take advantage of the liberal liquor laws. The flip side, however, is that the more frequented beaches tend to be plagued by gangs of drunks at weekends and public holidays; the state also has more than 60,000 registered alcoholics – ten times the national average.

Beer is consumed in vast quantities. The biggest-selling brand, emblematic of Goa, is the local brand Kingfisher ("Most Thrilling Chilled!"), but Kings is also drinkable, and San Miguel (brewed under licence in Bombay and nowhere near as good as its Spanish namesake) is also ubiquitous, although more expensive. The slightly bitter and unpleasant aftertaste in all Indian beers is caused by **glycerine**, a preservative which you can remove by pressing your middle finger over the mouth of the bottle and turning it upside down in a glass of water: when you remove your finger under water, the glycerine, which is heavier, will flow out of the bottle into the glass.

Few visitors acquire a taste for the traditional Goan tipple, **feni**, but locally produced spirits, known by the acronym IMFL (Indian-made Foreign Liquors), are generally palatable when mixed with soda or some kind of soft drink. Dozens of types of whisky are sold in bars, alongside Indian gin, vodka, rum and brandy; stick to big-name brands (such as Honeybee brandy and Old Monk rum) and you shouldn't go far wrong.

In addition to spirits, Goa produces several varieties of **wine**, including a popular sparkling medium dry known as Vinho Espumoso, or Vinicola. You can buy this and other brands such as Grover, imported from the Bangalore area and reputedly the best wine produced in India, in large general stores in Panjim, Mapusa and Margao, and in most upscale restaurants, but they tend to be expensive and poor value for money by comparison with prices and standards in most European countries (UK included). The same applies to Goan **port**.

Communications and the media

There is no need to be out of touch with the rest of the world while you're in Goa. The mail service is pretty reliable (if a little slow), international phone calls are surprisingly easy and Internet/email facilities are available everywhere. In addition, there are a number of decent English-language newspapers, and more people and places than you might imagine have access to English-language satellite TV.

Mail services

Mail can take anything from six days to three weeks to get to or from Goa, depending on where you are and the country you are mailing to; ten days is about the norm. Most **post offices** are open Monday to Friday 10am–5pm and Saturday 10am–noon, but town GPOs keep longer hours, usually Mon–Sat 9.30am–1pm & 2–5.30pm. **Stamps** are not expensive, but you'll have to stick them on yourself as they tend not to be self-adhesive (every post office keeps a pot of evil-smelling glue for this purpose). You can also buy stamps at some big hotels. Aerogrammes and postcards cost the same to anywhere in the world. Ideally, you should also have mail franked in front of you; stamps are sometimes peeled off and resold by unscrupulous clerks.

Poste restante services throughout the state are pretty reliable, though exactly how long individual offices hang on to letters is largely at their own discretion; for periods of longer than a month, it makes sense to ensure your mail is marked with your expected date of arrival. Letters are filed alphabetically; in larger offices, you sort through them yourself. To avoid misfiling, your name should be printed clearly, with the surname in large capitals and underlined, but it is still a good idea to check under your first name too, just in case. Have letters addressed to you c/o Poste Restante, GPO (if it's the main post office you want), and the name of the town and state. Don't forget to take ID with you to claim your mail. The American Express office in Panjim also keeps mail for holders of their charge card or traveller's cheques. Having **parcels** sent to you in Goa is not a good idea, as they often go astray. If you do have one sent, get it registered.

Sending a parcel from Goa can be a performance. First take it to a tailor and agree a price to have it wrapped in cheap cotton cloth (which you may have to buy yourself), stitched up and sealed with wax. Next, take it to the post office, fill in and attach the relevant customs forms (it's best to tick the box marked "gift" and give its value as less than Rs1000 or "no commercial value", to avoid bureaucratic entanglements), buy your stamps, see them franked and dispatch it. Parcels should not be more than a metre long, nor weigh more than 20kg. Surface mail is incredibly cheap, and takes an average of six months to arrive – it may take half, or four times that, however. It's a good way to dump excess baggage and souvenirs, but don't send anything fragile this way.

As in Britain, North America and Australasia, books and magazines can be sent more cheaply, unsealed or wrapped around the middle, as **printed papers** ("book post"). Remember that all packages from India are likely to be suspect at home, and searched or X-rayed: don't send anything dodgy.

Telephones

Privately run phone offices with **international direct-dialling** facilities are very widespread. Advertising themselves with the acronyms STD/ISD (standard trunk dialling/international subscriber dialling), they are extremely quick and easy to use; some stay open late into the evening. Both national and international calls are dialled direct. If the number takes some time to register, try pressing the star

International calls

To call Goa from abroad, dial the international access code, followed by 91 for India, 832 for Goa, then the number you want.

To call abroad from Goa, dial the international access code (00), followed by the country code, then the area code (minus the initial zero if there is one), then the number you want.

	From India:	To India:
UK	☎00 44	☎00 91
Irish Republic	☎00 353	☎00 91
US and Canada	☎00 1	☎011 91
Australia	☎00 61	☎0011 91
New Zealand	☎00 64	☎00 91

button first, which should switch the set to faster digital mode. Bills are paid at the end when you've finished all your calls.

India is one of the most **expensive** countries in the world from which to make international calls. The per-minute rate for the UK and North America is currently around Rs8, although this may fall if government plans to open the market up to private companies materialize. There are no cheap-rate times for ISD (international) calls. Note that hotels often charge wildly inflated rates for telephone calls.

Home country direct services are now available from any STD/ISD phone to the UK, the USA, Canada, Ireland, Australia, New Zealand and a growing number of other countries. These allow you to make a collect or telephone credit card call to that country via an operator there. If you can't find a phone with home country direct buttons, you can use any phone toll-free, by dialling 000, your country code, and 17 (except Canada which is 000-167).

Alternatively, get the person you're phoning to ring you back (telephoning India from abroad is a lot cheaper than the other way around). Some STD/ISD booths charge Rs3–5 per minute for this service, known as **"call-back"**.

To reduce congestion on the overloaded Indian telephone system, many larger businesses and hotels use several phone numbers, with only the final digit changing. In such cases we've denoted the range of numbers with a dash: ☎123456–9. If you don't get through on the first number (☎123456), work your way through the sequence until you do (☎123457, 123458, 123459).

Mobile phones

Most **mobile phone** network providers offer coverage in India, although unless you've a top-of-the-range package you'll have to contact them to get it switched on; there may be a charge for this. You are also likely to be charged extra for incoming calls or texts when abroad, as the people calling/texting you will be paying the usual rate. To retrieve messages while you're away, ask your provider for a new access code, as your home one won't work in Goa.

For further general information about using your phone abroad, check out ☯www.tele-comsadvice.org.uk/features/using_your_mobile_abroad.htm.

Internet and email

Internet and **email** facilities are accessible to the general public throughout the state, usually at special cybercafés, though many hotels and STD booths offer this service as well. Charges are around Rs20–60 per hour for browsing and email, and extra for printing. Connection speeds vary from place to place, but are generally slow by Western standards. For the fastest connection times, avoid early evenings, Sunday afternoons, and Monday mornings. Power cuts are another constant hassle. When you arrive at a cybercafé check to ensure they have a UPS machine, which powers the computer when the electricity is down. The best ones have batteries lasting up to an hour.

If you're planning to be away from home for more than a fortnight, you may want to set up a **free email** account before you leave. This takes five or ten minutes, costs nothing and allows you to receive electronic mail wherever you are in the world. All you have to pay is the cybercafé's charges after you've finished using their machine. The Hotmail service (@www.hotmail.com) is phenomenally popular, but due to the volume of traffic through this server, smaller Web-based email providers such as Yahoo (@www.yahoo.com) tend to be quicker and less prone to interruptions. To sign up, access the Internet, key in the site address and follow the instructions.

The media

Goa has three English-language daily **newspapers**: the *Navhind Times*, which tends to support the political establishment of the day, and the more independent *Herald* and *Gomantak Times*. These locally published broadsheets all dish up a uniformly dry diet of regional and national news, with very limited coverage of foreign affairs. If you want to read about what's happening in the rest of the world, the international pages of **Indian newspapers** such as the *Times of India*, *Indian Express* or, better still, the *Independent*, are more informative. Alternatively, look for a **foreign paper or magazine**: the *Herald Tribune*, *Time*, *Newsweek*, *Le Monde*, *Der Spiegel,* the *Guardian*, and a range of British tabloids are sold in Panjim's two bookshops (see p.81), and at tourist shops in the major resorts several days after publication.

Anyone keen to learn more about Goan current affairs should also look out for the excellent **monthly magazine** *Goa Today*, which spotlights local issues and features extracts of Goan fiction.

BBC World Service radio can be picked up on short wave, although reception quality is highly variable. The wavelength also changes at different times of the day. In the morning, try 5965Khz (49m/5.95–6.20Mhz) or 9605Khz (31m/9.40– 9.90Mhz); in the afternoon, 9740Khz (31m/9.40–9.90Mhz) or 11750Khz (25m/11.70Mhz). A full list of the World Service's many frequencies appears on the BBC website (@www.bbc.uk/world-service).

The Indian government-run **TV** company Doordarshan, which broadcasts a sober diet of edifying programmes, has found itself unable to compete with the onslaught of mass access to **satellite TV** in Goa, with illegal use of cables ensuring that one satellite dish can serve dozens of homes at an affordable price. The main broadcaster in English is Rupert Murdoch's Star TV network, which incorporates the BBC World Service, the Hindi-film-oriented Zee TV, and a couple of American soap and chat channels.

Festivals and holidays

Goa abounds with all kinds of festivals and holidays – Hindu and Christian, national and local – and the chances of your visit coinciding with one are high. Religious celebrations range from exuberant *Zatras*, when Hindu deities are paraded around their temple compounds in huge wooden chariots, to modest *festas*, celebrating the patron saint of a village church. Secular events are less common, although Carnival, which involves a cast of thousands, is the state's largest cultural event. Christmas also enjoys a high profile: travellers from all over South Asia converge on Goa for the Yuletide revelries, when local people traditionally consume prodigious quantities of pork, sweets and *feni* – the hallmark of most Goan festivals.

While Christian events follow the Gregorian calendar introduced by the Portuguese, the dates of Hindu celebrations vary from year to year according to the lunar cycle, with key rituals reserved for the full-moon (*purnima*) or new-moon (*ama*) periods. However, ascertaining exactly when any given temple is holding its *Zatra* can be difficult. If you're keen to see a major Hindu festival, ask for precise dates at the GTDC tourist office in Panjim, as it arranges transport to most major events for pilgrims.

Public holidays

On **public holidays**, banks and government offices close, but not restaurants or private businesses such as money-changers.

Republic Day (Jan 26). India's national day is marked with military parades and political speeches.

Independence Day (Aug 15). India's largest secular celebration, on the anniversary of its Independence from Britain in 1947.

Mahatma Gandhi's Birthday (Oct 2). A sober commemoration of Independent India's founding father.

Liberation Day (Dec 17). The anniversary of Nehru's expulsion of the Portuguese from Goa in 1961 is a low-key public holiday, with military parades and the occasional air force fly-past.

Christmas Day (Dec 25).

Festivals

Movable dates

Ramadan The start of a month when Muslims may not eat, drink or smoke from sunrise to sunset, and should abstain from sex.

Id-ul-Fitr Muslims' feast to celebrate the end of Ramadan.

January to mid-March

Festa dos Reis (Jan 6). Christians flock to Remedios Hill, Quelim (near Cansaulim, Salcete) for the state's main Epiphany celebration, during which three young boys, decked in brocaded silk and wearing crowns, ride to the hilltop chapel on white horses. Similar processions take place in the Franciscan church at Reis Magos, near Panjim (see p.125), and at Chandor (see p.187).

Bandeira festival (mid-Jan). Emigrant workers from Divar island (see p.104) return home for the local patron saint's day, and march through the village waving the flags of their adopted countries and firing pea shooters.

Shantadurga festival (Jan) A solid silver image of Shantadurga is carried in procession over the hills from Fatorpa to Cuncolim. The event, one of the most famous and well-attended religious festivals in the state, is known as the "Procession of the

Umbrellas" because it is led by twelve colourful umbrellas carried on tall poles by youths smeared with red powder.

Carnival (Feb/March). Three days of *feni*-induced mayhem centring on Panjim (see p.77) marking the run-up to Lent.

Shigmo (Feb/March). Goa's version of the Hindu Holi festival – held over the full-moon period to mark the onset of spring – includes processions of floats, music and dance, in addition to the usual throwing of paint bombs; these can permanently stain clothing, so don't go out in your Sunday best.

Shivratri (Feb/March). Anniversary of Shiva's creation dance (*tandav*), and his wedding day. Big *pujas* are held at Shiva temples all over the state, and many Hindus get high on *bhang* – a milk and sugar preparation laced with ground cannabis leaves.

Mid-March to May

Easter (March/April). Christ's Resurrection is celebrated with fasting, feasting, and High Mass held in chapels and churches across Goa.

Procession of the Saints (March/April). Twenty-six life-size effigies of saints, martyrs, popes, kings, queens and cardinals are paraded around Goa Velha (see p.84) on the first Monday of Easter week. This solemn religious event is accompanied by a lively fun fair.

Our Lady of Miracles (Milagros) (April/May). Mapusa's main church (see p.122) is the venue for a big *tamasha*, or fair, held sixteen days after Good Friday and connected with the Hindu goddess Lairaya, whose worshippers also flock here to pay their respects.

Igitun Chalne (May). *Dhoti*-clad devotees of Lairaya enter trances and walk over hot coals in fulfilment of thanksgiving vows. This famous fire-walking ritual only takes place in Sirigao, Bicholim *taluka*.

Music Festival (May). Local rock, pop and jazz bands strut their stuff at the Kala Academy, Panjim.

June–August

Sanjuan (June 24). The feast day of St John, or Sao Joao (corrupted in Konkani to "Sanjuan"), is celebrated all over Goa, but is particularly important in the coastal villages of Cortalim, Arambol (see p.163) and Terekol (Pernem; see p.167). Youngsters torch straw dummies of "Judeu", representing St John's baptism (and thus the death of sin). In addition, the day includes processions of revellers in striped pants, and lots of drunken diving into wells to retrieve bottles of *feni*.

Sangodd (June 29). Slap-up *sorpatel* (roast pig) suppers mark the *festa* of St Peter, the patron saint of fishers. Boats are tied together to make floating stages on which extravagantly costumed actors and musicians perform traditional dramas for audiences assembled on the river banks. The biggest events take place in the villages of Orda, Saipem and Candolim, Bardez *taluka*.

Ganesh Chaturthi (late June). Giant effigies of the elephant-headed Hindu deity Ganesh, god of peace and prosperity, are displayed in elaborately decorated household and neighbourhood shrines, then taken through the streets to the river or sea for holy dips.

Janmashtami (Aug). Ritual bathing in the Mandovi River off Divar island (see p.104), near Old Goa, to celebrate Krishna's birthday.

September–December

Dusshera (Sept/Oct). A nine-day Hindu festival (usually with a two-day public holiday) associated with Rama's victory over Ravana in the *Ramayana*, and the goddess Durga's over the buffalo-headed Mahishasura. Celebrations include the construction of large effigies, which are burnt on bonfires with

fireworks, and performances of *Ram Lila* ("Life of Rama") by schoolchildren.

Fama (Oct). Colva's miracle-working "Menino Jesus" statue (see p.193), normally locked away in the village church, is exposed to large crowds of pilgrims from all over Goa on the second Monday of October.

Diwali (Oct/Nov). Five-day "festival of lights" to celebrate Rama and Sita's homecoming – an episode in the *Ramayana*. The event features the lighting of oil lamps and firecrackers, the giving and receiving of sweets, and the hanging of paper lanterns outside Hindu houses.

Feast of St-Francis Xavier (Dec 3). Tens of thousands of Catholics file past the tomb of SFX and attend open-air Mass outside. All of Goa turns up, dressed to the nines, at some point in the week-long festival.

Christmas (Dec 24/25). Goan emigrants return home for the state's most important festival, which is celebrated by both Hindus and Christians. *Missa de Galo*, Midnight Mass (literally "cockerel mass" because it sometimes carries on until dawn), marks the start of festivities. Meanwhile, tourist ravers party in Anjuna. Christmas Day is a public holiday.

Cultural hints and etiquette

Cultural differences extend to all sorts of little things. While allowances will usually be made for foreigners, visitors unacquainted with Goan customs may need a little preparation to avoid causing offence or making fools of themselves. The list of dos and don'ts here is hardly exhaustive: when in doubt, watch what the Goan people around you are doing.

Dress

The most common cultural blunder committed by foreign visitors to Goa concerns **dress**. People accustomed to the liberal ways of Western holiday resorts often assume it's fine to stroll around town in beachwear: it isn't, as the numerous stares and giggles that follow tourists who walk through Panjim, Margao or Mapusa shirtless or in a bikini top demonstrate. Ignoring local norms in this way will rarely cause offence, but you'll be regarded as very peculiar. This is particularly true for women (see "Women travellers", p.59), who should keep legs and

breasts well covered in all public places. It's OK for men to wear shorts, but swimming togs are only for the beach, and you shouldn't strip off your shirt, no matter how hot it is. None of this applies to the beach, of course, except in the most remote coastal villages, where local people may not necessarily be used to Western sunbathing habits (see also p.56).

Eating and the right-hand rule

Another minefield of potential faux-pas has to do with **eating**. In Goa (although not, as a rule, in tourist restaurants), this is traditionally done with the fingers, and requires a bit of practice to get absolutely right. Rule one is: eat with your right hand only. In Goa, as right across Asia, the left hand is for wiping your bottom, cleaning your feet and other unsavoury functions (you also put on and take off your shoes with your left hand), while the right hand is for eating, shaking hands and so on.

This rule extends beyond food too. In general, do not pass anything to anyone with your left hand, or point at anyone with it either; and Goans won't be impressed if you put it in your mouth. In general, you should accept things given to you with your right hand – though using both hands is a sign of respect.

The other rule to beware of when eating or drinking is that your lips should not touch other people's food. When drinking out of a cup or bottle to be shared with others, don't let it touch your lips, but rather pour it directly into your mouth. This custom can be difficult to get the hang of, but it protects you from things like hepatitis. It is also customary to wash your hands before and after eating.

Visiting temples and churches

Non-Hindus are welcome to visit Goan **temples**, but you're expected to observe a few simple conventions. The most important of these is to dress appropriately: women should keep their shoulders and legs covered, while men should wear long trousers or *lunghis*. Always remove your shoes at the entrance to the main hall (not the courtyard), and never step inside the doorway to the shrine, which is strictly off limits to everyone except the *pujaris*. Photography is nearly always prohibited inside the temple, but OK around the courtyard. Finally, if there is a passage (*pradakshena*) encircling the shrine, walk around it in a clockwise direction.

It's also always a good idea to dress respectably when visiting **churches**, and to leave a small donation for the upkeep of the building when you leave.

Other possible gaffes

Kissing and embracing are regarded in Goa as part of sex: do not do them in public. It is not even a good idea for couples to hold hands. Be aware, too, of your **feet**. When entering a private home – especially a Hindu one – you should normally remove your shoes (follow your host's example); when sitting, avoid pointing the soles of your feet at anyone. Accidental contact with one's foot is always followed by an apology.

Finally, always ask someone's permission before taking their **photograph**, particularly in or around temples. If you photograph a hawker, flower-seller or any other low-income itinerant vendor on the beach, it is not impolite to offer them a tip.

Meeting people

Like most Indians, Goans are generally very garrulous and enjoy getting to know their visitors. You'll often be quizzed about your background, family, job and income by locals. Questions like these can seem baffling or intrusive to begin with, but such topics are not considered "personal", and it is completely normal to ask people about them. Asking the same things back will not be taken amiss – far from it. Being curious does not have the "nosy" stigma in Goa that it does in the West.

Things that Goans are likely to find strange about you are lack of religion (you could adopt one), travelling alone, being part of an unmarried couple (letting people think you are married can make life easier), and staying in cheap hotels when, as a tourist, you are obviously rich. You will probably end up having to explain the same things many times to many different people; on the other hand, you can ask questions too, so you could take it as an opportunity to ask things you want to know about Goa.

Shopping and souvenirs

The streets and lanes of Goa's coastal resorts are glutted with handicraft boutiques and makeshift market stalls that offer inexhaustible shopping possibilities. You'll also be approached at regular intervals on the beach by hawkers selling everything from tropical fruit and bamboo flutes to head massages and papier-mâché boxes. These migrant vendors travel to the region from other parts of India, spending on average six months camped by the sea before returning home, or heading off to the Himalayan hill stations for the summer. The stuff they sell is generally expensive by Indian standards, but seems amazingly cheap if you arrive directly from Europe.

Where to shop

Deservedly the most famous place to **shop** in Goa is the flea market in **Anjuna** (see p.148). Just about everyone with something to sell – whether a dog-eared paperback or a heavy silver ankle bracelet – makes their way on Wednesday morning to the palm-shaded market ground, which has to be among the most exotic shopping locations in the world. Its only drawback is that the

---

Hawkers

Hawkers are a feature of beach life in all but the most remote resorts these days, and you'll be pestered by a steady stream of them in the course of any day. The large majority are kids from Karnataka, flogging cheap cotton clothes, coconuts and cold drinks, but you'll also come across Kashmiris selling papier-mâché boxes, Rajasthani girls with sacks of dodgy silver jewellery, Tamil stone carvers, buskers, painted bulls led around by their turbaned, oboe-blowing owners, and, most distinctive of all, Lamani tribal women from the Gadag-Hubli-Hampi area, with their coin necklaces, cowrie-shell anklets and rainbow-coloured mirrorwork.

Initially, this parade can be a novel distraction. The hawkers are usually polite and pleasant to chat with; and it is, after all, convenient to have a slice of melon or fresh pineapple cut for you just when you fancy one. Eventually, though, the constant attention will start to wear your patience, and you'll find yourself experimenting with different ways to shake off the hawkers, who, given half the chance, will congregate in tight huddles around you. An "I've-been-here-a-while-already" tan helps, as does feigning sleep or burying yourself in a book. Failing that, a stern shake of the head or wave of the hand should send the vendor on his or her way. Occasionally, however, one comes along who won't take no for an answer, in which case you'll either have to buy something (which will inevitably attract every other hawker on the beach) or else start shouting – neither of which is likely to bring you much peace and quiet the following day.

The best ploy if you're going to spend much time on the same beach is to hook up with one or two hawkers, and always do "beesness" with them; that way, the others will more often than not leave you alone. And in case you start losing your temper, remember that the hawkers live off the few rupees' mark-up they make on the stuff they sell; they're not here out of choice, but from economic necessity. Most are either landless peasants fleeing poverty in the countryside, or else refugees from exploitative labour on construction sites and brick works in the cities. They may also have a hard time working the beaches in Goa, regularly getting beaten up by the police (hawking is technically illegal in the state), or for not paying *baksheesh* to local shack owners.

prices tend to be high, but mostly because of the mad money some tourists are prepared to part with for trinkets.

If you miss the flea market, you'll find virtually the same assortment of stalls in **Mapusa** on Friday mornings (see p.122). This weekly bazaar is also more typically Goan, with fish, fruit, vegetables and other fresh produce sold alongside tourist goods.

In addition, souvenirs are sold on the **beaches** by itinerant hawkers, a large percentage of whom seem barely old enough to walk let alone haggle. Conducted at an unhurried pace in the shade of an old fishing boat, buying and selling can be a sociable pastime, although make one purchase and you'll be bothered non-stop by bands of other hopeful hawkers.

The kind of **places not to shop** if you are bargain hunting are the posh Kashmiri handicraft boutiques, particularly those located in, or near, an upmarket hotel: you can pick the same stuff up at the flea market at fairer prices. Also, avoid going anywhere near a shop with a taxi driver. Cabbies in Goa make most of their money from emporiums who pay them **commission** for bringing customers, and then a percentage of the money they subsequently spend there. This, of course, is added on to the cost of whatever you're buying.

Bargaining

Wherever you shop (with the exception of general stores), you will almost always be expected to **haggle**. Bargaining is very much a matter of personal style, but should always be lighthearted, never acrimonious. There are no hard and fast rules – it's really a question of how much something is worth to you. It's a good plan, however, to have an idea of how much you want to pay.

Don't worry too much about initial prices. Some people suggest paying a half or less of the opening price, but it's a flexible guideline depending on the shop, the goods and the shopkeeper's impression of you. You may not be able to get the seller much below the first quote; on the other hand, you may end up paying as little as a tenth of it – this is particularly true of beach hawkers. If you bid too low, you may be hustled out of the shop for offering an "insulting" price (a

typically Kashmiri ploy), but this is all part of the game, and you will no doubt be welcomed as an old friend if you return the next day.

Don't start haggling for something if in fact you know you don't want it, and never let any figure pass your lips that you are not prepared to pay. It's like bidding at an auction. Having mentioned a price, you are obliged to pay it. If the seller asks you how much you would pay for something, and you don't want it, then say so. And never go shopping with a tout, who will get a commission on anything you buy, which means a higher price to you.

What to buy

Just about the only thing souvenirs on sale in Goa these days have in common is that they nearly all come from India, manufactured for the tourist market in other parts of the country and imported by the traders who sell them. Nor do you often come across bona fide Goan goods, or articles that aren't available in some form back home. The one consolation is that everything costs a lot less than it does in London or New York.

Goan goods

Goans generally lack the competitive business edge of their Indian neighbours, and thus tend to leave souvenir selling to migrant vendors from out of state. This, in part, explains the dearth of authentically **Goan souvenirs** on offer in the resorts. You can, however, pick up some exportable local produce. The most ubiquitous speciality on offer is **cashew nuts** – the state's number one cash crop. They come in a variety of sizes, whether salted, dry-roasted, loose or packaged.

The other typically Goan souvenir is a bottle of **feni** (see p.44), widely available in bars and liquor stores, or through your guesthouse owner: the best stuff is distilled in the coastal villages and kept for local consumption.

Karnatakan goods

Among the most distinctive souvenirs are those touted by the Lamanis, an ethnic

Hunt for traditional handicrafts in Goa and you'll sadly find little more than the odd shell lampshade collecting dust in the lobby of a government hotel. This paucity of local handicrafts is largely attributable to the persecution of indigenous arts during the Portuguese era, when those Goan artists not employed making fittings and furniture for opulent stately homes fled the region.

One isolated pocket of consummate craftsmanship lies 15km north of the Goan border in the Maharashtran town of **Sawantwadi**. In the Darbar ("Audience") Hall of the local maharaja's palace, surrounded by old weapons, hunting trophies and a bust of Queen Victoria, a handful of ageing artists are all that survives of a once thriving lacquerware industry based on the production of traditional Indian **playing cards**, or **ganjifa**. Unlike their counterparts in Western countries, different types of packs come in different sized suits: eight (known as "Moghul", or *Changkanchan* in Konkani); nine (*Navagraha*, after the "nine planets" frequently enshrined in Hindu temples); ten (*Dasavatara*, after the God Vishnu's "ten incarnations"); twelve (*Rashi*, after the signs of the zodiac), and even sixteen or 24 in the eastern Indian state of Orissa. The mythological and astrological themes also provide the subject matter for the *ganjifa's* rich decoration, meticulously hand-painted according to designs that have been passed down through generations.

Sawantwadi is one of very few places in India where *ganjifa* are still made. Up until the last century, several families in the village were employed manufacturing them, but by 1959, when the local maharaja decided to revive the lacquer industry in the town, only one man could be found who still painted cards (at a rate of two packs per year). Today, four men work full time producing *ganjifa*, in addition to chess sets, board games and furniture, but the art form is definitely in decline. Most of what they make is exported for sale in other parts of the country or abroad; the sheer amount of time needed to paint a full pack puts the cards beyond the pocket of most Indians.

For foreign tourists, however, a set of *ganjifa* makes a beautiful, and affordable, souvenir. Painted in vibrant reds, saffrons and blues, the cards feature ocean-churning tortoises, man-lions, sacred boars, dwarves, axe-wielding or elephant-headed gods, princes and winged griffons, to name but a few of the designs drawn from Hinduism's weird pantheon. Most packs cost in the range of Rs750–950, although the most elaborate sell for Rs2650.

As little of Sawantwadi's produce finds its way to Goa, to purchase any you'll have to travel up there yourself, which you can do by train (the town lies on the Konkan Railway), or by taxi. Either way, it is advisable to arrange a visit in advance through Sawantwadi Lacquerwares, at The Palace, Sawantwadi, Maharashtra 416510 (☎02363/72010). When you arrive, look for the lake in the middle of town; the palace lies on its eastern shore, accessed via an imposing gateway and long drive.

Photographs of Sawantwadi *ganjifa* appear on the website of the International Playing Card Society at ⓦwww.pagat.com/ipcs/pattern/.

group from **Karnataka**. Easily recognizable by their multicoloured tribal garb, these hawkers are members of a semi-nomadic low-caste minority who traditionally lived by transporting salt across the Deccan Plateau. These days, the women and girls make most of the family money through the sale of **textiles** and cheap **jewellery**, carefully tailored for the tourist trade. Their rainbow cloth, woven with geometric designs and inlaid with cowrie shells or fragments of mirror and mica, is fashioned into shoulder bags, caps and money belts. Their jewellery, however, is more traditional, made with coral beads, old Indian coins and low-grade silver. If you haggle hard and can put up with all the shouting and tugging that inevitably accompanies each purchase, you can usually pick up this Karnatakan stuff at bargain prices.

Kashmiri goods

Forced to leave their homeland after the ongoing political unrest there killed off most of the tourist traffic, the **Kashmiris** are the most assiduous traders in Goa. If you get dragged into one of their shops, chances are it's a **carpet** they really want to sell you. Kashmiri rugs are among the best in the world, and you can get yourself one at a decent price in Goa (though you can also get ripped off if you're not careful). A pukka Kashmiri carpet should have a label on the back stating that it's made in Kashmir, what it's made of (wool, silk or "silk touch" – wool combined with a little cotton and silk to give it a sheen), its size, density of knots per square inch (the more the better), and the name of the design. To tell if it really is silk, scrape the carpet with a knife and burn the fluff – real silk shrivels to nothing and has a distinctive smell. Even producing the knife should cause the seller of a bogus silk carpet to demur.

The best way to make sure a carpet reaches home is to take it away and post it yourself; a seller may offer to post it to you and bill you later, which is fair enough, but be aware that your carpet will be sent immediately, whatever you say, and if you use a credit card, your account will also be billed immediately, whatever is said.

The Kashmiris' other specialities are **leather clothes**, Himalayan **curios** and lacquered **papier-mâché**, which they make into pots, fussy little boxes and even baubles for Christmas trees. The most relaxed places to check out the full range are the Anjuna flea market or Mapusa's Friday-morning market; venture into one of their little shops and you'll find it difficult to get out.

Other goods

The **Tibetans'** central Asian features look almost as foreign in Goa as those of their Western customers, but these laid-back Himalayan traders have carved out a niche for themselves in the resorts selling reproduction Buddhist **curios**. Their other stock in trade is **silver jewellery**, which is sold by weight. In principle, the price per gram is fixed (Tibetans claim they hate haggling), but in practice you can usually knock down the rate, which also varies according to how elaborate the piece is, and how much turquoise, coral or lapis lazuli has been added to it. However, the prices of **Himalayan handicrafts**, the Tibetans' other line, are generally more flexible. Whatever they tell you, though, none of the prayer wheels, brass Buddhas, *tsampa* bowls or *thangkas* (religious paintings on cloth) are antiques, and few actually come from the mountains: most are made in refugee camps in Old Delhi.

Browsing Anjuna or Mapusa market, you'll come across the odd apprentice stone carver from South India, taking time out to flog miniature **devotional statues**. These make great souvenirs, but they don't always come cheap: even a small piece cut from malleable soapstone takes hours of painstaking work. However, they also do a brisk trade in more affordable *trompe l'oeil* pendants. Touted as lucky talismans, these usually take the form of small Shiva faces which, when turned upside down or flipped over, look the same. Also worth keeping an eye open for are **woodcarvings** of gods from the South Indian state of Kerala; ones of the elephant-headed deity Ganesh, god of peace and prosperity and the overcomer of obstacles, are always a favourite.

Handicrafts from the western Indian states of **Gujarat** and **Rajasthan** crop up in most souvenir shops. Beautiful block-printed and appliqué bed covers are this region's forte, along with miniature paintings and elaborate mirrorwork textiles. You may also be shown gemstones from Jaipur, and elaborate silver jewellery, although it's never easy to tell fakes from the genuine articles.

Anjuna's flea market is awash with **clothes** made and sold by the village's transient Western population. These look a lot less incongruous on a Goan beach than back home, but are popular with tourists keen to kit themselves out for the big beach parties. **Rave gear** in drug-inspired, day-glo colours features prominently, as do dresses and shirts fashioned from Balinese batiks, and woven or mirrorwork waistcoats. Anjuna is also the place to pick up those trendy wrap-around Thai trousers you see everywhere, along with *tangas*, the G-strings beloved of posey racketball players.

Crime and personal security

While the vast majority of visitors to Goa never encounter any trouble, tourist-related crime is definitely more prevalent than in any other parts of the country. Theft is the most common problem – usually of articles left unattended on the beach or in rented houses. Don't assume your valuables are safe in a padlocked room, either. Break-ins, particularly on party nights, are on the increase in the main resorts.

Most people carry their passports and traveller's cheques in concealed money belts, but guesthouses and hotels will often have some kind of **safe-deposit facility** where you can store your valuables. Don't, however, be tempted to use the Bank of Baroda's safe-deposit service in Anjuna, Calangute and Mapusa, as stuff has reput-

Child prostitution in Goa

Fears that Goa is fast becoming a playground for paedophiles were realized in 1996, when one local priest and a foreign expat, Freddy Peats (who had been running an orphanage for two decades in Margao), were arrested for sex offences. Several other similar cases involving foreigners are awaiting trial, and evidence of organized paedophile rings with networks abroad has been accumulated by Interpol with the help of local police.

An undercover investigation was recently undertaken in India by NAWO (the National Alliance of Women's Movements), and revealed that around half of the prostitutes in Goa were girls between the ages of 11 and 15. Many claimed they were driven into the trade by poverty; others were sold by their parents to clear debts. The same research also showed that child prostitution was not merely confined to the traditional red-light districts, but had spilled onto Goa's beaches in recent years. So far, however, there have been very few convictions, mainly because of the ease with which offenders are able to bribe their way out of trouble, or jump bail. Until 1997, foreign paedophiles also knew that they were immune from prosecution in their home countries for offences committed against children in India. However, a new law was recently passed in the UK to facilitate their repatriation; in July 2000, the legislation was used by Interpol to arrest a British man in London for sex offences allegedly committed in Goa. Stiffer anti-paedophile laws were also passed in the state itself in 2003, since when sexual abuse of children carries a three- to ten-year prison sentence. In addition, hoteliers are now obliged by law to inform police if they suspect such offences are taking place on their premises.

Because child prostitution centres on the coastal resorts, you may come into direct contact with it during your holiday, and wonder what course of action to take if you do. It's never easy to be one hundred percent sure that what you're seeing is actually child prostitution, but if you see a foreign man, or men, with Indian girls or boys on the beach, and if their behaviour towards the children is more attentive than seems normal, alert the local police. You may also be tempted to photograph the suspect, but bear in mind that by taking the law into your own hands in this way you may be putting yourself and your travelling companions at risk.

An international response to the problem of child sex tourism is being co-ordinated from the UK by the **ECPAT** (formerly **The Coalition on Child Prostitution and Tourism**), and you can contact them at their base at The Stable Yard, Broomgrove Rd, London SW9 9TL ☎020 7501 8927 or via ⊛www.ecpat.net.

edly gone missing from these places in the past. It's also a good idea to keep a separate record of the numbers of your traveller's cheques, together with a note of which ones you've cashed, and the papers and telephone numbers necessary for replacing them if they are stolen.

Police

The Goan **police** – recognizable by their blue berets, white shirts and blue trousers – have become a major hassle for tourists over the past few years. **Corruption**, which originally crept in as a reaction to low pay and late salaries but has since evolved into a form of institutionalized racketeering, is the root of the problem. Indeed, the pickings in India's premier tourist state are rumoured to be so rich that officers routinely pay large backhanders of around Rs2 *lakh* (£2,600/$3,900) to be posted here. Over the past few years, some have even turned to old-fashioned robbery, the most publicized case being that of one Constable Digambar Naik, who was suspended for stealing £500 from a British tourist at Dabolim airport.

However, the way foreigners most often find themselves on the wrong side of the law is by **driving** around without a valid international driver's licence (see p.33). Even if you have one, though, the cop that waved you over will probably find another excuse to extract Rs100 or so *baksheesh*, usually for the absence of insurance papers or a helmet (even though it is not illegal to ride in Goa without one). The simple solution is to avoid police posts like the plague, which means travelling through towns such as Panjim, Mapusa and Margao, and to the Anjuna flea market, by public transport or on foot.

Nudity

Nudity is illegal in Goa, mainly because visitors in the past all too often ignored local sensibilities, forgetting or wilfully ignoring the fact that the state is part of India. In case tourists miss the "NO NUDISM" signs posted at the entrances to most beaches, police regularly patrol the busier resorts to ensure that decorum is maintained. If you are tempted to drop your togs, check that there are no families within eyeshot. No one is likely to object openly, but when you consider that wet Y-fronts and saris are about as risqué as beachwear gets for most Indians, you'll understand why men in G-strings and topless women cause such a stir (see p.49 for more on Goan sensibilities).

Travellers with disabilities

Disability is far more common in India than Europe and North America; many conditions that would be curable in the West are permanent disabilities here because people simply can't afford the treatment. Goa is no exception, although the number of disabled people begging for alms on the streets and outside temples is considerably less than in neighbouring states.

For travellers with **impaired mobility** Goa can present major problems. State-of-the-art wheelchairs and accessible toilets are virtually non-existent, and the streets of Panjim, Mapusa and Margao are full of all sorts of obstacles that would be hard for a blind person or wheelchair user to negotiate independently. Kerbs are often high, and pavements uneven and littered. There are also pot holes all over the place, and very little room on roadsides. Few of the resorts have any kind of walkways for pedestrians, and in a wheelchair you'll struggle to keep out of the way of passing traffic – a particular menace along the Calangute–Baga strip.

As for **hotels**, some of the five-stars have ramps for the movement of luggage equipment, but if that makes them accessible to wheelchairs, it's by accident rather than design.

On the positive side, you'll find Goans likely to be very helpful if, for example, you need their help getting on and off buses or up stairs. Taxis and rickshaws are easily affordable and very adaptable; if you rent one for a day, the driver is certain to help you in and out, and perhaps even around the places you visit. The same goes for any guides you might employ.

Contact one of the specialist organizations listed below for further advice on planning your trip. Otherwise, some package companies, such as Somak (see p.13), go out of their way to cater for travellers with disabilities, but it's essential to contact the operator and discuss your needs in detail with them before booking. You should also ensure you're covered by any travel insurance you take out.

Contacts for disabled travellers

UK and Ireland

Irish Wheelchair Association Blackheath Drive, Clontarf, Dublin 3 ☎01/818 6400, ⊛www.iwa.ie. Useful information provided about travelling abroad with a wheelchair.

RADAR (Royal Association for Disability and Rehabilitation) 12 City Forum, 250 City Rd, London EC1V 8AF ☎020/7250 3222, minicom ☎020/7250 4119, ⊛www.radar.org.uk. A good source of advice on holidays and travel.

Tripscope Alexandra House, Albany Rd, Brentford, Middlesex TW8 0NE ☎0845/758 5641, ⊛www.tripscope.org.uk. This registered charity provides a national telephone information service offering free advice on UK and international transport for those with a mobility problem.

US and Canada

Access-Able ⊛www.access-able.com. Online resource for travellers with disabilities.
Directions Unlimited 123 Green Lane, Bedford Hills, NY 10507 ☎1-800/533-5343 or 914/241-1700. Travel agency specializing in bookings for people with disabilities.
Mobility International USA 451 Broadway, Eugene, OR 97401 ☎541/343-1284, ⊛www.miusa.org. Information and referral services, access guides, tours and exchange programmes. Annual membership $35 (includes quarterly newsletter).
Society for the Advancement of Travelers with Handicaps (SATH) 347 5th Ave, New York, NY 10016 ☎212/447-7284, ⊛www.sath.org. Non-profit educational organization that has actively represented travellers with disabilities since 1976.
Wheels Up! ☎1-888/38-WHEELS, ⊛www.wheelsup.com. Provides discounted airfare, tour and cruise prices for disabled travellers, and publishes a free monthly newsletter. Comprehensive website.

Australia and New Zealand

ACROD (Australian Council for Rehabilitation of the Disabled) PO Box 60, Curtin ACT 2605; Suite 103, 1st Floor, 1–5 Commercial Rd, Kings Grove 2208; ☎02/6282 4333, TTY ☎02/6282 4333, ⊛www.acrod.org.au. Provides lists of travel agencies and tour operators for people with disabilities.
Disabled Persons Assembly 4/173–175 Victoria St, Wellington, New Zealand ☎04/801 9100 (also TTY), ⊛www.dpa.org.nz. Resource centre with lists of travel agencies and tour operators for people with disabilities.

India

India Rehabilitation Co-ordination A–2 Rasadhara Co-operation Housing Society, 385 SVP Rd, Mumbai 400004 ☎040/2404 2143.

Travelling with children

Parents are often put off the idea of travelling to Goa by the potential risks of holidaying in a tropical climate, but provided you take some common-sense precautions, the region and its beaches provide a perfectly salubrious, in fact ideal, environment for families with little ones.

Goans adore kids and you'll be welcomed all the more warmly if you bring yours. The majority of tourists are either unmarried or of middle to retiring age, so the appearance of Western children always generates lots of interest and contact with local parents, especially if you stay in a small, family-run hotel or guesthouse.

The most obvious thing to watch out for is the Indian **sun**, which can roast young, sensitive skin at any time of the day or year. Come armed with sun hats and plenty of maximum-factor block. Generally, the beaches are gently shelving and safe for kids to splash about in, but always be wary of **undertow**, which can arise at certain phases of the tide even in relatively shallow water, and sweep away feet from beneath small children. Another hazard along the shoreline are fishermen's rejects, discarded from hand nets on the sand: never allow your children to mess with jelly fish or sea snakes (especially the black-and-white striped variety) – they may not be completely dead.

Goan **dogs**, ubiquitous on beaches, are as a rule benign and friendly, but may not take kindly to the attentions of a toddler: bear in mind that if they're bitten they'll have to have a rabies jab. Bites and stings, however, are less of a worry than the common mosquito and the concomitant risk of **malaria**. Always ensure your kids are well protected by prophylactic tablets, or at the very least DEET-based repellent in the evenings, and that they're well covered by a net throughout the night. Special small nets

> If your child should need **medical attention** at any stage, try to arrange an appointment with Dr Lily Sequeira, Goa's foremost paediatrician, who has a surgery in Panjim, contactable through the *Panjim Inn* ☎0832/222 6523.

for babies' cots are sold at local markets and may be available through your hotel or guesthouse.

Formula milk and jars of baby food are available at supermarkets in the resorts, as are disposable **nappies**; you'll find international brands such as Pampers and Huggies are a good deal cheaper, but they're not easy to get hold of away from the main towns. Staying in less developed coastal villages, you should come with enough stuff to see you through, and be prepared to cook for yourself as your kids may not take to the spicy meals prepared by Goan families. Rented houses nearly always have some kind of **self-catering** area, if not a fully equipped kitchen, though don't expect much more at the budget end of the market than a sink and marble worktop. Mid-range places should come with a decent-sized gas hob, pans, crockery and cutlery.

Most **hotels and guesthouses** will provide an extra bed for a small additional charge (usually less than 25 percent of the room rate). Bigger hotels are also likely to be able to provide cots, but check first (through your tour operator if you're on a package holiday).

Women and sexual harassment

Compared with other regions of India, Goa is an easy-going destination for women travellers: incidents of sexual harassment are relatively rare, and opportunities to meet local women frequent. At the same time, it is important to remember that significant cultural differences still exist, especially in those areas where tourism is a relatively recent phenomenon.

Problems, when they do occur, invariably stem from the fact that many Western travellers do a range of things that no self-respecting Goan woman would consider: from drinking alcohol or smoking in a bar-restaurant, to sleeping in a room with a man to whom they are not married. Without compromising your freedom too greatly, though, there are a few common-sense steps you can take to accommodate local feelings.

The most important and obvious is **dress**. Western visitors who wear clothes that expose shoulders, legs or cleavage do neither themselves nor their fellow travellers any favours. Opt, therefore, for loose-fitting clothes that keep these areas covered. When travelling alone on public transport, it is also a good idea to sit with other women (most buses have separate "ladies' seats" at the front). If you're with a man, a wedding ring also confers immediate respectability.

Appropriate behaviour for **the beach** is a trickier issue. The very idea of a woman lying semi-naked in full view of male strangers is anathema to Goans. However, local people in the coastal resorts have come to tolerate such bizarre behaviour over the past two or three decades, and swimsuits and bikinis are no longer deemed indecent, especially if worn with a sarong. **Topless bathing**, on the other hand, is definitely out of the question (see "Nudity", p.56), even though you'll doubtless encounter bare breasts on the more hippified beaches. One very good reason to keep your top on is that it confounds the expectations of men who descend on Goa in large parties from outside the state expressly to ogle women, enticed by the prospect of public nudity.

Not surprisingly, the beaches are where you're most likely to experience **sexual harassment**, known in Goa as "Eve teasing". Your **reaction** to harassment is down to you. Verbal hassle is probably best ignored, but if you get touched it's best to react: the usual English responses will be well enough understood. If you shout "don't touch me!" in a crowded area, you're likely to find people on your side, and your

Rape

Rape is probably less of a danger in Goa than in most Western countries, but the number of sexual assaults on women travellers has seen a marked increase over the past few seasons, to the extent that a pamphlet entitled "Rape Alert" was posted around the resorts in 1996–97 by women tourists urging fellow travellers to take care at night. Among the incidents that provoked this was the 1996 attack on a 33-year-old British woman in Anjuna by two men, one of whom was her taxi driver. In another incident in March 1997 (also in Anjuna) two Swedish women were gang raped by seven or eight men on their way home from a beach party; their motorbike was stopped by assailants armed with sticks and knives, and a male companion was forced at knife-point to witness the rape.

Wherever you're staying, therefore, take the same common-sense precautions as you would at home: keep to the main roads when travelling on foot or by bicycle, avoid dirt tracks and unfrequented beaches unless you're in a group, and when you're in your house after dark, ensure that all windows and doors are locked.

assailant shamed. Touching up a Goan woman would be judged totally unacceptable behaviour, so there's no reason why you should put up with it, either.

On the positive side, spending time with **Goan women** can be a delight. Public transport can be a good meeting ground, as can shops and guesthouses, which are often run by women. On the beach, you'll also find yourself frequently mobbed by women hawkers from Karnataka and Rajasthan. Such encounters are, of course, motivated primarily by commercial interest, but can be rewarding nonetheless.

Directory

Airport departure tax Airport tax should technically be included in the price of your ticket these days, but the rules change from year to year and it makes sense to check in advance, through your travel agent or tour operator (or holiday company rep once in Goa), just in case you have to hang on to some rupees to hand over at Dabolim prior to departure.

Body-piercing and tattoos Western body-piercers and tattooists ply their trade in several Goan resorts. Most are conscientious when it comes to using sterilized needles, but you should check first or you could run the risk of contracting HIV.

Cigarettes Various brands of cigarettes, including imported makes such as Rothmans and Benson and Hedges, are available in Goa. More expensive imported rolling tobacco, including Golden Virginia, Duma and Samson, are sold at Anjuna flea market and some stalls around Colva, although it is advisable to bring your own papers as the indigenous Capstans are thick and don't stick very well, while imported Rizlas are expensive. One of the great smells of India is the *bidi*, the cheapest smoke, made with low-grade tobacco wrapped in a eucalyptus leaf.

Contraceptives Oral contraceptives are available over the counter at most pharmacies in Goa. Indian condoms are less reliable than those in the West, so stock up at duty-free.

Duty-free allowance Anyone over 17 can bring in one US quart (0.95 litre – but nobody's going to quibble about the other 5ml) of spirits, or a bottle of wine and 250ml spirits; plus 200 cigarettes, or 50 cigars, or 250g tobacco. You may be required to register anything valuable on a Tourist Baggage Re-export Form to make sure you take it home with you, and to fill in a currency declaration form if carrying more than US$10,000 or the equivalent.

Electricity Generally 220V 50Hz AC, though direct current supplies also exist, so check before plugging in. Most sockets are European-style double round-pin but sizes vary. British, Irish, Australian and New Zealand plugs will need an adaptor, preferably a universal one; American and Canadian appliances need a transformer, too, unless multi-voltage. Power cuts and voltage variations are very common.

Gay and lesbian life Homosexuality is not generally open in Goa, and anal intercourse is actually an offence under the Indian penal code, while laws against "obscene behaviour" are used to arrest gay men cruising or liaising anywhere that could be considered a public space; lesbianism is much more clandestine. It isn't surprising, therefore, that gay and lesbian life in the state is very low-key. The tourist scene is also very straight-oriented, although one or other of the beach cafés at Ozran Vagator (see p.152) usually becomes a hangout for gay visitors during the season.

Laundry In Goa, no one goes to the laundry: if they don't do their own, they send it out to a *dhobi wallah*. Wherever you are staying, there will be either an in-house *dhobi wallah*, or one very close by to call on. The *dhobi wallah* will take your dirty washing to a *dhobi ghat*, a public clothes-washing area (the bank of a river for example), where it is shown some old-fashioned discipline: separated, soaped and given a damn good thrashing to beat the dirt out of it. Then it is hung out to dry in the sun and, once dried, taken to the ironing sheds where every garment is endowed with razor-sharp creases and then matched to its rightful owner by hidden cryptic markings. Your clothes will come back from the *dhobi wallah* absolutely spotless, though this kind of violent treatment does take it out of them: buttons get lost and eventually the cloth starts to fray.

Massage The art of massage has been practised in India since ancient times, and masseurs, carrying a bag of oils and a towel, regularly offer their services on the beach. Their trade does not have the seedy connotations it sometimes does in the West, although women should definitely think twice before accepting a rubdown from a man.

Opticians Glasses and contact lenses can be made up in Goa to exactly the same standards as in Europe and the US, but for a fraction of the cost. Panjim, Calangute, Mapusa and Margao all have large, air-con opticians. Just take along your specs (or a prescription).

Photography Beware of pointing your camera at anything that might be considered "strategic", especially Dabolim airport, and anything military, even bridges, stations and main roads. Remember, too, that some people prefer not to be photographed, so it's wise to ask before you take a snapshot of them – and only common courtesy after all. Camera film is widely available in Goa (but check the date on the box), and it's pretty easy to get films developed, though they don't always come out as well as they might at home. Prices are broadly similar to those in the West, with the exception of slide film, which is harder to get hold of and considerably more expensive.

Smoking According to the Goa Prohibition of Smoking and Spitting Act 1997, it is ille-

Things to take

Many things are of course easy to find in Goa and cheaper than at home, but here is a miscellaneous and rather random list of items you should consider taking with you:

❑ A padlock (to lock rooms in budget hotels)
❑ A universal electric plug adaptor and a universal sink plug (few sinks or bathtubs have them)
❑ A mosquito net
❑ A roll of adhesive tape (for blocking up holes in mosquito nets)
❑ A sheet sleeping bag
❑ A small flashlight
❑ Earplugs (for street noise in hotel rooms and music on buses)
❑ High-factor sunblock
❑ A pocket alarm clock (for any early-morning departures)
❑ A multi-purpose penknife
❑ A needle and some thread (dental floss is better for holding baggage together)
❑ Plastic bags (to sort your baggage, make it easier to pack and unpack, and keep out damp and dust)
❑ Tampons (those available in Goa are not so wonderful)
❑ Multi-vitamin and mineral tablets
❑ A stick of glue (for fixing stamps to letters and postcards)
❑ A motorcycle helmet with a visor or goggles (if you plan to rent a bike)
❑ A sealable water bottle

gal to smoke, chew or spit tobacco in public places. Although you're unlikely to witness any police enforcement of this draconian law, it has successfully eradicated cigarette advertising from the state.

Time Goa is 5hr 30min ahead of London, 10hr 30min ahead of New York, 13hr 30min ahead of LA, and 4hr 30min behind Sydney; however, summer time in those places will vary the difference by an hour.

Toilets Toilets in most mid-range and upmarket hotels are of the standard Western-style "sit-down" type, and generally clean. In some budget guesthouses and bars, however, Asian facilities are the norm – these involve getting used to the squatting posture. Paper, if used, should go into the bucket provided rather than down the loo.

Indians instead use a pot of water and their left hand, a method you may prefer to adopt, but if you do use paper, keep some handy – it isn't usually supplied, and it might be an idea to stock up before going too far off the beaten track as it is not available everywhere. In most villages, "pig toilets" are more common (see p.38). Believe it or not, these tend not to smell as bad as conventional ones. They are also more environmentally sound, as they use less water.

Yoga Goa is a perfect place to come to study yoga, and dozens of schools have opened in the past three or four years to cater for the growing demand. However, it can be hard to know which offer truly expert tuition. For some pointers, see our Yoga listings on pp.134, 151 & 166.

Guide

Guide

Panjim and Central Goa

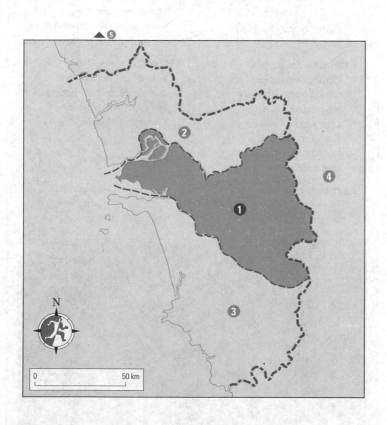

CHAPTER 1 # Highlights

✳ **Panjim Inn** One of Goa's few bona fide heritage hotels, situated in the heart of the capital's frayed colonial quarter. **See p.73**

✳ **Viva Panjim** Down-to-earth, traditional Goan food in a gorgeous Portuguese-era square. **See p.79**

✳ **Old Goa** The former Portuguese capital retains some of Asia's most spectacular churches, as well as Saint Francis Xavier's incorruptible corpse. **See p.87**

✳ **Crocodiles** Take a boat ride out to view freshwater crocs basking in the mangrove swamps of the Cambarjua Canal. **See p.103**

✳ **Spice plantations** Star apples, nutmeg, cardamom, pineapples and mangoes are some of the exotic produce of the fruit and spice plantations reachable in an easy day-trip inland. **See p.108**

✳ **Hindu temples** The woods around Ponda shelter dozens of Hindu temples, in a typically Goan hybrid style. **See p.110**

✳ **Dudhsagar Falls** A bumpy jeep ride through the jungle takes you to India's second-highest falls. **See p.116**

1

Panjim and Central Goa

The wedge-shaped tract of land between the Mandovi and Zuari rivers encompasses the whole gamut of Goan landscapes, from the palm-fringed paddy fields of the coast, through the wooded valleys of the interior, to the dense forests and hills of the Western Ghats.

Bounded in the east by the Cambarjua Canal, **Tiswadi** *taluka* has been the most densely populated district in the region since ancient times, from when its name (meaning "land of thirty villages") derives. It is technically an island, linked to the rest of Goa by a network of concrete road bridges and rusty river ferries. Known as the *Velhas Conquistas* (Old Conquests), this was the first area to be colonized by the Portuguese, whose former capital at **Old Goa** remains the state's premier historical site. The ruined town's modern counterpart, **Panjim** – officially known as Panaji – lies 10km west on the left bank of the Mandovi, its colonial-era houses, civic buildings and ships well deserving a day away from the beach. A short detour to **Pilar**'s seventeenth-century seminary and nearby **Talaulim**'s imposing parish church of Santana can also be rewarding. Other incentives to explore inland include the picturesque islands of **Chorao**, site of Goa's only bird reserve, and **Divar**, whose main village, Piedade, harbours a crop of elegant Portuguese villas and a stately hilltop church.

Hidden among the hills of **Ponda** *taluka*, southeast of Panjim, is Goa's largest concentration of **Hindu temples**. Built away from the town in the fifteenth and sixteenth centuries to escape persecution by the Portuguese, these architectural oddities, which fuse Hindu, Muslim and European Renaissance styles, are often visited en route to the **spice plantations** dotted around the unprepossessing district headquarters, Ponda town, or as part of a longer tour to the wildlife reserves further east. Of these, the **Bhagwan Mahaveer Sanctuary** is much the most interesting. In addition to some dramatic scenery, it boasts India's biggest waterfalls, **Dudhsagar**, and the last remaining medieval temple in Goa, the Mahadeva *mandir* at **Tamdi Surla**, in Sanguem *taluka*.

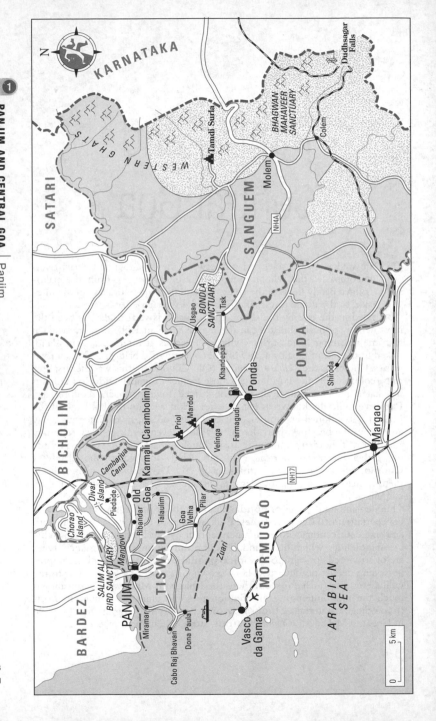

Panjim

Take any mid-sized Portuguese town, add a sprinkling of banana trees and auto-rickshaws, drench annually with torrential tropical rain, and leave to simmer in fierce humid sunshine for at least one hundred and fifty years, and you'll end up with something similar to **PANJIM**. The Goan capital has a completely different feel from any other Indian city. Stacked around the sides of a lush terraced hillside at the mouth of the Mandovi River, its skyline of sloping red-tiled roofs, whitewashed churches and mildewing concrete apartment blocks has more in common with Lisbon than Lucknow. The lingering European influence is most evident in the small squares and back lanes of the town's old quarters, **Fontainhas** and **Sao Tomé**. Here, Portuguese is still the lingua franca, the shopfronts sport names like José Pinto and de Souza, and the women wear tailored knee-length dresses that would turn heads anywhere else in India.

While most domestic tourists base themselves in Panjim, foreign visitors rarely see more of the town than its busy bus terminal, which is a pity. Although you can completely bypass the capital when you arrive in Goa – by jumping off the train or bus at Margao (for the south) or Mapusa (for the northern beach resorts), or by heading to the coast from the airport – it's definitely worth spending some time here – if only a couple of hours en route to the ruined former capital at Old Goa, 10km east, or the Hindu temples, further east around Ponda. Sights are thin on the ground, but the palm-lined squares and atmospheric old quarters, with their picturesque Neoclassical houses and Catholic churches, make a pleasant backdrop for aimless wandering.

Some history

The earliest mention of **Panjim** crops up in a Kadamba inscription, dated 1107, in which the settlement, then a handful of fishers' huts surrounded by dunes and swampland, is referred to as **Pahajani**, "land that does not flood". Recently, philologists have contested that the name may be derived from the Urdu *panch ima afsugani* – later corrupted by the Portuguese to *ponji* – meaning "five enchanted castles", a reference to the five hilltop forts erected here by **Muslim invaders** during the fourteenth century. Boasting 55 cannons, these were installed to guard the mouth of the Mandovi River, along with a fortified waterfront palace erected by Yusuf 'Adil Shah, the first Sultan of Bijapur. However, the defences failed to repel the Portuguese, who took the forts prior to the main assault on Ela (Old Goa), after which the site was used as a military embarkation point and customs post.

The Dominicans founded a college here in 1584, and convents and *hidalgos'* (noblemen's) houses sprang up in the seventeenth century, but Panjim remained little more than a scruffy colonial outpost of sailors and Kunbi fishing families until the lethal malaria epidemic of 1759. Leaving Old Goa to the mosquitoes, the then governor converted Panjim's waterfront Muslim palace into a splendid residence, and by the early nineteenth century the town had eclipsed its predecessor upriver. Governor **Dom Manuel Port'e Castro** (1826–35), dubbed Panjim's "Founding Father", was largely responsible; he initiated the large-scale land drainage and construction project when the town acquired most of its grand civic buildings, squares, schools and roads. **Nova Goa**, as it was then known, became the territory's capital in 1843. Given its (more politically correct) Marathi name, **Panaji**, in 1961, the town expanded rapidly after Independence, yet never reached the unmanageable proportions of other Indian state capitals: compared with Mumbai or Bangalore, its uncongested streets today seem easy-going and pleasantly parochial.

Arrival

European charter planes and domestic flights from Mumbai, Bangalore, Kochi (Cochin), Delhi, Chennai (Madras) and Tiruvananthapuram (Trivandrum) arrive at Goa's **Dabolim airport** (see p.173), 29km south of Panjim on the outskirts of Vasco da Gama. Pre-paid taxis into town from here (45min;

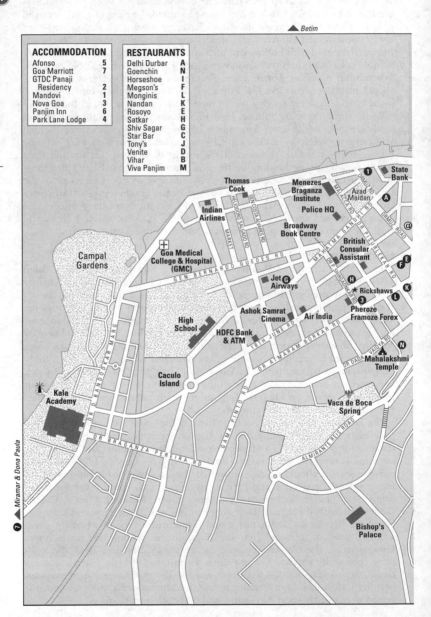

ACCOMMODATION	
Afonso	5
Goa Marriott	7
GTDC Panaji	
Residency	2
Mandovi	1
Nova Goa	3
Panjim Inn	6
Park Lane Lodge	4

RESTAURANTS	
Delhi Durbar	A
Goenchin	N
Horseshoe	I
Megson's	F
Monginis	L
Nandan	K
Rosoyo	E
Satkar	H
Shiv Sagar	G
Star Bar	C
Tony's	J
Venite	D
Vihar	B
Viva Panjim	M

Miramar & Dona Paula

Rs475), booked at the counter in the forecourt immediately outside the arrivals hall, can be shared by up to five people.

Arriving on the Konkan **Railway** from Mumbai, Bangalore or Kerala, the nearest station to Panjim is Karmali (Carambolim), 10km east of Panjim on the edge of Old Goa; buses and taxis (Rs200) queue outside to ferry passengers into town.

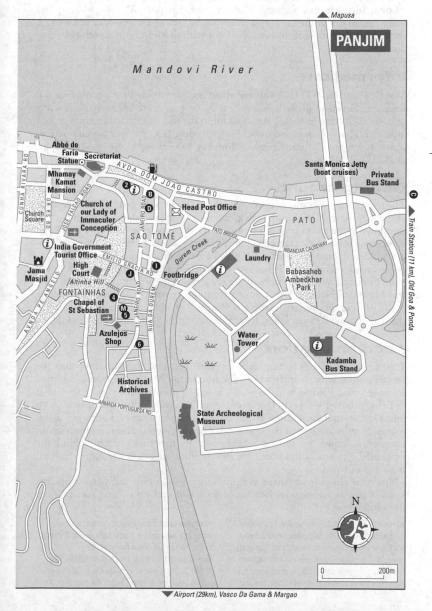

▲ *Mapusa*

PANJIM

M a n d o v i   R i v e r

Abbé de
Faria
Statue
Secretariat
AVDA DOM JOAO CASTRO
Mhamay
Kamat
Mansion
Church
Square
Church of
our Lady of
Immaculer
Conception
SAO TOMÉ
India Government
Tourist Office
EMILIO GRACIA RD
Jama
Masjid
High
Court
Altinho Hill
FONTAINHAS
Chapel of
St Sebastian
Azulejos
Shop
Historical
Archives
ARMADA PORTUGUESA RD
State Archeological
Museum

Santa Monica Jetty
(boat cruises)
Private
Bus Stand
Head Post Office
PATO BRIDGE
PATO
Ourem Creek
RIBANDAR CAUSEWAY
Laundry
Footbridge
Babasaheb
Ambedkhar
Park
Water
Tower
Kadamba
Bus Stand

CUNHA RIVARA RD
OR RS RD
JOSE TAICAO ROAD
31 JANEIRO ROAD
AVND PE ANGELO
31 JANEIRO ROAD
RUA DA OUREM

▶ *Train Station (11 km), Old Goa & Ponda*

N

0   200m

71

▼ *Airport (29km), Vasco Da Gama & Margao*

Long-distance government **buses** pull into Panjim at the town's busy Kadamba bus stand, 1km east of the centre in the district of Pato; private inter-state buses arrive a short way further north at the new stand under the Mandovi road bridge. It takes around ten minutes to walk from here across Ourem Creek to Fontainhas, where there are several budget hotels. If you plan to stay in the more modern west end of town, flag down a motorcycle taxi or jump into an auto-rickshaw at the rank outside the Kadamba station concourse.

Local buses from Calangute, Baga, Anjuna, Chapora, Mapusa, Margao and Vasco also arrive at the Kadamba interstate bus stand. Destinations are written above the relevant platform and called out with machine-gun rapidity by con-ductors.

Information

The Goa Tourism (GTDC) **information** counter inside the concourse at the Kadamba bus stand (daily 9.30am–1pm & 2–5pm; ℡0832/222 5620, ⒲www .goa-tourism.com) is useful for checking train and interstate bus timings, but little else. More efficient and helpful is the Indian Government **tourist office**, across town on Church Square (Mon–Fri 9.30am–6pm, Sat 9.30am–1pm; ℡0832/222 3412).

Getting around

The most convenient way of **getting around** Panjim is by **auto-rickshaw**, with virtually no journey within the town costing more than around Rs30; either flag one down at the roadside or head for one of the ranks dotted around town. Even cheaper are motorcycle taxis (aka "pilots"), distinguished by their ballcaps and yel-low mudguards; the fare from the Kadamba bus stand to Fontainhas is Rs15.

The only local **buses** likely to be of use to visitors run to Dona Paula from the main bus stand, via several stops along the esplanade (including the Secretariat) and Miramar beachfront; the journey from the centre out to Dona Paula costs Rs10. If you feel up to taking on Panjim's anarchic traffic, rent a bicycle (Mon–Sat only; Rs5 per hour) from the stall up the lane opposite the GPO.

Accommodation

The majority of Goa's Indian visitors prefer to stay in Panjim rather than the coastal resorts, which explains the huge number of hotels and lodges crammed into the town. Finding a place to stay is only a problem during the festival of St Francis (Nov 24–Dec 3), Dusshera (Sept/Oct) and during peak season (from mid-Dec to mid-Jan), when tariffs double. At other times, hotels try to fill rooms by offering substantial discounts. The most atmospheric options are in Fontainhas, down by Ourem Creek, and in the back streets behind the esplanade. The rest of the hotels are mostly bland places in the more modern, west end of town.

Note that **check-out times** in Panjim vary wildly. Find out what yours is as soon as you arrive, or your holiday lie-in could end up costing you an extra day's room rent.

Afonso St Sebastian Chapel Square, Fontainhas ℡0832/222 2359. Recently refurbished colonial-era house in a picturesque backstreet. Spotlessly clean, cool en-suite rooms, friendly owners and rooftop terrace with views. Single occupancy avail-able. Rates soar to Rs800 at Christmas, but are

otherwise low for the level of comfort and loca-tions. The best choice if your budget won't stretch to the Panjim Inn down the road. ❸
Goa Marriott Miramar beach ℡0832/243 7001, ℡246 3034, ⒲www.marriott.com. Huge five-star out on the edge of town, facing the mouth of the

Tours and cruises

GTDC (ⓦ www.goa-tourism.com) and several private companies run a range of **bus tours** around the state. Pitched primarily at domestic visitors, they tend to be conducted at breakneck pace, cramming a dozen or so stops into a long day and leaving you far too little time to enjoy the sights. The only one really worth considering is the two-day "Dudhsagar Special", which covers Old Goa, several temples, Bondla, Tambdi Surla and the Dudhsagar falls, with an overnight stay at Molem (Sat & Sun only, depart 9am, return 6pm the next day; Rs500). For booking and information, go to the GTDC *Panaji Residency*, near the Secretariat (ⓣ 0832/222 7103).

A popular alternative to watching the sunset from a beach bar – at least for most Indian tourists – is an evening **river cruise** along the Mandovi. GTDC runs two return trips every day from Santa Monica jetty, directly beneath the Mandovi road bridge: the first at 6pm, and the second at 7.15pm. Aim for the earlier one, as it usually catches the last of the sunset. Snacks and drinks are available, and the Rs100 price includes a display of Konkani and Portuguese dance accompanied by folk singers in traditional Goan costume. Two-hour "Full Moon" cruises also leave daily at 8.30pm, regardless of the lunar phase. Operating in direct competition to GTDC are Emerald Waters' cruises from the quay outside the *Mandovi Hotel*. In addition to evening departures (daily 5.45pm, 7pm, 8.15pm & 9.30pm; Rs150), also with live folk music and dance, and a bar, they offer longer sightseeing trips during the day. The "Rome of the Orient Special" (Mon, Wed, Thurs & Sat depart 1pm, return 5pm; Rs300) heads up the Mandovi River to Old Goa via Ribandar, with a guided tour of the monuments and free cocktails. Another cruise sails across Mormugao Harbour to Grande Island (Sun depart 10am, return 5pm; Rs800), where the launch pulls in for a few hours of swimming on a deserted beach. Finally, the "Backwater Cruise" (Tues depart 10am, return 5pm; Rs650) takes you upriver from Old Goa and down the Cambarjua Canal to the rarely visited St Estevam Island.

Bookings for the GTDC cruises can be made through their agents, Goa Sea Travels, opposite the *Tourist Hostel*. Emerald Waters' ticket counter is opposite the *Mandovi Hotel*. Alternatively, buy your ticket at the counters behind the jetty, underneath the Mandovi bridge.

Mandovi. Predictably formulaic, and not a great location for a package holiday (despite what the brochures might suggest), but large and luxurious, with all the mod cons you'd expect. ❾

GTDC Panaji Residency Avda Dom Joao Castro ⓣ 0832/222 3396 or 222 7103. Spacious rooms in an amorphous government-run hotel next to the main road and river. Not at all inspiring, but good value. ❹–❺

Mandovi Dr D Bandodkar Rd ⓣ 0832/242 6270–3, ⓕ 222 5451. Overlooking the waterfront with river and roofscape views, this was formerly the town's grandest hotel and a real Goan institution. Evelyn Waugh and Graham Greene stayed here when it was being built in the early 1950s, but it's been badly neglected in recent years and now offers poor value for money, despite the plum location. Dull beige decor and no pool. ❾

Nova Goa Dr Atmaram Borkar Rd ⓣ 0832/227 7226–8, ⓕ 222 4958, ⓦ www.hotelnovagoa .com. Panjim's brightest, newest top-class hotel in the heart of the shopping area and with the usual comforts, plus bath tubs and a pool. Popular

mainly with visiting Portuguese and corporate clients. ❼

Panjim Inn E-212, 31 Janeiro Rd, Fontainhas ⓣ 0832/222 6523, ⓕ 222 8136, ⓦ www .panjiminn.com. Grand colonial-era town house, now managed as an upmarket but homely hotel, with period furniture, sepia family photos, balconies and a common verandah, where meals and drinks are served to guests. An even more beautiful Hindu house across the road, Panjim Pousada, renovated by the same owner, offers the chance to sample what Panjim must have felt like a century ago, with a leafy inner courtyard and huge breadfruit tree overhanging the rear verandah. Easily the best place in its class. ❻–❼

Park Lane Lodge Near Chapel of St Sebastian ⓣ 0832/222 7154, ⓔ pklaldg@goatelecom.com. Cramped but clean family guesthouse in old colonial-style house. Pepper and coffee plants add atmosphere to a narrow communal terrace, and there's a TV lounge upstairs; also safe deposit facilities, Internet access, laundry service and good off-season discounts. ❹

The Town

Until a little over a decade ago, most visitors' first glimpse of Panjim was from the decks of the old Bombay steamer as it chugged into dock at the now-defunct ferry ramp. These days, however, despite the recent inauguration of the Konkan railway, the town is most usually approached by road – from the north via the huge ferro-concrete bridge that spans the Mandovi estuary, or from the south on the NH7, which links the capital with the airport at Vasco da Gama. Whatever your approach, you'll have to pass through the suburb of **Pato**, home of the main Kadamba bus terminal, before crossing Ourem Creek to arrive in Panjim proper. West of **Fontainhas**, the picturesque Portuguese quarter, the commercial centre's grid of long straight streets fans out west from Panjim's principal landmark, **Church Square**. Further north, the main thoroughfare, **Avenida Dom Joao Castro**, sweeps past the post office and **Secretariat** building before bending west along the waterfront towards the nearby beach resort of Miramar.

Panjim's few conventional sights are all grouped in the east end of town. A good route stringing them together heads along the esplanade from the Secretariat to the **Menezes Braganza Institute**, and then south to Church Square via **Azad Maidan**, winding up with an amble through the old quarters.

Church Square

The leafy rectangular park opposite the Government of India tourist office, known as **Church Square** or the **Municipal Gardens**, forms the heart of Panjim. Originally called the Jardim de Garcia da Orta, after a famous sixteenth-century physician, it used to harbour a bust of Portuguese explorer Vasco da Gama, but this was pulled down after Independence, transferred to the museum in Old Goa and replaced with India's national emblem: three Ashokean lions mounted on an abacus decorated with a wheel, symbolizing "strength and unity in diversity".

Presiding over the east side of the square is Panjim's most distinctive and pho-togenic landmark, the toothpaste-white Baroque **Church of Our Lady of the Immaculate Conception** (Mon–Sat 9am–1pm & 3.30–6pm, Sun 10.30am–1pm & 6.15–7pm). Standing at the head of a criss-crossing laterite walkway, between rows of slender palm trees, it was built in 1541, when the town was no more than a swamp-ridden fishing village, for the benefit of sailors arriving here from Lisbon. The weary mariners would stagger up from the quay to give thanks for their safe passage before proceeding to the capital at Old Goa – the original home of the enormous bell that hangs from the central gable. The second largest in the state, this was salvaged from the ruins of the Augustinian Monastery on Holy Hill and installed here in a specially enlarged belfry, erected in 1871 at the same time as the steps. The interior of the church is dominated by a splendid gilt reredos dedicated to Our Lady. On feast days, the original beams of the vaulted ceiling above it are festooned with strings of blue and white flowers to match the outside of the church.

North of Church Square

The road that runs northeast from the church, Rua José Falcao, brings you out at the riverside near Panjim's oldest surviving building. With its sloping tiled roofs, carved-stone coats of arms and wooden verandahs, the stalwart **Secretariat** looks typically colonial. Yet it was originally the summer palace of Goa's sixteenth-century Muslim ruler, the 'Adil Shah. Fortified with 55 cannons and a saltwater moat, its defences did not, however, deter Alfonso de

Abbé de Faria

José Custodio de Faria was born in Candolim, Bardez, on May 20, 1756, the son of a down-at-heel seminarian and a local landowner's daughter. When this marriage ended in 1771, José's mother ran off to a nunnery, and his father took him to Lisbon, where the pair soon gained the patronage of the king, Dom José I. Faria senior eventually rose to become confessor to the king's daughter but fell out of favour in 1779, accused of whipping up sedition among Goan expats in Lisbon. José, too, was linked with the rebels and fled to Paris soon after.

While in the French capital, Faria developed an interest in the occult science of *magnétisme*, or hypnosis. Aided by his exotic dark skin, ascetic dress and Goan-Brahmin credentials, the young priest started up a course in a school hall on the Rue Clichy, attracting a large and predominantly female following, but his "performances" enraged the clergy and scientific establishment, who spread rumours that Faria was taking advantage of his women students and patients. These attacks on his reputation brought a premature end to his career and, in 1819, Faria died penniless – on the very day his now famous treatise on hypnosis, *De la cause du sommeil lucide* ("On the Causes of Lucid Sleep"), was published.

Faria's enduring contribution to the modern science of psychology is his insistence that hypnotic trances were not produced by body fluids, but by suggestion, which opened up the notion of the unconscious mind. Largely forgotten in both Paris and his native Goa, his memory is most vividly preserved in Alexandre Dumas' novel *The Count of Monte Cristo*, in which he appears as a mad monk rotting away in the dungeons of the Château d'If off the coast of Marseille.

Albuquerque, whose troops stormed the building in 1510, then converted it into a temporary rest house for the territory's governors, who used to overnight here en route to and from Europe. Following the viceroy's move from Old Goa in 1759, the palace, by this time known as the Idalcaon's Palace (from *Adil Khan*, a Portuguese corruption of 'Adil Shah), became the official viceregal residence, which it remained until the completion of the even grander mansion at Cabo, near Vasco da Gama, in 1918. Today, the Secretariat is the home of the Goan State Legislature (pending the completion of a still grander building on the north bank of the river), which explains the presence of so many shiny chauffeur-driven Ambassador cars, and the armed guards at the door.

Standing on the opposite side of the main road to the Secretariat is one of Panjim's last surviving examples of vernacular Hindu architecture. The 250-year-old **Mhamay Kamat mansion** was the home of a wealthy family of merchants. Former owners of one of the three largest brokering houses in western India, the Mhamays exerted considerable influence over the rulers of neighbouring princely states (some of whom were in debt to them), and controlled a vast business empire based on the trade of Pakistani opium, African slaves, textiles and, more improbably, socks, which they had made by the inmates of a high-security prison on an island south of Goa. After the family business went bust, the mansion was sold off piecemeal, and now accommodates nearly one hundred people, as well as around twenty shops. It's not officially open to visitors, but walk through the main portico into the colonnaded inner courtyard (*raj angan*), and you'll probably find someone to show you around.

Just west of the mansion stands Panjim's most striking **statue**. Glaring fixedly down from his pedestal, a long-haired, haggard-faced man is bent with his hands stretched over the supine body of a curvaceous woman, unconscious at his feet. Contrary to appearances, this peculiar portrait is not a scene from some lascivious nineteenth-century melodrama, but a memorial to one of Goa's more illustrious sons, the **Abbé de Faria** – priest, revolutionary, and the founding father of modern hypnotism (see box p.75). When he saw it in the 1960s, Graham Greene aptly described the figure as " . . . pouncing like a great black eagle on his mesmerized female patient."

An even more impressive edifice than the Mhamay Kamat mansion is the **Menezes Braganza Institute** (Mon–Fri 9.30am–1.15pm & 2–5.30pm; free) now the town's Central Library, which stands behind the esplanade, 1km west of the Secretariat past the Abbé de Faria statue. Among the colonial leftovers in this grand Neoclassical building, which was erected as part of the civic makeover initiated by the Marquis of Pombal and Dom Manuel de Portugal e Castro in the early nineteenth century, are the panels of blue-and-yellow-painted ceramic tiles, known as *azulejos*, lining the lobby of the west (Malacca Road) entrance. These larger-than-life illustrations depict scenes from Luis Vaz Camões' epic poem, *Os Luisiades*. The tone of the tableaux is intentionally patriotic (valiant Portuguese explorers being tossed on stormy seas and a nobleman standing defiantly before a dark-faced Raja of Calicut), but the tale was, in fact, intended as an invective against the Portuguese discoveries, which Camões rightly believed was milking his mother country dry and leaving its crown easy prey for the old enemy, Spain.

Immediately south of the library building lies the parched grass square of **Azad Maidan**, fringed by tall trees and centred on a weed-choked pavilion of Corinthian pillars salvaged from the rubble of Old Goa. Built in 1847 to protect the huge brass statue of Alfonso de Albuquerque (now housed in the state archeological museum in Old Goa), the pavilion was made into a memorial to Goan freedom fighter Dr Tristão de Braganza Cunha after Independence.

Fontainhas and Sao Tomé

Panjim's oldest and most interesting district, **Fontainhas**, lies immediately west of Pato, overlooking the banks of the oily green Ourem Creek. The district, or ward (*waddo*), was laid out on land reclaimed during the late eighteenth century by a Goan expatriate known as "the Mossmikar" because he had amassed his fortune in the African colony of Mozambique. From the footbridge that cuts between the Kadamba bus stand and town centre, a dozen or so blocks of Neoclassical houses rise up the sides of **Altinho Hill**. Many have retained their traditional coat of ochre, pale yellow, green or blue – a legacy of the Portuguese insistence that every Goan building (except churches, which had to be kept white) should be colour-washed after the monsoons.

At the southern end of the neighbourhood, the pristine whitewashed **Chapel of St Sebastian** is one of many Goan *igrejas* to remain faithful to the old colonial decree. It stands at the end of a small square where Fontainhas' Portuguese-speaking locals hold a lively annual street *festa* to celebrate the Feast of Our Lady of Livrament in mid-November. The eerily lifelike crucifix inside the chapel formerly hung in the Palace of the Inquisition in Old Goa. Unusually, Christ's eyes are open – allegedly to inspire fear in those being interrogated by the Inquisitors. It was brought to Panjim in 1812, after the Inquisition had been suppressed in Goa, and installed in the Secretariat, finally coming to rest here a little over a century later when the viceroys had decamped to Cabo. The most atmospheric time to visit is during early morning Mass, which begins at 6.45am.

A short way north of the chapel, just beyond the *Park Lane Lodge*, begins a flight of old laterite steps leading up Altinho Hill to Panjim's best-preserved nineteenth-century building, the **High Court of Mumbai (Bombay) in**

Goa. Stripped of fancy pilasters, eaves, corbels and decorative frames, the edifice typifies the functional aesthetic that prevailed during the Pombal era, when Lisbon and the great Brazilian cities were rebuilt by the Portuguese. Overlooked by mature palm trees, its elegantly arched windows and high pitched Mangalorean tiled roofs today evoke the twilight of the Lusitanian empire better than any other civic structure in the town.

Carnival

Panjim's chaotic three-day **Carnival**, held during late February and early March, is the state's most famous festival. Introduced by the Portuguese as a means to let off steam before Lent, it has been celebrated with gusto in Goa since the eighteenth century, and now draws tens of thousands from around India and abroad. In recent years, however, the colourful parade forming its centrepiece has been the cause of controversy, as its organizers are accused of vulgarizing Goan culture for crude commercial gain.

The **origins** of Carnival date back to the hedonistic religious festivals of ancient Greece and Rome. The festival was later exported to the Spanish and Portuguese colonies, where black slaves infused it with a healthy dose of African panache. Known in Konkani as *Intruz* (a corruption of the Portuguese word *Entrudo*, from the Latin *Introito*, meaning the start of Lent), Goa's carnival was grafted on to an indigenous tradition of local village festivals in which *khells*, or **satirical folk plays**, were – and still are – performed.

Following the centuries-old model, Panjim's Carnival is kicked off on **Sabato Gordo** ("Fat Saturday") by the entry into the town of King Momo, who reads a decree ordering his subjects to forget their worries and "be happy". This unleashes three days of music, masked dance and general mayhem, accompanied by exuberant cross-dressing, mock battles fought with bags of sawdust or flour and water, known as *cocotes*, and *assaltos* or trick-or-treat-style raids on neighbours' kitchens.

Condemned by the Goan government as "colonial", the festivities were suspended following Independence but lately have enjoyed something of a revival, spurred on by injections of funds from local businesses, national liquor and cigarette manufacturers, and five-star hotel chains. Such **commercialism** angers many Goans, who claim it runs counter to the spirit of Carnival, which traditionally inverts and satirizes the prevailing power structures. Worse still, in many people's eyes, is the gradual **vulgarization** of the event, which has become closely associated in the popular Indian imagination with licentious behaviour, particularly among local women. The prime propagators of this myth are lurid feature films of the Hindi cinema that regularly include scenes of seduction and sexual intrigue set against a Goan Carnival backdrop. Nor, according to one Goan women's group, have such misconceptions been dispelled by official Carnival publicity, which actively promotes such unrepresentative images of women.

Over the past four or five years, other pressures have somewhat diminished the colours of Carnival, which has seen a marked decline in popularity. Foremost among these was the **Church's pronouncement** of 1993 that Catholic girls should not take part in the main parades. A **ban on alcohol** use by all participants rendered the processions even more lacklustre, as has the municipality's insistence that floats should illustrate worthy, but essentially dull, themes, such as 1996's "Health for All by the Year 2000" – hardly a party winner.

In spite of the controversy, the main Saturday parade continues to draw large numbers of revellers to the Goan capital, while Goans all over the state avidly watch the event on television. However, if you plan to come to Panjim yourself, travel here for the day only, as hotels tend to be fully booked weeks in advance. It's also a good idea to bring plenty of film, and expect to get plastered in paint and sludge, hurled in balloon bombs by gangs of rowdy teenagers.

Sao Tomé ward is the other old quarter, lying north of Fontainhas on the far side of Emilio Gracia Road. This is the area to head for if you fancy a bar crawl: the narrow streets are dotted with dozens of hole-in-the-wall taverns, serving stiff measures of rocket-fuel *feni* under strip lights and the watchful gaze of colourful Madonnas. Drinks are cheap in these places, but you'll probably feel less conspicuous in the neighbourhood's best-known hostelry, the *Hotel Venite* (see p.79), at the north end of Janeiro Road.

South of Church Square

South of Church Square, the only landmark in a featureless jumble of concrete is the multicoloured **Mahalakshmi temple**, dating from the early eighteenth century and the first Hindu shrine established in Panjim during Portuguese rule. Behind it, a flight of stone steps climbs through shady woods to the top of Altinho Hill, where the grandest of Panjim's old colonial houses languish in overgrown gardens. Among the few not suffering from terminal neglect is the **Bishop's Palace**, where the Pope stayed during his 1989 visit to Goa.

The State Archeological Museum

The most noteworthy feature of Panjim's **State Archeological Museum** (Mon–Fri 9.30am–1.15pm & 2–5.30pm) at the far end of Ourem Creek, near the Kadamba bus stand, is its imposing size, which stands in glaringly inverse proportion to the scale of the collection inside. In their bid to erect a structure befitting a state capital, Goa's status-obsessed bureaucrats ignored the fact that there was precious little to put in it. The only rarities to be found amid the lame array of temple sculpture, hero stones and dowdy colonial-era artefacts are a couple of beautiful **Jain bronzes** rescued by Customs and Excise officials from smugglers and, on the first floor, the infamous Italian-style **table** used by Goa's Grand Inquisitors, complete with its original, ornately carved tall-backed chairs. On your way out, look out too for the photos of the prehistoric rock carvings at Kajur and Usgalimal, lining the walls of the main entrance hall. Their discovery in a remote corner of the state in 1993 effectively redrew the Konkan coast's archeological map by proving that more than twelve thousand years ago – well before the arrival of settled agriculturists from the north – the region supported a population of hunter-gatherers.

Eating and drinking

Catering for the droves of tourists who come here from other Indian states, as well as fussy, more price-conscious locals, Panjim is packed with good **places to eat**, from hole-in-the-wall fish-curry-rice joints to swish air-conditioned restaurants serving top-notch Mughlai cuisine. In a week you could feasibly attempt a gastronomic tour of the subcontinent without straying more than five minutes from Church Square. Most eating places are connected to a hotel, but there are also plenty of other independently run places offering quality food for far less than you pay in the coastal resorts. Vegetarians are particularly well catered for at the numerous South Indian-style cafeterias (known locally as "*udipi* restaurants") that have sprung up in recent years. Most open at around 7am to provide breakfast for early-rising office *wallahs*. Beer, *feni* and other spirits are available in all but the purest "pure veg" places.

Delhi Durbar Mahatma Gandhi Rd, behind the *Hotel Mandovi*. A provincial branch of the famous Mumbai restaurant, and the best place in Panjim – if not all Goa – to sample traditional Mughlai cuisine of mainly meat steeped in rich, spicy sauces (try their superb *rogan ghosh* or melt-in-the-mouth chicken *tikka*). For vegetarians, there's a generous choice of fresh veg dishes, including a delicious *malai kofta*. Beer and spirits available. Most main dishes are pricey at around Rs120, but this place is well worth a splurge.

Goenchin Off Dr Dada Vaidya Rd. Glacial a/c and dim lighting, but (along with *Sweet and Sour* in Vasco – see p.174) this is the best and most authentic Chinese food to be found in Goa. Count on Rs400 per head.

Horseshoe Rua de Ourem, Fontainhas. The town's only Portuguese-Goan restaurant, serving a limited, but very reasonably priced, menu of old standards such as *caldo verde* soup and grilled sardines. The food is so-so, but the decor and atmosphere make this a worthwhile option. Most main dishes around Rs70.

Megson's Next to *Rosoyo*, 18 June Rd. The state's top deli, with a great selection of traditional Goan foods: spicy sausages, prepared meats, tangy cheese from the Nilgiris, olive oil, and the best *bebinca* you can buy (ask for Linda brand).

Monginis Dr Atmaram Borkar Rd. A recently opened, highly air-conditioned pastry shop that does great choc-chip cake, date-and-walnut cup sponges and English-style homemade biscuits. Take away, or eat in on a little marble mezzanine floor.

Nandan Ground floor of *Rajdhani* hotel, Dr Atmaram Borkar Rd. The classiest *thali* joint in town, with comfortable upholstered furniture and a/c. They offer a choice of Gujarati, Punjabi, South Indian or Chinese meals – all pure vegetarian.

Rosoyo 18 June Rd. Run by *Megson's*, this busy little fast-food joint is the place to sample tasty, hygienic Bombay-style street food: crunchy *bhel puri* (crispy fried noodles served cold with lime, coriander and chopped onion) or delicious *pau bhaji* (spicy tomato and potato-based mush dished up with a blob of butter and a fluffy Portuguese bread roll). They also serve wonderful Gujarati snacks such as *thepla* – *chappatis* griddle-cooked with curry leaves and cummin, and served with South Indian *chatni* – plus a full range of shakes and ice creams. You'll be hard pushed to spend Rs50 here.

Satkar 18 June Rd. Newest and much the most congenial of Panjim's numerous South Indian snack joints. They do a huge range of dishes, including Chinese and North Indian, but most people go for their fantastic *masala dosas* and piping hot, crunchy *samosas* – the best in town.

Shiv Sagar MG Rd. Smarter than average snack café that does a brisk trade with Panjim's middle classes for its consistently fresh, delicious pan-Indian food and fresh fruit juices. The northern dishes aren't so great, but their South Indian menu is superb (try the delicious *palak dosa*, made with spinach). A/c "family" mezzanine upstairs. No alcohol.

Star Bar 4km west in Ribandar. Rough-and-ready café-bar on the riverside, frequented mostly by local students from the nearby management college. Worth braving the spit-and-sawdust atmosphere, long waits and lack of toilets for the wonderfully traditional Goan seafood, which is all melt-in-the-mouth fresh and comes pan-fried in firey rechead and millet crumbs. Try their amazing mussels (dzob) and bring plenty of mozzie repellent. Most dishes Rs40–65.

Tony's Emilio Gracia Rd/31 Janeiro Rd, Fontainhas. Blue-painted street stall run by retired footballer and his wife, who serve up the freshest, tastiest and most authentic Goan food in town. Dishes (see Glossary on p.341 for explanations) change daily, but they usually do sublime fish cutlets, mince rissoles, chicken *xacuti*, chilli beef, *sorpatel* and – on Saturdays only – perfect *sanna*, made with real palm *toddi*. Ask for a helping of *feijoada* and some of their fresh *poee*. Around Rs30 per person for a filling meal; no veg options. Takeaway only.

Venite 31 Janeiro Rd. With its wooden floors and romantic, candle-lit balcony seats, this tourist-oriented place used to be worth coming to Panjim for in itself, but things have gone drastically downhill since the original owner sold up and it's now best avoided.

Vihar Around the corner from *Venite*, on Avenida Dom Joao Castro. One of the best South Indian snack cafés in Panjim, and more conveniently situated than its competitors if you're staying in Fontainhas. Try their tasty *rawa masala dosas* or cheese *uttapams*. The only drawback with this place is the traffic noise, so avoid it during rush hours.

Viva Panjim 178 Rua 31 de Janeiro, behind Mary Immaculate High School, Fontainhas ☎ 0832/242 2405. Traditional Goan home cooking – xacutis, vindaloo, prawn balchao, cafreal, amotik and delicious freshly grilled fish – served by a charming local lady in an atmospheric colonial-era backstreet. This place should be your first choice for dinner if you're staying in Fontainhas.

Shopping

Goans love to grumble about how bad Panjim is for **shopping**, but in recent years, largely thanks to tourism and the input of Gulf money, the capital's commercial centre has picked up a lot and boasts several shops worth a trip to town for.

Top of your souvenir hunting list should be **cashew nuts**, sold in bulk from a string of stores along 18 June Road. Zantye's, available at several different outlets, are generally regarded as the best brand, but they've plenty of competition. The nuts themselves, which are the state's most lucrative foreign export after iron ore, are as good as any in the world. They come in various qualities and sizes, salted or plain, with and without shells, and are sold pre-packed at fixed prices. If you're not convinced of how delicious they are, ask for a small taster packet.

Goan **feni**, the ideal accompaniment for dry-roasted cashews, is also sold at numerous liquor shops along 18 June Road. Souvenir bottles tend to come covered in horrendous shell confections, but you can buy the same stuff a lot more cheaply in plain plastic or glass containers.

As nearly all "Goan handicrafts" are imported, authentic artisanal items are thin on the ground. The only truly traditional Goan souvenirs available are **azulejos**, Portuguese painted tiles, which you'll find at a tiny gallery tucked down a sidestreet just outside the Chapel of St Sebastian in Fontainhas. Most are quickly rendered, kitsch vignettes of "typical" Goan scenes, but they also do Baroque door numbers and decorative plaques exactly like the ones you see around Fontainhas. While in the area, have a nose, too, around the Geetanjali Gallery in the *Panjim Pousada* (part of the *Panjim Inn* – see Accommodation), which displays (and markets) original **paintings** by local artists.

Sosa's, a little air-conditioned boutique around the corner next door to the *Horseshoe* restaurant at E-245 Rua de Ourem, stocks the town's best selection of Goan **designer clothes**, ranging from glamorous ethnic frocks to loose, Portuguese-style cotton shirts. If they don't have what you want in your size, ask if they can arrange to have one made to measure.

The coastal resorts are full of young **tailors** who can run off baggy pyjama trousers and shirts on their old Singer sewing machines, but if you're after anything more serious – such as Indian *kurtas* or suits – Panjim is a safer bet. One of the town's top stitchers (at least for men's clothes) is Chandu Tailors, down a small arcade (ask for the Sai Baba temple) opposite the National Cinema, just off Church Square. The best source of traditional Indian textiles is the nearby government Khadi Grammodyog, opposite *Rajdhani Hotel* on Dr Atmaram Borkar Rd, which sells various kinds of hand-spun cotton for next to nothing and bolts of wonderful pure silk.

For conventional Western **men's wear**, both ready made and made-to-measure, a dependable outlet with a huge range is Bharne Creations on Cunha Rivara Rd, just north of the Municipal Gardens. The main shop stocks boxed shirts by major British brands (made in India, of course) sold at half the price you'd pay at home; and they have a subsidiary branch around the corner with a selection of quality material to choose from.

Other good buys in the town (although strictly speaking not Goan at all) are the wonderful tribal *dokra* (lost-wax) metal items, leather sculpture and textiles (mostly block-printed and batik) sold at Mrignayanee in the Kadamba bus stand. This new emporium, set up by the state government of Madhya Pradesh to provide employment for some of its poorest inhabitants, is run along the lines of an Oxfam shop, with recycled newspaper bags instead of plastic (made by blind victims of the Bhopal gas disaster) and strictly fixed prices.

Out at Ribandar, 5km east of town on the road to Old Goa, **Camelot** is a swish lifestyle emporium with a range of traditional Indian furniture and textiles, as well as expensive clothes by renowned Indian designers such as Wendell Rodricks and Savio Jon. See also our write-up of lifestyle galleries on p.139.

Finally, anyone suffering withdrawal symptoms from their local shopping mall should head for the road behind the *Mandovi Hotel*, near *Delhi Durbar* restaurant, where a handful of international retailers – Levis, Benetton and Reebok among them – sell familiar products at lower prices than back home. The same applies to watchmakers, Titan, who've a swish outlet on 18 June Road, along with several pricey sunglasses manufacturers.

Listings

Airlines Air France, Air Seychelles, American Airlines, Biman Bangladesh, Gulf Air, Kenyan Airways, Royal Jordanian, Sri Lankan Airlines, all c/o Jetair, Rizvi Chambers, 1st Floor, H Salgado Rd ☎0832/222 2438, 222 6154 or 222 3172; Air India, *Hotel Fidalgo*, 18 June Rd ☎0832/222 4081; Alitalia, Globe Trotters International, G-7 Shankar Parvati Bldg, 18 June Rd ☎0832/243 6702, ☎222 9678; British Airways, DKI Airlines Service, 2 Excelsior Chambers, MG Rd ☎ & ☎222 4573; Indian Airlines, Dempo House, Dr D Bandodkar Road ☎0832/222 4081; Jet Airlines, Sesa Ghor, ECD Plaza, next to GTDC *Panjim Residency*, Pato ☎0832/224 3147 or 222 1476; Sahara Airlines, Ground Floor, Livein Appts, General Bernard Guedes Rd ☎0832/223 7346 or 223 0237.

Banks and ATMs The most efficient places in Panjim to change money are: Thomas Cook, near the Indian Airlines office, at 8 Alcon Chambers, Devanand Bandodkar Rd (Mon–Sat 9am–6pm, Oct–March also Sun 10am–5pm); and the Pheroze Framroze Exchange Bureau on Dr P Shirgaonkar Rd (Mon–Sat 9.30am–7pm & Sun 9.30am–1pm). Unlike most private companies, the latter's rates are competitive and they don't charge commission on either currency or traveller's cheques. The HDFC Bank on 18 June Rd has a handy 24hr ATM, where you can make withdrawals using Visa or Mastercard. Changing money in the regular, government-run banks tends to take a lot longer: the Bank of Baroda (where you can draw money on Visa cards), is on Azad Maidan.

Books The bookshops in the *Hotel Fidalgo* and the *Hotel Mandovi* stock English-language titles, including paperback pulp fiction and guides, but the best selection of Goa-related books is at the Broadway Book Centre, on Dr P Shirgaonkar Rd, off MG Rd, which sells a great range of old stuff in facsimile editions and lots of architecture and photographic tomes in hardback – at discounted prices.

British Consular Assistant The British High Commission of Mumbai has a Consular Assistant in Panjim (see p.17): Shilpa Sarah Caldeira's office is on the third floor of 302 Manguirish Building (opposite Gulf Supermarket), 18 June Rd ☎0832/222 8571, ☎223 2828.

Hospital Panjim's Government Hospital, in the west of town at the far end of Avda Dom Joao Castro, is grim and overstretched; if you're able to travel, head for the more modern and better-equipped Goa Medical College (aka GMC) ☎0832/222 3010, 222 3026 or 222 3658, 7km south on NH17 at Bambolim. Ambulances (☎102) are likely to get you there a lot less quickly than a standard taxi.

Internet access A couple of Panjim's hotels offer Internet access to residents, including the *Park Lane Lodge* and the *Panjim Inn*. In addition, a couple of Internet bureaus can be found on the west side of Church Square.

Laundry The hole-in-the-wall laundry on the south side of Pato Road, between the bus stand and Pato Bridge (Mon–Sat 9.30am–8.30pm), cleans clothes within 24 hours. The only place open on a Sunday is the pricey dry cleaner's in GTDC's *Tourist Hostel* on Avda Dom Joao Castro.

Music and dance Regular recitals of classical Indian music and dance are held at Panjim's school for the performing arts, the Kala Academy in Campal, at the far west end of town on Dr D Bandodkar Road. For details of forthcoming events, consult the boards in front of the auditorium or the listings page of local newspapers. The best place to shop for cassettes and CDs, both Indian and Western, is VP Sinari's, which has two branches: one opposite the Secretariat, and the other near the Bombay Bazaar mall on 18 June Rd. For musical instruments, including excellent-value Hoffner and Gibson copy guitars, mandolins and cases, as well as tabla, sitar and hand drums, call at Pedro Fernandes & Cia, 19 Avda Dom Joao Castro, next door to the *Vihar* restaurant, near the Head Post Office.

Petrol The main petrol pump in Panjim is on Ava Dom Joao Castro, just east of the Secretariat building; the fuel sold here is dependably clean. There's also a good pump across the river in Betim – riders without international licences are advised to park up there and catch the ferry over the Mandovi to avoid Panjim's ubiquitous traffic police.

Pharmacies Hindu Pharma, near the tourist office on Church Square ☎0832/222 3176, stocks a phenomenal range of Ayurvedic, homeopathic and allopathic medicines.

Police The Police Headquarters is on Malaca Road, central Panjim. In an emergency, call ☎100.

Poste restante Panjim's reliable poste restante counter (Mon–Sat 9.30am–1pm & 2–5.30pm) is at the Head Post Office, 200m west of Pato Bridge. Note that to get your stamps franked (the only way to ensure they won't get peeled off and resold by some unscrupulous clerk), you have to walk around the back of the building and ask at the office behind the second door on the right. Indian postal regulations insist that parcels have to be stitched in cotton and sealed; this can be done at the Deepak store, on the corner of the next block north from the post office.

Travel agents AERO Mundial, Ground Floor, Hotel Mandovi, Dr D Bandodkar Rd ☎0832/222 3773; Menezes Air Travel, Rua de Ourem ☎ & ☎0832/222 2214. For air tickets, try MGM International, Mamai Camotim Building (near the Secretariat).

Moving on to Mumbai (Bombay)

If you're heading north to **Mumbai**, the quickest and easiest way is **by plane**. Seven or eight flights leave Goa's Dabolim airport daily. One-way fares range from $63 with Indian Airlines, or $93 with Sahara, to $103 with Jet. In addition, Air India operates a service to Mumbai which few people seem to know about, so you can nearly always get a seat on it (the one drawback is that you have to check in three hours before departure as Air India is an international carrier). Wherever possible, try to book tickets directly through the airline (for addresses see "Listings" on p.81). Private agents charge you the dollar fare at poor rates of exchange, although when you take into account the cost of the taxi and hassle involved in travelling to the airline office, the net saving of booking direct may seem irrelevant.

Since the inauguration of the **Konkan Railway** in 1996, journey times to Mumbai from Goa have been slashed from twenty-four to twelve hours. Two services run daily, the most convenient of them being the Konkan–Kanya Express (#0112), which departs from Margao at 6pm, arriving at CST (still commonly known as "Victoria Terminus", or "VT") at 5.55am the following day. The other fast train from Margao to Mumbai CST is the Madgaon–Mumbai Express (#0104), departing at 10.30am and arriving at 9.45pm.

The cheapest, though most nightmarish, way to get to Mumbai is by **night bus**, which takes fourteen to eighteen hours, covering 500km of rough road at often terrifying speeds. Fares vary according to levels of comfort, and luxury buses arrive two or three hours sooner. Book Kadamba bus tickets at their offices in the Panjim and Mapusa bus stands (daily 9–11am & 2–5pm); private companies sell theirs through the many travel agents immediately outside the bus stand in Panjim, and at the bottom of the square in Mapusa. The most popular private service to Mumbai, and the most expensive, is the 24-seater run by a company called Paulo Travels. A cramped berth on this bus (which bizarrely you may have to share) costs Rs600, and it is worth pointing out that women travellers have complained of harassment during the journey. For tickets, contact Paulo Holiday Makers, near the Kadamba bus stand, Panjim (☎0832/222 3736), or at Hotel Nanutel, opposite Club Harmonia, Margao (☎0832/272 1516). Information on all departures and fares is available from Goa Tourism's counter inside Panjim's bus stand (see p.72).

Miramar

Panjim's esplanade continues west through the swish suburb of Campal, with its grand colonial residences (and their modern concrete counterparts), before swinging south past the *Marriott* hotel towards the beach at **MIRAMAR**. If this were anywhere else but Goa, you might be tempted to spend an afternoon here, enjoying two kilometres of sand and views across Aguada Bay. As it is, the beach's noisy bus parties and over-zealous peanut *wallahs* make it far less attractive than most of the other resorts in easy reach of the capital. If all you want is a quick escape from Panjim to watch the sunset, however, the south end of Miramar beach, fifteen minutes' walk from the bus park, is fine. At this time of day, the only people you see are fishermen fixing their nets under the palm trees, and the odd café owner staring hopefully up the beach from an empty terrace.

Buses to Miramar leave every fifteen minutes from Panjim's Kadamba stand. You can also pick them up from the steamer jetty north of Church Square, and at various points along the waterfront. Travelling in the other direction, they stop just off Miramar's main roundabout. For a review of the *Marriott*, see p.73.

Dona Paula

Nestled 9km southwest of Panjim on the south side of the rocky, hammer-shaped headland that divides the Zuari and Mandovi estuaries, **DONA PAULA** takes its name from a viceroy's daughter who threw herself off the cliff here when refused permission to marry a local fisherman. Today, the views from the top of the peninsula over Miramar beach and Mormugao Bay are pleasant enough, but the village itself – a swanky suburb and upmarket beach resort – is characterless and commercialized, and not somewhere you'd choose to spend much time unless you're staying in one of the campus hotels that have mushroomed here in recent years.

Due to its proximity to Panjim, Dona Paula is a popular stop on GTDC bus tours of the area and tends to be heaving in season with crowds of visitors. Taking advantage of this transient trade, stalls laden with tasteless T-shirts and "I Love Goa" straw hats line the old fishing jetty, from where a small ferry shuttles across the bay to Mormugao harbour four times a day (20min). There's nothing much to see from the other side, but the trip is great fun, as the rusty old tub pitches and rolls past the container ships and sand dredgers moored at the mouth of the Zuari. The bluff behind Dona Paula's ferry jetty is crowned with a mock acropolis, below which stands Baroness von Leistner's white-washed sculpture, *Image of India*, depicting a couple staring wistfully in opposite directions – the man towards the past and the woman to the nation's future.

Crouched on the westernmost tip of the headland, known as **Cabo Raj Bhavan**, is the official residence of the Governor of Goa, Daman and Diu. The site, a viceregal seat since 1918, used to be occupied by a Portuguese fort, erected in the seventeenth century to guard the entrance to Goa harbour, whose cannons crossed fire with those of Aguada to the north and Mormugao to the south. These days, nothing remains of the old citadel, but you can still visit the small Our Lady of Cabo church, founded by the Portuguese in 1541, while from the road beyond the Institute of Oceanography you can see the ruins of the small **military cemetery** built by the British at the time of their brief occupation of the Cabo during the Napoleonic wars – a move intended to deter the French from invading Goa.

Practicalities

Regular **buses** run from Panjim to Dona Paula until around 9pm, dropping passengers at the roundabout below the Institute of Oceanography, where you can usually pick up an auto-rickshaw into town. Mini-van **taxis** hang around outside the four main resort hotels, situated along the road to the jetty and 1km further east in the once sleepy hamlet of **Vainguinim**, where you'll find the five-star *Cidade de Goa* (T0832/222 1133, F222 3303; ➒), designed by the famous Goan architect Charles Correa (Arundhati Roy's former husband). With its two pools, shopping arcades, tennis courts, sauna, gym and watersports facilities, this is the village's premier resort complex, where a room will set you back upwards of $245 per night. Overlooking a small and relatively inaccessible beach, it's sheltered on one side by a wooded headland, and on the other by an old laterite wall. Behind the *Cidade de Goa*, the more modest *Hotel Villa Sol* (T0832/222 5852; ➏) also has sea-facing air-conditioned rooms, a pool and sun terraces. Dona Paula's two remaining **luxury hotels** are both on the opposite side of the bay above the jetty, and cater exclusively for package tourists. The secluded *Prainha* (T0832/222 4162, F222 9959; ➐) offers simple but comfortable chalets with balconies, and easy access to a quiet sandy cove to the north. The same is true of the *Dona Paula Beach Resort*, aka *O Pescador* (T0832/222 7955, F222 1371; ➑), the most tastefully designed of the bunch, with ersatz Portuguese blocks around a central lawn and pool, and some rooms with air conditioning and sea views.

All of the places listed above have pricey à la carte **restaurants** that welcome non-residents. For a drink, steer clear of the raucous, messy cafés along the waterfront in favour of the *Crosshill*, at the top of the village, overlooking the roundabout below the Institute of Oceanography, which is quieter and has a sociable garden.

Goa Velha

Blink during the breakneck journey between Panjim and Dabolim airport on the NH17, and you will probably miss **GOA VELHA**. Yet this roadside village, dotted among the paddy fields 9km southeast of the capital, was, until the emergence of Ela (Old Goa) during the fifteenth century, southwest India's wealthiest city and busiest port.

Govapuri, or Gopakkapttana (later Gova), was founded in 1054 by the Kadamba ruler Jayakeshi I, who moved his capital here from Chandrapura – now Chandor in Salcete *taluka* – to exercise more control over the movement of maritime traffic through the busy harbour. Import duties and taxes creamed off this lucrative trade (in Arabian horses, Chinese silks and southeast Asian spices) financed the construction of sumptuous palaces, temples and a well-planned city with its own charitable institutions. The period of prosperity survived two Kadamba rebellions, brutally put down by their Chalukyan overlords, but not the arrival in Govapuri of the Sultan of Delhi's army in 1312. Following a lengthy siege – witnessed and vividly described in his memoirs by the great Arab traveller, Ibn Battuta – the Goan kings fled back to Chandrapura. Thereafter, the city witnessed a series of bloody sackings as it changed hands between the Muslim Bahmani dynasty and the Hindu Vijayanagars. It was finally left to rot in 1470, after the Zuari River silted up and receded, leaving the harbour high and dry.

The Procession of the Saints

The Procession of the Third Franciscan Order, better known as the **Procession of the Saints**, is one of the highlights of the state's religious calendar. Borne on the shoulders of local devotees, dozens of life-size effigies of saints, martyrs, popes, kings, queens and cardinals are paraded around the village of Goa Velha on the first Monday of Easter week, watched by a huge crowd.

The tradition was instigated in the seventeenth century by the Franciscans as an attempt to reverse the decline in morals afflicting the colony at that time. Once the libertines and ruffians of Old Goa had clapped eyes on such striking symbols of piety and self-sacrifice, they would – or so it was hoped – give up their licentious lifestyles and embrace the teachings of Christ. The event caught on, and by the eighteenth century a total of 65 lavishly attired statues, encrusted with gold and precious stones, took part in the procession. However, when the religious orders were suppressed in 1835, it was banned and many statues destroyed. Not until the end of the nineteenth century was the parade finally revived, using money donated by the Franciscans.

Today, after delivering the Sermon of St Francis in the Church of St Andrew in Goa Velha, a priest orders a heavy black curtain to be drawn back, revealing the assembled effigies for the first time. Mounted on floats, the 26 figures are then carried into the square and around the village by members of **confrades**, "religious brotherhoods" formed out of the medieval trades guilds (ie to preserve caste divisions). Along the way, onlookers duck under the floats to receive the blessings of the saints. In their wake march representatives of the clergy, local villagers, schoolchildren chanting rosaries and, finally, members of the Third Franciscan Order. The procession draws to a close with a candle-lit Mass outside the church, the statues arranged in a semicircle.

Although the parade itself is essentially a solemn affair, the funfair that accompanies it certainly isn't. Togged out in their Sunday-best *shirtings*, *suitings* and silk dresses, busloads of visitors descend on Goa Velha for the festival and for an auspicious glimpse of the 26 statues, displayed for the two days following the parade in St Andrew's Church.

Precious little of ancient Govapuri remains in Goa Velha, save for the ruins of the original harbour walls, which local fishermen sometimes see protruding through the mud of the estuary at low tide (the museum in Pilar – see below – displays a couple of photos of these). However, if you pull off the highway just before entering the village (from the Panjim side), at the De Souza general store, and follow the lane running into the *toddi* grove between the Kadesh Gas shop and mechanic's yard, you'll eventually come across the only in situ remnant of the once great city: a tubular, perfectly carved Kadamba **millstone** used for extracting coconut oil (the dynasty's chief export), which must have been too heavy, or too useful, to move; ask for the "*fatrar*".

Pilar

The seminary at **PILAR**, resting on the edge of a thickly wooded hill 12km southeast of Panjim and a couple of kilometres from Goa Velha, is one of the two theological colleges that survived out of the four founded by the Portuguese (the other is at Rachol). Established by the Capuchins in 1613, it was abandoned after the expulsion of the religious orders in 1835, but restored 22 years later by the Carmelites. Although it boasts a well-preserved seventeenth-century church and a small museum, the seminary, which is now run as a training college for Christian missionaries, isn't a particularly inspiring tourist destination, and most of its visitors come on pilgrimages. However, if you are passing on the nearby NH17, the superb views over the Zuari estuary are worth a quick detour. Any of the Panjim–Cortalim–Vasco buses will drop you at the turn-off on the main road, from where it is possible to take a short cut through the modern wing of the seminary to a flight of old steps that lead up the hill.

The **Church of Our Lady of Pilar**, at the bottom of the car park, is entered through a stately whitewashed Baroque facade, whose gable is inscribed with the seminary's foundation date, 1613. Deeply carved tombstones of Portuguese *hidalgos* line the floor of the entrance porch, to the right of which stands the **tomb of Father Angelo D'Souza**, head of Pilar seminary from 1918 until 1927, and regarded by Goan Christians as a de facto saint. Ranged around a tiny garden, the cloisters inside are decorated with rather clumsily restored seventeenth-century frescoes. Look out, too, for a didactic pictorial depiction of the history of the world, drawn by a missionary in the 1940s for the "speedy and easy instruction of Indians, children and uneducated people."

The priming of young Goan priests for this proselytizing work continues in the large 1950s-style college at the top of the hill. Run by the Mission Society of St Francis Xavier, it occupies the site of an ancient Shiva temple, the Goveshwar *mandir*, from which the name Goa is believed to derive. The Konkani name for the hill itself was *rishincho mellavo*, or "meeting place of the holy men", suggesting this has been one of the region's most sacred sites for thousands of years. All that remains of the former Hindu shrine, however, is a stone-lined tank, which now supplies the seminary orchards. Fragments of pottery and temple sculpture unearthed in the gardens or found submerged in the seminary wells are informatively displayed on the first floor in the small **museum** (Mon–Sat 8am–1pm & 2.30–6pm, Sun by request; admission free), along with a splendid *Simhalanchana*, the Kadambas' traditional lion emblem (in modern times adopted by the state bus company), a beautiful bas relief of St Mary Magdalen carved in 1733 featuring symbols of the four great Indian religions, and a copy of the first Maharathi translation of the Gospels.

The first floor of the building also houses a **chapel** dominated by a set of vibrant stained-glass windows, while the roof terrace a couple of storeys higher up affords fine panoramic views south over the Zuari River towards Vasco, and north across the lush rice fields and palm groves of Tiswadi. Visible to the northeast is the mildewing hulk of Santana Church at Talaulim.

Talaulim

Lost deep in the heart of Tiswadi *taluka*, the village of **TALAULIM**, 4km north of Pilar, would feature on few maps were it not for the enormous **Church of Santana** (St Anne) that looms from its northern edge. Boasting the most spectacular facade outside Old Goa, it is difficult to get to without your own transport, as buses from the capital only run every two hours. With a car or motorcycle, however, you can tie Talaulim into a neat loop with Old Goa, Pilar and Panjim, 7km northwest.

The original church on the site was founded in the sixteenth century after reports that a vision of the Virgin Mary's mother, St Anne, had appeared before local villagers in the form of an old woman with a hat and walking stick. In

1695, a much grander replacement was erected, modelled on the Augustinian Monastery in Old Goa, of which only a single ruined belfry now remains.

Years of neglect have taken their toll on this building, too, but it is still an impressive sight. Rising in five stages, the mighty whitewashed facade is composed of a Baroque gable (featuring a statue of St Anne as its centrepiece), flanked by a pair of square towers and positively bristling with pinnacles, shell motifs and balustrades. Sadly, much of the detail higher up is currently lost under a shroud of black mildew and weeds, although the Portuguese Fundaçao Oriente plan to restore the church in the near future.

To visit the lofty interior, you'll have to summon the key keeper – most easily done by yanking the rusty wire dangling from the belfry, which tolls the bell (if he still doesn't come, ask at the house down the lane leading from the unpainted west wall of the church). Most of the fittings, furniture and decor preserved inside – including an imposing reredos and carved wood pulpit – date from the eighteenth and nineteenth centuries. On your way out look for the tiny dark corridor, running parallel to the main wall, which is still used for hearing confessions.

Old Goa

Soaring high above the surrounding canopy of riverine palm groves, the colossal, cream-painted cathedral towers, belfries and domes of the former Portuguese capital, nowadays known as **OLD GOA**, are by far and away the state's most impressive historical monuments, and collectively one of the finest crops of Renaissance architecture in the world. In its heyday, *Goa Dourada*, "Golden Goa", 10km east of Panjim, was the largest, richest and most splendid city in Asia. With a population of around 300,000 in the 1500s (greater than either Lisbon or London at the time), it sprawled south from a grand civic centre and bustling port on the banks of the Mandovi River to within a stone's throw of the Zuari estuary, and west as far as Ribandar: a maze of narrow twisting streets, piazzas, ochre-washed villas and imposing Baroque churches.

These days you need a fertile imagination indeed to picture Old Goa as it must have looked in the sixteenth and seventeenth centuries. The vast suburbs have disappeared without trace, reduced to rubble and reclaimed by the jungle, leaving a mere dozen or so churches and convents marooned amid the Archeological Survey of India's carefully manicured lawns. Granted World Heritage status by UNESCO, the site attracts busloads of foreign tourists from the coast and Christian pilgrims from around India in roughly equal numbers. While the former come primarily to admire the gigantic facades and gilt altars of Old Goa's beautifully preserved churches, the main attraction for the latter is the tomb of **St Francis Xavier**, the renowned sixteenth-century missionary, whose remains are enshrined in the **Basilica of Bom Jesus**.

If you're staying at one of the nearby resorts and contemplating a day-trip inland, this is the most obvious and accessible option. Thirty minutes by road from the state capital, Old Goa is served by **buses** every fifteen minutes from Panjim's Kadamba bus stand (30min); alternatively, hop into an auto-rickshaw or rent a taxi. All the main package tour companies also offer Old Goa as an optional excursion, while GTDC slots its main highlights into several of their sightseeing tours, starting in Panjim, Mapusa, Vasco, Margao or Colva; further details and tickets for these are available at any GTDC hotel or information counter.

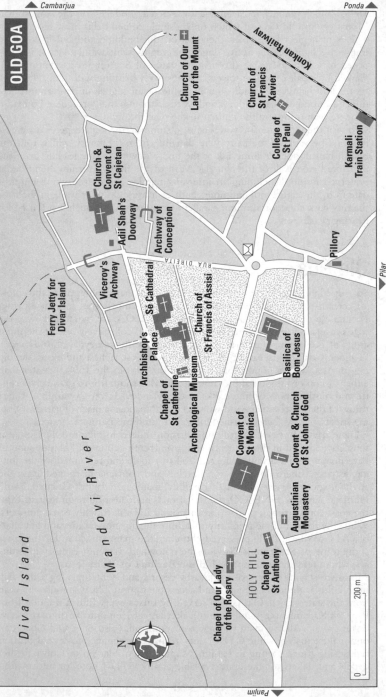

OLD GOA

- Cambarjua
- Ponda

Konkan Railway

Church of Our Lady of the Mount

Church of St Francis Xavier

College of St Paul

Karmali Train Station

Church & Convent of St Cajetan

Adil Shah's Doorway

Archway of Conception

Viceroy's Archway

Sé Cathedral

RUA DIREITA

Church of St Francis of Assisi

Pillory

Pilar

Ferry Jetty for Divar Island

Archbishop's Palace

Archeological Museum

Chapel of St Catherine

Basilica of Bom Jesus

Mandovi River

Divar Island

Convent of St Monica

Convent & Church of St John of God

Augustinian Monastery

HOLY HILL

Chapel of St Anthony

Chapel of Our Lady of the Rosary

N

200 m

0

- Panjim

Some history

The earliest recorded occupation of Old Goa was at the beginning of the twelfth century, when the local Hindu king founded a brahmin colony, or *brahmapuri* here. Known as **Ela**, the settlement later expanded under the Vijayanagars, but was occupied by the Bahmani Muslims after they razed the former Hindu capital of Govapuri (now Goa Velha) further south. Eventually, Ela became the second city of the ruler of Bijapur, **Yusuf 'Adil Shah**, following the break-up of the Bahmani kingdom towards the end of the fifteenth century. Encircled by fortified walls and a deep moat, Ela's grandest building was the 'Adil Shah's palace, whose lofty minarets once dominated the town, but of which only a lone-standing doorway now remains.

Goa's fabled golden age began in 1510 with the appearance of the Portuguese. Commanded by **Alfonso de Albuquerque**, a squadron of warships moved in to mop up the remnants of a Muslim fleet it had previously engaged off Kerala, then seized the town to use it as a base for operations along the Malabar coast. The Portuguese were able to profit from the lucrative local trade in horses and spices, and as the wealth poured in, so did immigrants – by the end of the sixteenth century, some 2500 new arrivals every year replenished a population constantly depleted by disease. With them came missionaries from various religious orders, encouraged by the colonial government as a "civilizing influence" on both the natives and famously licentious colonials. This process was hastened by the arrival in 1542 of **Francis Xavier**, and by the dreaded Holy Office, better known as the **Inquisition**, for whose trials and bloody *autos da fé* the colony later became notorious.

Beneath the outward gloss of piety, however, Goa was fast developing a reputation for **decadence**. Accounts by European travellers of the day record that adultery, drunkenness and prostitution were rife, although ultimately natural and economic factors rather than vice were to bring about the city's decline. The original site was swampland, a perfect breeding ground for malaria-carrying mosquitoes. Bad drainage caused drinking water to become infected by raw sewage, and more than half the city's inhabitants died during the **epidemics** of 1543 and 1570, with a further 25,000 perishing in the first thirty years of the seventeenth century. To compound the health problems, the Mandovi started to silt up, preventing ships entering the harbour. Finally, after the Portuguese trade monopoly had been broken by the British, French and Dutch, **Viceroy Conde do Alvor** ordered the administrative capital to be shifted to Mormugao. This scheme was eventually dropped in favour of a move upriver to Panjim, but the damage to Old Goa had already been done, and most of the houses were demolished to provide masonry for the new capital. When the chronicler Abbé Cottineau de Kloguen passed through in 1827, he remarked with dismay that "nothing remains of the city but the sacred; the profane is entirely banished".

Arrival and orientation

Arriving by **bus**, you'll be dropped off just south of the main square, which is flanked by the Basilica of Bom Jesus to the south, and the Sé Cathedral, Church of St Francis Assisi and archeological museum to the north. The main highlights all lie within comfortable walking distance of here and can be seen in two to three hours. The logical place to start any tour of the site is at its northeast corner, where the **Viceroy's Archway** marks the traditional entrance to the city from the Mandovi riverfront. Head south from here along the **Rua Direita**, Old Goa's principal thoroughfare, and you'll pass the chief monuments in more or less chronological order, winding up at the Basilica, the spiritual hub of Old Goa. It's also well worth making an additional foray west to **Holy Hill**, site of some of the city's oldest and architecturally most important buildings, and east to the hilltop Church of Our Lady of the Mount, which commands the best view of the old city and its environs. However long you spend exploring the site, be sure to bring a sun hat and plenty of drinking water, as the heat and humidity can be ferocious.

The site

Throughout its most prosperous period in the sixteenth and early seventeenth centuries, Old Goa could only be reached by river. This remains the most spectacular approach to the site, although the vast majority of visitors now travel up the Mandovi from Panjim by road, crossing a three-kilometre-long causeway, the **Ponte de Linhares**, built by slaves in 1633 and reputedly still the longest bridge in South Asia.

Originally, the riverbank was lined with the city's grandest *palacios* and mansions, which contemporary oil paintings show were painted a uniform white, with high-pitched terracotta-tiled roofs and austere fortified facades. Today, none of these remain, although you can get some idea of what they looked like from the Archbishop's Palace, described below, and the gorgeous Casa dos Colçao at nearby Ribandar, 5km west on the roadside (not open to visitors), which you pass en route to Old Goa from Panjim. Having docked at the main quay (now a barge refitting yard), new arrivals would enter the city walls via the pompous Viceroy's Archway, the only fragment of the walls still standing. Made from a mixture of red laterite and green granite, the gate was erected in

The architecture of Old Goa

Exuding the spirit of imperial self-confidence typical of its day, the architecture of Old Goa is resolutely European, inspired by contemporary Italian fashions rather than the indigenous traditions which it supplanted. The high point of the colony's building boom, in the early seventeenth century, coincided with the end of the Renaissance in Europe and the beginning of the **Baroque era** with its predilection for twisting scrollwork, chubby winged cherubs, lashings of gilt and generally over-the-top ornamentation. In part, this shift was a reaction against the restrictive conventions of the past, but it also served the purposes of missionaries by providing awe-inspiring spectacles to impress new converts. You only have to step inside the Basilica of Bom Jesus to get some idea of the impact such splendour must have had on local people more used to modest monochrome stone temples.

The other architectural style represented at Old Goa is more particularly Portuguese. Named after its principal patron, King Manuel (1495–1521), the **Manueline movement** celebrated the achievements of the Portuguese discoveries by incorporating nautical motifs, such as anchors and ropes, into the buildings' design. Few examples of this style have survived, but you'll get a sense of it from the main doorway of the Church of St Francis of Assisi, next to the museum, or the Church of Our Lady of the Rosary on Holy Hill.

Although many of Old Goa's churches feature decorative details carved from **basalt** (reputedly brought to Goa as ballast in the ships that sailed from Lisbon, but more probably quarried at Bassein, near Mumbai), virtually all of Old Goa's churches were made of local laterite. As this porous red-brown stone eroded badly during the annual monsoons, a thick coat of lime whitewash, made from crushed clam shells, was traditionally applied over the top, and renewed after each rainy season. Nowadays, a far less appealing off-white paint is used, but the principle remains the same, as you'll see if you come here in September or early October, when the buildings are invariably still covered with streaks of black mildew.

1599 by Viceroy Francisco da Gama as a memorial to the achievements of his grandfather, the famous explorer Vasco da Gama, whose statue and coat of arms feature on the river-facing side. On the opposite facade, a Bible-carrying figure stands with its feet on the neck of a cringing native, symbolizing the victory of Christianity over "paganism".

Once under the archway, people would head along the Rua Direita (so named because it was allegedly the only straight street in town), towards the civic centre, passing the main bazaar, customs house, foundry and arsenal en route. Only sleepy palm groves line the road today, but when French adventurer François Pyrard walked down it after being shipwrecked in the Maldives in 1608, he was overwhelmed by the Rua Direita's cosmopolitan prosperity: "on both sides [are] many rich lapidaries, goldsmiths, and bankers, as well as the richest and best merchants and artisans in all Goa: Portuguese, Italians, Germans and other Europeans."

The Church and Convent of St Cajetan

The distinctive domed **Church of St Cajetan**, just south of the Viceroy's Archway, was erected between 1612 and 1661 by the Theatine Order. Sent to India by Pope Urban VIII, the priest-missionaries were refused entry to their original destination, the Sultanate of Galconda, and settled instead in Goa, where they built themselves this miniature replica of St Peter's in Rome, naming it after the founding father of their order.

Like St Peter's, the church's dome, the only one remaining in Old Goa, is partially obscured from below by a grand Neoclassical facade, pierced by a Corinthian portico and flanked by a pair of square-turreted towers – the only concession made by the Italian architect to local Portuguese taste. Inside, the cross-plan of the building centres on a slab of stone concealing a well, thought to be a remnant of the Hindu temple that formerly stood on the site. St Cajetan is also renowned for its fine **woodcarving**, notably the decoration of the pulpit, and the panels surrounding the high altar dedicated to La Divina Providencia. Behind this, a free-standing reredos rests on top of the crypt where the embalmed bodies of Portuguese governors were once kept in lead coffins before they were shipped back to Lisbon. Forgotten for over thirty years, the last batch (of three) was only removed in 1992 on the eve of the state visit to Goa of Portuguese President Mario Soares.

Adjoining this church is the **Convent of St Cajetan**, recently renovated and now used as a theological college for newly ordained priests. Immediately to its west, a lone-standing grey basalt **doorway**, raised on a plinth and reached by a flight of five steps, is all that remains of the once-grand Islamic **palace of 'Adil Shah**, ruler of Goa until the arrival of the Portuguese. Prior to the construction of the new viceregal Fortress Palace on the waterfront, the building was occupied by the ruling viceroys. Thereafter the Inquisition took it over, converting its basement into dungeons. It was here that the Inquisitor and his household lived and worked, while below, suspected heretics such as the Frenchman Dellon (see "The Goan Inquisition" box p.94) were held and tortured. It was also here that the infamous Inquisitors' table resided.

Sections of the palace still stood when the governor decamped downriver to the swish suburb of Panelim in 1754, but these were eventually pulled down for use in the construction of Panjim. Ironically, the Muslim doorway may also have been made from plundered masonry. The decorative work on the lintel is typically Hindu, indicating that the stone must have come from an older temple erected nearby, although the scrollwork was clearly a later Portuguese addition.

△ The Church of St Francis of Assisi, Old Goa

The main square and Sé Cathedral

Old Goa's **main square**, originally known as the Terreiro de Gales, was formerly used for public hangings, cockfights and as a Portuguese military parade ground. These days, however, its well-watered lawns serve as a picnic spot for bus parties. A stern notice warns visitors (or more particularly "couples") not to "commit unholy acts" in the grounds, under threat of imprisonment or a hefty Rs5000 fine. It is presumably to enforce this rule that the bizarrely named "Heritage Police", distinguished by their navy-blue uniforms, patrol the site from old-style canvas tents pitched nearby.

Dominating the square's north side is the mighty sixteenth-century **Sé Cathedral**, the episcopal seat of the Archdiocese of Goa and the largest church in Asia. Envisaged by its founder, Viceroy Redondo, as "a grandiose church worthy of the wealth, power and fame of the Portuguese who ruled the seas from the Atlantic to the Pacific", it took eighty years to build. Work on the interior was beset by financial problems and only completed in 1652, when Portuguese fortunes were already in decline. The shortfall was raised from the sale of land belonging to Goan Hindus who died without having converted to Christianity, while foundations were dug into the ruins of a mosque.

Although designed for the Dominican Order, the cathedral takes its cue from Jesuit architecture. The one typically Goan inclusion was the two square **bell towers** flanking the main facade. The campanile still standing on the south side – the other collapsed after being struck by lightning in 1776 – houses the largest bell in Asia, the legendary *Sino do Ouro* or "**Golden Bell**", famed for its mellow tone. During the Inquisition, its tolling announced the start of Goa's gruesome *autos da fé*, held in the square in front of the Sé (now a lawn), to which suspected heretics would be led from the Palace of the Inquisition's dungeons opposite.

The main entrance opens onto an awe-inspiring **interior**, in which rows of huge pillars separate the broad barrel-vaulted nave from its side aisles. Ahead, the magnificent reredos rises above the main altar to the ceiling, contrasting sharply with plain white surroundings. Deeply carved and layered with gold leaf, it features six finely painted panels depicting scenes from the life and martyrdom of **St Catherine**, to whom the Sé is dedicated, suffused by light from the lofty side windows. The one on the top left shows her debating philosophy with foreign scholars. Opposite, she awaits execution for her heresy, before being beheaded in the bottom-left panel. Finally, in the bottom-right panel, her headless body is carried away by angels to Mount Sinai. The spiked wheel on which St Catherine was tortured (whence "Catherine Wheel" fireworks) is also depicted. In 1065 this became the symbol of the Order of Knights of St John, formed to protect the holy relics after St Catherine's corpse was disinterred in Alexandria, where she was executed, and taken to Sinai.

The small shrine nearest the altar on the north wall, known as the Chapel of St Anne, houses relics of the Blessed Martyrs of Cuncolim, whose plucky mission to convert the Muslim court of Moghul emperor Akbar resulted in their execution. Also much revered is the **Cruz dos Milagres**, or "Miraculous Cross", two chapels further down, which pilgrims petition to cure sickness. Housed behind an opulently carved wooden screen, the cross, which allegedly grew from a braid of palm leaves planted in a rock by a local priest, stood in a Goan village until an apparition of Christ was seen hanging from it in 1619. The chapel next to the entrance (also on the north side) contains another famous holy object: the **font** that St Francis Xavier used to baptize new converts.

The Archbishop's Palace

Adjoining the Sé Cathedral, of which it is an exact contemporary, the **Archbishop's Palace** is unique as the last surviving civil building of colonial Goa's golden era. Though in a lamentable state of disrepair, its steeply inclined roofs and white facade still perfectly embody the solidity and imposing strength of the so-called "chã" style of architecture, derived from military con-

The Goan Inquisition

Written histories of Goa are rife with accounts of atrocities committed by the Portuguese. None, however, compare with those perpetrated in the name of Christianity by the dreaded **Santo Officio**, or "Holy Office'. Better known as the **Inquisition** (from the Latin verb *inquiro*, "to inquire into"), the dreaded tribunal became the most brutal, systematic and macabre instrument of cultural bigotry ever devised by a European colonial power. As one eighteenth-century historian put it, "(the) Holy Office combined all that the ferocity of savages and the ingenuity of civilized man had till then invented".

The original targets of the Inquisition were not, as is often assumed, Hindus, but *Christianos nuevos* ("new Christians") – mainly Iberian Jews and Muslims who had been forcibly converted during the religious persecution of the medieval era, but who had since lapsed into their former faiths. Jews, in particular, had fled in large numbers to the new colonies of Africa, South America and Asia, where they had become the dominant mercantile community. It was to complain of their lax religious ways that Francis Xavier wrote to King Joao III of Portugal in 1546, encouraging him to dispatch the Holy Inquisition to Goa, which he duly did four years later, in 1560.

By this time, the religious intolerance that had been making life difficult for the *Christianos nuevos* in Europe had also infected attitudes to local Hinduism in the *Estado da India*. Temple worship had been banned, shrines destroyed and brahmin priests banished. With the arrival of the two Grand Inquisitors and their spies from Lisbon, however, the range of "crimes" for which one could be imprisoned broadened considerably. Substances and plants connected with Hindu ritual – turmeric powder (*haldi*), basil (*tulsi*) leaves, incense or marigolds – were banned, as was cooking rice "without salt"; wearing a *dhoti* or *choli* (sari top); selling arms or horses to Muslims; sodomy ("the unnameable sin"); and refusing to eat pork. Other offences that could land their perpetrators a long stretch of hideous incarceration – or worse – included astrology, alchemy or polygamy.

Goa being the most notoriously licentious and decadent European enclave in Asia, it wasn't long before the Inquisition's jails began to fill. Deep in the bowels of the Holy Office HQ (known to terrified locals as simply *Orlem Ghor*, "Big House"), suspects would be tortured into confessing their heresy. Among the devices used for such purposes were, according to one record, "stretching racks, thumbscrews, leg crushers, holy water, burning sulphur, candles, quicklime and spiked wheels over which the victims were drawn with weights on their feet".

The only surviving first-hand account of the Goa Inquisition is attributed to a French physician named **Charles Dellon**, who found himself at the mercy of the Santo Officio in 1673, aged 24. His alleged crime was blasphemy; he'd supposedly mocked certain Christian rituals and criticized the Inquisition itself (although the fact that he'd seduced the Governor of Daman's mistress can't have helped him any). Dellon languished in solitary confinement, without light or sanitation, for a total of three years while his case was debated. In the end, his life was spared, but not before he'd twice attempted suicide (by trying to slash his wrists with a sharpened coin) and endured one of the infamous **autos da fé** – literally "trials of faith" – staged every few years by the Inquisition.

His blow-by-blow account of this ordeal, in which he and 150 others were paraded in front of the city before being told whether or not they would be burned to

structions of the day, of which the most extreme example was the Viceroy's Fortress Palace (Palacio da Fortaleza), which has since vanished without trace. Presenting their most austere aspect to the river, these two fortified palaces formerly dominated the skyline of the waterfront, appropriately enough for a city perennially under threat of attack.

These days, the Archbishop's Palace, sandwiched between two of Old Goa's

death, remains a spine-chilling read, not least for its depiction of the grotesque theatricality with which the whole event was enacted. On the morning of the trial, a petrified Dellon, crippled by a "universal and violent trembling", was handed long black-and-white-striped robes to wear. Over these was tied a thigh-length yellow tabard, called a *sambenito*, emblazoned with the cross of St Andrew. Heretics accused of the most heinous crimes ("sorcery", or "*crimen magicae*") were required to don similar grey robes, known as *samarras*, bearing images of their heads engulfed in flames and tormented by trident-wielding devils. To complete the ensemble, tall mitres (*carocha*) daubed with ghoulish images and slogans were placed on the prisoners' heads.

From the dungeons, the accused were marched barefoot to the Great Hall of the Holy Office, where each was allotted a "Godfather" – a kind of warder drawn from the aristocracy. Among the pews, coffin-like boxes and dummies were held aloft by Inquisition agents – these were the remains and effigies of heretics who had died in captivity, or else been condemned posthumously. With the great bell of the Sé Cathedral tolling in the background, the procession would then be led by Dominican friars carrying banners and a huge crucifix across Terreiro de Gales square to the Church of Saint Francis of Assisi, watched by huge crowds of onlookers.

Inside the church, the terrified assembly knelt in front of the Viceroy and Grand Inquisitor, while the Augustinian prelate delivered a sermon. When he'd finished, the judgements were read aloud. Dellon was sentenced to five years of galley slavery in Lisbon, while two of his fellow prisoners were to be burned at the stake beside the Mandovi.

Before embarking on his voyage back to Europe, the Frenchman had to swear on oath that he would never speak of what had happened to him at the hands of the Santo Officio in Goa. Ten years later, however, he reneged on this promise. One of the most harrowing accounts of captivity ever written, his *Relation de l'Inquisition de Goa* (see "Books" p.331), first published in Paris in 1687, was an immediate bestseller. Translations into English, German and Dutch appeared the following year, to glowing reviews by key Enlightenment figures such as Voltaire (who lifted material from it for *Candide*) and Montesquieu. As a result, *Relation* contributed in no small part to the eventual suppression of the regime it described with such amazing exactitude.

Until 1774 – the point up to which detailed records survive – 16,176 people (an average of 75 per year) were arrested by the Goa Inquisition. The majority of these were Hindus, although of those condemned to death, 71 percent were *Christianos nuevos* of Jewish descent. Its activities were curtailed towards the end of the eighteenth century, but the Inquisition was not fully repealed until 1814, as part of a treaty between the Portuguese and British.

Few remnants of this gruesome chapter in Goa's history survive. The Palace of the Inquisition was pulled down during the shift of the capital upriver, and most of its written records incinerated in 1814. You can, however, sit at the old table used by the Inquisitors for their grim deliberations (see p.78), while the crucifix that formerly hung above it – rendered with open eyes to instil fear into the heart of the accused – can still be seen in a small chapel in Fontainhas, Panjim (see p.76).

great churches, is often overlooked by visitors, not least because the ASI (Archeological Survey of India), whose neglect of the building seems likely to result in its imminent collapse, do little to advertise its existence. If you want to have a nose around, you'll have to bully or bribe the caretaker into letting you.

Old nineteenth-century photos show that the city-facing side of the building was originally enclosed by a low wall which surrounded a garden. This has been dismantled, but the two grand **entrance porches** remain intact. The one on the right (as you look at the building) is original, complete with red decorative frescoes lining the side walls, among the last remaining paintings of their kind left in Goa. The other porch is believed to date from the eighteenth century. During the Portuguese heyday, guards in blue livery would have stood on the steps, as they did in the viceroy's palace and most *hidalgo* houses. Inside, the two huge rooms originally served as an antechamber and audience hall for the archbishop. Both retain their exquisitely carved wooden corner **beams**, intricately decorated with designs of unmistakably Hindu origin.

The Church of St Francis of Assisi

The **Church of St Francis of Assisi**, sandwiched between the cathedral and archeological museum, dates from 1661 but stands on the site of an earlier convent church founded by Franciscans at the beginning of the sixteenth century. Elements of this first building were incorporated into the later one, probably to save money. They include the splendid Manueline doorway, whose heavy ornamentation stands out incongruously against an otherwise plain classical facade. Typical nautical themes include navigators' globes flanking the trefoil arch and a Greek cross above the royal coat of arms, which used to adorn the sails of Vasco da Gama and other Portuguese explorers' ships.

The interior of the church is no longer used for worship, and has a much older and more faded feel than its neighbours. Sculpted tombstones of Portuguese *hidalgos* pave the floor of the nave, while the walls and ceilings are plastered with frescoes and floral patterns rendered in delicate green, pink, yellow and gold. These latter designs are particularly well executed, perhaps because their Islamic style – derived from the Muslim-influenced art of Spain and Portugal – may have been familiar to local Goan artists. Less successful, but still of interest, are the painted wooden panels lining the chancel next to the high altar, which illustrate the life and teachings of St Francis. As part of extensive renovation work currently being undertaken in this church, new, elaborately carved panels have been installed on the walls flanking the altar, crafted by local artisans using traditional motifs. Finally, the gilt reredos, which envelops the east wall of the church, centres on two large figures of St Francis and Jesus, beneath which are inscribed the vows of the Franciscan Order: "Poverty, Humility and Obedience".

The archeological museum

A wing of the old Franciscan monastery adjacent to the Church of St Francis of Assisi was converted in 1964 into Goa's main **archeological museum**, exhibiting a modest selection of pre-colonial sculpture, coins and manuscripts, as well as Portuguese artefacts. Presiding over the main entrance hall is a huge sixteenth-century bronze statue of Alfonso de Albuquerque, the military commander who conquered Goa in 1510. The statue stood in Old Goa but was later shifted to Panjim's municipal square, where it remained until Independence in 1961. A left turn takes you into the **Key Gallery**, where the exhibition of Hindu sculpture is dominated by the bronze figure of one-eyed, sixteenth-century Portuguese poet Luis Vaz Camões, holding a copy of his epic *Os Lusiades*, which was written during his sojourn in Goa. The statue used to form the focal point of the square outside the museum, between the Sé Cathedral and Basilica of Bom Jesus. However, the finest piece of sculpture is an intricately carved thirteenth-century standing icon of Vishnu flanked by his consort, Lakshmi, and the winged gryphon Garuda (directly in front of you as you enter). The images arching above the Preserver of the Universe's head are of his ten *avatars*, or incarnations. Also worth a close look are the nearby hero stones, carved as memorials to Hindu warriors who died bravely in battle. The best of these (right of the Vishnu sculpture) shows a king on his throne, surrounded by attendants, with the naval engagement in which he was killed depicted below.

Reached via the stairs at the far end of the Key Gallery, the **first floor** of the museum is given over mainly to a collection of sixty paintings of Portuguese governors. Beginning with the 1527 portrait of Dom João Castro and ending with the right-wing Portuguese dictator Salazar, who was in power at the time of Goa's liberation, most have seen some heavy-handed renovation and are of little artistic merit, although they provide a vivid account of formal dress over the centuries – much of it stiflingly unsuitable for the Goan climate. Before moving on, hunt out the wonderful seventeenth-century oil paintings on wood of missionaries and *padrés* meeting sticky ends at the hands of Moluccan natives and wild Hindus, hung in the corner of the far gallery.

The stairs near to these lead to the monastery cloisters, renovated in 1707 and now the main **sculpture gallery**. Alongside a handful of Islamic inscriptions and hero stones stand several *sati* stones dating from the Kadamba period. These marked the spot where a widow committed suicide by throwing herself on her husband's funeral pyre. *Sati* was outlawed during the British Raj but still occurs – albeit very rarely – in more traditional parts of India, notably Rajasthan. A memorial to a martyr of a different kind is encased in the northwest corner of the courtyard. The centrepiece of this small shrine is a carved stone pillar from Chennai (Madras) in which a fragment of the lance that reputedly skewered the apostle St Thomas (who first brought Christianity to India) was once embedded.

The Chapel of St Catherine

The small but historically significant **Chapel of St Catherine** stands on a stretch of sloping ground immediately west of the museum, hemmed in by palm groves and dense vegetation. An inscription etched on one of its bare laterite walls recalls that the present structure was built in the seventeenth century on the spot where Albuquerque first entered the Muslim city on St Catherine's Day in 1510. In fact, it replaced an older mud-and-straw church erected by the Portuguese commander as an act of thanksgiving soon after his victory. The building that superseded this was granted cathedral status by a Papal Bull of 1534, which it retained until the construction of the Sé. Architecturally, St Catherine's is important because its twin-towered facade provided the prototype for the Sé, and thus inaugurated a distinctively Goan style of church design.

The Basilica of Bom Jesus

Site of the world-famous mausoleum of St Francis Xavier, the **Basilica of Bom Jesus**, on the south side of the main square, is India's most revered and architecturally accomplished church, and the logical place to wind up a tour of

St Francis Xavier in Goa

Visit almost any church or Christian house in Goa, and you're certain to find an image of the state's patron saint, **Francis Xavier**, known locally, and with considerable affection, as **"Goencho Sahib"**. The "Apostle of the Indies" was born on April 6, 1506, the son of aristocrats in Navarre, Spain. In his late teens he left for Paris, where he studied for the priesthood at the Sorbonne. There he met fellow Basque nobleman and future mentor (St) **Ignatius Loyola** (1491–1556), who, after his ordination in 1534, recruited Xavier, along with five other young priests, to be founder members of the evangelical "Society of Jesus" (*Compañía de Jesús*), later known as the **Jesuits**.

Around this time, reports were reaching the Lisbon court of the dissolute lifestyle being led by Portuguese expatriates in Goa. The king, Dom João III (1521–57), appealed to the Jesuits for help to reverse this moral decline, and when one of the original candidates fell ill, Francis Xavier was asked to lead the mission. He and his delegation arrived a year later, on May 6, 1542, and immediately set to work saving the souls of Goa's wayward colonials.

Xavier founded several churches, schools, a university and printing press, and ordained dozens of priests during his first five months. Then he sailed south to evangelize the lapsed Catholic Parava pearl fishers of the Malabar Coast, where miracles like curing the sick and raising the dead with a touch of his crucifix helped him notch up a staggering 30,000 conversions, before heading further east for Malacca and the Spice Islands.

Another brief spell in Goa was followed by two years in Japan, where Xavier tried unsuccessfully to convert the Shinto Buddhists. This was to be his last mission, for, on December 3, 1552, he died of a fever while trying to sneak into China. His body was buried on the deserted island of Sancian, near the mouth of the Canto River, coated with quicklime to hasten its decomposition. However, when the grave was reopened three months later, the corpse was in perfect condition. Reburied in Malacca, it was exhumed again after five months and found to be still incorrupt.

Old Goa. Work on the building was completed in 1605, sixteen years after the Jesuits were first granted leave to construct a convent on the same spot. In 1964, it became the first church in South Asia to be promoted to a Minor Basilica, by order of Pope Pius XII, and today forms the main focus for Christian worship in the old colonial capital.

The design of the Basilica is believed to be derived from the Gesù, the Jesuits' headquarters in Rome, and, with its idiosyncratic blend of Neoclassical restraint and Baroque extravagance, is typical of the late Renaissance, with a sumptuous **facade**, the most ornate in Goa, culminating in the intricately carved and disproportionately large central pediment at the top. This is dominated by the IHS motif, standing for *Iaesus Hominum Salvator* ("Jesus Saviour of men") – a feature of all Jesuit churches. Unusually for Goa, neither the facade nor the rest of the building is whitewashed, although plans are afoot to cover the soft red stone again as the monsoon rains have begun to blur some of the stonework. The erosion is particularly evident on the north wall, where you can admire the impressively sturdy buttresses that prop up the Basilica.

Spanned by a stark, lofty wooden ceiling, the **interior** is positively plain compared with the facade, but no less impressive, dominated by a massive gilt altarpiece and a huge central statue of St Ignatius Loyola, founder of the Jesuit Order, accompanied by the Infant Jesus. As you pass through the main doorway, look for two blue plaques attached to the pillars beneath the choir gallery, commemorating (in Latin and Portuguese) the inauguration of the Basilica in 1605. Midway down the nave on the north wall (opposite the sumptuously decorated main pulpit) stands a memorial to **Dom Jeronimo Mascarenhas**,

The arrival of Xavier's body in Goa, in March 1554, was greeted by a vast and euphoric crowd. But the church would not formally acknowledge the miracle until a medical examination had been carried out by the viceroy's physician to ensure the corpse had not been artificially preserved. The medic declared the skin firm and the intestines intact, then asked a Jesuit priest to stick his finger into a hole in the chest. When the finger was withdrawn, it was smeared with blood that was "smelt and found to be absolutely untainted".

Francis Xavier was eventually canonized in 1622 and his body installed in the **Basilica of Bom Jesus**, but not before bits of it had been removed by relic hunters: in 1614, his right arm was dispatched to the pope in Rome (where it allegedly wrote its name on a pile of papers), a hand to Japan and parts of the intestines to southeast Asia. Other relics found their way into private homes, such as the Perreira-Braganza mansion in Chandor, whose family shrine boasts St Francis Xavier's diamond-encrusted fingernail (see p.188). Much the most macabre mutilation, though, occurred in 1634 when a Portuguese noblewoman, Dona Isabel de Caron, bit off the little toe of the corpse's right foot. Supposedly, so much blood spurted into the woman's mouth that it left a trail all the way to her house and she was found out.

Once every ten years, the saint's body is carried in a three-hour ceremony from the Basilica of Bom Jesus to the Sé Cathedral, where visitors file past, touch and photograph it. During the last Exposition, from November 23, 1994 until January 7, 1995, an estimated two million pilgrims flocked for *darshan* (ritual viewing) of the corpse, these days a shrivelled and somewhat unsavoury spectacle. The event, rumoured to be the last, was managed with military precision by the Goan Tourist Police, amid paranoid delusions that Pakistan's Inter Services Intelligence (ISI) were planning to steal the relic. However, the 48-day festival passed off without a hitch, and stallholders did a brisk trade in day-glo plastic Francis Xaviers, dashboard Madonnas and other religious kitsch.

whose will financed the construction of this church: its panels depict heroic episodes from his career as Captain of Cochin. Swathed in lush gold leaf, the gigantic **reredos**, filling the far end of the nave, remains the Basilica's most arresting feature, with spiralling scrollwork, extravagantly carved panels, statues and pilasters illuminated for maximum effect.

The Basilica's main claim to fame, however, is to be found in the south transept, the **mausoleum of St Francis** (immediately to the right as you leave the Basilica through the door on the right of the main altar). This was installed in 1698, a century and a half after his death, gifted to the Jesuits by the last of the Medicis, Cosimo III (1670–1723), Grand Duke of Tuscany, in exchange for the pillow on which the saint's head was laid to rest. It took Florentine sculptor Giovanni Batista Saggini a decade to design and was made from precious marble and coloured jaspers specially shipped from Italy. Set in the base are four superbly crafted **bronze panels** illustrating scenes from the life of the saint: preaching in the Moluccas; baptizing converts; swimming to escape the natives of Moro; and on his deathbed. The huge silver casket mounted on the plinth contains what is left of the body, although it was not part of the Medici endowment but made earlier by Goan silversmiths in 1659. Its sides were originally encrusted with precious stones, but these have long since disappeared.

From the tomb, a corridor leads behind the main altar to the **Sacristy** (daily except Fri 9am–noon & 2–5.30pm), renowned for its beautifully carved wooden door and stone door jamb. On display inside are several chests containing clerical regalia, along with one of St Francis Xavier's toes, which fell off the corpse in 1890. Stairs lead from here, via a room full of garish modern paintings of "Goencho Sahib" (see box), to a first-floor gallery where you get a good bird's-eye view of the glass-topped casket and its contents.

The pillory

Goa's **pillory** formerly stood smack in the centre of the city's main square but now occupies a quiet site southeast of the Basilica, overgrown with weeds in front of a mildew-covered concrete house. This pair of grey basalt columns, plundered from the ruins of a Hindu temple and mounted on a stepped plinth, once sported a set of iron rings to which criminals were bound, before being flogged and left to dangle for the edification of marketgoers.

The whipping post loomed large in the picaresque life story of one **Fernão Lopes**, a former Portuguese prisoner conscripted to fight with Albuquerque's original expeditionary force. Following the first rout of Muslim Ela, those soldiers who had acquitted themselves bravely in battle were given members of the 'Adil Shah's *zenana*, or harem, as a reward. Contemporary chronicles record that these men became known as *casados*, literally "married", and were subject to widespread derision and harassment for their relations with women deemed to be racially inferior. When clerics declared the alliances immoral, and the administration started arresting the Bijapuri women and handing them over to other men, some of the *casados* – including Lopes – defected to the nearby Muslim outpost at Banastarim, on the far bank of the Mandovi, in order to remain with their wives.

The move backfired, however, after Albuquerque's decisive counterattack of 1510, when Banastarim was captured. Included in the terms of the Muslim surrender was an agreement to hand over the Portuguese "traitors", who were swiftly tried and sentenced to torture by mutilation. The twenty or so *casados* were then lashed to pillories where they had their noses, ears, right hands and left thumbs removed. Half of them died from the wounds, but those who didn't were released and ordered out of Goa (one eventually made it all the way to Cochin, where he is said to have worked as a gravedigger).

Among the surviving *casados* was Lopes, who the chroniclers surmise must have had a wife and child in Portugal, because at the first opportunity he set sail on a ship bound for Lisbon. He never made it, however. For reasons that have remained a mystery, Lopes jumped ship at the deserted island of **Santa Helena** (the St Helena of Napoleon's later exile) ". . . and refused to continue the journey". With clothes and supplies left for him on the beach by his companions, he holed up in a cave and somehow, with only four fingers on his left hand, managed to survive a year until a second passing ship dropped off a consignment of provisions, tools, seeds and chickens.

Over the next two decades, it became customary for Portuguese crews to pause at Santa Helena en route to the Indies to see how Lopes was faring – a tradition that over time blossomed into the full-scale colonization of the island. However, Portugal's own true-life Robinson Crusoe was not left to live out his remaining days in peace. Instead, he was seized and forcibly returned to Lisbon. He only returned to Santa Helena to die in 1546, after travelling to Rome to plead for absolution from the pope.

Holy Hill (Monte Santo)

Anyone not totally churched out by this stage should head west up the lane leading from the bus stand to take in the cluster of monuments on **Holy Hill**. Nestled amid thick tropical vegetation, the first building encountered, to the left of the road, is the **Convent and Church of St John of God**, a late-seventeenth-century building abandoned after the suppression of the religious orders in 1835. The **Convent of St Monica**, opposite, was at one time the only nunnery in the entire colony. Dating from 1601–27, it burned down in 1636, but was completely rebuilt the following year. These days, the triple-storeyed building looks the worse for wear, with weeds choking its buttressed walls and eroded Baroque stonework, but it is still occupied by nuns from the Mater Dei Institute. You can ask to be shown around the convent by ringing the bell at the main entrance; note the deeply carved Manueline-style reliefs here. Inside, cloisters and a sunken courtyard enclose a small octagonal garden called the **Vale de Lirio**. Although in a dishevelled state, the convent's church, next door, is also worth a quick look, mainly for its fine pulpit and the blue-painted tilework near the altar – the peculiarly Portuguese art form, rare in Goa, known as *azulejo*. The **cross** behind the high altar is believed to be miraculous; it's said that in 1636 the Christ figure opened its eyes and blood dribbled from its crown of thorns. A row of enigmatic black-faced statues, known as the Black Virgins, once stood beside the main altar. For centuries, iconographers and liturgists argued about where they may have come from and how significant they were, until it was discovered that their black colour was ingrained soot from the countless candles that had been lit at their feet.

At one time the grandest building in the colony, Holy Hill's melancholic **Augustinian Monastery**, opposite St Monica's, now lies in ruins, though the partially collapsed belfry remains one of the city's most distinctive sights. The monastery was founded when the Augustinians first arrived in Goa in 1572, and was enlarged using a grant from the King of Portugal thirty years later. However, when the orders were expelled, the monastery and church were deserted and soon became derelict. The spectacular facade finally collapsed in 1942, but its bell was salvaged from the rubble and installed in Panjim's Church of Our Lady of the Immaculate Conception (via Fort Aguada), where it is still in use today. Other vestiges that have come to light here are the skeletons of nine Portuguese dignitaries. They were unearthed in a dig funded by the government of the former Soviet state of Georgia, which wanted to find the bones of the martyr Guativanda Deopoli, a Georgian princess murdered by her husband, Shah Abbas I of Persia, for converting to Christianity. After swearing allegiance to the Roman Church and renouncing her marriage vows, Guativanda (aka Katevan), Queen of Ghurgistan, was allegedly tortured and put to death by drowning. When her body was exhumed four months later, however, it was said to have given off a "pleasant perfume". The Augustinian missionaries present took this as a sign that Guativanda's untimely death was a martyrdom, and managed to smuggle her corpse back to Goa, where it was entombed here in the monastery. Yet despite historical references to the precise site of the tomb, no female remains have so far been found.

Continue up the lane past the ruins and you'll soon arrive at the beautifully restored **Chapel of St Anthony**, commissioned in the fifteenth century by Albuquerque and renovated by the Portuguese the year they were finally kicked out of Goa by Nehru. St Anthony is the patron saint of the Portuguese armed forces, which partly explains why the statue inside the chapel was granted the honorary rank of army captain. The painted figure used to be taken to the Treasury every year in a grand procession to collect its wages – a tradition discontinued by one of the governors, but quickly reinstated after he was nearly killed in an accident on St Anthony's Day.

To reach Holy Hill's most interesting monument, rejoin the path that runs in front of St Monica's church and follow it west as far as a small clearing. A plaque on the southwest corner of the **Church of Our Lady of the Rosary** records that from this vantage point above the Mandovi, Alfonso de Albuquerque followed the fortunes of the fateful battle of 1510. Erected by him soon after, in fulfilment of a victory vow, the original church was where St Francis Xavier preached on arrival here in 1542. Its successor, completed in 1549, is the oldest complete building in Old Goa, and the sole surviving church "Goencho Sahib" is likely to have visited in person. It also forms the state's best example of Manueline architecture, with unusual rounded towers, tall windows and rope mouldings. Its cruciform interior is unremarkable, except for the marble tomb of **Catarina a Piró**, believed to be the first European woman to set foot in the colony. A commoner (the *Nobilaria*, the Portuguese book of lineage, described her as an "ordinary woman"), she eloped here to escape the scandal surrounding her romance with Portuguese noble-man Garcia de Sá, who later rose to be governor of Goa. Under pressure from no less than Francis Xavier, Garcia eventually married her, but only *in articulo mortis* as she lay on her deathbed. Her finely carved tomb, set in the wall beside the high altar, incorporates a band of intricate Gujarati-style ornamentation, probably imported from the Portuguese trading post of Diu. Garcia's more modest gravestone lies in front of the main altar. Catarina's daughter Leonor outlived her and gained a reputation in the colony as a paragon of virtue (in marked contrast to her beautiful mother, whom high society always considered wanton). After swimming to safety from a shipwreck on the African coast, Leonor buried herself up to her neck in the sand and starved to death rather than submit to the ravages of the natives, as she supposed her companions had.

The Church of Our Lady of the Mount

Crowning a thickly wooded hilltop to the east of the city, the **Church of Our Lady of the Mount**, recently restored to its former glory by the Portuguese government, is one of Old Goa's least accessible monuments, but one well worth making the effort to see. The best time to visit is towards the end of the day, when the **views** west over the tops of the city's Baroque facades and bell towers, silhouetted against the setting sun, are something to savour. The best way to get there is to follow the Cambarjua road, turning right up a narrow lane when you reach a small bar. This motorable track winds up the hill, peter-ing out at a car park, from where a flight of old steps runs the rest of the way (see map on p.88).

Our Lady of the Mount was one of three churches founded by Albuquerque after his victory over the Muslim ruler of Goa. The 'Adil Shah's army also mus-tered on this hilltop prior to their counter-assault on the city in 1510, as recorded by a plaque attached to the west wall of the church. Little of interest is to be found inside, but you could hunt around in front of the main altar for the tombstone bearing a skull and crossbones, which belongs not to a pirate, but to the Portuguese architect **Antonio Alvares Pereira**, who designed the original church.

Chorao and Divar islands

Marooned amid mangrove swamps, shifting sandbanks and waterlogged paddy fields in the Mandovi estuary, the islands of **Chorao** and **Divar** are very rarely visited by tourists in spite of their proximity to Panjim. But if you want to get a taste of rural Goa and haven't time to venture far from the coast, a trip across the river en route to or from Old Goa is worth considering. Passing through a string of tranquil farming hamlets, their peaceful (and mainly flat) lanes are perfect for cycling, in spite of the cuttings and huge concrete bridges of the Konkan Railway that dominate the landscape hereabouts.

A recommended route loops from the Ribandar ferry jetty to the Shri Saptakoteshwar temple at **Naroa**, and back across Divar to Old Goa, and remains a pleasant way to pass an afternoon, taking a leisurely three to four hours by bicycle (or one and a half hours by motorbike). Alternatively, nip across the Mandovi River from Old Goa to **Piedade**, Divar's largest village, to visit the hilltop **Church of Our Lady of Compassion**, whose terrace affords stunning views south over the former capital and upriver to Panjim.

Chorao Island

Most of the western spur of sleepy **CHORAO ISLAND**, reached by ferry from Ribandar, 5km east of Panjim (every 15min, 6am–10pm; Rs2), has been turned into the **Dr Salim Ali Bird Sanctuary**. Fringed by a dense wall of mangrove swamps, the roadless reserve, which you can only get close to by boat, is home to a healthy and varied population of coastal birds, as well as flying foxes, jackals and the odd crocodile. The grey-brown mud flats around the sanctuary are also a good place to spot one of the region's more unusual fish, the bulbous-headed mudskipper, which, as its name implies, can often be seen leaping through the silt.

From the ferry crossing, the road heads north through a series of small Hindu settlements, some of them made of mud and thatch, to **Chorao village**, a picturesque scattering of Portuguese-style villas grouped below a whitewashed

Mandovi "muggers"

The silt banks and tidal waters of the Mandovi River, east of Panjim around Chorao and Divar islands, are home to a small population of crocodiles known in Konkani as *magars*, later corrupted by the British to "muggers". Writing in the sixteenth century, the chronicler João de Barros insisted that the crocs, which he said … were so enormous as to devour whole bullocks and upset large boats", were first introduced by the 'Adil Shah of Bijapur "as a guard against surprise attacks and the escape of slaves". Regardless of whether or not they were bred by the Bijapuris, the famously rapacious reptiles are known to have been put to use by the Portuguese in just as grisly a fashion: unwanted Muslim prisoners of war and, later, convicted criminals, were thrown to them alive. Their numbers have dropped perilously low over the past two or three decades, but you can still see the odd mugger basking on mud banks and sliding through the mangrove shallows of Chorao. Further east, where the Cambarjua Canal meets the Mandovi, a chemical plant overlooking the river also receives occasional visits from the crocs, who allegedly swim up an effluent duct and roll onto their backs on the factory's lawns.

Based just outside Candolim in north Goa, a company called **Southern Birdwing** offers **crocodile-spotting** trips along the Mandovi and Cambarjua canal. The all-in price of Rs990 includes pick-up from any hotel along the Candolim–Calangute–Baga belt, a six-hour guided boat ride, drinks, lunch and drop-off back at your hotel. Reservations can be made at numerous agents in the resorts; alternatively, contact Neil Alvares or Harvey D'Souza at 94B Bairro Forta Waddo, Nerul, Bardez 403 114 ☎0832/221 1814 or 221 1957, ⊛www.southernbirdwing.com. The same outfit also runs excellent **bird-watching** trips along the same route, to look for the extremely rare white-collared kingfishers (*Halcyon chloris*), who nest amid the mangroves of the Cambarjua.

church. Bear right at the fork in the road here, and you'll eventually drop down the far side of the hill to the northern edge of the island. A bridge, surrounded by palm-fringed rice paddy, marks the border of Tiswadi and Bicholim *talukas*. To reach the Shri Saptakoteshwar temple at Naroa, turn right at the next junction and continue until you reach the main road, where you should turn left. A right turn here will take you downhill to the ferry crossing for Divar.

Divar Island

Encircled by the silt-laden waters of the Mandovi River, **DIVAR ISLAND** (from the Konkani *dev*, "god", and *vaddi*, "place") was an important religious centre in pre-colonial Goa, with one of western India's most powerful *Shivalingams*. This was smuggled to nearby Naroa, across the river, during the time of the Inquisition (when 1510 islanders were forcibly converted in a single mass event), but the church that now stands on its former hilltop site, together with the crop of elegant old Portuguese-style houses in the village below, easily warrant a short foray north from the ruins of Old Goa.

The island can only be reached by **ferry**: from the south via Old Goa's jetty (every 15min; free), or from the north at Naroa (every 20–30min; free). After crossing a broad flood plain, dotted with drainage ditches and wooded hillocks, both roads converge on the island's main settlement, **Piedade**. The village, dominated from on high by its striking church, exudes a lazy, prosperous feel. Its leafy lanes, winding through the shade of an old forest, harbour dozens of elegant and immaculately painted Portuguese villas, with typically Goan *balcões* flanking their deep verandahs, and names like "Vivenda Fernandes" and "Saudades".

If you are wondering why most of Divar's inhabitants seem to be women, this is because a large number of its menfolk work abroad. Every January, however, the prodigal sons return home to take part in the **Festa das Bandeiras** ("Flag Festival"), during which they parade around the village waving the flags of their adopted countries. The event is thought to derive from a much older pre-Christian harvest ceremony, in which villagers used to mark the limits of their territory by marching around its boundaries brandishing weapons.

The Church of Our Lady of Compassion

Perched atop the hill above Piedade, the **Church of Our Lady of Compassion** occupies the site of an ancient Hindu temple that was destroyed by Muslims in the late fifteenth century. Chunks of masonry from the building were incorporated into the first Christian structure erected here, reportedly seen by Albuquerque from his ship when he returned to Goa for the last time in 1515. It was enlarged ten years later, although the present building, designed by a Goan priest, dates from the early eighteenth century.

Tucked away to the south side of the church is a remnant of the illustrious Kadamba era, when this hilltop was a sacred Hindu site. A tiny walled **cemetery**, which the resident priest will unlock for you, encloses a chapel converted from the former Hindu shrine. The deity was whisked away before the arrival of the Muslims, but the carving and painted plaster decoration on the ceiling is original, as is the fragment of ornate stone tracery in the window, carved about the same time as the foundation of the Tamdi Surla temple near Molem, in Sanguem *taluka*.

Its monuments aside, the best thing about Piedade is its superb panoramic **views**. Little wonder the region's ancient inhabitants chose this spot. Sitting on the terraces of the GTDC's recently laid out **Children's Park**, south of the church, you can take in a wide sweep of scenery, from the shadow of the Western Ghats on the horizon, to the rice fields and tangled tributaries of the Mandovi River, flowing west past Panjim into the Arabian Sea. This is also a good place from which to admire the remains of Old Goa, whose gigantic belfries tower above the carpet of palm trees to the south.

Ponda

Characterless, chaotic **PONDA**, 28km southeast of Panjim and 17km northeast of Margao, is Ponda *taluka's* administrative headquarters and main market town, but not somewhere you're likely to want to hang around. Straddling the busy Panjim–Bangalore highway, the NH4, its ugly ferro-concrete centre is permanently choked with traffic, and may well leave you wondering why you ever left the coast. Of the few visitors who stop here, most do so en route to the nearby Hindu temples or wildlife reserves further east, or to take a quick look at Goa's best-preserved sixteenth-century Muslim monument, the **Safa Masjid**, 2km west on the Panjim road.

Until the road through the town was upgraded in the 1970s, Ponda was little more than a sleepy rural settlement, eclipsed by the port of Durbhat, 7km southwest on the Zuari River. Conquered by the Portuguese shortly after Albuquerque arrived in Goa at the beginning of the sixteenth century, its first real claim to fame was as the capital of Muslim rebel leader Abdullah, Prince of Bijapur, who plotted from here to overthrow his brother, Ibrahim 'Adil Shah, in 1555. The rebellion was nipped in the bud by the Bijapuri-Vijayanagar army, after which the town, along with its two forts (now in ruins), became a Muslim outpost on the edge of Christian Goa. It was only returned to the Portuguese by the Hindu King Sunda in 1791, following more than a century of Maharatha rule.

Ponda today is enjoying something of a boom, fuelled by its proximity to some of the state's largest iron ore mines. This prosperity has spawned a rash of small factories and industrial estates on the outskirts, as well as a rapid increase in size; swollen by a flood of immigrants from neighbouring Karnataka, the predominantly Hindu population has more than doubled over the past decade.

The Safa Masjid

Ponda's **Safa Masjid**, 2km west of the town centre in a district known as Shapur, is renowned less for its architecture than for being one of only two sixteenth-century Islamic monuments in Goa to survive the excesses of the Inquisition. Built in 1560 by the Bijapuri ruler Ibrahim 'Adil Shah, it presides over a complex that once included extensive formal gardens and a large palace, but which now lies in ruins beside the Panjim–Bangalore highway. Without your own transport, the easiest way to get there is by auto-rickshaw from Ponda's main bus stand.

Capped with a more recent pointed terracotta tile roof, the Safa Masjid's rectangular **prayer hall** rests atop a high plinth, its whitewashed walls decorated with elegant Islamic arches. Surrounding the building are the stumps of several octagonal pillars where a covered courtyard once provided shade for worshippers. The interior, still in use, is plain except for the blind Bijapuri arches of the *mihrab*, or prayer wall, facing west towards Mecca.

The decoration around the sides of the **ablutions tank**, unusually situated to the south of the prayer hall rather than outside its main entrance, mirrors that of the mosque, suggesting that the two were contemporary. A superstition holds that it is dangerous to swim in the murky green water because of the hidden tunnels that are supposed to connect it with a smaller reservoir nearby – not that the soapy kids splashing around the shallows seem in the least deterred. Some locals also claim that the Safa Masjid is connected by secret underground passages to a ruined hilltop fort 2km north of here, although none have yet been discovered.

Practicalities

Ponda is served by regular **buses** from both Panjim (via Old Goa), and Margao, and lies on the main route east to Karnataka. The town's Kadamba bus stand is situated in the middle of town on the main square, next to the auto-rickshaw rank.

There are plenty of **places to stay** if you get stuck here. Best of the budget lodges is the *Padmavi* (no phone; ❷) at the top of the square. For more comfort, try the *President* (☎0832/233 5122 or 233 5037; ❸–❹), a short rickshaw ride up the Belgaum road, which has large, clean en-suite rooms, some with air conditioning. More upmarket is the three-star *Atash* (☎0832/231 3224, ℱ231 3239; ❺), 4km northwest on the NH4 at Farmagudi, where the comfortable air-conditioned rooms have satellite TV, and there's also a restaurant and car parking facilities. However, the best mid-range deal within striking distance of Ponda has to be GTDC's *Hill Retreat* (☎0832/231 2932; ❸), also at Farmagudi (look for the signpost on the roundabout below the Shivaji memorial), whose en-suite chalets, stacked up the side of a steep hill overlooking the highway, are spacious, clean and reasonably priced. There's also a small terrace restaurant serving a standard menu of spicy mixed cuisine.

Decent **places to eat** in Ponda itself are few and far between, although the *Sanman* on the main square is fine for a pit stop, offering a good selection of inexpensive South Indian-style snacks. A five-minute walk up the main Belgaum road from the square, the no-nonsense *Gomantak* is deservedly more popular, with a non-veg menu that includes mountainous fish *thalis* and piping hot *channa batura*. If you fancy eating somewhere a little smarter, try the *Hotel President*'s dimly lit but air-conditioned restaurant, just up the lane, where tasty Chinese, Mughlai and vegetarian main courses cost around Rs65.

Ponda's main **service station** is 1km northeast of the square on the Belgaum road. The shop opposite stocks basic motorbike spares.

Around Ponda

Scattered among the lush valleys and forests **around Ponda** are a dozen or so **Hindu temples** founded during the seventeenth and eighteenth centuries, when this hilly region formed a Christian-free buffer zone between Portuguese Goa and the Hindu-dominated hinterland. Although the temples themselves are fairly modern by Indian standards, their deities are ancient and held in high esteem by both local people and the thousands of pilgrims from Maharashtra and Karnataka who travel here on special "*Darshan* tours" to see them.

The temples are concentrated in two main clusters: the first to the north of Ponda on the busy NH4, and the second deep in the countryside around 5km west of the town. You would have to be an avid templophile indeed to see more than half a dozen in a day. Most people only manage the **Shri**

Manguesh and **Shri Mahalsa** between the villages of Mardol and Priol, which both lie a stone's throw from the main highway and are among the most interesting temples in the state. Any of the regular **buses** that run between Panjim and Margao via Ponda drive past these. The others are further off the beaten track, although they are not hard to find on motorbikes: the locals will wave you in the right direction if you get lost. Ponda's auto-rickshaw *wallahs* also know the way, but expect to be charged for waiting time.

The Shri Manguesh temple

Shri Manguesh *mandir*, 9km north of Ponda near the village of **Priol**, is one of the largest, wealthiest and most frequently visited temples in Goa. Its principal deity, a stone *Shivalingam*, was first brought here in the sixteenth century from its previous hiding place on the south bank of the Zuari River at Curtolim, although the present building was erected over two hundred years later. During the time of the Inquisition, devotees from the Old Conquests area used to creep across the Cambarjua Canal under cover of darkness to worship here, knowing that torture, imprisonment or even execution awaited them if caught.

Amid lush forest at the foot of a steep hillside, the temple is now approached in a more leisurely fashion via a raised walkway through waterlogged paddy fields – land given to the temple by the local rajah in the eighteenth century. A flight of steps, lined by flower and incense *wallis*, leads to the main entrance, overlooking a large water tank whose ornamental brickwork is picked out with whitewash. The courtyard inside, hemmed in by ugly modern *argashallas*

Spice plantations

An essential ingredient in Goa's notoriously fiery cuisine, and prized for centuries by European palates as meat preservers and flavouring agents, spices were one of the region's principal exports long before Vasco da Gama left the Malabar Coast with a *caravela* full of pepper in 1499. Nowadays, they are grown, along with other cash crops such as cashews, tropical fruit and areca nuts, in several large **spice plantations** around Ponda.

Many of the big package tour companies these days offer pre-booked excursions to the spice farms, combining them with a visit to one or more of the Hindu temples nearby. The tours usually kick off with an introductory talk (and a stiff "peg" of cashew *feni*), followed by a stroll through the orchards. In keeping with a centuries-old system developed by strictly vegetarian Brahmin farmers, the plantations are divided into three tiers of terraces, stacked up a well-irrigated hillside. Planted at the top in the shade of flowering trees are spindly areca palms, coconuts, mangoes and jackfruit. Below these come breadfruit, star apples, banana trees, cinnamon and nutmeg; finally, at the bottom, are pineapple and cardamom.

Being herded around with a busload of fellow tourists may not be your idea of a perfect day out, but the spice plantation tours do offer a hassle-free way to sample the beautiful interior of Goa, which few visitors on package holidays get to see. However, if you'd prefer to visit independently, head for the **Tropical Spice Plantation**, 6km north of Ponda just off the Ponda–Mardol road at A-14 Arla Bazar, Keri (℡0832/234 0329), where guided tours are run daily for Rs300. Visits typically last a couple of hours and include a copious Goan lunch.

(pilgrims' hostels) and offices, is dominated by a seven-storey *deepmal*, the most impressive lamp tower in Goa.

The temple itself, painted ochre, blue and white, is a kitsch concoction of Moghul-style domes, Baroque balustrades and pilasters piled around the sides of a grand octagonal sanctuary tower. Its principal deity, Shiva, in his benefi-cent form, Manguesh, presides over a silver shrine, flanked by a solid gold idol and lit by oil lamps.

Before you leave, pay your respects to the ancient stone *devtas* housed in the **subsidiary shrines** to the rear of the main building (from left to right: Lakshmi Narayan, Satiri and Mulkeshwar), and the gigantic ceremonial chari-ots (*raths*), put to use during the annual *Zatra* festival, which are stored in the northwest corner of the compound.

The Shri Mahalsa temple

Like Shri Manguesh, the **Shri Mahalsa** temple, 7km northwest of Ponda, originally stood in Salcete, but was destroyed in the sixteenth century during a siege by 'Adil Shah's Muslim army after a platoon of Portuguese soldiers had taken refuge in it. The deity survived, having previously been smuggled across the Zuari River to **Mardol**, where it was installed in a new temple. This has been rebuilt or renovated on several occasions since: the last time in 1993–95, when a shiny new *mandapa*, or pillared porch, was added and the courtyard paved with finest Karnatakan marble.

Crowned by rising tiers of red pyramidal roofs, the distinctly oriental Shri Mahalsa is noted for its fine woodcarvings, especially on the pillars supporting the eaves of the main *mandapa*, set above beautiful floral panels. Inside, an ornate ceiling spans deeply carved and brightly painted images of Vishnu's ten incarnations, or *avatars*. The presiding deity here is Vishnu's consort, the black-faced goddess Mahalsa (aka Lakshmi, goddess of wealth and prosperity), who peers out from her silver shrine, swathed in red and yellow silk.

Standing beside the seven-storey, pink- and white-painted *deepmal* in the courtyard is an unusual brass **lamp pillar**. The column, erected in 1978, symbolizes the Hindu *Axis Mundi*, Mount Kailash, which the gods placed on the back of Vishnu's second incarnation, the tortoise Kurma (featured at the base of the pillar), prior to his epic plunge into the Primordial Ocean. The dive was performed to rescue all the treasures of the world lost in the Great Flood. When Kurma reached the bottom of the sea, a cosmic serpent was coiled around the mountain and then pulled, churning the oceans and forcing their contents to the surface. Among the goodies that came to light were a jar of immortality-giving nectar, the *Amrit Samovar*, and Vishnu's consort, Lakshmi. The Preserver's winged vehicle (*vahana*), the half-man half-eagle Garuda, crowns the top of the pillar, whose oil lamps are lit every Sunday evening.

West of the temple, a flight of steps drops down to a laterite-lined water tank, overlooked by a large sacred *peepal* tree. The opposite (east) gateway, leading from the courtyard to the main road, is surmounted by a pagoda-roofed musicians' gallery (*naubhat khanna* or *sonddio*), where the instruments used during Shri Mahalsa's *pujas*, Sunday evening promenades and annual *Zatra* are stored.

The Shri Lakshmi Narcenha temple

Crouched on the side of a steep, densely wooded hill, the secluded **Shri Lakshmi Narcenha** *mandir* at **Velinga**, 3km southwest of Mardol, is one of the more picturesque temples around Ponda. To find it, turn west where the main highway begins its climb up to Farmagudi, and follow the road for 1500m until it reaches Velinga village. The path to the temple starts at the top of the grassy square, in the centre of which stands a modern concrete shrine.

Transferred here from Salcete in 1567, the Lakshmi-Narcenha *devta* housed inside this temple, a conventional eighteenth-century structure surrounded by neat lawns and pilgrims' hostels, is Vishnu in his fourth incarnation as the man-lion Narashima, aka Narayan. However, his shrine and the brightly painted assembly hall leading to it (lined with images of Vishnu's various *avatars*) are of less interest than the beautiful water tank at the far end of the courtyard. Fed by an eternal spring, this is fringed by a lush curtain of coconut palms, and entered (from the opposite side) via a grand ceremonial gateway. Its stepped sides, used by locals as communal bathing- and *dhobi-ghats*, are ornamented with rows of Islamic-arched niches. The squat tower behind is a musicians' gallery.

The Shri Naguesh temple

From the main intersection at Farmagudi, dominated by a statue of the Maharatha leader Shivaji, a narrow back road winds sharply down the sides of a sheltered valley, carpeted with cashew trees and dense thickets of palms, to the **Shri Naguesh** temple at **Bandora**, 4km northwest of Ponda. If you are working your way north, note that this temple can also be approached via the road that starts opposite the Shri Shantadurga *mandir* near Quela (see below).

Established at the beginning of the fifteenth century and later renovated by the Maharathas, Shri Naguesh is older than most of its neighbours, although stylistically very much in the same mould, with the usual domed *shikhara*, or terracotta-tiled roofs, and gaudy Goan decor. Lying in its entrance porch is a stately black **Nandi** bull, vehicle of the temple's chief deity, Shiva, here known

Stick to the former Portuguese heartland of Bardez, Salcete and Tiswadi *talukas*, and you'd be forgiven for thinking Goa was exclusively Christian. It isn't, of course, as the innumerable brightly painted Hindu temples hidden amid the lush woodland and areca groves of more outlying areas confirm. The oldest-established and best-known **devuls** (from the Sanskrit word meaning "house of God") lie well away from the coastal resorts, but are worth hunting out. Apart from being some of South Asia's quirkiest sacred buildings, they are the main focus of religious life for the state's Hindu majority, offering the chance to experience at first hand traditions that have endured here for over 1500 years.

Goa's first temples were made of wood and mud brick, and later of stone, during the rule of the Kadamba dynasty, between the fifth and fifteenth centuries AD. Fragments of sculpture and masonry unearthed on the site of the ancient capital, Govapuri (see p.84), suggest these were as skilfully constructed as the famous monuments of the neighbouring Deccan region. However, only one, the richly carved Mahadeva temple at **Tamdi Surla** in east Goa (see p.115), has survived. The rest were systematically destroyed, first by Muslim invaders, and later by the Portuguese. To ensure that the deities themselves did not fall into the hands of iconoclasts, many were smuggled away from the Christian-dominated coastal area to remote villages in the interior, which explains why the greatest concentration of temples in Goa today is among the dense woodland and hidden valleys of Ponda *taluka*, southeast of Panjim.

Architecture

The design of Goan temples has altered dramatically over the centuries, yet without ever ditching the four fundamental features of Hindu architecture. Symbolizing the Divine Mountain from which the sacred River Ganges flows into the world, the **sanctuary tower**, or *shikhara*, rises directly above the **shrine room**, or *garbhagriha*, where the *devta* is housed. This inner sanctum is the most sacred part of the building: only the strictly vegetarian brahmin *pujari*s (high-caste priests) can cross its threshold, after performing acts of ritual purification. The **main shrine**, flanked by those of the two *pariwar devtas* (accessory deities) and surrounded by a circumambulatory passage (*pradakshena*), is approached through one or more pillared assembly halls, called *mandapas*, which are used for congregational worship and ritual recitals of music and dance. When the halls are full, the crowds spill outside on to the *prakara*, or courtyard. Finally, adjacent to most temples you will also find a stepped **water tank**, or *tirtha*, in which devout worshippers bathe before proceeding to the shrine.

In addition to these basic components, Goan temples boast some unusual features of their own – some necessitated by the local climate, or the availability of building materials, others the result of outside influences. The impact of

as Naguesh. Once inside, your eye is drawn to the multicoloured wood-carvings that run in a continuous frieze along the tops of the pillars. Famous all over Goa, these depict scenes from the Hindu epic *Ramayana*, in which the god Rama (Vishnu's seventh incarnation), with the help of Hanuman's monkey army, rescues his wife Sita from the clutches of arch demon Ravana. After the great battle, the couple are reunited back home in Ayodhya, as shown in one of the last panels. The silver-doored **sanctum** (*garbhagriha*), flanked by subsidiary shrines dedicated to Lakshmi-Narayan (left) and the elephant-headed Ganesh (right), houses a Shiva *devta*. If you're lucky, you may see it flooded with holy water – a costly ritual performed to cure sickness. Opening onto the courtyard are a couple of accessory shrines. The one on the south side harbours

European/Portuguese architecture (inevitable given the fact that the majority of Goan temples were built during the colonial era, but ironic considering the Portuguese destroyed the originals) is most evident on the exterior of the buildings. Unlike conventional Hindu temple towers, which are curvilinear, Goan *shikharas*, taking their cue from St Cajetan's Church in Old Goa, consist of octagonal drums crowned by tapering copper domes. Hidden inside the top of these is generally a pot of holy water called a **poornakalash**, drawn from a sacred Hindu river or spring. The sloping roofs of the *mandapas*, with their projecting eaves and terracotta tiles, are also distinctively Latin, while the glazed ceramic Chinese dragons often perched above them, originally imported from Macau, add to the colonial feel. Embellished with Baroque-style balustrades and pilasters, Islamic arches, and the occasional bulbous Moghul dome, the sides of larger temples also epitomize Goan architecture's flair for fusion.

Always worth looking out for inside the main assembly halls are **woodcarvings** and panels of **sculpture** depicting mythological narratives, and the opulently embossed solid silver doorways around the entrance to the shrines, flanked by a pair of guardians, or *dwarpalas*. The most distinctively Goan feature of all, however, has to be the **lamp tower**, or *deepmal*, an addition introduced by the Maharathas, who ruled much of Goa during the seventeenth and eighteenth centuries. Also known as *deep stambhas*, literally "pillars of light", these five- to seven-storey whitewashed pagodas generally stand opposite the main entrance. Their many ledges and windows hold tiny oil lamps that are illuminated during the *devta*'s weekly promenade, when the temple priests carry the god or goddess around the courtyard on their shoulders in a silver sedan chair known as a *palkhi*.

Near the *deepmal* you'll often come across an ornamental plant pot called a **tulsi vrindavan**. The straggly sacred shrub growing inside it, *tulsi*, represents a former mistress of Vishnu whom his jealous consort Lakshmi turned into a plant after a fit of jealous pique. Hindus also regard a number of trees as auspicious, including the *peepal*, with its spatula-shaped leaves, and the majestic *banyan*, both of which can invariably be found in the temple courtyard, surrounded by circular pedestals, and bristling with red pennants and small shrines.

Zatras

The most spectacular processions of the year occur during the annual **Zatra** celebrations, when the temple *devta*, together with his or her two principal accessory deities, is hauled around the precinct in a colossal and ornately carved octagonal wooden chariot, or **rath**. The grand promenades, which attract large crowds of locals but few foreign visitors, are accompanied by cacophonic trumpet blasts and drumming from the temple musicians, whose instruments are stored in special galleries known as *sonddios*.

a *lingam* carved with the face of Shiva – a rare form of the god known as Mukhaling. The temple **tank**, whose murky green waters are teeming with fish, is also worth a look, if only to hunt for the donatory inscription (on the wall beside the steps) recording the foundation of the temple in 1413.

The Shri Shantadurga temple

Standing with its back to a wall of thick forest and its front facing a flat expanse of open rice fields, Shri Shantadurga is Goa's largest and most famous temple, and the principal port of call on the region's Hindu pilgrimage circuit. Western visitors, however, may find its heavily European–influenced architecture less than exotic, and barely worth the detour from Ponda, 4km northeast. If you are pushed for time, skip this one and head straight for the temples further north at Mardol and Priol, described above.

From the row of souvenir and cold drink stalls along the roadside, steps lead to Shri Shantadurga's main entrance and courtyard, enclosed by offices and blocks of modern pilgrims' hostels, and dominated by a brilliant-white, six-storey **deepmal**. The russet- and cream-coloured temple, crowned with a huge domed sanctuary tower, was erected by the Maharatha Chief Shivaji's grandson, Shahu Raja, in 1738, some two centuries after its presiding deity had been brought here from Quelossim in Mormugao *taluka*, a short way inland from the north end of Colva beach.

The **interior** of the building, dripping with marble and glass chandeliers, is dominated by an exquisitely worked silver screen, embossed with a pair of guardian deities (*dwarpalas*). Behind this sits the garlanded Shantadurga *devi*, flanked by images of Vishnu and Shiva. According to Hindu mythology, Durga, another name for Shiva's consort, Parvati, the goddess of peace, resolved a violent dispute between her husband and rival god Vishnu, hence her position between them in the shrine, and the prefix *Shanta*, meaning "peace", that was henceforth added to her name.

After paying their respects to the goddess, worshippers generally file along the passage leading left to the subsidiary shrine where Shantadurga sleeps. Also worth a look before you leave are the *devi*'s colossal *raths*; during the annual February *Zatra* festival held here, these elaborately carved wooden chariots are pulled around the precinct by teams of honoured devotees.

The Shri Ramnath temple

Thanks to the garishly outsize entrance hall tacked onto it in 1905, the **Shri Ramnath** temple, 500m north up the lane from Shri Shantadurga, is the ugly duckling of Ponda's monuments. The only reason you'd want to call in here is to view the opulently decorated silver screen in front of the main shrine, the most extravagant of its kind in Goa. Brought from Lutolim in Salcete *taluka* in the sixteenth century, the *lingam* housed behind it is worshipped by devotees of the Shaivite and Vaishnavite sects of Hinduism, Shri Ramnath being the form of Shiva propitiated by Lord Rama before he embarked on his mission to save Sita from the clutches of the evil Ravana.

Khandepar

Hidden deep in dense woodland near the village of **KHANDEPAR**, 5km northeast of Ponda on the NH4, is a group of four tiny free-standing rock-cut **cave temples**, gouged out of solid laterite some time between the ninth and tenth centuries AD. They are among Goa's oldest historical monuments but are also virtually impossible to find without the help of a guide or knowledgeable local: ask someone to show you the way from the Khandepar crossroads, where the **buses** from Ponda pull in.

Set back in the forest behind a slowly meandering tributary of the Mandovi River, the four caves each consist of two simple cells hewn from a single hillock. Their tiered roofs, now a jumble of weed-choked blocks, are thought to have been added in the tenth or eleventh centuries, probably by the Kadambas, who converted them into Hindu temples. Prior to that, they were almost certainly Buddhist sanctuaries, occupied by a small community of monks. Scan the insides of the caves with a torch (watching out for snakes), and you can make out the carved pegs used for hanging robes and cooking utensils; the niches in the walls were for oil lamps. The outer cell of cave one also has lotus medallions carved onto its ceiling, a typically Kadamban motif that was added at roughly the same time as the stepped roofs.

The Bondla Sanctuary

Of Goa's four nature reserves, the **BONDLA SANCTUARY** (daily except Thurs 9.30am– 5.30pm; tickets, sold at the gate, cost Rs4, with additional charges of Rs5 for cars, Rs5 for cameras and Rs10 for camcorders), 52km east of Panjim on the border of Ponda and Sanguem *talukas*, is the least appealing. Encompassing a mere eight square kilometres of mixed deciduous and ever-green forest, its centrepiece is a seedy zoo whose cramped enclosures are guaranteed to disappoint any animal enthusiast hoping to see fauna in the wild. On the plus side, Bondla is set amid some magnificent **scenery**. Draped with lush jungle, a spectacular ridge of hills rises to the southeast, roamed by herds of *gaur* (Indian bison), black-faced *langur*, jackals, monkeys, wild boar, several species of deer, pythons, some gargantuan spiders and a handful of elusive leopards. The park is also a bird- and butterfly-spotter's paradise, boasting enough rare species to warrant a lengthy stop if you're on an ornithological tour of the region.

Approached from the west via the crossroad settlement of **Usgao**, the park gates open onto a surfaced road which drops down to a car park and café. Nearby, a small **Interpretation Centre** (daily except Thurs 9.30am–1pm & 2–5.30pm) gives a rundown of Bondla's flora and fauna, and displays natural curiosities that include a whale skeleton. Most visitors proceed from here to the **zoological and botanical gardens,** lured by the promise of elephant rides and the chance to ogle a captive lion or tiger, although its mangy macaques and big cats cooped up in pens are distressing, and you'd be better to head along the lane leading south from the car park. Fording several streams, this road is impassable during the monsoons, but at other times is a safe and scenic short cut to the more inspiring Bhagwan Mahaveer Sanctuary (see below) and the railhead for the Dudhsagar waterfalls at Colem, 25km south-east.

Practicalities

Unless you take a taxi, the easiest way to get to the park is to take a **bus** from Panjim or Margao to Ponda, and then jump into a taxi or auto-rickshaw for the remaining 13km. Alternatively, catch any bus heading east on the NH4 from Panjim or Ponda towards Molem, and get off at Bondla's nearest road-head, **Tisk**, 11km south, where you can pick up the Forest Department's special **minibus** service (Mon–Wed, Fri & Sat depart 11am & 7pm, Sun depart 10.30am & 7pm; Rs10).

Accommodation in Bondla is limited to the Forest Department's plain but pleasant *Tourist Cottages* (❶–❹), tucked away under the trees near the park gates, which has a dozen self-contained chalets and some cheap dormitory beds. Rooms here can be hard to come by, especially on weekends and public holidays, so it's a good idea to make an advance reservation through the Forest Department's head office in Panjim, on the ground floor of Junta House (opposite the *Hotel Fidalgo*), Swami Vivekanand Road (☎0832/222 4747). The only other places to stay within striking distance are GTDC's *Dudhsagar Resort* at Molem, 17km southeast, or at Ponda (see p.106).

Moderately priced Goan, Indian and Chinese **food** is available at *The Den* restaurant in Bondla, next door to the *Tourist Cottages*.

The Bhagwan Mahaveer Sanctuary

Bounded in the north by the mountains of the Karnatakan border, the **BHAGWAN MAHAVEER SANCTUARY** encompasses 240 square kilometres of semi-evergreen and moist deciduous woodland, peppered with clearings of parched yellow savannah grass and the occasional mud and palm-thatched tribal village. The thick tree cover harbours a diverse array of **wildlife**. However, unless you are prepared (and equipped) to spend days trudging along unmarked forest trails, you will be lucky to see more action than the odd squirrel, as animal numbers were decimated by hunters and poachers during the colonial era. Since the creation of the sanctuary, many species have recovered, but the woods are still eerily quiet compared with reserves elsewhere in India.

Easily Bhagwan Mahaveer's most famous attraction, and an increasingly popular destination for package tour groups, are the **Dudhsagar waterfalls** in the far southeast corner of the park, which can only be reached by a memorable jeep or train journey through some amazing scenery. To get to Bondla's other well-known sight, you will also need your own transport. The **Mahadeva temple** at Tamdi Surla, Goa's best-preserved ancient monument, lies at the dead end of a windy back road, crouched at the foot of the Western Ghats. Also worth considering if you have your own car or motorcycle, and plan to spend a night or two in the park, is a visit to **Devil's Canyon**, a picturesque river gorge near Molem. Permission must first be obtained from the park warden, in the **Interpretation Centre** (daily 9.30am–5.30pm), 100m beyond the police check-post, who will unlock the barrier and give you directions. The canyon itself is a popular picnic spot, particularly during the monsoon season, even though its river is rumoured to be infested with the ominously named "mugger" crocodiles (see p.103). Another reason not to swim here are the notoriously treacherous undercurrents, which claimed the lives of two picnickers in October 2000. Around the end of the monsoons, if water levels are high, you may find the canyon closed to visitors as a result.

This far-flung corner of Goa is also the homeland of the **Dhangars**, whose traditional livelihood of nomadic buffalo herding is currently under threat from deforestation, forcing many to take up settled agriculture or migrate to the towns. Alcoholism is also something of a problem among the Dhangars, and the sight of men lying comatose by the roadside clutching an empty bottle is all too common in more remote districts of the park.

Practicalities

The main jumping-off point for the Bhagwan Mahaveer Sanctuary is **Molem**, a fly-blown cluster of truckers' *dhabas*, *chai* stalls and liquor shops grouped around a crossroads, 28km east of Ponda on the NH4. Only 10km from the Karnatakan border, this is also the site of a busy police and customs **checkpoint**, and the logical place to stock up on fuel if you are heading east by car or motorcycle; note that you are not technically allowed across the Goan border with a rented bike, although it is usually possible to *baksheesh* your way past the checkpoint. The nearest railhead is 5km south at the village of **Colem**, served by four or five daily passenger **trains** from Vasco, Margao and Chandor; beyond Colem, the track remains closed pending the completion of conversion work. All **buses** bound for Belgaum, Hubli, Bangalore and Hospet (for Hampi) also stop at Molem, and there are several daily local services from Ponda. **Transport around the park** (which for most visitors means a return trip to Tamdi Surla, or to the train station) is limited to the handful of auto-rickshaws and jeeps that ply their trade on the Molem crossroads.

The only **accommodation** inside – or anywhere near – the sanctuary is GTDC's *Dudhsagar Resort* (☎0832/261 2238; ❸) at Molem. A campus of octagonal concrete bungalows scattered under the trees, 200m beyond the police post, this roadside motel is clean and comfortable enough, with attached shower-toilets, running water, fans and verandahs in all of its rooms, several of which are air-conditioned. The woodland around it is especially good for bird-watching.

The *Dudhsagar Resort*'s multi-cuisine **restaurant** offers far less inspiring food than the more congenial *Karibou*, on Colem road, which serves fresh, tasty Goan and continental menus, and stays open late.

Tamdi Surla

Six or seven hundred years ago, the Goan coast and its hinterland were scat-tered with scores of richly carved stone temples. Only one, though, came through the Muslim onslaught and religious bigotry of the Portuguese era unscathed. Erected in the twelfth or thirteenth century, the tiny **Mahadeva temple** at **TAMDI SURLA**, 12km north of Molem in the far northeastern corner of Sanguem *taluka*, owes its survival to its remote location in a tranquil clearing deep in the forest at the foot of the Western Ghats, which enfold the site in a sheer wall of impenetrable vegetation. To get there, head north from the Molem crossroads and bear right when you reach the fork in the road after 3km. The next right turn, 2km further north, is signposted. From here on, the route is winding but easy to follow and very scenic, passing through a string of picturesque villages and long stretches of woodland. If you are coming from Ponda on the NH4, note that it is quicker to approach Tamdi Surla via the hamlet of Sancordem: turn left off the highway 5km east of Tisk and carry on until you reach the fork mentioned earlier.

Why the Kadamba dynasty, who ruled Goa between the tenth and fourteenth centuries, chose this out-of-the-way spot remains a mystery: no traces of set-tlement have been unearthed in the vicinity, nor did it lie near any major trade route. Yet the temple, dedicated to Shiva, was clearly important, built not from malleable local laterite but the finest weather-resistant grey-black basalt, carried across the mountains from the Deccan plateau and lavishly carved in situ by the region's most accomplished craftsmen. Their intricate handiwork, which adorns the interior and sides of the building, is still astonishingly fresh and stands as a poignant memorial to Goa's lost Hindu architectural legacy.

Facing east – so that the rays of the rising sun light its deity at dawn – the temple is composed of a *mandapa*, or pillared porch, with three stepped entrances, a small *antaralhaya* (vestibule) and *garbhagriha* (shrine) surmounted by a three-tiered sanctuary tower, or *shikhara*. The tower's top section has col-lapsed, giving the temple a rather stumpy appearance, but the carving on its upper sections is still in good shape. As you walk around, look out for the beau-tiful **bas-reliefs** that project from the sides. Punctuating the four cardinal points, these depict the gods of the Hindu trinity, Shiva (north), Vishnu (west) and Brahma (south), with their respective consorts featured in the panels above. In addition, bands of delicate carving pattern the sides of the porch, capped with an oddly incongruous roof of plain grey sloping slabs.

After a purifying dip in the river immediately east of the temple, reached via a flight of old stone *ghats* (sacred steps), worshippers would proceed to the main **mandapa** for *darshan*, the ritual viewing of the deity. In its centre stands a headless Nandi bull, Shiva's *vahana* (vehicle), surrounded by four matching columns, one of whose bases bears a relief of an elephant trampling a horse – thought to symbolize the military might of the Kadamba dynasty. The building's finest single piece of stonework, however, has to be the intricate lotus motif carved out of the *mandapa's* ceiling. Flanked by four accessory deities that include a damaged dancing goddess (left) and an elephant-headed Ganesh (right), the pierced-stone screen surrounding the door of the vestibule comes a close second. The shrine itself houses a stone *Shivalingam*, mounted on a pedestal.

Dudhsagar Falls

Measuring a mighty 600m from head to foot, the famous **waterfalls** at **DUDHSAGAR**, near the easternmost edge of Sanguem *taluka* on the Goa-Karnataka border, are the second highest in India, and a spectacular enough sight to entice a steady stream of visitors from the coast into the rugged Western Ghats. After pouring across the Deccan plateau, the headwaters of the Mandovi River form a foaming torrent that fans into three streams, then cascades down a near-vertical cliff face, streaked black and dripping with lush foliage, into a deep green pool. The Konkani name for the falls, which literally translated means "sea of milk", derives from clouds of mist kicked up at the bottom when the water levels are at their highest between October and December.

Overlooking a steep, crescent-shaped head of a valley carpeted with pristine tropical forest, Dudhsagar is set amid appropriately dramatic scenery, making the Jeep journey there an unforgettable experience. On arrival at the falls themselves, spanned by an old viaduct, you'll probably be pestered by lads offering to show you the way to the river and to protect you from the monkeys that scamper around the place trying to pilfer food from picnickers. The path is steep and slippery in places, but you won't need a guide to find it: just head back along the rails from the train platform and turn right when you reach the gap between the two tunnels. After a fifteen-minute scramble, the trail emerges at a shady **pool** hemmed in by large grey-brown boulders – an ideal spot for bathing. If you want to escape the large groups that congregate here, clamber over the rocks a little further downstream, where there are a number of more secluded places to swim and watch the amazing butterflies and kingfishers that flit past.

A more strenuous way to while away a few hours before catching the Jeep back is the climb to the head of the falls. This arduous ninety-minute hike is relentlessly steep and impossible to follow without the help of someone who knows the path, but well worth the effort for the superb views from the top.

Dudhsagar practicalities

The best time to visit Dudhsagar is immediately after the monsoons, from October until mid-December, although the falls flow well into April. Unfortunately, the train line, which climbs above the tree canopy via a series of spectacular cuttings and stone bridges, only sees two services per week in each direction (Tues & Sat; depart Margao 7.21am), neither of them returning the same day. As a result, the only practicable way to get there and back is by four-wheel-drive **jeep** from **Colem** (reachable by train from Vasco, Margao and Chandor, or by taxi from the north coast resorts for around Rs1250). The cost of the onward thirty- to forty-minute trip from Colem to the falls, which takes you across rough forest tracks and two or three river fords, is around

Rs300–400 per person; the drive ends with an enjoyable fifteen-minute hike, for which you'll need a sturdy pair of shoes. Finding a Jeep-*wallah* is easy; just turn up in Colem and look for the "Controller of Jeeps" near the station. However, if you're travelling alone or in a couple, you may have to wait around until the vehicle fills up, or else fork out Rs2000 or so to cover the cost of hiring the whole Jeep yourself. Note that it can be difficult to arrange transport of any kind from Molem crossroads, where regular taxis are in short supply.

In recent years, GTDC, a number of large resort hotels and some package holiday companies have also been offering Dudhsagar as an **excursion**. The all-in price of the trip, which starts at the crack of dawn and finishes around 8pm, usually includes the minibus or taxi fare to Colem, the Jeep trip to and from Dudhsagar, guides and a packed lunch. If you rent a car, it's also possible to combine a visit to Dudhsagar with a detour to the Mahadeva temple at Tamdi Surla.

Travel details

By train

For details of trains to Mumbai from Goa on the new Konkan Railway, see p.82.
Colem to: Chandor (2 weekly; 1hr); Margao (2 weekly; 1hr 40min); Vasco da Gama (2 weekly; 2hr).

By bus

Panjim to: Arambol (12 daily; 1hr 45min); Baga (every 30min; 45min); Calangute (every 30min; 40min); Candolim (every 30min; 30min); Chaudi (hourly; 2hr 15min); Dona Paula (every 15min; 20min); Goa Velha (every 15min; 30min); Gokarna (2 daily; 5hr 30min); Hampi (2 daily; 9–10hr); Mapusa (every 15min; 25min); Margao (every 15min; 55min); Miramar (every 15min; 15min); Molem (5 daily; 1hr 45min); Mumbai (6 daily; 14–18hr); Old Goa (every 15min; 20min); Pernem (6 daily; 1hr 15min); Pilar (every 15min; 30min); Ponda (hourly; 50min); Vasco da Gama (every 15min; 50min).
Ponda to: Margao (hourly; 40min); Molem (5 daily; 1hr).

By ferry

Divar to: Naroa (every 20min; 5min).
Old Goa to: Divar Island (every 15min; 5min).
Panjim to: Betim (every 15min; 5min).
Ribandar to: Chorao (every 15min; 5min).

2

North Goa

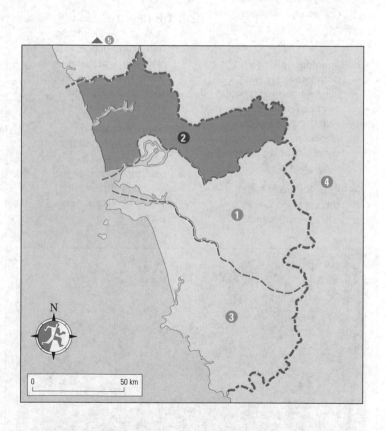

CHAPTER 2   # Highlights

✳ Sunset at Fort Aguada
Superb views of the
coast from the ramparts
of Goa's largest citadel.
See p.126

✳ Boat excursions Dolphin-
spotting tours, trips in
luxury catamarans, and
cruises on a Chinese
junk all run off the north
coast. **See p.133**

**✳ Sangolda, near
Calangute** This two-
hundred-year-old palacio
has been beautifully con-
verted into an upscale
emporium – Goa's most
stylish shopping oppor-
tunity. **See p.139**

**✳ Ingo's Saturday Night
Bazaar** Far cooler in
every sense than the

Flea Market, and the
best place for souvenir
hunting. **See p.143**

✳ Anjuna Flea Market A
riot of goods, sellers and
colours from all over
India, slap on the beach.
See p.148

✳ The Nine Bar, Vagator
Optimum venue for Goa
Trance and dance, com-
plete with whopping
sound system and an
appropriately blissful
view. **See p.154**

✳ Terekol An historic
Portuguese fort that's
been renovated as a
parador-style hotel, with
luminous interiors and
sweeping vistas. **See
p.167**

2

North Goa

B eyond the mouth of the Mandovi estuary, the Goan coast sweeps **north** in a near-continuous string of beaches, broken only by the odd salt-water creek, rocky headland and three tidal rivers – the northernmost of which, the Arondem, still has to be crossed by ferry. The most developed resorts in this district, known as **Bardez** *taluka*, all lie within a half-hour drive of Panjim. Spread behind a seven-kilometre strip of golden sand,

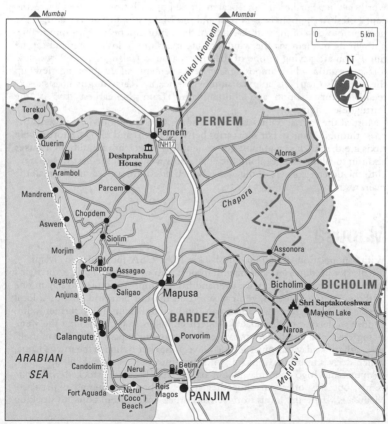

Candolim, Calangute and Baga are the centres of the tourist boom. Formerly infamous for the colonies of hippies who gathered there during their annual winter migration from the Himalayas, these three villages now heave during high season with British charter tourists, busloads of day-trippers from out of state and Kashmiri handicraft merchants.

The "scene", meanwhile, has drifted further north to **Anjuna**, the next sizeable village up the coast from Baga, where most of the Christmas–New Year full-moon parties take place. Scattered around paddy fields behind a white-sand beach, this picturesque settlement is also renowned for its Wednesday **flea market**, where you can buy anything from Tibetan prayer wheels to cutting-edge techno tapes. Further north still, **Vagator** and **Chapora** are the preserve of long-stay travellers who hole up in simple houses and huts until the onset of summer. Accommodation of any kind is thinner on the ground once you cross the Chapora River from Bardez into the mainly Hindu *taluka* of **Pernem**. The only place with anything resembling a tourist scene this far north is the fishing community of **Arambol**, which hosts a small contingent of mostly long-staying budget travellers.

The **interior** of north Goa – through Bardez and Pernem to Bicholim and Satari *talukas* – harbours few sights likely to entice you from the coast, although the colourful Friday market at **Mapusa**, Bardez's largest town, is definitely worth a visit. Further off the beaten track but of historical interest are the Saptakoteshwar temple near **Naroa** and the Maharatha fort at **Terekol**, at the northernmost tip of the state. Neither of these monuments ranks as unmissable, but getting to them via the winding back roads of the lush hinterland can be fun. If you are staying in one of the resorts around Calangute, the Portuguese fort at **Aguada**, whose imposing laterite battlements afford stunning views up the coast, also warrants an excursion, while nearby **Reis Magos** boasts a sixteenth-century bastion and church dating from the earliest days of the Portuguese colony.

Most of the tourist traffic arriving in north Goa is siphoned off towards the coast through Mapusa. For short trips between towns and resorts, **motorcycle taxis** are the quickest and most convenient way to get around, although **buses** also run to all the villages along the coast. However, much the best way to travel to the quieter corners of the area is by rented motorcycle, available at all the main resorts.

Mapusa

With a population of 35,000, ramshackle **MAPUSA** (pronounced "Mapsa"), the district headquarters and main transport hub of Bardez *taluka*, is the state's third largest town. If you arrive overland from Mumbai and plan to stay in one of the north Goan resorts, you can jump off the bus here and pick up a local service straight to the coast, rather than continue to Panjim, 13km further south. A dusty collection of dilapidated modern buildings scattered around the west-facing slope of a low hill, Mapusa is of little more than passing interest in itself, although on Friday mornings it hosts a lively **market** (whence the town's name, which derives from the Konkani words for "measure", *map*, and "fill up", *sa*).

Anjuna and Ingo's Saturday Night bazaar may be better stocked with souvenirs, but this offers an altogether more authentic shopping experience. Mapusa is where the locals from across Bardez and Pernem come to stock up

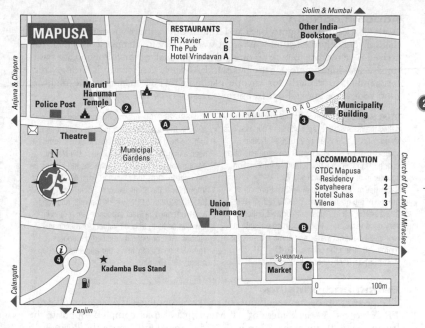

on essentials, from fresh fish, fruit and veg to scooter parts and football shirts. The majority of stall-holders are women from the surrounding villages, squatting in the shade of torn umbrellas. Local specialities to look out for include strings of spicy Goan sausages (*chouriço*), bottles of *toddi* spirit and the large green plantains grown in the nearby village of Moira. For **books**, check out the wonderful Other India Bookstore (☎0832/226 3305; ✉oib@goatelecom.com), hidden away behind Mapusa Clinic, which holds a vast range of titles relating to ecology, the environment and Goa in general; a full stock list is available via email.

Whatever you're looking for in Mapusa market, it's a good idea to arrive as early in the morning as possible to beat the heat; after 11am temperatures can be stifling.

Practicalities

Arriving by **motorbike**, bear in mind that the police in Mapusa tend to stop tourists to check their documents on market day; if you don't have a valid licence, park up well before the centre and walk the last stretch, or catch the bus. Traffic can be overwhelming on Fridays, and you should make a note of your registration number, as the bike parking areas along the main routes get filled with hundreds of lookalike vehicles by mid-morning, which can make it difficult to find yours again when you come to leave.

Buses drop passengers at the main Kadamba stand, just below the town's square, the **Municipal Gardens**, where there's a dependable petrol pump and ranks of motorcycle "pilots" touting for trade. If you're travelling in by taxi, ask to be dropped somewhere where you'll easily be able to meet up with your driver again afterwards, such as outside the GTDC *Mapusa Residency*.

Accommodation

With Candolim, Calangute, Baga and Anjuna only a short bus or taxi ride away, the only conceivable reason you might want to stay in Mapusa would be if you arrived here too late to pick up onward transport. All of the following are within easy walking distance of the bus stand. Advance reservation is strongly recommended, particularly for anyone planning to pull in during the night, as most rooms are booked out to business travellers by late afternoon.

GTDC Mapusa Residency On the roundabout below the main square, opposite the Kadamba bus stand ☎0832/226 2794 or 226 2694. Nothing special, but the en-suite rooms are large and clean enough, and there's a helpful tourist information counter in the lobby. Some a/c. ③

Satyaheera Opposite the Municipal Gardens at the top of the main square ☎0832/226 2849 or 226 2949. Much the most comfortable option, and very good value, with well-appointed en-suite rooms, 24-hour hot water, and some a/c. Ask for a room overlooking the square. ③–④

Hotel Suhas Near Other India Bookstore

☎0832/226 2700. A large, no-frills lodge tucked away in the back streets above the main square, and the best fall-back if the *Vilena* is full. To find it, head along the lane up the hill past the Maruti (Hanuman) temple, and take the second turning on the right towards the Mapusa Clinic. ②–③

Vilena Near the Municipality building, Feira Baixa Rd ☎0832/226 3115. Run-of-the-mill, mid-range hotel, offering the least expensive a/c rooms in town, in addition to good-value, clean economy options, with or without attached bathrooms. There's also a dimly lit a/c bar and small rooftop restaurant. ②–④

Eating and drinking

The perfect pitstop between bouts of market shopping is the beguilingly dated *FR Xavier* café in the middle of the Municipal Market complex (opposite the banana section), which has been here (and changed little) since the Portuguese era. The waiters leave heaped baskets of scrumptious veg patties and beef "chops" (rissoles) on your table, billing you for what you eat at the end. Apart from the fresh fruit and juice bars dotted around town, the other commendable place to eat and drink Indian food is the *Hotel Vrindavan*, on the east side of the main square, which dishes up Mapusa's best inexpensive South Indian snacks – *masala dosas, wadas, pakoras* and the like – along with an impressive range of ice creams, sundaes and shakes. On the main road directly opposite the north side of the market complex, *The Pub* has a high terrace from which you can survey the lively comings and goings over an ice cream or cold beer, and they serve main meals and a range of tourist-oriented snacks.

Naroa

The one monument in Bicholim *taluka* worth going out of your way to see is the secluded **Shri Saptakoteshwar temple** at **NAROA**, 5km south of the district headquarters. Ensconced in a thickly wooded valley amid well-watered areca plantations and *toddi* groves, this remote shrine is most easily reached from the south via Divar Island, from whose north shore a **ferry** chugs across the Mandovi River.

The temple **deity** here, a ferocious aspect of the god Shiva in the form of a *lingam* (see p.344), has a long and turbulent history. Cast from seven separate metals ("an alloy of the unalloyable"), it is believed to have been made by seven sages, known as the Saptarishis, after Shiva himself had appeared to them at the end of a seventy-million-year fast. Patronized during the fourteenth century by the Kadamba royal family, the shrine housing it, at Narve on Divar Island, was demolished in 1560 by the Portuguese – its masonry plundered to build the church in Piedade – after which the *lingam* was used as a well shaft until a party of Hindu marauders managed to rescue it. The idol was then smuggled across the river to Bicholim, where it was installed in a brand-new temple and revamped in 1668 by the Maharatha rebel leader, Shivaji.

With its shallow Moghul dome mounted on an octagonal drum, sloping tiled roofs, European-style *mandapa*, or assembly hall, and tall lamp tower, the present structure is regarded by art historians as the prototype of the modern Goan temple. Its **interior** is plain by Indian standards. Vaulted arches line the marble-floored hall, entered beneath an equestrian mural of Shivaji, and although the wood-panelled shrine lacks the conventional embossed silver surround, its glaring-eyed golden *devta* is very fine.

Betim and Reis Magos

The concrete road bridge across the Mandovi River linking Panjim with the north bank collapsed on July 5, 1986, killing several people and sparking off a heated row about corruption in the government and the construction industry. The disaster was doubly embarrassing for those responsible, as the bridge had been in use for a lot less time than it had taken to build. Its replacement fared even worse, falling apart before it was even finished. The present structure, completed in 1992, looks sturdy enough, but if you are not convinced, jump on the ferry that shuttles between Panjim's old steamer jetty and the fishing and boat-building settlement of **BETIM**, 1km west of the bridge. Straddling the busy back road to Candolim and Calangute, the village is inundated with traffic during the day; the only incentive to stop here is a small Sikh temple, or **Gurudwara**, whose yellow Moghul domes and saffron pennant are visible from the opposite shore.

After winding past Panjim's **fishing dock** and through a string of ribbon developments, the coastal road veers inland to a small market crossroads. A Hindu tree shrine, 20m before this in the middle of **Verem**, marks the turning to **REIS MAGOS**, 3km west of Betim bazaar. It's not on a bus route, but you can get there easily enough by motorcycle taxi from the main road if you're not up to walking. Visible from across the river in Panjim, Reis Magos **church** (Mon–Sat 9am–noon & 4.30–5.30pm) was built in 1555 and taken over soon after by Franciscan friars, charged with missionary responsibility for the colony at the time, who founded a small seminary here. Historians believe the original church was constructed on the ruins of an old Hindu temple, and the two bas-relief lion figures flanking the steps at the ends of the balustrades lend credence to this theory, being a typical feature of Vijayanagar temple architecture in the fourteenth and fifteenth centuries. A further indication of the site's former prominence is the Portuguese royal family's coat of arms, featured below the crucifix at the top of the gabled facade. Two viceroys are also buried inside the church: one at the west entrance, the other to the north of the nave. The best preserved of the tombstones, both still in crisp condition with their Portuguese and Latin inscriptions clearly legible, is that of **Dom Luis de Ataide**, renowned as the hero of the 1570 siege of Old Goa, in which a force of 7000 defenders managed to keep an army of 100,000 Muslims (with 2000 elephants) at bay for ten months. The centrepiece of the church's elaborately carved and painted **reredos**, behind the high altar, is a multicoloured wood relief showing the Three Wise Men – or *Reis Magos*, after whom the village is named – bearing gifts to the baby Jesus. Each year, this scene is re-enacted in the **Festa dos Reis Magos**, held in the first week of January, during Epiphany.

Crowning the sheer-sided headland immediately above the church, Reis Magos **fort** was erected in 1551 to protect the narrowest point at the mouth of the Mandovi estuary. Like the 'Adil Shah's palace on the opposite bank, converted by the Portuguese after Albuquerque's defeat of the Muslims, it formerly accommodated viceroys and other dignitaries newly arrived from, or en route to, Lisbon, and in the early eighteenth century proved a linchpin in the wars against the Hindu Maharathas, who were never able to take it. These days, the bastion, surrounded by sturdy laterite walls studded with typically Portuguese turrets, is used as a prison and not open to the public, but you can clamber up the stony slope to the ramparts for the views over the river.

Nerul (Coco) beach

Continuing west along the coast road for another 3km you pass the turning for **NERUL BEACH**, better known these days as "**Coco beach**". Gently inclined palm trees there certainly are, but in every other respect the new tourist name for this old, mainly Hindu fishing settlement is misleading. Due to the beach's proximity to Panjim at the mouth of the Mandovi estuary, the sand and water are dubiously discoloured and few prudent tourists venture into the water beyond their knees.

If you come here at all it will probably be for lunch on one of the dolphin- or croc-spotting **boat trips** out of Candolim (see p.133), or to party at the *Coco Beach Bar*. Set up by the ever entrepreneurial owners of *Tito's* in Baga, this place may well offer the only bona fide **beach party** you'll experience during your stay, thanks to the recent ban on amplified music after 10pm (see p.155). Gifts of books and uniforms to the village school have effectively circumvented the curfew and local objections, making this the liveliest place in the state on **Sunday nights**, when the music continues until dawn. The drinks are reasonably priced, the sound system is hefty and there's unlimited dance space on the hard sand at the top of the beach, beneath a large bar terrace lit by lanterns and fairy lights. The crowd – a mixture of locals, teenagers from Mumbai and Bangalore and young British charter tourists – is also relaxed, and the atmosphere less edgy than *Tito's*.

To reach Coco beach from Candolim or Calangute, head south down the strip until you reach the main Panjim turning (opposite *Casa Sea Shell* in Candolim), and follow the road over the river bridge as far as Nerul market (the first village you come to); take a right turn here and go straight across the junction when you reach the church, from where the bar is signposted.

Fort Aguada

West of Reis Magos and Nerul, a long peninsula extends into the sea, bringing the seven-kilometre-long Calangute beach to an abrupt end. **FORT AGUADA**, which crowns the rocky flattened top of the headland, is the largest and best-preserved Portuguese bastion in Goa. Built in 1612 to guard the northern shores of the Mandovi estuary from attacks by Dutch and Maharatha raiders, its name derives from the presence inside of several freshwater springs – the first source of drinking water available to ships arriving in Goa after the long sea voyage from Lisbon. On the north side of the fort, a rampart of red-brown laterite juts into the bay to form a jetty between two small sandy coves; the gigantic cannon that once stood on it covered a blind spot in the fortification's defences. In the late 1970s, this picturesque spot, known as **Sinquerim beach**, was among the first places in Goa to be singled out for upmarket tourism. Today the *Fort Aguada Beach Resort* still overlooks the beach from the lower slopes of the promontory: a sprawling agglomeration of chalets, swimming pools and overwatered lawns that local environmental groups have been campaigning against for years. Only recently, however, have their efforts been rewarded. Following a protracted legal battle, the Goan High Court forced the hotel's owners, Taj Group, to demolish structures built within the protected coastal zone.

The fort

The extensive ruins of the **fort**, formerly encircled at sea level by battlements (of which only fragments now remain), can be reached by road: head south past the Taj village towards Nerul, and turn right after about 1km when you see a lane striking uphill through the woods. Before reaching it, you pass the palace of diamond and rubber tycoon Jimmy Gazdar, on your left, overlooking the bay (and prison) from the steep hillside. A monumentally kitsch pile of pink

---

Forts

Crowning river mouths and hilltops along the whole length of the state, Goa's crumbling red-black **forts** stand as evocative reminders of the region's colonial past, dating from an era when this was a remote European trading post on the margins of a vast maritime empire. Laterite, the hard, heavily pitted stone used to build them, was quarried locally and proved an efficient foil for the heavy weapons being developed in the sixteenth and seventeenth centuries, at the high watermark of Portuguese power in Asia.

The castles of medieval Europe were no match for improved gunpowder and cast-iron cannonballs, so the Portuguese, under the guidance of an Italian architect, Filipo Terzi, strengthened Goa's defences by erecting forts with low, thick walls, filled with cushions of earth and built at an angle to deflect shot. The large, V-shaped bastions, added to the battlements, were designed both to deflect incoming fire and to give greater range for the huge Portuguese revolving cannons.

Inside, buildings were chiselled out of solid rock, and the level of the ground around them was lowered to give extra defensive height. Underneath, store rooms and arsenals were excavated, interconnected by a network of narrow tunnels and corridors, such as those still visible in Fort Aguada. These often led to concealed safe moorings at sea level – essential supply lines in times of siege. The whole was then encircled by deep dry moats and ditches to waylay foot soldiers and cavalry, though the Portuguese most feared attack from the sea by their trade rivals, the British and Dutch. The latter did penetrate the Mandovi estuary in 1604, but it was from the land that the most decisive invasion of the territory came, sixty years later, when the army of the Hindu Maratha leader, Shivaji (see p.293), poured virtually unopposed through a poorly defended interior border.

As the threat of attack diminished through the eighteenth and nineteenth centuries, the Portuguese forts gradually fell into disrepair, and today most of them, like the one at **Rachol** in Salcete have been completely reclaimed by vegetation, or their masonry plundered for building material. Only a handful of bastions remain intact, their walls, ditches and discarded cannons choked with weeds. Of these, **Fort Aguada** is by far the most impressive, with **Chapora**, also in north Goa, a close second. Other forts worth visiting include **Terekol**, in the far north of the state, and windswept **Cabo da Rama** in the south.

marble staircases, spiral pillars, follies and fountains, it was the brainchild of Goa's most famous architect, Gerard da Cunha. Visitors are not welcome, but you can see what it looks like behind the high retaining walls by getting hold of a copy of Taschen's *Indian Interiors* (see "Books", p.332), which includes photos of the palace's over-the-top interiors.

From "Jimmy's Palace", the surfaced road runs the length of the ridge to an impressive square-shaped **citadel**, joined to an anchorage, jetty and storehouses on the south side of the headland. Since World War II, these have served as Goa's largest prison, **Fort Aguada Jail**, whose population includes those foreigners arrested for drug offences. Ringed by thick battlements, the heart of the fort, directly above the prison, was protected by two hundred cannon and a deep dry moat, which you still have to cross to get inside. Steps lead down from the middle of the courtyard within to an enormous vaulted **cistern** capable of storing ten million litres of fresh water.

The other unusual feature of the fort is a four-storey Portuguese **lighthouse**, erected in 1864 and the oldest of its kind in Asia. Scaled via a spiral staircase, the oddly stumpy structure surveys the vast expanse of sea, sand and palm trees of Calangute on one side, and the mouth of the Mandovi to Cabo Raj Bhavan and the tip of the Mormugao peninsula on the other. Superseded by a modern lighthouse only in 1976, it used to house the colossal bell salvaged from the ruins of the monastery of St Augustus in Old Goa, which now hangs in Panjim's Our Lady of the Immaculate Conception.

Aguada's **Church of St Lawrence**, which you pass on your left before reaching the citadel on the road, is dedicated to the patron saint of sailors, whose statue presides over the high altar's reredos, clutching a model ship. Normally, the Portuguese erected churches outside their forts' battlements so as not to give the enemy a potential stronghold within firing distance of the inner defences, but Aguada was so sprawling it was deemed safe to site the shrine here. The overall design proved eminently successful: this was the only Portuguese fort in Goa never conquered during more than 450 years of colonial rule.

Candolim

Compared with Calangute, 3km north along the beach, **CANDOLIM** (from the Konkani *kandoli*, meaning "dikes" – a reference to the system of sluices that the area's first farmers used to reclaim the land from the nearby Nerul marshes) is a surprisingly sedate resort, attracting mainly middle-aged package tourists from the UK and Scandinavia. Over the past five years or so, its ribbon development of hotels and restaurants has sprouted a string of multistoreyed holiday complexes, and during peak season the few vestiges of authentically Goan culture that remain here are drowned under a deluge of Kashmiri hand-

Candolim beach has seen a spate of **drownings** over the past couple of years. The undertow here has always been strong at certain phases of the tide, but the currents rarely proved treacherous until June 6, 2000, when the 61,000-tonne bulk carrier, the **MV River Princess**, ran aground just off Sinquerim. Since then, the ship's owners, its insurers and the Goan government have been embroiled in a dispute over who should foot the bill for salvaging the vessel, leaving the River Princess to lurch deeper into the sand. Meanwhile, eddies and whirlpools whipped up around its hull have claimed lives each season.

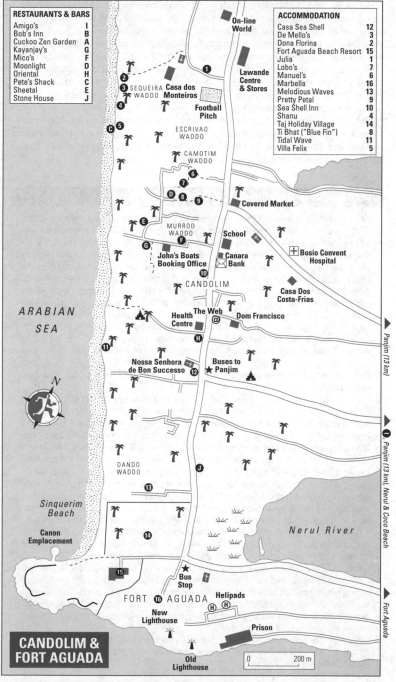

▲ **Ⓐ**, **Ⓑ** & Calangute (2 km)

RESTAURANTS & BARS

Amigo's	I
Bob's Inn	B
Cuckoo Zen Garden	A
Kayanjay's	G
Mico's	F
Moonlight	D
Oriental	H
Pete's Shack	C
Sheetal	E
Stone House	J

ACCOMMODATION

Casa Sea Shell	12
De Mello's	3
Dona Florina	2
Fort Aguada Beach Resort	15
Julia	1
Lobo's	7
Manuel's	6
Marbella	16
Melodious Waves	13
Pretty Petal	9
Sea Shell Inn	10
Shanu	4
Taj Holiday Village	14
Ti Bhat ("Blue Fin")	8
Tidal Wave	11
Villa Felix	5

On-line World

Lawande Centre & Stores

SEQUEIRA WADDO   Casa dos Monteiros

Football Pitch

ESCRIVAO WADDO

CAMOTIM WADDO

Covered Market

MURROD WADDO

School

John's Boats Booking Office

Canara Bank

Bosio Convent Hospital

CANDOLIM

Casa Dos Costa-Frias

The Web @

ARABIAN SEA

Health Centre

Dom Francisco

N

Nossa Senhora de Bon Successo

Buses to Panjim

DANDO WADDO

Sinquerim Beach

Nerul River

Canon Emplacement

Bus Stop

FORT AGUADA

Helipads

New Lighthouse

Prison

Old Lighthouse

0   200 m

CANDOLIM & FORT AGUADA

▶ *Panjim (13 km)*

▶ **Ⓘ**, *Panjim (13 km), Nerul & Coco Beach*

▶ *Fort Aguada*

icraft stalls, luridly lit terrace cafés and shops crammed with postcards and beachwear. Long gone are the days when this was a tranquil bolt hole for burgundy-clad *sanyasins* from the Rajneesh *ashram* at Pune. Now the beach where they used to pull yoga poses on empty sands is lined with sun beds, parasols and shack cafés, and the surf sees more jet-skis and paragliders than fishing boats. The main road that runs through the village, revamped for a Commonwealth heads of state visit in the 1980s, is also busy with traffic, much of it decrepit private buses careering towards Calangute at death-defying speeds.

On the plus side, Candolim has lots of pleasant places to stay, many of them tucked away down quiet sandy lanes and better value than comparable guest-houses in nearby Calangute, making this a good first stop if you've just arrived in Goa and are planning to head further north after finding your feet. It also harbours several wonderful old **mansions**.

Portuguese palacios in Candolim

Anyone with an eye for old **Indo-Portuguese architecture** will find plenty of inspiration among the shady palm groves of Candolim's outlying *waddos*, where several stately *palacios* recall the era when this ranked among the most affluent of Goa's villages. In the seventeenth and early eighteenth centuries, when malaria and cholera were decimating the population of the capital, those wealthy families who could afford to buy land built grand new houses in this more salubrious seaside district. Among them were the **Pintos**, a powerful dynasty infamous for fomenting a rebellion against the Portuguese in 1787. Marshalled by a priest called Father Couto, 47 disaffected clerics, soldiers and local grandees (including several Pintos), exasperated by the racial discrimination that was rife in the colonial administration at the time, assembled in the Pintos' house to prepare a coup against the regime in Panjim. However, the Portuguese governor got wind of the impending revolution and dispatched troops to arrest the culprits, who were promptly shipped off for two decades of imprisonment in Portugal, or – in the case of the lowly troops – hanged and quartered.

The house where the so-called **Pinto Revolt** took place collapsed long ago, but others dating from this period still stand and are well worth hunting out. In the north of Candolim, the **Casa dos Monteiros** is an outstandingly well-preserved, late-seventeenth-century rural *palacio*, of a kind that has virtually disappeared. The Monteiros, once among the richest and most influential families in Goa, were linked to the Pintos through marriage, and it is thought this house is similar to the one their inlaws lived in at the time of the 1787 revolt. It stands within a low enclosure wall, facing a small chapel, **Nossa Senhora dos Agonizantes** (Our Lady of Dying), opened by a special papal bull in 1714. Divided by ornamental pilasters, the oyster-shell windows of the mansion's three facades are capped by beautifully proportioned triangular pediments, typical of the period but now extremely rare in Goa.

Candolim's other oldest *palacio*, the **Casa dos Costa-Frias**, stands further north, not far from the Bosio Hopital, and also belonged to relatives of the Pintos. Built in the early eighteenth century, it boasts a wonderful whitewashed gateway with moulded Corinthian columns and a pediment crowned by a cross. The facade, the north side of which was recently renovated, is equally impressive, with a full set of sliding oyster-shell blinds, surmounted by elegant stone-carved scroll-work. Behind the house (facing the road), the family **chapel** also dates from the early eighteenth century, although the twisting pillars flanking its doorway hark back to the more exuberant Manueline style of the sixteenth.

Both of these *palacios* are still inhabited by descendants of their original occupants and are thus **not open to visitors**, but no-one will mind you admiring them from outside the enclosure walls.

Practicalities

Buses to and from Panjim stop every ten minutes or so at the stand opposite the *Casa Sea Shell*, in the middle of Candolim. A few head south here to the *Fort Aguada Beach Resort* terminus, from where services depart every thirty minutes for the capital via Nerul village; you can also flag them down from anywhere along the main drag to Calangute. **Taxis** are ubiquitous. During the season, however, there is often a dearth of **motorcycles for rent** here, and you may find yourself having to search for a bike in Calangute (see p.136).

Accommodation

Candolim is charter holiday land, so **accommodation** tends to be expensive for most of the season. That said, if bookings are down you can pick up some great bargains here. Listed below are a handful of well-situated places that have no connection with the charter companies, and in which rooms may be reserved by email or fax.

Inexpensive

Julia Escrivao Waddo ☎0832/227 7219. At the north end of the village, with comfortable en-suite rooms, tiled floors, balconies, a relaxing, sociable garden, and easy access to the beach. ❸

Lobo's Camotim Waddo ☎0832/227 9165. In a peaceful corner of the village, this is a notch up from *Manuel's* opposite, with larger rooms, a long common verandah on the ground floor and very friendly owners. ❷

Manuel's Camotim Waddo ☎0832/227 7729. Small family guesthouse that's been around for years and is welcoming, clean and cheap, although somewhat boxed in by other buildings. All rooms have fans and attached shower-toilets. ❷

Ti Bhat ("Blue Fin") Camotim Waddo ☎0832/227 5291. Five basic rooms, some of them rather stuffy, but otherwise pleasant enough, run by a pair of friendly brothers, Cajie and Savio. Among the cheapest options in the area. ❷

Mid-range

Casa Sea Shell Fort Aguada road, near *Bom Successo* ☎0832/247 9879, ✉ seashellgoa@hot-mail.com. A newish block with its own pool, picturesquely situated beside a small chapel. The rooms are large, with spacious tiled bathrooms, and the staff and management welcoming and courteous. If they're full ask for a room in the identical and slightly cheaper (but pool-less) *Sea Shell Inn* (same phone) up the road. ❹

De Mello's Escrivao Waddo ☎0832/227 7395. Gaudy pink-and-orange place in the dunes that takes the overspill from the (pricier) *Dona Florina* next door. Smallish rooms with not very private balconies, but only a stone's throw from the beach and very quiet. ❸

Dona Florina Monteiro's road, Sequeira Waddo ☎0832/227 5051 or 227 7398, ☏227 6878,

✉ donaflorina@sify.com. Large, ten-year-old guesthouse in a superb location, overlooking the beach in the most secluded corner of the village. Sanyasins from the Rashneesh ashram from Pune have long been its mainstay, hence the higher than usual rates – worth paying if you want idyllic sea views. No car access. ❸–❹

Marbella Sinquerim ☎0832/227 5551, ☏227 6509. Individually styled suites and spacious rooms (from Rs1000) in a beautiful house built to resemble a traditional Goan mansion. The decor, fittings and furniture are gorgeous, especially in the top-floor "Penthouse" (Rs1700), and the whole place is screened by greenery. Unashamedly romantic and well worth splashing out on. ❻

Melodious Waves Dando Waddo ☎0832/247 9711, ☏241 7211, ⊕www.melodiouswaves.com. A dozen recently built rooms with balconies in a quiet location, well back from the main road and two minutes through the dunes from a relatively peaceful stretch of beach. Tariffs reflect its proximity to the *Taj*, though still good value. ❹

Pretty Petal Camotim Waddo ☎0832/227 6184. Not as twee as it sounds: very large, modern rooms, all with fridges and balconies, and relaxing, marble-floored communal areas overlooking lawns. Their top-floor apartment, with windows on four sides and a huge balcony, is the best choice, though more expensive. ❹

Sea Shell Inn Fort Aguada road, opposite the Canara Bank ☎0832/277 6131 or 227 1555, ✉ seashellgoa@hotmail.com. Homely, immaculately clean rooms in a roadside hotel; safe-deposit lockers, laundry facility and a popular terrace restaurant. The tariff includes use of a nearby pool – a very good deal. ❹

Shanu Escrivao Waddo ☎0832/227 6899, ✉ shanu.candolim@vsnl.com. Large, well-appointed rooms, some on the dark side, but right on the dunes. The best of them are in a block adjacent to the main building called "Sea Pearl". ❸–❹

Tidal Wave Vaddy Candolim, just down the lane from *Casa Sea Shell* ☎0832/227 6884, ℮newmanwarren@rediffmail.com. Lovely sea-facing rooms in a recent construction right behind the beach. Those in the newest block are more spacious and have kitchenettes for long lets. The very hospitable Newman family have their own shack nearby. ❹

Villa Felix Escrivao Waddo ☎0832/227 5289. Clean, breezy guesthouse in a peaceful location well away from the road. Try for room #7, from whose large balcony you can watch the sun set over the sea. The same family also rents nice apartments for longer stays at reasonable rates. ❸–❹

Expensive

Fort Aguada Beach Resort Sinquerim beach ☎0832/227 6201, ℻227 6044, ℠www.tajhotels.com. Five-star opulence in

sprawling, hermetically sealed vacation campus with huge pool, health club and courtesy vehicles to ferry you around. Three categories of rooms: the "standard" ones in the main block (from around $200) overlook the beach; next up are self-contained "cottages" (from $220); and top of the hill, amid abundant vegetation, is the *Hermitage* (around $400 for 2 people), comprising cosy laterite bungalows with their own gardens (#515 is pick of the bunch). Pools, but no private beach. Note that their already sky-high tariffs double at Christmas. The complex has infringed upon environmental laws. ❾

Taj Holiday Village Sinquerim beach ☎0832/227 6201, ℻227 6044, ℮village.goa@tajhotels .com. Supposedly modelled on a "traditional Goan village", but more like a typical Thai five-star resort complex, save for the *balcões* and pitched tiled roofs. Absurdly expensive and lacking atmosphere, but slap on the beach and highly exclusive. Doubles from $150–355. ❾

Eating and drinking

Candolim has an amazingly eclectic choice of **places to eat**, ranging from rough-and-ready seafood shacks on the beach to the full five-star monty at the Taj. The British palate is particularly well catered for, down to greasy English breakfasts and Yorkshire pudding Sunday lunches. Bear in mind that Calangute and Baga also lie well within range.

Amigo's 3km east of Candolim at Nerul bridge. Well off the beaten track and rarely patronized by tourists, this down-to-earth riverside shack, tucked away under the bridge, is famous locally for its superb fresh seafood, served straight off the boats on stone tables. Fish curry and rice is their stock in trade, but they also do stuffed pomfret, calamari chilli-fry, red snapper and, best of all, Jurassic-sized crabs in butter-garlic sauce. Count on Rs150 for the works, with drinks.

Caravella *Fort Aguada Beach Resort*, Sinquerim. The *Taj's* flagship restaurant, overseen by Goa's most renowned chef, Urbano de Rego, is *the* place to sample the cream of local seafood. With views of the beach and old Portuguese ramparts, you can tuck into piles of fresh lobster *balchao*, *pomfret recheado*, tiger prawns *peri peri*, and oysters with fresh coriander, all fished locally. The wine list is as good, too, but brace yourself for a whacking bill: with fish as a main, count on Rs750–1000 for three courses, or Rs1500 if you order lobster.

Casa Sea Shell *Casa Sea Shell* hotel. This is the place to head for top-notch tandoori (from a real charcoal-fired oven) and North Indian dishes, although they also offer a good choice of Chinese and European food, served on a hotel patio next to an illuminated fountain. Excellent service and

moderate prices. Don't miss the to-die-for Irish coffee.

Cuckoo Zen Garden Authentic Taiwanese and Japanese evening meals, including melt-in-the-mouth (and scrupulously hygienic) sushi, miso and tofu, made with imported ingredients and served on Oriental porcelain. To find it, turn down the lane just south of *Bob's Inn* (towards the sea), and then first right, and first left after that. Closed Sat.

Kayanjay's Murrod Waddo. Flame-coloured cocktail bar cum barbecue restaurant, run by a gang of enthusiastic local lads. The decor's studiously "Lounge", complete with three-piece suite. Grilled fish and meat dishes (mostly around Rs200) dominate the menu; and the Planters Punch is a must.

Mico's Murrod Waddo. Succulent barbecued meats and seafood are the speciality of this unpretentious new restaurant, set around a Portuguese-era house just off the main road. They also serve a range of tasty, healthy starters (including great satay chicken, houmous and tsatsiki), tender steak in whisky sauce and a great Thai-style green curry. Main courses from Rs120 (for Indian veg),to Rs500 (for a grilled fresh lobster).

Moonlight Camotim Waddo. Homely little multi-cuisine restaurant, well away from the main strip, run by a welcoming couple, Santana and Theresa

Pires. Theresa honed her culinary skills at the *Taj*, and her repertoire ranges from traditional Goan to traditional British. Their roast-beef-and-Yorkshire-pudding Sunday lunch gets rave reviews, and there's an informal barbecue on Wednesday evenings, with imported wines (advance reservation recommended). Jools Holland numbers among the regulars.

Oriental Opposite the Health Centre, Fort Aguada Rd. Sumptuous Thai cuisine prepared by master chef Chawee, who turns out eighteen house sauces to accompany choice cuts of seafood, meat and poultry, as well as plenty of vegetarian options. Be sure to try their signature starter, *soom tham* (papaya salad). At around Rs450–600 for three courses, it's superb value for cooking of this standard. Enthusiasts can attend cookery classes here (Mon 2–5pm; Rs1100, including a five-course dinner).

Pete's Shack Escrivao Waddo. One beach shack that deserves singling out because it's always in the same spot, professional and serves great Italian-style salads (Rs100–300), with real olive oil, mozzarella and balsamic vinegar. All the veg is carefully washed in chlorinated water first, so the food is safe and fresh. The same applies to their moderate range of seafood and sizzler main courses.

Sea Shell *Sea Shell Inn*, Fort Aguada road. A congenial terrace restaurant in front of an old colonial-era *palacio* decked with green fairy lights. Sizzlers, spaghetti bolognaise and beef steaks are their specialities, but they do a range of seafood, Indian and Chinese dishes, as well as delicious cocktails. Not as pricey as it looks, either (with most mains Rs175–300).

Sheetal Murrod Waddo. One of the few restaurants in Goa specializing in authentic Mughlai

Boat trips and cruises from Candolim

Still riding high a decade after a BBC TV plug, **John's Boat Cruises** (℡0832/247 9780, ℮johnsboats@rediffmail.com), run by an entrepreneurial former fisherman, have cornered Candolim's lucrative dolphin- and croc-spotting market with their "No Dolphins, No Pay" policy, and British-safety-standard lifejackets. The four- to five-hour trips start at 9am from "John's HQ" in Murrod Waddo (see map, p.129), and cost Rs600 per head (which includes food, drink and taxi pick-up from your hotel). Book in advance. The same outfit has also acquired a splendid **Keralan rice boat** in which they run two-day tours (with one night on board) of the backwaters around the Mandovi estuary and Cambarjua canal – prime crocodile country. Again, the price (around Rs3350 per head) includes all meals and transfers. Contact John's new office in Murrod Waddo (near *Mico's* restaurant) for more details.

Budget alternatives to these tours (Rs330 for dolphin trips, or Rs1000 for croc spotting on the Cambarjua) are offered by Daytripper, whose bright hoardings line the main road in Gaura Waddo, north of Candolim.

At the opposite end of the range, you can go for luxury cruises on a **catamaran**, the *Viva Fiesta*, owned by the couple that run the *Fiesta* restaurant in Baga. The eleven-metre British-built vessel is powered by twin 60 horse-power Mercedes engines and can cruise at 8 knots. A half-day spin on it up the north Goan coast costs Rs850, or Rs450 for a shorter sunset cruise in the evening.

Fiesta also owns a magnificent **Chinese junk** from Hong Kong, called the *Precious Dragon*, which cruises daily off Fort Aguada and Calangute beach. All the food served onboard is gourmet Mediterranean prepared by *Fiesta's* chefs. At Rs1000 per head, prices (which include transport to and from the boat, meals, drinks and loan of sports fishing gear) are higher, but this is a unique opportunity to sail in an historic Asian vessel, complete with replica maps and navigational instruments from the era of the Ming dynasty.

The ultimate sea cruise offered by the *Fiesta* crew, however, is a three-night, four-day **dive sailing adventure** on board a 27-metre racing catamaran, the *Enterprise*. Former holder of the transatlantic record, the huge yacht can sail at 10 knots. Starting in Goa, trips run south to prime dive sites in the crystal clear waters off the Lakshadweep archipelago, 120 miles off the coast of Kerala.

For tickets and more details of *Fiesta's* cruises contact Maneck Contractor at *Fiesta* restaurant, near *Tito's* in Baga (see p.142).

cusine – the creamy, Persian-influenced style of cooking elaborated by the Moghul rulers between the fifteenth and eighteenth centuries in India. Served in copper *karais* with braziers by a team of snappy waiters dressed in traditional shalwars, the menu features a long list of chicken, mutton and vegetarian dishes steeped in rich sauces. Try the wonderful *murg malai* (chicken in cashew nut paste topped with cream) or equally delicious *dal mughali* (black lentils, kidney beans and small cubes of paneer with ginger). Count on Rs250–300 per head, plus drinks.

Stone House South end of Fort Aguada Rd ☎0832/247 9909. Blues-nut Chris D'Souza hosts this lively, low-lit bar-restaurant, spread in front of a gorgeous bare-laterite Goan house. Prime cuts of beef and kingfish, served with scrumptious baked potatoes, are their most popular dishes. Blues enthusiasts should come just for the CD collection. Most mains under Rs200.

Listings

Classical Indian dance On Saturday nights, the *Tamarind Tree Restaurant* in the *Dom Francisco Hotel* stages first-rate music and dance performances. Recitals of traditional Indian dance are also given on Tuesday evenings at the Kerkar Art Gallery in Calangute (see p.139).

Foreign exchange There are plenty of places to change money in Candolim, but the rates offered by the banks and foreign exchange bureaux up in Calangute, notably Wall Street Finances and the Bank of Baroda (see p.139), are more competitive.

Internet access A string of places along the main road advertise email and Internet access. At the time of writing, rates were around Rs40 per hour, with the exception of The Web, opposite the Candolim Health Centre, which for some inexplicable reason charges exactly double what everyone else does. Online World, opposite the Lawande Centre, has by far the fastest connection.

Travel agent Davidair (☎0832/227 5003–4, ✉davidgoa.goatelecom), on the left side of the main road as you leave Candolim in the direction of Calangute, has been established for over a decade and is very efficient. It's also one of the few agents licensed to sell charter tickets to Manchester and Gatwick, which it frequently does for as little as £150. Also recommended for Agra/Delhi excursions.

Yoga A former student of Yogarcharya BKS Iyengar, Maggie Hughes (aka Yoga Rashnu) is a world-class teacher who winters in Goa, working from her first-floor studio, opposite *Sonesta Inn* at the north end of Candolim – take the turning on the left between *Bob's Inn* and Davidair (there's a sign pointing the way). Drop-in classes start at 8am and cost Rs200. Beginners are welcome. For further details, contact ☎0832/227 6887 or go to ⊚www.maggiehughes.com.

Calangute

A 45-minute bus ride up the coast from the capital, **CALANGUTE** is Goa's busiest and most commercialized resort and the flagship of the state government's bid for a bigger slice of India's package-tourist pie. In the 1970s and early 1980s, this once-peaceful fishing village epitomized Goa's reputation as a safe haven for hedonistic hippies. Indian visitors flocked by the busload from Mumbai and Bangalore to giggle at the tribes of dreadlocked Westerners lying naked on the vast white sandy beach, stoned out of their brains on local *feni* and cheap *charas*. Calangute's flower-power period has, however, long passed.

The charter boom, combined with a huge increase in the number of Indian visitors for whom this is Goa's number one resort, has placed an impossible burden on Calangute's rudimentary infrastructure. Each year, as another crop of construction sites blossoms into resort complexes, what little charm the village has retained gets steadily more submerged under ferro-concrete and heaps of garbage. Hemmed in by four-storey buildings and swarming with traffic, the market area, in particular, has now taken on the aspect of a typical ramshackle Indian town of precisely the kind that most travellers used to come to Goa to get away from.

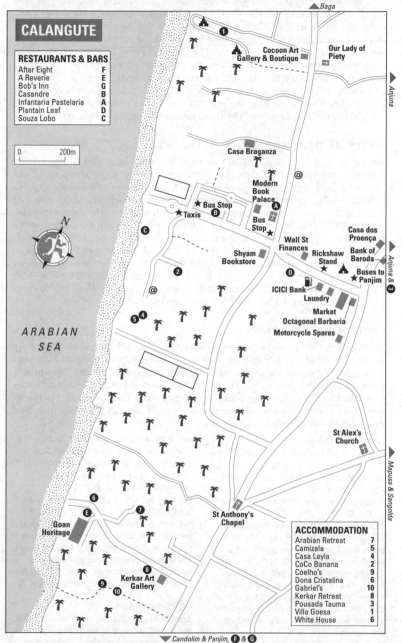

CALANGUTE

RESTAURANTS & BARS

After Eight	F
A Reverie	E
Bob's Inn	G
Casandre	B
Infantaria Pastelaria	A
Plantain Leaf	D
Souza Lobo	C

0   200m

N

▲ *Baga*

Cocoon Art
Gallery & Boutique

Our Lady of
Piety

▶ *Anjuna*

Casa Braganza

Modern
Book
Palace   **A**

★ Bus Stop
★ Taxis   **B**
               Bus
               Stop

C

Casa dos
Proença

Wall St
Finances   Rickshaw   Bank of
                Stand   Baroda

Shyam   Buses to
Bookstore   **D**   Panjim

ICICI Bank   Laundry

               Market
Octagonal Barbaria
Motorcycle Spares

2

5 4

*ARABIAN
SEA*

St Alex's
Church

▶ *Anjuna & 3*

▶ *Mapusa & Sangolda*

6
E
7
Goan
Heritage

St Anthony's
Chapel

8
Kerkar Art
Gallery

9
10

ACCOMMODATION

Arabian Retreat	7
Camizala	5
Casa Leyla	4
CoCo Banana	2
Coelho's	9
Dona Cristalina	6
Gabriel's	10
Kerkar Retreat	8
Pousada Tauma	3
Villa Goesa	1
White House	6

▼ *Candolim & Panjim,* **F** & **G**

The **pollution** problems are compounded by an absence of adequate provision for waste disposal and sewage treatment, insufficient electricity supply (blackouts are routine in the tourist season) and ever-increasing water consumption levels. In May 1998, a survey revealed that septic tanks and run-offs of hotel waste had finally contaminated the ground water. Another worrying sign that Calangute has already started to stew in its own juices has been a dramatic rise in **malaria** cases: Virex, and the potentially more serious Falciparum strain, are now both endemic here, and rife during the early part of the season.

In short, this is somewhere to avoid if you possibly can; the only reasons to endure the chaos are to shop for essentials in the well-stocked market, and to eat: Calangute boasts some of the best **restaurants** in the whole state.

Arrival and getting around

Buses from Mapusa and Panjim pull in at the small bus stand in the market square at the centre of Calangute. Some continue to Baga, stopping at the crossroads behind the beach en route. **Taxis** hang around the little sandy square behind GTDC's grim *Calangute Residency*, next to the steps that drop down to the beachfront itself. Also ask around here if you want to rent a **motorcycle**. Rates are standard (Rs150–200 per day for a 100cc Yamaha); the nearest **service station** ("petrol pump") is five minutes' walk from the beach, back towards the market on the right-hand side of the main road. For the past few years, following the owner's arrest for adulterating the petrol with kerosene, it has been closed but plans are afoot to open it under new management; until then you'll have to ride to Mapusa or Betim (on the riverfront opposite Panjim) for clean petrol. **Bicycles** are widely available from around Rs50–60 per day.

Accommodation

Calangute is chock-full of **places to stay**, and demand only outstrips supply in the Christmas–New Year high season, and at Diwali; at other times, it pays to haggle a little over the tariff, especially if the place looks empty. Nowhere is far from the shore, but sea views are more of a rarity. The top hotels are nearly all gleaming white, exclusive villa complexes with direct beach access. High-season rates in such places are staggeringly steep (if you can get a room), as they cater almost solely for package tourists.

Inexpensive

Camizala 5-33B Maddo Waddo ☎0832/227 9530 or 227 6263. Lovely, breezy little place with only four rooms, common verandahs and sea views. About as close to the beach as you can get, and the waddo is very quiet. Cheap considering the location. ❷–❸

Casa Leyla Maddo Waddo ☎ & ℱ0832/227 6478. This is a great place if you're a family looking for somewhere with plenty of space for a longish let, say of at least one week. The rooms are huge and well furnished, with fridges, kid-friendly beds and chairs, and basic self-catering facilities, while the house itself, whose upper storey sits in the palm canopy, is set deep in the secluded fishing ward, behind the quietest stretch of the beach. ❸

Coelho's Just south of *Golden Eye*, near the ice factory, Gauro Waddo ☎0832/227 7646. Twelve,

very spacious rooms in a large new house, on the peaceful (sea-facing) side of the village, 2min from the beach. Individual balconies, and a wonderful roof terrace with sea views. A good fallback if *Gabriel's* next door is full. ❸

Gabriel's Next door to *Coelho's*, Gauro Waddo ☎0832/227 9486, ℱ227 7484, ℮fele@rediffmail.com. A congenial, quiet guesthouse midway between Calangute and Candolim, run by a lovely family who go out of their way to help their guests. Shady garden, pleasant views across the *toddi* dunes, a top little restaurant and very close to the beach. The best value in its category for miles. ❸

Mid-range

Arabian Retreat Gauro Waddo ☎0832/227 9053, ℱ222 1467, ℮arabianretreat@yahoo.com. Large rooms in a new block of flats with balconies on both sides (those on the first floor are best), swathed in greenery and shaded by areca palms. A/c available. Only Rs650 per double, but rising to Rs1200 in Dec to mid-Jan. ❹

CoCo Banana 1195 Umta Waddo ☎ & ℗0832/227 6478, down the lane past *Meena Lobo's* restaurant. Very comfortable, spacious chalets, all with bathrooms, mosquito nets, extra-long mattresses and verandahs, around a central garden. Run by a very sorted Swiss-Goan couple who have been here for years. ❹–❺

White House 185/B Gauro Waddo, near *Goan Heritage* ☎0832/227 7938, ℗227 6509. Immaculate, large rooms in modern block close to the beach, with balconies, bathrooms and some views. They also offer spacious four-room apartments for Rs1200 per night. If full, try the equally comfortable (and much cheaper) *Dona Cristalina* along the lane (☎0832/229 7012). ❺

Expensive

Kerkar Retreat Gauro Waddo ☎0832/227 6017, ℗227 6308. Colour themed rooms, artfully deco-rated with original paintings, Goan *azulejos* and designer furniture creating an effect that's modern, but definably Goan. You pay for the decor here more than the roadside location. ❼

Pousada Tauma Porba Waddo ☎0832/227 9061, ℗227 9064, ⓦwww.pousada-tauma.com. New luxury resort complex, comprising double-storey laterite villas ranged around a graceful pool, in the middle of Calangute, but screened from the din by lots of vegetation. Understated decor and antique furnishings, and a very exclusive atmosphere, preserved by five-star prices. Their big draw is a first-rate Keralan Ayurvedic health centre (open to non-residents). From $200 per night. ❾

Villa Goesa Cobra Waddo ☎0832/227 7535, ℗227 6182, ⓔalobo@goatelecom.com. A stone's throw from the beach and very swish, set around a lush garden of young palms and lawns. Rooms are on the small side for the price, and the bathrooms are ceilinged closets, so a little stuffy. Occasional live music and a cocktail bar. All rooms have balconies. ❼

The Town

The road from the **town** to the beach is lined with handicraft boutiques and Tibetan stalls selling Himalayan curios and jewellery. The quality of the goods on offer – mainly Rajasthani, Gujarati and Karnatakan textiles – is dubious and so are the prices. Haggle hard and don't be afraid to walk away from a heavy sales pitch – the same stuff crops up every Wednesday at Anjuna's flea market. The **beach** itself is nothing special – its sand shelves steeply but is more than large enough to accommodate the huge numbers of visitors. Most of the action centres on the scruffy beachfront below GTDC's unsightly *Calangute Residency*, where crowds of Indian women in saris and straw hats stand around watching their sons and husbands frolic through the surf in their underpants. Nearby, stray cows nose through the rubbish left by the previous bus party, while an endless stream of ice cream and fruit sellers, *lunghi wallahs*, ear cleaners and masseurs tout for trade.

Given the numbers of whisky-swilling Indian men that stumble around here, you'd have to have thick skin indeed to want to sun-bathe, or even swim, any-where near the beachfront if you're a woman. To escape the melee, head fifteen minutes or so south, towards the rows of old wooden boats moored below the dunes at Maddo Waddo (literally "toughies' quarter").

At the other end of the village's social hierarchy, one of Calangute's wealthiest families in the early eighteenth century built an extraordinary mansion, the **Casa dos Proença**, which still stands just north of the market area, beyond the Bank of Baroda. Its most distinctive feature is a wonderful tower-shaped verandah the sides of which are covered in screens made from oyster shells (*carepas*). The gallery is surmounted by a grand pitched roof, designed to funnel the air entering the room through the windows and other openings towards the ceiling – an ingenious natural air-conditioning system that was in time adopted all over the Portuguese empire. Dating from the early nineteenth century, Calangute's other wonderful old *palacio* is the **Casa Braganza**, on the first lane north of the *Infanteria Pastelaria* café.

Another oddity worth hunting out is the old octagonal **customs post**, presiding over the crossroads at the centre of the market. During the Portuguese era, a string of these curious structures was erected along the coastal route to monitor trade and traffic and to deter smugglers. Only a few are left standing (at nearby Siolim and Assolna, in the south); this specimen now serves as a barber's shop (*barbaria*). One of the traditional pleasures of Calangute market (at least for men) is to have a shave or haircut inside it, watching the progress of your tonsure in the mirrors lining its eight walls.

Eating and drinking

Ever since *Souza Lobo* opened on the beachfront to cater for Goan day-trippers in the 1930s, Calangute has been somewhere people come as much to eat as for a stroll on the beach, and even if you stay in resorts elsewhere you'll doubtless be tempted down here at some stage for a meal – whether in the famous *Plantain Leaf* South Indian canteen in the main bazaar, or one of the swankier restaurants on the outskirts. For other options in the area, see the accounts of Baga (p.142) and Candolim (p.132).

After Eight Gauro Waddo, midway between Calangute and Candolim, down a lane leading west off the main road, between the Lifeline Pharmacy and a small chapel. Superb gourmet restaurant run by two ex-*Taj* (Mumbai) whizz kids, in a quiet garden. Steaks are their most popular dish, but chef Chakraborthy has a sublime touch with seafood, served with original, delicate sauces blending Bengali and Italian influences (try the *rahu*, a local river fish, in balsamic vinegar and mustard); for veggies there's baby-corn milles feuilles; and they do a memorable chocolate mousse. Most main courses around Rs175–225.

A Reverie Next to *Hotel Goan Heritage*, Gauro Waddo ☎0832/228 2597. Akritee and Virendra Sinh set new standards for the area when they co-founded *After Eight*. Both the menu and decor of this, their new venture, are more romantic and extravagant still, but remain within reach of most budgets (around Rs500 per head, plus drinks – a steal given the quality of the food). The dishes are all original, with eclectic influences, and beautifully presented: try the mushrooms with marjoram and fresh parsley sauce, or chicken breast stuffed with pistachio mousseline.

Casandre Beach road. Housed is a smartly renovated Portuguese-era home, with a deep verandah fronting the main drag. The menu here is gigantic, but the seafood specials listed on a blackboard tend to be the best bets. Try their delicious baby kingfish panfried in Szechwan sauce. Mains Rs100–150.

Gabriel's *Gabriel's* guesthouse, Guara Waddo. Authentic Goan cooking (pork *sorpotel*, chicken *xacuti*, stuffed squid and prawn masala), and very popular Italian dishes (with homemade pasta) served on a cosy roof terrace well away from the main road. A tiny bit pricier than average for a budget place (most mains around Rs80) but worth it, and the espresso coffee is excellent. Only five tables, so come early and expect a long-ish wait as the spices are hand-ground.

Infantaria Pastelaria Next to St John's Chapel, Baga road. Roadside terrace café run by *Soua Lobo's* that gets packed out for its stodgy croissants, freshly baked apple pie and traditional Goan sweets (such as *dodol* and homemade *bebinca*). Top of the savoury list, though, are the prawn and veg patties, which locals buy by the box load.

Plantain Leaf Market area. The best *udipi* restaurant outside Panjim, where waiters in Argentinian football strip serve the usual range of delicious dosas and other spicy snacks in a clean, cool marble-lined canteen, with relentless background *filmi* music. Try their definitive *idly-wada* breakfasts, delicious *masala dosas* or the filling set *thalis* (Rs40).

Souza Lobo On the beachfront. A Calangute institution since the 1930s, even though the food – served on gingham tablecloths by legions of fast-moving waiters in matching Madras-checked shirts – isn't always what it used to be. Stuffed crab, full baby kingfish and crepe Souza are the house specialities. Most main dishes Rs100–150.

Nightlife

Calangute's **nightlife** is surprisingly tame for a resort of its size. All but a handful of the **bars** wind up by 10pm, leaving punters to prolong the short evenings back at their hotels, find a shack that's open late, or else head up to Baga (see p.143). The area's only noteworthy alternative is the **West End Club**, on a hilltop just outside Saligao, 4km inland from St Anthony's church. A couple of years ago, this place looked set to eclipse *Tito's*, but it's since gone downhill and is often empty. Admission costs Rs100, and drinks are charged at average bar prices.

Closer to the market area, *Bob's Inn*, between Calangute and Candolim, is a famous old bar, renowned above all for its extrovert owner, who claims with some justification to have been Goa's first hippy. He was certainly around when the flea market started up, and was instrumental in organizing some of the legendary parties of the 1970s, as were several of his regulars. Seated around the long wooden table in the middle of the bar, under a portrait of Goa's most famous hippy, "Jungle Barry" (who's no longer with us), these ageing heads love to do nothing more than reminisce about the good old days, between bouts of backgammon and serious drinking.

Finally, don't miss the chance to sample some pukka Indian culture while you are in Calangute. The **Kerkar Art Gallery**, in Gauro Waddo, at the south end of town (℡0832/227 6017, Ⓦwww.subodhkerkar.com), hosts evenings of **classical music and dance** every Tuesday from 6.45 to 8.30pm, held in the back garden on a sumptuously decorated stage, complete with incense and evocative candlelight. The recitals, performed by students and teachers from Panjim's Kala Academy, are kept comfortably short for the benefit of Western visitors, and are preceded by a short introductory talk. Tickets, available in advance or at the door, cost Rs250. See also Candolim listings, p.134.

Listings

Art and lifestyle galleries The excellent Kerkar Art Gallery (Mon–Sat 9.30am–7pm; free), at the southern edge of Calangute, exhibits and sells original paintings, sculpture and crafts by local Goan artists. Further north on the Baga road, the Cocoon Art Gallery is a smart boutique with designer clothes by Wendell Rodricks and hand-painted *azulejos*. For quality ethnic Indian furniture, textiles and traditional ornaments, head 4km east of Calangute on the CHOGM road to Sangolda (Mon–Sat 10am–7.30pm), housed in a magnificently restored 200-year-old *palacio*. The project was set up by French fashion stylist Claudia Derain and her husband, Hari Ajwani (who own the *Nilaya Hermitage*; see p.142), and is well worth taking time to visit for the architecture alone, even if you can't afford the prices. Immediately next door, Saudades is another lifestyle emporium in an old Portuguese-era mansion that deserves a browse, although its reproduction antiques aren't in the same league as its neighbour's.

Banks If you need to change money, head for Wall Street Finances (Mon–Sat 9.30am–6pm), opposite the petrol pump and in the shopping complex on the beachfront, who exchange cash and traveller's cheques at bank rates. At the Bank of Baroda (Mon–Fri 9.30am–2.15pm, Sat 9.30am–noon, Sun 9.30am–2pm), just north of the market on the Anjuna road, you can make encashments against Visa cards; commission is one percent of the amount changed, plus Rs100 for the authorization phone call. The ICICI Bank in the main market has a 24-hour ATM.

Books The Shyam (aka Rama) secondhand book-shop, where the main Baga road bends north, stocks a vast range of paperbacks in several languages, including English, French, German, Dutch, Swedish and Japanese, but is a real rip-off. For new books, including a particularly good selection of bird field guides, try *Modern Book Palace*, just off the beach road.

Opticians Romano's have two branches: one in the main market area (on the north side of the road), and another on the south side of town on the Candolim road. As with most quality Goan opticians, they can make up prescription glasses for a fraction of what you'd pay at home.

Baga

BAGA, 10km west of Mapusa, is basically an extension of Calangute; not even the locals agree where one ends and the other begins. Lying in the lee of a rocky, wooded headland, the only real difference between the two is that the scenery here is marginally more varied and picturesque. A small river flows into the sea at the top of the village, below a broad spur of soft white sand scattered with fishing boats, from where a dirt track strikes across an open expanse of rice paddy towards Anjuna.

Until the early 1990s, few buildings stood at this far northern end of the beach other than a handful of old red-tiled fishers' houses nestling in the dunes.

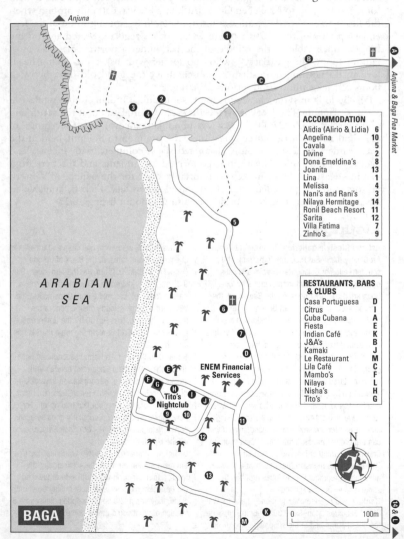

ACCOMMODATION

Alidia (Alirio & Lidia)	6
Angelina	10
Cavala	5
Divine	2
Dona Emeldina's	8
Joanita	13
Lina	1
Melissa	4
Nani's and Rani's	3
Nilaya Hermitage	14
Ronil Beach Resort	11
Sarita	12
Villa Fatima	7
Zinho's	9

RESTAURANTS, BARS & CLUBS

Casa Portuguesa	D
Citrus	I
Cuba Cubana	A
Fiesta	E
Indian Café	K
J&A's	B
Kamaki	J
Le Restaurant	M
Lila Café	C
Mambo's	F
Nilaya	L
Nisha's	H
Tito's	G

ENEM Financial Services

Tito's Nightclub

ARABIAN SEA

Anjuna

Anjuna & Baga Flea Market

N

BAGA

0   100m

Boats to the Anjuna flea market

Every Wednesday, **boats** leave Baga beach for the flea market at Anjuna from around 9am until just before sunset. How much you pay for the twenty-minute trip depends on how many passengers the fishermen manage to cram on board, but it usually works out the same as a motorcycle taxi. If you go, pack your cameras and any valuables in a plastic bag. Accidents occasionally happen when the fishermen load their vessels to the gunwales and then try to save time and fuel by cutting through a narrow channel between two rocks – straightforward enough on calm days, but a hair-raising stunt when the sea is choppy.

Since the package boom, however, Baga has developed more rapidly than anywhere else in the state and today looks less like a Goan fishing village than a small-scale resort on one of the Spanish costas, with a predominantly young, charter-tourist clientele to match. Initially the locals, who'd been expecting the travel agencies to bring groups of smart middle-aged couples with bulging wallets, were more astonished by the bar brawls and lewd behaviour of the British lager louts than they had ever been by the naked hippies of previous decades. But businesses were quickly tailored to give the new breed of hard-drinking, low-spending party seekers what they wanted, with the result that Baga's **nightlife** is far and away the most consistently full-on in Goa.

So if you're looking for peace and quiet, forget it and head further north. Once across Baga's ugly concrete **box bridge**, the hotels, handicraft shops and restaurants give way to a more tranquil hinterland of coconut plantations peppered with Hindu farming hamlets. This area has also recently acquired a couple of huge hotels – most of them in flagrant violation of building rules limiting the height and size of new structures – but at least you don't feel quite so boxed in as you do in the village proper.

Accommodation

With most of the strip along the main road and its side lanes given over to handicraft boutiques, bars and restaurants, **accommodation** can be in short supply when the season's in full swing, but at other times usually keeps up with demand. Some of the nicest cheap guesthouses and rooms for rent lie on the quieter north side of the river, favoured by long-staying travellers, although these are like gold dust in peak season.

If you come around Christmas and New Year, watch out for "compulsory gala dinner supplements" or some similarly named ruse to slap stiff surcharges (typically of around Rs750 per head) on to your room tariff.

Inexpensive

Angelina Near *Tito's*, Saunta Waddo ☎0832/227 9145. Spacious, well-maintained rooms with large tiled bathrooms and big balconies, off the road but still in the thick of things. Particularly good value out of peak season. A/c available. ❸

Divine Near *Nani's & Rani's*, north of the river ☎0832/227 9546. Run by fervent Christians (the signboard features a burning cross and bleeding heart), the rooms are on the small side, but clean; some have attached shower-toilets. ❸

Joanita Baga road ☎0832/227 7166. Clean, airy rooms with attached baths and some double beds, around a quiet garden. A good choice if you want to be in the village centre but off the road. ❸

Lina North of the river ☎0832/228 1142. Baga's most secluded guesthouse, deep in a peaceful palm grove on the edge of dense woodland. Quiet, with only four simple en-suite rooms, and cheap for the area. ❸

Melissa 620 Anjuna Rd ☎0832/227 9583. Eight recently built rooms in a clean, quiet block on the north side of the river, all with attached shower-toilets. Good off-season discounts, too. ❸

Nani's and Rani's North of the river ☎0832/227 6313 or 227 7014. A handful of red-tiled, white-washed budget cottages in a secluded garden behind a huge colonial-era house. Fans, some attached bathrooms, well-water, outdoor showers and Internet facility. ❷–❹

Sarita Just south of Tito's Lane ☎0832/227 9087. Half-a-dozen sea-facing en-suite rooms, built in 2002. Those on the lower floor are smaller, but with larger verandahs than the much nicer top-storey ones. Friendly management and very close to the liveliest stretch of the beach. ❸

Villa Fatima Baga road ☎0832/227 7418, ⓔfatima@goatelecom.com. Thirty-two attached rooms in a large, three-storey hotel centred on a sociable garden terrace. Their rates are reasonable, varying with room size. All rooms have attached bathrooms. Popular mainly with young backpackers. ❷–❸

Zinho's 7/3 Saunta Waddo ☎0832/227 7383. Tucked away off the main road, close to *Tito's*. Half a dozen modest size, clean rooms above a family home. Near to the beach and good value. ❸

Moderate to expensive

Alidia (Alirio & Lidia) Baga road, Saunta Waddo ☎0832/227 6835 or ☎ & ℻0832/227 9014, ⓔalidia@goaworld.com. Attractive modern chalet rooms with good-sized verandahs looking on to the dunes. Double or twin beds. Quiet, friendly and the best deal in this area. ❸–❹

Cavala On the main road ☎0832/227 7587 or 227 6090, ℻227 7340, ⓦwww.cavala.com. Modern hotel in tastefully traditional mould, with a

pool surrounded by banana groves; spacious twin-bedded rooms, and separate balconies, but a little close to the road for comfort. ❻–❼

Dona Emeldina's Sauto Waddo ☎0832/227 6880. Pleasantly old-fashioned cottages with verandahs opening on to lawns, run by a garrulous Portuguese-speaking lady. A bargain in low and mid-season (Rs550–650), but pricey over Christmas, due to its proximity to the party enclave – a dubious distinction. If she's fully booked, check out her other place, the cheaper but less appealing *Baga Queen* nearby. ❺

Nilaya Hermitage Arpora Bhati ☎0832/227 6793–4 or 227 5187–8, ℻227 6792, ⓔnilaya@goatelecom.com. Set on the crest of a hilltop 6km inland from the beach, with matchless views over the coastal plain, this place ranks among India's most exclusive hotels, patronized by a very rich international jet set (Richard Gere and Demi Moore are rumoured to have stayed here). On site are a steam room, gym, clay tennis court, and a restaurant. Rooms from around $280 ($450 at Christmas) for two, including meals and airport transfers. ❾

Ronil Beach Resort Baga road ☎0832/227 6101, ℻227 6068. Large three-star with ersatz Portuguese apartments overlooking two small pools, and a swish restaurant. Right in the thick of things, but only five minutes from the beach. ❽

Eating and drinking

Nowhere else in the state offers such a good choice of quality eating as Baga. Restaurateurs – increasing numbers of them European expats or refugees from upper-class Mumbai – vie with each other to lay on the trendiest menus and most romantic, stylish gardens or terraces. It's all a very far cry indeed from the beach-shack culture that held sway only five or six years ago.

Casa Portuguesa Baga road. Traditional Portuguese and Goan food served by candlelight inside a romantic colonial villa, or alfresco on a leafy lawn. The food isn't what it used to be and – at around Rs650 for three courses with drinks – is ludicrously overpriced, but it remains so popular they enforce time limits on tables. Given the quality of the competition, it's hard to understand the place's enduring appeal.

Citrus Tito's Lane. The first pure-vegetarian fine-dining restaurant in Goa, created by former animal-rescue supremo, Nicholas Maddocks. Starters include delicious cashew rissoles with satay sauce; creamed pumpkin croquettes and roquefort brik are pick of the mains (from Rs150); and they do real Italian coffee.

Fiesta Tito's Lane ☎0832/227 9894. Run by the glamorous but improbably named Yellow and

Maneck Contractor, Baga's most extravagantly decorated restaurant enjoys a perfect spot at the top of a long dune, with sea views from the verandah of a 1930s house. The menu's Mediterranean-Portuguese, and as delectable as the decor. Try their buffalo mozzarella salad or smoked aubergine pâté for starters, followed by paella, moussaka or the wonderful house pizzas. Most mains around Rs200. Reservation recommended.

Indian Café Just down the lane from *Le Restaurant*. Traditional home-cooked South Indian snacks – dosas, idlys, and wadas, with fiery sambar, green chutney and delicious fresh fruit lassis – dished up on a verandah of an old Goan house. A lot more relaxing than the *Plantain Leaf* in Calangute, and much cheaper.

J&A's Baga Creek ☎0832/227 5274, ⓦwww.littleitalygoa.com. Mouthwatering, authentic Italian food (down to the imported Parmesan, sun-dried tomatoes and olive oil) served in the gorgeous candle-lit garden of an old fisherman's cottage. They offer an innovative range of salads and antipasti (the carpaccio of beef is sublime), a choice of sumptuous pasta dishes, wood-fired pizzas and tender steaks for mains, with Ayesha's melt-in-the-mouth baked lemon cheesecake to round things off. At the time of writing there were rumours that the restaurant might be moving to the *Cavala Hotel* for 2003–2004. Count on Rs400–500 per head plus drinks. Reservation recommended.

Le Restaurant Baga road. Stylish French gastronomy with a fun atmosphere, whipped up by the three Gallic partners. Go for the prawns with filo-wrapped mushrooms or crispy sardines with basil coulis and vanilla-scented mashed potato. There are also plenty of equally refined dishes for vegetarians and a sublime dessert menu. Count on around Rs400 per head, plus drinks, and be sure to book as they don't open every night.

Lila Café Baga Creek. Laid-back bakery-cum-snack-bar, run by a German couple who've been here for decades. Their healthy homemade breads

and cakes are great, and there's an adventurous lunch menu featuring spinach à la crème, aubergine pâté and smoked water buffalo ham. Open 8am–8pm.

Nilaya Arpora Bhati, 6km inland ☎0832/227 6793. Two gourmet chefs, one Sri Lankan and the other French, preside over this unique hilltop restaurant, in the ultra-luxurious designer hotel of the same name (see "Accommodation"). Their four-course menus, dominated by seafood, chicken and vegetarian dishes, cost in the range of Rs650–950 per head, depending on the ingredients, which are all fresh and local, or organically grown by a Dutchman from Karnataka. A good place for a one-off celebration.

Nisha's Tito's Lane ☎0832/227 7588. This little restaurant, occupying a sandy terrace just down from *Tito's*, can't be beaten for simply prepared seafood – snapper, kingfish, tiger prawns and lobster – flame-grilled or tandoori-baked to perfection in front of you by chef Frankie Almon and his crew. Freshness counts more here than fancy sauces. For starters, try calamari in chilli oil with lemon. Most mains a reasonable Rs250–300.

Nightlife

That Baga's nightlife has become legendary in India is largely attributable to one club, *Tito's*. Lured by TV images of sexy dance wear and a thumping sound-and-light system, hundreds of revellers each night descend on its long narrow terrace to drink, shuffle about and watch the action, the majority of them men from other states who've come to Goa as an escape from the nar-

Saturday night bazaars

One of the few genuinely positive improvements to the north Goa resort strip in recent times has been the **Saturday Night Bazaar**, held on a plot midway between Baga and Anjuna. The brainchild of an expat German called Ingo, it's run with great efficiency and a sense of fun that's palpably lacking these days from the Anjuna Flea Market. The balmy evening temperatures and pretty lights are also a lot more conducive to relaxed browsing than the broiling heat of mid-afternoon on Anjuna beach; moreoever, the laid-back ambience is preserved with a "three-strikes-and-out" ban on hassling customers, which means you can even walk past the normally full-on Lamani women unmolested.

Although far more commercial than its predecessor in Anjuna, many old Goa hands regard this as far truer to the original spirit of the flea market. A significant proportion of the stalls are taken up by foreigners selling their own stuff, from reproduction Indian pop art to antique photos, the latest Trance party designer wear, hand-polished coconut shell art and techno DJ demos. There's also a mouthwatering array of ethnic food concessions to choose from and a stage featuring live music from around 7pm until midnight, when the market winds up. Admission is free.

Somewhat confusingly, a **rival** but inferior Saturday night market in much the same mould has opened nearby, closer to Baga by the riverside. Spurned by the expatriate designers and stallholders, this one's not a patch on Ingo's, though, no matter what your taxi driver may tell you.

row moral confines of life at home. For Western women, in particular, this can sometimes make for an uncomfortably loaded atmosphere, although since a recent facelift (and a hike in door charges), *Tito's* seems to have put the era of Kingfisher-fuelled brawls behind it. New theme bars and clubs are also popping up each year, offering increasingly sophisticated alternatives.

For anyone who's been travelling around the rest of the country, Baga by night – complete with drunken karaoke, toga parties and all the garishness of a Saturday in British clubland – can come as an unpleasant shock. So, too, can the traffic congestion on Fridays and Saturdays; if you venture down here by motorbike on the weekend, park up well away from Tito's Lane or you might find yourself literally jammed in until the small hours.

For more on the area's nightlife, see the accounts of Calangute (p.139) and Anjuna (p.150).

Bars and clubs

Cuba Cubana 82 Xim Waddo, Arpora Hill ⓦ www.clubcubana.net. Glam new club on a forested hilltop inland from Baga, spread around an underlit open-air pool. Its high entrance charge (Rs400 for men; Rs300 for women; or Rs600 per couple) buys you unlimited drinks from a well-stocked bar – a policy intended to keep out the low-spending riff raff from down on the strip. R&B, Hip Hop and Garage (they purposely stay well away from Techno) played on a small a/c dance floor. Fri, Sat & Sun 9.30pm–5am.
Kamaki Tito's Lane, Saunta Waddo. Big screen sports and a state-of-the-art karaoke machine account for the appeal of this air-conditioned, Brit-dominated bar just up the lane from Tito's. Rs100 cover charge sometimes applies.

Mambo's At the end of Tito's Lane, Saunta Waddo. Large, semi-open air bar with wooden decor and a big circular counter, that gets packed out most nights in season with a lively, mixed crowd. Once again, karaoke is the big draw, though drinks cost well above average, and they slap on a Rs200 admission charge after 11pm.
Tito's Tito's Lane, Saunta Waddo. Following a recent makeover, Goa's number one nightspot looks smarter and enjoys a better behaved clientele than it has for years, although it's still male-dominated. Occasional cabarets, fashion shows and guest DJs feature through the season. Admission prices vary for men; no charge for women. Open 8pm–late Nov–Dec; and until 11pm out of season.

Listings

Football Well worth checking out on Sunday afternoons is the regular football match between visiting British tourists and resident Kenyan students, held on the wastegrounds between Baga and the concrete box bridge. Kickoff is around 3pm.
Foreign exchange ENEM Financial Services, on the main road opposite *Hotel Beira Mar* (daily 8am–9pm), changes traveller's cheques and cash

at 1.5 percent below current bank rates. You'll get a more competitive rate at Wall Street Finances or any of the banks down in Calangute market (see p.139).
Travel agent Lina, 3/22 Villa Nova, on the main road near the *Casa Portuguesa* ☎ 0832/227 6196, ☏ 227 6124.

Anjuna

With its fluorescent painted palm trees and infamous full-moon parties, **ANJUNA**, 8km west of Mapusa, is Goa at its most Alternative. Fractal patterns and day-glo lycra may have superseded cotton kaftans, but most people's reasons for coming are the same as they were in the 1970s: drugs, dancing and lying on the beach. Depending on your point of view, you'll find the headlong hedonism a total turn-off or heaven-on-sea. Either way, the scene looks here to stay, despite repeated government attempts to stamp it out, so you might as well get a taste of it while you're in the area, if only from the wings, with a day-trip to the famous **flea market**.

The season in Anjuna starts in early November, when most of the long-staying regulars show up, and it peters out in late March, when they drift off again. During the Christmas and New Year rush, the village is inundated with a mixed crowd of round-the-world backpackers, refugees from the English club scene, and revellers from all over India, lured by the promise of the big **beach parties**. A large contingent of these are young **Israelis**, on a short fuse after three years of national service. Outside peak season, however, Anjuna has a surprisingly simple, unhurried atmosphere – due, in no small part, to the shortage of places to stay. Most visitors who come here on market day, or for the raves, travel in from other resorts. That said, a couple of large package tour hotels have appeared over the past couple of years, and this is bound to radically alter the

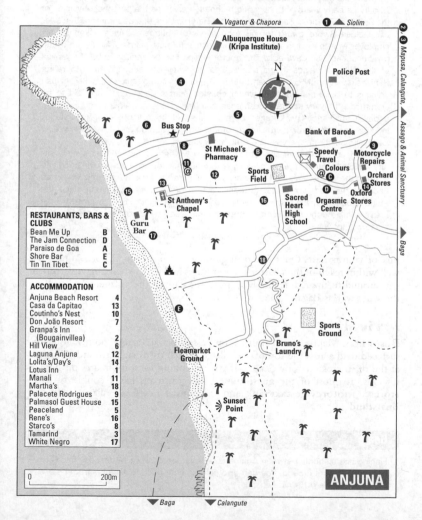

▲ Vagator & Chapora   ❶ ▲ Siolim

Albuquerque House
(Kripa Institute)

Police Post

N

❹

❺

Bus Stop ❻

❽

St Michael's
Pharmacy

Bank of Baroda

Speedy
Travel
Colours

Motorcycle
Repairs ❾

❿

Sports
Field

Orchard
Stores

Oxford
Stores

Orgasmic
Centre

❶❶
@

❶❷

❶❺

❶❸

St Anthony's
Chapel

❶❻

Sacred
Heart
High
School

Guru
Bar

❶❼

❶❽

Sports
Ground

Bruno's
Laundry

Fleamarket
Ground

Sunset
Point

RESTAURANTS, BARS & CLUBS

Bean Me Up	B
The Jam Connection	D
Paraiso de Goa	A
Shore Bar	E
Tin Tin Tibet	C

ACCOMMODATION

Anjuna Beach Resort	4
Casa da Capitao	13
Coutinho's Nest	10
Don João Resort	7
Granpa's Inn (Bougainvillea)	2
Hill View	6
Laguna Anjuna	12
Lolita's/Day's	14
Lotus Inn	1
Manali	11
Martha's	18
Palacete Rodrigues	9
Palmasol Guest House	15
Peaceland	5
Rene's	16
Starco's	8
Tamarind	3
White Negro	17

0   200m

ANJUNA

▼ Baga   ▼ Calangute

The Anjuna jinx

One reason Anjuna may have been spared the sprawling development that today blights most of Baga and Calangute is an old dictum prophesying bad luck for the owners of any construction with an upper storey. Every villager knows of the curse, and few, if any, have ignored it, despite the lucrative spread of concrete further down the coast. Express even the slightest scepticism and you'll be reminded of numerous cases, including the huge abandoned hulk just past *Starco's* crossroads, whose owners were beset with financial difficulties from the time they started work on the first floor.

No one knows where the curse originated. Less superstitious villagers suggest it may be derived from years of experience building on Anjuna's sandy soils. This, however, doesn't explain the bizarre runs of misfortune that appear to have dogged those who have erected "ground-plus-one" structures over the centuries.

Among the most notorious victims of the curse was one Dr Manuel Albuquerque, who in the early years of the twentieth century served as the personal physician of the Sultan of Zanzibar, Sayeed Khalifa 'bin Haruba. On being decorated with a special Golden Sword award for his long service, Albuquerque was asked by his employer what he would like as a gift of thanks for safeguarding the health of the royal household so devotedly. The doctor replied that he wanted to build a replica of the Sultan's palace in his native Goa, to where he soon planned to retire. Permission was duly granted, and Albuquerque recruited a team of crack Zanzibari artisans to build his mansion, which boasted marble floors and was said to be crammed with ivory statues and Macao porcelain. However, Albuquerque's family, bedevilled by various misfortunes, bore no heirs and the building, though still standing (just north of *Starco's* crossroads on the way to Vagator) and covered in yellow and white paint, now serves as a drug rehabilitation centre.

An acid test for whether or not the Anjuna jinx will endure into the twenty-first century will be the fate of the huge luxury resort currently taking shape on the headland north of the village. Funded by the owner of Oxford Stores and a team of absentee backers, the complex is the grandest act of hubris seen in Anjuna since the Albuquerque mansion. Environmental groups and villagers keen to preserve the area's relative tranquillity secretly hope the nemetic powers of the mysterious old curse will not wane.

mix of visitors here. Only ninety minutes' drive from the airport, Anjuna lies well within reach of the charter transfer buses and if, or when, the government gets around to upgrading the road from the capital, the village could well go the same way as Baga.

Arrival

Buses from Mapusa and Panjim drop passengers at various points along the surfaced road across the top of the village, which turns right towards Chapora at the main crossroads by *Starco's*. If you're looking for a room, get off here as it's close to most of the guesthouses. The crossroads has a couple of small **stores**, a **motorcycle taxi** rank, and functions as a de facto village square and **bus stand**.

Boats

Fishing boats shuttle between Anjuna and Baga beach every Wednesday from just below the market ground. You can also catch a boat back to Arambol from here in the evening; see p.164.

Accommodation

Most of Anjuna's very limited **accommodation** consists of small unfurnished houses. Finding one is a problem at the best of times, but in peak season it's virtually impossible. By then, all but a handful have been let to long-staying regulars who book by post several months in advance. Budget travellers who arrive hoping to find one on spec will probably have to make do with a room in a guesthouse at first. Higher-spending visitors are nowadays spoiled for choice, with the appearance in recent years of a couple of classy designer hotels.

Inexpensive

Anjuna Beach Resort De Mello Waddo ☎0832/227 4499, ✉fabjoe@goa1.dot.net.in. Fifteen spacious, comfortable rooms with balconies, fridges, attached bathrooms and solar hot water in a new concrete building. Those on the upper floor are best. Good value. ❸

Casa da Capitao Near St Anthony's Chapel ☎0832/227 3832. Three basic but spruce, purple-painted rooms amid lots of greenery, and with large sit-outs, slap in the centre of the village. Slightly better than the nearby *Omkar.* ❷

Coutinho's Nest Soronto Waddo ☎0832/227 4386. Small, very respectable family guesthouse on the main road, in the centre of Anjuna. Their immaculately clean rooms are among the village's best budget deals. Shared shower-toilets only. ❷

Hill View De Mello Waddo ☎0832/227 3235. One of the newer and more pleasant budget places, run by a landlady who puts her Israeli guests into a separate "unbreakable" block. Quiet location, and good value. ❷

Lolita's/Day's Behind Orchard Stores ☎0832/227 4526 or 227 3289. A handful of simple, large rooms with high tiled roofs and attached shower-toilets, run by the affable Darryl Days. The pricier one has an air cooler, fridge and cable TV. Peaceful, despite its proximity to the road. Bookable through Joel's Mini Store next door. ❸

Manali South of *Starco's* ☎0832/227 4421, ✉manali@goatelecom.com. Anjuna's best all-round budget guesthouse has simple rooms opening on to a yard, fans, safe deposit, money changing, library, Internet connection, a sociable terrace-restaurant and shared bathrooms. Very good value, so book in advance. ❷

Palmasol Guest House Praia de St Anthony, behind middle of beach ☎0832/227 3258, ✉222 2261. Huge, comfortable rooms in an immaculately kept old house very near the beach. The larger ones have running water, verandahs, cooking space and a relaxing garden; cheaper alternatives in the back yard. ❸

Peaceland Sorranto Waddo ☎0832/227 3700 or 227 3441. Simple budget rooms in two blocks (the newer ones are worth the Rs100 extra), run

by a charming local couple and a pair of friendly dogs. ❸

Rene's Opposite Sacred Heart High School, Monteiro Waddo ☎0832/227 3405 or 9822 /483798. Cool, well-ventilated rooms behind a family home. Welcoming hosts and pleasantly secluded, though quite a trog across the fields from the beach. ❷

Starco's On the crossroads. No phone. Some of the cheapest rooms in Anjuna: very basic, but well-maintained, clean and screened from the racket outside. Excellent value if you're happy with basic amenities. ❷

Mid-range to expensive

Don João Resort Soronto Waddo ☎ & ✉0832/227 4325, ⓦwww.goacom.com/hotels /donjoao.html. An unsightly multistorey hotel, slap in the middle of the village. Aimed squarely at the charter market (there's a small pool), but the suites are large, with sitting rooms, kitchenettes and balconies, and cheap for the area. ❸–❺

Granpa's Inn (Bougainvillea) Gaunwadi ☎0832/227 3270, ✉227 4370, ⓦwww.goacom.com/hotels/granpas. Lovely 200-year-old house set in lush gardens, with a pool and shady breakfast terrace. The en-suite rooms are large and have high ceilings; the suites are even nicer. Ashtanga yoga on site; and there's a billiards table. Very popular, so book well ahead. ❺

Laguna Anjuna De Mello Waddo ☎0832/227 4305, ⓦwww.lagunaanjuna.com. Swish alternative resort designed by Dean D'Cruz, the architect responsible for the *Nilaya Hermitage* (see p.142). Set amid a garden of banana and mango trees, it comprises 25 colourfully decorated, domed laterite "cottages" with wooden rafters and terracotta tiles, grouped behind a convoluted pool. Restaurant, pool room and bar. ❾

Lotus Inn Zor Waddo ☎0832/227 4015, ✉227 4189, ✉lotusinn@goatelecom.com. On the leafy northern limits of Anjuna, tucked away down a maze of narrow lanes: ten swish suites and six double rooms (on the small side for the price), all with a/c, centred on a good sized pool. ❻

Water shortages

Anjuna has, thanks to the extra inhabitants it attracts over the winter, become particularly prone to **water shortages**. These tend not to affect many visitors, as the drought only begins to bite towards the end of March when the majority have already left. For the villagers, however, the problem causes genuine hardship. Use well water very sparingly and avoid water toilets if possible – traditional "dry" ones are far more ecologically sound.

Martha's 907 Montero Waddo ☎ 0832/227 4194, ⓔ mpd8650@hotmail.com. Eight immaculate en-suite rooms, including two pleasant houses, run by a warm and friendly family. Basic amenities include kitchen space, fans and running water (solar-heated). Pleasant location. ❹

Palacete Rodrigues Near Oxford Stores, Mazal Waddo ☎ 0832/227 3358, ⓦ palaceterodrigues @hotmail.com. Two-hundred-year-old residence converted into an upmarket guesthouse. Carved wood furniture, and a relaxed, traditional Goan feel. Single occupancy available and there are three good-value economy options in a separate block around the back. ❹–❺

Tamarind Kumar Waddo ☎ 0832/227 4319, ⓕ 227 3363, ⓔ tamarind9@sify.com. Pleasant stone-lined rooms with relaxing sit-outs opening on to a small pool. Some way inland, they lay on complimentary transfer buses to the beaches. Other noteworthy attributes include a full-size billiards table and Goa's largest doberman (friendly). Mostly booked by charter companies, but worth trying for a vacancy. ❺

White Negro 719 Praia de St Anthony, south of the village ☎ 0832/227 3326, ⓔ mjanets@goatelecom.com. A row of twelve spotless back-to-back chalets catching the sea breeze, all with attached bathrooms, tiled floors, safe lockers and mozzie nets. Quiet, efficient and good value. ❹

The beach and flea market

Anjuna **beach** is no great shakes by Goan standards, with a dodgy undertow and even dodgier groups of whisky-filled Indian men in constant attendance. A small, pretty and better sheltered cove at its far southern end is where Anjuna's mostly Israeli, frisbee-throwing tourists hang out during the day, Trance thumping away from the shacks behind it. North of here, the sand broadens, running in an uninterrupted kilometre-long stretch to a low red cliff. The village bus park lies on top of this high ground, near a crop of small cafés, bars and Kashmiri handicraft stalls where, every lunchtime, tour parties from Panjim pull in for a beer.

The flea market

Anjuna's Wednesday **flea market**, held in the coconut plantation behind the southern end of the beach, is the hub of Goa's alternative scene and *the* place to indulge in a spot of souvenir shopping. A few years back, the weekly event was the exclusive preserve of backpackers and the area's seasonal residents, who gathered here to smoke *chillums* and to buy and sell clothes and jewellery they probably wouldn't have the nerve to wear anywhere else: something like a small pop festival without the stage. These days, however, everything is more organized and mainstream. Pitches are rented out by the metre, drugs are banned and the approach roads to the village are choked solid all day with air-conditioned buses and Ambassador cars ferrying in tourists from resorts further down the coast. Even the beggars have to pay *baksheesh* to be here.

The range of goods on sale has broadened, too, thanks to the high profile of migrant hawkers and stall-holders from other parts of India. Each region or culture is allotted its own corner. At one end, Westerners congregate around racks of rave gear, Techno tapes, designer beachwear and clapped-out old Enfields sporting "For Sale" signs. Nearby, hawk-eyed Kashmiris sit cross-

△ Anjuna beach

legged beside trays of silver jewellery and papier-mâché boxes, while trendily dressed Tibetans preside over orderly rows of prayer wheels, turquoise bracelets and sundry Himalayan curios. Most distinctive of all are the Lamani women from Karnataka, decked from head to toe in traditional tribal garb, selling elaborately woven multicoloured cloth, which they fashion into everything from jackets to money belts, and which makes even the Westerners' party gear look positively funereal. Elsewhere, you'll come across dazzling Rajasthani mirrorwork and block-printed bedspreads, Keralan woodcarvings and a scattering of Gujarati applique.

What you end up paying for this exotic merchandise largely depends on your ability to **haggle**. Lately, prices have been inflated as tourists not used to dealing in rupees will part with almost anything. Be persistent, though, and cautious, and you can usually pick things up for a reasonable rate.

Even if you're not spending, the flea market is a great place just to sit and watch the world go by. Mingling with the suntanned masses are bands of strolling musicians, mendicant sadhus, fortune-telling bulls and snake charmers.

Eating and drinking

The beach shacks tend to be overpriced by comparison with those elsewhere in the state (especially on flea market days, when they hike their prices) but many will feel the location is worth paying for. Responding to the tastes of its alternative visitors, the village also boasts a crop of quality wholefood cafés serving healthy veg dishes and juices. If you're hankering for a taste of home, call in at the **Orchard Stores** on the eastern side of the village, which, along with its rival **Oxford Stores**, directly opposite, serves the expatriate community with as vast range of pricy imported delights such as Digestive biscuits, Marmite and extra-virgin olive oil. They also offer delicious coffee and fresh croissants.

Bean Me Up On the main road through the village. India's one and only American-run tofu joint – the last word in Goan gourmet healthy eating. Try their delicious Thai-style tempeh in spicy cashew sauce. Main courses (around Rs175) come with steamed spinach, fresh brown bread and hygienically washed salads. And there's a tempting range of vegan desserts (the banana pudding with soya whip's a winner).

The Jam Connection Opposite *Tin Tin Tibet*. Fresh, interesting salads (with real organic rocket and garden herbs), mocha and espresso coffee, homemade ice cream and all-day breakfasts,

served in a lovely garden. You can lounge on bamboo easy chairs or on tree platforms. Daily except Weds 11am–7pm.

Martha's Breakfast Home *Martha's* guesthouse, 907 Montero Waddo. Secluded, very friendly breakfast garden serving fresh Indian coffee, crepes and delicious waffles.

Tin Tin Tibet Near Oxford Stores. Well-established budget café, serving the usual budget-travellers' grub, plus Tibetan specialities (*momos* and *thukpa*), and some Israeli dishes. Worth a try if only for the fried banana with cashew nuts.

Nightlife

Anjuna no longer deserves the reputation it gained through the early 1990s as a legendary rave venue, but big **parties** are still held here from time to time, especially around the Christmas–New Year full-moon period. Smaller events may also happen in off-track locations (such as "Disco Valley" behind Vagator beach) whenever the organizers can muster the increasingly large pay-offs demanded by local police.

First stop for confirmed Techno heads should be the **Paraiso de Goa**, aka **Paradiso**, at the far north end of Anjuna beach. Partly owned by the government, this place epitomizes the new, more above-board face of Goa Trance.

Presiding over a dance space surrounded by spacey statues of Hindu gods and Tantric symbols, visiting DJs spin text-book Trance for a mainly Israeli crowd. It's all a bit commercial, but even the now legendary Goa Gill, one of the leading free-party hosts of the 1980s and 1990s, has given the club his seal of approval by playing here. Paradiso keeps to a sporadic timetable, but should be open most nights from around 10pm; admission charges are Rs200–400, depending on the night.

Along similar lines, but with free admission, is the **Nine Bar**, above Vagator beach, and the nearby **Primrose Café** (both reviewed on pp.154–5). Down on the beach proper, the **Shore Bar** used to be *the* place to hangout after the flea market, attracting hundreds of people for sunset, but it has fallen out of favour over the past couple of years and now lacks the atmosphere of the *Nine Bar*.

Listings

Books On the floor above Oxford Stores is Anjuna's best-stocked bookstore, selling both new and secondhand titles.

Foreign exchange The *Manali Guest House* and Oxford Stores **change money** (at poor rates). The Bank of Baroda on the Mapusa road will make encashments against Visa cards, but doesn't do foreign exchange, nor is it a good place to leave valuables, as thieves have previously climbed through an open window and stolen a number of "safe custody" envelopes.

Internet access *Manali Guest House* offers Internet access for Rs40 per hour, but Colours, next to Speedy Travel, has a much faster connection and a/c for the same price.

Laundry Bruno's Laundry, in St Michael's Waddo on the south side of the village.

Motorcycle repairs Anjuna's two motorcycle repair workshops are both up the road from the Oxford Stores. The smaller one, further back from the roadside, is more helpful. Fuel and some spares, such as inner tubes and spark plugs, can be bought from the store on the *Starco's* crossroads.

Pharmacy St Michael's Pharmacy, Soronto Waddo, near the *Starco's* crossroads, is open 24hr during the season.

Photography Oxford Stores stocks and processes colour print film.

Post office The post office is just off the Mapusa road, 1km inland, with an efficient poste restante counter.

Travel agents MGM (☎0832/227 4317), Traveland (☎0832/227 73207) and Connexions (☎ & ☎0832/227 74347) are east of *Starco's* on the main Mapusa road; Speedy Travel (☎0832/227 3266) lies between the post office and *Rose Garden Restaurant*. All are reliable and efficient.

Yoga The Purple Valley Yoga Centre (☎www .yogagoa.net) gives classes in Ashtanga yoga, as taught in Mysore by Sri K Pattabhi Jois, at their studio in the garden of the *Hotel Bougainvillea*; all levels of ability are catered for. Drop-in classes cost Rs400, or Rs3000 if you book ten in advance, and they also offer two-week retreats in a purpose-built *shala* (yoga studio) in some nearby woods. For expert Iyengar-style yoga tuition, contact Erson Viegas at his studio in nearby Arpora (☎0832/227 7993); see also the listing for Maggie Hughes under "Yoga" on p.134.

Vagator

Barely a couple of kilometres of clifftops and parched grassland separate Anjuna from the southern fringes of its nearest neighbour, **VAGATOR**. Spread around a tangle of leafy lanes, this is a more chilled, undeveloped resort that appeals, in the main, to Israeli and northern European Trance heads, who hole up for the full season in ramshackle old Portuguese bungalows or cheap guesthouses.

With the red ramparts of Chapora fort looming above it, Vagator's broad sandy **beach** – known as "**Big Vagator**" – is undeniably beautiful. However, a peaceful swim or lie on the sand is out of the question here as it's a prime stop

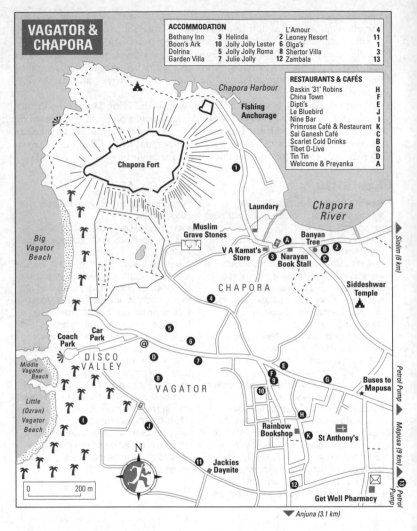

VAGATOR &
CHAPORA

ACCOMMODATION
Bethany Inn   9   Helinda   2   L'Amour   4
Boon's Ark   10   Jolly Jolly Lester 6   Leoney Resort   11
Dolrina   5   Jolly Jolly Roma 8   Olga's   1
Garden Villa   7   Julie Jolly   12   Shertor Villa   3
                                            Zambala   13

RESTAURANTS & CAFÉS
Baskin '31' Robins   H
China Town   F
Dipti's   E
Le Bluebird   J
Nine Bar   I
Primrose Café & Restaurant   K
Sai Ganesh Café   C
Scarlet Cold Drinks   B
Tibet O-Live   G
Tin Tin   D
Welcome & Preyanka   A

Chapora Harbour

Fishing
Anchorage

Chapora Fort

Laundary

Chapora
River

Muslim
Grave Stones

V A Kamat's
Store

Banyan
Tree

Narayan
Book Stall

Siddeshwar
Temple

CHAPORA

Big
Vagator
Beach

Coach
Park

Car
Park

DISCO
VALLEY

Middle
Vagator
Beach

VAGATOR

Buses to
Mapusa

Little
(Ozran)
Vagator
Beach

Rainbow
Bookshop

St Anthony's

N

Jackies
Daynite

Get Well Pharmacy

0   200 m

Siolim (6 km)

Petrol Pump

Mapusa (9 km)

Petrol Pump

Anjuna (3.1 km)

for bus parties of domestic tourists, which ensures a steady stream of whisky-swilling Maharashtran men. Far better, then, to head to the next cove south. Backed by a steep wall of crumbling palm-fringed laterite, **Ozran** (or "Little") **Vagator beach** is more secluded and much less accessible than either of its neighbours. To get there, walk ten minutes from Big Vagator, or drive to the end of the lane running off the main Chapora–Anjuna road (towards the *Nine Bar*), from where a footpath drops sharply down to a wide stretch of level white sand (look for the mopeds and bikes parked at the top of the cliff). At the far southern edge of the beach, a sculpted face stares contemplatively out of a rock, and a freshwater spring trickles through a lush tangle of vegetation into a shady pool at the foot of the cliff – ideal for washing off the salt after swimming.

Practicalities

Buses from Panjim and Mapusa, 9km east, pull in every fifteen minutes or so at the crossroads on the far northeastern edge of Vagator, near where the main road peels away towards Chapora. From here, it's a one-kilometre walk over the hill and down the other side to the beach. The *Primrose Café*, on the south side of the village, has a **foreign exchange** licence (for cash and traveller's cheques) but their rates are well above those on offer at *Jackie's Daynite* shop (see map). If you need medical attention, contact Dr Jawarhalal Henriques at Zorin, near the petrol pump in Chapora (℗0832/227 4308).

Accommodation

Accommodation in Vagator revolves around a couple of pricey resort hotels, family-run budget guesthouses and dozens of small private properties rented out for long periods. Once again, **water** is in very short supply here, and you'll be doing the villagers a favour if you use it frugally at all times.

Bethany Inn Next to the Chapora crossroads ℗0832/227 3731, ⓔbethany@goatelecom.com. Seven immaculately clean rooms with fridges, balconies and attached bathrooms. Tastefully furnished, and efficiently managed by two young brothers, originally from Pune. Internet access available (Rs50/hr). ❸–❹

Boon's Ark Near *Bethany Inn* ℗0832/227 4045. New-ish place just off the crossroads at the top of the village. Pleasant, clean and well run. ❹

Dolrina North of the road near the beach ℗0832 /227 4896. Nestled under a lush canopy of trees, Vagator's largest budget guesthouse is owned by a friendly Goan couple and features attached or shared bathrooms, a sociable garden café, individual safe deposits and roof space. Single occupancy rates, and breakfasts available. ❸

Garden Villa Beach road ℗0832/227 3571, ⓔgarden@goatelecom.com. Two categories of rooms: the older ones are better value than the ones in the newer block. All spacious and cool, with tiled floors and large bathrooms. Also has a friendly café showing video movies daily at 7.30pm. ❸

Jolly Jolly Lester Halfway between the crossroads and Big Vagator beach ℗0832/227 3620. Eleven pleasant doubles with tiled bathrooms, plus a small restaurant, set in a lovingly kept garden and surrounded by woodland. Single occupancy possible. ❸

Jolly Jolly Roma Just off the main beach road ℗0832/227 3620 or 227 3001.Very smart, good-sized chalet rooms with sit-outs; laundry, forex and a small library for guests. ❹

Julie Jolly South side of the village ℗0832/227 3357. Recently revamped and now among the most pleasant places in Vagator, on the edge of the leafy belt, within easy reach of Ozran beach. All rooms are newly tiled and well aired. Self-caterers can stay in larger suites with sitting rooms and kitchettes. ❷–❸

L'Amour North side of village, on a hillside above Chapora ℗0832/277 4180. Immaculately clean, tiled en-suite rooms in a block newly built by Gulf returner. Quiet, well run and fantastic value if tariffs are held. ❷

Leoney Resort On the road to Disco Valley ℗0832/227 3634, ℗227 3595, ⓔromi@goatelecom.com. Smart chalets and pricier (but more spacious) octagonal "cottages" on sleepy side of village, ranged around a pool. Restaurant, laundry, lockers and foreign-exchange facilities. A comfortable option. No advance bookings Dec–Jan. ❺–❻

Zambala 1639 Deul Waddo ℗0832/227 3479 or 238 2352, ⓦwww.zambala.org. Fifteen smart little rooms surrounding a shady courtyard. Formerly an Israeli-chillum dive, but now British-run with clean sheets and honest prices. The best value all-round budget place in the area. ❷

Eating, drinking and nightlife

Vagator's travellers' scene has spawned a bumper crop of **restaurants**, as well as the usual rash of shacks down on the beach. With the exception of *Le Bluebird*, none are all that innovative, but they're a cut well above the dives in Chapora. The place to head for a sundowner is the **Nine Bar**, on the clifftop above Ozran beach, where big Trance sounds attract a fair-sized crowd for sunset, especially on Wednesdays after the flea market. Encircled by a fortress-style

2

The dark side of the moon

Hedonism has figured prominently in European images of Goa from the mid-sixteenth century, when mariners and merchants returned to Lisbon with tales of unbridled debauchery among the colonists. The French traveller François Pyrard was first to chronicle this as moral decline, in a journal littered with accounts of wild parties and sleaze scandals.

Following the rigours of the Inquisition, a semblance of morality was restored, which prevailed through the Portuguese era. But traditional Catholic life in Goa's coastal villages sustained a rude shock in the 1960s with the first influx of **hippies** to Calangute and Baga beaches. Much to the amazement of the locals, the preferred pastime of these would-be sadhus was to cavort naked on the sands together on full-moon nights, amid a haze of *chillum* smoke and loud rock music blaring from makeshift PAs. The villagers took little notice of these bizarre gatherings at first, but with each season the scene became better established, and by the late 1970s the **Christmas and New Year** parties, in particular, had become huge events, attracting thousands of foreign travellers.

In the late 1980s, the local party scene received a dramatic face lift with the coming of Acid House and Techno. Ecstasy became the preferred dance drug as the dub-reggae scene gave way to rave culture, with ever greater numbers of young clubbers pouring in for the season on charter flights. Goa soon spawned its own distinctive brand of psychedelic music, known as **Goa Trance**. Distinguished by its multilayered synth lines and sub-bass rhythms, the hypnotic style combines the darkness of hard Techno with an ambient sentiment. Cultivated by artists such as Goa Gill, Juno Reactor and Hallucinogen, the new sound was given wider exposure when big-name DJs Danny Rampling and Paul Oakenfold started mixing Goa Trance in clubs and on national radio back in the UK, generating a huge following among music lovers who previously knew nothing of the place which had inspired it.

The **golden era** for Goa's party scene, and Trance, was in the early 1990s, when big raves were held two or three times a week in beautiful locations around Anjuna

---

laterite wall that's open to a great chill-out terrace and the sea on one side, the dancing starts after dark and keeps going until the bar closes around 10pm. At this point, there's a general exodus over to the nearby **Primrose Café**, which offers much the same atmosphere, without the views.

Baskin "31" Robbins, near *Primrose Café*. Thirty-one flavours of melt-in-the-mouth American ice cream. The nut crunch is to die for.

China Town Next to *Bethany Inn.*. For the past few seasons, this small roadside restaurant, tucked away just south of the main drag, has been the village's most popular budget place to eat, serving particularly tasty seafood dishes in addition to a large Chinese selection, as well as all the usual Goa-style travellers' grub.

Dipti's On the Mapusa road. Extraordinary magic mushroom plastic art meets Ajanta-mural-decor is the hallmark of this cosy bar, which serves a full Indian–Goan–Chinese–continental menu. It's also a friendly place for a quiet cocktail.

Jolly Jolly Lester Halfway between the village crossroads and Big Vagator beach. Small restaurant attached to the guesthouse offering a good selection of inexpensive seasonal seafood, salads and tasty Western-style veg dishes.

Le Bluebird On the road out to the *Nine Bar*. Tucked away in the most appealing corner of the village is Vagator's famous French-run restaurant, which serves classier-than-average Gallic food – pepper steak in brandy sauce, prawns in coconut, squid in white wine and garlic – at traveller-friendly prices (around Rs300 for three courses, plus wine). Seafood is their strong point, but they offer a better range of veg dishes than you'd find in a real French restaurant, as well as crepes, Bordeaux claret and champagne (around Rs2000 per bottle).

Nine Bar Above Ozran beach. Boasting a crystal Trance sound system, this clifftop café enjoys a prime location, with fine sea views from its terrace through the palm canopy, where Nepali waiters serve up cold beer and the usual range of budget travellers' grub to a generally spaced out clientele.

and Vagator. UV and fluoro gear appeared and for a few years the authorities turned a blind eye to the growing scene. Then, quite suddenly, the plug was pulled. For years, drug busts and bribes provided the notoriously corrupt Goan cops with a lucrative source of *baksheesh*. But after a couple of drug-related deaths, a series of sensational articles in the local press and a decision by Goa Tourism to promote upmarket over backpacker tourism, the police began to demand impossibly large bribes – sums that the organizers (many of them drug dealers) could not hope to recoup. Although the big New Year and Christmas events continued unabated, smaller parties, hitherto held in off-track venues such as "Disco Valley" behind Middle Vagator beach and the "Bamboo Grove" in south Anjuna, started to peter out, much to the dismay of local people, many of whom had become financially dependent on the raves and the punters they pulled in to the villages.

Against this backdrop, the imposition during the run up to the Y2K celebrations of an **amplified-music ban** between 10pm and 7am seemed to sound the death knell for Goa's party scene. Reports in the international media that India's rave-era was at an end were, however, premature. Three years on, the scene survives, albeit in a more mainstream style, with a batch of established, above-board clubs – notably the **Nine Bar** and **Paradiso** – providing permanent venues and big sound systems for the first time in Goa. As predicted by many locals at the time, the ban has had little impact beyond the pockets of local police, who use it as a pretext to lever bribes out of bar owners. Parties now take place as often as they did before.

All the same, if you've come here expecting an Indian equivalent of Ko Pha Ngan or Ibiza-on-the-Arabian Sea, you'll be sorely disappointed. Only over Christmas and New Year do really big parties take place, and these are a far cry from the free-and-easy events that once filled the beaches and bamboo groves of Anjuna on full-moon nights.

See also "Nightlife", p.154.

They've recently enlarged the place to accommodate a dance floor and chill-out area.

Primrose Café and Restaurant On the southern edge of the village. Goa's posiest café-bar livens up around 10pm and serves tasty German wholefood snacks, light meals and cakes, as well as cocktails.

Tibet O-Live East side of the village, on the main road. Run by a team of friendly young lads from Darjeeling, this place shuttles between Manali in the summer and Goa in the winter, and has earned a strong reputation in both for its ultra-tasty, inexpensive pizzas. They also serve top fried *momos* (the spinach and cheese ones are best).

Tin Tin West side of the village, near the clifftop car park. Large and lavishly decorated, and crammed with a mainly young package tourist clientele, hence the higher-than-average prices, which the expat British co-owner justifies with a popular "big portions" policy. The menu is exhaustive, but best bets are the dishes of the day chalked on boards. Mains from Rs150 to 350.

Chapora

Crouched in the shadow of a Portuguese fort on the opposite, northern side of the headland from Vagator, **CHAPORA**, 10km from Mapusa, is busier than most north coast villages. Dependent on fishing and boat-building, it has, to a great extent, retained a life of its own, independent of tourism. The workaday indifference to the annual invasion of Westerners is most evident on the main street, lined with as many regular stores as travellers' cafés and restaurants. It's highly unlikely that Chapora will ever develop into a major resort, either. Tucked away under a dense canopy of trees on the muddy southern shore of a river estuary, it lacks both the space and the white sand that have pulled crowds to Calangute and Colva.

If you have your own transport, however, Chapora is a good base from which to explore the region: Vagator is on the doorstep, Anjuna is a short ride to the south, and the ferry crossing at Siolim – gateway to the remote north of the state – is barely fifteen minutes away by road. The village is also well connected by bus to Mapusa, and there are plenty of bars and cafés to hang out in during the evenings, when the main street is clogged with what looks like the contents of half a dozen Amsterdam coffee shops. The one real drawback with staying here is the general grubbiness of the accommodation on offer, which tends to be booked for long periods to an unchanging crowd of hard-drinking, heavy-smoking old heads.

The fort

Chapora's chief landmark is its venerable old **fort**, most easily reached from the Vagator side of the hill. At low tide, you can also walk around the bottom of the headland, via the anchorage, and the secluded coves beyond it, to Big Vagator, then head up the hill from there. The red-laterite bastion, crowning the rocky bluff, was built by the Portuguese in 1617 on the site of an earlier Muslim structure (whence the village's name – from Shahpura, "town of the Shah"). Intended as a border watch post, it fell to various Hindu raiders during the seventeenth century, among them the Maharatha chieftain Sambhaji, whose troops local legend claims were able to scale the precipitous walls with the aid of giant monitor lizards. Known as *ghorpad* in Konkani, these metre-and-a-half-long reptiles are said to be able to climb and support the weight of a man when wedged into a hole or between crenellations; they inflate themselves and will allegedly starve to death before relinquishing their grip.

The fortress was finally deserted by the Portuguese in 1892, after the territory's frontiers had been forced further north into the *Novas Conquistas* region. Today, it lies in ruins, although you can still see the heads of two tunnels that formerly provided supply routes for besieged defenders, as well as a scattering of Muslim **tombstones** ringed by an enclosure on the southern slopes of the hill, believed to be relics of pre-colonial days. However, the main incentive to climb up here are the superb **views** from the bastion's weed-infested ramparts, which look north across the estuary to Morjim. From a doorway on the north-west side of the fort, you can also follow a **footpath** downhill to a bluff that affords an even more dramatic panorama; it's a perfect spot to watch the sunset, and if you're lucky you might catch sight of the wild jackals that live in the scrub surrounding it.

Practicalities

Direct **buses** arrive at Chapora three times daily from Panjim, and every fifteen minutes from Mapusa, with departures until 7pm. **Motorcycle taxis** hang around the old banyan tree at the far end of the main street, near where the buses pull in. Air, train, bus and catamaran **tickets** may be booked or reconfirmed at Soniya Tours and Travels, next to the bus stand.

Chapora also boasts a better-than-average general **store**: in addition to basic provisions such as food and kerosene, V.A. Kamat's, at the west end of the main street, stocks sun cream, colour film, postcards and other tourist essentials.

Finally, anyone running short of reading material should head for the tiny Narayan Books, next door to *Baba Restaurant* on the main street, which rents out, sells and part-exchanges **secondhand books** in a range of languages.

Accommodation

If you want to check into a cheap guesthouse while you sort out more permanent **accommodation**, best bet is the basic *Shettor Villa* (☎0832/227 4335; ❷–❸), off the west side of the main street. Nearly all its rooms, ranged around a sheltered back yard, come with fans and running water. They're good value, but often booked to regulars, in which case try the *Helinda* (☎0832/227 4345; ❷–❸), at the opposite end of the village, which has rock-bottom options and a couple of more comfortable rooms with attached shower-toilets, or *Olga's* (☎0832/227 4355), a rudimentary, but clean and quiet little guesthouse on the west side of the village towards the fishing anchorage.

Eating and drinking

Finding somewhere to **eat** in Chapora is easy: just take your pick from the crop of inexpensive little cafés and restaurants on the main street. The popular *Welcome*, halfway down, offers a reasonable selection of cheap and filling seafood, Western and veg dishes, plus relentless reggae and techno music and backgammon sets. The *Preyanka*, nearby, is in much the same mould, but has a few more Indian and Chinese options. Alternatively, try the restaurant at the *Helinda* guesthouse, which specializes in *tandoori* fish and chicken. If you're suffering from chilli-burn afterwards, *Scarlet Cold Drinks* and the *Sai Ganesh Café*, both a short way east of the main street, knock up deliciously cool fresh-fruit milkshakes.

Siolim

Although one of the state's largest villages, with a population nudging 12,000, **SIOLIM**, like nearby Chapora, has been spared the tourist-led development that has ravaged the coastline around Calangute, 10km south, thanks to its distance from the beach. Spread under a rich canopy of palm trees, its collection of gorgeous colonial-era houses still exudes an air of Portuguese bourgeois prosperity. Siolcars love to remind you that their village has traditionally dominated the region's cultural and sporting life, having spawned a steady stream of soccer and hockey stars, as well as musicians (most recently pop supremo and film music composer Remo Fernandes; see box). Siolim's other boast is that it is the source of the world's best *feni* – a claim hotly contested by the residents of Palolem, in the south.

Life in the village revolves around two centres of gravity. On its south side, at the foot of the road descending from Anjuna and Assagao, a busy little market area clusters around the crossroads in front of an ostentatiously Corinthian **Church of Saint Anthony**, one of the oldest Christian shrines in the region. The church's fame dates from the sixteenth century, when it was the scene of two miracles witnessed by the entire congregation. The second bazaar, known as **Tar**, lies five minutes' drive north, grouped around the concrete landing ramp on the Chapora River, from where the ferries (three per hour) chug back and forth to Chopdem. To do so, they have to navigate around the concrete supports of the massive new **roadbridge** which nowadays carries most traffic across the river. En route, you can pull over to enjoy the views across the estuary, where groups of locals can usualy be seen up to their necks in water gathering clams (*tisreo*) from the river bed with their feet.

Siolim Zagor

While much of India has had to learn to live with the spectre of religious violence, Goa's Christians and Hindus, despite the sabre-rattling of their respective right-wing politicians, manage to co-exist peacefully and in a spirit of mutual respect unsurpassed on the subcontinent. Emblematic of this communal harmony, and indeed the richness of Goa's melting pot culture in general, is **Siolim's** extraordinary **Zagor festival,** held on the first Sunday after Christmas.

Although ostensibly a Christian celebration, coinciding with the feast day of Nossa Senhora de Guia, the night-long event blends together elements from both religions. It centres on a small Hindu shrine, housed under a *peepal* tree down a lane near the ferry ramp. This sacred spot is associated with an important local deity called **Zagoryo,** believed to be the guardian of the village dams (*bunds*) which hold the river off the rice paddy. During the festival, each household makes offerings to Zagor to give thanks and ensure the village is protected from flooding over the coming year: the Christians give candles, the Hindus give oil, and both offer cakes of pressed rice called *pohe*.

The festivities, however, start with a sombre candle-lit **procession** through Siolim, in which an effigy of Zagor is carried around the various *waddos* of the village, stopping at wayside crosses and shrines along the way to receive offerings. Everyone then gathers at a *mand*, or sacred arena, in a Catholic house for a **dance drama**. The actors in this ancient ritual, assuming hereditarily assigned roles, are always drawn from two old Siolim families: the Shirodkars (Hindus) and D'Souzas (Catholics). It enacts stories from the legend of the Zagor deities, of which there were traditionally twelve (*bara*) in the area (whence "Bardez", from *bara-desh*, or "twelve districts"). At dawn, when the play is complete and the priests have recited mantras and Christian scriptures to invoke the god's protection, Zagor is carried amid much pomp back to his shrine, where offerings of roasted maize, *feni* and fermented rice pikelets (called *sanna*) are placed before his small domed shrine.

Traditionally, local satirists used to take over at this point, performing **zupatteos**, songs poking fun at politicians, priests and anyone else who deserved to be taken down a peg or two. These days, however, the culmination of Zagor tends to be a Konkani *tiatr* play, followed by a set of crowd-pleasing Konkani classics from local rock star Remo Fernandes, who was born and still lives in Siolim (see p.157).

Aside from being a model of religious tolerance, Zagor is a great spectacle and enormous fun. Surprisingly few tourists participate, but foreigners are welcomed enthusiastically, to both the religious dance drama and the resolutely secular, *feni*-fuelled party that succeeds it.

Accommodation and eating

The village has only one **hotel**, an elegantly converted *palacio* called *Siolim House* (T0832/227 2138, F227 2323, Wwww.siolimhouse.com; ❽). Located just past the crossroads, a short way down the back (riverside) route to Chapora, the three-hundred-year-old building used to belong to the governor of Macao, but fell into disrepair and was virtually derelict when its present London/Delhi-based owners acquired it. Today, the *palacio* numbers among the tiny handful of hotels in the state that capture the period feel of the Portuguese era, with romantic, beautifully furnished rooms and suites ranged around a central pillared courtyard. Individually styled and named after old Portuguese trading centres, they are priced from US$45–65, depending on the time of year and size of the room; the more expensive ones are huge, with bathtubs, gorgeous oyster-shell windows and four-poster beds. Mod cons have been kept to a minimum (no a/c, minibars or televisions), but there's a twelve-metre pool in the garden, and an unobtrusive restaurant serving fine Goan food.

Other than *Siolim House*'s pricey restaurant, the only commendable **place to eat** in Siolim is the spit-and-sawdust *Hotel de Jakin*, the locals' favourite little *pao bhaji* joint in the market opposite the church. It fills up to bursting on Sundays in particular, when its owner, Camil Raimundo, dishes up his famous *sorpatel*, mopped up with delicious fresh *sanna* made from local *toddi*.

Pernem and the far north

Bounded by the Chapora and Arondem rivers, **Pernem** is Goa's northernmost district and one of its least explored regions. Apart from the fishing village of **Arambol**, which during the winter plays host to a large contingent of hippy travellers seeking a rougher, less pretentious alternative to Anjuna and Vagator, the beautiful Pernem coastline of long sandy beaches, lagoons and coconut plantations is punctuated with few settlements equipped to cope with visitors. However, the wonderfully picturesque journey north to **Terekol fort**, on the Maharashtran border, can easily be covered in a day-trip.

Before the Portuguese took over Pernem in 1778, the Chapora River marked the border between old Christian Goa (the *Velhas Conquistas*) and wider Hindu India. The two-and-a-half centuries of colonial rule that preceded the acquisition of the *Novas Conquistas*, of which Pernem was a part, ensured this divide was as much cultural as political, and even today the transition between the two is clearly discernible. Once across the river, most villages are grouped around brightly painted, colonnaded temples, the calendars in the provision stores sport images of Ganesh or Lakshmi rather than Our Lady, and the women tend to wear saris instead of dresses.

Travelling north from Siolim, the entrepot to Pernem proper is the far side of the new road bridge at **Chopdem**. Head straight on for 200m or so until you arrive at a T-junction. A right turn here will take you along the quick route to Arambol; bear left, and you'll end up in Morjim.

Morjim

Viewed from Chapora fort, **MORJIM** (or **Morji**) appears as a dramatic expanse of empty sand sweeping north from a surf-lashed spit at the river mouth. Behind it, broken dunes are backed by a dense patch of palms and casuarina trees, sheltering a mixed Hindu-Christian village whose inhabitants still live predominantly by fishing and farming. Bypassed completely by the main road to Arambol, their settlement has remained a relative backwater. Only in the last couple of years, in anticipation of the development that is bound to accompany completion of the new Siolim–Chapora bridge, have shacks and small guesthouses begun to creep along the sand.

Even so, comparatively few tourists venture up here, and the beach remains essentially a place of work for the hand-net and outrigger fishers who live behind it. They make their living mainly from small mackerel and sardines, most of which are dried and sold as fertilizer for palm trees. However, with fish stocks diminishing annually, the future of the industry in the area looks bleak. Only five years ago, forty men were employed full time pulling the nets; now, barely half that number turn out in the morning to begin four hours of hard hauling.

Most of the net pullers live at the south end of Morjim beach, known locally as **Temb**. The area attracted some rare media attention recently when a

The turtle wind

When a strong and steady on-shore breeze blows through the night in early November at Morjim, the locals call it a **turtle wind** because such weather normally heralds the arrival of Goa's rarest migrant visitors: the **olive ridley marine turtles** (*Lepidochelys olivacea*).

For as long as anyone can remember, the spoon-shaded spit of soft white sand at **Temb**, the southern end of Morjim beach, has been the nesting ground of these beautiful sea reptiles. Each winter, a succession of females emerge from the surf during the night and, using their distinctive flippers, crawl to the edge of the dunes to lay their annual clutch of 105–115 eggs. Just over two months later, the fresh hatchlings clamber out and crawl blinking over their siblings to begin the perilous trek back to the water, guided into the sea by reflected moonlight.

Little more is known about how these enigmatic creatures spend the rest of their long lives (turtles frequently live for over a century), but it is thought that the females return to the beaches where they were born to lay their own eggs. Some have been shown to travel as far as 4500 km to do this.

Once a thriving species, with huge populations spread across the Pacific, Atlantic and Indian oceans, the olive ridley is nowadays endangered. Aside from a wealth of traditional predators (such as crows, ospreys, gulls and buzzards, who pick off the hatchlings during their dash for the sea), the newborns and their parents are vulnerable to a host of threats from humans. In Morjim, as in most of Asia, the eggs are traditionally considered a delicacy and local villagers collect them to sell in Mapusa market. Many (perhaps as many as 35,000 worldwide) are killed accidentally by fishermen, caught up in fine shrimp nets or attracted by squid bait used to catch tuna. Floating litter, which the hapless turtles mistake for jellyfish, has also taken its toll over the past two decades, as have tar balls from oil spills, which coat the animals' digestive tracts and hamper the absorption of food. The growth of tourism poses an additional danger: electric lights behind the beaches throw the hatchlings off course

Calcutta-based businessman announced plans to site a three-star hotel there, having acquired nearly 50,000 square metres of land. Concerned that the building work and subsequent tourist influx would hasten the end of their already ailing industry, the local fishers got together with a Goan environmental group to oppose the plans. Offers from the developers of a new road, fishing jetty and money to renovate their chapel were spurned, and a march was organized to storm the municipality buildings in Pernem and Panjim. Eventually, amid accusations of intimidation and threats of violence on both sides, the hotel chain backed down, but with a huge sum invested, it seems unlikely they will give up on the project.

Judging by the ease with which developers have overridden environmental laws and local opposition elsewhere in the state, it would seem the best hope of preserving Temb's peace and quiet lies not with the machete-wielding fishers but with the handful of **turtles** who nest there each winter (see box). If they continue to show up in growing numbers, this side of the beach, at least, should be designated as a nature sanctuary, which will effectively block any future construction.

Practicalities

Few of the buses running north to Arambol pass through Morjim, making it difficult to reach without your own transport. Most visitors come here by taxi or motorbike. From the north side of the bridge at Chopdem, turn left at the T-junction and follow the road along the bank of the Chapora. After roughly

as they scuttle towards the sea, and sand compressed by sunbathers' trampling feet damages nests, preventing the babies from digging their way out at the crucial time.

On average, only two out of a typical clutch of more than one hundred survive into adulthood to reproduce. In Goa, the resulting decline has been dramatic. Of the 150 nesting females that used to return each year to Morjim, for example, only five showed up in 1997–8.

However, under the auspices of the Forest Department, a new scheme has been launched to revive turtle populations. Locals are employed to watch out for the females' arrival in November and guard the nests after the eggs have been laid until they hatch. You'll see them camped under palm-leaf shades on the beach, with the nests fenced in and marked by Forest Department signs. One of the main reasons the fishing families at Temb have so enthusiastically espoused the initiative is that its success promises to bring about the creation of an official **nature sanctuary** at Morjim, blocking forever plans to build unwanted tourist resorts on their beach.

So far, the government-led conservation attempt seems to have been successful. In 2000–01, almost 2500 hatchlings were monitored at Morjim and a further 2500 at Goa's other turtle-nesting site, **Galjibag**, in the south (see p.212).

Watching the nesting turtles is an unforgettable experience, although one requiring a certain amount of dedication, or luck. No one knows for sure when an olive ridley female will turn up, but with a strong turtle wind blowing at the right time, the chances are good. Much more predictable are the appearances of the hatchlings, who emerge exactly 54 days after their mothers laid the eggs. If you ask one of the wardens looking after the nests, they can tell you when this will be.

For more on international attempts to save marine turtles, including the massive synchronized *arribida* (arrival) of around 200,000 at the Bhita Kanika Sanctuary, Orissa, on the east coast of India, visit the website of the World Wildlife Fund ⓦwww.wwf.org.

1.5km you arrive at a fork near a sheltered inlet, where a right turn will take you into Morjim bazaar; go left here, and you'll eventually end up at a sandy turning circle at Temb, behind a row of shacks – the easiest access point for the far end of the beach. To pick up the scenic back road to Arambol, however, you should take the road that veers right shortly after the bazaar turn-off, and follow this past the church and community hall. From here it runs in a more or less straight line all the way up the coast, punctuated by a string of signs indicating the way to small guesthouses and beach shacks.

The village's limited **accommodation** lies at the head of a lane peeling west off this road, in Vithaldas Waddo. Look for a blue signboard for *Britto's* (☎0832/278 4245; ❷), a cheap and friendly guesthouse tucked away 200m behind the beach, with simple rooms and a handful of bamboo treehouses. Facilities here are basic, but the Brittos are very hospitable. They also run a small shack restaurant during high season, serving delicious Goan fish curry, fried sardines and other seafood. Next door is the much less enticing *Goan Café/Lobo's Paradise* (☎0832/224 6394; ❷), with bamboo huts and a handful of basic rooms.

Keep heading down the lane towards the sea, instead of following the sand track to *Britto's*, and you'll arrive at a relatively undeveloped beachfront area. The best restaurant here, if not in the entire district, is the British–Belgian-run *Olive Ridley*, where you can dine on locally caught rock fish in light sauces and copious fresh rocket salad. Prices are on the high side for the area, but the food is of a correspondingly high standard and the atmosphere – with a wood-filled, lantern-lit interior open to the sea – conducive to lazing around and working your way through their tempting dessert list (the chocolate mousse is in a league of its own).

Early signs that Morjim is starting to succumb to the attentions of the Mumbai jet set include the incongruous *Other Side*, just down the lane from *Olive Ridley*. With its chic lighting and water features, this place would look less out of place in downtown Colaba than a Goan fishing village, and perhaps not surprisingly sees few punters. The opening night in 2002 was a surreal affair, with Bollywood film stars jetting in and yachts moored off the beach, watched with bemusement by the local fishermen.

Aswem

At the northern limits of Morjim, where the village's wooden fishing fleet is beached, stands a clump of eroded black rocks and a solitary white crucifix, around which locals harvest mussels at low tide each evening. Beyond it, the coast empties completely save for a handful of shacks and the odd palm-leaf hut encampment, nestling in the shade of small *toddi* plantations and tangles of prickly cactus. With the completion of the bridge, this stretch of coast, known as **ASWEM**, is bound to be transformed, but for the time being, plovers and gulls still well outnumber tourists.

If you're after peace and solitude during the day, it's best to avoid the collection of shack restaurants and handicraft hawkers who congregate beneath the laterite bluff at the far northern end of Aswem beach, to which groups of tourists are brought by boat or minibus on package excursions from other resorts. When the trippers have gone home, however, this can be a pleasantly peaceful spot.

Hidden on the far side of a winding creek overlooking the beach, is a wonderfully secluded hideway owned by local photographer Denzil Sequeira. He rents out *Elsewhere*, an impeccably restored three-bedroom period house, complete with a chef and waiters plus a cheaper alternative, a row of three exclusive, self-contained architectural tents called *Otter Creek*. Opening on to the river, each tent has a hot shower, four-poster bed and fan; weekly bookings only; ⓦwww.aseascape.com, or via the UK-based agency, Lazy Days (see p.13).

Mandrem

The next village up the coast, **MANDREM**, is also showing signs of low-key development, most of it in a small but lively riverside enclave behind the dunes known as **Junasa Waddo**. Top of the range is the functional *Mandrem Beach Resort* (☎0832/229 7115, Ⓕ227 9238, ⓦwww.prazeresgroup.com; ❹), to date the northernmost outpost of charter tourism in Goa. Its en-suite rooms are spacious and light, and have good-sized individual balconies. A quirkier alternative, with colourfully decorated rooms, relaxing cane furniture and large verandahs, is the River Cat Villa (☎0832/229 7346 or 98230/92107, Ⓕ0832/229 7375, Ⓔerinoopeter7@yahoo.com; ❹), whose rates are a notch lower than the *Beach Resort's* (some of the rooms share bathrooms and toilets). Budget travellers would do better asking around the village, back towards the main road, where *Merryland Paradise* (☎0832/229 7440; ❶–❷), has rock-bottom rooms, leaf "cottages" and some treehouses that are a bit close together for comfort. *Line Guest House* (☎0832/229 7935; ❷), nearby, has four basic en-suite rooms close to the beach, but without views.

All three of these places offer **food**, but the most congenial restaurant in Junasa Waddo is the *Oasis*, near the *River Cat Villa*, where you can eat top tandoori

❷

seafood on a lovely terrace overlooking the river. For *pao-bhaji* breakfasts, you'll have to head back into Mandrem village, 3km along the main road to Arambol, where there's a great little *udipi* restaurant serving all the usual Goan snacks and *thali* rice-plate meals at lunchtime. This busy little bazaar also has the area's best stocked provisions **stores** and a cheap **laundry** (above the jeweller's shop in the small courtyard just off the main street; Rs5 per item of clothing).

Pernem

For the majority of bleary-eyed bus travellers who roll through it on the long haul from Mumbai, **PERNEM**, the district headquarters, is another of those nameless settlements you pull into at some unearthly hour of the night and only stay in long enough for the bus driver to grab a packet of *bedees* and a glass of *chai*. Heaped around a crossroads on the NH17, it functions as a service station and as a market for the dozens of small farming villages scattered across the surrounding rice terraces and *toddi* groves.

The town, 2km south of the Maharashtran border, is also renowned as the site of Goa's grandest Hindu mansion, **Deshprabhu House**, set amid shady woodland 1km northeast of the bazaar – the home of a wealthy land-owning family who sided with India during the Independence struggle with Portugal, and were thus allowed to keep their property after 1961. The present incumbent, Jitendra Deshprabhu and his family, still live in their grand ancestral seat, which presides over a huge estate encompassing some two dozen or so villages. It can be reached by following the main road east from Pernem bazaar, and turning left when you see a grand mock-Moghul archway at the end of a long drive.

Deshprabhu House can only be visited by prior appointment, most easily made through your hotel (if you're staying in one) or the tourist office. Built in the nineteenth century, the pink-painted mansion comprises sixteen courtyards and a dozen or so different wings, which once accommodated some 14,000 soldiers, cavalry and artillery, as well as ceremonial elephants and their mahouts. It also houses a **temple** and a small **museum** where you can study portraits and photographs of Deshprabhus past, along with other family heirlooms such as a pair of silver palanquins. You'll also be shown photos of Goa's first ever car, imported by the rajah during the 1920s, despite the fact the region had no surfaced roads at the time. Frustrated at not being able to ride his beloved limousine, he eventually got rid of the vehicle by palming it off on a visiting Portuguese viceroy.

Passing through Pernem bazaar, you cannot fail to notice the town's other well-known monument. The entrance to the turquoise-painted **Shri Bhagwati temple**, which stands on a raised square of dusty red dirt just above the crossroads, is flanked by a pair of colossal multicoloured elephants. Its deity, a ferocious form of Shiva's consort Parvati hewn from jet-black rock, presides over a modern shrine; the fragments of pedestals and pillars scattered over the forecourt date from a much older Kadamba structure.

Arambol (Harmal)

The largest coastal village in Pernem district, and the only one really geared up for tourism, is **ARAMBOL** (or Harmal), 32km northwest of Mapusa. If you're happy with basic amenities but want to stay somewhere lively, this might be your best bet. The majority of foreigners who stay here tend to do so for the season, and over time a close-knit expat community (of mostly ageing hippies who've been coming for years) has grown up, with its own alternative health facilities, paragliding school, yoga gurus and wholefood cafés.

②

Crime in Arambol: a warning

Ever since the psychopathic Czech serial killer Thomas Gross stabbed to death three fellow tourists on Lakeside beach in 1983, Arambol has been notorious for crime. Violent attacks are very rare indeed, but you should keep alert to the possibility of **theft**, which has become an everyday occurrence here in the season. Dozens of tourists have lost their passports and money in recent years (long sticks through the window grilles seems to be the usual ploy), so make sure your valuables are locked somewhere secure when you go out, particularly at night. Women should also be aware that incidents of sexual harassment are annoyingly common, notably at the weekends, when jeeploads of drinkers from outside the state hang around the beaches.

Modern Arambol is scattered around an area of high ground west of the main coast road, where most of the buses pull in. From here, a bumpy lane runs downhill to the more traditional fishing quarter, clustered under a canopy of widely spaced palm trees. The village's two **beaches** are beautiful and still relatively unexploited – thanks to the locals, who a few years back managed to block proposals put forward by a local landowner to site a sprawling five-star resort. The main one lies 200m farther along the lane the British contingent call "Glastonbury Street". Strewn with dozens of old wooden boats and a line of tourist café-bars, the gently curving bay is good for bathing, but much less picturesque than its neighbour around the corner.

To reach Paliem (aka "**Lakeside**" beach), follow the track over the headland to the north. Beyond a rather insalubrious smelling, rocky-bottomed cove, the trail emerges onto a broad strip of soft white sand hemmed in on both sides by steep cliffs. Behind it, the **freshwater Paliem Lake** extends along the bottom of the valley into a thick jungle. Hang around the banks of the murky green water for long enough, and you'll probably see a fluorescent-yellow human figure or two appear from the bushes at its far end. Fed by boiling hot springs, the lake is lined with sulphurous mud, which, when smeared over the body, dries to form a surreal, butter-coloured shell. The resident hippies swear it's good for you and spend much of the day tiptoeing naked around the shallows like refugees from some obscure tribal initiation ceremony – much to the amusement of Arambol's Indian visitors.

Practicalities

Buses to and from Panjim (via Mapusa) pull into Arambol every thirty minutes until noon, and every ninety minutes thereafter, at the small bus stop on the main road. A faster private **minibus** service from Panjim arrives daily opposite the *chai* stalls at the beach end of the village. **Boats** leave here every Wednesday morning for the ninety-minute trip to the flea market at Anjuna. Tickets should be booked in advance from the *Welcome Restaurant* by the beach (Tues–Sun 8–9am & 8–9pm; Rs150), which also rents out motorcycles (Enfields and 100cc Yamahas). The **post office**, next to the church, has a poste restante box. A couple of places in the village **change money**: Delight, on the east side of the main road, and Tara Travel, directly opposite, where you can also reconfirm and book air and catamaran tickets.

Accommodation

Standards of tourist accommodation in Arambol lag well behind the rest of the state, although there are signs of improvement, with a crop of new, family guesthouses beginning to appear on the south side of the village in **Modlo** and

Girkar waddos. The warren of narrow sandy lanes behind the north end of the beach, known as **Khalcha Waddo**, has a dozen or so places to stay, but – with the exception of those listed below – these are uniformally cramped and grotty.

Ave Maria House #22 Modlo Waddo ☎0832/229 7674 or 229 7724, ⓔavemaria@satyam.net.in. Arambol's largest guesthouse, offers good-value rooms, with or without bathrooms, and a sociable rooftop restuarant in a three-storey modern building. It's tricky to find: turn left on to a *kutchha* track where the main road through the south side of the village makes a sharp right bend. ❷
Famafa Khalcha Waddo ☎0832/229 2516–7, ⓔfamafa_in@yahoo.com. Large, ugly concrete place just off "Glastonbury Street"; popular with Israelis, and correspondingly rowdy, but it usually has vacancies and is very close to the beach. ❸
God's Gift House #411 Girkar Waddo ☎0832/222 9239. Variously priced, sizeable rooms, all tiled

and with comfortable sit-outs. Some also have living rooms and kitchens. A nice family and cheap rates. Marred only by the unsightly rubbish strewn around the communal well in front of it.
Ivon's Girkar Waddo ☎0832/229 2672. Immaculately clean, tiled rooms, all attached and fronted by good-sized balconies opening on to a well-groomed family compound. The pick of the bunch. ❷
Priya Modlo Waddo ☎0832/229 2661, ⓔzdmello@hotmail.com. Welcoming ten-roomed guesthouse, hidden away behind *Ave Maria*.
Residensea North end of the beach ☎0832/229 2413, ⓔpkresidensea_37@hotmail.com. Leaf huts crammed close together with minimal facilities and inflated rates. You pay for the location. ❸

Eating, drinking and nightlife

Thanks to its annually replenished pool of expatriate gastronomic talent, Arambol harbours a handful of unexpectedly good **restaurants** – not that you'd ever guess from their generally lacklustre exteriors. The village's discerning hippy contingent cares more about flavours than fancy decor, and prices reflect the fact that most of them eke out savings to stay here all winter. If you're on a really rock-bottom budget, stick to the "rice-plate" shacks at the bottom of the village. *Sheila's* and *Siddi's* tasty *thalis* both come with *puris*, and they have a good travellers' breakfast menu of pancakes, eggs and curd. *Dominic's*, also at the bottom of the village (near where the road makes a sharp ninety-degree bend), is renowned for its fruit juices and milkshakes, while *Sai Deep*, a little further up the road, does generous fruit salads with yoghurt.

Evenings in Arambol tend to revolve around the café-restaurants and whichever bar is hosting **live music**. Free jam sessions alternate between *Loeki's*, just off the lane leading to the beach ("Glastonbury Street"), on Sunday and Thursday evenings, and the *Mango Tree*, a little further up the same lane, on Tuesdays and Fridays. Standards vary with whoever happens to blow in, but there have been some memorable impromptu gigs held here over the past few seasons. Of the late drinking venues down on the beach, the Sudanese-run *Babylon* is the most enduring and closes only when the last punters have staggered home. Newcomer *Dreamcatcher* (see below) lays on occasional small party evenings with guest DJs.

On Sunday mornings, don't miss Axel and Lucie's **Indian classical concert** held at the *Double Dutch Café*, which starts around 11am. Drawn from the Kala Academy in Panjim, the musicians – normally sitar and tabla players – are professional players of a high standard.

Double Dutch Half-way down the main street on the right (look for the yellow signboard). Axel and Lucie's chilled café, spread under a palm canopy in the thick of the village, is the hub of alternative Arambol (viz their "Bullshit Info" notice board). Famous above all for its melt-in-the-mouth apple pie (possibly the best in the world), it also does a

tempting range of home-baked buttery biscuits, cakes, healthy salads and sumptuous main meals, including fresh buffalo steaks and proper nasi goreng.
Dreamcatcher South end of beach. Currently the most sophisticated shack on the strip, run by a team of cool young dudes from Delhi. They knock

up a range of tasty snacks and salads in the day, some main meals in the evening and host occasional small parties with guest DJs.

Fellini's Just off the lane as you approach the beach ("Glastonbury Street"). Italian-run restaurant serving delicious wood-fired pizzas (Rs80–140), and authentic pasta/gnocchi with a choice of over twenty sauces.

Relax Inn North end of the beach. Top-quality seafood straight off the boats and unbelievably authentic pasta (you get even more of the expat

Italians in here than *Fellini's*). Try the vongole clam sauce. Inexpensive.

Silver Sand Opposite Arambol chapel, on the south side of the village. Another deceptively ordinary streetside café whose charming owners, local couple Rufin and Santan, specialize in fresh seafood (including Chapora calamari), homemade pasta, ratatouille for vegans and popular chocolate cake, baked daily. The espresso's top notch, too, and there can be queues at breakfast for Rufin's homemade pineapple jam.

Sports and holistic therapies

Posters pinned to palm trees and café notice boards around Arambol advertise an amazing array of activities you can take part in during your stay, from sand surfing to reiki. A good place to get a fix on what's happening is the *Double Dutch* "Bullshit Info" corner, with email addresses and meeting details for just about everyone who does anything.

For the more adventurous, there's **paragliding** from the clifftops above Lakeside beach, run by a German outfit who've been here for several seasons. The cost of the flight includes all the equipment you'll need and full instruction. At the opposite end of the beach, an English expat called Douglas Rankin has **watersports** gear for rent, including kite buggies, boogie and sail-boards, and two-metre sandboards for speeding on the hard sand further south towards Mandrem. Everything costs Rs200–250 per hour. You can usually find Douglas at the *Dreamcatcher* or on the beach somewhere – look for his kites.

Each season, an army of holistic therapists also offer their services and run courses in Arambol, making this a great place to learn new skills. Look out for Iyengar-qualified **yoga** teacher Sharat (ⓦ www.hiyogacentre.com), who holds five-day classes on the beach (Rs1000). Prospective students usually have to sign up by Wednesday lunchtime. For reiki and massage, contact Lucie and her colleagues at the *Double Dutch Café*.

Terekol

North of Arambol, the sinuous coast road climbs to the top of a rocky, undulating plateau, then winds down through a swathe of thick woodland to join the River Arondem, which it then follows for 4km through a landscape of vivid paddy fields and coconut plantations dotted with scruffy red-brick villages. The tiny enclave of **TEREKOL**, the northernmost tip of Goa, is reached via a clapped-out car ferry (every 30min from 6.30am to 9.30pm; 5min; Rs2–3) from the hamlet of Querim, 45km from Panjim. Before you reach the jetty, however, keep your eyes peeled for a turning on the left (marked with white painting on the road surface), which leads across the fields to a gorgeous beach, backed by firs.

After the long and scenic drive, the old **fort** that dominates the estuary from the north bank of the Arondem is a bit of an anticlimax. Hyped as one of the state's most atmospheric historic monuments, it turns out to be little more than a country house marooned on a lonely, sun-parched hillside, with the red-dusty smokestacks of the giant USHA iron-ore complex smouldering in the background. The fort was built by the Maharathas at the start of the eighteenth century, but taken soon after by the Portuguese, who held on to it more or less continuously until they were ousted by Nehru in 1961. Nothing much of any importance ever happened here, except in 1825, when the liberal Goan governor general, Dr Bernardo Peres da Silva, used it as a base for an armed insurrection against the Portuguese – the first of several such rebellions. The governor's own troops mutinied at the eleventh hour, however, and were massacred by their colonial overlords. Thereafter, Terekol disappeared into obscurity until 1954, when a band of Goan Gandhi-ites (*satyagrahas*) hoisted an Indian tricolour over the ramparts in defiance of Portuguese rule.

If your visit coincides with the arrival of a guided tour, you may well get a chance to look around the gloomy interior of the **Chapel of St Anthony**, in the fort's claustrophobic cobbled square; at other times it's kept firmly locked.

Practicalities

The few visitors who venture up to Terekol tend to do so by motorbike or taxi, heading back at the end of the day to the relative comfort of Calangute or Baga. If you run out of fuel, it's useful to know that the nearest **petrol station** is at Arambol, though be warned that it frequently runs out of gas and closes. One of GTDC's daily tours from Panjim (see p.73) comes up here, as does one daily Kadamba **bus** from the capital; alternatively, the 7am bus from Siolim pulls in at the Querim ferry an hour later.

Accommodation is offered at the recently revamped *Fort Tiracol* (℡0832/226 8258; ❾), the Goan equivalent of a Spanish parador. Designed by the owners of the *Nilaya Hermitage* and Sangolda lifestyle gallery at Saligao (see p.139), it comprises seven rooms, all sparsely decorated in traditional ochre and white, with wrought-iron furniture and gorgeous Indian textiles. Rooms start at Rs4015, which includes full-board for two people. For the best of the views, climb up to the "lounge bar" (open to non-residents), on whose terrace you can enjoy authentic Goan cooking and what must rank among the finest seascapes in southern India.

If you're staying at the *Fort Tiracol*, you should be offered the use of their guest boat to cross the river. Otherwise jump on the **ferry**, although be warned that at low tide it isn't able to clear the sandbanks, in which case you can either backtrack 5km east down the main road to a second and more dependable ferry crossing, or else negotiate a price to be taken over by one of the boatmen who hang around the jetty.

Travel details

For details of services on the new Konkan Railway, which runs through northeastern Goa, see p.82.

By bus

Arambol to: Mapusa (every 30min; 1hr); Panjim (12 daily; 1hr 45min).
Baga to: Calangute (every 15min; 5min); Candolim (every 15min; 15min); Panjim (every 15min; 45min).
Calangute to: Panjim (every 30min; 40min).
Candolim to: Panjim (every 15min; 30min).
Mapusa to: Anjuna (hourly; 30min); Arambol (12 daily; 1hr 45min); Baga (hourly; 30min); Bicholim (hourly; 1hr); Calangute (hourly; 45min); Chapora (every 30min; 30–40min); Mumbai (24 daily; 14–18hr); Panjim (every 15min; 25min); Pernem (6 daily; 1hr 45min); Vagator (every 30min; 25–35min).

By ferry

Betim to: Panjim (every 15min; 5min).
Querim to: Terekol (every 30min, except at low tide; 5min).

South Goa

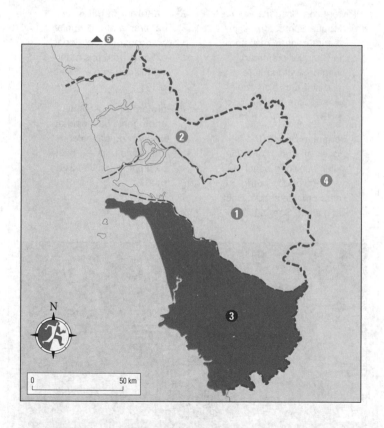

CHAPTER 3 # Highlights

✳ **Colonial architecture, Margao** Preserved in the region's main market town are streets of charismatic Portuguese-era houses and churches. **See pp.178–181**

✳ **Menezes-Braganza House** Sumptuous eighteenth-century mansion in Chandor crammed with original furniture and antiques from the Portuguese heyday. **See p.187**

✳ **Benaulim beach** The loveliest stretch of a 25-kilometre-long beach, where wooden outriggers provide shade. Best at sunset. **See p.198**

✳ **Usgalimal** Venture deep into Goa's sparsely populated southeast to see these prehistoric rock carvings, etched on to a laterite riverbank. **See p.190**

✳ **Chandranath Hill** A panorama of the whole of the lush Salcete coast extends from this magical hilltop temple. **See p.191**

✳ **Palolem** An irresistibly photogenic bay, backed by swaying palms and Thai-style huts – a backpackers' paradise. **See p.207**

3

South Goa

Arriving by plane at Dabolim airport, just outside the industrial city of **Vasco da Gama**, first impressions of south Goa can be unpromising. Once clear of the terminal, a parched laterite plateau stretches inland, scarred by the chimney stacks, agro-chemical plants and workers' slums of the Mormugao peninsula. Only after dropping down the flank of the headland towards the coast does the palm canopy reassert itself, spreading southwards in a lush belt that's edged by a magnificent expanse of shimmering sand and surf.

The string of resorts and luxury hotel complexes lining 25-kilometre-long **Colva beach** marked the southernmost limit of tourism in Goa until a decade or so ago, when travellers started to explore the hilly coast beyond the **Cabo da Rama** headland. Crossing the *cabo* at **Karmali Ghat** (see p.xii), a superb vista opens up ahead over the tops of the cashew bushes to reveal a succession of exquisite sandy bays, sheltered by the forested slopes of the Sayadhri hills. The most beautiful of them all, **Palolem**, has over the past decade become a fully-fledged backpackers' playground, attracting a greater number of tourists than anywhere else in the south.

With **Colva**, formerly the region's principal resort, patronized by domestic rather than foreign tourists, the European charter enclave has shifted south to **Cavelossim** and the farthest extremity of Colva beach, **Mobor**. In between, **Benaulim** remains a pleasantly uncrowded village with a distinctively Christian-Goan atmosphere, despite the recent appearance amid its paddy fields of large Mumbai-owned time-share complexes. Even at the height of the season locals still well outnumber visitors and there's plenty of space on the vast beach, making this an ideal first footfall if you've just stumbled off the plane.

A ten-minute drive inland from Benaulim, south Goa's main market and transport hub is **Margao** – district headquarters of Salcete *taluka* – from where metalled roads fan west to the coast and east across fertile farmland to the Zuari River. Scattered over the plain around the town are dozens of picturesque villages, many harbouring colonial-era **country houses**. These, together with Margao market and the magical hilltop **Chandranath temple**, provide the main focus for day-trips inland.

Staying in south Goa, you'll soon grow familiar with the distant wail of the **Konkan Railway** trains trundling up and down the coast. The line, completed only in 1997, has done more than anything else to transform the complexion of this formerly remote region, bringing ever increasing numbers of visitors from the Indian metropolises – now an easy overnight journey away. With this new influx have come big developers' bucks and a new lease of life for the large-scale luxury resort hotels that punctuate the coastline. Staying in one of

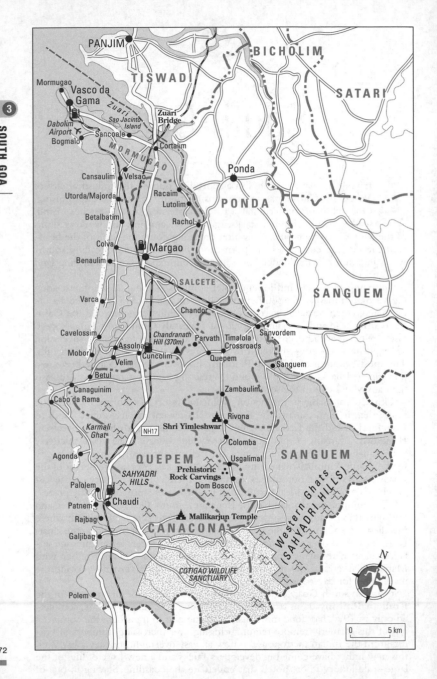

PANJIM

TISWADI

BICHOLIM

SATARI

Mormugao

Vasco da
Gama

Zuari

*Sao Jacinto
Island*

**Zuari
Bridge**

*Dabolim
Airport*

Sancoale

Cortalim

Bogmalo

MORMUGAO

Ponda

PONDA

Cansaulim

Velsao

Racaim

Utorda/Majorda

Lutolim

Betalbatim

Rachol

Colva

Margao

Benaulim

SALCETE

Varca

Chandor

SANGUEM

Cavelossim

Assolna

*Chandranath
Hill (370m)*

Parvath

Timalola
Crossroads

Sanvordem

Mobor

Cuncolim

Quepem

Sanguem

Velim

Betul

Canaguinim

Zambaulim

Cabo da Rama

*Karmali
Ghat*

NH17

Shri Yimleshwar

Rivona

Agonda

QUEPEM

Colomba

*SAHYADRI
HILLS*

Usgalimal

SANGUEM

Palolem

**Prehistoric
Rock Carvings**

Patnem

Chaudi

Dom Bosco

Rajbag

Mallikarjun Temple

Galjibag

CANACONA

Western Ghats
(SAHYADRI HILLS)

*COTIGAO WILDLIFE
SANCTUARY*

Polem

N

0   5 km

③

these, you'll be sharing the poolside with Maharashtran industrialists and honeymooning dot-com couples from Bangalore, in addition to the more familiar blend of German, Scandinavian and British sun seekers.

Vasco da Gama

VASCO DA GAMA (commonly referred to as "Vasco"), 29km by road southwest of Panjim, sits on the narrow western tip of the Mormugao peninsula, overlooking the mouth of the Zuari River. This strategically important site was first acquired by the Portuguese in 1543, and by the end of the century was one of the busiest ports on India's west coast. When the city of Old Goa was threatened by the Maharathas in 1685, its women, children and noncombatant men were moved here and interned for safe-keeping in **Mormugao fort**, erected on the top of the headland to control the movement of ships in the estuary. Today, the bastion lies deserted and in ruins, but the modern town that spills around the bay to its east continues to prosper. A large proportion of Vasco's 150,000-strong population are immigrants from neigh

Dabolim airport

Dabolim, Goa's only airport, lies on top of a rocky plateau, 4km southeast of Vasco da Gama. Although it has recently acquired a new terminal building, this run-down navy aerodrome is a far cry from the sophistication of Western airports, with the shells of old Russian military aircraft rotting outside camouflaged hangars, and construction workers and civilian ground traffic moving freely across the runway between flights. Less interesting are the immigration formalities, which generally take upwards of one hour as ranks of khaki-clad officials scrutinize, stamp and recheck passports and disembarkation slips.

In the **arrivals hall** you'll find the State Bank of India's equally slow **foreign-exchange desk**, which opens to meet flights but isn't entirely dependable. If you use it, ask for an encashment certificate and carefully count your notes and check their figures. From the hectic arrivals' concourse outside the main exit, tourists are whisked off by their reps to air-conditioned buses, while other travellers head for the pre-paid **taxi counter**. Fixed fares to virtually everywhere in the state are displayed behind the desk; pay here and give the slip to the driver when you arrive at your destination.

Facilities in Dabolim's first-floor **departures hall** include another pint-size State Bank of India (Mon, Tues, Thurs & Fri 10.30am–1.30pm, Sat 10.30am–noon), a sub post office and branches of several domestic airlines: Indian Airlines (daily 7.15am–2pm; ☎0832/251 2788), Sahara Airlines (daily 9.30am–5pm; ☎0832/251 0043) and Jet (daily 9.30am–5pm; ☎0832/254 0029 or 254 1354). There's a very ordinary and overpriced cafeteria, too, but it doesn't open in time for early morning domestic departures, so if you're looking for a filling breakfast, head across the road from the front of the terminal building to the staff canteen, where you can grab piping hot *bhaji pao* and *batata wada* for a few rupees. Finally, don't forget that if you're leaving Goa by international charter you may have to pay **airport tax** before checking in; check the current situation with your travel agent or tour operator when you purchase your ticket.

Anyone **visiting** the airport, or meeting arrivals, should note that a Rs20 visitor ticket (on sale at the hatch next to the main ground-floor exit) will buy you entrance to the foyer of the air-conditioned arrivals hall – worth paying to escape the heat and crowds outside.

bouring states. Drawn here by the prospect of employment in the town's iron-ore and barge-building yards, many end up living in the slum encampments that have grown over the past decade on the outskirts.

Dominated by the unsightly storage tanks of Hindustan Petroleum's oil refin-ery, Vasco is unremittingly drab, industrial and seedy (Goa's red light district lines the south of the town around Bainha Bay), and no place to spend time if you can help it. With the state's principal railhead now moved to Margao, the only conceivable reason you might end up here is by getting lost on the way to or from the airport. Apart from a browse around the small **bazaar**, crammed into the narrow streets northwest of the main square, there's absolutely noth-ing to see or do in the town. If you've time to kill, jump in a taxi or auto-rick-shaw, or rent a bicycle from the stall on the square, and head off to Bogmalo beach, 8km southeast.

Practicalities

Vasco is laid out in a grid, bordered by Mormugao Bay to the north and by the train line on its southern side. Apart from the cluster of oil storage tanks, the town's most prominent landmark is the **train station** at the south end of the main Dr Rajendra Prasad Avenue.

Thanks to its business city status, Vasco boasts a better-than-average batch of **hotels**. None see many foreign tourists and so do not hike their tariffs during the winter season. Of the budget places, the *Annapurna* (☎0832/251 3375 or 251 3715; ❷) on Dattatreya Deshpande Road is the most pleasant, with a good restaurant downstairs serving pure-veg South Indian and Punjabi-style *thalis*. If it's full, the recently renovated *GTDC Vasco Residency* (☎0832/251 3119; ❸), off Swatantra Path near the station, is the best fallback. The town's top hotel, complete with 68 air-conditioned rooms, plush bars, three restaurants and a courtesy coach to the airport, is *La Paz* (☎0832/251 2121, ☞251 3302, ⓦwww.hotellapazgardens.com; ❼) also on Swatantra Path. *La Paz* also has the swish Oriental restaurant, *Sweet and Sour*, serving a huge selection of Cantonese, Mandarin and Szechwan dishes; most mains are priced between Rs200–300.

Around Vasco da Gama

The industrial zone **around Vasco da Gama** is best avoided, but if you've time to kill en route to or from **Dabolim airport**, secluded **Bogmalo**, a short ride by taxi from the town centre, offers the closest beach. Heading east of the town towards the Zuari bridge and Panjim, you pass tiny **Sao Jacinto island**, its old Portuguese lighthouse poking above the canopy of coconut palms, and **Sancoale**, where the decaying fragment of a once massive Baroque church facade looms above the estuary's southern shore.

Bogmalo

Immediately south of the airport, the Mormugao peninsula's central plateau tumbles to a flat-bottomed valley lined with coconut trees. The sandy **beach** at the end of the cove, looking across the water to Sao Jorge island, is backed by a small resort that would have been a lot more picturesque were it not for the multi-storey five-star perched above it. Even so, compared with Calangute or Colva, **BOGMALO** is still a small-scale, relaxed holiday centre, with only a

Diving at Bogmalo

Bogmalo has a British-run dive school, which is one of the few places in India where you can do PADI-approved Open Water diving courses. Operating out of *Joet's Guest House*, at the far end of the beach, Goa Diving also offers guided dives to shipwreck sites and coral beds off the coast, and tuition for more advanced qualifications. The only potential drawback of diving here is the visibility, which fluctuates wildly from 25m to 2m. Prices range from Rs1500 for a one-tank guided dive, to Rs15,000 for the three-day PADI Open Water course. For more information, contact Goa Diving, House #145P, Chapel Bhat, Chicalim, near Bogmalo (☎0832/255 5117 or 255 5036).

handful of family-run hotels – the majority of them given over to British charter companies. Screened from the nearby industrial complexes by steep, green cliffs, the sand is clean and not too crowded, the water safe for swimming, and there are plenty of places to eat, drink and shop. Lying a stone's throw from Dabolim airport, it's also a convenient place to overnight if you're catching an early morning flight.

You'd have to be desperate for ways to kill time – or else exceptionally interested in aviation and marine warfare – to find much inspiration in the **Naval Air Museum**, at the top of the hill above Bogmalo (Tues–Sun 10am–5pm; Rs10), which details the history of the Indian Fleet Airarm with a motley collection of old jet aircraft dating back to the late 1940s.

Practicalities

As this is primarily a package tourist destination, walk-in **accommodation** is very limited and best booked ahead. Top of the range is the *Bogmalo Beach Resort* overlooking the cove (☎0832/255 6222, ℱ255 6236, ℮bbppr@goa1.dot.net.in; ❾), which offers formula five-star luxury, with all the trimmings, including a pool, gym and a large sun terrace. The hotel recently came under new management (for the third time in five years), whose only discernible impact has been on the prices: a double, with mandatory full board, at peak season will set you back Rs4000 per night. A stone's throw up the beach, *Sarita Guest House* (☎0832/255 5965, ℮www.goaorigin.com/saritas-guesthouse; ❺) is altogether more humble and much better value for money, with well-furnished, comfortable rooms and a terrace bar-restaurant. You're more likely to find a vacancy here than at nearby *Joet's* (☎0832/255 5036; ❺), which is invariably block-booked by charter companies. Non-residents are welcome to eat in their breezy restaurant, though, which serves excellent seafood and hosts popular local crooner "Newton" on Friday evenings after sunset. A kilometre or so inland, *Coconut Creek* (☎0832/255 6100; ❺) is a relative newcomer that gets rave reviews, for both its accommodation and its restaurant. Comprising ten double-storey chalets grouped around a pool, with hammocks strung between the trees, the well-shaded complex is run with great efficiency and style by British-Goan owners, Lynne and Nello.

The two remaining places to stay lie just outside Bogmalo, next to the naval base on the top of the hill. The longer-established of the pair is *Vinny's* (☎0832/255 5170; ❹–❺), a comfortable, efficient and friendly hotel that's popular with package tourists. The other good place is the *Raj Resort* next door (☎0832/255 5177, ℱ251 8854; ❹–❺). Run by a very hospitable Rajasthani owner, its rooms are spacious, light and clean, and the ground floor has a Mughlai-style restaurant with carved wood furniture, brass hookah pipes, curios and comfy cushions.

What Bogmalo lacks in places to stay it makes up for in **bars** and **restaurants**. Most of the places dotted along the beach depend on a steady trickle of refugees from the *Beach Resort*, and have whacked up their prices accordingly. The *Full Moon Kneipe*, outside the main hotel entrance, takes the lion's share of the overspill. Its menu of mainly seafood and chicken dishes, including locally caught tiger prawns and lobster, is predictably expensive, and the portions are not overly generous, but no one seems to mind. The *Sea Cuisine* opposite offers identical dishes and prices, but tends to be less crowded at lunchtimes. Further up the beach, *Joet's*, decked out in cheerful blue-and-white mosaic, occupies a prime spot and serves succulent, moderately priced seafood from its breezy terrace. Served on a gorgeous pool-side terrace, *Coconut Creek's* cuisine has a more international flavour, with live music and weekly salsa dance displays.

The north shore of Mormugao

Connecting Dabolim with Panjim, the road hugging the rocky south bank of the Zuari estuary is many visitors' first taste of Goa. Few people bother to break the journey along it, but the shoreline shelters a string of colonial landmarks dating from the earliest phase of Christian settlement in Goa. Behind them, lost in a dense tangle of undergrowth, lurk a handful of caves; pre-historic artefacts unearthed in them have indicated that this northern rim of the Mormugao peninsula was inhabited more than five thousand years ago.

Sao Jacinto

Connected to the shore by a causeway, **SAO JACINTO**, a wooded islet 7km east of Vasco da Gama, is marked by a picturesque whitewashed **chapel**, whose stone steps double up as a landing stage for the island's tiny population of *toddi* tappers. Beginning at the hamlet just beyond it, you can follow a path through the trees to a clearing at the top of the hill, presided over by another small **church** whose gable, nosing above the trees, is visible from the main road. An old **lighthouse** stands at the opposite end of the clearing from where the track drops down to Sao Jacinto village: an easy round walk of fifteen to twenty minutes.

Sao Antonio and Sancoale

A little over 1km further west along the coast road sits another tiny islet, **Sao Antonio**, joined to the shore by a narrow isthmus of land. Time your visit to coincide with low tide on Sunday afternoon and you'll be treated to one of the great spectacles of the Zuari, when hundreds of locals gather to forage for clams (*tisreo* in Konkani), submerged up to their waists in muddy water. As befits all the best Goan get-togethers, Sao Antonio's Sunday **clam hunt** is accompanied by much drunkenness and shouting. Afterwards, everyone sloshes home along the road to cook up their haul in a big *pulao*, flavoured with stone-ground chilli *rechad* and *toddi* vinegar.

When Jesuit missionary priests first reached Goa in 1560, their landfall lay a little way west of Sao Antonio at the hamlet of **Sancoale**. This historic occasion was commemorated with the construction of a magnificent church, **Nossa Senhora de Saude** (Our Lady of Health), completed in 1566 on the site of an earlier Hindu temple. Only a fragment of the facade is left standing, a fire having destroyed the rest of the building in 1834, but it's a supremely elegant chunk, embellished with decorative panels and fancy plaster work typical of early Christian-Goan architecture. Early morning is the best time to visit, when the monument's contours are picked out in shadow, lending to it a forlorn air. A red Archeological Survey sign flags the turning off the main road.

The sinking of the Ehrenfels

Mormugao Bay, the natural harbour at the mouth of the Zuari estuary, was the scene of one of the most bizarre and audacious episodes of World War II, immortalized in the Hollywood film *Sea Wolves*, starring Roger Moore and Gregory Peck, and by James Leasor's rip-roaring account, *The Boarding Party* (see "Books" in Contexts, p.331).

Following the outbreak of hostilities in 1939, one Italian and four German ships made a dash for Goa – at that time the nearest neutral port in the Arabian Sea. The vessels anchored in Mormugao harbour, safe in the knowledge that the Allies would not dare jeopardize their cosy relationship with Portugal by making an armed attack. While most of the Axis crews sat out the last years of the war on board ship, the radio operator of the 7752-ton *Ehrenfels* was kept busy with a transmitter hidden in the engine room, broadcasting details of Allied shipping movements to U-boats prowling the coast. This information, gleaned from an extensive network of agents all over India, was causing catastrophic losses for the Allies: 46 ships were sunk in the Arabian Sea in less than six weeks.

Eventually, the British traced the transmissions to the *Ehrenfels*, but were unable to intervene because of a potential political backlash (it was feared that any discovery of Allied troops in Goa might be deemed a violation of the colony's neutrality, provoking the Portuguese to side with Germany). The solution to this dilemma, devised by the top-secret Special Operations Executive (SOE), reads like a script from an old Ealing comedy. The five Italian and German ships were to be stolen or sunk by a team of veteran civilians recruited from the ranks of the Calcutta Light Horse, a gentlemen's regiment that was more a social club than a fighting unit. If captured, these men – a motley crew of middle-aged company directors, accountants, tea planters and jute merchants – could feasibly claim the raid was a drunken prank conceived while on leave in the Portuguese territory.

After a crash course in basic commando skills, the fourteen men were dispatched by train to Cochin, on the southwest coast of India. There they met up with an SOE officer and a plastic-explosives expert who, together with a hastily assembled Bengali crew, had sailed from Calcutta in an old mud dredger called *Little Phoebe* – the only seaworthy tub not already requisitioned by the British navy. Meanwhile, another member of the Calcutta Light Horse was covertly organizing diversions that would lure the German crews ashore on the night of the attack. These included a ritzy reception at the Portuguese governor's residence for the officers, and, for the rest of the crews, a week of complimentary hospitality in Mormugao's brothels, paid for by the British secret service.

The raid went off smoothly. As *Little Phoebe* chugged into Mormugao Bay during the small hours of March 9, 1943, its crew, clutching Sten guns and with faces blackened, could hear music and raucous laughter drifting across the water. Using long bamboo ladders, they crept aboard the *Ehrenfels* and began to dismantle its anchor chains. However, the Germans, who had been half expecting an assault, set off incendiary devices and kerosene bombs. During the ensuing commotion, valves in the ship's sides were opened and its holds flooded, though not before the raiders had destroyed the radio room. Keeping close to the shore to avoid the Portuguese search lights, *Little Phoebe* slipped out of the harbour, as the five Axis ships burned in its wake, having been scuppered by their crews.

Newspaper reports the next day claimed that German and Italian sailors had set fire to their own ships in desperation at their internment in Goa. No one knew the true cause of the sinkings until years later. Four of the Germans involved in the *Ehrenfels* incident raised enough money after the war to salvage their old ship and retired in Goa on the proceeds. One, known to everyone in Panjim simply as "Fritz", married a local woman and opened a clock and camera repair shop in the capital, where he worked until his death in 1997.

Margao

MARGAO (sometimes spelt **Madgaon**), the capital of prosperous Salcete *taluka*, is regarded as Goa's second city, even though it's marginally smaller than Vasco da Gama, 30km northwest. Surrounded by fertile farmland, the town has always been an important agricultural market, and was once a major religious centre, boasting a university with a library of ten thousand books, and dozens of wealthy temples and *dharamsalas* – however, most of these were destroyed when the Portuguese absorbed the area into their *Novas Conquistas* during the seventeenth century. Today, Catholic churches still outnumber Hindu shrines, but Margao has retained a markedly cosmopolitan feel, largely due to a huge influx of migrant labour from neighbouring Karnataka and Maharashtra.

If you are only in Goa for a couple of weeks and fancy a taste of urban India, a morning here should suffice. Clogged solid with slow-moving streams of auto-rickshaws, clapped-out buses, Ambassador cars, bicycles and handcarts, the town centre – a hotch-potch of 1950s municipal buildings and modern concrete blocks – simmers under a haze of petrol fumes and dust. The main reason most foreign visitors brave this melee is to shop in Margao's excellent **market**. While you're here, it's worth making a short rickshaw ride north to visit the **Church of the Holy Spirit**, in the heart of a run-down but picturesque colonial enclave, which is regarded as one of the finest specimens of Baroque architecture in Christian India.

The Town

For many travellers, what appeal Margao may have is frequently eclipsed by the lure of magnificent Colva beach, 6km west. But the town can be a pleasant place to wander around, at least once you've escaped the mayhem of the main square, the **Praça Jorge Barreto**. On its south side, facing the park, stands the stalwart **Municipal Building**, a red-washed colonial edifice erected in 1905 that now houses the town library.

The congested streets south of the square form the heart of Margao's **bazaar**. Most of the action revolves around a labyrinthine covered market, where you'll find everything from betel leaves and sacks of lime paste, to baby clothes, incense, spices and cheap Taiwanese toys heaped on tiny stalls. When the syrupy thick air in here gets too stifling, explore the streets around the market, among which is one given over to cloth merchants and tailors. Also worth checking out if you're looking to have clothes made is the excellent little government-run **Khadi Gramodyog** shop, on the main square (near the *Kamat*), which sells quality hand-spun cottons and raw silk by the metre, as well as ready-made traditional Indian garments.

The dusty square south of the covered market is the site of a small Shiva **temple** and is an atmospheric place to hang out at evening *puja* time, when local Hindus file past rows of flower *wallis* and beggars, sitting cross-legged on the floor, to leave offerings of coconuts and garlands at the shrine. If you're lucky, you may also catch an itinerant snake charmer putting his fangless cobras through their paces.

The Largo de Igreja

A five-minute rickshaw ride north of Praça Jorge Barreto up busy **Rua Abbé de Faria** (named after the Goan founder of modern hypnotism) lie the dishevelled remnants of Margao's colonial quarter. Once, this leafy suburb of colour-washed houses and tree-lined avenues must have been a peaceful enclave;

MARGAO

▲ Kadamba Bus Stand, Panjim & Ponda   ▲ Pilar, Lutolim & Ponda

0 ——————— 100m

BATISTA CANE RD

MASCARENHAS RD

"Seven Gables" House

Largo de Igreja

Church of the Holy Spirit

A V LOURENÇO RD

CALÇADA DE NOSSA SENHORA DE PIEDADE

Monte Hill

J.N. DE ALBUQUERQUE RD

BERNADO DA COSTA RD

ABBE DE FARIA RD

Hospital

Damodar Temple

PRIMITIVO HOSPICIO RD

RUA DA FATRE MIRANDA

Vibes

AV. CONCEIÇÃO

B P DA SILVA RD

DE PINTO RD

❶ ★ Paulo Travels (Hampi bus)

Confident Books

DA COSTA RD

RAFFAEL PEREIRA RD

N

Head Post Office

Ⓐ The Ghodge's

Poste Restante

Bus Stand

Excellency Tailor

Ⓑ @ Cyber Inn

Ⓒ

M. MENEZES RD

MIGUEL LOYOLA FURTADO RD

Praça Jorge Barreto

Khadi Shop

Bank of Baroda

❷

HDFC Bank

Ⓓ ★ Buses for Colva & Benaulim

Municipal Building

Music Shop

Ⓔ

LUIS MIRANDA RD

MARTIN DIAS RD

❸ ⓘ

Bazaar

Hindu Pharmacy

RUA DE CONSTANCIO ROQUE DA COSTA

IGNACIO DE LOYOLA RD

State Bank of India

Bobcards

Ⓕ

'T' Corner

RUA DA SAUDADES

Gandhi Market

Ⓖ

STATION ROAD

ACCOMMODATION

GTDC Mareao	
Residency	**3**
Nanutel	**1**
Woodlands	**2**

RESTAURANTS & CAFÉS

Banjara	**C**
Bombay	**F**
Gaylin	**A**
Kamat	**D**
Longuinho's	**E**
Shahi Darbar	**G**
Tato	**B**

BHARATKA HEGDE DESAI RD

Old Train Station (disused)

◀ Mumbai

◀ Vasco da Gama

◀ Colva & Benaulim

Train Station, Karnataka & South India ▶

▶ Quepem

▼ Karwar

nowadays, however, raucous traffic pours through on the main Panjim and Ponda roads, shattering the serenity of its central square, the **Largo de Igreja**.

Surrounded on three sides by some of the city's oldest houses, the square is dominated by the majestic **Church of the Holy Spirit (Espirito Santo)** (daily 6.30am–noon & 4–9pm), built in 1565 on the site of an ancient Hindu temple. This act of desecration, perpetrated by the infamous temple buster Diogo Rodrigues, Captain of Rachol Fort, must have enraged the local gods, for the first chapel erected here had to be rebuilt on several occasions after it was burned to the ground by marauding Muslims. The present structure, one of the finest examples of late-Baroque architecture in Goa, dates from 1675, by which time the Jesuit seminary founded next door had been moved to a safer spot at Rachol. Forming a striking contrast with the brilliant red exposed brickwork of its side and rear walls, the church's pristine white facade is flanked by a pair of square towers, crowned by domes. The **interior**, entered via a door on the north side, is equally impressive, with an elaborately carved reredos dedicated to the Virgin Mary, a gilded pulpit and an ornate stucco ceiling. As you leave, look out for the peacock motif moulded onto the wall of the north transept. Art historians claim this auspicious Hindu symbol, vehicle of Saraswati, the goddess of purification and fertility, was deployed to inspire awe among new converts as they filed into church.

The monumental **cross** in the middle of the square, standing in the shade of a giant mango tree, also dates from the late seventeenth century. Mounted on a wedding-cake-confection pedestal, it is carved with images from the Easter story, among them Judas' bag of blood money, a cockerel and a crown of thorns.

"Seven Gables" (Sat Banzam Gor)

Five minutes' walk northeast of Largo de Igreja, on the main Ponda road, stands one of Goa's grandest residences, **"Seven Gables"**. Originally the *palacio* sported a row of seven typically Goan high-pitched gables (whence its Konkani name, *Sat Banzam Gor*, which means "seven shoulders"). Now, only three of these remain, but the mansion – commissioned in 1790 by Sebastião da Silva, emissary and private secretary of the Portuguese viceroy – is still an impressive sight. Casual visits are not encouraged, but no one will mind you photographing the exterior from the roadside.

The house's red Rococo-style facade is beautiful, with oyster-shell windows, wrought-iron balconies and decorative scrollwork highlighted in limewash. If you're lucky enough to gain entry, you'll see Seven Gables' sweeping staircase, halfway up which stands a private chapel dedicated to St Anna, evocatively illuminated by a pair of side windows set at 45 degree angles. The da Silvas were among the first families in Goa permitted to celebrate Mass in their own home, so this oratory is an historical monument in its own right. Look out, too, for the painted terracotta busts framed by Classical pediments lining the stairwell – a feature lifted from seventeenth-century houses like the Costa Frias *palacio* in Candolim (see p.130). Upstairs, airy salons with suspended slatted wooden ceilings are dripping with Bavarian glass chandeliers, silverware and Chinese porcelain, as well as beautiful antique furniture, much of it imported from Bombay. One particularly opulent room also features some elaborate murals imitating red-and-gold brocaded damask wallpaper, offset by a black-and-white marble floor.

Monte Hill

For the best **views** of the town, head up the Calçada de Nossa Senhora de Piedade (Our Lady of Mercy), which winds from the hectic crossroads east of

Largo de Igreja to the top of **Monte Hill**. The small chapel overlooking the clearing at the end of the lane is always locked, but the fine views over Margao and Salcete's sand-fringed coastal plain – a solid swathe of palm forest broken by open patches of green paddy – make this ten- to fifteen-minute walk worthwhile. Blot out the modern concrete apartment blocks on the northern edge of town, and you can easily imagine what the old quarter, whose shaggy gardens and red-tiled rooftops spread from the foot of the hill, must have looked like two or three hundred years ago.

Practicalities

Margao's train station, the only stop in Goa for most long-distance express services on the Konkan Railway, lies 3km east of the centre. Several of the principal **trains** that pull into Margao do so at unsociable times of the night, but there's a 24hr information counter (☎0832/271 2790) and a round-the-clock, pre-paid taxi and auto-rickshaw stand outside the exit. Taxis to Benaulim cost Rs150, and Rs75-100 for an auto-rickshaw (not recommended as the road is bumpy in places). For details on ticket reservations, see "Listings" on p.182.

Arriving on long-distance government **buses,** you can get off either here or (at a more leisurely pace) at the main **Kadamba bus stand**, 3km further north, on the outskirts of town. This is also the departure point for interstate services to Mangalore, via Chaudi and Gokarn, and for services to Panjim and north Goa. If you're just passing through Margao, local private buses can whisk you off to Colva and Benaulim from in front of the *Kamat Hotel*, on the east side of Margao's main square. Paulo Travel's deluxe coach to and from Hampi departs from a lot next to the *Nanutel Hotel*, one kilometre or so south of the Kadamba bus stand on Padre Miranda Road.

GTDC's **information office** (Mon–Fri 9.30am–5.30pm; ☎0832/222 2513), which sells tourist maps and keeps useful lists of train and bus times, is inside the lobby of the GTDC *Margoa Residency*, on the southwest corner of the square.

Accommodation

With Colva and Benaulim a mere twenty-minute bus ride away, it's hard to think of a reason why anyone should choose to **stay** in Margao. If you do get stuck here, however, the safest choice is the GTDC *Margao Residency* (☎0832/271 5528; ❹), a comfortable mid-range place that recently had a major facelift. Just around the corner on Miguel Loyola Furtado Road, *Woodlands* (☎0832/272 1121; ❸) is a notch less pricey, but correspondingly more popular and rarely has vacancies. The only other commendable place in town is the swish *Nanutel* (☎0832/273 3176, ☎273 3175; ❺–❻), north of the main square on Padre Miranda Road. Pitched at visiting businessmen, it has 55 centrally a/c rooms and a small pool.

Eating and drinking

After a browse around the bazaar, most visitors make a beeline for *Longuinho's*, the long-established hang-out of Margao's English-speaking middle classes. If you are on a tight budget, try one of the South Indian-style pure-veg cafés along Station Road. A couple of these, notably the *Bombay Café*, open early for breakfast.

Banjara De Souza Chambers ☎0832/272 2088. This swish basement restaurant is the classiest North Indian joint outside Panjim, specializing in rich Mughlai and tandoori dishes. Tasteful wood and oil-painting decor, unobtrusive *ghazaal* background music, imported liquors and slick service. Most main courses around Rs100.
Bombay Café Station Road. Popular with office

workers and shoppers for its cheap veg snacks, served on tin trays by young lads in grubby cotton uniforms. Handy pitstop for the market.

Gaylin Behind Grace Church. Smart, air-conditioned Chinese restaurant serving a good selection of Cantonese and Szechwan dishes (mostly steeped in hot red Goan chilli paste). Count on around Rs175–250 for three courses; extra for drinks.

Kamat Praça Jorge Barreto, next to the Colva/Benaulim bus stop. The town's busiest *udipi* canteen, serving the usual South Indian selection, as well as hot and cold drinks. More hygienic than it looks, but *Tato* up the road is cleaner.

Longuinho's Opposite the *Tourist Hostel*, Luis Miranda Rd. Relaxing, old-fashioned café serving a selection of meat, fish and veg mains, freshly baked savoury snacks, cakes and drinks. The food isn't up to much these days, and the old Goan atmosphere has been marred by the arrival of satellite TV, but it's a pleasant enough place to catch your breath over a beer.

Shahi Darbar Station Rd. As its name implies, this is the place to come for meaty Muslim food. The traditional chicken biryanis (Rs40), scooped up with piping hot *rotis*, are fantastic.

Tato Tucked away up an alley off the east side of the Municipal Gardens square. The town's brightest and best South Indian café serves the usual range of hot snacks (including especially good samosas at breakfast time, and masala dosas from midday on). A bit cramped, but well worth the effort to find.

Listings

Banks Money-changing facilities are available at the State Bank of India (Mon–Fri 10am–2pm, Sat 10am–noon), off the southwest side of the square; the Bobcards office in the market sub-branch of the Bank of Baroda, on Station Road, does Visa encashments. However, transactions in both of these can be time consuming, and it is invariably quicker to change money at Paramount Travels (see "Travel agents" below), although the rates are not always as good. There's also a handy cash-point machine (ATM) at the HDFC Bank in Lorenz Mall, on the west side of Praça Jorge Barreto.

Books The Confident Bookstore, on Abbé de Faria Rd, stocks a reasonable range of fiction, and lots of (cheap) Indian editions of computer manuals.

Cashew nuts The only place we've come across in Margao that sells export-grade Zantye's cashew nuts – the best brand available – is The Ghodge's, Shop #2, Varde Valaulikar Rd, near *Gaylin* restaurant.

Dentist Dr Hubert Gomes, Ground Floor, Reliance House, nr Blue Theatre, opposite IDBI Bank and Global Trust Bank ☎0832/271 4370 or 273 6827.

Internet access CyberInn, behind Grace Church, is conveniently central; Klik, ten-minutes' walk east of the market on Station Rd, has a cheap ISDN connection, but can get very busy in the evenings.

Music shops Margao's best-stocked CD and cassette shop is *Vibes*, ten-minutes' walk north of the main square off Abbé de Faria Rd; the shop is actually on Custodio Pinho Rd, left off the main drag (as indicated by a signboard). If they don't have what you're looking for, VP Sinari's, on the first floor of a new mall on the east side of the square (near the *Mabai Hotel*), probably will. For cheap Konkani and Hindi pop compilations, check out the stalls in the market. Hoffner and Gibson copy guitars, mandolins and other Indian-made musical instruments are on sale at Pedro Fernandes & Cia, in the bazaar on Station Road (look for the sign above a doorway; the shop is up a flight of steps at the rear of the building).

Petrol Margao's main petrol pump is on the west side of the Praça Jorge Barreto.

Pharmacy Hindu Pharmacy, on J Ignacio de Loyola Rd, is the largest in town, with a huge range of traditional ayurvedic and homeopathic medicines, in addition to Western allopathic ones.

Photography Nowhere in Margao sells professional slide film, but you can have APS cartridges processed at the photography shop in the mall just next to *Longuinhos*.

Post office The GPO (Mon–Sat 9.30am–1pm & 2–5.30pm) is at the top of the Municipal Gardens, although its poste restante is in a different building, 200m west on the Rua Diogo da Costa.

Tailors Highly recommended by readers is Anthony Fernandes (aka "Excellency Tailor"), opposite *Tato* restaurant.

Tea An excellent range of top-quality Indian tea – an ideal, lightweight present to take home – is sold loose at 'T' Corner Tea and Coffee Merchants, Gandhi Market. Try their fine-grade Nilgiri orange pekoe.

Train reservations Located 3km east of town at the main train station, the Konkan Railway Company's reservation office (Mon–Sat 8am–4.30pm, Sun 8am–2pm) is divided between the ground and first floor; bookings for the superfast Rajdhani Express to Delhi are made at the hatch to the left of the main entrance. Tickets for trains to Mumbai, in particular, are in short supply

– so make your reservation as far in advance as possible, get here early in the day to avoid agonizingly long queues, and bring a book.

Travel agents Paramount Travels, at the Antonio Dias Building, next door to *Longuinhos* on Luis Miranda Rd ☎0832/273 1150 or 272 0112, ℻273 2572; Mon–Sat 9am–1.30pm & 3–6pm.

East of Margao

Dotted with wax-covered wayside shrines and whitewashed churches, the farming villages **east of MARGAO** form the eastern flank of Goa's Christian belt. Nestled among them are some evocative old colonial-era monuments that can be visited on day-trips from the coast. Stately-home hunters should head straight for **Lutolim**, in the northeast of Salcete *taluka*, where some of the state's most elegant old family houses languish behind rambling gardens. A short detour further east on the way takes you to **Rachol**, site of a sixteenth-century Jesuit seminary and a museum dedicated to Christian art. **Ponda**, Goa's main Hindu temple town, also lies just across the Zuari River from Lutolim, and is a worthwhile extension to this short foray north.

The area's remaining attractions are scattered to the southeast. Foremost among them is the famous Perreira-Braganza/Menezes-Braganza house at **Chandor**, renowned as Goa's most splendid mansion, whose subsiding walls harbour a horde of eighteenth-century antiques. With your own transport, it's possible to head further east into the hilly interior, taking in the Hindu temple at **Zambaulim** en route to **Rivona**'s ancient Buddhist hermitage and, still deeper into Sanguem *taluka*, the remote **prehistoric rock-art** site at **Usgalimal**. Alternatively, loop south from Chandor and round off the day watching the sunset from the top of **Chandranath Hill**, near Parvath, with its sixteenth-century Shiva temple and superb panoramic views over the coast.

Rachol

The Catholic **seminary** at **RACHOL**, 7km northeast of Margao, rises proudly from the crest of a laterite hillock, surrounded by the dried-up moat of an old Muslim **fort** and rice fields that extend east to the banks of the nearby Zuari River. During the early days of the Portuguese conquests, this was a border bastion of the Christian faith, perennially under threat from Muslim and Hindu marauders. Today, its painstakingly restored sixteenth-century church and cloistered theological college, one wing of which has recently been converted into a museum, lie in the midst of the Catholic heartland. The seminary itself harbours nothing you can't see on a grander scale in Old Goa, but is definitely worth a quick trip from the main road en route to Lutolim, 4km further north. Blue-painted Holy Family **buses** run here every hour or so from Margao's city bus stand, dropping passengers immediately below the church.

Rachol seminary

Rachol seminary was founded in 1580 by the Jesuits after its predecessor at Margao had been ransacked by the Muslims. The institution originally comprised a hospital and school for the poor, as well as the theological college; it also boasted India's third-ever printing press, installed by Father Thomas Stephens, the first Englishman to set foot in the subcontinent. During its 58 years of service, the press published sixteen books, including the *Christian Purana* (1616), the first translation of the Gospels into an Indian language (Maharathi).

Built in 1576 – and renovated several times since – the seminary's splendid **church**, dedicated to St Ignatius Loyola, is in excellent condition. Its richly carved and gilded main altarpiece, enlivened with touches of turquoise, cream and brown, features a uniformed figure of **St Constantine**, the first Roman emperor to convert to Christianity, and now revered as the protector of women against widowhood. Fragments of his bones, sent here from Rome in 1782, are enshrined near the main doorway, along with a small glass vial that originally contained a sample of the saint's blood. One reredos behind the altar holds a beautifully carved statue of the infant Jesus, found on the coast of Africa and brought to Goa by a Jesuit priest, who installed it in his church in Colva, where it was reputed to have miraculous powers until being moved to Rachol.

No visit to Rachol seminary is complete without a tour of the college proper. Knock at the doorway to the right of the church, and a guide will show you up a flight of stairs – lined with fragments of Hindu sculpture unearthed during the construction of the seminary – to a first-floor corridor. Punctuated by huge oyster-shell windows, this looks down onto a spacious courtyard whose paving stones conceal an ancient **water tank** – a remnant of the Shiva temple that formerly stood on the spot. You'll also be shown the seminarians' living quarters and wood-panelled studies, a library full of dusty leather-bound tomes in Latin and Portuguese, portraits of Goan bishops past and present, and old class photographs of Indian seminarians and their European teachers. Whereas the college used to open its doors to young men not intending to take up Holy Orders, today it prepares its pupils exclusively for the priesthood with a seven-year course in philosophy and theology.

Rachol's **Museum of Christian Art** (Tues–Sun 9am–1pm & 2–5pm; Rs5) was established in 1991 by the Indian National Trust of Architecture and Cultural Heritage and the Gulbenkian Foundation of Portugal, who financed extensive restoration of the building. Assembled in its light and airy ground-floor hall is a sizeable collection of antique Roman Catholic art objects, ranging from large silver processional crosses to pocket-size ivory ornaments, damask silk clerical robes and some fine wooden icons, mostly dating from the seventeenth and eighteenth centuries. Among the quirkier exhibits is a mobile Mass kit, designed for Goa's missionaries and peripatetic Jesuit priests.

Rachol fort

Before the evangelization of Goa during the sixteenth century, Rachol hill was encircled by an imposing **fort**, built by the Muslim Bahmani dynasty that founded the city of Ela (Old Goa). Taken from the Sultan of Bijapur by the Hindu Vijayanagars in the fifteenth century, it was ceded to the Portuguese in 1520 in exchange for military help against the Muslims. One hundred cannons once nosed over the battlements, but when, during the late eighteenth century, the borders of the territory were pushed back further east into the *Novas Conquistas* area, these were redeployed and the fort eventually abandoned. Today, the red-, yellow- and white-stone archway that spans the road below the seminary is the only fragment left standing. You can, however, follow the course of the old **moat** around the base of the hill, along with the resident herd of water buffalo.

Lutolim

Dotted around the tree-lined lanes of **LUTOLIM**, 10km northeast of Margao, are several of Goa's most beautiful colonial *palacios*, dating from the heyday of the Portuguese empire, when this was the country seat of some of the territory's

The stately homes of Goa

The **stately homes of Goa** are scattered throughout its rural heartland and along the coastal belt of Salcete. Most date from the early eighteenth century, when the Portuguese were raking off handsome profits from their African colonies and the gold and gemstone trade with Brazil. However, their owners were not generally Europeans, but native Goans: wealthy merchants and high-ranking officials who were granted land as golden handshakes. Kept afloat by rent from their estates, these families weathered the decline of the empire to emerge as a powerful aristocracy, frequently intermarrying to preserve their fortunes. Many, however, had their estates confiscated and parcelled out to former tenants after Independence in 1961. Deprived of their chief source of income, some now struggle to maintain their rambling properties, living in one wing and selling off heirlooms to pay for renovation work on the others. In such cases, donations from visitors for the upkeep of the buildings are gratefully received.

The architecture of Goa's eighteenth-century stately homes was heavily influenced by European tastes, while remaining firmly rooted in a strong vernacular tradition. The materials and construction techniques mostly originated in India: red laterite for the walls and pillars, and local wood, overlaid with curved terracotta roof tiles from Mangalore (Karnataka). Many of the sumptuous furnishings, luxurious to the point of decadence, were imported: fine porcelain and silk came from China, Macao and Korea, cut glass and mirrors from Venice, chandeliers from Belgium and Germany, and tapestries from Spain or Portugal. Some furniture was also shipped here, but most was fashioned by Goan craftsmen out of rare rosewood brought from Ceylon or Africa. Among the finest examples of the furniture-maker's craft – and a feature of most Goan mansions still – are the chapels used to celebrate Mass and important religious festivals. Looking more like giant cupboards than shrines, these elaborately carved **oratories** often contain gilded altars and ivory statues of saints.

The exteriors of the houses, too, incorporate several peculiarly Goan features. Most distinctive of these is the pillared porch, or **balcão**. Surmounted by a pyramidal roof and flanked by a pair of cool stone benches, this is where Goan families traditionally while away sultry summer evenings. In larger houses, the *balcão* opens onto a covered verandah that extends along the length of a colour-washed Classical facade, whose Rococo mouldings and pilasters are picked out in white. Another typical Goan trait, noted by the traveller François Pyrard in the early seventeenth century, is the use of oyster shells instead of glass for windows. The wafer-thin inside layer of the shells was cut into rectangular strips and fitted into wood frames to filter the glare of the Goan sun. Sadly, most have long been replaced by glass, but you'll still come across them from time to time in more traditional villages, where the art of oyster-shell window-making survives.

Goa's most famous stately homes are situated in Salcete *taluka*, but you'll also find villas in other areas, especially **Piedade** (Divar Island), **Candolim**, **Calangute** and **Anjuna** in Bardez, Benaulim, **Colva** and **Majorda**. While some (such as the grand Perreira-Braganza and Sara Fernandes houses in Chandor) welcome walk-in visitors, others (notably the Miranda and Costa family homes in **Lutolim**, and "Seven Gables" in **Margao**) can only be seen by appointment, arranged through your hotel or the local GTDC tourist office.

wealthiest gentry. Lying just off the main road, the village is served by eight daily buses from Margao, which drop passengers on the square in front of a lopsided-looking church. The cream of Lutolim's architecture lies within walking distance of here, nestled in the woods, or along the road leading south. However, with the exception of Ancestral Goa's showpiece *palacio*, you shouldn't turn up at any of them unannounced; visits have to be arranged in advance (see box above).

A commendable place to refuel if you're in the area is *Fernando's Nostalgia*, a Goa theme **restaurant** on the main Ponda–Margao road, just outside Lutolim. Decked out with azulejos and Mario Miranda-esque murals, it's crammed with heritage clichés but fun nonetheless, and the food is scrupulously authentic. On a palm-shaded garden terrace, you can tuck into chicken *cafreal*, *ambotik* and fiery *xacuti*. For veggies there's *choulis ros*, a filling kidney bean stew, and deliciously smoky *sanna*, steamed rice cakes flavoured with fresh *toddi*; most main courses are priced under Rs75.

Miranda house

A dirt track peels left off the road running west from Lutolim's church square to the **Miranda house**, hemmed in by high walls and a tangle of tropical foliage. One of Goa's oldest stately homes, it was built in the early 1700s but renovated at the end of the nineteenth century, when cast-iron balconies, mosaic floors and a cool inner verandah were added. The mansion's present owner, a direct descendant of its original occupants, is the famous Goan cartoonist Mario João Carlos do Rosario de Brito de Miranda ("Mario" for short), who lives here with his wife, a former princess from the Hyderabadi royal family. As this is a family home, it is **not open** to visitors.

In past centuries the Mirandas made their money through cultivating areca, the palm from which betel nut derives, and several spindly specimens still stand outside the house, silhouetted against its plain Classical facade; the front door is crowned with the Miranda coat of arms (presented by King Dom Luís of Portugal in 1871). Unusually for a double-storey Goan house, the salons, chapel, living rooms and bedrooms all lie on the ground floor, fronted by a deep verandah.

Salvador Costa house

The elegant **Salvador Costa house**, ten minutes' walk west of the church square, dates from the late eighteenth century and, fronted by a beautiful pastel-painted verandah, has retained a distinctly *fin-de-siècle* feel, with stained-glass windows and fading sepia photographs of family members hanging on the walls. Its most famous feature, however, is an opulent **oratory**, gilded from floor to ceiling and crammed with ivory statues and candles, which the resident Senhora Costa Dias opens for prayers at noon. Also worth a close look if you are lucky enough to be granted a visit (call in advance through your hotel or tourist office) are the delicate mosaic floors, the finely carved four-poster in the master bedroom, and some exquisite pieces of Cantonese porcelain on polished table tops and rosewood chests of drawers.

Roque Caetan Miranda house

The **Roque Caetan Miranda house**, which stands on the roadside two minutes' walk south of the main square (back towards Margao), was built in 1846, at the height of the family's feud with the Ranes. The grandparents of the present owners had to flee for their lives at one stage, but the house and its contents came through intact. These days, it is maintained by two middle-aged sisters and a brother from Bangalore, who have renovated the property to attract groups of charter tourists from the coast. This involves slapping lots of gloss paint on to the walls and, regrettably, over hitherto polished antique furniture. The finest pieces are to be found in the splendid first-floor salon, which also contains a couple of cut-glass chandeliers and family portraits.

Ancestral Goa exhibition

Billed as "a centre for the preservation of art, culture and environment", Lutolim's **Ancestral Goa exhibition** (daily 9am–6pm; Rs20), near the Big Foot Dance Floor, a short way east of the village on the Ponda road, turns out to be a well-meaning, but ultimately dull, model village. The aim is to show a cross-section of Goan village life as it was a hundred years ago, with different miniature houses representing the different occupations and social classes, from fisher folk and fruit-*wallis* in the market to the grand Portuguese colonial homes of the land owners. An additional attraction is a giant fourteen-metre sculpture of **Sant Mirabai**, which the site's creators, proudly quoting the *Limca Book of Records*, claim is the "longest laterite sculpture in India".

Of more interest are the thirty-minute tours of the owner's ancestral home, the **Casa Araujo Alvares** opposite the main entrance (same hours; Rs100). Although evidently stripped of most of its antique furniture and fittings, the interior conveys a sense of what life must have been like for the Goan aristocracy during the swansong of the Portuguese empire. On the ground floor you'll be shown a hole in the wall, just wide enough for a musket barrel, which guarded the approach to apartments where the family hid during the Rane revolts of the late nineteenth century. The rebel Rajput clan, forced south from Rajasthan in the 1700s, played an important part in the Independence movement, but dabbled in a bit of banditry on the side, terrorizing this wealthy corner of Salcete.

Chandor

Thirteen kilometres east of Margao, across the fertile rice fields of Salcete, lies sleepy **CHANDOR**, a scattering of tumbledown villas and farmhouses ranged along shady tree-lined lanes, many of which sport a layer of fine red dust from the iron-ore trucks that thunder through. Between the late sixth and mid-eleventh centuries, this was the site of ancient *Chandrapura*, capital of the Kadamba dynasty, which ruled Goa until its conquest by the Vijayanagars in 1367. Known to medieval Arab cartographers as Zindabar, the city declined when the royal court decamped to Govapuri on the Zuari River in 1017, and crumbled completely after a sound sacking by the ruthless Muslim warlord Ghiyas-ud-din Tughluq three hundred years later.

Excavations carried out in Chandor in 1921, and more recently in 1999, revealed traces of a pre-Kadamba settlement. Tucked away in the north of the village (1km east of the square), the foundations of an ancient Shiva temple, marked by a blue sign, are believed to date from the third or fourth century AD. Among the finds yielded by the latest dig here were a copper donatory plaque, contemporary with the temple – the oldest piece of text ever discovered in Goa – and numerous fragments of two-thousand-year-old pottery. These have been removed to the state archeological museum in Old Goa, but a solitary headless Nandi bull, garlanded and smudged with vermilion powder by local Hindus, still stands *in situ*.

Perreira-Braganza/Menezes-Braganza house

In addition to its uninspiring ancient remains, Chandor is famous in Goa for the huge stately home that sprawls across the south side of its church square. Fronted by a spectacular Portuguese-style facade, the Perreira-Braganza/Menezes-Braganza house is stuffed with old furniture, paintings and porcelain, and makes Chandor one of the most rewarding day-trip destinations in South Goa. Visitors generally travel here by taxi, but you can also get to Chandor by bus from Margao (8 daily; 45min). It's generally fine to turn up without an appointment, but to ensure someone from the family is in to receive you, phone ahead (℡0832/278 4227 or 9822/160009).

Although parts of the house date from the 1500s when its owners were Hindus, most were built after the Braganza family had converted to Catholicism in the eighteenth century. Two separate wings were originally commissioned to accommodate the two sons and their wives. When no male heirs issued from either marriage, sons-in-law were drafted in for the daughters and granted inheritance rights on condition they adopt the Braganza title (hence the double-barrelled names). Descendants of both branches of the family still occupy their respective sides of the house; the most frequently visited of these is the left (east) wing.

The east wing

When he lived here as a boy, Senhor Alvaro de Perreira-Braganza, the elderly owner of the mansion's **east wing**, was pampered by twenty servants. Nowadays, however, he and his niece, Sharmila, who generally shows visitors around, can barely afford to shore up the gaping cracks to the rear of the building that widen after each monsoon. The long double-storeyed facade at the front, by contrast, is still in fine shape. Twenty-eight windows, each with its own wooden balustrades (made with weather-resistant shipbuilding timber specially imported from Holland), flank the main entrance. These were reputedly designed to catch the balmy Zephyr breezes, but now allow clouds of red dust to blow in from the road and settle on the polished floors and furniture inside. Reached via a grand staircase, the top floor comprises a series of plush interconnecting salons, reception rooms, dining halls and the family's private chambers, ranged around a central courtyard; the ground floor, now empty, used to accommodate the kitchen and servants' quarters.

The grandest room in the house, if not in all of Goa, is the **Great Salon**, or ballroom. Sumptuous crystal chandeliers hang from its ceiling, decorated with floral motifs overlaid with a crisscross pattern of painted zinc netting. The walls are beautifully marbled to match the floor and upholstery. Prominent among the pieces of furniture here is a pair of stately high-backed chairs, bearing the family crest, which were presented to the Perreira-Braganzas by King Dom Luís of Portugal.

The remaining rooms contain eighteenth-century furniture, much of it made from local *seeso* (martel wood), lacquered or inlaid with mother-of-pearl by craftsmen from the nearby village of Cuncolim. You may, in addition, be shown the Perreira-Braganza's private **chapel**, among whose treasures number relics of the Cuncolim Martyrs, and, more precious still, St Francis Xavier's gold-and-diamond-encrusted fingernail. Retrieved from a local bank vault, this now occupies pride of place on the main altar.

No admission fees are charged for visits to this half of the house, but its owners gratefully accept **donations** (Rs50 per person is adequate) towards costly restoration of the property and its contents.

The west wing

The design of the mansion's **west wing**, belonging to the Menezes-Braganza family and also open to visitors, mirrors that of its neighbour. Lovers of antiques, in particular, will drool over its superb collection of Chinese porcelain. Other highlights include several seventeenth- and eighteenth-century portraits of family members on glass, a pair of large ceramic elephants and a set of four matching conversation chairs, housed in the library. The five thousand or so leather-bound (and worm-eaten) tomes shelved here were mostly collected by Luis de Menezes-Braganza (1878–1938), a famous journalist and freedom fighter, whose offspring also became involved in the independence struggle (the Menezes-Braganzas were one of the few wealthy Christian families in Goa to actively oppose Portuguese rule). Forced into exile in 1950, they returned twelve years later and were astonished to find their home untouched, although the property had lapsed into a state of disrepair from which it is only now beginning to recover.

Visits to this half of the house should be arranged through the owners of the other, east wing on the day. An admission payment is requested, but not at fixed rates so check in advance with Sharmila what the appropriate amount should be.

Fernandes House

An air of charismatic dilapidation hangs over the **Fernandes House**, on the south side of the village as you head towards Zambaulim. One of the oldest surviving *palacios* in Goa, its core is of pre-conquest Hindu origin, overlaid by later accretions. Sara Fernandes, the present owner, receives visitors in the wonderful **salon** that extends the length of the building's first floor, abutting a bed chamber containing its original, ornately carved four-poster. The mansion's most outstanding feature, however, lies on the ground floor, accessed via a sinister trap door through the bottom of a false cupboard. Hidden in the bowels of the building below, a narrow passage fitted with disguised gun holes was where the family used to shelter when attacked by Hindu rebels and bandits such as the Ranes. This portion, recorded in a series of accomplished architectural plans drawn up recently by local students, is believed to be five hundred years old. Like most wealthy land-owning brahmins in the region, the Fernandes converted to Christianity soon after the Portuguese conquest in order to preserve their influence and power, but never entirely relinquished their traditional notions of caste, which were preserved in the layout of the house. Centred on an enclosed courtyard, with private access to the river behind, the original Hindu structure remained the heart of the building long after the more ostentatious European-influenced additions eclipsed it.

Visitors are welcome to call on Sara Fernandes any day of the week, but should telephone in advance (℡0832/278 4245). A **donation** of around Rs50 per head is expected.

Zambaulim and Rivona

Two historically significant religious sites, one Hindu, the other Buddhist, lie in the district of Sanguem, hidden in the foothills of the Western Ghats. Neither is of more than passing interest, but the road that leads to **Zambaulim** and **Rivona**, winding through the picturesque Pareda valley, makes a pleasant detour from Chandor, 10km northwest. Self-reliant travellers with their own transport may also want to press on further south into Sanguem *taluka* to visit Goa's most enigmatic archeological site, the fairly recently discovered prehistoric rock-art site at **Usgalimal**.

Zambaulim

If you're travelling from Chandor, head east from the church square until you reach a right turn in the main road. After approximately 4km, this brings you out at Tilamola crossroads; go straight on here for 3km to **ZAMBAULIM**, site of the **Shri Damodar temple**, which stands to the right of the road below a dusty square. The precinct, an important Hindu pilgrimage centre, was rebuilt in the 1950s and 1960s, supplanting a typically Goan-style *devul*, or temple, with a polychrome concrete eyesore loosely inspired by the architecture of medieval Orissa in northeast India. The building may be modern, but its presiding deity, a manifestation of Shiva, is centuries old. The idol is also associated with a well-known legend in which the son of a wealthy local landowner and his bride were murdered on their wedding day by a gang of thugs hired by a jealous suitor. A temple was erected in Margao to mark the tragedy, but this was pulled down by the Portuguese to make way for their Church of the Holy Spirit. The *lingam*, however, was smuggled to this out-of-the-way spot, where it is still enshrined beside an image of Lakshminarayan.

Rivona

RIVONA, a small rice-farming hamlet 3km southeast along the road from Zambaulim, lies in the middle of nowhere and would be unremarkable if it weren't for a pair of rock-cut caves hidden in the wooded hills behind it. Nicknamed the **Pandava caves,** these served as cells for a small community of Buddhist monks in the seventh century and are buried in the forest outside the village, carved out of a slab of overhanging laterite. To find them, follow the road through Rivona until it sweeps into a sharp bend; a signpost marked "Shri Sansthan Gokarn" points left up a dirt track (accessible by motorbike) to the caves, which nestle in the shade of an old tamarind tree hung with strips of auspicious red cloth as votive offerings.

The main opening to the caves is at the bottom of the rock, next to a small stepped well and ablutions tank. Flanked by a sixteenth-century bas-relief of the Hindu monkey god Hanuman, this leads, via a low-roofed tunnel, to the cell on the upper level, although you're better off peering in from the opposite side as the excavations are pitch-black and infested with snakes.

Also worth a look while you're in Rivona is the **Shri Yimleshwar temple**, located on the edge of the village near the turn-off for the caves. The shrine, which houses an old *Shivalingam*, is architecturally undistinguished, but enjoys a picturesque situation, its olive-green and terracotta-red sanctuary tower rising from swathes of terraced rice paddy.

The Usgalimal rock carvings

In 1993, archeologists scouring sparsely populated Sanguem *taluka* for traces of prehistoric settlement hit the jackpot when villagers at **Usgalimal**, around 16km south of Rivona, told them of some mysterious rock carvings in the forest nearby. The team was led to a bend in the River Kushawati outside the village, where a gently sloping shelf of laterite was coated in a layer of mud swept downstream by the monsoon floods. When this was cleared away, it became clear the rock had been extensively carved with spirals, lines and images of bulls and human figures. At the time, no one knew quite when these enigmatic marks had been etched into the rock, but they are now thought to date from the Upper Paleolithic or Mesolithic eras, between twenty and thirty thousand years ago, which makes this one of the most important prehistoric sites in western India.

The ASI (Archeological Survey of India) has recently erected a signboard on the roadside to advertise the existence of the carvings at Usgalimal, which, although nowhere near as spectacular as the figurative rock art in southern France, aboriginal Australia or even central India, will nevertheless appeal greatly to anyone with even a passing interest in prehistory. If you are tempted to look for them, be prepared for a bit of an adventure: the site, hidden behind an old iron-ore mine, lies a fair way from the coast, along winding backroads that are punctuated with few settlements. The directions below, however, should get you there.

Coming from Chandor, ask for directions to the **Timalola crossroads**, on the main Margao–Sanguem highway, where you should head straight on towards Zambaulim and Rivona. From the latter, continue south and through the hamlet of **Colomba**, until you see the round, green and red ASI sign on the roadside. This points the way along a dirt track that skirts an ore heap and, later, a giant flooded pit, before dropping downhill towards a large areca plantation. The carvings can be seen on the uneven shelf of rock lining the near bank. If you're having trouble, ask a local for the *fatrar koree-lee cheetra*, "rock carvings" in Konkani.

Spread over an area of 500 square metres, the rock art comprises around one hundred distinct figures, mostly figurative depictions of animals – zebu bulls, bison, deer and antelope. Some show wound marks, or have spears and harpoons stuck in their sides; others are of the X-ray type, showing anatomical details. They must have been carved using tools made from flint, which is harder than laterite.

Alongside the animals are a number of less distinct human figures, the most impressive of which is a "dancing woman", shown with her left arm resting on her hip and her leg raised. Other female forms have small figures next to them which archeologists think represent placentas or babies.

The best-preserved and most striking of all the carvings, though, are the shapes dubbed as **triskelions** – circular mazes of seven concentric furrows, roughly 15cm wide and 2–3cm deep, centred on what could be symbolically rendered cobra heads. Dr P. P. Shirodkar, who led the team of archeologists who first rediscovered the site, has suggested it might have been used for time measurement (though he did not venture to suggest why the Usgalimal hunter-gatherers would have wanted to measure time). Just beyond it lies a small reservoir and metre-wide canal, which is thought to have been excavated to channel and collect excess water during the monsoon.

Parvath

In the far southeastern corner of Salcete *taluka*, the semicircular ridge of **Chandranath Hill** blisters out of the coastal plain, cloaked with deep green forest. The solitary **Shri Chandeshwar (or Bhutnath) temple** crowning it at **PARVATH**, 12km southeast of Margao on the main Quepem road, affords superb views from its 370-metre summit. A road winds up the north flank of the hill through a series of switchbacks to the shrine, revealing impressive glimpses of the Goan hinterland through the cashew trees. At the top, a vista of sand-fringed *toddi* forest, sprinkled with small villages, opens up to the west – a panorama at its most serene around dusk, when the sun sinks into the sea behind a haze of wood-smoke produced by the cooking fires on the plain below.

According to an ancient Sanskrit inscription, a temple has stood on this magical spot for nearly 2500 years, ever since a large meteorite landed here. However, the present building, dedicated to Shiva, is comparatively modern, dating from the late 1600s. The only part of the shrine that is definitely a vestige of the Vedic age is its cavernous inner sanctum, hollowed from a rock around which the site's seventeenth-century custodians erected a typically Goan-style structure, capped with a red-tile roof and domed sanctuary tower.

The road up Chandranath Hill peters out at a small car park just below Parvath, from where a long flight of steps (fashioned from discarded slabs of twelfth-century buildings) leads steeply up to the temple. Having paid the requisite penance in sweat, pilgrims arrive puffing and panting at the main entrance for *darshan*, or the ritual viewing of the god. Inside, a wild-eyed golden Chandreshwar deity, Shiva as "Lord of the Moon", stares out from an ornately decorated sanctum, wrapped in brocaded silk. His accessory deities, or *pariwar devtas* – medieval images of Shiva's consort and son, Parvati (west) and elephant-headed Ganesh (east) respectively, sculpted in stone – are housed in small niches to the rear of the shrine. This circumambulatory passage, which you should walk around in a clockwise direction, hugs the base of the boulder that forms the temple's heart.

Similar-sized chunks of rock are scattered around the dusty clearing outside, along with fragments of masonry from previous temples sited here, including a small **Nandi bull** that lies discarded among the rubble opposite the main entrance. The graffiti-splattered boulder to the south of the clearing can be climbed, and is a good place from which to admire the views west out to sea and south across the Assolna estuary to the Cabo da Rama headland.

Practicalities

You'll need your own **transport** to get to Parvath, as there are no buses up the hill and too little traffic for hitching to be viable. Travelling from Margao, look for a right turn across the fields about a kilometre beyond the main Chandor junction (marked by a yellow sign in Hindi).

Colva beach

Spectacular **COLVA BEACH**, 6km west of Margao, constitutes the longest unbroken stretch of white sand in the state, spanning 25km from the Mormugao peninsula in the north to Cabo da Rama (Cape Rama) in the south. Lined by a deep band of coconut plantations, it sweeps south to the horizon, seemingly empty save for an occasional rank of wooden outriggers or a fleet of trawlers bobbing in the middle of the bay. However, appearances from this distance are deceptive. Nestling under the lush tree cover is a string of fishing settlements and *toddi* tappers' hamlets, interconnected by a network of sandy tracks and lanes that feed onto a busy north–south highway. Over the past decade or so, several of these settlements have been developed for tourism, and now dozens of concrete hotels have displaced more traditional dwellings amid the dunes and open patches of rice paddy.

Colva, at the middle of the beach, is the area's main tourist trap, sucking in the lion's share of southern Goa's domestic tourist trade. Its rash of hotels and beach bars peters out further north, but erupts again at **Majorda**, where several luxury five-stars rise from the surrounding fields. Lying in the shadow of the ugly (and potentially lethal) Zuari Agro Chemical plant (see p.311), this top end of the beach is less appealing than the middle section south of Colva, where **Benaulim** holds plentiful budget accommodation, most of it overlooking unspoilt paddy and coconut groves. Further south still, the largely empty beach features a series of jarring cultural juxtapositions, as fishing settlements stand cheek-by-jowl with a string of mega-luxurious resorts. The most intrusive of these occur around **Varca**, **Cavelossim** and **Mobor**, where a long spit of soft white sand noses into the Assolna estuary, forming a natural border between Salcete and Quepem *talukas*.

Although a couple of **buses** each day run from Vasco da Gama along the coast road to Colva village (via Dabolim airport), the most straightforward way

Colva's miraculous "Menino" Jesus

Local legend has it that the statue of **"Menino" (or "Baby") Jesus** in the church of Igreja de Nossa Senhora de Piedade was discovered by a Jesuit missionary, Rev Father Bento Ferreira, in the mid-seventeenth century. The priest and his party had been shipwrecked off the coast of Mozambique and, having swum to safety, spotted a flock of vultures circling a stack of rocks ahead. The object of their attention was a statue of the baby Jesus, washed ashore after being dumped into the sea by Muslim pirates.

When Father Ferreira was posted to Colva in 1648, he took the statue, by now a minor miracle worker, with him. Installed on an appropriately grand altar, it quickly acquired cult status, drawing large crowds of devotees for the annual *Fama* ("fame") festival when the image was ritually exposed for public veneration. However, disaster struck following the suppression of the religious orders in 1836. Forced to flee, the Jesuits took the Menino with them to the seminary at Rachol (see p.184), along with a considerable hoard of jewellery and cash. Naturally, the villagers were furious and petitioned the head of the Jesuit Order in Rome for its return. When he pleaded "finders, keepers", they took their grievance to the viceroy, and, when that failed, to the king of Portugal, Dom João V, who promptly wrote to the governor general of Goa insisting the statue be sent back. It wasn't, however, so the disgruntled villagers gave up and commissioned a copy, which they adorned with a gold and diamond ring that had dropped off the original while it was being moved to Rachol. The old statue, meanwhile, mysteriously lost its powers, much to the chagrin of the Jesuits and the evident satisfaction of the inhabitants of Colva, who claimed its healing abilities had been concentrated in the ring and transferred to their replica.

Today, the mark-two Menino still cures the sick, who flock here every year on the second Monday in October for the *Fama* festival – the only time the image is removed from the church's triple-locked vaults. After being paraded in a solemn procession around the building, it is stripped of its finery and dipped in the nearby river, while pilgrims eagerly scoop cupfuls of the water for good luck. They then file past the statue, installed for the day on the high altar, leaving behind wax limbs, eyes, stomachs and other disembodied bits and pieces as petitions (these are later melted down by the priests, remoulded and resold). Among other religious souvenirs you'll come across if you're in Colva for the event are *medidas*, lengths of string the same height as the magical statue, which devotees believe contain a sample of its miraculous properties.

to approach Colva beach is through **Margao**, from where regular buses and a busy fleet of auto-rickshaws and taxis service most of the coastal settlements. Having found your feet, the best way to get around the area is by rented **bicycle**. The hard sand exposed at low tide supports heavy Indian cycles, allowing you to make the most of the hawker-free stretches between resorts.

Colva

A hot-season retreat for Margao's moneyed middle classes since long before Independence, **COLVA** is the oldest and largest – but least appealing – of south Goa's resorts. Its leafy outlying *waddos*, or wards, are pleasant enough, dotted with colonial-era *palacios* and ramshackle fishing huts, but the beachfront is dismal: a lacklustre collection of concrete hotels, souvenir stalls and fly-blown snack bars strewn around a bleak central roundabout. Each afternoon, busloads of visitors from out of state mill around here after a paddle on the crowded foreshore, pestered by postcard *wallahs* and the little urchins whose families camp on the outskirts. The ambience is not improved by heaps of rubbish dumped in a rank-smelling ditch that runs behind the beach, nor by the

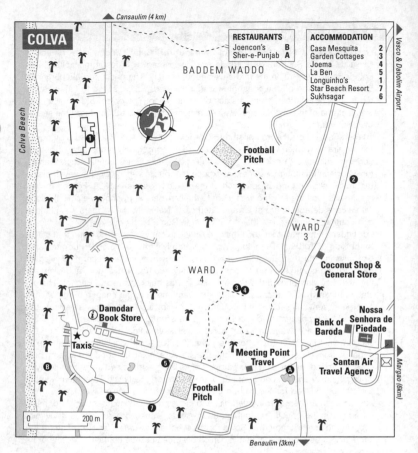

stench of drying fish wafting from the nearby fishing village. If, however, you steer clear of this central market area, and stick to the cleaner, greener outskirts, Colva can be just about bearable. Swimming is relatively safe (the local life-guards are more for show than anything else), while the sand, at least away from the beachfront, is clean.

Colva is nowadays better known for its beach than its parish church, yet the whitewashed **Igreja de Nossa Senhora de Piedade** ("Our Lady of Mercy"), founded in 1630 and rebuilt in the eighteenth century on the village square, houses one of Goa's most venerated cult objects: the miraculous statue of "Menino" Jesus (see box, p.193).

Arrival

Buses leave Margao every fifteen to thirty minutes for Colva (from outside the *Kamat Hotel* on Praça Jorge Barreto), dropping passengers at the main beach-front and at various points along the main road. The thirty- to forty-minute trip costs virtually nothing, but can be a real endurance test towards the end of the day when the conductors pack on punters like sardines. Far better to jump in an **auto-rickshaw** for Rs75, or squeeze into a shared **taxi**. Heading in the opposite direction, from Colva to Margao, these pick up passengers at the entrance to the beach, along the main road leading to the village, and from the crossroads 200m west of the church. The fare costs between Rs10 and Rs15, depending on the number of people the driver manages to cram in. Regular mini-van and Ambassador taxis line up on the north side of the beachfront, next to the public toilets, and outside several of the upmarket resort hotels, including the *Silver Sands* and *Penthouse*.

Accommodation

Colva these days attracts far more low-budget domestic visitors than foreign tourists, and accommodation standards have fallen drastically as a result. Aside from a handful of former hippy haunts in the relatively green and peaceful enclave of "Ward 4", and a couple of conspicuously upscale charter resort hotels dotted along the main road, it is genuinely hard to single out many places you'd want to spend time. Only a short drive away, Benaulim is far nicer and, on the whole, a lot cheaper, too.

Casa Mesquita 194 Vasco road, Ward 3 ☎0832/ 278 8173. Large rooms, with rickety four-poster beds (if you're lucky) but no fans or attached shower-toilets, in a fading old colonial-style house. Mosaic-floored verandahs add to the Old World atmosphere. A touch grubby, but cheap and full of period atmosphere. ❶–❷

Garden Cottages Ward 4 ☎0832/278 0776. Immaculately maintained, attractive budget guest-house in Colva's most tranquil quarter. Spacious en-suite rooms with fans, and a garden. Very popular and excellent value, so book ahead. ❷

Joema Ward 4. No phone. Established in 1973, which probably makes it the oldest guesthouse in Colva. They've since added four small and simple but scrupulously clean attached rooms around the back. Easy, friendly Goan family atmosphere, with kids and pigs charging around, and a relaxing café-restaurant from mid-November. ❷

La Ben On the beach road. ☎0832/278 8040, ℱ278 8105. Neat, clean, and good value at this price, though better known for its rooftop restau-

rant. ❸–❺

Longuinho's North of the beachfront ☎0832/278 8068, ℱ0832/278 8070, ⓔlbresort@goatelecom.com. Swish campus hotel with lawns opening on to the beach. Most rooms have a/c and sea views, and there's an in-house travel agent and foreign exchange desk. Good-value half-board deals. ❻

Star Beach Resort near the football ground. ☎0832/278 8166 or 278 0092, ⓔstarbeachresortgoa@yahoo.com. Spacious rooms in a new complex, with a large pool, Ayurvedic health centre and inexpensive a/c. Not such a great deal at the beginning of the season, but they only increase their rates by Rs100 over Christmas. ❻

Sukhsagar Opposite the *Penthouse* restaurant. ☎0832/272 1888, ℱ273 1666, ⓔsukhsagar@goatelecom.com. Nothing special from the outside, but its en-suite rooms are clean, light and airy, and the best deal in this price range. There's also a pleasant palm-shaded garden to relax in. Some a/c. ❺–❻

Eating and drinking

When the season is in full swing, Colva's beachfront sprouts a row of large seafood **restaurants** on stilts, some of them very ritzy indeed, with tablecloths, candles and smooth music. The prices in these places are top-whack, but the portions are correspondingly vast and standards generally high. Travellers on tight budgets are equally well catered for, however, with a sprinkling of **shack-cafés** at the less frequented ends of the beach, and along the Vasco road.

Joencon's Second restaurant south from the beachfront. The classiest of Colva's beach restaurants. Agonizingly slow service and pricey, but the food is superb: try their flamboyant fish sizzlers, mouthwatering *tandoori* sharkfish or Chinese and Indian vegetarian specialities.

La Ben's On the beach road. Pleasant rooftop restaurant in the guesthouse of the same name, with a predictable, moderately priced menu and

sea views. A good sunset spot.

Sher-e-Punjab Near the main crossroads, between the beachfront and church. Offshoot of the popular Panjim Punjabi joint, serving an exhaustive menu of inexpensive, deliciously spicy Indian food. Butter chicken is their signature dish, but there are plenty of tasty vegetarian options too, and their naan bread is possibly the best in the village.

Nightlife

Catering for an uncomfortable mixture of boozy Indian men from out of state and young European charter tourists, Colva's **nightlife** is less than enticing these days, despite the presence at the south end of the beach of Goa's few surviving "discos". *Splash* boasts a big MTV satellite screen and music to match, with a late bar and dance floor that livens up around 10pm. Less sophisticated than *Mambo's* and *Tito's* in Baga, however, it can be unpleasant for women.

Listings

Books Damodar Book Store, shop no. 4 on the beachfront, stocks a good selection of reasonably priced secondhand paperbacks in English. They will also part-exchange any books you've finished with, and have the best range of postcards in Colva. In addition, *Men Mar*, on the Vasco road, keeps a cabinet of well-thumbed paperbacks in a variety of languages, which they rent to travellers at fixed rates that cover a refundable deposit.

Foreign exchange Meeting Point Travel (see "Travel agents" below), or Bridge the World, next to the post office and church.

Motorcycle rental Along with Benaulim, Colva is the best place in south Goa to rent motorcycles. Ask around the taxi rank, or in front of *Vinson's Hotel*, where 100cc Yamahas are on offer at knock-down rates. Their owners will advise you to avoid Margao as the approach road passes the police post (see below).

Petrol Sold by the mineral-water bottle from a little house behind the Menino Jesus College, just east of *William's Resort* – the only fuel stop in Colva. The nearest bona fide petrol pump (one that sells unadulterated petrol) is in the middle of Margao, but don't be tempted to venture in unless you have a full international driving licence and your motorcycle's registration and insurance documents.

Post office Colva's sub-post office, opposite the church in the village, has a small but reliable poste restante box.

Travel agents The two most reliable agents in Colva are Meeting Point Travel (☎0832/272 3338, ℻273 2004), between *William's Resort* and the crossroads, and Sanatan Air Travel Agency, S-15 Sanzgiri Arcade, near Colva church (Mon–Sat 9.30am–7pm; ☎ & ℻ 0832/222 5876); both book and reconfirm domestic and international flights, and arrange deluxe bus and train tickets to other parts of India, including Hampi.

North of Colva

North of Colva, the sand stretches for 12km to meet the Mormugao peninsula, overshadowed by the pressurized storage tanks of Zuari Agro's giant fertilizer plant. Seepages from this complex, dubbed by Goan green groups as "an industrial time bomb", caused ground water pollution and the death of tonnes of fish here during the mid-1970s; its presence overlooking one of the world's most beautiful beaches is a continued source of controversy.

Another debate rages over the luxury hotels that loom above the dunes and well-irrigated paddy fields of **BETALBATIM**, **MAJORDA** and **UTORDA** villages, 4–7km north of Colva. Local environmentalists assert that the immense amount of water needed to maintain their lawns and swimming pools causes dry-season shortages for villagers. While the litigation cases against the hotel owners crawl through Goan courts, package tourists continue to flock here, along with yuppies from other states.

The presence of the big five-stars seems to have inadvertently shielded the area immediately inland from other kinds of development, with the result that once out of sight of the resort complexes, you find yourself in a pleasantly uncongested, traditional belt that will appeal greatly to anyone seeking peace and quiet within walking distance of the beach. Of the three, Betalbatim is the best bet for independent travellers, with a handful of well-furnished, more comfortable than average guesthouses in large family homes. The same village also harbours one of Goa's best restaurants, *Martin's Corner* (see opposite), famous for its delicate and tasty traditional Goan cuisine.

The other reason to venture up here is to hunt out the splendid old **palacios** belonging to the region's *Goenkars*, or landlords, built during the Portuguese era. None is open to casual visitors, but, as ever, nobody minds you admiring them from outside. At Betalbatim, next to the turning for *Nanu's Resort*, stands one of the grandest, the eighteenth-century **Casa Walfrido Antão**, whose yellow-washed facade boasts some fine oyster-shell windows, surmounted by particularly exuberant late-Baroque surrounds. The double-storeyed **Casa dos Piedade Costas** at Majorda, visible from the main road, is older still, dating from the early seventeenth century when the more austere, so-called "châ" ("plane") school of architecture predominated. Built in traditional style around a large inner courtyard, the house is entered via a side doorway, enabling the Portuguese ladies to pass and dismount from their palanquins without being seen. Attached to this is an early-seventeenth-century chapel, facing a well and an ornamental cross.

Another 4km north, midway between the villages of **Cansaulim** and **Velsao**, look for a low bridge under the railway, below which a lane leads west off the main road (marked by a blue sign for "Aldeia Dona Lina") and then veers north to the wonderful **Casa dos Roldão de Souza** (aka "Maison Rodesa"). Built at the beginning of the twentieth century, its handsome yellow, white and blue facade features unique window surrounds which, despite their misleadingly jazzy star-shaped arches, are thought to take their cue from sixteenth-century Manueline architecture. Like most of the old *palacios* in the area, this one is uninhabited these days, its owners having shifted to Margao, leaving the place to be looked after by an elderly retainer.

Practicalities

Transfer **buses** whisk newly arrived charter tourists from Dabolim airport to Betalbatim, Majorda and Utorda's resorts, but a couple of buses each day also run between Colva and Cansaulim, a busy village on the train line at the far north end of the beach. Fleets of shiny new Maruti-van **taxis** also hang around outside the big **hotels**. These luxury resorts cater for the lion's share of foreign visitors, although dotted along the approach roads to them are a string of smaller family-run places, mostly patronized by former package tourists returning for longer stays on smaller budgets.

For **eating,** head for the justly famous *Martin's Corner* **restaurant**, tucked away two minutes' drive off the main Colva–Vasco road (follow the sign just north of Betalbatim centre, or ask any cab driver). Ten years ago, Mrs Martin started out cooking no-nonsense fish curry, rice and chilli-fry for local taxi drivers, while their passengers were off eating inferior food for ten times the price in nearby hotels. The secret soon got out, however, and today she presides over one of the largest and most popular restaurants in the region, while her food remains superb. Seafood and chicken dishes are the speciality and the main reason to come here, though they also do a full menu of quality Indian, Chinese and continental dishes. Highlights include fish *caldin*, a superior version of UK curry house *korma*, and chicken *cafreal*, best enjoyed with a naan bread straight out of the oven. If you're splashing out, go for the lobster in garlic-butter sauce. It's open for lunch and dinner; no reservations necessary.

Accommodation

Coconut Grove Rabn Waddo, Betalbatim ☎0832/ 288 0123, ℱ288 0124, ⊚www.goacom.com /hotels/coconutgrove. Newest in this area's rank of ritzy resorts, with 35 rooms set amid lush lawns

right behind the beach, plus a pool. ⑥ **Kenilworth Resort** Majorda ☎0832/275 4180, ℱ275 4183, ℮kbrgoa@satyam.net.in. A five-star hotel stuck out on a limb, but lavishly refurbished under its new management, with 57 luxurious rooms and a huge new pool right behind the beach. ⑧

Majorda Beach Majorda ☎0832/275 4871, ⓕ275 4382, ⓔmbr.goa@rma.sprintrpg.ems .vsnl.net.in. One of India's most opulent resort hotels, boasting indoor and outdoor pools, tennis and squash courts, a sauna, health club, large sun terrace and billiards room. Peak season rates soar for walk-in clients, though they offer discounts for longer stays. ⑨

Manuelina House #4, Thond Waddo, Betalbatim ☎0832/273 0655. The nicest and homeliest guesthouse hereabouts, just behind *Ray's*, with very large en-suite rooms and an airy communal verandah. They also have a pleasant self-catering apartment, equipped with a small kitchen and spare bedroom. Very good value. ③–③

Nanu Resort Betalbatim ☎0832/270 1401–3, ⓕ273 4428, ⓦwww.nanuindia.com. Smart cottages set around lawns and an oblong pool, on one of the quieter stretches of the beach. Brace yourself for an ominous-sounding "Compulsory Christmas Dinner" if you're here then. Otherwise rooms from Rs2500. ⑧

Ray's Betalbatim ☎0832/273 8676. Four neat, airy rooms above a modern Goan family house. Well back from the beach, but easily accessible by road. Look for the signs before *Nanu Resort*. ③–③

Benaulim

According to Hindu mythology, Goa was created when the sage Shri Parasurama, Vishnu's sixth incarnation, fired an arrow into the sea from the top of the Western Ghats and ordered the waters to recede. The spot where the shaft fell to earth, known in Sanskrit as Banali ("place where the arrow landed") and later corrupted by the Portuguese to **BENAULIM**, lies in the dead centre of Colva beach, 7km west of Margao. Fifteen years ago, this atmospheric fishing and rice farming village, scattered around the coconut groves and paddy fields between the main Colva–Mobor road and the dunes, had barely made it onto the backpackers' map. Since the completion of the nearby Konkan Railway, however, large numbers of big-spending, middle-class Indians have started to holiday here in the luxury resorts and time-share apartment blocks which now line the outskirts. As a result, some of the village's *sossegarde* feel has been lost, but time your visit well (avoiding Diwali and the Christmas peak season), and Benaulim is still hard to beat as a place to unwind. The seafood is superb, accommodation and motorbikes cheaper than anywhere else in the state, and the beach breathtaking, particularly around sunset time, when its brilliant white sand and churning surf reflect the changing colours to magical effect.

Shelving away almost to Cabo da Rama on the horizon, the beach is also lined with Goa's largest, and most colourfully decorated, fleet of **wooden outriggers**, and these provide welcome shade during the heat of the day. Hawkers, itinerant masseurs and fruit *wallahs* appear at annoyingly short intervals, but you can usually escape them by renting a bike and pedalling south on the hard tidal sand.

Arrival

Buses from Margao, Colva, Varca, Cavelossim and Mobor roll through Benaulim every fifteen to thirty minutes, dropping passengers at the Maria Hall

Cobra warning

You'll rarely see a villager in Colva or Benaulim crossing a rice field at night. This is because paddy is prime territory for **snakes**, especially cobras. If you do intend to cut across the fields after dark, take along a strong flashlight, make plenty of noise and hit the ground ahead of you with a stick to warn any lurking serpents of your approach.

For more information on what to do if bitten see Basics, p.24.

Colva ▲   Airport & Vasco da Gama ▲

RESTAURANTS

Durigo's	A
Hawaii	G
Johncy's	B
Malibou	F
Palmira's	C
Satkar	D
Seshaa's	E

Bank of
Baroda

Pharmacy

GK Tourist
Centre

Cycle
Hire   Laundry

Taxis

Shacks

New Horizons
(Travel Agent)   General Store

Buffalo Plot

Shacks

*Lotus
Lake*

Prawn
Farm

MANZIL
WADDO

VAS
WADDO

Margao ▶

MARIA HALL CROSSROADS

ACCOMMODATION

Anthy's	4
Camilson's	1
Caphina	6
Carina	15
Caroline Guest House	8
Egee	17
Furtado's Beach House	3
L'Amour	7
Libra Cottages	12
Liteo Cottages	11
O Manqueiro	16
O Palmar	9
Oshin	14
Palm Grove	13
Paul Rina Tourist Home	10
Simon Cottages	5
Succorina Cottages	19
Taj Exotica	18
Xavier's	2

0   100m

JACK'S CORNER

Manthan Gallery

▼ ⑱ & ⑲   Cavelossim & Mobor ▼

crossroads. Ranged around this busy junction are two well-stocked **general stores**, a couple of locals' café-bars, a **bank**, **pharmacy**, **laundry** and the **taxi- and auto-rickshaw rank**, from where you can pick up transport 2km west to the beach, or back into Margao.

Accommodation

Aside from the unsightly time-share complexes and five-stars that loom in the fields around the village, most of Benaulim's **accommodation** consists of small budget guesthouses, scattered around the lanes 1km or so back from the beach. The majority are featureless annexes of spartan tiled rooms with fans and, usually, attached shower-toilets; the only significant difference between them is their location. The best way to find a vacancy is to hunt around on foot or by bicycle, although if you wait at the Maria Hall crossroads or the beach-front with luggage, someone is bound to ask if you need a room. Of the more comfortable mid-range places, the most desirable are tucked away north of the village in Sernabatim (technically in Colva, but within easy cycling distance).

Inexpensive

Anthy's Sernabatim ☎0832/277 1680, ℮anthysguesthouse@rediffmail.com. Technically in Colva, but one of the few places hereabouts actually located on the beach. Well-maintained rooms, with tiny bathrooms, breezy verandahs, in-house Keralan ayurvedic massage centre and the sea on your doorstep. ❸

Caphina Beach road ☎0832/271 0573. Nine spacious, spotless rooms with verandahs, in the middle of the village, five minutes' walk down the lane from the beachfront. ❷

Egee Vas Waddo ☎0832/277 0422. Half a dozen nicer-than-average budget rooms on first floor above a family house, in the quiet southern half of the village. ❷

Furtado's Beach House Sernabatim ☎0832/277 0396. Slap on the beach, with en-suite rooms and road access. Very popular, mainly with refugees from Colva's charter hotels, but a good fallback if nearby *Anthy's* is full.❸

Libra Cottages Vas Waddo ☎0832/277 0598. Standard budget place, but a bit brighter than usual, with a floor of economy options and a nice new house for rent around the back. Very good value. ❷

Liteo Cottages Opposite the tailor's shop, on the beach road ☎0832/277 0576. Very large, clean rooms (all en-suite and with balconies) in the centre of the village. Hardly the most inspiring location, but good value. ❸

O Manqueiro Vas Waddo ☎0832/277 0408. Dependable budget guesthouse in the secluded south of the village. Their best rooms (Rs250 per double) are in the recently constructed "Millennium" block, and have small balconies and new beds and mattresses – as opposed to rooms above the family house next door (Rs150), which are very basic indeed. ❷

O Palmar Opposite *L'Amour* ☎0832/277 1836–7, ℮opalmar@goatelecom.com. A row of slightly shabby sea-facing chalets, virtually on the beach, and with their own verandahs. Those at the rear are the most appealing, as they're not plagued by wind-blown rubbish from the beachfront. ❸

Oshin Mazil Waddo ☎0832/277 0069, ℮inaciooshin@rediffmail.com. Large, triple-storey complex set well back from the road, with views over the tree tops from the top-floor balconies. Spacious and clean, with en-suite bathrooms. A notch above most places in this area, and very good value.❸

Paul Rina Tourist Home Vas Waddo ☎0832/277 0591. Good-sized rooms, secluded balconies and attached shower-toilets in a modern house next to the beach road. A notch up from the standard budget places, and worth the little extra cost. If full, try the cheaper but equally pleasant *Caroline Guest House* (☎0832/277 0590) opposite. ❷

Simon Cottages Sernabatim Ambeaxir ☎0832/277 0581. Currently among the best budget deals in Benaulim: huge rooms, all with shower-toilets and sit-outs, opening on to a sandy courtyard in a secluded spot on the unspoilt north side of the village. ❷

Succorina Cottages House #1711/A, Vas Waddo ☎0832/277 0365. Immaculate rooms in a new-ish house, 1km south of the crossroads in the fishing village, with glimpses of the sea across the fields. You'll need at least a bicycle to stay here, but it's a perfect place to get away from the tourist scene. ❷

Xavier's Sernabatim ☎0832/277 1489, ℮jovek @goatelecom.com. Impeccably maintained rooms in small "resort", set very close to the beach amid a lush garden, although well away from the village. All rooms have private terraces. If they don't have vacancies, try the equally pleasant *Camilson's* (☎0832/277 1694 or 277 1696, ℮camilsons @hotmail.com) next door. ❸–❺

Moderate to expensive

Carina Tamdi-Mati, Vas Waddo ☎0832/271 0573, ℱ271 1400, ℮carinabeachresort@yahoo .com. This good-value, upmarket hotel lies in a tranquil location on the south side of Benaulim and has a pool, garden and bar-restaurant. Some a/c. ❻–❼

L'Amour On the beachfront ☎0832/277 0404, ℱ277 0578. Benaulim's longest established hotel is a comfortable thirty-room cottage complex, with terrace restaurant, travel agent, money-changing and some a/c. No single occupancy. ❸–❺

Palm Grove Tamdi-Mati, 149 Vas Waddo ☎0832/ 277 0059 or 277 1170, ℮palmgrovecottages @yahoo.com. Secluded hotel surrounded by beautiful gardens, with a luxurious new block around the back (Rs600–800), some a/c, a pleasant terrace restaurant and friendly management. A bike ride back from the beachfront, but by far the most pleasant place in its class. ❸–❺

Taj Exotica Cal Waddo ☎0832/270 5666, ℱ273 8916, ℮www.tajhotels.com. It's a sad reflection on the corrupt state of Goan politics that one of India's highest profile hotel chains was "allowed" to build this sprawling five-star complex slap on the last remaining empty stretch of Colva beach, in total violation of environmental laws. Its generator alone makes more noise and smoke than the combined population of nearby Vas Waddo, and the per-head water consumption required to keep the huge lawns and golf course going must approach that of the entire village. Doubles from around $220–430 per night (plus taxes). ❾

△ Boat at Benaulim

Eating and drinking

Benaulim's proximity to Margao market, along with the presence of a large Christian fishing community, means its **restaurants** serve some of the most succulent, competitively priced seafood in Goa. The best shacks flank the beachfront area, where *Johncy's* catches most of the passing custom. However, you'll find better food at lower prices in the smaller joints further along the beach, which seem to change owners and chefs annually; the only way to find out which ones offer the best value for money is to wander past and see who has the most customers: *Hawaii* is one that has maintained its high reputation over several seasons.

Durigo's 2km north of Maria Hall. This is the locals' favourite place to eat, serving traditional Goan seafood of a kind and quality you rarely find in the shacks: try their succulent barramundi (*chonok*), lemon fish (*modlo*) or mussels (*dzob*). Marinated in spicy, sour *rechead* sauce and pan-fried in ground millet, it's twice as tasty and half the price of anywhere else in the area, although some will find the no-frills, male atmosphere a bit off-putting – in which case, follow the example of the village's middle classes and order a takeout.

L'Amour On the beachfront and part of the hotel of the same name. Just about the slickest restaurant in Benaulim, serving an exhaustive multi-cuisine dinner menu (most main meals Rs80–150). With background noise limited to chinking china and hushed voices, it's also a relaxing place for breakfast: fresh fruit, muesli, yoghurt and pancakes.

Malibou On the lane leading south through Vas Waddo, near the *Palm Grove* hotel. Cosy little corner café-restaurant that's a popular late-night drinking spot. Attentive service, fresh seafood and

they have a *tandoor* to bake *pomfret*, kebabs and spicy chicken.

Palmira's Beach road. Benaulim's best tourist breakfasts: wonderfully creamy, fresh set curd, copious fruit salads with coconut, real espresso coffee, warm local bread (*bajri*) and smiling service.

Palm Grove At the hotel of the same name, Tamdi-Mati, Vas Waddo. Mostly Goan seafood, with some Indian and continental options, served in a smart new garden pagoda against a backdrop of illuminated trees. Not the cheapest place in the village, but many consider the atmosphere worth the extra.

Satkar Maria Hall crossroads. No-frills locals' *udipi* canteen on the crossroads that's the only place in Benaulim where you can order regular Indian snacks – samosas, masala dosas, hot pakoras and spicy chickpea stew (*channa*) – at regular Indian prices. And the *bhaji pao* breakfast here is a must.

Seshaa's Maria Hall crossroads. Local lads' café up near the crossroads. Gloomy and a bit cramped, but great for pukka Goan *channa bhaji* and, best of all, deliciously flaky veg or beef patties.

Listings

Bike rental Signs offering bicycles and motorbikes for rent are dotted along the lane leading to the sea: rates are standard, descending in proportion to the length of time you keep the vehicle. Worth bearing in mind if you're planning to continue further south is that motorbikes are much cheaper to rent (and generally in better condition) here than Palolem, where there's a relative shortage of vehicles.

Foreign exchange If you need to change money, the most convenient places are GK Tourist Centre and New Horizons, at the crossroads in the village centre, and the *L'Amour Beach Resort*, which in principal offers the same rates as Thomas Cook. With a Visa card, you can also make encashments at the Bank of Baroda (Mon–Fri 9.30am–2.30pm, Sat 9.30am–12.30pm), on Maria Hall crossroads. Otherwise, the nearest foreign exchange facilities are at Margao and Colva.

Internet access GK Tourist Centre, on the crossroads west of Maria Hall, has lots of machines and blissfully cool air-conditioning, but the connection

is slower than New Horizons opposite. Rates in Benaulim are pretty standard (around Rs40).

Lifestyle gallery Manthan, just south of Benaulim's Holy Trinity Church, on the main road in Mazil Waddo. Displayed to great effect in a recently restored Portuguese-era residence, its range of antique furniture, Christian art, pottery, sculpture and oil paintings is the finest in south Goa.

Petrol You can buy petrol, sold by the litre, from a table at the roadside, two minutes' walk south down the road leading to the *Royal Palm Beach Resort*, but it tends to be badly laced with solvent and smokes badly. The best place to buy is in Margao (see p.182).

Travel agents International and domestic flights can be booked, altered or reconfirmed at the highly efficient New Horizons (☎0832/277 1218, ☎0821 /277 0634, ✉dokl@goatelecom.com), opposite the GK Tourist Centre. They also have access to special train quotas on the Konkan Railway, although you have to book in person for these.

South of Benaulim

South of Benaulim, the main road, running parallel with Colva beach, passes through a string of small settlements dominated by outsize whitewashed churches. Bumpy back lanes peel west at regular intervals, winding across the rice fields to the fishing hamlets huddled in the dunes, and to the secluded luxury resort hotels that punctuate the beach. By the time you reach **Cavelossim**, gateway to the package enclave and trawler anchorage of **Mobor**, the palm cover has all but petered out, while the pale green profile of the Sahyadri Hills beckons to the southeast.

Unless you're booked into one of the big resorts or are following this more tranquil coast road south in preference to the hectic Margao–Chaudi highway (NH17), there's little reason to venture into the far southwest corner of Salcete *taluka*. Away from the beach, the scenery is flat and monotonous, and, once you've reached Cavelossim and Mobor, it's blighted by large hotel complexes.

Varca

The row of beached wooden fishing boats 2km south of Benaulim belongs to a community of Christian fishers at **VARCA**, whose palm-thatch shelters line the foot of the dunes. Of the tourists who pedal past, few stay longer than a couple of hours, crashed in the shade of an outrigger. The only blot on the otherwise unspoilt landscape around Varca is the clutch of luxury **hotels** proliferating amid the dunes. The most secluded of these is the *Resorte de Goa* (℡0832/274 5066, ℱ274 5310, ⓦwww.resortgoa.com; ❽), comprising 56 rooms and a small campus of chalets clustered around a pool and sun terrace, with two bars and two restaurants (for guests only). Further south, the palatial *Renaissance Goa Resort* (℡0832/274 5200–7, ℱ274 5225, ⓔitstimefor@renais-sancegoa.com; ❾), a member of the Marriott chain complete with Goa-themed atrium lobby, is an altogether more ostentatious affair, dominating the fields for miles. Facilities, which include one of only two casinos in Goa, are what you'd expect from an international-style five-star resort.

Cavelossim

CAVELOSSIM, 11km south of Colva, straddles the coast road and is the last major settlement in southwest Salcete. A short way beyond the village's picturesque church **square**, a narrow lane veers left (east) across an open expanse of paddy fields to the Cavelossim–Assolna **ferry crossing** (every 20min, with last departures at 8.30pm from Cavelossim and 8.45pm from Assolna; Rs2), near the mouth of the Sal River. Make the crossing at low tide, and you'll probably see scores of men wading up to their necks in the water, collecting clams, mussels and oysters from the river silt. The discovery that the bed of the Sal between here and nearby Betul was phenomenally rich in **shellfish** was only made a few years back. Present stocks are expected to last for another season or two, although the boom may be brought to a premature end if the Directorate of Fisheries presses ahead with plans to dredge the river for the benefit of trawler fishers.

A short way west of the main road near Varca, the *Hotel Dona Sa Maria*, in Tamborim Waddo (℡0832/274 5290 or 274 5673, ℱ287 1559, ⓦdonasamaria.com; ❺), is the most congenial place to stay hereabouts. It's a laid-back little place with helpful staff, a small pool, restaurant and friendly family atmosphere. In the dunes and salt pans nearby, a huge concrete arrow used to serve as target practice for the Indian navy's squadron of ageing fighter jets, but seems to have become redundant over the past couple of seasons.

Beyond the *Dona Sa Maria*, the road continues in the direction of the beach, where a huge resort and apartment complex, *Colonia José Menino* (T0832/222 4485, F222 5042, Ekylesai@goa1.net.in; ⑤), languishes in the dunes. Since several European charter companies pulled out of the venture, standards appear to have dropped and the rooms aren't all that well maintained. A much more cheerful option is the family-run guesthouse, *Mariner's Inn* (T0832/274 5732; ❸), which offers immaculate rooms and self-contained apartments.

Mobor

The tract of rolling dunes backing the southern limits of Colva beach come to an abrupt end at **MOBOR**. Tapering into the Sal estuary, this remote spit of sand serves Goa's largest concentration of purpose-built luxury resorts, pitched as much at wealthy Indian clients as northern European tourists. Great controversy attended the development in its early days, but the environmentalists seem to have given up trying to stem the rising tide of concrete, which now includes air-con shopping malls and fast-food outlets. Whatever the rights or wrongs of individual cases, few would deny that the sprawling campuses – complete with golf courses, enormous pools and, in one case, a monumentally kitsch mock sailing ship – do nothing to enhance the area's natural beauty.

Set against a backdrop of receding hills, the beach itself is largely screened from the resorts by the few surviving trees. A row of large shack restaurants and sun beds lines up beneath them, whose owners lay on firework parties on alternate nights in season to attract punters, but otherwise life here is mellow given the potential number of tourist beds in the area.

Accommodation

Dona Sylvia Mobor T0832/287 1321, F287 1320. A huge charter hotel with 176 rooms, including some two-storey cottages, grouped around a pool. Accused by environmentalists of destroying sand dunes to improve the view. Rooms from $240 per night. ❾

Gaffino's Mobor T0832/287 1441 or 287 1430, F273 0635. The smallest of Mobor's hotels is a friendly family-run place: sixteen immaculate rooms (with river views), and a small restaurant. Great value considering the cost of other accommodation in the area. ⑤

Haathi Mahal Mobor T0832/287 1101, F287 1139, Wwww.haathimahal.com. The newest and flashiest of Mobor's resorts is geared squarely for domestic tourists, although it does boast an "authentic Cornish pub". Tariffs start around Rs5700 per double. ❾

Holiday Inn Near the *Leela Palace*, Mobor T0832/287 1303, F287 1333, Wwww

.holidayinngoa.com. Formulaic four-star hotel with 170 luxury rooms and suites, two restaurants, a coffee shop, tennis court, gym and pool. Very near the beach. Rooms start at $140 per night. ❾

Leela Palace Mobor T0832/287 1234, F287 1352, Wwww.leelapalace.com. This massive resort is the largest and most luxurious hotel in the state, if not in all India. It's also the environmentalists' big green meany, accused of felling *toddi* trees, displacing locals, dumping sewage into the river and polluting ground water. Set amid 45 acres of gardens, facilities include seven multi-cuisine restaurants, a huge pool, casino and unrivalled sports facilities. Golf carts take you to your chalet. US$270–1400. ❾

Sao Domingo's Mobor T0832/287 1649, 287 1461 or 98221/68432, Wwww.saodomingosgoa .com. Spruce new place near the river, with fifteen large, light and pleasantly furnished rooms opening onto separate balconies. Good value. ⑤

Assolna

Turn left when you ride off the ferry, and a winding lane will lead you to the middle of **Assolna** bazaar, lining the main Margao–Karnatak highway. The village holds a well-preserved collection of colonial-era mansions; none are officially open to visitors, but you can view them from the roadside. The oldest, **Casa dos Costa Martins**, stands a short way south of the crossroads, where a side lane turns right at a 45-degree angle. Overlooking the junction from behind a tall screen of trees, the mansion is still occupied and well maintained. It's arranged around a square central courtyard, and preserves many features from the old Hindu patio house that must have preceded its conversion to a Christian *palacio* in the seventeenth century. The entrance doorway is particularly striking, surmounted by a peacock-tail fan made from oyster shells (*carepas*) – a typically Hindu motif.

Canacona taluka

Ceded to the Portuguese by the rajah of Sund in the Treaty of 1791, Goa's far south – **Canacona** *taluka* (from the Kannad for "forest full of bison") – was among the last parts of the territory to be absorbed into the *Novas Conquistas*, and has thus retained a distinctly Hindu feel: multicoloured *tulsi* plant pots stand outside its red-tiled village houses, while stray cows wander freely across the roads. The area also boasts some outstanding scenery. Set against a backdrop of the jungle-covered **Sahyadri Hills** (an extension of the Western Ghat range), a string of pearl-white coves and sweeping beaches scoops its indented coastline, enfolded by laterite headlands and colossal piles of black boulders.

The finest of them is **Palolem**, whose beautiful curved bay supports a tourist scene that's more full-on than anywhere else in south Goa. Opinion tends to be divided over whether the village has been irrevocably spoiled by the volume of visitors it receives these days, but the beach alone is worth the trip down here, especially at sunset time. A more peaceful alternative lies a twenty-minute ride drive north at **Agonda**, a village whose economy remains firmly rooted in its traditional fishing and *toddi*-tapping economy, despite the recent arrival of the **Konkan Railway**, which since 1997 has connected this formerly remote corner of Goa with Mumbai and south India by fast express trains. The region's other main transport artery is the NH17, which cuts through the middle of the district headquarters, **Chaudi**. Bus services between here and Margao are frequent; off the highway, however, bullock carts and bicycles far outnumber motor vehicles. The only way to do the area justice, therefore, is by motorcycle, although it's a good idea to rent one further north and drive it down here as few are available *in situ*.

Travelling south in a taxi or with your own transport, the best route to take is not the NH17 – a perilous undertaking even on quiet days – but the back-road winding along the coast via Assolna and the scruffy fishing settlement of **Betul**, from where an atrociously potholed road climbs a series of laterite headlands. The Portuguese carved out a border post on the tip of the most prominent of these, **Cabo da Rama**, the ruined ramparts of which provide fine views back up the coast.

Cabo da Rama

Cabo da Rama (Cape Rama), the long bony finger of land that juts into the sea at the south end of Colva Bay, takes its name from the hero of the Hindu epic, the *Ramayana*, who, along with his wife Sita, holed up here during his exile from Ayodhya – one of several such sacred sites in central and southern India. This one, however, is more grandiose than most, commanding spectacular views north over the length of Colva beach, and down the sand-splashed coast of Canacona. The easily defensible promontory was crowned by a **fort** centuries before the Portuguese wrested it from the local Hindu rulers in 1763. They erected their own citadel soon after, but this now lies in ruins, lending to the headland a forlorn, world's end feel.

A small coconut wholesaler stands close to the turning for Cabo da Rama on the coast road, 7km east of the village – look for the circular, green and red Archeological Survey signpost. If you're travelling by bus from Margao (4–5 daily; 1hr 30min), you'll be dropped outside the fort's **gatehouse**. Once inside, either turn right and scale the battlements, where a crumbling turret still houses a couple of rusty old Portuguese cannons, or else head straight on past the chapel, swathed in colourful bougainvillea bushes, towards the west end of the peninsula. Until 1955, the bastion housed a prison; now its only habitable building is a lonely government **observation post**, occupied from time to time by a couple of young scientists from Dona Paula's Institute of Oceanography, who are marooned here for weeks on end until a chopper swoops in to rescue them.

From the bungalow, a steep path passes through a gap in the boundary walls to a narrow ridge, eventually emerging from the wooded bluff beyond at the windswept tip of the cape. The sea views from this serene spot are superb, but be careful while clambering over the boulders stacked above the shoreline – a few years ago, a lad from the nearby village fell to his death here while hunting pigeons.

The one and only **place to stay** at Cabo de Rama is John Fernandes' bar (☎0832/267 6259; ②), 2km from the fort on the roadside. Facilities are very basic, but John and his wife are very welcoming hosts, serving mackerel hauled fresh from the sea each evening with hand nets.

Agonda

AGONDA can only be reached along the winding coast road from Assolna and Cabo da Rama, or by driving north for around twenty minutes from Palolem. No signposts mark the turning and few of the tourists that whizz past pull off here, but the beach is superb – albeit with a strong undertow that weak swimmers should be very wary of. Finding a patch of shade can be a problem, too, unless you head for the cluster of smooth brown boulders at the bottom end, beyond which the village's fishing fleet shelters in a sandy cove.

Agonda has not always been as tranquil as it appears today. In 1982, a dozen absentee landlords sold the palm groves behind the beach to a Delhi-based hotel chain, backed, according to rumours at the time, by the former PM Rajiv Gandhi and his (now-widowed) Italian wife Sonia. Construction work began soon after on the *Seema Hotel*, a luxury resort complex and eighteen-hole golf course, but soon floundered when local *toddi* tappers refused to vacate the plot, claiming the hotel would ruin their traditional livelihoods. The tenants even threatened to defend their land rights by force, and daubed a rock in the middle of the bay with the slogan: "Your tourists will never be safe here". The project was never completed. Embroiled in costly court cases, the developers eventually backed down (rumours at the time suggested Rajiv's business partner "diverted funds") and left a huge unfinished concrete hulk languishing in the woods, to be claimed by a troupe of monkeys.

Practicalities

Facilities for visitors are minimal but adequate. At present, there are only a handful of **places to stay**, mostly grouped at the south end of the beach. Pick of the bunch is *Dercy's* (☎0832/264 7503; ③), whose rooms are exceptionally clean and comfortable, with tiled floors and good-sized bathrooms. Those on the first floor (front side) have a common sea-facing verandah that catches the breezes; you can lie in bed and hear the waves crashing only 100m away. The garrulous proprietor, Inacino, and his wife, also run a cheerful little terrace restaurant serving mainly seafood, bought from the village fishermen fresh each day. Strung with weaver birds' nests, it has a warm family atmosphere and is less expensive than the next best option down the lane, the *Dunhill Beach Resort* (☎0832/264 7604, ✉dunhill-resort@rediffmail.com; ❸). All the rooms here are en suite with small verandahs opening onto a sandy enclosure, and guests can use their Internet connection. There are quite a few small places offering accommodation beyond *Dunhill's*, both in leaf huts behind the beach and in concrete annexes. *Eldfra* (☎0832/264 7378; ❷) offers room of various sizes, most of them with attached shower-toilets but no sit-outs.

If you want to get away from the tourist scene altogether, head a kilometre or so north to the opposite end of Agonda beach, where the *Sea View* (☎0832/264 7548; ❷–❸) is the most appealing option, comprising three mud-and-thatch huts with cow-dung floors (a lot more fragrant than they may sound) and decent beds. They're ultra basic, but clean and secluded, and right on the beach. A short way south of here, *Forget Me Not* (no phone; ❸) has bamboo huts and sturdier stone-built rooms, and would be all right if it weren't for the indifferent staff, overall grubbiness and ambitious tariffs.

Chaudi

CHAUDI (aka Chauri, or Canacona), 33km south of Margao, is Canacona district's bustling headquarters. Packed around a junction on the main Panjim–Mangalore highway, it is primarily a transport hub, of interest to visitors mainly because of its proximity to Palolem, 2km west. Buses to and from Panjim, Margao and Karwar in Karnataka *taluka* trundle in and out of a scruffy square on the main street, where taxis and auto-rickshaws wait to ferry passengers to the villages scattered across the surrounding fields. The new **train** station stands 1.5km northeast of town; auto-rickshaws usually meet services, but you may have to share one with other passengers.

If you spend much time in Palolem, you're sure to nip into Chaudi to shop for provisions, or simply soak up its gritty Indian atmosphere, which comes as a bit of a shock after the dreamy beaches nearby. The small covered **market** is an essential source of fresh fruit and vegetables; several stalls sell stoves, cooking equipment and other hardware, while the excellent *udipi* **restaurant**, a short way south of the main crossroads, is one of the few places for miles where you can eat pukka South Indian food: try their filling Rs15 *thalis*, or spicy fried *pakora* and samosas – all freshly prepared, and piping hot if you come around 5pm. They also do delicious *lassis*, sweetened with traditional syrups.

Palolem

Nowhere else in peninsula India conforms so closely to the archetypal image of a paradise beach as **PALOLEM**, 35km south of Margao. Lined with a swaying curtain of coconut palms, the bay forms a perfect curve of golden sand, arcing north from a giant pile of boulders to the spur of Sahyadri Ghat, which tapers into the sea draped in thick forest. For those foreigners who found their way here before the mid-1990s, however, Palolem is most definitely a paradise lost these days. With the rest of Goa largely carved up by package tourism, this is where the majority of India's foreign travellers come for a beach break from the road, and the numbers can feel overwhelming in peak season, when literally thousands of people spill across the beach. Behind them, an unbroken line of shacks and Thai-style bamboo- and palm-leaf huts provide food and shelter that grows more sophisticated (and less Goan) with each season – not least because many of the businesses here are now run, if not owned, by expatriates.

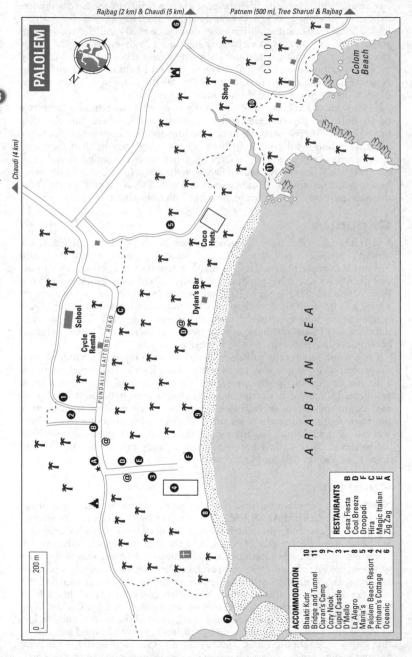

Rajbag (2 km) & Chaudi (5 km) ▲

Patnem (500 m), Tree Sharuti & Rajbag ▲

C O L O M

Colom Beach

Chaudi (4 km) ▲

N

6

Shop

10

11

5

Coco Huts

School

Cycle Rental

Dylan's Bar

C

D @

P U N D A L I K   G A I T O N D I   R O A D

A R A B I A N   S E A

1

2

B

9

A

D

E

F

@

@

3

4

8

7

0   200 m

RESTAURANTS

Cesa Fiesta	B
Cool Breeze	D
Droopadi	F
Hira	C
Magic Italian	E
Zig Zag	A

ACCOMMODATION

Bhakti Kutir	10
Bridge and Tunnel	11
Ciaran's Camp	9
Cozy Nook	7
Cupid Castle	3
D'Mello	1
La Alegro	8
Maria's	5
Palolem Beach Resort	4
Pritham's Cottage	2
Oceanic	6

3

Basically, Palolem in full swing is the kind of place you'll either love at first sight or want to get away from as quickly as possible. If you're in the latter category, try smaller, less frequented Patnem beach, a short walk south, where the shack scene is more subdued and the sand emptier. Further south still, Rajbag, around half-an-hour's walk from Palolem, used to be one of Goa's last deserted beaches until a vast, seven-star luxury hotel resort was recently built slap behind it.

Arrival

Frequent **buses** run between Margao and Karwar (in Karnataka) via Chaudi (every 30min; 2hr), the nearest railhead to Palolem. The train station lies a short way north of town. Rickshaws from there, or Chaudi market, cost around Rs50, or Rs100 for a taxi. Alternatively, get off at the Char Rostay ("Four-Way") crossroads, 1.5km before Chaudi, and walk the remaining kilometre or so to the village. Regular buses also go all the way to Palolem from Margao; these stop at the end of the lane leading from the main street to the beachfront. The last bus from Palolem to Chaudi/Margao leaves at around 4.30pm; check with the locals for the precise times, as these change seasonally.

Accommodation

The local municipality's strict enforcement of a rule banning new concrete construction in Palolem has ensured that most of the village's accommodation consists of simple palm leaf **huts** or "tree houses". Apart from the more snazzily set up places listed below, there's very little difference between the camps: check in to the first that takes your fancy and reconnoitre the rest of the beach at leisure when you've found your feet. The other option is to look for a **room** in a family home. Most, although not all, of these also have limited shared washing facilities and pig toilets. The easiest way to find a place is to walk around the palm groves behind the beach with a rucksack; sooner or later someone will approach you. Rates vary from Rs100 to Rs250 per night, depending on the size of the room and the time of year.

The vast increase in visitor numbers in Palolem has been blamed for the severe water shortages that have afflicted Canacona district over the past three years. The municipality seems unwilling or unable to do anything about the problem, so the onus falls on tourists to **use as little water as possible** during their stay. One of the most effective ways you can do this is to **avoid water toilets**, which dump a colossal quantity of untreated sewage into often poorly manufactured septic tanks below the ground. Traditional pig loos, still common in the village, are a far cleaner, greener option.

Bhakti Kutir On the headland above Colom fishing village ☎0832/264 3460 or 264 3472, ℻264 3469, ✉bhaktikutir@yahoo.com. Eco-friendly, ersatz tribal huts equipped with Western amenities (including completely biodegradable chemical toilets), in a secure, leafy compound five minutes' walk from the south end of Palolem beach. Beautifully situated and sensitively designed to blend with the landscape by German-Goan owners. ❸–❺

Bridge and Tunnel South side of the beach ☎0832/264 2237 or 264 3296, ✉sera_goa @rediffmail.com. More atmospheric than usual hut camp, with Thai-style bamboo structures dotted on and around the boulder hill overlooking the end of the beach. There's also a chill-out area and bar in a glade by the riverside. ❸–❸

Ciaran's Camp Middle of the beach ☎0832/264 3477 or 264 4074, ✉johnciaran@hotmail.com. One of Palolem's longest established hut camps: twenty structures, sharing five toilets, equipped with fans, mozzie nets, mirrors and tables. Free library, laundry, bar, restaurant and safe lockers. ❷

Cozy Nook North end of the beach, near the island ☎0832/264 3550. After *Bhakti Kutir*, this is the most attractively designed set up in the village, comprising 25 bamboo huts (sharing 7 toilets, but with good mattresses, mozzie nets, safe lockers and fans) opening on to the lagoon on one side and the beach on the other – an unbeatable spot, which explains the higher than average tariffs (Rs600 for one with attached shower-toilet; Rs300 without). ❷–❸

Cupid Castle On the road to the beachfront ☎0832/264 3326 or 264 5013, ⓔgraciasjon @yahoo.com. An original name, but these rooms are characterless, and a little too close to the beachfront for comfort. Nonetheless, they're clean, spacious, and have attached bathrooms. ❷–❸

D'Mello Pundalik Gaitondi Road ☎0832/264 3057. A mix of attached and non-attached rooms on three storeys, some in a concrete annexe set back from the main road. Well maintained, and most have balconies. ❸

La Alegro North side of the beach ☎0832/264 4261. En-suite rooms slap on the beach. Very basic and not all that well kept, but the location's great. The same owner also has five more (cheaper) identikit rooms around the back, as well as a clutch of slightly larger ones on PG Road. ❸

Maria's South of the village, near the *Classic* restaurant ☎0832/264 3732 or 264 3856, ⓔselvin16@yahoo.com. Five simple rooms opening onto an orchard of banana, fruit and spice trees. All with attached shower-toilets, and very

friendly management. Nice little bar-restaurant, ISD phone and Internet access on site. A good deal. ❷

Palolem Beach Resort On the beachfront ☎0832/264 3054, ⓕ264 3054, ⓔyogesh@goa1.dot.net.in. Twin-bedded canvas tents, each with their own locker, lights and fans, grouped under a shady *toddi* grove in a walled compound. In addition, there's a handful of small en-suite rooms. The big drawback here is noise from the busy terrace restaurant. ❸–❸

Pritham's Cottages Next door to *Cupid Castle* ☎0832/264 3320. One of the larger, newer and more appealing blocks of budget rooms in the centre of the village: they're bigger than average (all attached), on two storeys with a common verandah. Central, but quiet. ❷

Oceanic Tembi Waddo ☎0832/264 3059, ⓦwww.hotel-oceanic.com. A relative newcomer that, strictly speaking, is in Colom, a 10min walk inland from the beach; you can also get here via the backroad to Chaudi. Owned and managed by a resident British couple, its rooms are very tastefully fitted out, with large mozzie nets, blockprinted bedspreads and bedside lamps. There's also a brand new pool on a wooded terrace behind, and a quality restaurant. ❸

Eating and drinking

Palolem's **restaurants** and **bars** reflect the cosmopolitan make-up of its visitors. Each year, a fresh batch of innovative, ever more stylish places open, most of them managed by expats. Standards and prices have both increased greatly as a consequence. For those on tight budgets, there are a couple of cheap and cheerful **bhaji stalls** outside the *Beach Resort*, and the *Hira Restaurant* in the village proper, where you can order tasty and filling breakfasts of *pao bhaji*, fluffy bread rolls, omelettes and chai for next to nothing. Alternatively, rent a bike for a couple of hours and cycle out to the excellent *Udipi Hotel* in Chaudi, which serves delicious dosas, potato *wadas*, samosas, rice-plate meals and other South Indian standards at local prices.

Bhakti Kutir Between Palolem beach and Colom fishing village at the guesthouse. Laid-back terrace café-cum-restaurant with sturdy wooden tables and a German-bakery-style menu. Cooked dishes here are pricey (mains around Rs150), but delicious (their omelettes are made with imported cheese), and the ingredients are usually local and organically produced.

Casa Fiesta Pundalik Gaitondi Rd. Funky expat-run place on the main drag, offering an eclectic menu of World cuisine: houmous, Greek salad, Mexican specialities and fish *pollichatu*; mains (mostly under Rs150) come with delicious roasties.

Cool Breeze Beach road. Co-run by a British couple, this is currently among the classiest restaurants in the village. Their tandoori chicken and

seafood, in particular, have set new standards for Palolem, and the prices are reasonable. Come early, or you could face a long wait for a table.

Cozy Nook Far north end of the beach at the guesthouse. Wholesome Goan-style cooking served on a small terrace that occupies a prime position opposite the island. Their filling set four-course dinners (7–9pm; Rs125) are deservedly popular, offering imaginative and carefully prepared dishes such as pan-fried fish, aubergine with shrimps and fresh beans. They also do a tasty veg equivalent (Rs100), as well as a full seafood, North Indian curry and snack menu.

Droopadi Beach front. This place enjoys both a top beachfront location and Palolem's best Indian chef, who specializes in rich, creamy Mughlai dishes and tandoori fish. Go for the superb *murg makhini* or one of the paneer options. With most main courses around Rs100, their prices are low, too, considering the quality of the cooking.

Hira Pundalik Gaitondi Road. Tiny locals' café at the south end of the village, serving "cheap and best" *bhaji*–bread breakfasts, good South Indian-style filter coffee and freshly fried samosas, with a complimentary *Navhind Times* passed around if you're lucky.

Magic Italian Beach road. By general consensus, south Goa's number one Italian, serving home-made ravioli and tagliatelle, along with scrumptious wood-fired pizzas (Rs110–140).

Maria's South side of the village, attached to the guesthouse. Authentic Goan food, such as chicken vindaloo, fried calamari and spicy vegetable side dishes, prepared entirely with local produce and served alfresco on a terrace. Maria's garrulous

husband, Joseph, serves a mean *feni*, too, flavoured with cumin, ginger or lemongrass.

Oceanic Colom, in the guesthouse of the same name. Chilled terrace restaurant, set well back from the beach but worth the walk for the better-than-average food and background music (the owner's an ex-Womad sound man). North and South Indian dishes are the chef's forte (especially *dum aloo Kashmiri* and butter chicken), but they also do great red and green Thai curries, and a tempting selection of freshly baked desserts (including lemon-and-ginger cheesecake and banoffee pie) and coffee liqueur. Check the specials board for dishes of the day. Occasional live music.

Zig Zag Pundalik Gaitondi Road. A Keralan-British co-project, offering particularly strong South Indian food (the only place in Palolem that does), in addition to veg, meat and fish dishes prepared with light, mild sauces and fresh herbs. Mains under Rs150.

Listings

Bike rental A stall halfway along the main street charges the princely sum of Rs5 per hour (with discounts for longer periods).

Foreign exchange Several agents in Palolem are licensed to change money. Sarken Tours inside the *Nature Restaurant* and LKP Forex in the *Beach Resort* offer the best rates.

Internet cafés The best ones are clustered around the bus stop.

Safe deposit For those wishing to stash valuables while they're here, *Lalita Enterprises*, on the main beach road, offers lockers for Rs15 per day.

Telephones The village has a dozen or more STD/ISD telephones: avoid the one in the *Beach Resort*, which charges more than double the going rate for international calls, and head for the much cheaper booths 100m down the lane (next to the bus stop).

Colom

A stony path threads its way through the boulders and *toddi* groves at the south end of Palolem beach to the Hindu hamlet of **COLOM**, clustered around the rocky shore of two palm-shaded coves. Several families here rent out huts and rooms to travellers, and there are a handful of small cafés where you can buy drinks and snacks, but these are the only discernible trickle-down from Palolem.

Tucked away in the woods at the top of a low rise as you enter Colom, *Tree Shanti* (T0832/264 4460, Esaritagita7@rediffmail.com; ❷) is a small family guesthouse, run by a couple of feisty sisters, Gita and Sarita Komarpunt. The seven rooms are spartan, and share a single toilet and shower, but this is a fun place to stay with a friendly atmosphere that's a world away from Palolem's hut camps. For more privacy, you might want to ask for a room at the *Boom Shankar* bar (T0832/264 4035; ❷), on the southern edge of Colom, where the path rounds the headland to Patnem. Scattered up the palm-covered headland behind the bar are fifteen small houses and rooms for rent, most of them with individual bathrooms and toilets; they're peaceful, secluded and some have gorgeous views.

Patnem

The broad white beach beyond Colom, known as **PATNEM**, is equally peaceful, although less safe to swim from than Palolem, with a fair undertow at certain phases of the tide. Behind it, straggly casuarina trees shade a string of shacks, some of which rent out palm-leaf huts to backpackers. Pick of the **accommodation** here, though, has to be *Home* (☎0832/264 3916; ❸–❺), a smart white-and-blue painted annexe with a pitch-tiled roof, midway down the beach. Run by a Swiss-British couple, its rooms are simply but elegantly furnished, with flowing mozzie nets, white cotton sheets and cosy little touches that justify the higher-than-average tariffs. It's extremely popular, so book in advance. Five minutes' behind the beach on the roadside, *Sea View* (☎0832/264 3110; ❷–❹) offers a range of clean rooms: simple, old-fashioned ones in a little block around the back of the main building, and smarter, marble-lined modern ones with large balconies and bathrooms. Their restaurant, occupying a sandy terrace behind, is better than it looks and not at all expensive for the area, serving particularly good tandoori. Finally, the *Molyma*, 1km inland (☎0832/264 3028, ℻264 3081; ❸); is a large and somewhat maudlin place whose clientele consists mostly of Karnatakan men up on booze tours for the weekend.

Rajbag and Talpona

RAJBAG beach stretches in an unbroken sweep south of Patnem to the mouth of the Talpona River. Sadly, a 280-room, seven-star holiday complex, the *Bharat-Hilton*, was nearing completion when we last passed through and will certainly ruin the tranquillity of what was hitherto a gem of a beach when it opens.

It's possible to press on even further **south from Rajbag**, by crossing the Talpona via a hand-paddled passenger ferry, which usually has to be summoned from the far bank. Once across, a short walk brings you to **Talpona beach**, backed by low dunes and a line of straggly palms, where you'd be (un)lucky to come across another tourist. From there, assuming you haven't already succumbed to sunstroke and dehydration, you can cross the headland at the end of Talpona beach to reach Galjibag (see below).

Galjibag

One of Goa's most remote beaches, **GALJIBAG**, 16km south of Chaudi, can be reached on foot if you continue south from Talpona across a low headland. Alternatively, heading south on the NH17, take a right turn after the large double-river bridge. The approach to the beach, fringed by wispy fir trees, hugs the south bank of the Talpona River, passing a string of Hindu hamlets and a massive new railway bridge. The village, sandwiched between two estuaries, is devoid of tourist facilities, but its tranquil beach is refreshingly unspoilt. It is also one of only two remote spots in Goa where the rare **olive ridley marine turtle** nests. Villagers have traditionally harvested the eggs laid in the sand by the females, who return each year in early November to the same spot, but the Forest Department now strictly protects the turtles from poaching in an attempt to arrest their decline. During the breeding season you'll see their nests fenced off and marked with flags. In the winter of 2000–01, 33 pregnant females returned and almost 2500 baby turtles successfully hatched here – a ten-fold increase on the previous year.

Cold drinks, alcoholic and otherwise, are available at Galjibag's only **café**, tucked away in the *toddi* groves 50m north of the village church.

The Mallikarjun temple

Few non-Hindu visitors make it to the **Mallikarjun temple**, 7km northeast of Chaudi (look for the signpost off the NH17). Yet this small Shiva shrine is one of Goa's oldest – not that you'd know it from the outside, which is awash with concrete and coloured paint. Its interior, however, has largely escaped heavy-handed renovation, thanks to a ban imposed by the Department of Archeology. Some of the finest surviving art is to be found in the assembly hall or *mandapa*, whose stocky pillars writhe with sculpted musicians, dancers and floral motifs. At the far end, an elaborately embossed door jamb opens on to the inner sanctum, where a *Shivalingam* with a metallic mask is enshrined.

The inland route to Rivona

A few kilometres beyond the turn-off for the Mallikarjun temple, a Forest Department checkpoint on the left of the NH17 marks the start of what is arguably **Goa's most scenic road**. Taking you through pockets of fragrant forest into the heart of the mountains, it penetrates the jungle wilderness separating Canacona from Quepem *taluka*, eventually joining up with the main road to Rivona. With a motorbike, you can use it to reach the extraordinary **stone-age rock carvings** at Usgalimal (see p.190), and then press on north towards Timola and Chandor, where the main road connects the interior with Margao and the coastal highway. This circuit makes a memorable drive, but don't underestimate the remoteness of some of the terrain: the *ghat* section, in particular, is rough in places and a long way from the nearest village if you run out of fuel or water.

The following directions should help you find your way, but always check your progress with any woodcutters, forest wardens, and cattle herders you meet along the route.

From the checkpoint and turning off NH17 south of Malikarjun, the road crosses open cultivated land before passing through a couple of villages to begin the climb, via a series of sharp switchbacks, into the mountains. By the time you reach the pass, the jungle – and profusion of bird and insect life – is impressive, while odd gaps in the tree cover reveal wonderful panoramas over the hidden valleys on the far side of the hills. Beyond the col, however, the road surface deteriorates rapidly and should not be attempted on anything less than a 100cc motorcycle (you'll never make it back up again on a moped). Dropping down through a further 12km of uninhabited forest, it passes another forest checkpoint, and then forks: bear left at the first junction, and left again at the second (where there's a school). A third left turn soon brings you to the hamlet of **Dom Bosco**, site of a large boys' school. Continue straight along this road, past an iron-ore mine, and you'll eventually pass the marked turning for the rock carvings (on your left), exactly 13km from Timola crossroads – a route described in reverse on p.189.

Cotigao Wildlife Sanctuary

The **Cotigao Wildlife Sanctuary**, 10km southeast of Chaudi, was established in 1969 to protect a remote and vulnerable area of forest lining the Goa–Karnataka border. Encompassing 86 square kilometres of mixed deciduous woodland, the reserve is certain to inspire tree lovers, but less likely to yield many wildlife sightings: its tigers and leopards were hunted out long ago, while the gazelles, sloth bears, porcupines, panthers and hyenas that allegedly lurk in the woods rarely appear. You do, however, stand a good chance of spotting at least two species of monkey, a couple of wild boar and the odd gaur (the primeval-looking Indian bison), as well as plenty of exotic birdlife. Best visited between October and March, Cotigao is a peaceful and scenic park that makes a pleasant day-trip from Palolem, 12km northwest. Any of the buses running south on the NH-14 to Karwar via Chaudi will drop you within 2km of the gates. However, to explore the inner reaches of the sanctuary, you really need your own transport. The wardens at the reserve's small **Interpretative Centre**, where you have to pay your entry fees (Rs5, plus Rs50 for a car, Rs10 for a motorbike; Rs25 for a camera permit), will show you how to get to a 25-metre-high treetop watchtower, overlooking a **waterhole** that attracts a handful of animals around dawn and dusk. You can also stay here at a rather unprepossessing little room (Rs200 per night), in the compound behind the main reserve gates. Food and drink may be available by prior arrangement, and there's a shop at the nearest village, 2km inside the park.

More inspiring accommodation is to be found at a secluded riverside location on the edge of Cotigao. Hidden away in a working spice plantation, *Pepper Valley* (☎0832/264 2370; ❸) comprises a row of simple huts on the river bank, shaded by a canopy of areca palms, with cashew bushes and yam plants growing around. Facilities are basic for the money (Rs300 per double), but this is a lovely spot to chill out for an evening. To find it, turn left at the Cotigao Interpretative Centre then follow the road for 500m until you see a signboard indicating a motorable track off to the left.

Polem

A stone's throw from the state border, **POLEM**, 30km south of Chaudi, is Goa's southernmost beach, and sufficiently secluded to have been overlooked even by the sand-hopping hippies heading between Goa and Gokarn, in Karnataka. The hundred-metre strip of smooth white sand, enfolded by a pair of rocky headlands, is immaculately clean and unspoilt, and visited regularly by dolphins and white-bellied fish eagles. However, it's not the most welcoming of places, possibly because the principal source of income for the villagers is smuggling and illegal liquor. Westerners sunbathing and swimming can expect a frosty reception from the locals.

It is possible to get to within striking distance of Polem by **bus** from Panjim, Margao or Chaudi: catch any service heading south down NH17 to Karwar (every 30min), and get off 2km before the border at the *Milan Bar* (you'll know you've overshot the turning if you see a petrol station on the left). The owner

Crossing the Goa–Karnataka border

If you're heading south from Goa towards Jog Falls or the Hindu pilgrimage town of Gokarn (covered in Chapter 4, p.217), you'll have to cross the state border at a road barrier a short way before the river bridge, near the town of Karwar. For travellers on buses, or in cars, this is a straightforward procedure; you probably won't even have to fill in the requisite form. Anyone who is crossing into Karnataka on a rented motorbike, however, can expect some **hassle from the police**. The standard routine is to take your passport, scrutinize it with a very stern face, and then inform you that you can't continue south because of some directive from Panjim. Of course, this is all a ploy to extract *baksheesh*, and like it or not, you'll probably have to shell out at least Rs100 to continue. Curiously enough, the cops are honest when it comes to recognizing you on the return trip, and will politely wave you through the barrier after you sign the ledger in their office.

of this roadside café will show you the path leading across the paddy fields to Polem, a pleasant fifteen-minute walk.

Travel details

By train

Chaudi to: Gokarn (1 daily; 1hr 30min); Margao (3 daily; 50min).
Margao to: Chaudi (3 daily; 50min); Colem (2 weekly; 1hr 40min); Delhi (1–2 daily; 26hr–35hr); Ernakulam/Kochi (5 daily; 12hr–15hr 40min); Gokarn (1 daily; 2hr 10min); Hospet (2 weekly; 8hr 30min); Mangalore/Kanakadi (5 daily; 4–6hr); Mumbai (3 daily; 12hr); Thiruvanantapuram (2 daily; 16hr 15min); Udupi (4 daily; 3hr 40min); Vasco da Gama (4–6 daily; 40min).
Vasco da Gama to: Colem (2 weekly; 2hr); Hospet (2 weekly; 9hr); Margao (2 weekly; 40min).

By bus

Benaulim to: Cavelossim (hourly; 20min); Colva (every 30min; 20min); Margao (every 30min; 15min); Mobor (hourly; 25min).
Chaudi to: Gokarn (1 daily; 3hr); Karwar (every 30min; 1hr); Palolem (2 daily; 15min).
Margao to: Agonda (4 daily; 2hr); Benaulim (every 15–30min; 15min); Chaudi (every 30min; 1hr

40min); Cabo da Rama (4 daily; 1hr 40min); Cavelossim (8 daily; 30min); Chandor (8 daily; 45min); Colva (every 15–30min; 20–30min); Gokarn (1 daily; 4hr 30min); Hampi (1 daily; 10hr); Karwar (every 30min; 2hr); Lutolim (8 daily; 30min); Mangalore (5 daily; 7hr); Mapusa (10 daily; 2hr 30min); Mobor (8 daily; 35min); Mumbai (2 daily; 16–18hr); Panjim (every 30min; 1hr 30min); Pune (1 daily; 12hr); Rachol (every 2hr; 30min).
Vasco da Gama to: Bangalore (1 daily; 16hr); Bogmalo (hourly; 20min); Colva (2 daily; 30min); Mangalore (2 daily; 11hr); Margao (every 15min; 1hr); Panjim, via Sao Jacinto (every 15min; 45min–1hr); Pilar (every 15min; 30min).

By plane

Dabolim airport (Vasco da Gama) to: Bangalore (2 daily; 1 hr 30min–2hr 25min); Chennai (2 weekly; 3hr); Cochin (2 weekly; 1hr); Delhi (4 weekly; 2hr 25min); Hyderabad (4 weekly; 2hr 55min); Mumbai (3–6 daily; 40min).

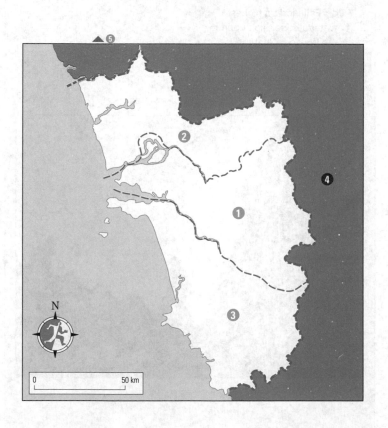

Around Goa

CHAPTER 4

Highlights

✳ **Hampi** Ruined palaces, wild monkeys, hilltop temples and a serene riverine setting combine to create one of Asia's most memorable destinations. See p.224

✳ **Jog Falls** India's highest waterfalls, set high up in the Western Ghat mountains. See p.233

✳ **Gokarn** Bustling Hindu pilgrimage town with heaps of atmosphere, close to a string of lovely beaches. See p.234

Around Goa

G oa's towns and coastal resorts may induce a certain culture shock when you first arrive, but they are far from representative of the rest of the country, and many visitors are tempted across the state border into neighbouring **Karnataka**, beyond the limits of Portuguese colonial influence, for a taste of the "real" India. Even if you're only here for two weeks, it's perfectly feasible to do this. Indeed, a foray through the forests of the Western Ghats to the **Deccan plateau** – with its open vistas of dark-soiled, rolling plains – or south down the lush **Konkan coast** may well provide some of the most vivid experiences of your trip. And don't let the prospect of long overland journeys deter you. A number of southwest India's most exotic sights lie a mere day's drive from Goa, set amid landscapes that differ wildly from the palm groves and paddy fields of the coast. Moreover, travelling to them can be fascinating and fun, yielding glimpses of everyday life in both remote, rural villages and the sprawling cities just beyond Goa's eastern border.

The single greatest incentive to venture away from the beaches has to be the extraordinary ruined city of **Vijayanagar**, better known as **Hampi**. Situated eight and a half hours by train east of the coast, this vast archeological site harbours the remains of palaces, temples and bazaars dating from the fifteenth and sixteenth centuries, when this was the capital of a huge Hindu empire – in its heyday among the largest and most powerful in Asia. The city was destroyed by Muslim armies in 1565, but enough finely carved stone buildings survive to occupy interested visitors for days. Hampi's setting is impressive too: an otherworldly jumble of smooth boulders, piled in colossal heaps around the banks of the Tungabhadra River, with banana plantations and rice paddies cutting swathes of green through the rocky terrain. People travel the length of India to see Hampi, and few visitors from Goa return disappointed.

The other obvious target for a trip out of state, the Hindu pilgrimage town of **Gokarn**, 154km south of Margao, is a less well-established stop on the tourist trail. This might well change as tourist traffic on the Konkan Railway increases, but for the time being, the majority of Gokarn's foreign visitors are backpackers taking time out from long tours of India. They come both for the heady religious atmosphere of the town, which harbours a couple of major temples and plenty of attractive vernacular architecture, and to laze on the exquisite beaches to the south, some of which are still only accessible on foot.

En route to Gokarn, a worthwhile side trip is the journey through the hills and forests of the Ghats to **Jog Falls**, the highest waterfalls in India. Tourist facilities and public transport services in the adjacent village are minimal (most Indians visit only for the day), but the scenery is dramatic and the road trip across the mountains an adventure.

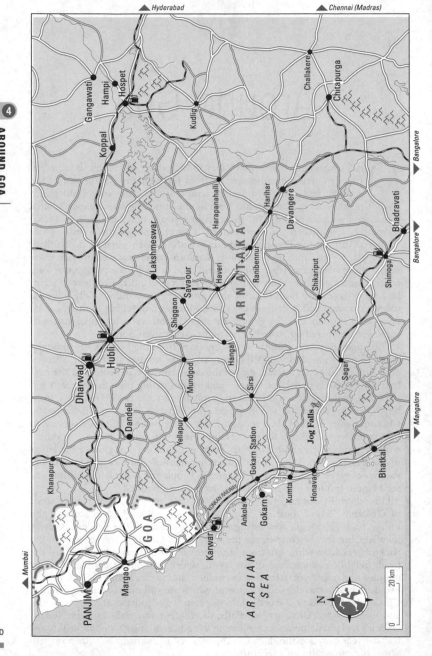

Now that the Konkan Railway is fully functional, travelling along the coast between Goa and Gokarn is straightforward, with fast and regular services from Margao and Chaudi. Running in tandem with the rail route, the recently revamped coastal highway is also well served by buses from towns in Goa. The same is true of the main eastbound road artery crossing the Western Ghats to **Hospet**, the nearest sizeable town to Hampi. You'll find a full rundown of transport services to the destinations covered in this chapter at the beginning of the relevant accounts, and there's a summary in "Travel details" on p.238.

Hospet

Charmless **HOSPET**, 345km east of Margao, is of little interest except as a springboard for the ruined city of Vijayanagar (Hampi), 13km northeast. If you want somewhere fairly comfortable to sleep, it makes sense to stay here and catch a bus or taxi out to the ruins the following morning. Otherwise, hole up in Hampi itself, where the setting more than compensates for the basic facilities.

Getting there

The most stress-free and economical way to reach Hospet from Goa is the twice-weekly **train** service from **Margao**. The Vijaywada Express (#7228) departs every Wednesday and Saturday at 7.20am, arriving just over eight and

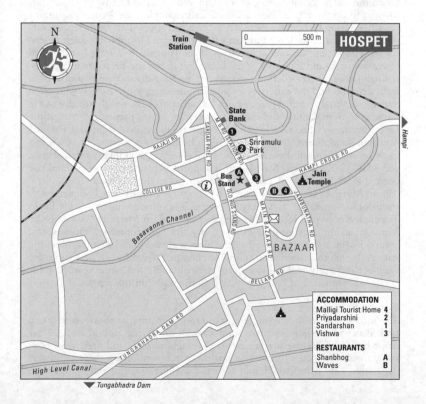

a half hours later at 4.05pm. Take the Saturday one and you can spend Sunday exploring Hampi then catch the train back on Monday morning (at 8.50am); the only other Goa-bound service (#7227) leaves on Thursdays (also at 8.50am).

Fares range from just under Rs90 for a seat in ultra-basic, crowded second class (where the toilets are pretty grim and you'll more than likely be pestered constantly by buskers, beggars and sundry other well-wishers) to around Rs460 for more comfortable, cleaner first-class non-a/c, which has open windows and plenty of room. Splash out Rs650 and you can travel second-class air-conditioned – the most comfy option, but with the disadvantage of tinted, double-glazed windows that you can barely see through. In both first-class non-a/c and second-class a/c, delicious, freshly cooked meals (vegetarian or non-vegetarian) may be ordered; they arrive neatly packed in foil trays, cost next to nothing and are accompanied by regular rounds of tea and coffee.

Tickets can be bought on the day at either point of departure. Arrive at Margao by at least 6.30am, as the "queues" are invariably more like rugby scrums. Alternatively, pay a little extra for a travel agent to book the ticket on your behalf.

All in all, this a wonderful rail journey, taking you through one of the wildest stretches of the Western Ghats, including the Dudhsagar Falls area (see p.116), where the train actually crosses the white water. Once over the mountains, the landscape changes dramatically, first to dry forest and then vast plains striped with cotton fields.

By bus

Given the cost and convenience of the train, you'd have to be a bit of a masochist to want to do the trip by **bus**, although many people consider the discomfort worth enduring to have an extra day or two in Hampi. Two or three clapped-out government buses leave **Panjim's** Kadamba stand (platform 9) each morning for Hospet, the last one at 10.30am. Brace yourself for a long, hard slog; all being well, it should take nine or ten hours, but delays and breakdowns are frustratingly frequent. Travellers unaccustomed to long-distance road journeys in India may also find the experience somewhat nerve-racking, as the drivers often attempt seemingly suicidal manoeuvres, swinging onto the rough margins of the highway to overtake or avoid oncoming vehicles. This is particularly true of the faster private services, which you'll see advertised on boards around Panjim's main bus stand; they may get you there an hour or two sooner, but you're less likely to enjoy the trip because of the breakneck speeds. **Tickets** for Kadamba and KSRTC (Karnatakan State Road Transport Corporation) services should be booked at least one day in advance at the hatches in the bus stand.

From **Margao**, you can also travel to Hampi on a **night bus**, complete with pneumatic suspension and sleeper berths. The service, operated by Paulo Travels, leaves from a lot next to the *Nanutel Hotel* on Margao's Rua da Padre Miranda, at 6pm, arriving in Hampi early the next morning. **Tickets** cost around Rs400 and can be bought from most reputable travel agents around the state. Although the coach is comfortable enough, the coffin-like berths can get very hot and stuffy, making sleep very difficult; moreover, some women readers have complained of harassment during the night on this service.

By car

The most comfortable way of getting to Hospet/Hampi, of course, is to take a **taxi**. Rates vary wildly, but you should count on paying around Rs1000 per day, which includes the driver's meals, overnight charges and fuel. Most taxi-*wallahs* will offer you a "fixed rate" for the trip, but in reality these are always negotiable; after Mumbai, Hampi is their most lucrative run and competition for punters is stiff, so haggle hard over the price, and do this yourself rather than relying on your hotel or guesthouse owner.

Hospet practicalities

Hospet's **railway station** is 1500m north of the centre. At the main entrance, you'll probably be greeted by a volley from rickshaw-*wallahs* wanting to take you to Hampi, but the road there is horrendously pot-holed making the twenty- to thirty-minute trip a lot more comfortable (and quicker) by local bus. These leave roughly every half-hour from the main **bus stand**, 250m south of the train station down MG (Station) Road (jump on a cycle-rickshaw for Rs10–15). Government (KSRTC and Kadamba) services from Goa pull in here from 6pm to 8pm, depending on departure times. Paulo Travels' luxury overnight coach from Goa stops outside the *Hotel Priyadarshini* on MG Road, where they have a booking office. For for the adventurous, Bullet **motorbikes** are available to rent (or buy) from Bharat Motors (℡0839/424704) near *Rama Talkies*.

The **tourist office** in Hospet is at Rotary Circle (Mon–Sat: June–March 10am–5.30pm; April & May 8am–1.30pm; ℡0839/428537), a couple of blocks west of the bus stand on College Road, but it's pretty useless. For bus and train timings, you're better off checking at the stations.

Traveller's cheques and cash may be exchanged at the State Bank of Mysore (Mon–Fri 10.30am–2.30pm & Sat 10.30am–12.30pm), next to the tourist office, and cash only at the State Bank of India (same hours) on Station Road. Full **exchange facilities** are available at the *Hotel Malligi*, while Neha Travels (℡0839/425838) at the Elimanchate Complex, next to the *Hotel Priyadarshini* on MG Road, also changes any currency and traveller's cheques, and advances money on credit cards.

Accommodation and eating

By far the most popular place to stay in Hospet is the versatile *Malligi Tourist Home*, with something to suit most budgets, but the *Priyadarshini* is also good value and nearer the railway station.

There's little to do in the town itself, so you'll probably pass a fair amount of time **eating**, drinking and crowd-watching. Many of the hotels have good dining rooms, but in the evening, the upscale though affordable *Waves*, a terrace restaurant in the *Malligi* complex, is the most congenial place to hang out, serving tandoori and chilled beer from 7pm to 11pm (bring lots of mosquito repellent). *Shanbhog*, an excellent little South Indian *udipi* restaurant next to the bus station, is a perfect pit stop before heading to Hampi, and opens early for breakfast.

Karthik Pampa Villa, off MG Road ℡0839/424938, ℱ420028. A new, characterless block featuring unremarkable rooms but with a surprise around the back in the form of an extraordinary nineteenth-century stone villa housing two huge suites. ❸–❼

Malligi Tourist Home 6/143 Jambunatha Rd, 2min walk east of MG Road (look for the signs) and the bus stand ℡0839/428101, ℮malligihome @hotmail.com. Friendly, well-managed hotel with cheaper, clean, comfortable rooms (some a/c) in the old block and two new wings across the lawn, with luxurious air-conditioned options. There is also a great new swimming pool (Rs25/hr for non-residents) in their Waves complex beneath the

restaurant/bar plus billiards and massage facilities. The alfresco *Madhu Paradise* restaurant/bar in the old block serves good veg food, and they have an efficient travel service. ❸–❽

Priyadarshini MG Road, up the road from the bus stand, towards the railway station ℡0839/428838. Rooms from rock-bottom singles to doubles with TV and a/c (some balconies). Large, and bland, but spotless and very good value. They have two good restaurants: the veg *Naivedyam* and, in the garden, non-veg *Manasa*, which has a bar. Their travel desk also handles bus and train tickets. ❷–❺

Pushpak Lodge near bus stand, MG Road ℡0839/421380. With basic, but clean, attached rooms, this is the best rock-bottom lodge. ❷

Hampi (Vijayanagar)

The ruined city of **Vijayanagar**, "the City of Victory" (also known as **HAMPI**, the name of a local village), spills from the south bank of the Tungabhadra River, littered among a surreal landscape of golden-brown granite boulders and leafy banana fields. According to the *Ramayana*, the settlement began its days as Kishkinda, ruled by the monkey kings Vali and Sugriva and their ambassador, Hanuman. The weird rocks – some balanced in perilous arches, others heaped in colossal, hill-sized piles – are said to have been flung down by their armies in a show of strength.

Between the fourteenth and sixteenth centuries, this was the most powerful Hindu capital in the Deccan. Travellers such as the Portuguese chronicler Domingo Paez, who stayed for two years after 1520, were astonished by its size and wealth, telling tales of markets full of silk and precious gems, beautiful, bejewelled courtesans, ornate palaces and joyous festivities. However, in the

second half of the sixteenth century, the dazzling city was devastated by a six-month Muslim siege. Only stone, brick and stucco structures survived the ensuing sack – monolithic deities, crumbling houses and abandoned temples dominated by towering *gopuras* – as well as the sophisticated irrigation system that channelled water to huge tanks and temples.

Thanks to the Muslim onslaught, most of Hampi's monuments are in disappointingly poor shape, seemingly a lot older than their four or five hundred years. Yet the serene riverine setting and air of magic that lingers over the site, sacred for centuries before a city was founded here, make it one of India's most extraordinary locations. Even so, mainstream tourism has thus far made little impact: along with bus loads of Hindu pilgrims, and sadhus who hole up in the more isolated rock crevices and shrines, most visitors are budget travellers straight from Goa. Many find it difficult to leave, and spend weeks chilling out in cafés, wandering to whitewashed hilltop temples and gazing at the spectacular sunsets.

The **best time to come** to Hampi, weather-wise, is from late October to early March, when daytime temperatures are low enough to allow long forays on foot through the ruins. It does start to get busy over Christmas and New Year, however, and from early January for a month or so the site is invaded by an exodus of (mostly Israeli) travellers from Goa, though the general tourist downturn means it has been less crowded in recent years than during the late-Nineties peak; still, if you want to enjoy Hampi at its best, come outside peak season.

Some history

The rise of the **Vijayanagar empire** seems to have been a direct response, in the first half of the fourteenth century, to the expansionist aims of Muslims from the north, most notably Malik Kafur and Mohammed-bin-Tughluq. Two Hindu brothers from Andhra Pradesh, Harihara and Bukka, who had been employed as treasury officers in Kampila, 19km east of Hampi, were captured by the Tughluqs and taken to Delhi, where they supposedly converted to Islam. Assuming them to be suitably tamed, the Delhi sultan despatched them to quell civil disorder in Kampila, which they duly did, only to abandon both Islam and allegiance to Delhi shortly afterwards, preferring to establish their own independent Hindu kingdom. Within a few years they controlled vast tracts of land from coast to coast. In 1343 their new capital, Vijayanagar, was founded on the southern banks of the River Tungabhadra, a location long considered sacred by Hindus. The city's most glorious period was under the reign of **Krishna Deva Raya** (1509–29), when it enjoyed a near monopoly of the lucrative trade in Arabian horses and Indian spices passing through the coastal ports.

Thanks to its natural features and massive fortifications, Vijayanagar was virtually impregnable. In 1565, however, following his interference in the affairs of local Muslim sultanates, the regent Rama Raya was drawn into a battle with a confederacy of Muslim forces, 100km away to the north, which left the city undefended. At first, fortune appeared to be on the side of the Hindu army, but there were as many as 10,000 Muslims in their number, and loyalties may well have been divided. When two Vijayanagar Muslim generals suddenly deserted, the army fell into disarray. Defeat came swiftly; although members of his family fled with untold hoards of gold and jewels, Rama Raya was captured and suffered a grisly death at the hands of the sultan of Ahmadnagar. Vijayanagar then fell victim to a series of destructive raids, and its days of splendour were brought to an abrupt end.

Practicalities

Buses from Hospet terminate close to where the road joins the main street in

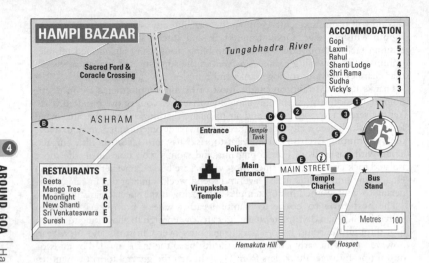

HAMPI BAZAAR

Tungabhadra River

ACCOMMODATION
Gopi	2
Laxmi	5
Rahul	7
Shanti Lodge	4
Shri Rama	6
Sudha	1
Vicky's	3

Sacred Ford &
Coracle Crossing

ASHRAM

Entrance
Temple Tank

Police

Main Entrance

MAIN STREET

Temple Chariot

Bus Stand

Virupaksha Temple

RESTAURANTS
Geeta	F
Mango Tree	B
Moonlight	A
New Shanti	C
Sri Venkateswara	E
Suresh	D

N

0 Metres 100

Hemakuta Hill   Hospet

Hampi Bazaar, halfway along its dusty length. A little further towards the Virupaksha temple, the **tourist office** (Mon–Sat 10am–5.30pm; ☎0839/441339) can put you in touch with a **guide** but not much else. Shankar (✉shankarlax@yahoo.com), the most friendly and knowledgeable guide in the area, runs a convenience store just behind the office. Most visitors coming from Hospet organize a guide from there.

Rented **bicycles**, available from stalls near the lodges, cost Rs5 per hour or Rs30–40 for a 24-hour period. Bikes are really only of use if you're planning to explore Anegondi across the river – accessible by **coracle** for Rs5 – you can also rent bicycles at Kamalapuram for Rs50 per day. Rickety **motorbikes and scooters** can be rented for Rs150–200 per day from Neha Travels who have three outlets in Hampi; the main office is at D131/11 Main Street (daily 9am–9pm; ☎0839/441590). They can also **change money** (including traveller's cheques) but at lowish rates, advance cash on credit cards and they book airline and **train tickets** as well as run **luxury buses** to Bangalore and luxury sleeper coaches to Goa; although these drop people off right in Hampi Bazaar, you have to pick them up from Hospet thanks to the powerful taxi/rickshaw mafia.

Run by Shri Swamy Sadashiva Yogi, the Shivananda Yoga Ashram overlooking the river, past the coracle crossing, offers courses in **yoga** and **meditation** as well as homeopathy.

Accommodation

If you're happy to make do with basic amenities, Hampi is a far more enjoyable place to stay than Hospet, with around fifty congenial **guesthouses** and plenty of cafés to hang out in after a long day in the heat. As you wander through the lanes, you may find yourself solicited by local residents offering rooms in their own homes. Staying in the village also means you can be up and out early enough to catch the sunrise over the ruins – a mesmerizing spectacle. Some travellers shun Hampi Bazaar for the burgeoning community of lodges at **Virupapuragadda** across the river, or the more comfortable *Kiskinda Resorts* at Hanomana Halli, 2km from Anegondi, which has been the scene of several raves. Outside of **high season**, which lasts for six weeks starting around Christmas, you may well get a substantial discount on the room rates quoted below.

Gopi Guest House A short walk down the lanes behind *Shanti* ☏ 0839/441695. There's a pleasant rooftop café here, and all ten rooms have attached baths. ❷

KSTDC Mayura Bhuvaneshwari Kamalapuram, 2.5km from Hampi Bazaar ☏ 0839/441574. The only remotely upscale place to stay within reach of the ruins. The modern block with clean en-suite rooms and competitively priced a/c rooms is agreeable enough. There's a pleasant garden, a good restaurant and a bar serving cold beers, but it feels detached from Hampi Bazaar and the village lacks charm. ❸–❹

Laxmi Just behind the main drag ☏ 0839/441728. A friendly guesthouse with clean rooms and shared baths. ❶

Rahul Guest House South of Main Street, near the bus stand ☏ 0839/441648. Now has some new attached rooms in addition to the small and spartan old ones, which share rudimentary washing and toilet facilities. Pleasant shaded café. ❶–❸

Sai Plaza Virupapuragadda ☏ 0853/387017. Nine attractive double attached huts, set around a pleasant landscaped garden. ❷

Shanti Lodge Just north of the Virupaksha temple ☏ 0839/441568. Follow the lane around the side of the temple enclosure, and the lodge is 30m further on the right. Run by the affable yoga guru, Mr Shivaram, this is still a real favourite, comprising a dozen or so twin-bedded cells ranged on two storeys around a leafy inner courtyard. It's basic (showers and toilets are shared), but spotless, and all rooms have fans and windows. Roof space is also available if the lodge is fully booked. ❶

Shri Rama Guest House Next to the Virupaksha temple ☏ 0839/441219. Rock-bottom attached rooms mainly for Hindu pilgrims, but foreigners are also welcome. ❶

Sudha Guest House At the east end of the village, near the river. Very friendly and pleasantly situated family operation, with cool attached rooms downstairs and smaller ones upstairs. Very good value and mozzie nets are provided. ❶

Umashankar Lodge Virupapuragadda ☏ 0853/387028. One of the better places to stay across the river. Small, but clean, attached rooms set round a lush lawn. ❶

Vicky's At the end of the lane furthest northeast from the temple ☏ 08394/41694. Small clean rooms, some with attached bath. Friendly and especially popular for its rooftop restaurant. ❷

Eating

During the season, Hampi spawns a rash of travellers' cafés and temporary tiffin joints, as well as a number of laid-back snack bars tucked away in more secluded corners. As a holy site, the whole village is supposed to be strictly vegetarian but one or two places bend the rules. Among the many **restaurants** in the bazaar, firm favourites with Western tourists, serving a predictable selection of pancakes, porridge, omelettes and veggie food, include *Geeta* and *Sri Venkateswara*, both on Main Street. The *New Shanti Restaurant* opposite *Shanti Lodge* is another typical travellers' joint, renowned for its fresh pasta and soft cheese. The friendly *Suresh*, behind the *Shri Rama Tourist Home*, serves delicious *shak-shuka* on banana leaves and is a good place for breakfast.

You can also get filling *thalis* and a range of freshly cooked snacks in the *Rahul Guest House*. The *Moonlight*, a thatched café overlooking the river and the coracle jetty, offers bland but wholesome veg food and has a pleasant location a short walk past the *Shanti*. However, the prize for Hampi's best all-round café has to go to the *Mango Tree*, hidden away in the banana plantations beyond the coracle jetty and the Shivananda Yoga Ashram. The food is fairly run-of-the-mill, but the relaxing riverside location is hard to beat. Across the river in Virupapuragadda, and the most popular hangout with Israelis, is *Third Eye*, perched on the ridge to the left of the coracle jetty; it churns out pasta, bland curries and Israeli favourites. You can also get authentic Western-style bread and **cakes** through *Shanti Lodge*; place your order by early evening, and the cakes and pies are delivered the following day.

The site

Although spread over 26 square kilometres, the ruins of Vijayanagar are mostly concentrated in two distinct groups: the first lies in and around **Hampi**

Admission charges

Admission to some of the best preserved of Hampi's archeological sites – namely the Vitthala temple and Lotus Mahal – is by **ticket**. Issued by the ASI at the entrances between 8am and 4pm and valid for one day only, the pass gains you entry to both sites, as well as the Royal Enclosure and Zenana complex surrounding the Lotus Mahal, and officially costs US$5 – or its rupee equivalent – for foreigners, and Rs10 for Indians. You'll probably be approached by characters outside the gates offering significantly reduced rates; they're local guides who've got together with the Survey ticket-*wallahs* to run a nice little scam which gets you in for less (a lot less if you haggle hard), and allows them to pocket the fee.

Bazaar and the nearby riverside area, encompassing the city's most sacred enclave of temples and *ghats*; the second centres on the **royal enclosure** – 3km south of the river, just northwest of **Kamalapuram** village – which holds the remains of palaces, pavilions, elephant stables, guardhouses and temples. Between the two stretches a long boulder-choked hill and a swathe of banana plantations, fed by ancient irrigation canals.

Frequent buses run from Hospet to Hampi Bazaar and Kamalapuram, and you can start your tour from either; most visitors prefer to set out on foot or bicycle from the former. After a look around the soaring **Virupaksha temple**, work your way east along the main street and riverbank to the beautiful **Vitthala temple**, and then back via the **Achyutaraya** complex at the foot of Matanga Hill. From here, a dirt path leads south to the royal enclosure, but it's easier to return to the bazaar and pick up the tarred road, calling in at **Hemakuta Hill**, a group of pre-Vijayanagar temples, en route.

On KSTDC's whistle-stop **guided tour**, it's possible to see most of the highlights in a day. If you can, however, set aside at least two or three days to explore the site and its environs, crossing the river by **coracle** to **Anegondi** village, with a couple of side hikes to hilltop viewpoints: the west side of Hemakuta Hill, overlooking Hampi Bazaar, is best for sunsets, while **Matanga Hill** offers what has to be one of the world's most exotic sunrise vistas.

Hampi Bazaar and the Virupaksha temple

Lining Hampi's long, straight main street, **Hampi Bazaar**, which runs east from the eastern entrance of the Virupaksha temple, you can still make out the remains of Vijayanagar's ruined, columned bazaar, partly inhabited by today's lively market. Landless labourers live in many of the crumbling 500-year-old buildings.

Dedicated to a local form of Shiva known as Virupaksha or Pampapati, the functioning **Virupaksha temple** (daily 8am–12.30pm & 3–6.30pm; Rs2) dominates the village, drawing a steady flow of pilgrims from all over southern India. Also known as **Sri Virupaksha Swami**, the temple is free for all who come for *arati* (worship; daily 6.30–8am & 6.30–8pm) when the temple has the most atmosphere. The complex consists of two courts, each entered through a towered *gopura*.

A colonnade surrounds the inner court, usually filled with pilgrims dozing and singing religious songs. On entering, if the temple elephant is around, you can get him to bless you by placing a rupee in his trunk. In the middle the principal temple is approached through a *mandapa* hallway whose carved columns feature rearing animals. Rare Vijayanagar-era paintings on the *mandapa* ceiling include aspects of Shiva, a procession with the sage Vidyaranya, the ten incarnations of Vishnu, and scenes from the *Mahabharata*.

△ Hampi

The sacred **ford** in the river is reached from the Virupaksha's north *gopura*; you can also get there by following the lane around the impressive temple **tank** and past *Shanti Lodge*. A *mandapa* overlooks the steps that originally led to the river, now some distance away. **Coracles** ply from this part of the bank, just as they did five centuries ago, ferrying villagers to the fields and tourists to the far bank. The path through the village eventually winds to an impressive ruined bridge, and on to the hilltop Hanuman shrine – a recommended round walk described on p.231.

Matanga Hill

The place to head for sunrise is the boulder hill immediately east of Hampi Bazaar. From the end of the main street, an ancient paved pathway winds up a rise, at the top of which the magnificent Tiruvengalanatha temple is revealed. The views improve as you progress up **Matanga Hill**, at the top of which a small stone temple provides an extraordinary vantage point. Be warned, however, that over the years there have been a number of **muggings** early in the morning along this path, and that you're advised to walk in a group.

The riverside path

To reach the Vitthala temple from the village, walk east along the length of Hampi Bazaar. Fifty metres or so before the end, a path on the left, staffed at regular intervals by conch-blowing sadhus and an assortment of other ragged mendicants, follows the river past a café. Beyond at least four Vishnu shrines, the paved and colonnaded **Achutya Bazaar** leads due south to the **Tiruvengalanatha temple**, whose beautiful stone carvings – among them some of Hampi's famed erotica – are being restored by the ASI. Back on the main path again, make a short detour across the rocks leading to the river to see the little-visited waterside **Agni temple** – next to it, the Kotalinga complex consists of 108 (an auspicious number) tiny *linga*, carved on a flat rock. As you approach the Vitthala temple, to the south is an archway known as the **King's Balance**, where the rajas were weighed against gold, silver and jewels to be distributed to the city's priests.

Vitthala temple

Although the area of the **Vitthala temple** (daily 8am–4pm; $5 [Rs10]; ticket also valid for the Lotus Mahal on the same day) does not show the same evidence of early cult worship as Virupaksha, the ruined bridge to the west probably dates from before Vijayanagar times. The bathing *ghat* may be from the Chalukya or Ganga period, but as the temple has fallen into disuse it seems that the river crossing (*tirtha*) here has not had the same sacred significance as the Virupaksha site. Now designated a World Heritage Monument by UNESCO, the Vitthala temple was built for Vishnu, who according to legend was too embarrassed by its ostentation to live there.

The open *mandapa* features slender monolithic granite **musical pillars** which were constructed so as to sound the notes of the scale when struck. Today, due to vandalism and erosion from being repeatedly beaten, heavy security makes sure that no one is allowed to touch them. Guides, however, will happily demonstrate the musical resonance of other pillars on an adjacent structure. Outer columns sport characteristic Vijayanagar rearing horses, while friezes of lions, elephants and horses on the moulded basement display sculptural trickery – you can transform one beast into another simply by masking one portion of the image.

In front of the temple, to the east, a stone representation of a wooden processional **rath**, or chariot, houses an image of Garuda, Vishnu's bird vehicle. Now cemented, at one time the chariot's wheels revolved.

Anegondi and beyond

With more time, and a sense of adventure, you can head across the Tungabhadra to **ANEGONDI**, a fortress town predating Vijayanagar and the city's four-teenth-century headquarters. The most pleasant way to go is to take a *putti*, a circular rush-basket coracle, from the ford 1500m east of the Vitthala temple; the *puttis*, which are today reinforced with plastic sheets, also carry bicycles.

Forgotten temples and fortifications litter Anegondi village and its quiet sur-roundings. The ruined **Huchchappa-matha temple**, near the river gateway, is worth a look for its black, stone, lathe-turned pillars and fine panels of dancers. **Aramani**, a ruined palace in the centre, stands opposite the home of the descendants of the royal family; also in the centre, the **Ranganatha temple** is still active.

A huge wooden temple chariot stands in the village square. To complete a five-kilometre loop back to Hampi from here (best attempted by bicycle), head left (west) along the road, winding through sugar cane fields towards the sacred **Pampla Sarovar**, signposted down a dirt lane to the left. The small temple above this square bathing tank, tended by a *swami* who will proudly show you photos of his pilgrimage to Mount Kailash, is dedicated to the goddess Lakshmi and holds a cave containing a footprint of Vishnu. If you are staying around Anegondi, this quiet and atmospheric spot is best visited early in the evening during *arati* (worship).

Another worthwhile detour from the road is the hike up to the tiny white-washed **Hanuman temple**, perched on a rocky hilltop north of the river, from where you gain superb views over Hampi especially at sunrise or sunset. The steep climb up to it takes around half an hour. Keep following the road west for another 3km and you'll eventually arrive at an impressive old **stone bridge** dating from Vijayanagar times. The track from the opposite bank crosses a large island in the Tungabhadra, emerging after twenty minutes at the sacred ford and coracle jetty below the Virupaksha temple in Hampi Bazaar. This rewarding round walk can, of course, be completed in reverse, beginning at the sacred ford. With a bike, it takes around three hours, including the side trips outlined above; allow most of the day if you attempt it on foot, and take plenty of water.

Hemakuta Hill and around

Directly above Hampi Bazaar, **Hemakuta Hill** is dotted with pre-Vijayanagar temples that probably date from between the ninth and eleventh centuries (late Chalukya or Ganga). Aside from the architecture, the main reason to clamber up here is to admire the **views** of the ruins and surrounding countryside. Looking across the boulder-covered terrain and banana plantations, the sheer western edge of the hill is Hampi's number-one sunset spot, attracting a crowd of blissed-out tourists most evenings, along with a couple of entrepreneurial *chai-wallahs* and little boys posing for photos in Hanuman costumes.

A couple of interesting monuments lie on the road leading south towards the main, southern group of ruins. The first of these, a walled **Krishna temple complex** to the west of the road, dates from 1513. Although dilapidated in parts, it features some fine carving and shrines.

Hampi's most-photographed monument stands just south of the Krishna temple in its own enclosure. Depicting Vishnu in his incarnation (*avatar*) as the Man-Lion, the monolithic **Narashima** statue, with its bulging eyes and crossed legs strapped into yogic pose, is one of Vijayanagar's greatest treasures.

The southern and royal monuments

The most impressive remains of Vijayanagar, the city's **royal monuments**, lie some 3km south of Hampi Bazaar, spread over a large expanse of open ground. Before tackling the ruins proper, it's a good idea to get your bearings with a visit to the small **Archeological Museum** (daily except Fri 10am–5pm; free) at Kamalapuram, which can be reached by bus from Hospet or Hampi. Turn right out of the Kamalapuram bus stand, take the first turning on the right, and the museum is on the left – two minutes' walk. Among the sculpture, weapons, palm-leaf manuscripts and painting from Vijayanagar and Anegondi, the highlight is a superb scale model of the city, giving an excellent bird's-eye view of the entire site.

To walk into the city from the museum, go back to the main road and take the nearby turning marked "Hampi 4km". After 200m or so you reach the partly ruined massive **inner city wall**, made from granite slabs, which runs 32km around the city, in places as high as 10m. The outer wall was almost twice as long. At one time, there were said to have been seven city walls; coupled with areas of impenetrable forest and the river to the north, they made the city virtually impregnable.

Just beyond the wall, the **citadel area** was once enclosed by another wall and gates of which only traces remain. To the east, the small *ganigitti* ("oil-woman's") fourteenth-century **Jain temple** features a simple, stepped pyramidal tower of undecorated horizontal slabs. Beyond it is **Bhima's Gate**, once one of the principal entrances to the city, named after the Titan-like Pandava prince and hero of the *Mahabharata*. Like many of the gates, it is "bent", a form of defence that meant anyone trying to get in had to make two ninety-degree turns. Bas-reliefs depict such episodes as Bhima avenging the attempted rape of his wife, Draupadi, by killing the general Kichaka. Draupadi vowed she would not dress her hair until Kichaka was dead; one panel shows her tying up her locks, the vow fulfilled.

Back on the path, to the west, the plain facade of the fifteen-metre-square **Queen's Bath** belies its glorious interior, open to the sky and surrounded by corridors with 24 different domes. Eight projecting balconies overlook where once was water; traces of Islamic-influenced stucco decoration survive. Women from the royal household would bathe here and umbrellas were placed in shafts in the tank floor to protect them from the sun. The water supply channel can be seen outside.

Continuing northwest brings you to **Mahanavami-Dibba** or "House of Victory", built to commemorate a successful campaign in Orissa. A twelve-metre pyramidal structure with a square base, it is said to have been where the king gave and received honours and gifts. From here he watched the magnificent parades, music and dance performances, martial arts displays, elephant fights and animal sacrifices that made celebration of the ten-day Dusshera festival famed throughout the land. Carved reliefs decorate the sides of the platform. To the west, another platform – the largest at Vijayanagar – is thought to be the basement of the **King's Audience Hall**. Stone bases of a hundred pillars remain, in an arrangement that has caused speculation as to how the building could have been used; there are no passageways or open areas.

The two-storey **Lotus Mahal** (daily 8am–4pm; $5 [Rs10]; ticket also valid for the Vitthala temple on the same day), a little further north and part of the **zenana enclosure**, or women's quarters, was designed for the pleasure of Krishna Deva Raya's queen: a place where she could relax, particularly in summer. Displaying a strong Indo-Islamic influence, the pavilion is open on the ground floor, whereas the upper level (no longer accessible by stairs) contains windows and balcony seats. A moat surrounding the building is thought to have provided water-cooled air via tubes.

Beyond the Lotus Mahal, the **Elephant Stables**, a series of high-ceilinged, domed chambers, entered through arches, are the most substantial surviving secular buildings at Vijayanagar – a reflection of the high status accorded to elephants, both ceremonial and in battle.

Walking west of the Lotus Mahal, you pass two temples before reaching the road to Hemakuta Hill. The rectangular enclosure wall of the small **Hazara Rama** ("One thousand Ramas") temple, thought to have been the private palace shrine, features a series of medallion figures and bands of detailed friezes showing scenes from the *Ramayana*.

Jog Falls

Hidden in a remote, thickly forested corner of the Western Ghats, **Jog Falls**, 240km northeast of Mangalore, are the highest **waterfalls** in India. These days, they are rarely as spectacular as they were before the construction of a large dam upriver, which impedes the flow of the River Sharavati over the sheer red-brown sandstone cliffs. However, the surrounding scenery is stunning at any time, with dense scrub and jungle carpeting the mountainous terrain. The views of the falls from the scruffy collection of *chai* stalls on the opposite side of the gorge are also impressive, unless, that is, you come here during the monsoons, when mist and rain clouds envelop the cascades. Another reason not to come here during the wet season is that the extra water, and abundance of leeches at this time, make the excellent **hike** to the floor valley dangerous. So if you can, head up here between October and January, and bring soild footwear. The trail starts just below the bus park and winds steeply down to the water. Confident hikers also venture further downriver, clambering over boulders to other pools and hidden viewpoints, but you should keep a close eye on the water level and take along a local **guide** to point out the safest path.

Practicalities

The easiest way to reach Jog Falls from Goa is to jump on the Konkan Railway's "KR01 Down" train from Margao (departs 1.50pm) or Chaudi (departs 2.20pm) to **Honavar** (arrives 4pm), and change there on to a bus; the onward journey between Honavar and Jog takes around two and a half hours. There is also one direct bus per day from Gokarn (5hr). Timetables for services heading in the opposite direction (to leave Jog), can be checked at the **tourist office** in the *Tunga Tourist Home* (Mon–Sat 10am–5.30pm), which also helps arrange **cars** or Jeeps for rent.

Accommodation

Accommodation at Jog Falls is very limited, so if you plan to stay book ahead. For those lucky enough to be granted a room, the *PWD Inspection Bungalow* (❶), on the north side of the gorge, has great views from its spacious, comfortable rooms, but is invariably full and has to be reserved in advance from the Assistant Engineer's office in Siddapur, 17km northeast. Across the falls on the main side of the settlement, the large concrete complex of the KSTDC *Mayura Gerusoppa* (☎0818/644732; ❷–❸), past the non-functioning public swimming pool, has vast rooms with fading plaster and bathrooms with rickety plumbing, but the staff are friendly and there's an adequate restaurant plus good views. Their annexe, the KSTDC *Tunga Tourist Home* at the bus stand, is more basic (❷) and doesn't have the garden or view. On the opposite side of the road the Karnataka Power Corporation also rents out its four comfy a/c rooms (☏0818/644742; ❹) when available. The youth hostel (❶), ten minutes' walk down the Shimoga road, has basic facilities but recent renovations have made it more appealing.

Eating

The KSTDC canteen next to the *Tunga Tourist Home* at the bus stand serves reasonable South Indian vegetarian **food** including *iddlis* and *dosas*. The KSTDC *Mayura Gerusoppa* has a more comfortable restaurant with a varied menu but still manages to remain uninspiring while the *chai* stalls around the square serve basic *thalis* and (eggy) snacks.

Gokarn

Set behind a broad white-sand beach, with the forest-covered foothills of the Western Ghats forming a backdrop, **GOKARN** (also spelled Gokarna), 154km south of Margao, is among India's most scenically situated sacred sites. Yet this compact little coastal town – a Shaivite centre for more than two millennia – remained largely "undiscovered" by Western tourists until the early 1990s, when it began to attract dreadlocked and didgeridoo-toting travellers fleeing the commercialization of Goa. Now, it's firmly on the tourist map, although the Hindu pilgrims pouring through still far outnumber the foreigners that flock here in winter.

Even if you've had your fill of beaches, Gokarn definitely deserves a trip down the coastal highway. A long-established pilgrimage place with a markedly traditional feel, it will give you a stronger taste of Hindu India than anywhere else in the region: shaven-headed Brahmins sit crosslegged on their verandahs murmuring Sanskrit verses, while pilgrims file through a bazaar crammed with religious paraphernalia to the sea for a holy dip. An added incentive is the superb scenery punctuating the journey here. Winding up thickly wooded spurs and headlands, the road regularly yields tantalizing glimpses of cobalt-blue bays, lined by unfeasibly white beaches where you'd be unlucky to run into another tourist all day.

Getting there

From Goa, the fastest and most convenient way to travel down the coast to Gokarn is via the **Konkan Railway**. At 1.50pm, train #KR001 Down leaves Margao, passing through Chaudi at 2.20pm en route to Gokarn, where it arrives at around 3.30pm. The station lies 9km east of Gokarn town itself, but buses and rickshaws are on hand to shuttle passengers the rest of the way. Heading in the other direction, the best train for Goa from Gokarn station, #KR002 Up, departs at 11.15am, arriving in Chaudi at 12.30pm and Margao at 1.05pm. As this is classed as a passenger service, you don't have to buy tickets in advance; just turn up at the station 30–45min before the departure time and pay at the regular ticket counter. However, it is always a good idea to check timings in advance, through any tourist office, travel agent or the KRC's website (⑩www.konkanrailway.com).

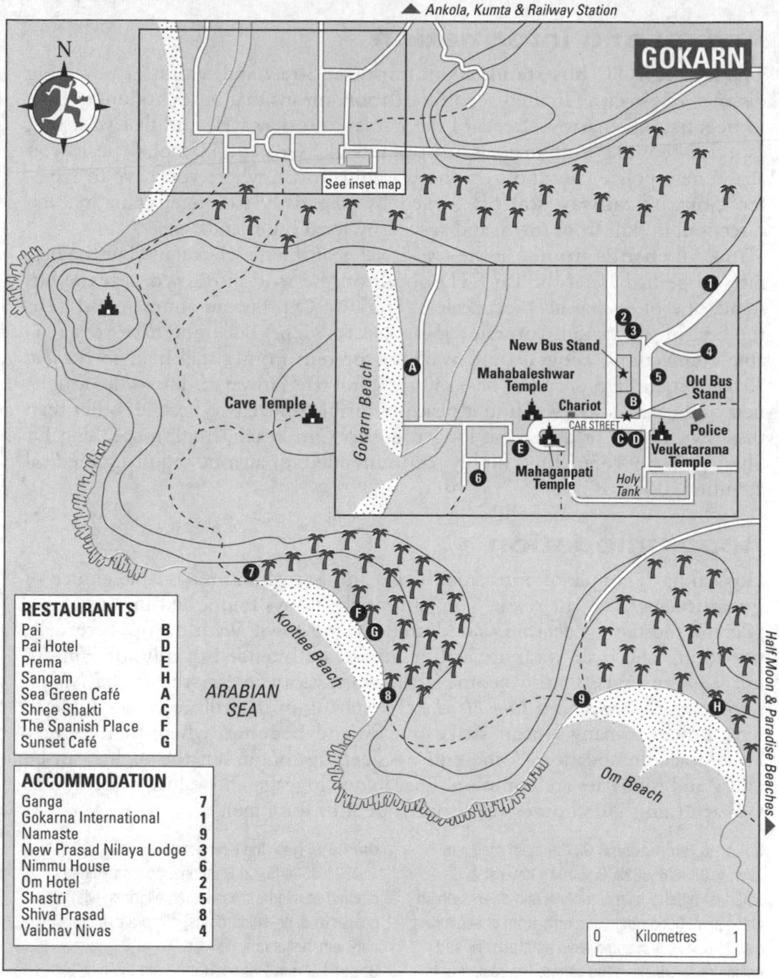
Ankola, Kumta & Railway Station
GOKARN
N
See inset map
Cave Temple
Gokarn Beach
New Bus Stand
Mahabaleshwar Temple
Chariot
Old Bus Stand
CAR STREET
Police
Veukatarama Temple
Mahaganpati Temple
Holy Tank
Kootlee Beach
ARABIAN SEA
Om Beach
Half Moon & Paradise Beaches
RESTAURANTS
Pai B
Pai Hotel D
Prema E
Sangam H
Sea Green Café A
Shree Shakti C
The Spanish Place F
Sunset Café G
ACCOMMODATION
Ganga 7
Gokarna International 1
Namaste 9
New Prasad Nilaya Lodge 3
Nimmu House 6
Om Hotel 2
Shastri 5
Shiva Prasad 8
Vaibhav Nivas 4
0 Kilometres 1

Buses take as much as two and a half hours longer to cover the same route. A direct service leaves Margao's interstate stand in the north of town daily at 1pm. You can also get there by catching any of the services that run between Goa and Mangalore, and jumping off either at Ankola, or at the Gokarn junction on the main highway, from where frequent private minibuses and *tempos* run into town. If you're planning to travel here from Hampi, it is also worth knowing that a daily government bus covers the route, in around ten hours.

The Konkan highway is straightforward **by motorcycle**, with a better-than-average road surface and frequent fuel stops along the way. Travelling on a rented bike also gives you the option of heading down sandy side lanes to explore some of the gorgeous beaches glimpsed from the road. The only drawback is crossing the border, which can involve a *baksheesh* transaction (see "Crossing the Goa–Karnataka border" box in Chapter 3, p.215).

Arrival and information

The new KSRTC **bus stand**, 300m from Car Street and within easy walking distance of Gokarn's limited accommodation, means that buses no longer have to negotiate the narrow streets of the bazaar. You may well find that your bus, especially coming from major tourist points like Goa and Hampi, deposits you at the new police checkpost on the way into town, where you have to register. Gokarn's **railway station**, served by one daily passenger train in each direction, is 9km from town, and served by local buses and *tempos*.

You can **change money** at the *Om Hotel* near the new bus stand but the best rates to be had are at the Pai STD booth on the road into town near the bus stand, one of several licensed dealers. The tiny Om bureau almost opposite is the best of the various **Internet** joints (all Rs40/hr) but none have very reliable connections. **Bicycles** are available for rent from a stall next to the *Pai Restaurant*, for Rs3 per hour or Rs30 for a full day. However, due to the roughness of the tracks you will find it near impossible to cycle to beaches other than the town beach, or along the long route to Om beach. English-speaking Dr Shastri (℡0838/656220) is highly recommended for anyone requiring medical attention.

Accommodation

Gokarn has a couple of bona fide **hotels** and a small but reasonable choice of **guesthouses**. As a last resort, you can nearly always find a bed in one of the pilgrims' hostels, or *dharamshalas*, dotted around town. With dorms, bare, cell-size rooms and basic washing facilities, these are intended mainly for Hindus, but Western tourists are welcome if there are vacancies: try the *Prasad Nilaya*, just down the lane from *Om Hotel*. After staying in the village for a couple of days, however, many visitors strike out for the **beaches**, where there is very limited accommodation. Some end up sleeping rough, but the nights can be chilly and robberies are common. Leave your luggage and valuables behind in Gokarn (most guesthouses will store your stuff for a fee).

Gokarna International On the main road into town ℡0838/656622. Gokarna's newest and smartest hotel, which is friendly and offers unbeatable value. Good range of rooms from cheap singles to deluxe a/c; some have bathtubs, TV and balconies overlooking the palms. The restaurants, one with bar, are more mediocre. ❷–❹

New Prasad Nilaya Lodge Near the new bus stand ℡0838/657135. A relatively new place with clean, bright, spacious rooms with attached baths and food to order. Very reasonable. ❶–❷

Nimmu House A minute's walk from the temples towards Gokarn beach ℡0838/656730, ©nimmuhouse@yahoo.com. Gokarn's best budget guesthouse, run by the friendly and helpful lady whose name it bears, with clean rooms (some with attached bath). The new block has very reasonable doubles; there are reliable left-luggage and Internet facilities and a peaceful yard to sit in. ❶–❷

Om Hotel Near the new bus stand ℡0838/656445. Conventional economy hotel pitched at middle-class Indian pilgrims, with plain, good-sized, en-suite rooms, some a/c, and a dingy bar-cum-restaurant. ❶–❷

Shastri Guest House 100m from the new bus stand ℡0838/656220. The best of the uniformly drab and run-down guesthouses lining the main street, this is a quiet place offering some rooms with attached bath, and rock-bottom single occupancy rates. ❷

Vaibhav Nivas Off the main road, five minutes from the bazaar ℡0838/656714. Friendly, cheap and justifiably popular place despite the tiny rooms, most with shared bathrooms. The new extension includes some rooms with attached bathrooms. Internet and left-luggage facilities available. ❶

The Town

Gokarn **town**, a hotchpotch of wood-fronted houses and red terracotta roofs, is clustered around a long L-shaped bazaar, its broad main road – known as **Car Street** – running west to the town beach, a sacred site in its own right. Hindu mythology identifies it as the place where Rudra (another name for Shiva) was reborn through the ear of a cow from the underworld after a period of penance. Gokarn is also the home of one of India's most powerful *shivalinga* – the **pranalingam** – which came to rest here after being carried off by Ravana, the evil king of Lanka, from Shiva's home on Mount Kailash in the Himalayas.

The *pranalingam* resides in Gokarn to this day, enshrined in the medieval **Shri Mahabaleshwar temple**, at the far west end of the bazaar. It is regarded as so auspicious that a mere glimpse of it will absolve a hundred sins, even the murder of a brahmin. Local Hindu lore also asserts that you can maximize the *lingam's* purifying power by shaving your head, fasting, and taking a holy dip in the sea before *darshan*, or ritual viewing of the deity. For this reason, pilgrims traditionally begin their tour of Gokarn with a walk to the beach, guided by their family *pujari*. Next, they visit the **Shri Mahaganpati temple**, a stone's throw east of Shri Mahabaleshwar, to propitiate the elephant-headed god Ganesh. Sadly, owing to some ugly incidents involving insensitive behaviour by a minority of foreigners, tourists are now banned from the temples, though you can still get a good view of proceedings in the smaller Shri Mahaganpati from the entrance.

The beaches

Notwithstanding Gokarn's numerous temples, shrines and tanks, most Western tourists come here for the beautiful **beaches** situated south of the more crowded town beach, beyond the lumpy laterite headland that overlooks the town.

To pick up the trail, head along the narrow alley opposite the south entrance to the Mahaganpati temple, and follow the path uphill through the woods. After twenty minutes, you drop down from a rocky plateau to **Kootlee beach** – a wonderful kilometre-long sweep of golden-white sand sheltered by a pair of steep-sided promontories. Despite appearances, locals consider the water here to be dangerous. The palm-leaf *chai* stalls and seasonal **cafés** that spring up here during the winter offer some respite from the heat of the midday sun, and some of them offer very basic **accommodation** in bamboo shacks. Two places have more solid, lockable brick or mud huts but are likely to be booked out by long-term visitors: the *Ganga*, to the right as you first approach the beach (℡0838/657195; ❶); and *Shiva Prasad* at the far end (℡0838/657150; ❶). *The Spanish Place* (owned by a lady from Spain), set behind a line of neatly planted palms midway down the beach, serves good pasta, sandwiches, sweets and creamy *lassis* in a relaxed atmosphere, and the nearby *Sunset Café* offers seafood, tasty sizzlers and other more basic meals. Freshwater has been a perennial problem but bottled water is widely available.

It takes around twenty minutes to hike over the headland from Kootlee to exquisite **Om beach**, so named because its distinctive twin crescent-shaped bays resemble the auspicious Om symbol. The advent of a dirt road from town means the coves are now frequented by a more diverse crowd than the hardcore hippy fringe whose exclusive preserve it used to be until the late-1990s. Hammocks and basic huts still populate the palm groves and about a dozen *chai* houses such as the laid-back *Sangam* provide ample food and drink, but the opening of the nicely landscaped *Namaste* (☎0838/657150; ❶) points to greater future development.

That said, it's unlikely the concrete mixers will ever reach Gokarn's two most remote beaches, which lie another twenty- to forty-minute walk over the hill. **Half-Moon** and **Paradise** beaches, are, despite the presence of one or two *chai* houses on each and the occasional shack, mainly for intrepid sun-lovers happy to pack in their own supplies. If you're looking for near-total isolation, this is your best bet.

Eating

Gokarn town offers a good choice of **places to eat**, with a string of busy "meals" joints along Car Street and the main road. Most popular, with locals and tourists, is the brightly lit *Pai Restaurant*, which dishes up fresh and tasty veg *thalis*, *masala dosas*, crisp *wadas*, teas and coffees until late. The other commendable "meals" canteen, around the corner on Car Street, is the similarly named *Pai Hotel*; it's much smaller, but their snacks are excellent, and the milk coffee delicious. *Shree Shakti Cold Drinks*, also on Car Street, serves mouthwatering fresh cheese, hygienically made to an American recipe and served with rolls, garlic and tomato; the friendly owner also makes his own peanut butter, and serves filling toasties and *lassis*. Round this off with an ice cream, either here or at any number of places along the road.

Every café does its own version of *gad-bads*, several layers of different ice creams mixed with chopped nuts and chewy dried fruit. One of the best is served at the tiny *Prema Restaurant* opposite the Mahabaleshwar temple's main gates, which has a traveller-friendly menu. The restaurant bar at the *Om* now does some Mexican and Italian dishes, as well as good fish, and is more pleasant if you can find a seat in the small courtyard rather than the dingy interior. Another decent eatery is the *Sea Green Café*, just behind the main town beach, which offers Tibetan and Nepali food, plus alcohol.

Travel details

By train
Gokarn to: Chaudi (1 daily; 1hr 15min); Kumta (1 daily; 20min); Honavar (1 daily; 30min); Margao (1 daily; 2hr).
Hospet to: Margao (2 weekly; 8hr 30min).

By bus
Gokarn to: Ankola (every 30min; 30min); Chaudi (1 daily; 2hr 30min); Hampi (1 daily; 10–11hr); Jog Falls (1 daily; 5hr); Karwar (4 daily; 1hr 30min); Margao (1 daily; 4hr); Panjim (1 daily; 5hr).
Hospet to: Gokarn (1 daily; 10hr); Hampi (every 30min; 20min); Panjim (2–3 daily; 10hr).

Mumbai

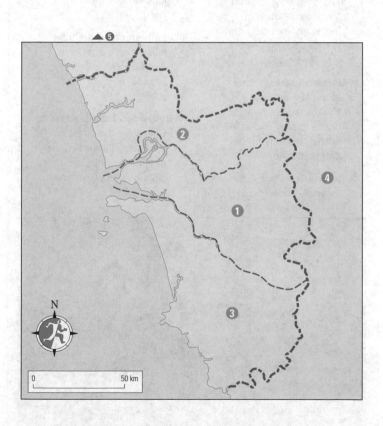

CHAPTER 5

Highlights

✳ **The Gateway of India** The departure-point for the last British troops leaving India, now a favourite spot for an evening stroll. See p.255

✳ **Prince of Wales Museum** The main enticement is the fine collection of Indian art, including erotic Gita Govinda paintings. See p.257

✳ **Maidans (parks)** Where Mumbai's citizens escape the hustle and bustle to play cricket, eat lunch and hang out. See p.259

✳ **Victoria Terminus** A fantastically eccentric pile, perhaps the greatest railway station ever built by the British. See p.261

✳ **The bazaars** A labyrinth of packed streets selling everything from gold wedding jewellery to junk left over from the Raj. See p.263

✳ **Elephanta Island** A magnificent rock-cut Shiva temple on an island in Mumbai harbour. See p.265

✳ **Bollywood blockbusters** Check out the latest Hindi mega movie in one of the city centre's gigantic air-con cinemas. See p.271

5

Mumbai

Ever since the opening of the Suez canal in the 1860s, the principal gateway to the Indian subcontinent has been **MUMBAI (Bombay)**, the city Aldous Huxley famously described as "the most appalling . . . of either hemisphere". Travellers tend to regard time spent here as a rite of passage to be survived rather than savoured. But as the powerhouse of Indian business, industry and trade, and the source of its most seductive media images, the Maharashtran capital can be a compelling place to kill time. Whether or not you find the experience enjoyable, however, will depend largely on how well you handle the heat, humidity, hassle, traffic fumes, relentless crowds and appalling poverty of India's most dynamic, westernized city.

First impressions of Mumbai tend to be dominated by its chronic **shortage of space**. Crammed onto a narrow spit of land that curls from the swamp-ridden coast into the Arabian Sea, the city has, in less than five hundred years since its "discovery" by the Portuguese, metamorphosed from an aboriginal fishing settlement into a sprawling megalopolis of over sixteen million people. Being swept along broad boulevards by endless streams of commuters, or jostled by coolies and hand-cart pullers in the teeming bazaars, you'll continually feel as if Mumbai is about to burst at the seams.

The roots of the population problem and attendant poverty lie, paradoxically, in the city's enduring ability to create wealth. Mumbai alone generates nearly forty percent of India's GNP, its port handles half the country's foreign trade, and its movie industry is the biggest in the world. Symbols of prosperity are everywhere: from the phalanx of office blocks clustered on Nariman Point, Maharashtra's Manhattan, to the expensively dressed teenagers posing in Colaba's trendiest nightspots.

The flip side to the success story, of course, is the city's much chronicled **poverty**. Each day, hundreds of economic refugees pour into Mumbai from the Maharashtran hinterland. Some find jobs and secure accommodation; many more (around a third of the total population) end up living on the already overcrowded streets, or amid the squalor of Asia's largest slums, reduced to rag-picking and begging from cars at traffic lights.

Mumbai/Bombay

In 1996 Bombay was renamed **Mumbai**, as part of a wider policy instigated by the ultra-right-wing Shiv Sena Municipality to replace names of any places, roads and features in the city that had connotations of the Raj. Mumbai is the Marathi name of the local deity, the mouthless "Maha-amba-aiee" (Mumba for short), who is believed to have started her life as an obscure aboriginal earth goddess.

MUMBAI

N

Airports

ARABIAN SEA

Haji Ali's Tomb

Mahalakshmi Temple

Crossword Bookshop

Breach Candy Hospital

Mahalakshmi Racecourse

Willingdon Golf Course

Municipal Dhobi Ghats

Veermata Jeejamata (Victoria & Albert) Museum

V J B Udyan (Victoria Gardens)

NATH PAI MARG (BEAY RD)

DR BABASAHEB AMBEDKHAR MARG

E S PANTANWALLA MARG

SANT SAVTA MARG (VICTORIA RD)

SANT JANU MARG

SETH MOTI SHAH RD

S B DIKHU MARG

SHIVDAS CHAMPS MARG

DR M BAIRU MARG

N M JOSHI MARG

SANE GURUJI MARG

SANE GURUJI MARG

KHADVE

MAHARAD CHOWK

BAPURAO JAGTAP MARG

MAULANA AZAD RD (NORTH)

MAULANA AZAD RD (SOUTH)

SIR J JEEJIBHOY RD

N M JOSHI MARG

NANDRAO NAIR MARG

Maratha Mandir Cinema

J BOMAN BEHRAM MARG

NAWAB TANK RD

Red Light District

Alfred Talkies

RAMCHANDRA BHAT

J Tata RD

Mumbai Central Inter-state Bus Stand

Mumbai Central

Bus Stop for Downtown

Grant Rd Railway Station

Opera House

SARDAR V PATEL RD

MAULANA SHAUKATALI (GRANT RD)

N DESAI RD

SARDAR V PATEL RD

KASHAVRO KHADE MARG

TADDEOR MARG

TARDEO RD

NAIK CHOWK

NANA CHOWK

DR G DESHMUKH MARG

KEMPS CORNER

BHULABHAI DESAI RD

S K BADODAWALA MARG

Mani Bhavan Mahatma Gandhi Museum

SITARAM PATKAR MARG

JAGANNATH SHANKARSHETH MARG

Babulnath Mandir Temple

DR BHADKAMKAR MARG

Towers of Silence

PM (Hanging) Gardens

Malabar Hill

Kamla Nehru Park

Chowpatty Beach

JAGMOHANDAS MARG

N DABHOLKAR MARG

BAL GANGADHAR KHER MARG

Jain Temple

Walukeshwar Temple

Banganga Tank

WALUKESHWAR MARG

MARINE DRIVE (NETAJI SUBHASH MARG)

MAHARISHI KARVE RD

Tarporevala Aquarium

Gymkhanas

Panjrapool Animal Sanctuary

Minara Masjid

MOHAMMED ALI RD

ABDUL REHMAN ST

JOHAR CHOWK

V P TAK MARG

NANDALAL MARG

R D'MELLO RD

NANDALAL JANI RD

Zaveri Bazaar

Jami Masjid

Crawford Market

Bhuleshwar Market

Mumba Devi Temple

MEMON ST

KALBADEVI RD

N A PURANDRE MARG

Metro Cinema (Buses to Goa)

MAHARISHI KARVE RD

Bombay Azad Hospital Maidan

Chatrapathi Shivaji Terminus (Victoria Terminus)

Chor Bazaar

G TANK RD

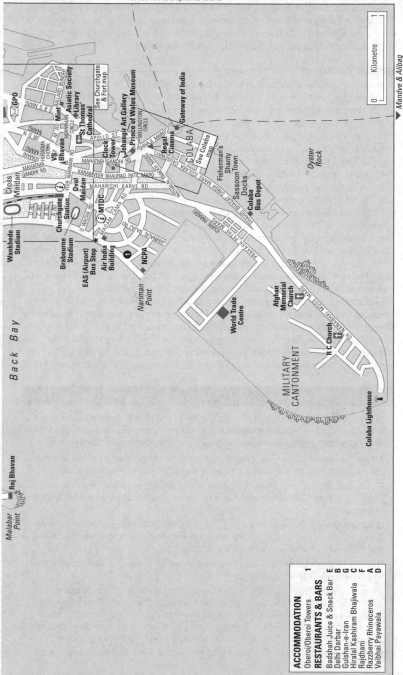

▲ *Launch to Elephanta Island*

GPO

Mint
Asiatic Society
Library

See Churchgate
& Fort map

St Thomas'
Cathedral

BALLARD BUNDER

S B S MARG

N O M RD

P M RD

CIRCLE

HORNIMAN

P K NARIMAN RD

SHOORJI VALLABHDAS MARG

APOLLO ST

Clock
Tower

Jehangir Art Gallery
Prince of Wales Museum

Gateway of India

WELLINGTON
CIRCLE

VS7
(Bhavan)

DINSHAW WACHA RD

SHAHID BHAGAT SINGH MARG

MSRTC

MAHATMA
GANDHI RD

MAHATMA GANDHI RD

Cross
Maidan

Oval
Maidan

MAHARISHI KARVE RD

KARAMVEER BHAURAO PATIL MARG

VEER NARIMAN RD

D WACHA RD

MADAM CAMA RD

JAMNALAL BAJAJ RD

COLABA

Regal
Cinema

See Colaba
map

Fisherman's
Shanty

Sassoon Town

Colaba
Docks

Colaba
Bus Depot

Oyster
Rock

Back Bay

Wankhede
Stadium

Churchgate
Station

MTDC

Brabourne
Stadium

EAS (Airport)
Bus Stop

Air India
Building

NCPA

*Nariman
Point*

World Trade
Centre

Afghan
Memorial
Church

R C Church

MAHARSHI KARVE RD

PRAKASH PETHE MARG

COLABE PARADE

DR NARIMAN ROAD ROOS MARG

MILITARY
CANTONMENT

Colaba Lighthouse

*Malabar
Point*

Raj Bhavan

▼ *Mandve & Alibag*

5

MUMBAI

| 0 | | Kilometre | 1 |

ACCOMMODATION			**1**
Oberoi/Oberoi Towers			
RESTAURANTS & BARS			
Badshah Juice & Snack Bar			E
Delhi Darbar			B
Gulshan-e-Iran			G
Hiralal Kashiram Bhajiwala			C
Rajdhani			F
Razzberry Rhinoceros			A
Vaibhai Payawala			D

However, while it would definitely be misleading to downplay its difficulties, Mumbai is far from the ordeal some travellers make it out to be. Once you've overcome the major hurdle of finding somewhere to stay, you may begin to enjoy its frenzied pace and crowded, cosmopolitan feel.

Some history

Mumbai originally consisted of seven **islands**, inhabited by small Koli fishing communities. The town of Puri on **Elephanta** is thought to have been the major settlement in the region, until King Bimba, or Bhima, sited his capital at Mahim on one island, at the end of the thirteenth century. In 1534, Sultan Bahadur of Ahmedabad ceded the land to the **Portuguese**, who felt it to be of little importance, and concentrated development in the areas further north instead. They handed over the largest island to the English in 1661, as part of the dowry when the Portuguese infanta Catherine of Braganza married Charles II; four years later Charles received the remaining islands and the port, and the town took on the anglicized name of Bombay (the name derives from the Mumba Devi deity who resided here long before the Portuguese came and corrupted it to "Bom Bahia", or 'Good Bay'). This was the first part of India that could properly be termed a colony; elsewhere on the subcontinent the English had merely been granted the right to set up "factories", or trading posts. Because of its natural safe harbour and strategic position for trade, the **East India Company**, based at Surat, wanted to buy the land; in 1668 a deal was struck, and Charles leased Mumbai to them for a pittance.

The English set about an ambitious programme of fortifying their outpost, living in the area known today as Fort. However, life was not easy. There was a fast turnover of governors, and malaria and cholera culled many of the first settlers. **Gerald Aungier**, the fourth governor (1672–77), began planning "the city which by God's assistance is intended to be built", and by the start of the eighteenth century the town was the capital of the East India Company. He is

---

Festivals in Mumbai

Mumbai has its own versions of all the major Hindu and Muslim **festivals**, plus a host of smaller neighbourhood celebrations imported by its immigrant communities. Exact dates vary from year to year; check in advance at the government tourist office.

Makar Sankranti (Jan). A celebration of prosperity, when sweets, flowers and fruit are exchanged by all, and kites are flown in the parks as a sign of happiness.

Elephanta Music and Dance Festival (Feb). MTDC-organized cultural event including floodlit performances by classical artists with the Shiva cave temple as a backdrop.

Gokhulashtami (July/Aug). Riotous commemoration of Krishna's birthday; terracotta pots filled with curd, milk-sweets and cash are strung from tenement balconies and grabbed by human pyramids of young boys.

Nowroz (July/Aug). The Parsi New Year is celebrated with special ceremonies in the Fire Temples, and feasting at home.

Ganesh Chathurthi (Aug/Sept). Huge effigies of Ganesh, the elephant-headed god of prosperity and wisdom, are immersed in the sea at Chowpatty Beach in a ritual originally promoted by freedom-fighters to circumvent British anti-assembly legislation. Recently it has seemed in danger of being hijacked by Hindu extremists such as the Shiv Sena, tingeing it more with chauvinism than celebration.

Nariel Purnima (Sept). Koli fishermen launch brightly decorated boats to mark the end of the monsoon.

credited with encouraging the mix that still contributes to the city's success, welcoming Hindu traders from Gujarat, Goans, Muslim weavers, and most visibly, the business-minded Zoroastrian **Parsis**.

Much of the British settlement in the old Fort area was destroyed by a devastating fire in 1803. The arrival of the **Great Indian Peninsular Railway** half a century or so later improved communications, encouraging yet more immigration from elsewhere in India. This crucial artery, coupled with the cotton crisis in America following the Civil War, gave impetus to the great Bombay cotton boom and established the city as a major industrial and commercial centre. With the opening of the Suez Canal in 1869, and the construction of enormous docks, Bombay's access to European markets improved further. **Sir Bartle Frere**, governor from 1862 to 1867, oversaw the construction of the city's distinctive colonial-Gothic buildings; the most extravagant of all, **Victoria Terminus** railway station – now officially Chatrapathi Shivaji Terminus or CST – is a fitting testimony to this extraordinary age of expansion.

As the most prosperous city in the nation, Bombay was at the forefront of the Independence struggle; Mahatma Gandhi used a house here, now a museum, to coordinate the struggle through three decades. Fittingly, the first British colony took pleasure in waving the final goodbye to the Raj, when the last contingent of British troops passed through the Gateway of India in February 1948. Since Independence, Mumbai has prospered as India's commercial and

The Dons

Criminals have always been a part of Mumbai's life, but the 1980s saw an intensification of **organized crime** in the city. Previously, gangsters had confined their activities to small-scale racketeering in poor neighbourhoods. After the post-1970s real-estate boom however, many petty "landsharks" became powerful godfather figures, or **dons**, with drug- and gold-smuggling businesses as well as involvement in extortion and prostitution. Moreover, corrupt politicians who employed the gangs' muscle-power to rig elections had become highly placed political puppets with debts to pay – a phenomenon dubbed **criminalization**. The dividing line between the underworld and politics grew increasingly blurred during the Nineties – in 1992, no less than forty candidates in the municipal elections had criminal records.

The gangs have also become integral in the dirty war between India and Pakistan, with Karachi-based Dawood Ibrahim heavily implicated with the Pakistani security services – he is thought to be behind the bombings of 1993 – and Bombay's leading don Chhota Rajan with the Indian forces. In fact, many see the bungling of Rajan's recent extradition from Thailand, and his subsequent escape from a guarded hospital room (he drugged his Thai police guards and climbed out of the window using his bed sheets) as payment for services rendered.

The late Eighties saw the entrance of the dons into **Bollywood**, when the rise of video and TV made regular film financiers nervous about investing in the industry. Mob money poured in and it's an open secret that the film industry is one of the favoured forms of money-laundering with the dons – rival films mysteriously put back their release dates in order to give mob-backed movies a clear run at the box office. In 2000, however, the authorities began to take action, and Bollywood mogul Bharat Shah (who usually has around ten billion rupees invested in films at any one time) was arrested for financial links to the Dawood Ibrahim gang.

However, Mumbai is still the playground for mafia gangs, each with their own personalities and legends. If you read any newspapers while you're in the city you won't escape this phenomenon; the media revels in the shocking and bloodthirsty exploits of the gangsters, and the unfolding sagas run like a Bollywood blockbuster.

cultural capital and this period has seen the population grow tenfold to more than sixteen million.

However, the resultant overcrowding has done little to foster relations between the city's various minorities, and the past two decades have seen repeated outbursts of communal tensions among the poorer classes. Strikes and riots paralysed the metropolis throughout the 1980s and early 1990s as more and more immigrants from other regions of the country poured in. The mounting discontent fuelled the rise of the extreme right-wing Maharashtran party, the **Shiv Sena**, founded in 1966 by the former cartoonist, Bal "the Saheb" Thackery, a self-confessed admirer of Hitler. Many people blamed Sena cadres for the orchestrating the appalling attacks on Muslims that followed in the wake of the Babri Masjid destruction in Ayodhya in 1992–93. Thousands were murdered by mobs as the city descended into anarchy for ten days.

Just as Mumbai was regaining its composure, disaster struck again. On March 12, 1993, ten massive **bomb blasts** ripped through the heart of the city, destroying key buildings (such as the Stock Exchange and Air India HQ) and killing 317 people. No one claimed responsibility, but the involvement of Muslim godfather Ibrahim Dawood and the Pakistani secret service was suspected. The city bounced back with characteristic ebullience, and the ensuing decade saw its rise as the capital of India's satellite TV industry: simpering MTV and Channel V "VJs" nowadays define Mumbai in the popular imagination of India's affluent middle classes every bit as strongly as its Bollywood stars have for decades in the eyes of the poor.

Arrival and information

Unless you arrive in Mumbai by train at **Chatrapathi Shivaji Terminus** (formerly Victoria Terminus), be prepared for a long slog into the centre. The international and domestic **airports** are north of the city, way off the map, and ninety minutes or more by road from the main hotel areas, while from **Mumbai Central** train or **bus station** you face a laborious trip across town. Finding a place to stay can be even more of a hassle; phone around before you set off into the traffic.

By air

Chatrapathi Shivaji (30km), Mumbai's busy **international airport**, is divided into two "modules", one for Air India flights and the other for foreign airlines. Once through customs and the lengthy immigration formalities, you'll find a 24hr State Bank of India exchange facility, rather unhelpful government (ITDC) and state (MTDC) tourist information counters, car rental kiosks, cafés and a prepaid taxi stand in the chaotic arrivals concourse. There's also – very usefully – an **Indian Railways booking office** which you should make use of if you know your next destination; it'll save you a long wait at the reservation offices downtown. If you're on one of the few flights to land in the afternoon or early evening – by which time most hotels tend to be full – it's worth paying on the spot for a room at the **accommodation booking desk** in the arrivals hall. All of the domestic airlines also have offices outside the main entrance, and there's a handy 24hr **left luggage** "cloakroom" in the car park nearby (Rs50 per day, or part thereof; maximum duration 90 days).

Many of the more upmarket hotels, particularly those near the airport, send out **courtesy coaches** to pick up their guests. **Taxis** are comfortable and not

Malaria warning

Due to the massive slum encampments and bodies of stagnant water around the **airports**, both Chatrapathi Shivaji and Santa Cruz are major **malaria** blackspots. Clouds of mosquitoes await your arrival in the car park, so don't forget to smother yourself with strong insect repellent before leaving the terminal.

too extravagant. To avoid haggling over the fare or being duped by the private taxi companies outside the airport, pay in advance at the taxi desk in the arrivals hall. The price on the receipt, which you hand to the driver on arrival at your destination, is slightly more than the normal meter rate (around Rs300 to Colaba or Nariman Point, or Rs100 to Juhu), but at least you can be sure you'll be taken by the most direct route. Taxi-*wallahs* invariably try to persuade you to stay at a different hotel from the one you ask for. Don't agree to this; their commission will be added on to the price of your room.

Internal flights land at Mumbai's more user-friendly **domestic airport**, **Santa Cruz** (26km to the north), which is divided into separate modern terminals: the cream-coloured one (Module 1A) for Indian Airlines, and the blue-and-white (Module 1B) for private carriers. If you're transferring directly from here to an international flight at Chatrapathi Shivaji, 4km northeast, take the free "fly-bus" that shuttles every fifteen minutes between the two. The Indian government and MTDC both have 24hr information counters in the arrivals hall, and there's a foreign exchange counter and accommodation desk tucked away near the first-floor exit. Use the yellow-and-black metered taxis that queue outside the exit. The touts that claim to be running a prepaid taxi system overcharge hugely – a journey to Colaba should cost around Rs300, no more.

Don't be tempted to use the **auto-rickshaws** that buzz around outside the airports; they're not allowed downtown and will leave you at the mercy of unscrupulous taxi drivers on the edge of vile-smelling Mahim Creek, the southernmost limit of their permitted area.

By train

Trains to Mumbai from most central, southern and eastern regions arrive at **Chatrapathi Shivaji Terminus or CST** (formerly **Victoria Terminus**, or VT), the main railway station at the end of the Central Railway line. From here it's a ten- or fifteen-minute ride to Colaba; taxis queue at the busy rank outside the south exit, opposite the new reservation hall.

Mumbai Central, the terminus for Western Railway trains from northern India, is further out from the centre; take a taxi from the main forecourt, or flag one down on the main road outside.

Some trains from south India arrive at more obscure stations. If you find yourself at **Dadar**, way up in the industrial suburbs, and can't afford a taxi (Rs450), cross the Tilak Marg road bridge onto the Western Railway and catch a suburban train into town, or take BEST bus #1 or #70 to Colaba, #66 to Central. **Kurla** station, where a few Bangalore trains pull in, is even further out, just south of Santa Cruz airport; taking a suburban train for Churchgate is the only reasonable alternative to a taxi (Rs250). From either, it's worth asking at the station when you arrive if there is another long-distance train going to Churchgate or Victoria Terminus shortly after – it's far preferable to trying to cram into either a suburban train or bus.

By bus

Nearly all interstate **buses** arrive at **Mumbai Central** bus stand, a stone's throw from the railway station of the same name. You have a choice between municipal black-and-yellow taxis, the BEST buses (#66, #70 & #71), which run straight into town from the stop on Dr DN Marg (Lamington Road), two minutes' walk west from the bus station, or a suburban train from Mumbai Central's local platform over the footbridge._

Most **Maharashtra State Road Transport Corporation** (MSRTC) buses terminate at Mumbai Central, though those from Pune, Nasik (and surrounding areas) end up at the **ASIAD** bus stand, a glorified parking lot near the railway station in **Dadar**.

Information

The best source of **information** in Mumbai is the excellent **Government of India tourist office** (Mon–Fri 8.30am–6pm, Sat 8.30am–2pm; ☎022/2203 3144, ✉gitobest@bom5.vsnl.net.in) at 123 M Karve Rd, opposite Churchgate station's east exit. The staff here are exceptionally helpful and hand out a wide range of leaflets, maps and brochures on both Mumbai and the rest of the country. There are also 24hr tourist **information counters** at Chatrapthi Shivaji (☎022/2832 5331) and Santa Cruz (☎022/2615 6600) airports.

Maharashtra State Tourism Development Corporation Ltd (**MTDC**) main office, on Madam Cama Road (Mon–Sat 8.30am–7pm; ☎022/202 6731), opposite the LIC Building in Nariman Point, can reserve rooms in MTDC resorts and also sells tickets for city **sightseeing tours**. Of these, the "City" tour (Tues–Sun 2–6pm; Rs70, not including admission charges) is the most popular, managing to cram the Prince of Wales museum, Marine Drive, the Hanging Gardens, Kamla Nehru Park and Mani Bhavan into half a day.

If you need detailed **listings**, ask at the tourist office in Churchgate for a free copy of the slick *Mumbai This Fortnight*, which is user-friendly and has a wealth of useful information, despite being a commercial venture. For **what's on** you're better off checking out the "The List" section of *Mid-Day* (Mumbai's main local rag), the "Metro" page in the *Indian Express*, or the "Bombay Times" section of the *Times of India*. All are available from street vendors around Colaba and the downtown area and cost Rs3–4.

City transport

Transport congestion has eased slightly since the opening of the huge flyover that now scythes straight through the heart of the city from just north of CST station. During peak hours, however, gridlock is the norm and you should brace yourself for long waits at junctions if you take to the roads by taxi, bus or auto. Local **trains** get there faster, but can be a real endurance test even outside rush hours.

Buses

BEST (Bombay Electric Supply and Transport; 24hr information line ☎022/2414 6262) operates a **bus** network of labyrinthine complexity, extending to the furthest-flung corners of the city. Unfortunately, neither route booklets, maps nor "Point to Point" guides (which you can consult at the tourist office or at newsstands) make things any clearer. Finding out which bus you need is difficult enough. Recognizing it in the street can be even more problematic, as the numbers are written in Maharathi (although in English on the sides). Aim, wherever possible, for the "Limited" services, which stop less frequently, and avoid rush hours at all costs. Tickets should be bought from the conductor on the bus.

Trains
Mumbai would be paralysed without its local **trains**, which carry millions of commuters each day between downtown and the sprawling suburbs in the north. One line begins at CST (VT), running up the east side of the city as far as Thane. The other leaves Churchgate, hugging the curve of Back Bay as far as Chowpatty Beach, where it veers north towards Mumbai Central, Dadar, Santa Cruz and Vasai, beyond the city limits. Services depart every few minutes from 5am until midnight, stopping at dozens of small stations. Carriages remain packed solid virtually the whole time, with passengers dangling precariously out of open doors to escape the crush, so start to make your way to the exit at least three stops before your destination. The apocalyptic peak hours are worst of all. Women are marginally better off in the "ladies carriages"; look for the crowd of saris and *salwar kamises* grouped at the end of the platform.

Taxis
With rickshaws banished to the suburbs, Mumbai's ubiquitous black-and-yellow **taxis** are the quickest and most convenient way to nip around the city centre. In theory, all should have meters and a current rate card (to convert the amount shown on the meter to the correct fare); in practice, particularly at night or early in the morning, many drivers refuse to use them. If this happens, either flag down another or haggle out a fare. As a rule of thumb, expect to be charged Rs6 per kilometre after the minimum fare of around Rs15, together with a small sum for heavy luggage (Rs5 per article). The latest addition to Mumbai's hectic roads is the **cool cab**, a blue taxi that boasts air-conditioning, and charges higher rates for the privilege (☎022/2824 6216).

Boats
Ferryboats regularly chug out of Mumbai harbour, connecting the city with the far shore and some of the larger islands in between. The most popular with visitors is the **Elephanta Island** launch (see p.265), which departs from the Gateway of India. Boats to **Mandve** (9 daily; 6.30am–6.15pm; 90min; Rs40), for Alibag, the transport hub for the rarely used **coastal route south**, leave from the Gateway of India.

Car rental
Cars with drivers can be rented per eight-hour day (Rs800–1000 for a non-a/c Ambassador, upwards of Rs1250 for more luxurious a/c cars), or per kilometre, from ITDC. They have an (occasionally) staffed counter at the Government of India tourist office and on the eleventh floor of the Nirmal Building at Nariman Point. Otherwise, go through any good travel agent (see p.276). Ramniranjan Kedia Tours and Travels (☎022/2437 1112) are recommended if you want to book a vehicle on arrival at Chatrapathi Shivaji international airport.

Accommodation

Finding **accommodation** at the right price when you arrive in Mumbai may be a real problem. Budget travellers, in particular, can expect a hard time: standards at the bottom of the range are grim and room rates exorbitant. The best of the relatively inexpensive places tend to fill up by noon, which can often mean a long trudge in the heat with only an overpriced fleapit at the end of it, so you should really phone ahead as soon as (or preferably well before) you arrive. Prices in upmarket places are further inflated by the state-imposed **"luxury tax"** (between four and thirty percent depending on how expensive the room is), and **"service charges"** levied by the hotel itself; such charges are included in the price symbols used in the following reviews.

Colaba, down in the far, southern end of the city, is where the majority of foreign visitors head first. A short way across the city centre, **Marine Drive**'s accommodation is generally a little more expensive, but more salubrious, with Back Bay and the promenade right on the doorstep. If you're arriving by train and plan to make a quick getaway, a room closer to **CST** (VT) station is worth considering. Alternatively, **Juhu**, way to the north near the airports, hosts a string of flashy four- and five-stars, with a handful of less expensive places behind the beach. For those who just want to crawl off the plane and straight into bed, a handful of overpriced options are also available in the suburbs around **Chatrapathi Shivaji** and **Santa Cruz** airports, a short taxi ride from the main terminal buildings.

Finally, if you would like to **stay with an Indian family**, ask at the government tourist office in Churchgate, or at their information counters at the airports, about the popular "paying guest" scheme. Bed and breakfast-style accommodation in family homes, vetted by the tourist office, is available throughout the city at rates ranging from Rs500 to Rs1200.

Colaba

A short ride from the city's main commercial districts, railway stations and tourist office, **Colaba** makes a handy base. It also offers more in the way of food and entertainment than neighbouring districts, especially along its busy main thoroughfare, **"Colaba Causeway"** (Shahid Bhagat Singh – SBS – Marg). The streets immediately south and west of the Gateway of India are chock-full of accommodation, ranging from grungy guesthouses to India's most famous five-star hotel, the *Taj Mahal Intercontinental*. Avoid at all costs the nameless lodges lurking on the top storeys of wooden-fronted houses along **Arthur Bunder Road** – the haunts of not-so-oil-rich Gulf Arabs and touts who depend on commission from these rock-bottom hostels to finance their heroin habits.

The hotels below are marked on the **map** of Colaba on p.256.

Aga Bheg's & Hotel Kishan Ground & 2nd Floor, Shirin Manzil, Walton Rd ☏022/2284 2227. *Aga Bheg's* has lurid pink walls and little wooden blue beds, though it's clean, cool and quiet. *Hotel Kishan's* more comfy a/c rooms are better value. ➍–➏
Bentley's 17 Oliver Rd ☏022/2284 1474, ☏2287 1846, www.bentleyshotel.com. Dependable old favourite in four different colonial tenements, all on leafy backstreets. Fairly well maintained and good value. ➏

Fariyas 25 Arthur Rd ☏022/2204 2911, ☏2283 4492, ☏www.fariyas.com. Compact luxury hotel, overlooking the Koli fishing bastee on one side, with all the trimmings of a five-star but none of the grandeur. From $175. ➒
Gorden House 5 Battery St, Apollo Bunder ☏022/2284 1828, ☏2287 2026, ☏www.ghhotel.com. Ultra-chic designer place behind the Regal cinema. Each floor is differently themed: "Scandinavian" (the easiest to live with),

"Mediterranean" and "American Country"; CD players in every room, but no pool. ❾

Godwin Jasmine Building, 41 Garden Rd ☎022/2287 2050, ℻2287 1592, ⓦwww.cyber-sols.com/goodwin. Top-class three-star with great views from upper floors (through tinted windows). The *Garden* (☎022/2283 1330, ℻2204 4290) next door is similar but slightly inferior. Both ❽

Gulf 4/36 Kamal Mansion, Arthur Bunder Rd (Haji NAA Marg) ☎022/2285 6672, ℻2283 2694, ⓔgulfhotel@hotmail.com. Seedy neighbourhood, but respectable and well kept, with clean modern rooms (though small windows). ❺

Harbour View Kerawalla Chambers, 3rd and 4th Floors, 25 PJ Ramchandani Marg ☎022/2282 1089, ℻2284 3020, ⓦwww.viewhotelinc.com. Comfortable, recently refurbished rooms and a popular rooftop coffee terrace, at the quiet end of the harbour front. Sea views cost extra. All rooms a/c. ❽

Lawrence 3rd Floor, 33 Rope Walk Lane, off K Dubash Marg, opposite Jehangir Art Gallery ☎022/2284 6318 or 5633 6107. Arguably Mumbai's best-value cheap hotel, close to the Jehangir Art Gallery. Six immaculate doubles (one single) with fans, and not-so-clean shared shower-toilet. Breakfast included in the price. Advance booking essential. ❸

Moti International 10 Best Marg ☎022/2202 5714. British-era building that's quiet and clean, though frayed around the edges, with original paint-ed woodwork and shabby coir carpets. The deluxe rooms are larger and come with fridges and TVs. ❻

Regent 8 Best Rd ☎022/2287 1854, ℻2202 0363, ⓔhotelregent@vsnl.com. Luxurious, interna-tional-standard hotel on small scale; all mod cons but smallish rooms. Good value in its bracket. ❽

Salvation Army Red Shield House, 30 Mereweather Rd, near the *Taj* ☎022/2284 1824. Rock-bottom bunk beds (Rs135) in cramped, stuffy dorms (lockers available), large good-value dou-bles (from around Rs600), and a cheap and socia-ble travellers' canteen. Priority given to women, but your stay is limited to one week or less. ❶–❹

Sea Shore 4th Floor, 1-49 Kamal Mansion, Arthur Bunder Rd ☎022/2287 4237. Among the best budget deals in Colaba. The sea-facing rooms with windows are much nicer than the airless cells on the other side. Friendly management and free, safe baggage store. Common baths only, though some rooms have a/c. If it's full try the wooden-parti-tioned rooms at the less salubrious *India* (☎022/2283 3769; ❹–❺) or the grubby but bearable *Sea Lord* (☎022/2284 5392; ❹–❻) in the same building. ❺–❼

Shelley's 30 PJ Ramchandani Marg ☎022/2284 0229, ℻2284 0385, ⓦwww.shellyshotel.com. Charmingly old-fashioned hotel in the colonial mould despite renovations to the rooms. Worth paying the extra Rs300 for sea-facing. ❼

Taj Mahal Intercontinental PJ Ramchandani Marg ☎022/2202 3366, ℻2287 2711, ⓦwww.tajhotels.com. The stately home among India's top hotels (see p.255), and the haunt of Mumbai's *beau monde*. Opulent suites in an old wing or a modern skyscraper, plus shopping arcades, outdoor pool, swish bars and restaurants. Rooms start at $335. ❾

YWCA 18 Madam Cama Rd ☎022/2202 5053, ℻2202 0445, ⓦwww.ywcabombay.com. Relaxing, secure and quiet hostel with spotless dorms, dou-bles or family rooms. Rate includes membership, breakfast and filling buffet dinner. One month's advance booking (by money order) advisable. ❼

Marine Drive and Nariman Point

At the western edge of the downtown area, Netaji Subhash Chandra Marg, or **Marine Drive**, sweeps from the skyscrapers of Nariman Point in the south to Chowpatty Beach in the north. Along the way, four- and five-star hotels take advantage of the panoramic views over Back Bay and the easy access to the city's commercial heart, while a couple of inexpensive guesthouses are worth trying if Colaba's cheap lodges don't appeal.

The hotels below are marked on the **map** on p.258, apart from the *Oberoi*, which is marked on pp.242–3.

Ambassador VN Rd ☎022/2204 1131, ℻2204 0004, ⓔambassador@vsnl.com. Ageing four-star whose scruffy concrete exterior and slightly worn furnishings are redeemed by its choice location, close to the sea and main shopping and café strip. Even if you're not staying, pop up to the revolving restaurant for the matchless city views. ❾

Bentley 3rd Floor, Krishna Mahal, Marine Drive ☎022/2281 1787. Run-down hotel on the corner of D Rd. No lift, no a/c, no attached bathrooms and no frills (except windows), but clean rooms, some of which have sea-facing balconies (the cheapest in the city). 24hr checkout, and breakfast included. ❹

Chateau Windsor 5th Floor, 86 VN Rd ☎022/
2204 4455, ℻2222 6459, ⊛www.chateauwind-
sor.com. Impeccably clean and central, with unfail-
ingly polite staff and a choice of differently priced
rooms in 1950s style. Very popular, so reserve well
in advance. ❼–❽

Marine Plaza 29 Marine Drive ☎022/2285 1212,
℻2282 8585, ⊛www.sarovarparkplaza.com. Ritzy
but small luxury hotel on the seafront, with retro-
Art-Deco atrium lobby, glass-bottomed rooftop
pool, and the usual 5-star facilities. Rooms from
around $300. ❾

Oberoi/Oberoi Towers Nariman Point ☎022/
2232 5757, ℻2204 3282, ⊛www.oberoihotels
.com. India's largest hotel, where Bill Clinton
stayed on his state visit, enjoys a prime spot overlooking Back Bay. There's little difference between
the two sections, which form a single complex.
Glitteringly opulent throughout, and the first choice
of business travellers, though lacking the heritage
character of the *Taj*. Rooms from $330 to $2200
per night. ❾

Around Victoria (Chatrapathi Shivaji) Terminus

Arriving in Mumbai at **CST** (VT) after a long train journey, you may not feel
like embarking on a room hunt around Colaba. Unfortunately, the area around
the station and the nearby GPO, though fairly central, has little to recommend
it. The majority of places worth trying are mid-range hotels grouped around
the crossroads of P D'Mello (Frere) Road, St George's Road and Shahid
Bhagat Singh (SBS) Marg, immediately southeast of the post office (5min on
foot from the station). CST (VT) itself also has **retiring rooms** (Rs150),
although these are invariably booked up by noon.

The hotels below are marked on the **map** on p.258.

City Palace 121 City Terrace ☎022/2261 5515,
℻2267 6897, ℮hotelcitypalace@vsnl.net. Large
and popular hotel bang opposite the station.
"Ordinary" rooms are tiny and windowless, but
have a/c, are perfectly clean and proudly sport
"electronic push button telephone instruments".
The pricier ones higher up the building have great
views over Nagar Chowk. ❹–❼

Grand 17 Shri SR Marg, Ballard Estate
☎022/2269 8211, ℻2262 6581, ⊛www.grand-
hotelbombay.com. British-era place out near the
old docks and former financial district. Their rooms
are mostly huge, but a bit institutional and overpriced: you pay for the heritage feel, which some
may consider worth the extra. ❽

Oasis 276 SBS Marg ☎022/2239 6570, ℻2266
9133 ℮hoteloasis@satyam.net. Unquestionably
the best-value budget place in this area. Non a/c
doubles from under Rs700: good beds, clean linen,
all en suite and with TVs, and very well placed for
CST station. ❺

Prince 34 Walchand Hirachand Rd, near Red Gate
☎022/2261 2809, ℻2265 8049. The best fallback
if *Oasis* is full: neat and respectable. Avoid the airless partition rooms upstairs. ❻

Railway 249 P D'Mello Rd ☎022/2261 6705,
℻2265 8049. Spacious, clean and friendly, and
the pick of the mid-range bunch around CST (VT),
though correspondingly pricey and with no a/c
options. ❻–❽

Around the airports

Hotels in the congested area around Chatrapathi Shivaji and Santa Cruz **airports** cater predominantly for transit passengers and flight crews, at premium
rates. If you can face the half-hour drive across town, head for **Juhu**, one of the
city's swisher suburbs, which faces the sea and is a lot less hectic. With its palm
trees, glamorous seaside apartment blocks and designer clothes stores, Juhu is
Mumbai's answer to Sunset Boulevard, though sunbathing and swimming are
out of the question, thanks to an oily slick of raw sewage that seeps into the
Arabian Sea from the slum bastis surrounding Mahim Creek to the south.
Wherever you stay, bookings should be made well in advance, by phone, fax or
email, and re-confirmed a couple of days before your arrival. Nearly all the
hotels below have courtesy buses to and from the terminal building, or at worst
can arrange for a car and driver to meet you (in which case check the tariff
beforehand). Travellers on lower budgets who need to overnight close to the

airport might also consider one of the Government of India's Paying Guest addresses, available via email: ⓔgitobest@bom5.vsnl.net.in.

Bawa International Near domestic airport, Vile Parle (East) ⓣ022/26113636, ⓕ2610 7096, ⓔbawaintl@vsnl.com. Nothing special, but spotlessly clean, efficient, modern and right next to Santa Cruz airport. ⑨

Holiday Inn Balraj Sahani Marg, Juhu ⓣ022/2693 4444, ⓕ2693 4455, ⓦwww.holidayinnbombay .com. Formulaic five-star – exactly what you'd expect from a *Holiday Inn*, and slap on the beach, with a decent-sized swimming pool. ⑨

Orchid 70-C Nehru Rd, Vile Parle (East) ⓣ022/ 2616 4040, ⓕ2616 4141, ⓦwww.orchidhotel.com. India's first "Eco-Five-Star", built with organic or recycled materials and non-VOC paints. Every effort is made to minimize waste of natural resources, with a water recycling plant and "zero garbage" policy. Even the coat hangers are made of compressed sawdust. Rooms from around $300. ⑨

Sea Princess Juhu Tara Rd, Juhu ⓣ022/2661 1111, ⓕ2661 1144, ⓦwww.seaprincess.com. The nicest of the five-stars overlooking Juhu beach. Cosy, recently refitted rooms (some with sea views) and a smart restaurant, in addition to small pool. ⑨

Samrat 3rd Rd, Khar, Santa Cruz East, near Khar railway station ⓣ022/2648 5441, ⓕ6249 3501, ⓔhotelsamrat@vsnl.com. Another comfortable transit hotel in a quiet suburban backstreet. No courtesy bus. ⑦

Shangri-La Nanda Parker Rd, Vile Parle East ⓣ022/612 8983. Dependable budget hotel near the domestic airport with lots of clean and basic a/c and non-a/c rooms, some refurbished, and a Chinese restaurant. The cheapest option in the area. ④–⑥

The City

Nowhere reinforces your sense of having arrived in Mumbai quite as emphatically as the **Gateway of India**, which, alongside its grandly gabled and domed neighbour, the *Taj Mahal Intercontinental*, stands as the city's defining landmark. Crowds of trippers congregate here on evenings and weekends, but early morning before the heat builds is the best time to be at the adjacent boat jetty if you're planning a trip across the harbour to the ancient rock-cut Shiva temple on **Elephanta Island**. Only a five-minute walk north, the **Prince of Wales Museum** (or the Chatrapati Shivaji Vastu Sanghralaya, as it was recently re-named) should be next on your list of sightseeing priorities, as much for its flamboyantly eclectic exterior as the art treasures inside. The museum provides a foretaste of what lies in store just up the road, where the cream of Bartle Frere's Bombay – the University and High Court – lines up with the open maidans on one side, and the boulevards of **Fort** on the other. The commercial hub of the city, Fort is a great area for aimless wandering, with plenty of old-fashioned cafés, department stores and street stalls crammed between the pompous Victorian piles. The innumerable banks and other financial institutions at the east end of Fort around **Horniman Circle** – site of the British era's oldest buildings, **St Thomas' Cathedral** and the old **town hall** – stand as reminders of the cotton boom prosperity of the late-nineteenth century. But for the fullest sense of why the city's Victorian founding fathers declared it *Urbs Prima in Indis*, you should visit **Victoria Terminus** (now re-named Chatrapathi Shivaji Terminus), the high watermark of India's Raj architecture.

Few visitors venture much further north than here unless they have to, but teeming **central Mumbai** certainly has its appeal. Beginning at **Crawford Market**, a quirky British structure crammed with fresh produce, you can press north into the thick of the intense **bazaar** district to visit the Mumba Devi temple from which the city took its name. Beyond lie the Muslim neighbourhoods, which encompass some of Mumbai's most interesting backstreet bazaars, as well as a serene little **Jain animal sanctuary**.

△ Sassoon docks, Mumbai

When the crush of city's central districts gets too much, an evening stroll along **Marine Drive**, bounding the western edge of the downtown area, is the ideal antidote. From there you can skirt Mumbai's most affluent enclave, Malabar Hill, to reach two important religious sites, the Hindu **Lakshmi temple** and Muslim **tomb of Haji Ali**.

One incentive to break out of Mumbai altogether is the thousand-year-old **Kanheri Cave** complex, carved from a forested hillside, which you can get to within striking distance of by train.

Colaba

At the end of the seventeenth century, **Colaba** was little more than the last in a straggling line of rocky islands extending to the lighthouse that stood on Mumbai's southernmost point. Today, the original outlines of the promontory (whose name derives from the Koli who first lived here) have been submerged under a mass of dilapidated colonial tenements, hotels, bars, restaurants and handicraft shops. If you never venture beyond the district, you'll get a very distorted picture of Mumbai. In spite of being the main tourist enclave and a trendy hang-out for the city's rich young things, Colaba has retained the distinctly sleazy feel of the bustling port it used to be, with dodgy moneychangers, dealers and pimps hissing at passers-by from the kerbsides.

The Gateway of India
Commemorating the visit of King George V and Queen Mary in 1911, India's own honey-coloured Arc de Triomphe, the **Gateway of India**, was built in 1924 by George Wittet, the architect responsible for many of the city's grandest constructions. It was originally envisaged as a ceremonial disembarkation point for passengers alighting from the P&O steamers, but – ironically – is today more often remembered as the place the British chose to stage their final departure from the country. On February 28, 1948, the last detachment of troops remaining on Indian soil slow marched under the arch to board the waiting troop ship back to Tilbury. Nowadays, the only boats bobbing about at the bottom of its stone staircase are the launches that ferry tourists across the harbour to Elephanta Island (see p.265).

Behind the Gateway
Directly behind the Gateway, the older hotel in the **Taj Mahal Intercontinental Hotel** complex (see p.251) stands as a monument to local pride in the face of colonial oppression. Its patron, the Parsi industrialist J.N. Tata, is said to have built the old *Taj* as an act of revenge after he was refused entry to what was then the best hotel in town, the "whites only" *Watson's*. The ban proved their undoing. *Watson's* disappeared long ago, but the *Taj*, with its grand grey and white stone facade and red-domed roof, still presides imperiously over the seafront, the preserve of visiting diplomats, sheikhs, businessmen and aircrew on expense accounts, and Mumbai's jet set. Lesser mortals are allowed in to sample the tea lounge, shopping arcades and vast air-conditioned lobby (a good place to cool down if the heat of the harbourfront has got the better of you).

From the *Taj*, you can head down the promenade, PJ Ramchandani Marg, better known as **Apollo Bunder** (nothing to do with the Greek sun god; the name is a colonial corruption of the Koli words for a local fish, *palav*, and quay, *bunda*), taking in the sea breezes and views over the busy harbour. Alternatively, Shivaji Marg heads northwest towards **Wellington Circle** (SPM Chowk), the hectic roundabout in front of the Art-Deco Regal cinema. The latter route

COLABA

Bombay
University

M G ROAD

Knesget
Eliyahoo
Synagogue

Rhythm
House
(A)

(B)

BORA BAZAAR LANE

SUBHASH
CHOWK

(C)

Max Mueller
Bhavan **(1)**

K DUBASH MARG

Secret-
ariat

HOPE ST

Jehangir
Art Gallery **(D)**

MAHATMA GANDHI RD

Prince of Wales
Museum

Bombay Natural
History Society

Institute of Science

S P Mukharji
Chowk
(Wellington Circle)

MADAM CAMA RD

Jet Airways **(2)**

Phillip's
Antiques

American
Express

Cottage
Industries
Emporium

SHIVAJI MARG

(E)

Sahakari
Bhandar

Regal
Cinema

BATTERY ST

COOPERAGE MARG

NATHALAL PAREKH MARG

(F)

RAJ KAVI GHUSHAN MARG

(H)

(3)

Bombay
Yacht Club

ARABIAN SEA

TULLOCH RD

(I)

Launch
Ticket
Booth

Launches to
Elephanta

NAWROJI F MARG

Gateway
of India

(J)

(K) (L)

MANDLIK MARG

Police
Station

(M)

SHAHID BHAGAT SINGH MARG (COLABA CAUSEWAY)

ORMISTON RD

(6) (5)

ORMISTON RD

(4)

(N)

(7)

Bus
Depot

(O)

BARROW RD

B BEHRAM MARG

HENRY RD

P J RAMCHANDANI MARG (APOLLO BUNDER)

WALTON RD

(8)

OLIVER ROAD

(9)

(P)

GARDEN RD

(10)

(11)

(12)

ARTHUR BUNDER RD (H N A MARG)

(13) (Q) (14)

(R)

STRAND RD

Strand
Cinema

(S)

(15)

Sassoon Docks

N

ACCOMMODATION

Aga Bheg's & Hotel Kishan	8
Bentley's	9
Fariyas	15
Gorden House	3
Godwin	10
Gulf	13
Harbour View	11
India	14
Lawrence	1
Moti International	6
Regent	5
Salvation Army	7
Sea Lord	14
Sea Shore	14
Shelley's	12
Taj Mahal Intercontinental	4
YWCA	2

RESTAURANTS, BARS, CAFÉS & CLUBS

All Stir Fry	3
Bademiya	I
Busaba	L
Café Mondegar	G
Café Samovar	D
Chetana	C
Churchill	P
Indigo	K
Kailash Parbat ("KP's")	S
Kamat	O
Kyber	B
Leopold's	J
Ling's Pavilion	H
Majestic	F
New Martin	R
Olympic Coffee House	M
Sea Lounge	N
Three Flights Up	E
Trishna	A
Voodoo Lounge	Q

takes you past the old **Bombay Yacht Club**, another idiosyncratic vestige of the Raj. Very little seems to have changed here since its smoky common rooms were a bolt hole for the city's *burra-sahibs*. Dusty sporting trophies and models of clippers and dhows stand in glass cases lining its corridors, polished from time to time by bearers in cotton tunics. If you want to look around, seek permission from the club secretary; accommodation is available only to members and their guests.

Southwards along Colaba Causeway

Reclaimed in the late-nineteenth century from the sea, the district's main thoroughfare, **Colaba Causeway** (this stretch of Shahid Bhagat Singh Marg), leads south towards the military cantonment. En route it passes the gates of the wholesale seafood market at **Sassoon Docks**, which provides an unexpected splash of rustic colour amid the drab urban surroundings. Koli fisherwomen, their cotton saris hitched dhoti-style, squat beside baskets of glistening pomfret, prawns and tuna, while coolies haul plastic crates of crushed ice over rickety gangplanks to the boats moored at the quay. The stench, as overpowering as the noise, comes mostly from bundles of one of the city's traditional exports, **"Bombay duck"**, drying on the trawlers' rigging. You may have been struck by Sebastião Salgado's powerful images of the docks in his book, *Work*, but in fact **photography** is strictly forbidden, as the market is close to a sensitive military area.

From the docks, hop on any bus heading south down Colaba Causeway (#3, #11, #47, #103, #123, or #125) through the cantonment to the **Afghan Memorial Church of St John the Baptist**, built (1847–54) as a memorial to the British victims of the First Afghan War. With its tall steeple and tower, the pale yellow church wouldn't look out of place in Worcester or Suffolk. If the door is unlocked, take a peep inside at the battle-scarred military colours on the wall and marble memorial plaques to officers who died in various campaigns on the Northwest Frontier.

Downtown Mumbai

The critic Robert Byron, although a wholehearted fan of New Delhi, was unenthusiastic about the architecture of **downtown Mumbai**, which he described as "that architectural Sodom". Today, the massive monuments of Empire and Indian free enterprise appear not so much ugly, as intriguing. Between them, you'll occasionally come across still more curious buildings, with facades flanked by what appear to be Mesopotamian griffins. These are old Zoroashtrian (Parsi) **fire temples** – or agiaries – erected by wealthy worthies in the late-nineteenth century. Few attract more than a trickle of ageing worshippers, and as a non-Parsi you won't be allowed inside, but they're a definitive Mumbai spectacle.

Prince of Wales Museum (Chatrapathi Shivaji Museum) and Jehangir Art Gallery

Set back from Mahatma Gandhi (MG) Road in its own grounds, the **Prince of Wales Museum of Western India** (Tues–Sun 10.15am–6pm; Rs150, Rs15 extra with camera), recently renamed as the tongue-twisting Chatrapathi Shivaji Vastu Sanghralaya, ranks among the city's most distinctive Raj-era constructions. Crowned by a massive white Moghul-style dome, it houses a superb collection of paintings and sculpture that you'll need several hours, or a couple of visits, to get the most out of. The building was designed by George

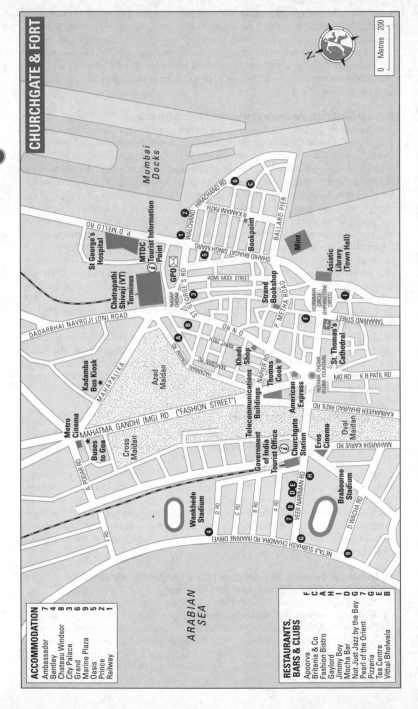

CHURCHGATE & FORT

5

0 Metres 200

Mumbai Docks

ARABIAN SEA

ACCOMMODATION
Ambassador 7
Bentley 4
Chateau Windsor 8
City Palace 3
Grand 6
Marine Plaza 5
Oasis 9
Prince 2
Railway 1

RESTAURANTS, BARS & CLUBS
Apoorva F
Britania & Co C
Fashion Bistro A
Gaylord H
Jimmy Boy I
Mocha Bar D
Not Just Jazz by the Bay 7
Pearl of the Orient G
Pizzeria G
Tea Centre E
Vithal Bhelwala B

Wittet, of Gateway of India fame, and is the epitome of the hybrid **Indo-Saracenic** style – regarded in its day as an "educated" interpretation of fifteenth- and sixteenth-century Gujarati architecture, mixing Islamic touches with typically English municipal brickwork.

The **central hall** provides a snapshot of the collection with a few choice Moghul paintings, jade work, weapons and miniature clay and terracotta figures from the Mauryan (third century BC) and Kushana (first to second century AD) periods.

The main **sculpture room** on the **ground floor** displays some fine fourth- and fifth-century heads and figures from the Buddhist state of Gandhara, a former colony of Alexander the Great (hence the Greek-style statues). Important Hindu sculptures include a seventh-century Chalukyan bas-relief from Aihole depicting Brahma seated on a lotus, and a sensuously carved torso of Mahisasuramaraini, the goddess Durga with tripod raised ready to skewer the demon buffalo.

The main attraction on the **first floor** has to be the superb collection of **Indian painting**, including illustrated manuscripts and erotic Gita Govinda paintings in the pre-Moghul Sultanate style. **Moghul schools** are well represented, too, with famous portraits and folios from the reign of Akbar (1556–1605)

European art – including a minor Titian and a Constable – is featured on the **second floor**, alongside a collection of weapons belonging to various Moghul emperors. The poorly lit **Indian textiles room** showcases brocaded saris, turbans, and intricately patterned antique Kashmiri shawls.

Technically in the same compound as the Prince of Wales Museum, though approached from further up MG Road, the **Jehangir Art Gallery** (daily 11am–7pm; free) is Mumbai's best-known venue for contemporary art, with five small galleries specializing in twentieth-century arts and crafts from around the world. You never know what you're going to find – most exhibitions last only a week and exhibits are often for sale.

Around Oval Maidan

Some of Mumbai's most important Victorian buildings flank the eastern side of the vast green **Oval Maidan**, where impromptu cricket matches are held almost every day (foreign enthusiasts are welcome to take part, but should beware the maidan's demon bowlers and less-than-even pitches). The dull yellow **Old Secretariat** now serves as the City Civil and Sessions Court. Indian civil servant G.W. Forrest described it in 1903 as "a massive pile whose main features have been brought from Venice, but all the beauty has vanished in transhipment". Inside, you can only imagine the originally highly polished interior, which no longer shines, but buzzes with activity. Lawyers in black gowns, striped trousers and white tabs bustle up and down the staircases, whose corners are emblazoned with expectorated paan juice, and offices with perforated swing-doors give glimpses of textbook images of Indian bureaucracy – peons at desks piled high with dusty beribboned document bundles.

Across A S D'Mello Road from the Old Secretariat, two major buildings belonging to **Mumbai University** (established 1857) were designed in England by Sir Gilbert Scott, who had already given the world the Gothic extravaganza of London's St Pancras railway station. Access through the main gates is monitored by caretakers who only allow you in if you say you're using the library. Funded by the Parsi philanthropist Cowasjee "Readymoney" Jehangir, the **Convocation Hall** greatly resembles a church. The **library** (daily

Dabawallahs

Mumbai's size and inconvenient shape create all kind of hassles for its working population – not least having to stew for over four hours each day in slow municipal transport. One thing the daily tidal wave of commuters do not have to worry about, however, is where to find an inexpensive and wholesome home-cooked lunch. In a city with a *wallah* for everything, it will find them. The members of the **Nutan Mumbai Tiffin Box Suppliers Charity Trust**, known colloquially, and with no little affection, as **"dabawallahs"**, see to that. Every day, around 1000 *dabawallahs* deliver freshly cooked food from 160,000 suburban kitchens to offices in the downtown area. Each lunch is prepared early in the morning by a devoted wife or mother while her husband or son is enduring the crush on the train. She arranges the rice, dhal, *subzi*, curd and *parathas* into cylindrical aluminium trays, stacks them on top of one another and clips them together with a neat little handle. This **tiffin box**, not unlike a slim paint tin, is the lynchpin of the whole operation. When the runner calls to collect it in the morning, he uses a special colour code on the lid to tell him where the lunch has to go. At the end of his round, he carries all the boxes to the nearest railway station and hands them over to other *dabawallahs* for the trip into town. Between leaving the wife and reaching its final destination, the tiffin box will pass through at least half a dozen different pairs of hands, carried on heads, shoulder-poles, bicycle handlebars and in the brightly decorated handcarts that plough with such insouciance through the midday traffic. Tins are rarely, if ever, lost – a fact recently reinforced by the American business magazine, *Forbes*, which awarded Mumbai's *dabawallahs* a 6-Sigma performance rating, the score reserved for companies who attain a 9.99999 percentage of correctness. This means that only one tiffin box in 6 million goes astray, in efficiency terms putting the illiterate *dabawallahs* on a par with bluechip firms such as Motorola.

To catch them in action, head for **CST (VT)** or **Churchgate** stations around late morning time, when the tiffin boxes arrive in the city centre. The event is accompanied by a chorus of "lafka! lafka!" – "hurry! hurry!" – as the *dabawallahs*, recognizable in their white Nehru caps and baggy pyjama trousers, rush to make their lunch-hour deadlines. Nearly all come from the same small village near Pune and are related to one another. They collect Rs150 from each customer, or around Rs5000 per month in total – not a bad income by Indian standards. One of the reasons the system survives in the face of competition from trendy fast food outlets is that *daba* lunches still work out a good deal cheaper, saving precious paise for the middle-income workers who use the system.

10am–10pm) is beneath the 79.2-metre-high **Rajabhai clock tower** which is said to be modelled on Giotto's campanile in Florence. Until 1931, it chimed tunes such as *Rule Britannia* and *Home Sweet Home*. It's worth applying for a visitor's ticket to the library (Rs5 a day, Rs10 for three days) just to see the interior. The magnificent vaulted wooden ceiling of the reading room, high Gothic windows and stained glass still evoke a reverential approach to learning.

Hutatma Chowk (Flora Fountain)

A busy five-point intersection in the heart of the Fort area, the roundabout formerly known as **Flora Fountain** has been renamed **Hutatma Chowk** ("Martyrs' Square") to commemorate the freedom fighters who died to establish the state of Maharashtra in the Indian Union. The chowk centres on a statue of the Roman goddess **Flora**, erected in 1869 to commemorate Sir Bartle Frere. It's hard to see quite why they bothered – the Raj architecture expert, Philip Davies, was not being unkind when he said, "The fountain was designed by a committee, and it shows."

Horniman Circle and the Town Hall

Horniman Circle, formerly Elphinstone Circle, is named after a pro-Independence newspaper editor. It was conceived in 1860 as a centrepiece of a newly planned Bombay by the then Municipal Commissioner, Charles Forjett, on the site of Bombay "Green". Forjett, a Eurasian, had something of a peculiar reputation; he was fond of disguising himself in "native" dress and prowling about certain districts of the city to listen out for seditious talk. In 1857, at the time of the First War of Independence (as it is now known by Indians; the British call it the Indian Mutiny), Forjett fired on two suspected revolutionaries from a cannon on the Esplanade (roughly the site of the modern maidans).

Flanking the east side of the circle, the impressive Doric Town Hall on SBS Marg houses the vast collection of the **Asiatic Society Library** (Mon–Sat 10am–7pm). Save for the addition of electricity, little has changed here since the institution was founded in the early eighteenth century, which makes it worth a visit even if you're not a bibliophile. Inside the reading rooms, lined with wrought-iron loggias and teak bookcases, scholars pour over mouldering tomes dating from the Raj. Among the 10,000 rare and valuable manuscripts stored here is a fourteenth-century first edition of Dante's Divine Comedy, said to be worth around $3 million, which the Society famously refused to sell to Mussolini. Visitors are welcome but should sign in at the Head Librarian's desk on the ground floor.

St Thomas' Cathedral

The small, simple **St Thomas' Cathedral** (daily 6.30am–6pm), on Tamarind Street, is reckoned to be the oldest British building in Mumbai, blending Classical and Gothic styles. After the death of its founding father, Governor Aungier, the project was abandoned; the walls stood 5m high for forty-odd years until enthusiasm was rekindled by a chaplain to the East India Company in the second decade of the eighteenth century. It was finally opened on Christmas Day 1718, complete with the essential "cannon-ball-proof roof". In those days, the seating was divided into useful sections for those who should know their place, including one for "Inferior Women".

St Thomas' whitewashed and polished brass-and-wood interior looks much the same as when the staff of the East India Company worshipped here in the eighteenth century. Lining the walls are memorial tablets to British parishioners, many of whom died young, either from disease or in battle.

Victoria Terminus (Chatrapathi Shivaji Terminus)

Inspired by St Pancras station in London, F.W. Stevens designed **Victoria Terminus**, the most barmy of Mumbai's buildings, as a paean to "progress". Built in 1887 as the largest British edifice in India, it's an extraordinary amalgam of domes, spires, Corinthian columns and minarets that was succinctly defined by the journalist James Cameron as "Victorian-Gothic-Saracenic-Italianate-Oriental-St Pancras-Baroque". In keeping with the current re-Indianization of the city's roads and buildings, this icon of British imperial architecture has been renamed **Chatrapathi Shivaji Terminus**, in honour of a Maratha warlord. However, the new name is a bit of a mouthful and the locals mostly still use **VT** (pronounced "vitee" or "wee tee") when referring to it.

Few of the two million or so passengers who fill almost a thousand trains every day notice the mass of decorative detail. A "British" lion and Indian tiger stand guard at the entrance, and the exterior is festooned with sculptures executed at the Bombay Art School by the Indian students of John Lockwood Kipling, Rudyard's father. Among them are grotesque mythical beasts, monkeys and plants and medallions of important personages. To minimize the sun's impact, stained glass was employed, decorated with locomotives and elephant images. Above it all, "Progress" stands atop the massive central dome.

An endless frenzy of activity goes on inside: hundreds of porters in red with impossibly oversize headloads; TTEs (Travelling Ticket Examiners) in black jackets and white trousers clasping clipboards detailing reservations; spitting checkers busy handing out fines to those caught in the act; *chai-wallahs* with trays of tea; trundling magazine stands; crowds of bored soldiers smoking *beed-is*; and the inexorable progress across the station of sweepers bent double. Amid it all, whole families spread out on the floor, eating, sleeping or just waiting and waiting.

Marine Drive and Chowpatty Beach

Netaji Subhash Chandra Marg, better known as **Marine Drive**, is Mumbai's seaside prom, an eight-lane highway with a wide pavement built in the 1920s on reclaimed land. Sweeping in an arc from the skyscrapers at Nariman Point in the south, the route ends at the foot of Malabar Hill and Chowpatty Beach. The whole stretch is a favourite place for a stroll; the promenade next to the sea has uninterrupted views virtually the whole way along, while the apartment blocks on the land side are some of the most desirable and expensive addresses in the city.

Just beyond the huge flyover at its northern end are a series of cricket pitches known as **gymkhanas**, where there's a good chance of catching a match any day of the week. A number are exclusive to particular religious communities. The first doubles as a swanky outdoor wedding venue for Parsi marriages; others include the Catholic, Islamic and Hindu pitches, the last of which has a classic colonial-style pavilion.

Chowpatty Beach

Chowpatty Beach is a Mumbai institution, which really comes to life at night and on Saturday. People do not come here to swim (the sea is foul) but to wander, sit on the beach, let the kids ride a pony or a rusty Ferris wheel, have a massage, get ears cleaned or picnic on *bhel puri* and cups of kulfi. For the last century or so, Gupta Bhelwallas's *bhel puri* stall has satisfied the discerning Mumbai palate with a secret concoction of the sunset snack; you'll find it amid the newly constructed "shack" to which the *bhel wallahs* were recently moved as part of the Municipality's bid to clean the beach up.

Once a year in September the **Ganesh Chathurthi** festival draws gigantic crowds to participate in the immersion of idols, both huge and small, of the elephant-headed god Ganesh.

Mani Bhavan Mahatma Gandhi Museum

A ten-minute walk north from the middle of Chowpatty Beach (along P Ramabai Marg), **Mani Bhavan**, at 19 Laburnum Rd (daily 9.30am–6pm), was Gandhi's Bombay base between 1917 and 1934. Set in a leafy upper-middle-class road, the house is now a permanent memorial to the Mahatma with an extensive research library. Within the lovingly maintained polished-wood interior, the walls are covered with photos of historic events and artefacts from the man's extraordinary life – the most disarming of which is a friendly letter to Hitler suggesting world peace. Gandhi's predictably simple sitting room-cum-bedroom is preserved behind glass. Laburnum Road is a few streets along from the Bharatiya Vidya Bhavan music venue on KM Munshi Marg – if coming by taxi ask for the nearby Gamdevi Police Station.

North of Chowpatty

Two of Mumbai's most popular religious sites, one Hindu, the other Muslim, can be reached by following Bhulabhai Desai Road **north from Chowpatty** as far as Prabhu Chowk, through the exclusive suburb of Breach Candy (bus #132 from Colaba). Alternatively, make for Mumbai Central and head due northwest to Vatsalabai Desai Chowk (also bus #132).

Mahalakshmi Mandir is joined to Bhulabhai Desai Road by an alley lined with stalls selling puja offerings and devotional pictures. Mumbai's favourite *devi*, **Lakshmi**, goddess of beauty and prosperity – the city's most sought-after attributes – is here propitiated with coconuts, sweets, lengths of shimmering silk and giant lotus blooms. Gifts pile so high that the temple *pujaris* run a money-spinning sideline reselling them. Their little shop, to the left of the entrance, is a good place to buy cut-price saris and brocades infused with lucky Lakshmi-energy. While you're here, find out what your future holds by joining the huddle of devotees pressing rupees onto the rear wall of the shrine room. If your coin sticks, you'll be rich.

Occupying a small islet in the bay just north of the Mahalakshmi is the mausoleum of the Muslim saint, Afghan mystic **Haji Ali Bukhari**. The tomb is connected to the mainland by a narrow concrete **causeway**, only passable at low tide. When not immersed in water, its entire length is lined with beggars who change one-rupee pieces into ten-paise coins for pilgrims. The prime sites, closer to the snack bars that flank the main entrance, near the small mosque, and the gateway to the **tomb** itself, are allocated in a strict pecking order. If you want to make a donation, spare a thought for the unfortunates in the middle. After all the commotion, the tomb itself comes as something of a disappointment. Its white Moghul domes and minarets look a lot less exotic close up than when viewed from the shore, silhouetted against the sun as it drops into the Arabian Sea.

The central bazaars

Lining the anarchic jumble of streets north of Lokmanya Tilak (formerly Carnac) Road, Mumbai's teeming **central bazaars** are India at its most intense. You could wander around here for days without seeing the same shop front twice. In practice, most visitors find a couple of hours mingling with the crowds in the heat and din quite enough. Nevertheless, the market districts form a fascinating counterpoint to the wide and Westernized streets of downtown, even if you're not buying.

In keeping with traditional divisions of guild, caste and religion, most streets specialize in one or two types of merchandise. If you lose your bearings, the best way out is to ask someone to wave you in the direction of **Mohammed Ali Road**, the busy road through the heart of the district (now surmounted by a gigantic flyover), from where you can hail a cab.

Crawford Market

Crawford (aka Mahatma Phule) **Market**, ten minutes' walk north of CST (VT) station, is an old British-style covered market dealing in just about every kind of fresh food and domestic animal imaginable. Thanks to its pompous Norman-Gothic tower and prominent position at the corner of Lokmanya Tilak Road and Dr DN Marg, the Crawford Market is also a useful landmark and a good place to begin a foray into the bazaars.

Before venturing inside, stop to admire the **friezes** wrapped around its exterior – a Victorian vision of sturdy-limbed peasants toiling in the fields designed by Rudyard Kipling's father, Lockwood, as principal of the Bombay School of Art in 1865. The **main hall** is still divided into different sections: pyramids of polished fruit and vegetables down one aisle, sacks of nuts or oil-tins full of herbs and spices down another. Around the back of the market, in the atmospheric wholesale wing, the pace of life is more hectic. Here, noisy crowds of coolies mill about with large reed-baskets held high in the air (if they are looking for work) or on their heads (if they've found some).

One place animal-lovers should definitely steer clear of is Crawford Market's **pet** and **poultry** section, on the east side of the building. You never quite know what creatures will turn up here, cringing in rank-smelling, undersized cages.

North of Crawford Market

The streets immediately **north of Crawford Market** and west of **Mohammed Ali Road** form one vast bazaar area. Ranged along both sides of narrow **Mangaldas Lane**, the cloth bazaar, are small shops draped with lengths of bright silk and cotton. Low doorways on the left open onto a colourful **covered market** area, packed with tiny stalls.

Eastwards along Mangaldas Lane from Carnac Road, the pale green-washed domes, arches and minarets of the **Jami Masjid**, or "Friday Mosque" (c.1800), mark the start of the Muslim neighbourhoods. **Memon Street**, cutting north from the mosque, is the site of the **Zaveri Bazaar**, the jewellery market where Mumabikars come to shop for dowries and wedding attire.

By the time the gleaming golden spire that crowns the **Mumba Devi temple**'s cream and turquoise tower appears at the end of the street, you're deep in a maze of twisting lanes hemmed in by tall, wooden-balconied buildings. One of the most important centres of Devi worship in India, the temple was built early in the nineteenth century, when the deity was relocated from her former home to make way for CST (VT) station. Mumba Devi's other claim to fame is that her name is the original root of the word "Bombay", as well as the official, Maharashtran version, "**Mumbai**".

Bear left at the temple and keep heading along the main bazaar for ten or fifteen minutes and you'll arrive at another important Hindu enclave, **Bhuleshwar**. The district is famous throughout the city for its colourful **phool galli** (flower lane), where temple goers buy luxurious garlands, lotus bundles and marigolds heaped in huge baskets. Of the 85 shrines said to be crammed into its lanes the most important is the **Bhola Ishtwar mandir**, the ancient Shiva temple around which this district is believed to have first grown up in the eighteenth century. Its odd mix of Gujarati, Rajasthani and Konkan architectural styles reflects the origins of the neighbourhood's first immigrants. Jain merchants also settled here from the northwest, erecting a pair of finely carved white marble temples – **Shantinath** and **Parshavanath** – tucked away down a narrow lane just off the next crossroads, Jayamber Chowk. Animal lovers should ask the way here to the nearby **Panjarapool animal sanctuary**, where around four hundred beautiful brown *gir* cows are cared for, along with a menagerie of pigeons, rabbits, chickens and ducks. You can purchase donatory bowls of grain and *ladoo* balls to feed them at reception, where stern faced Jain attendants enforce the strict no photography rule.

Chor Bazaar, Mutton Road and the red-light district

Jump in a taxi at the junction just down the lane from the Mumba Devi temple for the two-kilometre trip north to the other concentration of markets around **Johar Chowk**, just north of SP Patel Road. The most famous of these, **Chor** (literally "thieves") **Bazaar** (where vendors peevishly insist the name is a corruption of the Urdu *shor*, meaning "noisy"), is the city's largest **antiques-cum-flea market**. Friday, the Muslim holy day, is the best day to be here. From 9am onwards, the neighbourhood is cluttered with hawkers and hand-carts piled high with bric-a-brac and assorted junk. At other times, the antique shops down on **Mutton Road** are the main attraction. Once, you could hope to unearth real gems in these dark, fusty stores, but your chances of finding a genuine bargain nowadays are minimal. Most of the stuff is pricey Victoriana – old gramophones, chamber pots, chipped china – salvaged from the homes of Parsi families on the decline. The place is also awash with **fakes**, mainly small bronze votive statues, which make good souvenirs if you can knock the price down.

Press on north through Chor Bazaar and you'll eventually come out onto **Grant Road** (Maulana Shaukatali Road). Further north and west, in the warren of lanes below JB Behram Marg, lies the city's infamous **red-light district**. **Kamathipura's** rows of luridly lit, barred shop fronts, from where an estimated 25,000 prostitutes ply their trade, are one of Mumbai's more degrading and unpleasant spectacles. Many of these so-called **"cage girls"** are young teenagers from poor tribal areas, and from across the border in Nepal, who have been sold by desperate parents into **bonded slavery** until they can earn the money to pay off family debts.

Elephanta

An hour's boat ride from Colaba, the island of **ELEPHANTA** offers one of the more atmospheric escapes from the seething claustrophobia of the city – as long as you time your visit to avoid the weekend deluge of noisy day-trippers. Populated only by a small fishing community, it was originally known as **Gharapuri**, the "city of Ghara priests", until the island was renamed in the sixteenth century by the Portuguese in honour of the carved elephant they found at the port. Its chief attraction is its unique **cave temple**, whose massive **Trimurti** (three-faced) **Shiva sculpture** is as fine an example of Hindu architecture as you'll find anywhere.

"Deluxe" boats set off from the Gateway of India (Oct–May hourly 9am–2.30pm; Rs85 return including government guide); book through the kiosks near the Gateway of India. Ask for your guide at the caves ticket office on arrival – they take about thirty minutes. **Ordinary ferries** (Rs65 return), also from the Gateway of India, don't include guides, and are usually packed. The journey takes about an hour on either boat.

Cool drinks and souvenir stalls line the way up the hill, and at the top, the MTDC *Chalukya* restaurant offers food and beer, and a terrace with good views out to sea, but you cannot stay overnight on the island.

The Cave

Elephanta's impressive excavated eighth-century **cave** (9.30am–4pm; $5 [Rs5]), covering an area of approximately 5000 square metres, is reached by climbing more than one hundred steps to the top of the hill. Inside, the massive columns, carved from solid rock, give the deceptive impression of being structural. To the right, as you enter, note the panel of **Nataraj**, Shiva as the cosmic dancer. Though spoiled by the Portuguese who, it is said, used it for target practice, the panel remains magnificent; Shiva's face is rapt, and in one of his left hands he removes the veil of ignorance. Opposite is a badly damaged panel of Lakulisha, Shiva with a club (*lakula*).

Each of the four entrances to the simple square main **shrine** – unusually, it has one on each side – is flanked by a pair of huge fanged *dvarpala* guardians (only those to the back have survived undamaged), while inside a large *lingam* is surrounded by coins and smouldering joss left by devotees. Facing the northern wall of the shrine, another panel shows Shiva impaling the demon Andhaka, who wandered around as though blind, symbolizing his spiritual blindness. The panel behind the shrine on the back wall portrays the marriage of Shiva and Parvati. A powerful six-metre bust of **Trimurti**, the three-faced Shiva, who embodies the powers of creator, preserver and destroyer, stands nearby, and to the west a sculpture shows Shiva as **Ardhanarishvara**, half male and half female. Near the second entrance on the east, another panel shows Shiva and Parvati on **Mount Kailasha** with Ravana about to lift the mountain. His curved spine shows the strain.

The outskirts: Kanheri Caves

Overlooking the suburb of Borivli, 42km out at the northern limits of Mumbai's sprawl, are the Buddhist **Kanheri Caves** (daily 9am–5.30pm; $5 [Rs5]), ranged over the hills in virtually unspoilt forest. It's an interminable journey by road, so catch one of the many **trains** (50min) on the suburban line from Churchgate (marked "BO" on the departure boards; "limited stop" trains are 15min faster) to Borivli East. When you arrive, take the Borivli East exit, where a **bus** (for Kaneri Cave via SG Parles; Rs10), **auto-rickshaw** (about Rs60) or **taxi** (about Rs90) will take you the last 15km. Bring water and food as the stalls here only sell warm soft drinks.

Kanheri may not be as spectacular as other cave sites, but some of its sculpture is superb – though to enjoy the blissful peace and quiet that attracted its original occupants you should avoid the weekends. Most of the caves, which date from the second to the ninth century AD, were used simply by monks for accommodation and meditation during the four months of the monsoon, when an itinerant life was impractical. They are connected by steep winding paths and steps; engage one of the friendly local guides at the entrance to find your way about, but don't expect any sort of lecture as their English is limited. Due to a recent spate of muggings in some of the remoter caves, it is not advisable to venture off the beaten track alone.

In **Cave 1**, an incomplete *chaitya* hall (a hall with a stupa at one end, an aisle and row of columns at either side), you can see where the rock was left cut, but unfinished. Two stupas stand in **Cave 2**; one was vandalized by a certain N. Christian, whose carefully incised Times-Roman graffiti bears the date 1810. A panel shows seated Buddhas, portrayed as a teachers. Behind, and to the side, is the *bodhisattva* of compassion, Padmapani, while to the right the *viharas* feature rock-cut beds.

Huge Buddhas, with serenely joyful expressions and unfeasibly large shoulders, stand on either side of the porch to the spectacular **Cave 3**. Between them, you'll see the panels of "donor couples", thought to have been foreigners that patronized the community.

The sixth-century **Cave 11** is a large assembly hall, where two long "tables" of rock were used for the study of manuscripts. Seated at the back, in the centre, is a figure of the Buddha as teacher, an image repeated in the entrance, to the left, with a wonderful flight of accompanying celestials. Just before the entrance to a small cell in **Cave 34**, flanked by two standing Buddhas, an unfinished ceiling painting shows the Buddha touching the earth. There must be at least a hundred more Buddha images on panels in **Cave 67**, a large hall. On the left side, and outside in the entrance, these figures are supported by *nagas* (snakes representing *kundalini*, yogic power).

Eating

In keeping with its cosmopolitan credentials, Mumbai (and Colaba above all) is crammed with interesting **eating places**, whether you fancy splashing out on a buffet lunch-with-a-view from a flashy five-star restaurant, or simply tucking into piping-hot roti kebab by gaslight in the street.

Colaba

Colaba's cafés, bars and restaurants (see map on p.256) encompass just about the full range of modern Mumbai's gastronomic possibilities, from no-frills kerbside kebab joints and old Irani cafés to exclusive air-conditioned restaurants patronized by Bollywood stars and politicians. The majority – among them the popular travellers' haunt, *Leopold's* – are up at the north end of the Causeway.

All Stir Fry *Gorden House Hotel*. Build-your-own wok meal from a selection of fresh veg, meat, fish, noodles and sauces, flash-cooked in front of you (Rs150–200 per bowl). Trendy white, minimalist decor, glacial a/c, and snappy service.

Bademiya Behind the *Taj* on Tulloch Rd. Legendary Colaba kebab-*wallah* serving delicious flame-grilled chicken, mutton and fish steaks, wrapped in paper thin, piping hot *rotis*, from benches on the sidewalk. Rich families from uptown drive here on weekends, eating on their car bonnets, but there are also little tables and chairs if you don't fancy a takeaway.

Busaba 4 Mandlik Marg ☎022/2204 3779. Ultra-sophisticated bar-restaurant specializing in Asian cuisine (Thai curries, Tibetan staples and exotic green mango salads). One of *the* places to be seen (if you can't quite afford to eat at *Indigo*).

Churchill 103 Colaba Causeway. Tiny 26-seater Parsi diner, with a bewildering choice of curious dishes, mostly meat based and served in mild gravies alongside a blob of mash and boiled veg –

ideal if you've had your fill of spicy food. No alcohol. Main courses around Rs130.

Indigo 4 Mandlik Marg ☎022/2236 8999. Currently the city's most fashionable restaurant, and for once deserving of the hype. The cooking's Italian-based with a Konkan-Keralan twist (eg Kochi oysters with saffron ravioli). House flambée is extremely popular, as much more for its head-turning potential as anything else. Count on Rs750–1000 for three courses.

Kailash Parbat ("KP's") 1 Pasta Lane, near the Strand cinema. Uninspiring on the outside, but the *alu parathas* for breakfast, pure veg nibbles, hot snacks and sweets (across the road) are worth the walk. A Colaba institution – try their famous *makai-ka* (corn) *rotis*.

Kamat Colaba Causeway. Friendly little eatery serving unquestionably the best South Indian breakfasts in the area, as well as the usual range of southern snacks (*idly-wada-sambar*), delicious spring *dosas* and (limited) *thalis* for Rs30–85. The best option in the area for budget travellers with big appetites.

Street food

Mumbai is renowned for distinctive street foods – and especially **bhel puri**, a quintessentially Mumbai masala mixture of puffed rice, deep-fried vermicelli, potato, crunchy *puri* pieces, chilli paste, tamarind water, chopped onions and coriander. More hygienic, but no less ubiquitous, is **pao bhaji**, a round slab of flat bread stuffed with meat or vegetables simmered in a vat of hot oil, and **kanji vada**, savoury doughnuts soaked in fermented mustard and chilli sauce. And if all that doesn't appeal, a pit stop at one of the city's hundreds of **juice bars** probably will. There's no better way to beat the sticky heat than with a glass of cool milk shaken with fresh pineapple, mango, banana, *chikoo* (small brown fruit that tastes like a pear) or custard apple. Just make sure they hold on the ice – made, of course, with untreated water.

Restaurants, bars and cafés are listed below by district. The most expensive restaurants, particularly in the top hotels, will levy "service charges" that can add thirty percent to the price of your meal. **Phone numbers** have been given where we recommend you reserve a table for dinner.

Leopold's Colaba Causeway. Colaba's most famous – and overpriced – café-bar is determinedly Western, with a clientele to match. Three hundred items on the menu from scrambled eggs to "chilly chicken", washed down with cold beer (Rs120). There's also a bar upstairs.

Ling's Pavilion 19/21 Lansdowne Rd, behind the Regal cinema ☎022/2285 0023. Swanky Chinese restaurant: soft lighting, marble floors and gourmet Cantonese cuisine with most mains at Rs250 and up. If your budget can stretch to it, go for the house speciality, crab.

Majestic Near Regal cinema, Colaba Causeway. Large, cavernous South Indian joint patronized by off-duty taxi-*wallahs*, junior office staff and backpackers. The food is more fiery than average, and veggies should note the *sambar* is flavoured with mutton stock. Thalis from Rs40.

New Martin Near the Strand cinema, 11/21B Strand Rd. Unpromising Formica booths, but famed for delicious Goan dishes such as prawn *pulao*, sausages, pork vindaloo and spicy shark masala. Takeaways available.

Olympia Coffee House 1 Colaba Causeway. *Fin-de-siècle* Irani café with marble tabletops, wooden wall panels, fancy mirrors and a mezzanine floor for "ladies". Decor more alluring than the menu of greasy meat dishes, but nonetheless a quintessential Bombay experience.

The Sea Lounge *Taj Mahal Hotel*. Spacious 1930s-style lounge café on the first floor of the *Taj*. Come for afternoon tea or a late breakfast with a backdrop of the Gateway and harbour. Worth splashing out on for the atmosphere.

Downtown

The restaurants listed below are marked on either the Churchgate and Fort map on p.258 or the Colaba map on p.256.

Apoorva Vasta House (Noble Chambers), SA Brelvi Rd ☎022/2287 0335. Currently the city's most rated Mangalorean, hidden up a side street off Horniman Circle (look for the tree trunk wrapped with fairy lights). The cooking's completely authentic and the seafood – simmered in spicy coconut-based gravies – fresh off the boats each day. Try their definitive Bombay Duck or sublime prawn *gassi*. Women should note the ground floor doubles as a bloke-ish bar in the evenings.

Café Samovar Jehangir Art Gallery, MG Rd. Very pleasant, peaceful semi-open-air café, with varying menu of food and drink: *roti kebabs*, prawn curry, fresh salads and dhansak, chilled guava juice and beer.

Chetana 34 K Dubash Marg ☎022/284 4968. Painstakingly prepared Rajasthani/Gujarati food, including set *thalis* (Rs150) at lunchtime and numerous à la carte dishes – absolutely the last word in fine veg cuisine. Expensive, but not extravagant. Reserve for dinner.

Britania & Co Opposite the GPO, Sprott Rd, Ballard Estate. Definitive Parsi food and decor, at local prices (Rs40–75 for main dishes). Try their special "*berry pulao*" or Bombay duck. A real find, and there's a friendly resident rooster.

Jimmy Boy 11 Bank St, Vikas Bldg, off Horniman Circle ☎022/2270 0880. One of the few restaurants left where you can sample traditional Parsi wedding food (albeit in rather inauthentic a/c surroundings, to a Shania Twain soundtrack). Go for the Rs200 fixed menu (pomfret and green chilli sauce steamed in a banana leaf/mutton pulao with dhansak dal/dessert).

Khyber (sign not in English), opposite Jehangir Art Gallery, Kala Ghoda ☎022/2267 3227. Opulent Arabian Nights interior and uncompromisingly rich Mughlai/Punjabi cuisine, served by black-tie waiters. The chicken tikka is legendary, but their tandoori dishes and kebab platter are superb too. Count on Rs800–1000 per head for the works. Reservations essential.

Trishna 7 Ropewalk Lane, Kala Ghonda ☎022/2267 2176. Visiting dignitaries and local celebs from the President of Greece and Imran Khan to Bollywood stars have eaten here (as photos attest). Wonderful fish dishes in every sauce going, and prices to match the clientele (main courses from Rs450). Very small, so book in advance.

Vithal Bhelwala 5 AK Naik Marg (Baston Rd), close to CST (VT). Mumbai's favourite *bhel puri* outlet, open since 1875 and still doing a roaring trade. No less than 25 kinds of bhel are on offer, including one pitched at British plates, with "boiled veg and cornflakes". They also do delicious potato cutlets, served with crunchy puri and yoghurt. Handy for the movie houses and the station.

Churchgate and Nariman Point

The restaurants listed below are marked on the **Churchgate and Fort map** on p.258.

Gaylord VN Rd ☎022/2282 1259. Parisian-style terrace café in the heart of Mumbai. Tandoori, sizzlers and some Western food served inside; or wholemeal bread, baguettes and sticky buns from the patisserie counter. Most mains around Rs250–350.

Mocha Bar VN Rd. Chilled terrace café where you can order American-style coffees, Mediterranean mezes and outrageously expensive New World wines, crashed out on bolster cushions smoking fruit-flavoured tobacco on a hookah pipe.

The Pearl of the Orient *Ambassador Hotel*, VN Rd ☎022/2291131. Revolving Oriental restaurant in four-star hotel. The cooking's nothing special (and expensive at around Rs700 for three courses), but

the views over the city are extraordinary.

The Pizzeria Corner of Veer Nariman and Marine Drive. Delicious freshly baked pizzas served on newly renovated terrace overlooking Back Bay, or to take away. Plenty of choice, and moderate prices (Rs150–250 per pizza).

The Tea Centre Resham Bhavan, 78 VN Rd. Another vestige of colonial days which, despite a lavish new refit, has retained its Raj-era charm, with paddle fans, comfy furniture and waiters wearing old-style *pugris*. Fine tea is its *raison d'être*, but they also serve delicious Continental snacks (try their fluffy cheese omelettes) and cakes, as well as a good value "Executive Lunch" (Rs185).

Crawford Market and the central bazaars

The restaurants below are marked on the main Mumbai map on pp.242–243.

Badshah Juice and Snack Bar Opposite Crawford Market, Lokmanya Tilak Rd. Mumbai's most famous *falooda* joint also serves delicious *kulfi*, ice creams and dozens of freshly squeezed fruit juices. The ideal place to round off a trip to the market, though expect to have to queue for a table.

Delhi Darbar Corner of Maulana Shaukatali Rd (Grant Rd) and PB Marg (Falkland Rd), opposite Alfred Talkies. On the fringes of the red light district, but a must for lovers of authentic Mughlai cuisine. Waiters in Peshwari caps serve up superb flame-grilled chicken and mutton *shekh* kebabs, biryanis, pulaos and *the* house speciality, chicken tikka, rounded off with the creamiest *lassis* in Mumbai. Most dishes only Rs40–150.

Gulshan-e-Iran Palton Rd. Popular Muslim breakfast venue on the main road that does inexpensive biryanis, kebabs, chutneys and fresh bread. Open all day.

Hiralal Kashiram Bhajiwala Kumbhar Tukda, Bhuleshwar Market. Cheap restaurant serving great *farsan* savouries, including *ponk vadas* (millet and garlic balls), *batata vadas* (made with sweet potatoes) and *kand bhajis* (deep-fried purpleyam), all with a tasty, fiery chutney.

Rajdhani Mangaldas Rd (in the silk bazaar opposite Crawford market). Outstanding, eat-till-you-burst Gujarati *thalis* dished up by barefoot waiters to discerning aficionados. A little more expensive than usual, but well worth it.

Vaibhai Payawala 45 Guzer St, Bohri Mohalla. Aficionados of the "full English breakfast" should sample its Muslim Mumbaikar equivalent, the *bara handi*. Slow-cooked overnight in 12 pots sealed with flour dough, the dishes are all traditional meat delicacies, prepared the same way here for four generations. Enjoy them with rice or smoky-flavoured lamba pau bread from the adjacent bakery. Jump in cab to Bohri Mohalla and ask the way when you get there. Inexpensive.

Nightlife and entertainment

Mumbai never sleeps. No matter what time of night you venture out, there are bound to be others going about some business or other. The city has always led the **nightlife** scene in India and there are bars and clubs to suit every taste: jazz dens compete with salsa, tabla–dance fusions and funk. Mumbai's alternative but decidedly yuppie crowd meet at the *Ghetto Bar* before heading down to the gay, glitzy or groovy clubs around Colaba and Juhu.

Laughter clubs

On the principle that laughter is the best medicine, Mumbai doctor Madan Kataria has created a new kind of therapy: hasya (laughter) yoga. There are now over 300 **Laughter Clubs** in India and many more worldwide; around 50,000 people joined the Laughter Day celebrations in Mumbai in January 2003.

Fifteen-minute sessions start with adherents doing yogic breathing whilst chanting "Ho ho ha ha," which develops into spontaneous "hearty", "silent" and "swinging" laughter. Sessions mostly take place between 6am and 7am, a time that, according to the good doctor, "keeps you in good spirits throughout the day, energizes your body and charges you with happiness". There are many clubs in Mumbai itself: look for semi-circles of people holding their hands in the air and laughing on Juhu beach, or go to ⓦ www.laughteryoga.org for the full story.

Of course, Mumbai is also a cultural centre, attracting the finest **Indian classical music** and **dance** artists from all over the country. There are frequent concerts and recitals at venues such as: Bharatiya Vidya Bhavan, KM Munshi Marg (☎022/2363 0224), the headquarters of the international cultural (Hindu) organization; Cowasjee Jehangir (CJ) Hall opposite the Prince of Wales Museum (☎022/2282 2457); and the National Centre for the Performing Arts, Nariman Point (NCPA; ☎022/2288 3838).

Bars

Mumbai has an unusually easy-going attitude to **alcohol**; popping into a bar for a beer is very much accepted (for men at least) even at lunchtime. Chowpatty Beach and Colaba Causeway, where you'll find *Leopold's* and the *Café Mondegar*, form the focus of the travellers' social scene, but if you want to sample the pulse of the city's nightlife, venture up to Bandra and Juhu.

Café Mondegar Colaba Causeway. Draught beer by the glass or pitcher, imported beer and deliciously fruity cocktails in a small café-bar. The atmosphere is very relaxed, the music tends towards rock classics and the clientele is a mix of Westerners and students; murals by a famous Goan cartoonist give the place a nice ambience.

Leopold Pub 1st Floor, *Leopold's*, Colaba Causeway. Swanky, self-consciously Western-style bar-night-club, with bouncers, serving expensive beers to Mumbai's smart set. No single men admitted.

Not Just Jazz by the Bay Next to *The Pizzeria*, 143 Marine Drive. The official Channel V TV hang-out is a convenient place to crawl to after stuffing yourself with pizza. There's nightly live music, with both Indian and foreign artists performing, except on Sundays and Mondays when it's karaoke. Rs175 entrance; free Tues.

Nightclubs

The **nightclub** scene in Mumbai is the best in India and the late Nineties saw the rise of a funkier, groovier scene as the moneyed jet set began to hear the latest house, trance, fusion and funk that was hitting the decks in Goa and the West.

Most discos and clubs charge per couple on the door, and in theory have a "couples-only" policy. In practice, if you're in a mixed group or don't appear sleazy you won't have any problems. At the five-star hotels, entry can be restricted to hotel guests and members.

Fashion Bistro 16 Marzban Rd, next to Sterling Cinema. Mannequins display designer creations in one room, with a bar and tiny dance floor in another. Deafeningly loud Western chart-music with a Seventies and Eighties night on Fri. Rs250–400 cover charge per couple.

Razzberry Rhinoceros *Juhu Hotel*, Juhu Beach. Much UV lighting and a good-size dance floor playing trance (Fri), drum'n'bass (alternate Wed) and the latest Western sounds (Sat & alternate Weds). Also has live rock bands on Thursdays as well as occasional blues, jazz or reggae bands on

Sun. Cover charge Rs150–400 per couple and closes at 1.30am – though the coffee shop overlooking the beach stays open till 5 or 6am.

Three Flights Up 34 Shivaji Marg, near Cottage Industries Emporium, Colaba. Used to have the longest bar in Asia and, despite moving to new (smaller) premises in a converted *godown*, remains the biggest club in Mumbai. The music is Western disco, there's a no-smoking policy on the dance floor and fantastic a/c. Rs150/300 cover for men on weekdays/weekends; women free. No single men ("stags") admitted.

Voodoo Lounge Kamal Mansion, Arthur Bunder Rd, Colaba. Mumbai's premier gay bar, and one of the oldest watering holes in the city (it hosted gigs by the Stones, Led Zeppelin and Pink Floyd in the 1970s). The small dance floor livens up after 10am. Rs150 cover on Fri, Sat & Sun.

Bollywood

For anyone brought up on TV, it's hard to imagine the power that **movies** continue to wield in India. Every village has a cinema within walking distance and, with a potential audience in the hundreds of millions, the Indian film industry is the largest in the world, producing around 900 full-length features each year. Regional cinema, catering for different language groups (in particular the Tamil cinema of Chennai), though popular locally, has little national impact. Only Hindi film – which accounts for one-fifth of all the films made in India – has crossed regional boundaries to great effect, most particularly in the north. The home of the Hindi blockbuster, the "all-India film", is Mumbai, famously known as **Bollywood**.

To overcome differences of language and religion, the Bollywood movie follows rigid conventions and genres; as in myth, its characters have predetermined actions and destinies. Knowing a plot need not detract from the drama, and indeed, it is not uncommon for Indian audiences to watch films numerous times. Unlike the Hollywood formula, which tends to classify each film under one genre, the Hindi film follows what is known as a "masala format", and includes during its luxurious three hours a little bit of everything, especially romance, violence and comedy. Frequently the stories feature dispossessed male heroes fighting evil against all odds with a love interest thrown in. The sexual element is repressed, with numerous wet sari scenes and dance routines featuring the tensest pelvic thrusts. Other typical themes include male bonding and betrayal, family melodrama, separation and reunion and religious piety. Dream sequences are almost obligatory, too, along with a festival or celebration scene – typically Holi, when people shower each other with paint – a comic character passing through, and a depraved, alcoholic and mostly Western "cabaret", filled with strutting villains and lewd dancing.

Bollywood has moved closer to Hollywood in recent years, with **budgets** of tens of millions of dollars, foreign location scenes and a general increase in on-screen sauciness. The runaway success of the cricket movie *Lagaan*, which was partly tailored for foreign audiences and received huge acclaim abroad, further encouraged Mumbai's screen moghuls to be experimental. The result has been a long run of flops and huge losses for the industry, with a thirty percent drop in domestic box office receipts. Compounding the problems have been the rise of pirate videos and repeated mafia finance scandals. As Bollywood lurches into deeper crisis, the cadence of calls for a "return to basics" grows louder. Mumbai's Westernized film makers, the pundits insist, are becoming perilously detached from the tastes of their less sophisticated audiences across the country.

Visitors to the city should have ample opportunity to sample the delights of a movie. To make an educated choice, buy *Bombay* magazine, which contains extensive **listings** and reviews. Otherwise, look for the biggest, brightest hoarding, and join the queue. Seats in a comfortable air-conditioned cinema cost Rs40, or less if you sit in the stalls (not advisable for women). Of the two hundred or so **cinemas**, only eight regularly screen **English-language** films. The most central and convenient are the Regal in Colaba, the gloriously Art-Deco Eros opposite Churchgate station, the Sterling, the New Excelsior and the New Empire, which are all a short walk west of CST (VT) station.

Shopping

Mumbai is a great place to shop, whether for last-minute souvenirs, or essentials for the long journeys ahead. Locally produced **textiles** and export-surplus clothing are among the best buys, as are **handicrafts** from far-flung corners of the country. With the exception of the swish arcades in the five-star hotels, prices compare surprisingly well with other Indian cities. In the larger shops, rates are fixed and **credit cards** are often accepted; elsewhere, particularly dealing with street-vendors, it pays to haggle. Uptown, the **central bazaars** – see p.263 – are better for spectating than serious shopping, although the **antiques** and Friday flea market in the Chor, or "thieves" bazaar, can sometimes yield the odd bargain. The **Zaveri** (goldsmiths') **bazaar** opposite Crawford Market is the place to head for new gold and silver jewellery. The city features a number of swish modern **shopping centres**, including India's largest, Crossroads, at 28 Pandit MM Rd, near the Haj Ali mosque. **Tea** lovers should check out the *Tea Centre* on VN Rd (reviewed on p.269), which sells a wide range of quality tea, including the outrageously expensive "fine tippy golden Orange Pekoe" (Rs1000 per 250g).

Opening hours in the city centre are Monday to Saturday, 10am to 7pm. The Muslim bazaars, quiet on Friday, are otherwise open until around 9pm (or through the night during Ramadan).

Antiques

The **Chor Bazaar** area, and Mutton Street in particular, is the centre of Mumbai's **antique trade**. For a full account, see pp.264–5. Another good, if much more expensive, place is **Phillip's** famous antique shop, on the corner of Madam Cama Road, opposite the Regal cinema in Colaba. This fascinating, old-fashioned store has changed little since it opened in 1860. Innumerable glass lamps and chandeliers hang from the ceiling, while antique display cases are stuffed with miniature brass, bronze and wood Hindu sculpture, silver jewellery, old prints and aquatints. Most of the stuff on sale dates from the twilight of the Raj – a result of the Indian government's ban on the export by foreigners of items more than a century old.

In the **Jehangir Art Gallery** basement, a branch of the antiques chain Natesan's Antiqarts offers a tempting selection of antique (and reproduction) sculpture, furniture, paintings and bronzes.

Clothes and textiles

Mumbai produces the bulk of India's **clothes**, mostly the lightweight, light-coloured "shirtings and suitings" favoured by droves of uniformly attired office-*wallahs*. For cheaper Western clothing, you can't beat the long row of stalls on the pavement of MG Road, opposite the Mumbai Gymkhana. "**Fashion Street**" specializes in reject and export-surplus goods ditched by big manufacturers, selling off T-shirts, jeans, leggings, summer dresses and trendy sweatshirts. Better-quality cotton clothes (often stylish designer-label rip-offs) are available in shops along **Colaba Causeway**, such as Cotton World, down Mandlik Marg.

If you're looking for **traditional Indian clothes**, head for the Khadi Village Industries Emporium at 286 Dr DN Marg, near the Thomas Cook office. As Whiteaway & Laidlaw, this rambling Victorian department store used to kit all the newly arrived *burra-sahibs* out with pith helmets, khaki shorts and quinine tablets. These days, its old wooden counters, shirt and sock drawers stock dozens of different hand-spun cottons and silks, sold by the metre or made up as vests, *kurtas* or block-printed *salwar kamises*. Other items include the ubiquitous white Nehru caps, *dhotis*, Madras-check *lunghis* and fine brocaded silk saris.

Handicrafts

Regionally produced **handicrafts** are marketed in assorted state-run emporia at the World Trade Centre, down on Cuffe Parade, and along Sir PM Road, Fort. The quality is consistently high – as are the prices, if you miss out on the periodic holiday discounts. The same goes for the **Central Cottage Industries Emporium**, 34 Shivaji Marg, near the Gateway of India in Colaba, whose size and central location make it the single best all-round place to hunt for souvenirs. Downstairs you'll find inlaid furniture, wood- and metal-work, miniature paintings and jewellery, while upstairs specializes in toys, clothing and textiles – Gujarati appliqué bedspreads, hand-painted pillowcases and Rajasthani mirror-work, plus silk ties and Noel Coward dressing-gowns. **Mereweather Road**, directly behind the *Taj*, is awash with Kashmiri handicraft stores stocking overpriced papier-mâché pots and bowls, silver jewellery, woollen shawls and rugs. Avoid them if you find it hard to shrug off aggressive sales pitches.

Perfume is essentially a Muslim preserve in Mumbai. Down at the south end of Colaba Causeway, around Arthur Bunder Road, shops with mirrored walls and shelves are stacked with cut-glass carafes full of syrupy, fragrant essential oils. **Incense** is hawked in sticks, cones and slabs of sticky *dhoop* on the sidewalk nearby (check that the boxes haven't already been opened and their contents sold off piecemeal). For bulk buying, the hand-rolled, cottage-made bundles of incense sold in the Khadi Village Industries Emporium on Dr DN Marg (see p.258) is a better deal; it also has a handicraft department where, in addition to furniture, paintings and ornaments, you can pick up glass bangles, block-printed and calico bedspreads, and wooden votive statues produced in Maharashtran craft villages.

Books

Mumbai's English-language **bookshops** and bookstalls are well stocked with everything to do with India, and a good selection of general classics, pulp fiction and travel writing. Indian editions of popular titles cost a fraction of what they do abroad and include lots of interesting works by lesser-known local authors. If you don't mind picking through dozens of trigonometry textbooks, back issues of National Geographic and salacious 1960s paperbacks, the **street stalls** between Flora Fountain and Churchgate station can also be good places to hunt for secondhand books.

Bookpoint Indian Mercantile Chambers, R Kamani Marg, Ballard Estate ☎ 022/2269 6226. Excellent range of serious books on Indian religion, history, current affairs and literature and they stock the city's best collection of Victorian Orientalist tomes in facsimile. Discounts available on request.
Chetana 34 Dubash Rd (Rampart Row). Exclusively religion and philosophy.
Crossword Mahalakshmi Chambers, 22 Bhulabhai Desai Rd, Breach Candy ☎ 022/2492 2458. Mumbai's largest and most reputed retailer, a bus ride (#132) from the downtown area, near Mahalakshmi temple/Haji Ali's tomb. Open Mon–Fri 10am–8pm, Sat & Sun 10am–9pm.
Nalanda Ground floor, *Taj Mahal*. An exhaustive range of coffee-table tomes and paperback literature, though at top prices.
Pustak Bharati Bharatiya Vidhya Bhavan, KM Munshi Marg. Small bookshop specializing in Hindu philosophy and literature, plus details of Bhavan's cultural programmes.
Shankar Book-Stand Outside the *Café Mondegar*, Colaba Causeway. Piles of easy-reads, guidebooks, classic fiction, and most of the old favourites on India, at competitive rates.
Strand Next door to the Canara Bank, off PM Rd, Fort. The best bookshop in the city centre, with the full gamut of Penguins and Indian literature, sold at amazing discounts. A good place to buy hardback editions of new titles at knock-down prices.

Music

The most famous of Mumbai's many good **music shops** are near the Moti cinema along SV Patel Road, in the central bazaar district. Haribhai Vishwanath, Ram Singh and RS Mayeka are all government-approved retailers of traditional Indian instruments, including sitars, sarods, tablas and flutes. For **cassettes and CDs** the best outlet by far is Rhythm House, Subhash Chowk, next to the Jehangir Art Gallery. This is a veritable Aladdin's cave of classical, devotional and popular music from all over India, with a reasonable selection of Western rock, pop and jazz.

Listings

Banks and currency exchange The logical place to change money when you arrive in Mumbai is at the State Bank of India's 24hr counter in Chatrapathi Shivaji airport. Rates here are standard but you may have to pay for an encashment certificate – essential if you intend to buy tourist-quota train tickets or an Indrail pass at the special counters in Churchgate or CST (VT) stations. All the major state banks downtown change foreign currency (Mon–Fri 10.30am–2.30pm, Sat 10.30am–12.30pm); some (eg the Bank of Baroda) also handle credit cards and cash advances. Several 24hr ATMs handle international transactions, usually Visa, Delta and Mastercard. It's worth noting that there's often a limit on how much you can take out: it can be as low as Rs4000. ATM machines can be found at: Air India Building, Nariman Point and 293 DN Rd, Fort (Citibank); and 52/60 MG Rd, near Hutama Chowk, Fort. The fast and efficient American Express office (daily 9.30am–6pm; ☎022/2204 8291), on Shivaji Marg, around the corner from the Regal cinema in Colaba, offers all the regular services (including poste restante) to travellers' cheque- and card-holders and is open to anyone wishing to change cash. Thomas Cook's big Dr DN Marg branch (Mon–Sat 9.30am–7pm; ☎022/2204 8556), between the Khadi shop and Hutatma Chowk, can also arrange money transfers from overseas.

Airlines, domestic Alliance Air ☎022/2202 4142; Air India ☎022/287 6565, ☎www.airindia.com; Indian Airlines, Air India Building, Nariman Point (Mon–Sat 8.30am–7.30pm, Sun 10am–1pm & 1.45–5.30pm; ☎022/2202 3031); counter at the airport ☎022/2615 6850; Jet Airways, Amarchand Mansion, Madam Cama Rd ☎022/2285 5788, ☎www.jetairways.com; Sahara Airlines, Unit 7, Ground Floor, Tulsiani Chambers, Nariman Point ☎022/2283 5671.

Airlines, international Aeroflot, Ground Floor, 14 Tulsiani Chambers, Free Press Journal Rd, Nariman Point ☎022/2285 6648; Air France, Maker Chambers VI, 1st Floor, Nariman Point ☎022/2202 4818; Air India, Air India Building, Nariman Point ☎022/2202 4142; Air Lanka, 12-D, Raheja Centre, Nariman Point ☎022/2282 3288; Alitalia, Industrial Insurance Building, VN Rd, Churchgate ☎022/2204 5026; British Airways, 202-B Vulcan Insurance Building, VN Rd, Churchgate ☎022/2282 0888; Cathay Pacific, Bajaj Bhavan, 3rd Floor, 226, Nariman Point ☎022/2202 9561; Delta, Taj Mahal, Colaba ☎022/2288 5652; Egypt Air, Oriental House, 7 J Tata Rd, Churchgate ☎022/2282 4088; Emirates, 228 Mittal Chambers, Nariman Point ☎022/2287 1645; Gulf Air, Maker Chamber V, Nariman Point ☎022/2202 4065; Japan Airlines, Raheja Centre, Nariman Point ☎022/2283 3136; KLM, 7th Floor, 712 Acme Plaza, Andheri–Kurla Rd, opp. Sangam Cinema ☎022/2697 5959; Kuwait Airways, 86 VN Rd, Churchgate ☎022/2204 5331; Lufthansa, 1st Floor, Express Towers, Nariman Point ☎022/2230 1940; Pakistan International Airlines, Mittal Tower, B Wing, 4th Floor, Nariman Point ☎022/2202 1598; Qantas Airways,2nd Floor, Godrej Bhavan, Home St ☎022/2200 7440; Royal Nepal Airlines, 222, Maker Chamber V, Nariman Point ☎022/2283 6197; SAS and Thai Airways, Oberoi Towers, 11th Floor, Room 1120, Nariman Point ☎022/2230 8725; Saudia, Ground Floor, Express Towers, Nariman Point ☎022/2202 0199; South African Airways, Podar House, 10 Marine Drive, Churchgate ☎022/2284 2242; Syrian Arab Airlines, 7 Brabourne Stadium, VN Rd, Churchgate ☎022/2282 6043; TWA, Amarchand Mansion, M Carve Rd ☎022/2282 3080.

Ambulance ☎022/266 2913 or ☎101 for general emergencies or ☎105 for heart cases.

Airport enquiries Chatrapathi Shivaji International Airport ☎022/2836 6700. Santa Cruz Domestic Airport: Terminal 1A for Indian Airlines ☎022/2615 6633; 1B for all other airlines ☎022/2615 6600.

Consulates and high commissions Although the many consulates and High Commissions in Mumbai can be useful for replacing lost travel documents or obtaining visas, most of India's neighbouring states, including Bangladesh, Bhutan, Burma, Nepal and Pakistan, only have embassies in New Delhi and/or Kolkata (Calcutta) - see relevant city account. All of the following are open Mon–Fri: Australia, 16th Floor, Maker Tower "E", Cuffe Parade (9am–5pm; ☎022/2218 1071); Canada, 41/42 Maker Chambers VI, Nariman Point (9am–5.30pm; ☎022/2287 6027); China, 1st floor, 11 M.L. Dahanukar Marg (10am–4.30pm; ☎022/2282 2662); Denmark, L & T House, Narottam Moraji Marg, Ballard Estate (10am–12.45pm; ☎022/2261 4462); France, 2nd Floor, Datta Prasad, N Gamadia Cross Rd (9am–1pm & 2.30–5.30pm; ☎022/2495 0948); Germany, 10th Floor, Hoechst House, Nariman Point (8–11am; ☎022/2283 2422); Indonesia, 19 Altamount Rd, Cumbala Hill (10am–4.30pm; ☎022/2380 0940); Republic of Ireland, Royal Bombay Yacht Club Chambers, Apollo Bunder (9.30am–1pm; ☎022/2202 4607); Netherlands, Forbes Bldg, Chiranjit Rai Marg, Fort (9am–5pm; ☎022/2201 6750); Norway, Navroji Mansion, 31 Nathelal Parekh Marg (10am–1pm; ☎022/2284 2042); Philippines, 61 Sakhar Bhavan, Nariman Point (10am–1pm; ☎022/2202 4792); Singapore, 10th Floor, Maker Chamber IV, 222 Jamnal Bajaj Marg, Nariman Point (9am–noon; ☎022/2204 3205); South Africa, Gandhi Mansion, 20 Altamount Rd (9am–noon; ☎022/2389 3725); Spain, Ador House, 3rd floor, 6 K Dubash Marg, Kala Ghoda (10.30am–1pm; ☎022/2287 4797); Sri Lanka, Sri Lanka House, 34 Homi Modi St, Fort (9.30–11.30am; ☎022/2204 5861); Sweden, 85 Sayani Rd, Subash Gupta Bhawan, Prabhadevi (10am–12.30pm; ☎022/2436 0493); Switzerland, Maker Chamber IV, 10th floor, Nariman Point (8–10am; ☎022/2288 4563); Thailand, Malabar View, 4th floor, Dr Purandure Marg, Chowpatty Sea Face (9–11.30am; ☎022/2363 1404); United Kingdom, 2nd Floor, Maker Chamber IV, Nariman Point (8–11.30am; ☎022/2283 0517); USA, Lincoln House, 78 Bhulabhai Desai Rd (8.30–11am; ☎022/2363 3611).

Hospitals The best hospital in the centre is the private Mumbai Hospital (☎022/2206 7676), New Marine Lines, just north of the government tourist office on M Karve Rd. Breach Candy Hospital (☎022/2363 3651) on Bhulabhai Desai Rd, near the swimming pool, is also recommended by foreign embassies.

Internet access A couple of cramped 24hr places (Rs40/hr) can be found in Colaba, just round the corner from *Leopold's* on Nawroji F Marg, though it's worth paying the Rs5 extra at Access Infotech, located down a small alley further down Colaba Causeway on the left, which is faster and more comfortable.

Left luggage If your hotel won't let you store bags with them, try the cloakrooms at the airports (see p.246), or the one in CST (VT) station (Rs7–10 a day). Anything left here, even rucksacks, must be securely fastened with a padlock and can be left for a maximum of one month.

Libraries Asiatic Society (see p.261), SBS Marg, Horniman Circle, Ballard Estate (Mon–Sat 10.30am–7pm); British Council (for British newspapers), A Wing, 1st Floor, Mittal Tower, Nariman Point (Tues–Sat 10am–6pm); Alliance Française de Mombai, Theosophy Hall, 40 New Marine Lines; Max Mueller Bhavan, Prince of Wales Annexe, off MG Rd (Mon–Fri 9.30am–6pm). The KR Cama Oriental Institute, 136 Mumbai Samachar Marg (Mon–Fri 10am–5pm, Sat 10am–1pm), specializing in Zoroastrian and Irani studies, has a public collection of 22,000 volumes in European and Asian languages. Mumbai Natural History Society, Hornbill House (Mon–Fri 10am–5pm, Sat 10am–1pm, closed 1st & 3rd Sat of the month), has an international reputation for the study of wildlife in India. Visitors may become temporary members which allows them access to the library, natural history collection, occasional talks and the opportunity to join organized walks and field trips.

Pharmacies Real Chemist, 50/51 Kaka Arcade (☎022/2200 2497), and Royal Chemists, M Karve Rd (☎022/2534 0531), both close to Mumbai Hospital, are open 24hr. Kemps in the Taj Mahal also opens late.

Photographic studios and equipment The Javeri Colour Lab, opposite the Regal cinema in Colaba, stocks colour-print and slide film, as do most of the big hotels. A small boutique behind the florists in the Shakhari Bunder covered market does instant Polaroid passport photographs.

Police The main police station in Colaba (☎022/2285 6817) is on the west side of Colaba Causeway, near the crossroads with Ormiston Rd.

Postal services The GPO (Mon–Sat 9am–8pm, Sun 9am–4pm) is around the corner from CST (VT) Station, off Nagar Chowk. Its poste restante counter (Mon–Sat 9am–6pm, Sun 9am–3pm) is among the most reliable in India, although they trash the letters after four weeks. The much less efficient parcel office (10am–4.30pm) is behind the main building on the first floor. Packing-*wallahs* hang around on the pavement outside. DHL (☎022/2850 5050) have eleven offices in Mumbai, the most convenient being the 24hr one under the Sea Green Hotel at the bottom of Marine Drive.

Telephones and faxes STD booths abound in Mumbai. For rock-bottom phone and fax rates however, head for Videsh Sanchar Bhavan (open 24hr), the swanky government telecom building on MG Marg, where you can make reverse charge calls to destinations such as the UK, US and Australia. Receiving incoming calls costs a nominal Rs10. Numbers in the city change constantly, so if you can't get through after several attempts, try directory enquiries on ☎197.

Travel agents The following travel agents are recommended for booking domestic and international flights, and long-distance private buses where specified: Cox and Kings India Ltd, 271/272, Dr DN Marg ☎022/2207 3065, ⓦwwww.coxkings.com; Magnum International Tours & Travels, Frainy Villa, 10 Henry Rd, Colaba ☎022/2284 0016, ⓔmagnum.intnal@axcess.net.in; Sita World Travels Pvt Ltd, 8 Atlanta Building, Nariman Point ☎022/2286 0684, ⓔboml.sita@sma.springtrpg.ems.vsnl.in; Thomas Cook (see p.258).

Moving on from Mumbai

Most visitors feel like getting out of Mumbai as soon as they can. Fortunately, the city is equipped with "super-fast" services to arrange or confirm **onward travel**. All the major international and domestic **airlines** have offices in the city, the railway networks operate special tourist counters in the main reservation halls, and dozens of **travel agents** and road transport companies are eager to help you on your way by **bus**.

Travel within India

Mumbai is the nexus of several major internal flight routes, train networks and highways, and is the main transport hub for traffic heading towards South India. The most travelled trails lead north up the Gujarati coast to **Rajasthan** and **Delhi**; northwest into the **Deccan** via Aurangabad and the caves at Ellora and Ajanta; and south towards **Goa** and the **Malabar Coast**.

By plane

Indian Airlines and other **domestic carriers** – such as the more efficient Jet Airways – fly out of Santa Cruz to destinations all over India. Availability on popular routes should never be taken for granted. Check with the airlines as soon as you arrive; **tickets** can be bought directly from their offices (see p.274), via the Internet, or through any reputable travel agent.

In theory, it is also possible to book domestic air tickets abroad when you buy your original long-haul flight. However, as individual airlines tend to have separate agreements with domestic Indian carriers, you may not be offered the same choice (or rates) as you will through agents in Mumbai. Note, too, that Indian Airlines is the only company offering 25 percent discounts (on all flights) to customers under the age of thirty.

By train

Three main networks converge on Mumbai: the **Western Railway** (ⓦwww.westernrailway.com) runs to north and west India; the **Central Railway** (ⓦwww.centralrailway.com) connects Mumbai to central, eastern and southern regions; and the **Konkan Railway** (ⓦwww.konkanrailway.com) winds south down the coast to Goa, Mangalore and Kerala.

Nearly all services to Gujarat, Rajasthan, Delhi and the far north leave from **Mumbai Central** station, in the mid-town area. Second-class tickets can be booked here through the normal channels, but the quickest place for foreign nationals to make reservations is at the efficient tourist counter (no. 28) on the

Recommended trains from Mumbai

The services listed below are the most direct and/or the fastest. This list is by no means exhaustive and there are numerous slower trains that are often more convenient for smaller destinations. All the details listed below were correct at the time of writing, but departure times, in particular, should be checked when you purchase your ticket.

Destination	Name	No.	From	Frequency	Departs	Total time
Agra	Punjab Mail	#2137/38	CST	Daily	7.05pm	24hr 15min
Aurangabad	Devgiri Express	#1003	CST	Daily	9.05pm	7hr 45min
Bangalore	Chalukya Express	#1017	CST	Daily	10.05pm	24hr 15min
Bhopal	Firozpur Punjab Mail	#2137	CST	Daily	7.10pm	14hr
Chennai	Mumbai–Chennai Express	#6011	CST	Daily	2pm	24hr 45min
Delhi	Rajhani Express	#2951	MC	Daily	4.55pm	17hr
	Golden Temple Mail	#2903	MC	Daily	9.30pm	23hr 30min
Goa	Mumbai–Madgaon Express	#KR0111	CST	Daily	10.50pm	12hr
Hyderabad	Hussainsagar Express	#7001	CST	Daily	9.50pm	15hr
Jaipur	Mumbai–Jaipur Express	#2955	MC	Daily	6.50pm	18hr
Jodhpur	Ranakpur Express	#4708	Bandra	Daily	3pm	19hr 25min
Kochi* (Cochin)	Netravati Exp	#6345LTT (Kurla)		Daily	11.45am	26hr 40min
Kolkata (Calcutta/	Gitanjali Express	#2859	CST	Daily	6am	32hr 05min
Howrah)	Mumbai–Howrah Mail	#2809	CST	Daily	8.15pm	34hr 15min
Mysore	Sharavathi Express	#1035	CST	Daily	10.05pm	24hr 10min
Pune	Shatabdi Express	#2027	CST	Daily	6.40am	3hr 25min
Thiruvananthapuram (Trivandrum)	Netravati Exp	#6345	LTT	Daily	11.45am	31hr 30min
Udaipur	Saurashtra Express**	#9215	MC	Daily	7.45am	24hr 40min
Varanasi	Mahanagiri Express	#1093	CST	Daily	11.50pm	28hr 30min

*details also applicable for Ernakulam Town
**change at Ahmedabad to the Delhi Sarai Rohila Express #9944

first floor of the **Western Railway's booking hall**, next door to the Government of India tourist office in **Churchgate** (Mon–Fri 9.30am–4.30pm, Sat 9.30am–2.30pm; ℡022/2209 7577). This counter also has access to special "tourist quotas", which are released the day before departure if the train leaves during the day, or the morning of the departure if the train leaves after 5pm. If the quota is "closed" or already used up, and you can't access the "VIP quota" (always worth a try), you will have to join the regular queue.

Mumbai's other "Tourist Ticketing Facility" is in the snazzy air-conditioned **Central Railway booking office** to the rear of **CST** (VT) (Mon–Sat 8am–1.30pm & 2–3pm, Sun 8am–2pm; ℡022/2262 2859), the departure point for most trains heading east and south. Indrail passes can also be bought here, and there's an MTDC tourist information kiosk in the main concourse if you need help filling in your reservation slips.

Tickets for seats on the **Konkan Railway** can be booked at either Churchgate or CST booking halls; for more info on getting to Goa by rail, see p.278.

Just to complicate matters, some Central Railway trains to **South India**, including the fast Dadar–Madras Chennai Express #6063 to Madras, do not depart from CST at all, but from **Dadar station**, way north of Mumbai Central. Seats and berths for these trains are reserved at CST. Finally, if you're booking tickets to Kolkata (Calcutta), make sure your train doesn't leave from **Kurla station** (aka Lokmanya Tilak Terminus, or **LTT**), which is even more inconvenient, up near the airports. Getting to either of these stations on public transport can be a major struggle, though many long-distance trains from CST (VT) or Churchgate stop there and aren't as crowded.

Wherever you're heading, a good investment for anyone planning to do much rail travel is Indian Railways' indispensable *Trains at a Glance*, available from most station bookstalls for Rs25. You can also access **timetables** via the Internet at the websites listed above, and in some cases even book tickets online.

By bus

The main departure point for long-distance **buses** leaving Mumbai is the frenetic **Central bus stand** on JB Behram Marg, opposite Mumbai Central railway station. States with bus company counters here (daily 8am–8pm; ☎022/2307 6622) include Maharashtra, Karnataka, Madhya Pradesh, Goa and

---

Getting to Goa

Since the inauguration of the Konkan Railway, the best-value way to travel the 500km from Mumbai to Goa has been by **train**. However, tickets for the twelve-hour ride down the coast tend be in short supply, and virtually impossible to obtain at short notice, so it's best to try and book at home before setting off. Otherwise, you'll probably find yourself having to shell out for a **flight**. Considering how hellish the bus ride can be, and how hard getting hold of train tickets is, it's well worth paying the extra to travel by plane, which could save you days waiting around in Mumbai. Alternatively, consider heading south in stages, via Pune or southern Maharashtra.

By plane

At present, four airlines – Air India (🖰www.airindia.com), Indian Airlines (🖰www .indian-airlines), Jet Airways (🖰www.jetairways.com) and Sahara – operate between seven and eight daily services to Goa. Demand for seats can be fierce around Diwali and Christmas/New Year, when you're unlikely to get a ticket a short notice. At other times one or other of the carriers should be able to offer a seat on the day you wish to travel. If you didn't pre-book when you purchased your international ticket, check availability with the airlines as soon as you arrive; tickets can be bought directly from their offices (see "Listings" on p.274), via the Internet, or through any reputable travel agent in Mumbai, although bear in mind that an agent may charge you the dollar fare at a poorer rate of exchange than that offered by the airline company.

All Goa flights leave from Chatrapathi Shivaji Domestic Airport, 30km north of the city centre. One-way fares for the forty-minute journey start at $63 with Indian Airlines (the only carrier offering a reduced fare for under-30s) and rise to $93 with Sahara, or $103 with swisher Jet. In addition, Air India operates an Airbus service on Mondays and Thursdays for $105. Few people seem to know about this flight, so you can nearly always get a seat on it.

By train

The Konkan Railway line runs daily express trains from Mumbai to Goa. **Fares** for the twelve-hour journey from CST start at Rs273 for standard sleeper class, rising to Rs1250 for II class a/c or Rs2310 for luxurious I class a/c. However, these services are not always available at short notice from the booking halls at CST and Churchgate. If you're certain of your travel dates in advance (ie if you're flying into

Gujarat. Few of their services compare favourably with train travel on the same routes. Reliable timetable information can be difficult to obtain, reservations are not available on standard buses, and most long-haul journeys are gruelling overnighters. Among the exceptions are the deluxe buses run by MSRTC to Pune, Nasik and Kolhapur; the small extra cost buys you more leg-room, fewer stops and the option of advance booking. The only problem is most leave from the ASIAD bus stand in Dadar, thirty minutes or so by road or rail north of Mumbai Central.

Other possibilities for road travel include the "super-fast" **luxury coaches** touted around Colaba. Most are run by private companies, guaranteeing break-neck speeds and possible long waits for the bus to fill up. ITDC also operate similarly priced services to the same destinations, which you can book direct from their main offices downtown or through the more conveniently situated Government of India tourist office, 123 M Karve Rd, Churchgate. Two night buses leave Nariman Point every evening for the twelve-hour trip to **Aurangabad**, and there are morning departures to **Nasik** and **Mahabaleshwar**, which take six and seven hours respectively.

Mumbai and want to catch the train to Goa soon after arriving), consider **booking online** (at ⓦ www.konkanrailway.com). There are downsides to this: you're only enti-tled to relatively expensive three-tier a/c fares (Rs1250 one-way) and must make your booking between seven and two days before your date of departure – but all in all, online reservation is much the most convenient way to secure a seat than leav-ing it until you arrive in Mumbai. Alternatively, you could make the reservation through an Indian Railways agent in your home country.

Don't be tempted to travel "unreserved" class on any Konkan service as the jour-ney as far as Ratnagiri (roughly midway) is overwhelmingly crushed. The most con-venient of the Konkan services is the overnight Mumbai–Madgaon Express #KR0111 (10.50pm; 12hr) which departs from CST. The other, only slightly faster train is the Mandovi Express #KR0103, leaving at 7.05am (also from CST).

By bus

The Mumbai–Goa bus journey ranks among the very worst in India. Don't believe travel agents who assure you it takes thirteen hours. Depending on the type of bus you get, appalling road surfaces along the sinuous coastal route make eighteen to twenty hours a more realistic estimate.

Fares start at around Rs300 for a push-back seat on a beaten-up Kadamba (Goan government) or MSRTC coach. Tickets for these services are in great demand in season with domestic tourists, so book in advance at Mumbai Central or Kadamba's kiosks on the north side of Azad Maidan, near St Xavier's College (just up from CST station; ☎022/2262 1043). More and more private overnight buses (around 25 daily) also run to Goa, costing around Rs375–400 for a noisy front-engined Tata bus, Rs400–450 for an a/c bus with pneumatic suspension and on-board toilet, and Rs600–675 for a service with coffin-like sleeper compartments which quickly become unbearably stuffy. Tickets should be booked at least a day in advance through a reputable travel agent (see p.276), though it's sometimes worth turning up at the car park opposite the Metro cinema, Azad Maidan, where most buses leave from, on the off-chance of a last-minute cancellation. Make sure, in any case, that you are given both your seat and the bus registration number, and that you confirm the exact time and place of departure with the travel agent, as these frequently vary between companies.

Leaving India

In spite of its prominence on trans-Asian flight routes, Mumbai is no longer the bargain basement for **international air tickets** it used to be. Discounted fares are very hard to come by – a legacy of Rajiv Gandhi's economic reforms of the 1980s. If you do need to book a ticket, stick to one of the tried and tested agents listed on p.276.

All the major airlines operating out of Mumbai have offices downtown where you can buy scheduled tickets or confirm your flight; see p.274 for a list of addresses. The majority are grouped around Veer Nariman Road, opposite the *Ambassador Hotel*, or else on Nariman Point, a short taxi ride west of Colaba.

Travel details

Trains

Mumbai to: Agra (4 daily; 23hr 15min–27hr); Ahmedabad (4 daily; 7hr 10min–12hr); Aurangabad (2 daily; 7hr 45min); Bangalore (3 daily; 26hr 10min); Bhopal (4 daily; 14hr); Calcutta (see "Kolkata"); Chennai (3 daily; 24–29hr); Delhi (11 daily; 17–33hr); Hyderabad (2 daily; 15–17hr); Indore (1 daily; 14hr 35min); Jaipur (2 daily; 18–23hr); Jodhpur (1 daily; 19hr 25min; change at Ahmedabad); Kolhapur (3 daily; 11–12hr); Kolkata (Calcutta) (4 daily; 32–40hr); Madras (see "Chennai"); Nagpur (4 daily; 14–15hr); Nasik (15 daily; 4hr); Pune (25 daily; 3hr 25min–5hr); Thiruvananthapuram (2 daily; 42hr); Trivandrum (see "Thiruvananthapuram"); Udaipur (1 daily; 24hr 40min; change at Ahmedabad); Ujjain (1 daily; 12hr 25 min); Varanasi (2 daily; 29–36hr).

Buses

Only state bus services are listed here; for details of private buses, see p.279.

Mumbai Central to: Aurangabad (2 daily; 10hr); Bangalore (3 daily; 24hr); Bijapur (3 daily; 12hr); Goa (2 daily; 18–19hr); Indore (2 daily; 16hr); Ujjain (1 daily; 17hr).
ASIAD Dadar to: Kolhapur (4 daily; 10hr); Nasik (17 daily; 5hr); Pune (half-hourly; 4hr).

Flights

For a list of **airline addresses** and **travel agents**, see pp.274–276. In the listings below IA is Indian Airlines, AI Air India, JA Jet Airways, and SA Sahara Airlines.

Santa Cruz airport to: Ahmedabad (AI, IA, JA 5–7 daily; 1hr); Aurangabad (IA, JA 3 daily; 45min); Bangalore (IA, AI, JA, SA 10–12 daily; 1hr 30min); Bhopal (IA, JA 2 daily; 2hr 05min); Bhubaneshwar (IA 3 weekly; 2hr); Calcutta (see "Kolkata"); Chennai (IA, AI, JA 6–8 daily; 1hr 45min); Cochin (see "Kochi"); Delhi (IA, AI, JA, SA 33–36 daily; 1hr 55min); Goa (IA, AI, JA, SA 7–8 daily; 1hr); Hyderabad (IA, JA 6–12 daily; 1hr 15min); Indore (IA, JA 3 daily; 1hr 05min); Jaipur (IA, JA 4 daily; 1hr 35min); Jodhpur (IA, JA 2 daily; 2hr 10min); Kochi (IA, AI 1–3 daily; 1hr 45min); Kolkata (Calcutta; IA, AI, JA, SA 9–10 daily; 2hr 40min); Madras (See "Chennai"); Madurai (IA, 1 daily; 3hr 20min); Mangalore (IA, JA 2–3 daily; 1hr 15min); Nagpur (IA, JA 3 daily; 1hr 55min); Pune (IA, JA, SA 5 daily; 35min); Thiruvananthapuram (AA, IA, JA 2–3 daily; 2hr); Trivandrum (see "Thiruvananthapuram"); Udaipur (IA 2–3 daily; 1hr 10min); Varanasi (IA, SA 2 daily; 4hr 55min).

Contexts

Contexts

History

For most of the twentieth century, Goa's isolated position, separated from the rest of the subcontinent by jungle-covered mountains and tidal rivers, ensured it remained relatively detached from the influences that moulded modern India. This was, however, not always the case. Long before the Portuguese annexed the region at the beginning of the sixteenth century, the thriving Hindu city that flourished here on the Konkan belt, near the site of subsequent European settlement, was exposed to a wealth of outside influences, brought along with the caravans of spices, silk and precious stones from the interior and shiploads of horses from Arabia. Interaction over hundreds of years between the local merchants and their counterparts across Asia gave rise to a highly heterogeneous culture with diverse and far-reaching roots – a defining feature of the region's history since prehistoric times. Recent archeological evidence suggests that even the first settlers in Goa came from the far side of the mountains, and that it was they who originally introduced, from the subcontinent's distant northwest, the religious beliefs and practices that would eventually evolve into what the European colonizers would term "Hinduism".

Pre- and early history

According to Hindu mythology, **Goa** was originally created by **Parasurama**, the sixth incarnation of Vishnu (one of the Hindu trinity) following his victorious war with the *Kshatriya* warrior caste. As a reward for his victory, the god is said to have been granted the right to claim land where his brahmin caste could live forever in peace. The territory would be that defined by seven arrows fired from a mountaintop into the sea around South India. From the spots where they fell, the waters are said to have receded to form the brahmin homeland, known as Parasurama Kshetra ("Parasurama's Country"). One of these seven regions, midway down the west coast, was Govarashtra, and the fertile belt around it, Shurparaka Desh, "Land of the Winnowing Fan".

Historians have long interpreted this origin myth as some kind of transmission from ancient times, probably the period between 12,000 and 10,000 BC, when – as the presence of burnt shells and marine fossils in the red Goan soil confirms – a massive elevation of the coastal strip seems to have taken place. The Parasurama story could well refer to the intensive reclamation, drainage work and forest clearance carried out in the wake of these geological upheavals (*parasurm* means "axe") by the first farmers of the Konkan – migrants from the interior who were being displaced by the expansion from the northwest of the Aryan tribes.

Any notion that these first settled agriculturalists were Goa's aboriginal inhabitants, however, was firmly scotched in the 1990s by a series of dramatic **archeological discoveries**. Believed to date from the Upper Paleolithic era (100,000–10,000 BC), the extraordinary rock carvings at Usgalimal (see p.190), together with scattered stone implements recently unearthed in the hills around the headwaters of the Zuari River, near Dudhsagar Falls, prove the existence of a much older hunter-gatherer population. From their art, these forest-dwelling people seem to have venerated some kind of mother-goddess or fertility deity. Later rock art at the nearby Kajur stone circle, dating from the Megalithic period (1500 BC), suggests the beginnings of representative decision-making and elaborate funerary ritual.

Knowledge of farming techniques was imported by immigrants from the interior – either Aryans or those societies fleeing them – around 600 BC. It is from this period that the ancient Sanskrit names for Goa listed in the Hindu epic, *The Mahabharatha*, are thought to date. In addition to Parasurama's Govarashtra, the Konkan coastal strip – whose abundance of cows (*Go*) and beautiful cowgirls (*Gopikas*) are said to have entranced Lord Krishna – is alluded to as Goparashtra, Gopakapuri and Gopakapattana: "Cowherd Country".

The ancient Greeks, who traded right across the subcontinent and whose coins have been found throughout peninsular India, must have known of the existence of Goa, which they referred to as Melinda, but the first solid historical record of the region dates from the third century BC, when it formed a distant southwest province of the mighty **Mauryan empire**, based at Magadha in the Ganges Valley. Having filled the power vacuum that ensued from the break-up of Alexander the Great's empire in northwest India, the Mauryans expanded south to annex the Konkan coast, which Ashok, the second and greatest of the Mauryan emperors, renamed **Aparanta Desh**, or "Beyond the End". He also dispatched a Buddhist missionary of Greek origin, Dharmarakshita, to evangelize the locals. Based at rock-cut cave-temples positioned at junctions of the region's main trade routes, they preached the Buddhist doctrine of non-violence, encouraging the local tribes to give up blood sacrifice. Literacy and the use of the plough quickly took root as a result of their efforts, but the wider religious mission met with little success: when the empire collapsed after Ashok's death in 232 BC, brahmanical Hinduism reasserted itself as the region's predominant religion.

The Hindu Golden Age

A succession of powerful **Hindu dynasties** held sway over Goa for the next seven hundred years from their capitals elsewhere in India, installing puppet governors and exacting tribute from them in exchange for military protection. However, while the Bhojas, Silharas, Pallavas, Chalukyas and Rashtrakutas wrestled for control of southern India and the Deccan plateau, a home-grown dynasty emerged in Goa itself. Having declared independence from the Pallavas in 420 AD, the **Kadambas** gradually came to dominate the region, forging marital alliances with their powerful neighbours and founding a royal family that would endure well into the next millennium.

In 973, when the Kadambas' old allies and overlords, the Chalukyas, finally defeated their arch rivals, the Rashtrakutas, the Goan kings took this as their cue to oust the latter's governors from the capital, **Chandrapura** (see p.84), which they invaded by placing a fleet of ships side by side to form a bridge across the Zuari. Shortly afterwards, they shifted northwest to Govapuri on the banks of the river. Blessed with a deep harbour, the new Kadamba capital was perfectly placed to profit from the thriving maritime trade between the Malabar coast, Arabia and the Hindu colonies in Southeast Asia.

The move soon paid off. Within a decade, the Kadambas had amassed a fortune from the shipments of spices and horses that passed through their port, ploughing huge sums into civic building and the construction of exquisite stone temples throughout the kingdom, which by the reign of Jayakeshi II (1104–48) extended from just north of present-day Mumbai to the Malabar coast, and inland as far as the modern city of Belgaum. As a symbol of his might, the king adopted the figure of a roaring lion as his crest (an image that nowadays adorns the sides of the state bus company, Kadamba Transport, buses).

Muslim merchants from East Africa and Arabia were also encouraged to settle, and they added to the splendour by erecting mosques and villas in the capital. It was only a matter of time before such opulence attracted the attention of Muslim raiders who, during the eleventh and twelfth centuries, were pouring in ever greater numbers across India from the northwest. The old alliance with the Chalukyas had thus far protected Goa from Muslim incursions, but when the last ruler of the dynasty died in 1198, the kingdom lay exposed and vulnerable to attack from the Deccan.

Muslim invasions

The first **Muslim raids** on Goa took place late in the **tenth century**, orchestrated by the warlord Mahmud of Ghazni from Delhi. Directed mainly at the Kadambas' temples, which housed most of the region's treasure, the incursions grew more frequent and destructive as the twelfth and thirteenth centuries progressed, culminating with the iconoclastic excesses of **Ala ud-din Khalji**, the Sultan of Delhi, and Muhammed Tughluq. Successive sackings of Govapuri reduced it to ruins, and the beleagured Kadambas were forced to flee to their former capital at Chandrapura. This, too, was eventually destroyed, although not before Govapuri had been rebuilt.

The spirit of religious tolerance that prevailed between Goa's Arab merchants and their Kadamba hosts (even during the Muslim raids of the medieval era) vanished almost overnight in 1350 with the arrival of the **Bahmanis**. Driven by a new religious fanaticism, the invaders instigated a systematic persecution of the Hindus, smashing up temples and murdering priests. Many of the most sacred deities were smuggled to the safety of the interior, but nearly all of the ornately carved shrines were destroyed: only one – the tiny **Mahadeva Mandir** at **Tamdi Surla** in central Goa (see p.115), hidden in the forests at the foot of the Western Ghats – has survived.

The rise of Ela

This first period of Bahmani rule was short-lived, for in 1378, the Hindu **Vijayanagar** kings swept into the region across the Ghats from their capital at Hampi on the Deccan plateau. Exacting revenge for the earlier slaughter of their co-religionists by the Bahmanis, they massacred the Muslim inhabitants of the Goan capital, which the invaders occupied until it was counterattacked nearly a century later in 1470. This time the Bahmanis made sure of victory by launching a massive two-pronged invasion, with a vast army from the east and a navy of 120 warships from the sea.

The city they conquered, however, had already lapsed into decline. Blocked by silt, its once thriving harbour had been left high and dry, forcing the

Bahmanis to move to a more convenient location further north on the banks of the Mandovi River. Known as **Ela**, this new capital, erected on the site of a Hindu religious centre founded by the Vijayanagars, would soon become the wealthiest city on India's southwest coast.

The transformation of Ela from sleepy sacred site to prosperous port was masterminded by the **sultans of Bijapur**, who succeeded the Bahmanis in 1490. The rapidly expanding horse trade with Arabia enabled their first leader, **Yusuf Adil Shah**, to embark on a major building spree. During his short twenty-year rule, the sultan erected a huge mosque and a grand fort-palace overlooking the Mandovi, as well as a two-storey summer palace for his harem further upriver at a village called Pahajani.

The Portuguese discoveries

With the Moors ousted from the Iberian peninsula and Christendom established in the North African port of Ceuta in 1415, the crusading European superpowers began to seek fresh pastures in which to exercise their proselytizing zeal. The Americas, recently discovered by Columbus, provided the Spanish with potentially rich pickings, while the rival Portuguese turned their sights towards the African Gold Coast and beyond. Their initial goal had been to spread Christianity and locate the mythical Christian ruler Prester John, whom the Portuguese hoped would aid them in their quest against Islam in Africa.

The spy who never came home

Pub quiz historians will tell you that Vasco da Gama discovered the sea route to the Indies via the Cape of Good Hope, but he didn't. Nine years before the Portuguese admiral's historic crossing of the Indian Ocean, his compatriot **Bartolemeu Dias** became the first European to round the tip of Africa. That expedition, plagued by unfavourable winds and mutinous crews, was unable to progress much beyond the Cape, but unbeknown to Dias, a lone Portuguese spy had already made it to the "spiceries" of India before him, and was busy charting their maritime trade networks while Dias was heading back to Lisbon. History has all but forgotten his name, but had it not been for the Odyssean adventures of **Pêro de Covilhão**, da Gama would almost certainly never have reached Calicut in 1498.

Born in a mountain town on the Spanish border, Covilhão rose from poverty to become a knight in the Portuguese court through his outstanding aptitude for languages. Success on a string of minor diplomatic missions led to his first big break, when the king dispatched him to Morocco to repatriate the bones of a revered Christian martyr. It was here he learned Arabic and mastered the intricacies of Islamic culture and customs – knowledge that made him an obvious choice for the most daring espionage assignment of his era.

Covilhão's mission to India reads like the medieval equivalent of an airport thriller. His brief was to gather first-hand information about the spice ports of western India and to smuggle the reports back via a network of Jewish traders based in Egypt. To do this he had to adopt the disguise of an itinerant Muslim merchant, knowing that discovery would result in enslavement or death.

From the Aegean island of Rhodes, Covilhão and his partner Alphonso de Payva left Christendom for Alexandria and made their way south up the Nile to Cairo, and thence by camel caravan across the desert to the Red Sea. Selling Neapolitan honey to maintain their cover and pay for their passage, they reached Aden in August 1488, where their paths diverged: Payva's towards the interior of Africa in search of the

Later, however, the lure of cheap silk, pearls and spices overshadowed other motives, particularly after Bartolemeu Dias rounded the Cape of Good Hope in 1488, making a route across the Indian Ocean at last seem within reach. If this route could be opened up, it would bypass the much slower trans-Asian caravan trail, threatening the old Venetian-Muslim monopoly on Indian luxury goods and providing direct access to the spice islands of the Philippines – all of which meant potentially vast profits for any nation able to maintain maritime dominance.

As a result, the Portuguese were quick to throw their Spanish rivals off the scent and informed them that the Cape lay a good ten degrees further south than it did. This ruse made the voyage around the tip of Africa seem a lot less viable as a short cut to the spice islands, and contributed in no small part to the **Treaty of Tordesillas** of 1494, in which the Spaniards relinquished any claims to territories east of a dividing line set at 370 leagues west of the Cape Verde Islands, off the coast of West Africa.

Once rights to the world's seas had been carved up between the two Iberian nations, the way was open for the Portuguese to capitalize on their earlier efforts on the rim of the Indian Ocean. Aside from Dias' pioneering expedition, several secret voyages, of whose existence historians have only recently learned from old naval records, probed up the east coast of Africa. Meanwhile, Pêro de Covilhão (see box below), under cover as a Muslim merchant, infiltrated Arab and Indian trade networks and mapped the main ports of the Indian Ocean. The scene was thus set for the entry of Vasco da Gama, whose 1498 voyage from Lisbon to Calicut, on the west coast of India, marked the

mythical Christian ruler "Prester John", and Covilhão's via a dhow bound for Cannanore (Kannur in northern Kerala). The most prosperous spice market in Asia, Calicut, was only a short journey along the Malabar coast. Several Europeans had previously reached the city by land and returned with tales of its extraordinary wealth, but none had travelled there via the Indian Ocean. Meticulously noting everything he saw on hidden parchments and a secret chart given to him by King João's court cosmographers, Covilhão explored the length of India's rich west coast, from present-day Kerala to Goa, then under Muslim control, and on to the textile-producing state of Gujarat, from where he headed west across the Indus Delta to Persia via Hormuz.

Over the following years, Covilhão crisscrossed the Indian Ocean several times, always undercover and on the lookout for trade secrets. His search took him from the Horn of Africa to beyond the mouth of the Zambezi River, but after nearly three years he returned to Cairo, where he learned from two Jewish Portuguese agents, sent by the king to find out what had happened to him, that his erstwhile partner Payva had died in Ethiopia. Having handed over his chart and diaries (which were taken back to Lisbon and subsequently formed the basis of the maps used by Vasco da Gama), Covilhão escorted one of the emissaries to Hormuz, but when this was done chose, instead of returning home to his wife and children in Portugal, to continue to Mecca and thence to Abyssinia. However, a condition of entering the country at that time was that no visitor be allowed to leave it (lest its defences be compromised), and even the resourceful Covilhão saw it was futile to try. He may, of course, never have wanted to. Thirty years later in 1520, a Portuguese priest who'd managed to slip into Ethiopia encountered him in the royal court, where he had become a rich nobleman and personal friend of the empress. Granted land and given a wife, Covilhão had finally settled down to live out his old age in peace, far from the wide-ranging geopolitical upheavals his espionage adventures had brought about.

beginning of the colonial era. On his second and third expeditions, both marred by bloody encounters with his African and Indian hosts, Da Gama established permanent trade stations that would, in the course of the coming century, become the first European colonies in India. Before this was possible, however, the Portuguese would have to assert their control of the Indian Ocean's seaways. Since Da Gama's first crossing, the Europeans had been universally detested in East Africa and South Asia because of the atrocities they inflicted on local populations, and the major powers of southern India were eager to settle accounts.

The Battle of Diu

To counter the Portuguese naval threat in the Indian Ocean, the Ottoman Turks spent nearly a decade building a fleet of twelve ships at the head of the Red Sea. The Zamorin of Calicut, whose capital had been cannonaded and subjects mercilessly terrorized by da Gama and subsequent Portuguese traders, also wished to give the Christians a bloody nose, and sent a hundred light vessels north to join the Turks. Together they closed in on the Portuguese at Chaul (midway between modern Goa and Mumbai) in 1508, where a small fleet under the command of Dom Lourenco Almeida, son of the so-called viceroy of the *Estado da India*, was sheltering. In the ensuing engagement, the Portuguese flagship was sunk and its commander killed; the rest of the fleet limped south.

When news reached Almeida senior of his son's death, the viceroy swore revenge, but a year elapsed before he came within firing distance of the Muslim fleet at **Diu**, a strategically important island at the mouth of the Indus delta. From here, shipping to and from the textile-rich region of Gujarat could be controlled, as could trade into the Persian Gulf. Both sides must have known as they prepared for battle that whoever won would dominate the Indian Ocean for many years to come.

In the event, the superior firepower and manoeuvrability of the Portuguese ships prevailed, and the Muslim navy was squarely routed. To impress their triumph upon the local people, the Portuguese indulged in a characteristically gratuitous bout of blood-letting; whenever the fleet approached a town or city, prisoners taken in the battle were decapitated and their heads and limbs fired at close range into the centre of the settlements.

Albuquerque and the conquest of Goa

Eleven years after da Gama's first arrival in India, the Battle of Diu had ensured Portuguese control of the South Asian sea trade. This monopoly was maintained in a variety of ways. In addition to attacking and looting any Muslim ships, which the Christians considered fair game, they also decreed that anyone wishing to trade in the Indian Ocean carry a special permit, or **cartaz**, for which merchants had to pay huge sums. As the decade progressed, however, it became clear that some kind of permanent enclave was required from which to administer the huge volume of trade passing through Portuguese control. A site was needed for warehouses and sanatoriums where sick sailors could recuperate and ships could be repaired in dry docks on land.

The man who would oversee the creation of Portugal's first colony was not Francisco de Almeida, the victorious commander at the Battle of Diu and India's first viceroy, but his bitter rival, **Alfonso de Albuquerque**, whom Almeida rightly suspected had been earmarked by Lisbon for his job. A veteran of anti-Islamic crusades, Albuquerque had cut his teeth in North Africa and was so famous for his loathing of Muslims as for the strength of his own religious convictions. During Almeida's rule as viceroy, he kept a low profile, preferring to secure footholds on the African coast than the Indian. But after a string of exceptional military successes, notably in Muscat in 1507 and Hormuz the following year, he confronted the viceroy and demanded a transfer of power. Almeida was understandably incensed by this, and promptly incarcerated Albuquerque, until the latter was liberated by an emissary from Lisbon. The envoy, **Fernando Countinho**, had also brought with him instructions from the royal council that Albuquerque should capture the then Muslim port of Goa and establish a bastion there, while Countinho himself had orders to take Calicut, long a thorn in the side of Portuguese domination in the Indian Ocean. Together the two led a force south; both were nearly killed in the attack on Calicut, but slipped away to fight another day in Goa, where Turkish survivors of the battle of Diu had allegedly taken refuge. Aside from mopping up the remnants of a potentially troublesome fleet, the engagement would also fulfil Albuquerque's orders from Lisbon. When a Vijayanagar commander by the name of Thimmaya informed them that the local overlord was occupied fighting a war on the opposite side of his kingdom, and that Goa was thus poorly defended, the attack was launched.

The battle for Ela

The depleted Muslim garrison at Panaji fort was unprepared for the onslaught by the better-armed Europeans and capitulated without a fight. However, while the Portuguese were wondering what to do with their new acquisition, the chief minister and regent of the newly enthroned 13-year-old sultan of Bijapur, Ismail 'Adil Shah, ordered a massive counteroffensive. Albuquerque and his soldiers held out for a couple of weeks, but were eventually pushed back to the mouth of the Mandovi River, where, hemmed in by cannon-fire from Panaji fort and with supplies of food and water dwindling, they remained for three months, their only escape route blocked by heavy monsoon seas.

The storms eventually subsided and the Portuguese were able to retreat. Seeing this as a chance to slip back to Bijapur, the sultan and his ministers also withdrew, but left Goa inadequately defended, not suspecting that Albuquerque would attempt another assault with his impoverished force. The wily Portuguese commander, however, was able to galvanize his troops and mount a ferocious second attack on the city on November 25, 1510, St Catherine's Day, which, this time, resulted in a decisive victory. The European soldiers swarmed through Ela, routing the Muslims and strengthening its defences against the inevitable Bijapuri backlash. In his treatment of the survivors, Albuquerque, furious that the Muslim population of Goa had aided the 'Adil Shah's army in its attempt to retake the city, demonstrated the same predilection for atrocity he had so often shown in Morocco and East Africa. Three days before Christmas in a letter to King Manuel of Portugal, he wrote:

... for four days your men shed blood continuously. No matter where we found them, we did not spare the life of a single Muslim; we filled the mosques with them and set them on fire ... We found that 6000 Muslim souls, male and female, were dead, and many of their foot-soldiers and archers had died. It was a very great deed, Sire, well fought and well accomplished.

Work on fortifying the city progressed at an extraordinary pace and was completed by the time Albuquerque left Goa in 1513 to attack ports in the Red Sea and Persian Gulf. But the hitherto indefatigable commander suffered a bitter defeat at Aden, where he lost most of his soldiers in an ill-conceived siege, and found the establishment of a fort at Hormuz – his last significant contribution to the Portuguese empire in Asia – too much for his exhausted body. Leaving Hormuz in the care of his cousin, Albuquerque set sail for Goa knowing that his life was drawing to an end. The death blow came when, still moored in Panaji harbour, he received the news that another governor had been appointed in his absence. Apparently he said to himself, "Old man, oh for your grave! You have incurred the king's displeasure for the sake of his subjects, and the subjects' displeasure for the sake of the king!"

The 'Adil Shah launched a counterattack soon after Albuquerque's death four years later, but to no avail. Ela was by then securely under Portuguese control and would remain so for another 450 years.

Conversion to Christianity

The zeal with which the Portuguese had seized Ela from the Muslims did not subside after the conquest. Rather, it was channelled in another direction: the **dissemination of Christianity**, which both justified the colonial enterprise and endowed it with the air of a religious crusade.

Ela's Muslims fled from the city in 1510, but a large contingent of Hindus remained (Portugal's alliance with the Bijapuris' enemies, the Vijayanagars, had ensured their safety), and it was towards them that the first Christian **missionaries**, representatives of the Franciscan Order invited by the king of Portugal, directed their attention when they arrived. Under Albuquerque's administration, the Church was relatively tolerant, relying on persuasion rather than force to claim converts. The Governor also encouraged his soldiers to marry local women in the knowledge that the children of such alliances would be raised as Christians.

Such tactics proved effective but were deemed too liberal by Goa's first vicar general, whose arrival in 1532 signalled the start of a markedly more oppressive regime. Supported by the newly arrived zealous **Jesuits**, he passed a law in 1541 ordering the closure of all Hindu temples. This was followed four years later by the outlawing of collective worship of idols and the exiling of all brahmin priests. The proclamation also sparked off an orgy of iconoclasm, with more than 350 shrines plundered and razed across the territory.

Worse was to follow. In 1559, idols were banned from private houses, and the following year, the Tribunal of the Holy Office, better known as the **Inquisition**, descended on Goa to weed out anyone who dared deviate from the dogmas of the Roman Catholic Church. Imprisoned in the dungeons of the 'Adil Shah's former palace, suspects were subjected to appalling tortures that culminated in spectacular **autos da fé**, literally "acts of faith", when they would have to publicly recant their heresy before being condemned – usually to death or slavery (a fuller account of the Goan Inquisition appears on p.94).

Even two hundred years of the Inquisition, however, failed to eradicate Hinduism altogether. A large number of deities were smuggled into the Portuguese-free zone in the middle of the state, where they were enshrined in secret temples, tended by priests in exile and worshipped by devotees under cover of darkness, who risked their lives to pray. Many of these temples still exist in Goa, hidden in the woods and valleys of Pernem, Satari, Sanguem and Canacona *talukas*.

"Goa Dourada"

By the time the Inquisition arrived in Goa in 1560, the territory's Golden Age was already in full swing. Situated at the nexus of Asia's most prosperous trade routes, the city of Old Goa raked in vast profits from the shipment of spices to Europe and Arabian horses into the subcontinent, earning for it the nickname "**Goa Dourada**", or "Golden Goa". Taxes levied on the movement of goods through its port financed a prolific **building boom**, as dozens of splendid churches and cathedrals were erected in the capital – monuments worthy of Goa's role as the linchpin of Christianity in Asia.

Lured by the seemingly inexhaustible supply of heathen souls to save, representatives of various **religious orders** began to pour in to staff these lavish buildings, accompanied by an even greater deluge of **immigrants**. During the colony's heyday, an estimated 2500 people left Portugal each year, causing a chronic shortage of workers in the mother country and precipitating a recession there that would contribute in no small part to Goa's eventual decline. Many Portuguese emigrants perished during the sea voyage, but enough survived to swell the city's population to around 300,000 – bigger than either London or Lisbon at that time, in spite of the appalling **epidemics** that regularly decimated the city. The permanent population was further boosted by a transient contingent of soldiers, sailors and traders who came to seek their fortune.

Littered around the more salubrious suburbs of Asia's largest metropolis were the elegant villas and grand colonial residences of its **hidalgos**, or Portuguese nobility. The lifestyle led by this wealthy elite was, in spite of the Church's high profile, famously decadent. Accounts by contemporary travellers – notably the Frenchman François Pyrard, who visited Goa after being shipwrecked in the Maldives in 1608 – describe the rounds of unbridled debauchery that prevailed among Goa's aristocracy. Sexual mores were notoriously lax, with prostitution and adultery rife among both the upper and lower classes. Pyrard even claimed that wealthy women of the colony regularly used to drug their husbands with extract from the hallucinogenic *datura* plant: in small quantities, the substance induced sleep and memory loss, allowing them to facilitate their adulterous liaisons undetected.

When reports of this decadence finally filtered back to Lisbon, King Dom João III dispatched a party of young Jesuit priests to remedy the situation. Among them was **Francis Xavier** (see p.303), the most successful missionary of his day, who, after a brief sojourn as a seminary teacher in 1545, used the city as a base for his evangelical missions to the Malabar coast and the Moluccas in Southeast Asia. The saint's body, which for centuries remained miraculously free from signs of decomposition, is today enshrined in Old Goa's **Basilica of Bom Jesus**, the most magnificent of Goa's churches and spiritual nerve centre of Roman Catholicism in India. However, neither the Jesuits nor the Inquisition's subsequent crackdowns on Goa's licentious behaviour were to make much impact.

Decline

The writing was on the wall for Goa long before the source of its wealth – from total control of Asia's booming maritime trade – ran dry in the seventeenth century. The roots of the colony's **decline** lay in its ill-chosen location. Situated amid low-lying swampland, the city swarmed with malaria-carrying mosquitoes. In addition, outbreaks of cholera and typhoid were common, spread by the sewage that piled up and swilled through the streets during the rains. **Epidemics** plagued the city from the start, and by the late 1600s, its population had plummeted to less than a tenth of its previous peak. The Mandovi River had also begun to silt up, and ships were finding it increasingly difficult to dock at the quayside.

Ultimately, though, politics and not disease were to bring about the colony's eventual demise. The first blow was struck by the sultans of Bijapur. After 'Adil Shah's death in 1557, his son, Ali, negotiated an alliance between the region's five main Muslim nations against the Hindu Vijayanagars. This bore fruit eight years later when the Muslim coalition defeated their arch adversaries at the **Battle of Talikota**. The sack of the Hindu capital lasted for six months and furnished the attackers with enough booty to erect some of India's finest Islamic monuments in Bijapur. However, squabbles over the loot divided the Muslim league, although the Ahmednagar and Bijapuri dynasties stuck together to launch a combined attack on the Portuguese shortly after.

Following successful offensives against several trading posts and colonies further north, Goa was besieged by the Muslims in 1570: a fleet blockaded the port, while a massive army encircled the city itself, defended by a force of less than one hundred Portuguese soldiers and black slaves. The attack, however, failed. Bogged down in Goa's swamps, the invaders eventually succumbed to cholera and were forced to retreat after a year-long siege.

Further threats to Goa's survival followed as the struggle between European powers for trade supremacy in the region intensified. Foremost among the challengers to Portuguese maritime hegemony were **the Dutch**, whose lighter and more manoeuvrable ships easily outsailed the old-fashioned, ungainly Portuguese galleons. Mercantile rivalries were given an added edge by religious differences: determined not to allow Asia to be carved up by the proselytizing Roman Catholics, the Protestant Dutch systematically whittled away at Portugal's Oriental colonies, claiming the Moluccas in 1641, Ceylon in 1663, and Macao and several strongholds on the Malabar coast soon after. A further blow was dealt by the Persians when they captured Hormuz, at the entrance to the Gulf, to control the most direct route to Europe, while pepper-smuggling **privateers** found it increasingly easy to slip through the net cast by the Portuguese navy in the Indian Ocean.

With its trade monopoly broken, its port blocked by silt, its administration in tatters and its population decimated by disease, Goa was well and truly on its last legs by the end of the seventeenth century.

The Maharatha Wars 1664–1739

Meanwhile in the Deccan, a formidable new challenge to European ambitions in India was taking shape. From their homeland in the Northwestern Ghats, the Hindu **Maharathas**, led by the indomitable and militaristic **Shivaji**, were proving a thorn in the side of the mighty Moghul emperors, who ruled most of northern India at this time. For years, the Portuguese watched the skirmishes between these two native powers from the wings, but when Shivaji sacked the Moghul stronghold of Surat in 1664, both sides petitioned the Portuguese for support, and the viceroy found himself on the brink of involvement in the conflict.

He avoided commitment on this occasion, but was outmanoeuvred a couple of years later when a Moghul army massed on the Goan border and demanded safe passage through the territory, which it was reluctantly granted. This provided the ambitious new Maharatha chief **Sambhaji**, Shivaji's son, with precisely the excuse he needed to attack the Portuguese trading post of Chaul, a short way south of British Bombay. The Portuguese responded by attacking Ponda, recently seized by the Maharathas from the neighbouring rajah, but the offensive failed, with disastrous consequences for the Portuguese. No sooner had they retreated towards the Goan capital than the opposing Hindu army surged forward in an attack to annex chunks of Bardez and Salcete.

Outflanked and with no hope of reinforcements, the viceroy decided to appeal to God for help. Hurrying to the Basilica of Bom Jesus, he opened up the tomb of St Francis Xavier and placed inside it his viceregal regalia, putting the fate of the colony in the miracle-working hands of its patron saint. His faith proved well founded. Within days, the Moghuls appeared on the border, forcing the Maharathas to beat a hasty retreat.

War between the Hindu rebels and their Muslim overlords kept the two sides busy for the next couple of decades, but Goa found itself in the firing line again in 1737. The Maharathas, led this time by Sambhaji's son, **Shapu**, were besieging **Bassein**, a major Portuguese fort and coastal settlement north of Bombay. In order to waylay any potential Portuguese reinforcements, he also mounted a diversionary raid on Goa, seizing Margao and encircling the bastion at Rachol. Had Shapu realized just how weak the Goans had become since the last war, he would no doubt have pressed on to take the capital. However, fierce resistance at Bassein led him to overestimate the defensive capacity of his Portuguese adversaries, and the Maharatha leader opted for a truce. The **Treaty of May 1739** ceded control of Portugal's northern provinces (including Bassein but not Daman) to the Hindus, in exchange for the complete withdrawal of Maharatha forces from Goa. In addition, the Portuguese agreed to pay a hefty sum in **compensation**. This, coming in the wake of other territorial losses and financial setbacks inflicted by its European rivals, totally impoverished the territory, whose capital now lay virtually deserted and in ruins.

The Novas Conquistas

The Maharatha surrender let the Portuguese off the hook, but they found the humiliation hard to stomach and tried to regain the provinces lost in the treaty of 1739. However, both the Maharathas and the British, who had gained a number of important footholds on India's west coast (among them a couple of former Portuguese possessions), proved too powerful. Instead, Portugal sought to enlarge Goa as a way of boosting morale and compensating for their recent defeats. Bicholim and Satari, two rural districts to the west of Mapusa, were assimilated in 1780–81, and Pernem in the far north later that decade. Finally, in 1791, the rajah of Sunda handed over Ponda, along with Sanguem, Quepem and Canacona in the south. These acquisitions, known as the **Novas Conquistas** (New Conquests), were quickly integrated with the older established districts of Tiswadi, Bardez and Salcete – the **Velhas Conquistas** (Old Conquests) that formed a buffer zone around the capital – and the frontiers of modern Goa were finally fixed, maintained even after the colony was absorbed into India more than a century and a half later.

The British and French, meanwhile, were embroiled in the **Napoleonic Wars**, which spilled over into minor skirmishes along the coast of India. The Portuguese managed to remain neutral, but in 1798, the British thought it prudent to dispatch a small fleet to protect Goa against attack by the French and their South Indian ally, **Tipu Sultan of Mysore**. However, the Goan viceroy objected to this violation of Portuguese sovereignty and insisted the British withdraw. They did, but returned the following year, occupying the forts at Aguada and Cabo Raj Bhavan (where a small British military cemetery still lies; see p.83). This **British occupation** lasted a decade without ever escalating into a major conflict, for by now the British had tightened their grip on the rest of India, and the Portuguese, fearing that any provocation might result in the seizure of the Goan capital, chose to acquiesce.

The rise of Panjim

The **nineteenth century** was a period of great flux in Goa. Money was still trickling in from the gold and ivory trade with East Africa, but the capital had lapsed into irreversible decay, eclipsed by the Portuguese's more recently established colony of Brazil. When the Frenchman Abbé Cottineau visited Goa in 1822, he found only churches marooned in rubble and jungle, while Richard Burton, in his 1850 travelogue *Old Goa and the Blue Mountains*, remarked that the city was a scene of "utter destitution", its population " . . . as sepulchral-looking as the spectacle around them".

Disease and the decline of the empire had taken their toll, but the demise of the once proud metropolis was hastened by the departure of its few remaining inhabitants to a more salubrious site further west along the Mandovi. In a bid to escape the mosquitoes and ongoing cycles of pestilence that had afflicted Goa since its foundation three hundred years earlier, Viceroy **Conde de Alvor** proposed a move to Mormugao – the tip of a rocky peninsula west of the modern city of Vasco da Gama. Accordingly, civic buildings and houses in the old capital were demolished to provide masonry for the new location, and the colonial government prepared to decamp. However, the scheme was shelved in 1707 after de Alvor was posted back to Lisbon, leaving Old Goa in a shambolic state from which it would never recover.

At the start of the nineteenth century, **Panjim** was a small fishing settlement of around two hundred houses, with a decrepit Muslim fort, a handful of chapels and churches, and the 'Adil Shah's former summer palace presiding over its waterfront. However, its healthy position and proximity to both the open sea and the remains of Old Goa city made it an obvious candidate for the site of the colony's new capital. **Dom Manuel de Portugal e Castro**, viceroy between 1827 and 1835, is the man widely credited with Panjim's metamorphosis. He ordered the levelling of dunes and the draining of swamps around the town to create additional land for building, and oversaw the construction of the impressive administrative blocks that still stand in the centre today. By the mid-nineteenth century, Panjim had become a bustling town of tree-lined avenues and leafy seaside suburbs.

The independence movement

As the size of Panjim increased, so too did disenchantment with direct rule from Lisbon. Calls for Goa to be made a republic or be absorbed into British India were echoed in Portugal, which at this time was divided by civil war. When the fighting ended in 1834, the government of Queen Maria II sought to placate dissenters in the colony by bestowing the governorship of Goa on a Goan, nationalist **Bernado Peres da Silva**, whose brief it was to implement a programme of sweeping reforms. These, however, floundered because of fears that da Silva, being a local man, would bend too easily to pressures from political factions in the territory.

The mounting distrust culminated in a **coup** attempt by the Goan military. It was unsuccessful but led to the appointment of a new governor, the former viceroy and founding father of Panjim, Dom Manuel de Portugal e Castro. But even he was unable to stave off the series of further mutinies by the army that resulted in the bloody "**massacre of Gaspar Dias**", when, on May 4, 1835, the fort at Gaspar Dias was destroyed by rebel soldiers and the regiment posted inside it slain.

When the dust settled after the mutiny, the Portuguese remained in power, although drastic measures were now clearly required if the rising tide of disenchantment in Goa was to be stemmed. Frustration with Portuguese rule was felt most keenly by the Hindus, who were still treated as second-class citizens by the administration. Iniquitous colonial laws (some of which were introduced as late as 1910) denied them access to government jobs and positions of influence, even though many of the colony's most prosperous merchants and businessmen were Hindu.

Prominent politicians had successfully publicized Goa's plight in Europe, but it was through the local press that the fledgling **freedom movement** found its wings. In spite of stringent censorship laws, the newly created newspapers provided a platform for the separatists, whose ideas found favour among both the educated classes at home and influential Goan expatriates in Bombay.

However, after Portugal had itself been declared a republic in 1926, Goa's independence struggle sustained a major setback. For the next 46 years, Portuguese foreign policy was to be laid down by the right-wing dictator **Salazar**. Staunchly pro-colonial, he refused to relinquish control of Goa or Portugal's remaining possessions in Africa and Southeast Asia, even though the impoverished mother country could scarcely provide for itself, let alone prop up its flagging foreign territories.

Portugal's economic woes had another important **social consequence** for Goa. Throughout the twentieth century, hundreds of thousands of Goans were forced out-of-state and overseas – to Bombay, Bangalore and the Portuguese colonies in Africa – in search of work. Many men from poorer, low-caste fishing families also took jobs in the merchant marine and on cruise liners – a tradition that endures to this day among coastal communities.

Meanwhile, India's national independence struggle gathered momentum, culminating in the **British withdrawal** of 1947. Inevitably, the end of the Raj intensified demands for Portugal to "quit Goa". Inspired by Gandhi's philosophies of non-violent resistance, a dozen or more groups formed to agitate for Goan independence, but these failed to establish a unified front, riven by petty rivalries and political feuding. Nevertheless, hundreds of *satyagrahayas* ("freedom fighters") were imprisoned, tortured, shot or exiled to Africa and Portugal through the 1950s in Goa, as the Portuguese dictator struggled to shore up his rapidly crumbling hold over the colony.

Liberation

Outraged by reports of atrocities in Goa, India's first prime minister, **Jawaharlal "Pandit" Nehru**, openly encouraged civil disobedience in the colony. In March 1961, he sent a message of support to independence campaigners, denouncing Portuguese rule and urging Goans to fight "unremittingly" for liberation. Later, ostensibly in response to a build-up of Portuguese forces in the region, he ordered a massive movement of troops and battleships around Goa's borders. The previous year, India's prestige had received a bloody nose after China's invasion of Ladakh, in the Himalayas, and with an election pending, Nehru was in need of a foreign policy success to bolster his popularity.

Salazar, meanwhile, desperately tried to whip up international condemnation of India's claim on Goa by lobbying world leaders. John F. Kennedy was persuaded to write to Nehru, advising him not to use force to settle the dispute, while in London, the Portuguese ambassador reminded Macmillan of the Anglo-Portuguese Alliance of 1899, which obliged Britain to come to Portugal's aid in the event of an armed attack on Goa. But the British were determined not to become embroiled in a conflict with a Commonwealth state and kept their distance.

In the end, it was Salazar who gave Nehru the pretext he needed to invade, when Portuguese troops stationed at Anjediv Island (10km south of Goa) opened fire on Indian fishing boats. One month later, on December 17, 1961, Indian forces finally entered Goa and the other remaining Portuguese enclaves in India, Daman and Diu. Mounted in defiance of a United Nations resolution (subsequently vetoed by the Soviet Union), "**Operation Vijay**" met with only token resistance from the 1800 Portuguese troops stationed in the colony, with barely a shot fired on either side.

The offensive was heralded as an act of heroic "**liberation**" by India but met with a more ambivalent response in Goa itself. Many feared assimilation would result in a drop in the relatively high standards of living in the territory. The influx of immigrant workers from poorer states, as well as the army of troops and bureaucrats that descended from Delhi, also made Goans more acutely aware of how different they were from their neighbours.

Centuries of divide-and-rule politics from the Portuguese had the effect of accentuating social divisions rather than cultural similarities. To both colonizers and the colonized, Goa felt more like a conglomeration of separate communities – Hindus, Christians, Muslims, and dozens of castes and sub-castes – than a culturally homogeneous region. Notions of a definable "Goan identity" were thus either nebulous or, in the case of the Portuguese-speaking elite, based on the hackneyed, outdated image of "Goa Dourada" promoted by its European rulers. Now, however, with the Portuguese Raj replaced by an army of mustachioed troops and bland bureaucrats from distant Delhi, fears mounted that merger with the mother country might result in a loss of cultural identity.

The road to statehood

Recognizing Goa's cultural and historical distinctiveness, the Indian government immediately designated the former colony a **Union Territory**, with semi-independent status and its own ruling body, or Legislative Assembly. Within two years, Goa boasted its own popularly elected government, headed by the millionaire mining magnate, D.B. Bandodkar.

During the first two decades after liberation, sweeping **economic changes** transformed life in the territory beyond recognition, as it metamorphosed from a traditional colonial society to an industrial capitalist one. But the issue that most preoccupied the new leader and his electorate at this time was merger – the debate over whether or not to join the neighbouring state of Maharashtra.

In 1963, the ruling party, the **Maharashtrawadi Gomantak** (or MGP), came to office on a pro-merger platform, asserting that "Goan culture" was in essence a colonial myth and Konkani no more than an inferior dialect of Maharati; it also attacked the power of the upper caste *Goenkars* by championing rights of the lower landless castes. In opposition, the **United Goan Party** (UGP) stood vehemently against assimilation with Maharashtra, advocating greater autonomy and a more inclusive, less caste-based realpolitik.

These two parties dominated the fiercely fought campaign that preceded the **Opinion Poll** of January 16, 1967, when Goans were asked to vote for or against merger. After three days of intense nail-biting, a crowd of 25,000 gathered outside the Menezes Braganza Institute in Panjim to learn that 54 percent of the population had voted in favour of remaining a Union Territory. When it came to declaring their hand, Goa's Hindus had, contrary to the pundits' predictions, preferred the status quo. Integration with Maharashtra would have meant becoming a remote corner of a huge state, hence significantly fewer job opportunities and reduced government investment. Goa's liberal liquor laws, too, would have disappeared overnight, depriving tens of thousands of *toddi* tappers of their traditional livelihoods. In the end, it was probably these factors, rather than ideological ones, which swayed the day.

The pro-Goan lobby had triumphed by only a slim margin, but it was enough to bury the merger issue once and for all. After Bandodkar's death in 1973, when he was succeeded as chief minister by his daughter, **Shashikala Kakodkar**, the MGP found itself increasingly marginalized. Six years later, in the elections of 1979, it finally lost out to the Congress party, which has remained in power in Goa more or less until the present day.

In the 1980s, the status of **Konkani**, the language spoken by the majority of Goans but not that of government or education, formed the primary focus of debate over the territory's future. Spearheaded by the Konkani Porjech Avaz (KPA), campaigners agitated for it to be upgraded to an Official Language. The movement boiled over into riots in December 1986, provoking political upheavals and, two months later, the announcement from Delhi of the eagerly awaited Official Language Bill.

Indian states are drawn primarily along linguistic lines, thus the step from Official Language status to full-blown statehood is a small one in the subcontinent. Calls for Goa to be made the 25th state in the Republic of India soon came to dominate editorials in the notoriously emotive local press. As one commentator wrote at the time, "Konkani is the soul of the red soil of Goa. Statehood will be the body which will provide a home for the soul." The landmark decision was finally made on **May 31, 1987**, giving permanent acknowledgement from the central government to the region's distinct cultural identity.

Recent history

Throughout the 1990s, political life in the fledgling state was dogged by **chronic instability**. No fewer than twelve chief ministers held power over a succession of shaky, opportunistic coalitions, which saw standards of government plummet to depths hitherto unseen in the region. Elections were invariably followed by periods of deal cutting, in which old scores were settled and revenge exacted for past defections and betrayals. As a result, policy making was rendered near impossible, while **corruption** eroded the fabric of government.

Among the main beneficiaries of the ongoing chaos have been the right-wing Hindu nationalists, the **Bharatiya Janata Party** (BJP). In the past, their pro-merger stance made them unpopular with the Goan electorate – even Hindus – despite the party's dominance in the national arena. But at the time of writing, after substantial gains in three consecutive elections, the BJP enjoyed a safe majority of the seats in the Goan State Legislature, with Congress demoted to the opposition.

At the start of the twenty-first century, as massive inward investment, growing tourist numbers and ever-improving infrastructural links with the rest of India render Goa's borders more porous, the survival of the state as a culturally distinct region will doubtless depend on the extent to which its government is able to curb corruption and establish coherent, democratic policies. For the time being, at least, the chances of this happening seem remoter now than they have been since Independence.

The religions of Goa

Three great religions – Hinduism, Christianity and Islam – are represented in Goa, and they play a vital part in the everyday lives of the population. Indeed, some religious festivals, like Diwali and Easter, have become elevated to such a stature that they are among the region's main cultural events, while temples and churches provide a focus for social as well as devotional life.

Roughly speaking, **Christian** Goa encompasses the centre of the state: the coastal region of Tiswadi, Salcete and Bardez *talukas*. Known as the *Velhas Conquistas*, or Old Conquests, this area is still littered with whitewashed churches and wayside crosses, and its houses are very much in the Portuguese mould. The **Hindu** heartland lies in the hilly interior around the town of Ponda, and in areas in the far north and south of the state, known as the *Novas Conquistas*, or New Conquests, which retained a more obviously Indian feel. **Islam** has almost entirely died out in the state, with only a small remaining community.

However, even in outlying districts, it's not uncommon to find churches and temples side by side. For in spite of the systematic religious persecution of Portuguese times, the respective communities today live happily together, even, on occasions, participating in each others' religious festivals (Hindu and Christian neighbours, for example, commonly exchange sweets – *mithai* – for Diwali and Christmas). The two major faiths have also taken on many common traits: Goan temples incorporate features of Italian Renaissance architecture, while Christian worship frequently has the devotional air of Hindu rituals, with garlanded icons and prayers sung in Konkani.

Hinduism

The product of several millennia of evolution and assimilation, **Hinduism** was the predominant religion in Goa long before the arrival of Christianity, and is today practised by two-thirds of the region's population. Although underpinned by a plethora of sacred scriptures, it has no single orthodoxy, prophet, creed or doctrine, and thus encompasses a wide range of different beliefs. Its central tenet is the conviction that human life is an ongoing series of rebirths and reincarnations (*avatars*) that eventually leads to spiritual release (*moksha*). An individual's progress is determined by **karma**, very much a law of cause and effect, where negative decisions and actions impede the process of upward incarnations, and positive ones, such as worship and charitable acts, accelerate it. A whole range of deities are revered, which on the surface can make Hinduism seem mind-bogglingly complex, but with a loose understanding of the *Vedas* and *Puranas* – the religion's most influential holy texts – the characters and roles of the various gods and goddesses become apparent (see box on pp.300–301).

Castes in Hinduism

Every Hindu (from the Persian word for Indian) is born into a rigid social class, or **varna** (literally "colour", but sometimes referred to as **caste**), each with its own specific rules and responsibilities. In descending hierarchical order, the four *varnas* are: brahmins, known as *Bamons* in Konkani (priests and teachers), *Kshatriyas*, or *Chardos* (rulers and warriors), *Vaishyas* (merchants and cultivators) and *Shudras* (menials). Members of the first two classes, known as "twice-born", are distinguished by a sacred thread worn from the time of initiation, and are granted full access to religious texts and rituals; members of the fourth *varna* are occasionally excluded from some of India's most sacred shrines. Below all four categories, groups whose jobs involve "polluting" – coming in contact with dirt or death – such as undertakers, sweepers or leather

Hindu gods and goddesses

The Hindu pantheon is dominated by the primary gods **Shiva** and **Vishnu**, and to a lesser extent **Brahma**, the Creator, who collectively control the powers of destruction and preservation. Throughout India, Hinduism is organized around the two main sects – Vaishnavism and Shaivism – whose followers regard either Vishnu or Shiva as the pre-eminent deity. In Goa, however, you'll find images associated with both featuring in the same temple, although the central shrine and its accessory deities (*pariwar devtas*) will generally be from the same "family".

Shiva

Most temples in Goa are dedicated to **Shiva**, even though the all-powerful god of creation and destruction has never been incarnate on earth. Known in Goa by a variety of names (most commonly Manguesh, Naguesh or Saptakoteswara), he is often depicted with four or five faces, holding a trident, draped with serpents, and bearing a third eye in his forehead. In temples he is identified with the **lingam**, or phallic symbol, resting on the yoni pedestal, a representation of female sexuality. Whether a statue or a *lingam*, though, Shiva is always guarded by his faithful bull-mount, **Nandi**, and often accompanied by a consort, who assumes various forms and is looked upon as the vital energy, or *shakti*, that empowers him.

Vishnu

The chief function of **Vishnu**, the Pervader, is to keep the world in order, preserving, restoring and protecting. With four arms holding a conch, discus, lotus and mace, Vishnu (sometimes referred to in Goa as Vitthala, Narcenha or Narayan) is blue-skinned, and often shaded by a serpent, or is shown resting on its coils afloat the Primordial Ocean.

Vaishnavites, generally distinguishable by the two vertical lines of sandalwood paste on their foreheads, recognize Vishnu as the supreme Lord, and hold that he has manifested himself on earth nine times. These **incarnations** (*avatars*) have been as a fish (Matsya), tortoise (Kurma), boar (Varaha), man-lion (Narsingh), dwarf (Vamana), axe-wielding brahmin (Parasuram), Rama, Krishna and Buddha. Vishnu's future descent to earth as Kalki, the saviour who will come to restore purity and destroy the wicked, is eagerly awaited.

Vishnu's most important incarnation, however, was as **Krishna**. In this guise, he assumes different faces, but is most popularly depicted as the playful cowherd who seduces and dances with cowgirls (*gopis*), giving each the illusion that she is his only lover. He is also pictured as a small, chubby, mischievous baby, known for his butter-stealing exploits, who inspires motherly love in women. Like Vishnu, Krishna is blue and is often shown dancing and playing the flute.

Rama, Vishnu's other main *avatar*, is the chief character in Hinduism's most popular epic, the *Ramayana*. Born a prince in Ayodhya, he was denied succession to the throne by one of his father's wives, and was exiled for fourteen years, together with his wife Sita. The *Ramayana* details his exploits during these years, and his defeat of the demon king of Lanka, Ravana. When Rama was reinstated as king in Ayodhya, he put Sita through a "trial by fire" to prove that she had remained pure

workers, were traditionally classified as **Untouchables**, later renamed, following the campaign of Mahatma Gandhi, as *Harijans*, or "Children of God". Discrimination against this lowest stratum of society, called *Chamars* in Goa, is now a criminal offence, but "Untouchability" is by no means a thing of the past.

Within the four main *varnas* exist numerous sub-categories which usually, though no longer necessarily, denote a person's occupation. Each has a set place in a complex and rigid social hierarchy of Hinduism. In Goa, for example,

while in the clutches of Ravana. Sita passed the test unharmed, and is thus revered as the paradigm of female purity, honesty and faithfulness.

Durga

Durga, the fiercest of Hinduism's female deities, is an aspect of Shiva's more conservative consort, **Parvati** (the goddess of peace, known as Shantadurga in Goa), who is remarkable only for her beauty and fidelity. In whatever form, Shiva's consort is **shakti**, the primal energy that spurs him into action. Among Durga's many aspects (each one a terrifying goddess eager to slay demons) are Chamunda and Kali, but in all her forms she is Mahadevi, the "Great Goddess". Statues show her with ten arms, holding the head of a demon, a spear, and other weapons; she tramples demons underfoot, or dances over Shiva's body. A garland of skulls drapes her neck, and her tongue hangs from her mouth, dripping with blood.

Ganesh

Chubby and smiling, elephant-headed **Ganesh**, the first son of Shiva and Parvati, is invoked by Goan Hindus before almost every major undertaking (except funerals), and is the focus of one of the region's major religious festivals, Ganesh Chathurti. Seated on a throne or lotus, his image is often placed above temple gateways, in shops and houses; in his four arms he holds a conch, discus, bowl of sweets (or club) and a water lily, and he's nearly always attended by his vehicle, the rat. Credited with writing the epic poem the *Mahabharata* as it was dictated by the sage Vyasa, Ganesh is regarded as the god of learning, lord of success, prosperity and peace.

Lakshmi

The comely goddess **Lakshmi**, usually shown sitting or standing on a lotus flower, and known in Goa as Mahalsa or Mahalakshmi, is the goddess of wealth and the embodiment of loveliness, grace and charm. As Vishnu's consort, she appears in different aspects alongside each of his *avatars*. The most important of these are Sita, wife of Rama, and Radha, Krishna's favourite *gopi*. In some temples, she is shown with Vishnu, in the form of Lakshmi-Narayan.

Saraswati

The most beautiful Hindu goddess, **Saraswati**, the wife of Brahma, sits or stands on a water lily or peacock, playing the lute, *sitar* or *veena*. Associated with the mythical Indian river of the same name, she is seen as the goddess of purification and fertility, but equally revered as the inventor of writing, the queen of eloquence and goddess of music.

Hanuman

India's great monkey god, **Hanuman**, features in the *Ramayana* as Rama's chief aide in his fight against Ravana, the demon king of Lanka. Depicted as a giant monkey wielding a mace, Hanuman is the deity of acrobats and wrestlers, but is also seen as Rama and Sita's greatest devotee and an author of Sanskrit grammar.

members of the *Chardo* caste may be *borem munis* (literally "good people") or *sokol munis* ("low people"), while *Shudras* could be *shetkamti* (agricultural workers), *dhobis* (clothes washers), *dorjis* (tailors) or *render* (*toddi* tappers), depending on the traditional work undertaken by their family. As a rule, it is possible to ascertain a person's caste from their surname, but sub-caste is expressed through many other factors: which part of which village a person's family comes from, roles in temple rituals, food, dress and even political affiliation.

While it is certainly true that caste divisions are less marked in Goa than most other parts of India (in some states, such as Bihar and Rajasthan, inter-caste violence has taken on civil-war proportions), they remain influential, particularly in villages. For example, landowners (*Goenkars*) are invariably *Bamons*, or high *Chardos*, while the people who work their fields in exchange for a share of the rice harvest are nearly always *Shudras*. Government jobs have also tended to be taped up by *Bamons*, traditionally more literate and better educated than the lower castes, although the Delhi-imposed job reservation system – wherein sought-after positions, in both the civil service and government, are allocated according to quotas – has enabled greater representation for members of the so-called "Scheduled and Other Backward Castes" (SOBCs) in politics and public life. That said, post-Independence egalitarianism has had little impact in Hindu temples, whose ritual life and finances remain firmly in the control of the *Bamons*.

Temples

Religious life for Hindus revolves around the **temple**. Known as *devuls* or *mandirs* ("Houses of God") in Konkani, these sacred structures house the focal point of communal worship: the deity, or **devta**. Ranging from simple stones to solid-gold statues, cult objects are venerated not as mere symbols of divine power, but as actual embodiments of a particular god or goddess. The buildings in which they are enshrined also vary in scale and splendour according to how important the *devta* is: some are modest concrete affairs, while others are soaring multicoloured piles crammed full of finery.

The culmination of worship, or **puja**, is always the moment of **darshan**, or ritual viewing of the deity. After ringing a bell in front of the shrine, the worshipper steps forward, salutes the god or goddess (sometimes by prostrating him- or herself), and presents an offering of fruit, incense, flowers or money to the temple priest *(pujari)*. They are then given a spoonful of holy water (*tirtha*) and *prasad* – food (usually a sugary bonbon) – that has been blessed by the deity. Meanwhile, the bare-chested brahmin priests busy themselves with the daily round of readings and rituals: waking, bathing, dressing and garlanding the *devta*, chanting Sanskrit texts, and smearing vermilion paste (*tilak*) on the foreheads of worshippers.

Non-Hindus are welcome to **visit** Goan temples, but you're expected to observe a few simple conventions. The most important of these is to dress appropriately: women should keep their shoulders and legs covered, while men should wear long trousers or *lunghis*. Always remove your shoes at the entrance to the main hall (not the courtyard), and never step inside the doorway to the shrine, which is strictly off limits to everyone except the *pujaris*. **Photography** is nearly always prohibited inside the temple but allowed around the courtyard. Finally, if there is a passage (*pradakshena*) encircling the shrine, walk around it in a clockwise direction.

A more detailed account of Goan temples, including their historical background and a rundown of their chief architectural features, appears on p.110.

Christianity

Roman Catholicism was imposed on Goa by the Portuguese in the sixteenth century, spread by missionaries, and zealously upheld by the dreaded Inquisition, which weeded out heretics and ruthlessly persecuted any converts deemed to have lapsed into "pagan" ways (see p.94). The Inquisition's chief weapons were the infamous *autos da fé*, or "acts of faith", in which individuals suspected of heresy were tortured and, if found guilty, burnt at the stake. In later years, Hindus and Muslims were allowed to practise their religions openly, but by this time Christianity had firmly taken root, albeit in a form that retained too many indigenous traits to meet with Portuguese approval.

Today, just under a third of the total population is Christian, and the state trains priests and nuns in its seminaries and convents for service throughout India. At the head of the Catholic hierarchy in the region is the **Archbishop of Goa**, whose whitewashed palace stands at the top of Altinho Hill in the capital, Panjim; below him come the parish priests.

The spiritual heart of Christianity in Goa is the **Basilica of Bom Jesus** in Old Goa, which houses the sacred relics of **St Francis Xavier** – the region's patron saint. Every ten years, his corpse, which for centuries remained miraculously incorrupt, is exposed for public veneration: an event witnessed by tens of thousands of pilgrims. The annual Saint's Day in November also attracts huge crowds. Francis Xavier was against Indians entering the clergy, but his opposition was ultimately ignored, and the region's church has long been staffed by native Goans, some of whom are even in line for canonization.

On Sundays families flock to Mass togged out in their best clothes. Saints' days celebrating the patron saint of the village church also draw large congregations, as do the numerous religious festivals held around the state (see p.47). As you'll see if you come across one, these, and more routine church services, have a uniquely Goan atmosphere: violinists accompany the hymn singing, garlands adorn the Madonnas and high altars, and Mass is said in Konkani.

The most spectacular **Goan churches** are located in Old Goa, whose grandiose four-hundred-year-old cathedrals have earned for the site UNESCO World Heritage status. However, several other equally impressive buildings lie in less frequented parts of the state. Most are left open and can be visited freely, but in more out-of-the-way villages you may have to ask the local priest to unlock the doors for you. It's also a good idea to dress respectfully when visiting churches, and to leave a small donation for the upkeep of the building when you leave.

Our Lady of Health Vailankani

Even more prominent in the popular iconography of Christian Goa than Saint Francis Xavier is **Our Lady of Health Vailankani**, whose name and image you'll see displayed on buses and taxis everywhere. Goans who wish to make a special plea for divine intercession – to help overcome a serious illness, for example – will often travel to Our Lady's church, two or three days' long drive southeast in distant Tamil Nadu. The shrine was established in the early 1600s following a series of apparitions and miracles, and still attracts millions of worshippers each year, many of them Hindu and Muslim. Our Lady's mass appeal, however, displeases some of the clergy, who fear her popularity has begun to eclipse that of Jesus in the hearts of many Catholic Goans.

△ Carving in Old Goa church

Caste in Goan Christianity

Among the more notable differences between Goan Christianity and that practised by its former colonial overlords is the persistence of **caste**. During the religious persecution of the sixteenth and seventeenth centuries, Hindus faced a stark choice between conversion and escape across the border. Many took their temple deities and fled, but many more – including a significant number of those at the top of the social hierarchy, who were permitted to keep their land and wealth if they converted – stayed, exchanging their Indian surnames for Latin ones like Gomes and Barbosa. In Catholicism, where worship is largely communal, revolving around sharing of the Eucharist, the old Hindu concepts of pollution had no place and were quickly relinquished. However, belief in the importance of high and low birth persisted. This may have been because such ideologies sat comfortably with the Portuguese insistence on nobility and *pureza de sangue*, or "blood purity", which was jealously guarded by the European colonizers.

Today, caste remains a fundamental basis of social life for Goan Christians (even though few will readily admit to the fact). The same basic *varna* divisions apply, with former *Bamons* (brahmins) and *Chardos* at the top, and *Shudras* at the bottom. Greater occupational mobility since Independence has meant the lines between them may be blurred, but it is rare to find a parish priest or landowner (*Goenkar*) who's not from a *Bamon* or *Chardo* family, or a sharecropping field worker who isn't a *Shudra*.

Caste distinctions and status are preserved in numerous ways, most obviously through endogamous marriage (ie marrying only within one's caste), but also by adherence to a variety of less conspicuous customs. Writing of life in a small village in Salcete *taluka*, the anthropologist Rowena Robinson describes how caste among Christians in her study area was discernible through table manners and taste in music, diet and dress, with higher-caste families tending towards the European ways of their former rulers. *Chardo* women, for example, always wore *vistid* (dresses), whereas *Shudra* women mostly dressed in traditional *kepod*, or saris.

Among Goan Christians, however, the social hierarchy is most dramatically apparent in the life of the local parish church, particularly those occasions when the whole community comes together to worship or celebrate feasts, saints' days and marriages. During Sunday services, it is customary for higher-caste families to sit in the front pews of the church and lower-castes to stand at the back, while the *passe* celebration on Good Friday tends to be completely dominated by *Bamon* and upper *Chardo* families. In virtually all Christian villages, lower-caste people are also excluded from membership of the **fabrica** association, which oversees the maintenance of the church buildings, properties and finances. In addition, each church has its own **confrarias**, literally "brotherhoods", which organize feast days; needless to say, the *Chardos* and *Goenkars* join one *confraria*, running the most important festivals, while the *Shudras'* *confraria* gets to organize the minor feasts.

Charismatic Christianity

Since the early 1980s, charismatic Christianity has been on the increase in Goa and you may well encounter large open-air services held on specially erected stages. Focusing on teachings from the New Testament, charismatics believe that the power of the Holy Spirit can be accessed through prayer and used to heal or expel evil forces. Worship is far less formal and passive than conven-

Caste conflict in Cuncolim

The strength and complexities of **caste differences** in contemporary Goa have been vividly brought into focus by a recent conflict between the landowning *Goenkar* minority and their lower-caste *Shudra* neighbours in Cuncolim village, Salcete *taluka*.

The dispute hinges on ritual rights and privileges in the local church. For centuries, **religious life** in Christian Cuncolim – famous as the home of the five Jesuit priests martyred in their attempt to convert the Mughal emperor Akbar – has been dominated by members of the 3000-strong *Goenkar* community. Originally converts from the Hindu *Kshatriya* ("warrior") caste, the local landowners have traditionally claimed exclusive rights to be buried in the church cemetery, sing in the choir, lead the saints' day processions and don sacred red and white robes, known as *opa murca*, for important religious occasions. They have also, most critically, monopolized membership of the local confraternity – the Confraria do Santissimo Sacramento and Nossa Senhora de Saude – which organizes church festivals.

While traditionally upholding the dominance of the *Goenkars*, the Portuguese colonial administration and, **after Independence**, the Catholic Church had to be seen to promote greater equality and assert the rights of the lower castes. However, their efforts consistently met with stern rebuffs, provoking a more confrontational approach from the local *Shudras*.

A few years back, the low-caste villagers in Cuncolim held a funeral in the church cemetery, the first burial of a non-*Goenkar* there since the Church of Our Lady of Health was built in 1604. The following night, however, the body was exhumed, wrapped in cloth and dumped outside the church, on the road to the *Shudra* quarter. Firmly engrained pollution customs would have prevented *Goenkars* from carrying out the crime themselves, but no one in Cuncolim doubted that they were behind the outrage.

More recently, low-caste churchgoers from Cuncolim boycotted the saint's day feast and called on Goa's archbishop with a petition calling for greater equality in the management of their church.

What really fired the powder keg of Cuncolim's caste conflict, however, was the decision, by the new young, jeans-wearing village priest, Father Socorso Mendes, to admit two *Shudra* men into the Confraria. Immediately, a deputation of furious *Goenkars* stormed the priest's house, threatening to "cut him into pieces and send them to (his) mother" if the two weren't thrown out. When the priest refused, an angry mob formed a cordon around the church to demonstrate.

The stand-off was diffused by the intervention of senior clergymen, but the village has grown more divided since. The *Goenkars* have even gone so far as to lobby their Hindu counterparts in the village, arguing that if the lower orders are allowed to gain equal rights in the church, it is only a matter of time before the same happens in the nearby temple. The subsequent declaration of solidarity by the Hindu *Goenkars*, in turn, provoked a boycott of all their businesses in the village by members of the lower castes (both Christian and Hindu). Soon, the football and hockey teams and youth clubs all collapsed, as opposing castes refused to have anything to do with each other.

Cuncolim's problems are by no means exceptional. Throughout Goa, churches have become the arena in which growing tensions and changing political relations between castes are expressed. Recent decades have seen increased prosperity among *Shudras* and other lower castes, many of whom have raised their standard of living through reserved government jobs and wage employment abroad. This new-found affluence, and exposure to more democratic ways of life in the media and in other countries, has inevitably put the political disparities of traditional village life under pressure. The challenge for the Catholic Church in Goa now is how quickly it can adapt institutions originally devised to accommodate ancient Hindu beliefs to meet the expectations of its more equality-conscious congregations. Among many signals that it is failing to do so is the growing popularity of charismatic Christianity in the state (see below).

tional Christianity, with lots of singing and dancing and incidents of spirit possession or speaking in tongues. One interesting aspect of the movement is that its congregations tend to be drawn from predominantly *Shudra* and other low-caste families, perhaps as a backlash to their exclusion from more mainstream Christianity – a notion vehemently rejected by most charismatic priests, who do not acknowledge caste in any form.

Islam

Islam was originally brought to Goa in the eleventh century by Arab merchants, who played a pivotal role in maritime trade along the Malabar coast south of Goa. Encouraged by local Hindu rulers, wealthy Muslims erected mosques and put down roots in the region, practising their religion freely. However, this period of peaceful coexistence came to an abrupt end in the thirteenth century with the arrival from the northwest of marauders from Delhi and the Deccan. By the fourteenth century, an intolerant brand of Islam was in the ascendancy, as the raiders made permanent settlements, forcing out the Hindus, whom they regarded as heathen idol worshippers. The Bahmani conquests of the mid-1300s finally brought Goa under Muslim rule, with temples razed and their deities banished to the relatively inaccessible foothills of the Western Ghats.

While Hinduism weathered the religious persecution of the Portuguese era, Islam petered out almost completely in Goa, and today only a vestigial Muslim community remains. Distinguished by their half-beards and skullcaps on men, and on women by enveloping veils called *burqas*, or long shirts and pyjama trousers known as *shalwa-camises*, most live in and around Ponda, where the state's main mosque, the Safa Masjid, is located (see p.105).

Environmental issues in Goa

Impeded for decades by a near-bankrupt colonial administration, the pace of development in Goa has increased exponentially since Independence. Both light and heavy industries have mushroomed, tourism has boomed and the state's population has more than quadrupled – all of which has placed an enormous burden on the state's fragile natural environment. Deforestation, mining, sand extraction, overfishing, water use and tourism-related pollution all remain virtually impervious to central control. Goa's green activists, though small in number, have achieved remarkable success in bringing the environmental debate to the public, but the task they face is an uphill one. All too often dismissed as "backward" dissenters, they are consistently thwarted by bureaucracy, an inefficient legal system and political expedience, not to mention corruption, which is rife in many areas of public life.

Water

The most contentious environmental issue in Goa is the use and abuse of **water**. As the population continues to rise, augmented by immigrants from neighbouring states and an ever-growing annual deluge of foreign visitors, water is becoming increasingly scarce: in many coastal villages wells often run dry by late February. The problem is compounded by **pollution** from industrial plants and mines, and by **deforestation** of the interior, which interferes with the state's river systems.

Goa receives around two and a half metres of rain during the annual monsoon – more than double the national average. Yet the dry season is regularly accompanied by **droughts** affecting thousands of villagers. The main reason the wells and irrigation ducts dry up is that an estimated eighty percent of the annual rainfall flows straight into the sea. The response to the problem by the Indian government in the 1970s was to commission a series of **dams** at the foot of the Western Ghats to regulate the flow of water to the densely populated coastal plain. However, as is often the case with such large-scale engineering projects in India, the benefits reaped from the schemes have thus far proved scant reward for the huge sums of money invested in them, not to mention the displacement of thousands of villagers.

The **Selaulim Dam**, begun in south Goa in 1972 and long the *bête noire* of the Goan green lobby, exemplifies the potential drawbacks of dam-building as a response to the region's water problem. Plagued by financial setbacks and political scandals, the project ended up costing ten times its original estimate and fell more than five years behind schedule. In addition, it necessitated the clearance of seven square kilometres of virgin forest – exacerbating water shortages by causing soil erosion and an eventual drop in rainfall – and the relocation of 643 families, many of whom now endure substandard housing and soil that is too poor to farm. Another criticism of the dam is that its water was pumped to luxury resorts and a chemical plant on the coast years before it arrived in the towns of south Goa, while water promised to local farmers has yet to materialize.

Among the few beneficiaries of water shortages in Goa are the "**peddlars**" – private hauliers who tap communal wells and transport their contents in tankers to villages where the supply has been exhausted. Writs have been served to prevent this trade, but few peddlars have so far been brought to book: water transportation is so lucrative during the dry season that most can easily afford to pay off the local police.

The lowering of water tables on the coast, which has allowed many wells to become polluted with salt water, is frequently cited by the government as a reason to build more dams. Yet there has been little evidence that such projects actually alleviate the problem. In many cases, the promises of short-term financial gain for local companies or politicians turns out to be the real motive.

Tourism

Goa has been among India's leading **tourist destinations** since the early 1970s, when it first began to lure travellers off the trans-Asian "hippy trail". In these early days, the scene was decidedly low-key, with the majority of visitors staying in private family homes or makeshift huts on the beach. Luxury hotels were few and far between, concentrated on the north coast and a strip at the south end of Colva beach.

Goa's era as a hippy haven came to an end in 1987 when the then state governor announced a relaxation in the laws forbidding the construction of large five-star resort complexes. Hot on the heels of this came the much-publicized "Master Plan for Tourism". Henceforth, the government declared, backpacking budget travellers, who had hitherto formed the mainstay of tourism in the area, would be discouraged in favour of wealthier, high-spending package visitors.

Luxury vs budget tourism

Goa has indeed become firmly established on the package-tourist map, with charter flights bringing fortnighters into the state direct from Europe, and dozens of newly opened luxury hotels doing a roaring trade in villages that were formerly the preserve of budget travellers. However, beneath the glossy brochure images lurk a number of problems that belie the government's attempts to represent tourism as a godsend for Goa.

At the centre of the **local opposition to tourism** are the five-star hotels. Located within a stone's throw of the beach, many of these purpose-built resorts have wilfully ignored, or deviously circumvented, laws prohibiting construction within five hundred metres of the mean high-water mark. They are also water-intensive, with lush lawns, swimming pools, Western toilets, bathtubs and fountains to feed. Some obtain water by illegally tapping ground sources (thereby lowering alluvial levels and increasing the risk of saline pollution); others enjoy piped supplies while local villagers have to carry water from wells.

The impact of **luxury resorts** on the environment can be considerable in other ways, too: rubbish and untreated sewage may be dumped beside them, *toddi* trees felled to make room for new buildings, and sand dunes cleared for gardens. In some cases, the developers have even forcibly relocated local villagers, who have retaliated by picketing the offending hotels and mounting demonstrations in nearby towns. Accusations of **harassment** and physical intimidation against the ringleaders of such campaigns have also been reported. Nor do the resorts tend to bring many economic benefits to local people: profits invariably end up in Mumbai or Delhi, while their presence forces up the prices of food and housing.

Opposition to tourism from Goan pressure groups and the media is not directed solely at five-star resorts, either: budget travellers have also come in for flak. Critics complain about the threat to moral values posed by **nudity** on the beaches, and **drugs** have become a problem in some coastal villages. In addition, the presence of large numbers of budget travellers in out-of-the-way settlements may have a detrimental impact on the local environment: backpackers consume less water per day than the average package tourist, but they tend to stay for longer and thus place a protracted burden on scarce supplies. The price of food and other basic commodities has also risen dramatically in some budget tourist enclaves, where fish and fruit are beyond the means of low-income families during peak season.

The future

If mass tourism is allowed to develop unchecked in Goa, prospects are very bleak indeed. Unwilling to heed the hard-learned lessons of countries such as Spain, Thailand and Indonesia, local government and developers remain bent on making a fast buck, without investing adequately in the **future**. Such short-term vision could well have disastrous consequences.

Calangute, the state's most popular resort, typifies what happens when development runs out of control. Hotel complexes have been thrown up along the entire length of the beach, yet the village lacks a sewage treatment plant, provision for waste disposal and decent roads. In addition, many of the ritzy new resorts have been so hastily erected that they are certain to deteriorate badly over the next decade. By then, though, the village will be so built-up and polluted that the tourist trade will have moved on to fresh pastures: to less developed villages further up the coast at first, and later out of the region altogether.

The state's anti-tourism lobby is trying hard to highlight such dangers, filing writs against developers that ignore environmental laws, organizing demonstrations and publicizing their grievances at home and abroad; yet their efforts have failed to stem the flow of visitors or halt the inexorable spread of concrete along the coast. Foreign tour operators also remain impervious to local concerns. While paying lip service to green ideas in their brochures, many of the larger companies continue to patronize resorts that have been singled out for criticism by environmental groups, thereby encouraging the developers to build new ones in hitherto unspoilt areas.

It would be far from desirable for tourists to stop coming to Goa, as the livelihoods of too many local people already depend on the trade. In the long term, a small-scale and more environmentally friendly form of tourism is the only viable option. Village-style family guesthouses may not appeal to most package tourists, but at least they exact a lower cost on the environment; the income they generate also directly benefits the villagers, rather than property speculators and shareholders in distant cities. The trouble is that budget tourists are precisely the kind of visitors the government is seeking to discourage. What really stands in the way of sustainable tourism in Goa is the reluctance of policy-makers and law-enforcers to sanction changes from which they themselves will gain little, or nothing, in the short term.

Industry

Goa is a predominantly rural state, but a few isolated packets of heavy industry have sprung up over the past three decades, posing a serious threat to the environment and potential health risks for local people. The oldest-established and most controversial is the **Zuari Agro Chemical Fertilizer Plant** (ZAC) on the Dabolim plateau, near Vasco da Gama. Overlooking the north end of beautiful Colva beach, the factory first made headlines in the mid-1970s when toxic chemicals from it found their way into the water table, decimating fish populations and raising fears about the plant's overall safety. ZAC has been modernized since, but its productive capacity has increased enormously and environmentalists remain concerned about the risk of ammonia and other toxic gases escaping from its old-fashioned and poorly maintained storage tanks. In addition, **emissions** from the factory's chimney stacks are said to have affected the health of villagers nearby (ZAC, of course, vehemently denies this but continues to rotate staff lodged in the northeast side of the plant – downwind of the stacks – to more salubrious quarters every two years). Meanwhile, **tanker trucks** carrying loads of lethal chemicals routinely use local roads.

Another chemical plant to have sparked off controversy in Goa is the **Hindustan Ciba Energy** complex near Old Goa. Leakages of chlorine and other potentially dangerous compounds have been reported by villagers living nearby. A rerun of the Union Carbide gas tragedy in Bhopal may also have been narrowly averted here when a cylinder containing the lethal compound methyl chloride nearly ruptured.

Mining

Head into the hilly heart of Goa and you're bound to encounter a couple of open-cast ore **mines**. Forming gigantic red gashes across the landscape, these colossal industrial eyesores generate half of India's iron ore exports and more foreign currency than all of Goa's hotels and restaurants put together: around $170 million per annum, or ten percent of the state's GDP. Ninety percent of the ore goes to Japan (which funded the industry to begin with). Unfortunately, the mines also inflict untold damage on the region's ecology, causing **soil erosion** on a massive scale, destroying extensive tracts of forest and farmland, and leading to chronic **health problems** for local people.

The roots of the environmental problems lie in the nature of open-cast mining itself. To extract one tonne of ore, you have to dig up between two and three times that amount of surplus dirt; the thirteen million tonnes of iron and manganese ore that Goa exports every year leave around forty million tonnes of rock and soil waste in their wake, most of which gets dumped in massive heaps around the edges of the mines. With the onset of the monsoons, rainwater drains the **slag heaps** of their finer soil and flushes it into streams and rivers. These then clog up with **silt**, causing frequent floods in low-lying, rice-cultivating areas: paddy fields ruined for decades by slicks of red mud are nowadays a common sight in and around mining areas.

Since the late 1990s, several mines have actually been operating below the water table. To do this they have to pump out millions of gallons of ground water, which means more **water shortages** for local people. The response of the offending companies has been to supply water to the affected villages by tanker, thereby making the inhabitants dependent on the company's goodwill for one of their most fundamental needs.

Dust is another hazardous by-product of the mining industry. Travelling through the eastern Bicholim or Ponda *talukas*, you'll pass villages and stretches of forest completely covered in a pall of fine red dirt. This not only stifles vegetation; it also blows into houses, wells and people's food, and has caused a dramatic increase in respiratory disorders in towns such as Cuchorem-Sanvordem, whose train station is the hub of ore transportation in central Goa. To date, more than 35,000 cases of respiratory diseases have been reported in this district's health centre alone. Notwithstanding, a "scientist" working for the Dempo Mining Company, in an affadavit on the subject, claimed the disorders were caused by "flying cashew seeds" (local people have been growing cashew for thousands of years).

Mining companies in Goa have consistently ducked their environmental responsibilities, but they may soon be forced to clean up their act or face bankruptcy. Some Goan rivers have silted up to such an extent over the past few decades that the barges which transport the ore to Mormugao harbour, at the head of the Zuari estuary near Vasco da Gama, are only able to operate in the period after the rains, when water levels are highest (which explains why, if you stand on Candolim beach in October, the horizon is dominated by lines of floodlit dredgers and ore transport ships). Several mines have to shut down towards the end of the dry season. Spurred on by the example of a few large operators, the industry is now madly planting its tips with trees in an attempt to forestall the rate of the erosion. However, whether or not their efforts prove to be "too little, too late" remains to be seen.

Fishing

Around 40,000 Goans are directly dependent on **fishing** for a livelihood, the majority of them families who work in wooden outriggers or small fibreglass boats. Despite the introduction of outboard motors, their methods remain traditional and low-tech. This is particularly true of the hand-net fishermen you'll see on many Goan beaches, who join together in teams of twenty or thirty to haul in giant U-shaped nets laid in the shallows. Once landed, the catch is divided up according to each family's stake in the net (called a *rampon* in Konkani) and the sardines, mackerel and other smaller fish (used as fertilizer for coconut trees) are gathered by the women in baskets to be carried home.

Yields from this kind of fishing have diminished sharply over the past two or three decades, principally because of competition from larger, more modern and better-equipped **trawlers**. Ironically, these were introduced in the 1970s with large government subsidies aimed at boosting the protein in-take and living standards of disadvantaged coastal communities. In fact, few poor fishing families could afford the hefty down-payment required to secure the government loans, which were instead picked up by wealthy business people and industrialists. They, over time, have made huge profits, benefiting from grants by foreign governments and manufacturers eager to sell boats and engines, and obtain a cheap source of fish.

The results of this economic revolution have been three-fold: first, an increase in the price of fish (which is now largely beyond the pockets of most Goans); secondly, the virtual destruction of in-shore fishing as a viable livelihood; and thirdly, greater marine pollution. To combat such problems, Hindu and Christian in-shore fishermen from across the state got together and formed a union, the **Goenchea Rampon Karancho Ekrolte (GRKE)**. After much heated debate and occasional armed clashes between the two groups, a law was passed in the 1980s limiting the trawlers' fishing grounds to beyond a five-kilometre exclusion line.

CONTEXTS | Environmental issues in Goa

However, the fishing limit was never enforced and continues to be routinely ignored. The root of the government's inability to uphold the law and protect the rights of poor fishermen is that most representatives in the Goan State Legislature are firmly in the pockets of the trawler owners (if not trawler owners themselves). Just how ineffectual the law really is when set against such a powerful lobby was underlined in July 2000 when the High Court – responding to data on fish spawning supplied by the National Institute of Oceanography – imposed a blanket ban on mechanized fishing during the monsoon period. The decision, however, was effectively overturned only the following day by the State Legislature, which passed a bill prohibiting the court from ruling on the matter again.

The Konkan Railway

Few issues have provoked as much controversy in Goa over the past decade as the **Konkan Railway**, dubbed by the region's press as "The Chord of Dischord". Stretching 760km from the outskirts of Mumbai to the port city of Mangalore in Karnataka, the new line was conceived as the last missing link in the coastal route around peninsular India and a much needed fast track connecting densely populated Kerala with the Maharashtran capital.

Its **first year** of operation, however, was little short of disastrous: embankments sank into the silt, tunnels became waterlogged and blocked, landslides and rock falls caused constant delays, and there were two derailments and eight deaths on the line. Meanwhile, the company set up to build and run it, the Konkan Railway Company, teeters on the verge of insolvency. Goans are understandably puzzled as to how, in such a short time, such a high-profile project could run so hopelessly off the rails; the explanations currently coming to light hint at a web of corruption and incompetence on an awesome scale.

The Konkan Railway was first commissioned by V.P. Singh's Janata–BJP coalition government in 1990. No one had attempted to build a line along this route before because the Konkan coast is punctuated by a string of seemingly insurmountable **natural obstacles** – swamps, steep laterite spurs, ravines, estuaries and around two hundred rivers. But the government was on the lookout for a prestigious, vote-winning showpiece to shout about in the run-up to the 1994 elections, and devised a novel way to finance it.

Instead of stumping up taxpayers' money to be squandered by yet another bureaucracy-ridden department, the Ministry of Railways formed a separate company, the KRC, whose shares were bought entirely by the government and the four states who stood to benefit most directly from the new railway. More controversially, additional funds were raised by borrowing against the sale of tax-free bonds. The idea was that the KRC would oversee the construction of the line, run it for five years, and then hand it over to the government – a concept known as BOT ("Build, Operate and Transfer").

The next hurdle for the KRC was fixing a route. In Goa, the proposed **alignment** met with a barrage of objections from environmental groups. In addition to impinging on the historic monuments of Old Goa and causing widespread soil erosion and deforestation, the route was criticized because it was claimed that construction would interfere with traditional irrigation channels – impeding the flow of water across *khazans* (see p.317) – and allow the build-up of waste-infested water (perfect breeding grounds for malaria-carrying mosquitoes). A High Court enquiry was convened in July 1993, but the judge dismissed the environmentalists' case and, aside from a few minor amendments, ratified the original alignment.

No legal process could now prevent the spread of the red-dirt scar through Goa, and by late 1997, nearly four years later than planned, the first trains rattled through the region. The ride, however, has never been a smooth one. Even before the official opening, on Republic Day, January 1998, sections of the line had already subsided, forcing KRC engineers to attempt ineffectual "running repairs" (filling embankments with ballast), while the 1998 monsoon destroyed cuttings and blocked sections of the track with landslides.

It is now clear that most of these problems stemmed not from the inclement weather, as the KRC's spin doctors have tried to imply, but from innate weaknesses in the Konkan Railway's route. Prior to 1990, all train lines in the subcontinent were surveyed and constructed according to principles laid down in the Indian Railways Engineering Code, central to which was the assertion that low coastal land should be avoided whenever possible (lower ground meaning wetter soil, broader rivers and thicker hill bases, and thus unstable embankments, wider bridges and longer tunnels). During the alignment enquiry of 1993, it transpired that this code had formed the basis of a previous **survey** of the Konkan coast, conducted in 1972 by an Indian engineer, J.Y. Marathe. Following the contours of the Western Ghat hills, the route proposed was higher and further inland than the one subsequently adopted, and thus not only had far fewer bridges and tunnels but, significantly, managed to avoid the Konkan Railway's most impressive, and costly, engineering feats: the 6.5-kilometre Karabhude Tunnel, near Ratnagiri (said to be the longest tunnel in Asia), and a 64-metre-tall viaduct.

The existence of an old survey outlining in detail a cheaper, more technically sound alignment for the Konkan Railway begs the question of why the KRC opted for the one it did. Officially, the answer is that Marathe's route included too many curves for today's high-speed locomotives. It is more likely, however, that KRC's contractors wanted the more difficult route because they stood to make more money from it, building complicated bridges, cuttings and tunnels; and with such potentially vast profits at stake, the bribes paid to the politicians who gave them the final go-ahead would have been correspondingly huge. It may never be proven, but the Konkan Railway was probably doomed long before the diggers moved in.

The legacy of the government/KRC's dubious planning decisions is not only delays in services. Operational setbacks throughout the railway's short life have generated a colossal debt; vast sums are owed to banks (ANZ Grindlays recently bailed out the KRC to the tune of $120 million), contractors, suppliers and various electricity boards. Add to this running overheads and interest charges amounting to just under $3.5 million per day, and take into account the recent devaluation of the rupee, and you can see why one commentator recently remarked that "the [KRC's] creditors must be biting their nails".

One of the results of this spiralling debt situation is that the KRC has not been able to afford the state-of-the-art **locomotives** it had originally planned to buy, and which would have ensured average speeds on the line of around 160km per hour. Instead, old, poorly maintained trains and rolling stock have been drafted in from other Indian networks, travelling at average speeds of around 50km per hour, thus making a mockery of the KRC's original justification for routing the line the way it did.

How long the KRC can continue to operate under these conditions is anyone's guess. One thing is sure, though: at the end of the day it will be the Indian taxpayer who'll have to pick up the tab for the debacle. The debt to the environment will take a lot longer to repay.

Natural history

In spite of increased pressures on the rural landscape, Goa remains a state of beautiful and varied scenery with its own abundant and distinct flora and fauna. Many species have been hunted out or squeezed eastwards over the past fifty years, but enough survive to make a trip into the countryside worthwhile. Walking on less frequented beaches or through the rice fields of the coastal plain, you'll encounter dozens of exotic birds, while the hill country of the interior supports an amazing variety of plants and trees. The majority of Goa's larger mammals keep to the dense woodland lining the Karnatakan border, where three nature sanctuaries afford them some protection from the hunters and loggers who have wrought such havoc in this fragile forest region over the past few decades.

Geography

Rarely in India do you find such a wide range of different landscapes packed so tightly, or wilderness areas situated so close to modern towns and resorts, as in Goa. Broadly speaking, the state may be divided into three major **habitats**: the low-lying coastal plain, the laterite plateau country of the midland region, and the lush, forest-cloaked hills of the Western Ghats. Crammed into a fifty-kilometre-wide strip, these different terrains form a closely integrated ecosystem that is sustained by a tangle of rivers and tributaries meandering westwards into the Arabian Sea.

The **Western Ghats** (from the Sanskrit word for "sacred steps") are Goa's most important topographical feature. Running parallel to the coast at a mean elevation of between 900m and 1200m, the sheer mountains, which extend along the entire length of peninsular India, impede the path of the monsoon rain clouds as they sweep in from the southwest. The moist deciduous forest draped over their flanks thus acts like a giant sponge, soaking up the rainwater on which the region depends and channelling it down to the plains. **Deforestation** of this sparsely populated region – home to over 3500 different varieties of flowering plants (almost a third of India's total) and a rich assortment of mammals, birds, reptiles and insects – is a worsening problem: without the trees to modulate the flow of water, flooding and soil erosion are spoiling crops and destroying centuries-old irrigation systems.

From the foot of the Ghats, steep-sided **laterite plateaux** extend west, covered in scrub and savannah grasslands. Although the soil in this midland region is thin, the floors and sides of the many well-watered valleys are important agricultural zones, carpeted with fragrant cashew trees (the source of Goa's main cash crop) and areca groves. This is also the home of the state's largest **spice plantations**, as well as its lucrative iron- and manganese-ore mines, which form gigantic trenches of red against the green and yellow backdrop.

The majority of Goa's inhabitants live on the 105-kilometre-long **coastal strip**, whose fertile rice fields and coconut groves, together with a thriving fishing industry, provide the bulk of the region's food. The epicentre of the region's industry and tourism, this is also the most ecologically vulnerable area of Goa. Demand for new building space, and the shift away from traditional subsistence farming methods, have led to the drainage of wetlands and the destruction of many **mangrove swamps**, while the threat of pollution from chemical plants, power stations and sewage from the resorts looms ever larger (see "Environmental issues in Goa", p.308).

Land settlement and usage

Settled **agriculture** has been practised in Goa for over four thousand years. Prior to this, the region was inhabited by small groups of **semi-nomadic cultivators**, who cleared tracts of forest for their crops. This form of land use is still practised by tribal peoples (*adivasis*) in the most remote areas of Goa, where it is known as *kumeri*. The government has been trying for years to weed out the **kumeri** cultivators, arguing that shifting cultivation farming promotes soil erosion. However, recent studies have shown shifting cultivation to be well suited to the otherwise uncultivable hill country. The government's opposition to *kumeri* seems more motivated by greed than concern for the environment: kicking the *kumeri* cultivators off their traditional land means it can be clear-felled, its hardwood sold off at a profit, and then replanted with fast-growing and lucrative eucalyptus trees – a policy pursued even in so-called protected forest areas such as Cotigao (see p.213).

Shifting cultivation only accounts for a tiny percentage of land use in Goa. Most of the farmable land these days is given over to the production of **rice** or **coconuts**. The region's two main crops formerly met subsistence needs, but following the sudden surge in population caused by the arrival of the Portuguese, huge amounts of grain had to be imported from elsewhere in India. This forced the colonial administration to intensify production, which it did by introducing new farming methods (including high-yielding – but disease-prone – strains of rice) and a more strictly organized system of land tenure. The **communidades** system, originally devised by the Saraswat brahmins during the fifth century AD but refined under the Portuguese, placed control of all land not owned privately into the hands of the local villagers, who collectively granted the rights to farm it to the highest bidders. Proceeds from these auctions were then used to pay government taxes and maintain community properties (such as temples), while anything left over was divided up evenly among the male villagers. The replacement after independence of the *communidades* with the *panchayat*, or council system – a brainchild of the British – is often cited as a cause of environmental degradation in rural areas. With former *communidades* land now owned by the state, local villagers lack the incentive to protect it from unscrupulous developers.

Crops

Goa's main staple, **rice**, is grown in paddy fields (*cantors*) right across the coastal strip and on patches of flat ground between the laterite plateaux in the middle of the state known as *molloi*. Two different crops are planted: *sorondio* is sown during the monsoon in June and harvested in November, and *vangana* is cultivated during the dry season between October and February using irrigation water stored in reservoirs and ponds. Each stage of the process involves days sloshing around in thick mud or being bent double under blazing sunshine. Without such toil, though, many thousands of Goans would go hungry: rice is the mainstay of the rural economy, providing a livelihood for the state's landless sharecroppers and subsistence farmers.

Khazans

According to the *Skadna Purana*, an ancient Sanskrit scripture written sometime during the first half of the first millennium AD, the region now known as Goa was created when the sage Shri Parasurama, sixth incarnation of the god Vishnu, shot an arrow from the Western Ghats into the Arabian Sea, and then reclaimed the land where it fell. Scholars believe this myth derives from the colonization of the area by settled agriculturalists in the Vedic Age (around 1500 BC), and that Parasurama's arrow represents the process of land reclamation that ensued. Today, the saline flood plains lining Goa's tidal estuaries, known as **khazans**, have still not been submerged under sea water and remain the focus of the region's lowland economy. This fertile patchwork of paddy fields and palm grove enables local farmers to cultivate rice, fruit and vegetables and provide salt, fish and shells for the production of limewash.

Lying well below sea level, *khazans* are maintained by a complex system that has altered little over the past few millennia. The first lines of defence are the impenetrable **mangrove swamps** growing along the edges of Goa's estuaries, backed where necessary by sturdy laterite walls. Behind these, a grid of **bunds** – embankments made from mud, straw and areca poles – protect the fields, while sluice gates operate like valves to regulate the flow of water on to and off the land. As salt water kills off most crops, retention of fresh monsoon flood waters is essential for cultivation. However, on very low-lying *khazans*, where villagers plant only a single crop of rice, the sluices are left open for most of the year and the flooded fields used for fish farming.

Stable for centuries, the fragile ecology of the *khazans*, which comprise 180 square kilometres of Goa's coastal plain, is now under **threat** from a variety of sources. Large tracts of wetland have been drained and built on as urbanization gathers pace in the state, bringing with it increased amounts of sewage. Other causes of **pollution** include chemicals swept down from the iron-ore mines by stream, and oil swilled out of ships' bilges in the estuaries. The Konkan Railwayhas also carved a great red scar down the coastal plain, causing flooding in parts of Bardez, Bicholim, Salcete, Mormugao and around Ponda. However, the greatest potential risk to the *khazans* is posed by **poor land management**. A gradual breakdown in the indigenous *communidades* system of land tenure (see below) has led to increasingly widespread neglect of the ditches and sluice gates, and even their wilful destruction. Landless peasants not engaged in rice production have been known to illegally dynamite dykes so that the fields behind them may be used for more lucrative (but ecologically unsustainable) fish or prawn farming, a practice dubbed as **"bund busting"**.

The consequences of destroying the *khazans* are not only environmental. Flooded, polluted land is the perfect breeding ground for the *Culex vishnui* mosquito, carrier of the deadly disease Japanese encephalitis, which killed nearly one hundred people during the 1992 monsoons and may well have been what wiped out the population of Old Goa two hundred years ago. Hardliners in the environmental lobby prophesy that unless the *khazans* are protected, modern Goa could well go the same way.

Coconut cultivation, along with fishing, is the main moneymaker in many coastal villages. The principal derivative of this ubiquitous plant is its sap, or *toddi* – used to distil the local liquor, *feni* – but other parts are put to good use, too. The *copra* oil squeezed from the young nuts is used for cooking or sold to soap and cosmetic manufacturers; the coarse hair surrounding the shell produces fibre for rope, coir-matting and furniture upholstery; dried palm fronds make baskets, brooms and thatch; while the wood from fallen trees is used to make rafters for houses.

Further inland, you'll come across clusters of more spindly palm trees. More delicate than their coconut cousins, **areca trees** – the source of betel nuts that are ground and chewed by millions of Indians as *pan* – require constant irrigation and plenty of shade. Finally, alongside these are often planted fruit trees, most commonly mango (*ambo*), jackfruit (*ponos*), and cashews (*cazu*), whose fruit (which grows separately from the nut), produces a strong-smelling juice that Goans use to make *feni*.

Flora

Goa supports more than 3500 species of flowering **plants** – 27 percent of India's total – as well as countless lower orders of grasses, ferns and brackens. The greatest floristic diversity occurs in the Western Ghats, where it is not uncommon to find one hundred or more different types of trees in an area of one hectare. Many were introduced by the Portuguese from Europe, South America, Southeast Asia and Australia, but there are also a vast number of indigenous varieties which thrive in the moist climate.

Along the coast, the **toddi palm** predominates, forming a near-continuous curtain of lush foliage. Spiky **spinifex** also helps bind the shifting sand dunes behind Colva and Calangute beaches together, while casuarina bushes form striking splashes of pink and crimson during the winter months.

In the towns and villages of central Goa, you'll encounter dozens of beautiful **flowering trees** that are common in tropical parts of India but unfamiliar to most Europeans and North Americans. The **Indian laburnum**, or cassia, throws out masses of yellow flowers and long seed pods in late February before the monsoons. This is also the period when **mango** and **Indian coral** trees are in full bloom; both produce bundles of stunning red flowers.

Among the most distinctive trees that grow in both coastal and hill areas is the stately **banyan**, which propagates by sending out shoots from its lower branches. The largest-known specimen, recorded in neighbouring Maharashtra, had a staggering circumference of 577m. The banyan is also revered by Hindus and you'll often find small shrines at the foot of mature trees. Another tree regarded as sacred by Hindus (and by Buddhists, because Buddha is believed to have attained enlightenment beneath one), is the **peepal**, which has distinctive spatula-shaped leaves. Temple courtyards often enclose large *peepals*, usually with strips of auspicious red cloth hanging from their lower branches.

Tree lovers and botanists should not miss an opportunity to visit the **Western Ghats**, which harbour a bewildering wealth of flora, from flowering trees and plants to ferns and fungi. These are among Asia's densest rainforests. Sheltered by a leafy canopy that can rise to a height of twenty metres or more, buttressed roots and giant trunks tower above a luxuriant undergrowth of brambles, creepers and bracken, interspersed with brakes of bamboo. Common tree species include the **kadam**, **sisso** or martel, **kharanj** and **teak**, distinguished by its straight, bare trunk and broad leaves. There are dozens of representatives of the *Ficus*, or fig, family too, as well as innumerable (and ecologically destructive) **eucalyptus** and **rubber** trees, planted as cash crops by the Forest Department.

Mammals

During a fact-finding expedition to Goa in the 1970s, the eminent Indian naturalist Salim Ali complained the only animal he saw was a lone leopard cat lying dead at the roadside. For although the state harbours more than fifty species of **mammals**, visitors to the coast are unlikely to spot anything more inspiring than a monkey or tree squirrel. Most of the exciting **animals** have been hunted to the point of extinction, or else have fled into neighbouring Karnataka. The few that remain roam the dense woodland lining the Western Ghats, in the sparsely populated far east, glimpsed only by forest-dwelling tribespeople or enthusiasts prepared (and equipped) to spend several days and nights trekking through the jungle. Even so, it's nice to know they are still there, and if Goa's three **wildlife sanctuaries** are adequately protected over the coming decade, populations stand a strong chance of recovering.

One animal you definitely won't come across is the tiger, which has been completely hunted out. However, several kinds of **big cat** survived the depredations of the colonial era. Among the most adaptive and beautiful is the **leopard** or panther (*panthera panthus*), known in Konkani as the *bibto vag*. Prowling the thick forests of Sanguem and Canacona *talukas*, these elusive cats prey on monkeys and deer and occasionally take domestic cattle and dogs from the fringes of villages. Their distinctive black spots make them notoriously difficult to see amongst the tropical foliage, although their mating call (reminiscent of a saw on wood) regularly pierces the night air in remote areas. The **leopard cat** (*Felis bengalensis*), or *vagati* in Konkani, is a miniature version of its namesake, and more common. Sporting a bushy tail and round spots on soft buff or grey fur, it's about the same size as a domestic cat and lives around villages, picking off chickens, birds and small mammals. Another cat with a penchant for

Viewing wildlife in Goa

Of the state's main wildlife parks, the **Bhagwan Mahaveer Sanctuary**, 56km east of Panjim (see p.114), harbours the most impressive scenery and diverse fauna, with the **Cotigao Sanctuary** in south Goa (see p.213) coming a close second. **Bondla** (see p.113), near Ponda in central Goa, is more a zoo than wildlife park – a depressing spectacle of small cages and enclosures – although the variety of birdlife in this area can be astonishing. Ornithologists should also make time to take in the **Salim Ali Sanctuary** on Chorao Island (see p.103), a short way upriver from Panjim, where mangrove swamps and mud flats teem with waders and other water birds.

The **best time of year** for viewing wildlife is immediately after the monsoons, between October and January, when water levels are still high and temperatures cool enough for hiking. During the rainy season – roughly late June to September – off-track transport is frequently disrupted by flooding, and the larger reserves are closed to visitors. If you plan to do any serious wildlife-spotting, bring with you a pair of sturdy waterproof shoes or boots, a set of binoculars and a good field guide (those available in Goa are not so great; recommended titles are listed on p.334).

Guided wildlife viewing **trips** are offered in Goa by an enthusiastic and highly knowledgeable outfit called Southern Birdwing. In addition to their popular crocodile-spotting boat rides down the Mandovi (see p.103), the company operates birdwatching expeditions to Bondla and the Carambolim wetlands (Rs1250), and overnight tours into the interior to look for rare species of spiders, butterflies, moths and snakes. For more **information**, contact Southern Birdwing direct at 94 B, Bairro Forta Waddo, Nerul, Bardez, Goa 403 114, India; ☎0832/240 1814 or 240 2957, or visit their website ⊛www.southernbirdwing.com.

poultry, and one which Goan villagers occasionally keep as a pet if they can capture one, is the docile **Indian civet** (*Viverricual indica*), or *katanoor*, recognizable by its lithe body, striped tail, short legs and long pointed muzzle.

Wild cats share their territory with a range of other mammals unique to the subcontinent. One you've a reasonable chance of seeing is the **gaur**, or Indian bison (*Bos gaurus*), known in Goa as the *govo redo*. These primeval-looking beasts, with their distinctive sleek black skin and knee-length white "socks", forage around bamboo thickets and shady woods. The bulls are particularly impressive, growing to an awesome height of two metres, with heavy curved horns and prominent humps.

With its long fur and white V-shaped bib, the scruffy **sloth bear** (*melursus ursinas*), or *bhalu*, ranks among the weirder-looking inhabitants of Goa's forests. Sadly, it's also very rare, thanks to its predilection for raiding sugar-cane plantations, which has brought it into direct conflict with humans. Sloth bears can occasionally be seen shuffling along woodland trails, but you're more likely to come across evidence of their foraging activities: trashed termite mounds and chewed-up ants' nests. The same is true of both the portly **Indian porcupine** (*Hystix indica),* or *sal,* which you see a lot less often than the mounds of earth it digs up to get at insects and cashew or teak seedlings, and the **pangolin** (*manis crassicaudata*), or *tiryo*: a kind of armour-plated anteater whose hard grey overlapping scales protect it from predators.

Full-moon nights and the twilight hours of dusk and dawn are the times to look out for **nocturnal animals** such as the **slender loris** (*Loris tardigradus*). This shy creature – a distant cousin of the lemur, with bulging round eyes, furry body and pencil-thin limbs – grows to around twenty centimetres in length. It moves as if in slow motion, except when an insect flits to within striking distance, and is a favourite pet of Goa's forest people. The **mongoose** (*Herpestes edwardsi*) is another animal sometimes kept as a pet. Rudyard Kipling's "Rikitikitavi", known in Konkani as the *mongus*, keeps dwellings free of scorpions, mice, rats and other vermin. It will also readily take on snakes, which is why you often see it writhing in a cloud of dust with king cobras during performances by snake charmers.

Late evening is also the best time for spotting **bats**. Goa boasts four species, including the **fulvous fruit bat** (*Rousettus leshenaulti*), or *vagul* – so-called because it gives off a scent resembling fermenting fruit juice – **Dormer's bat** (*Pipistrellus dormeri*), the very rare **rufous horse-shoe bat**, and the **Malay fox vampire** (*Magaderma spasma*), which feeds off the blood of live cattle. **Flying foxes** (*Pteropus gigantus*), the largest of India's bats, are also present in healthy numbers. With a wingspan of more than one metre, they fly in cacophonous groups to feed in fruit orchards, sometimes falling foul of electricity cables on the way: frazzled flying foxes dangling from live cables are a common sight in the interior of Goa.

Other species to look out for in forest areas are the **Indian giant squirrel** (*Ratufa indica*), or *shenkaro*, which has a coat of black fur and red-orange lower parts. Two and a half times larger than its European cousins, it lives in the canopy, leaping up to twenty metres between branches. The much smaller **three-striped squirrel** (*Funambulus palmarum*), or *khadi khar*, recognizable by the three black markings down its back, is also found in woodland. However, the **five-striped palm squirrel** (*Funambulus pennanti*) is a common sight all over the state, especially in municipal parks and villages.

Forest clearings and areas of open grassland around Molem and Cotigao are grazed by four species of **deer**. Widely regarded as the most beautiful is the **cheetal** (*axis axis*), or spotted axis deer, which congregates in large groups around water holes and salt licks, occasionally wandering into villages to seek shelter from its predators. The plainer buff-coloured **sambar** (*cervus unicolor*) is also well represented, despite succumbing to diseases spread by domestic cattle during the 1970s and 1980s. Two types of deer you're less likely to come across, but which also inhabit the border forests, are the **barking deer** (*muntiacus muntjack*), or *bhenkaro*, whose call closely resembles that of a domestic dog, and the timid **mouse deer** (*Tragulus meminna*), or *pisoi*: a speckled-grey member of the *Tragulidae* family that is India's smallest deer, growing to a mere thirty centimetres in height. Both of these are highly secretive and nocturnal; they are also the preferred snack of Goa's smaller predators: the **striped hyena** (*Hyaena hyaena*) or *yeul*, **jackal** (*Canis aureus*) or *colo*, and **wild dog** (*Cuon alpinus*) or *deucolo*, which hunts in packs.

Long-beaked **dolphins** are regular visitors to the shallow waters of South Goa's more secluded bays and beaches. They are traditionally regarded as a pest by local villagers, who believe they eat scarce stocks of fish. However, this long-standing antipathy is gradually eroding as local people realize the tourist-pulling potential of the dolphins: Palolem beach, in Canacona, is where you're most likely to see one, although "Dolphin-Spotting" boat trips also operate out of Colva.

Finally, no rundown of Goan wildlife would be complete without some mention of **monkeys**. The most ubiquitous species is the mangy pink-bottomed **macaque** (*Macaca mulatta*), or *makad*, which hangs out anywhere scraps may be scavenged or snatched from unwary humans: temples and picnic spots such as Dudhsagar Falls in the Western Ghats are good places to watch them in action. The black-faced **Hanuman langur**, by contrast, is less audacious, retreating to the trees if threatened. It's much larger than the macaque, with pale grey fur and long limbs and tail. In forest areas, the langur's distinctive call is an effective early-warning system against big cats and other predators, which is why you often come across herds of cheetal grazing under trees inhabited by large colonies.

Reptiles

Reptiles are well represented in the region, with more than forty species of **snakes**, **lizards**, **turtles** and **crocodiles** recorded. The best places to spot them are not the interior forests, whose dense foliage makes observation difficult, but open cultivated areas: paddy fields and village ponds provide abundant fresh water, nesting sites and prey (frogs, insects and small birds) to feed on.

Your house or hotel room, however, is where you are most likely to come across Goa's most common reptile, the **gecko** (*Hemidactylus*), which clings to walls and ceilings with its widely splayed toes. Deceptively static most of the time, these small yellow-brown lizards will dash at lightning speed for cracks and holes if you try to catch one, or if an unwary mosquito, fly or cockroach scuttles within striking distance. The much rarer **chameleon** is even more elusive, mainly because its constantly changing camouflage makes it virtually impossible to spot. They'll have no problem seeing you, though: independently moving eyes allow them to pin-point approaching predators, while prey is slurped up with their fast-moving, forty-centimetre-long tongues. The other main lizard to look out for is the **Bengal monitor**. This giant brown speckled reptile looks like a refugee from *Jurassic Park*, growing to well over a metre in length, and used to be a common sight in coastal areas, where they basked on roads and rocks. However, monitors are often killed and eaten by villagers, and have become increasingly rare.

The monsoon period is when you're most likely to encounter **turtles**. Two varieties paddle around village ponds and wells while water is plentiful: the **flap-shell** (*Lissemys punctata*) and **black-pond** (*Melanochelys trijuga*) turtles, neither of which is endangered. Numbers of **marine turtles** (*Lepidochelys olivacea*), by contrast, have plummeted over the past few decades because villagers raid their nests when they crawl on to the beach to lay their eggs. This amazing natural spectacle occurs each year in Morjim and Galjibag, supervised by local wardens employed by the Forest Department to stamp out poaching. For more on Goa's **olive ridley** marine turtles, see pp.160–161.

An equally rare sight nowadays is the **crocodile**. Populations have dropped almost to the point of extinction, although the Cambarjua Canal near Old Goa, and more remote stretches of the Mandovi and Zuari estuaries, support vestigial colonies of **salt-water** crocs, which bask on mud flats and river rocks. Dubbed "salties", they occasionally take calves and goats, and will snap at the odd human if given half a chance. The more ominously named **mugger crocodile**, however, is harmless, inhabiting unfrequented freshwater streams and riversides around Devil's Canyon, near Molem (see p.114).

Snakes

There are 23 species of **snake** in Goa, ranging from the gigantic **Indian python** (*Python molurus*, or *har* in Konkani) – a forest-dwelling constrictor that grows up to four metres in length – to the innocuous **worm snake** (*Typhlops braminus*) or *sulva*, which is tiny, completely blind and often mistaken for an earthworm.

The eight **poisonous snakes** present in the region include India's four most deadly species: the cobra, the krait, the Russel's viper and the saw-scaled viper. Though these are relatively common in coastal and cultivated areas, even the most aggressive snake will slither off at the first sign of an approaching human. Nevertheless, ten thousand Indians die from snake bites each year, and if you regularly cut across paddy fields or plan to do any hiking, it makes sense to familiarize yourself with the following four or five species just in case: their bites nearly always prove fatal if not treated immediately with anti-venom serum, available at most clinics and hospitals.

Present in most parts of the state and an important character in Hindu mythology, the **Indian cobra** (*naja naja*), or *naga*, is the most common of the venomous species. Wheat-brown or grey in colour, it is famed for the "hood" it unfurls when confronted and whose rear side usually bears the snake's characteristic spectacle markings. Its big brother, the **king cobra** (*Naja hannah*), or *Raj nag*, is much less often encountered. Inhabiting the remote forest regions along the Karnatakan border, this beautiful brown, yellow and black snake, which grows to a length of four metres or more, is very rare, although the itinerant snake charmers that perform in markets occasionally keep one. Defanged, they rear up and "dance" when provoked by the handler, or are set against mongooses in ferocious (and often fatal) fights. The king cobra is also the only snake in the world known to make its own nest.

Distinguished by their steel-blue colour and faint white cross markings, **kraits** (*Bungarus coerulus*), locally known as *kaner* or *maniar*, are twice as deadly as the Indian cobra: even the bite of a newly hatched youngster is lethal. **Russel's viper** (*Viperi Russeli*), or *mandol*, is another one to watch out for. Distinguished by the three bands of elliptical markings that extend down its brown body, the Russel hisses at its victims before darting at them and burying its centimetre-long fangs into their flesh. The other common poisonous snake in Goa is the **saw-scaled viper** (*Echis carinatus*), or *phurshem*. Grey with an arrow-shaped mark on its triangular head, it hangs around in the cracks between stone walls, feeding on scorpions, lizards, frogs, rodents and smaller snakes. *Phurshems* also hiss when threatened; they produce the sound by rubbing together serrated scales located on the side of their head. Finally, **sea snakes** (*Enhdrina schistosa*), called *kusada* in Konkani, are common in coastal areas and potentially lethal, although rarely encountered by swimmers as they lurk only in deep water off the shore.

    Harmless snakes are far more numerous than their killer cousins and frequently more attractive. The beautiful **golden tree snake** (*Chrysopelea ormata*) or *kalingin*, for example, sports an exquisitely intricate geometric pattern of red, yellow and black markings, while the **green whip snake** (*Dryhopis nasutus*), or *sarpatol*, is stunning parakeet-green with a whip-like tail extending more than a metre behind it. The ubiquitous **Indian rat snake**, often mistaken for a cobra, also has beautiful markings, although it leaves behind it a foul stench of decomposing flesh. Other common non-poisonous snakes include the **wolf snake** (*Lycodon aulicus*) or *kaidya*, the **Russel sand boa** (*Eryx conicus*) or *malun*, the **kukri snake** (*Oligodon taeniolatus*) or *pasko*, the **cat snake** (*Boiga trigonata*) or *manjra*, and the **keelbacks** (*Natrix*).

Birds

You don't have to be an aficionado to enjoy Goa's abundant **birdlife**. As you travel around the state, breathtaking birds regularly flash between the branches of trees or appear on overhead wires at the roadside.

    Thanks to the internationally popular brand of Goan beer, the **kingfisher** has become the state's unofficial mascot: it's not hard to see why the brewers chose it as their logo. Three common species of kingfisher frequently crop up amid the paddy fields and wetlands of the coastal plains, where they feed on small fish and tadpoles. With its enormous bill and pale green-blue wing feathers, the **stork-billed kingfisher** (*Perargopis capensis*) is the largest and most distinctive member of the family, although the **white-breasted kingfisher** (*Halcyon smyrnensis*) – which has iridescent turquoise plumage and a coral-red bill – and the common, or **small-blue kingfisher** (*Aalcedo althis*), are more alluring.

    Other common and brightly coloured species include the green, blue and yellow **bee-eaters** (*Merops*), the stunning **golden oriole** (*Oriolus oriolus*), and the **Indian roller** (*Coracius bengalensis*), famous for its brilliant blue flight feathers and exuberant aerobatic mating displays. **Hoopes** (*Upupa epops*), recognizable by their elegant black-and-white tipped crests, fawn plumage and distinctive "hoo...po...po" call, also flit around fields and villages, as do **purple sunbirds** (*Nectarina asiatica*), and several kinds of bulbuls, babblers and drongos (*Dicrurus*), including the fork-tailed black drongo (*Dicrurus adsimilis*) – a winter visitor that can often be seen perched on telegraph wires. If you're lucky, you may also catch a glimpse of the **paradise flycatcher** (*Tersiphone paradisi*), which is widespread in Goa and among the region's most exquisite birds, with a thick black crest and long silver tail streamers.

    Goa's paddy fields, ponds and saline mud flats are teeming with **water birds**. The most ubiquitous of these is the snowy white **cattle egret** (*Bubulcus ibis*), which can usually be seen wherever there are cows and buffalo, feeding off the grubs, insects and other parasites that live on them. The **large egret** (*Ardea alba*) is also pure white, although lankier and with a long yellow bill, while the third member of this family, the **little egret** (*Egretta garzetta*), sports a short black bill and, during the mating season, two long tail feathers. Look out too for the mud-brown **paddy bird**, India's most common heron. Distinguished by its pale green legs, speckled breast and hunched posture, it stands motionless for hours in water waiting for fish or frogs to feed on.

The hunting technique of the beautiful **white-bellied fish eagle** (*Haliaeetus leucogaster*), by contrast, is truly spectacular. Cruising twenty to thirty metres above the surface of the water, this black and white osprey swoops at high speed to snatch its prey – usually sea snakes and mackerel – from the waves with its fierce yellow talons: an everyday sight in the more secluded coves of south Goa. More common birds of prey such as the **brahminy kite** (*Haliastur indus*) – recognizable by its white breast and chestnut head markings – and the **pariah kite** (*Milvus migrans govinda*) – a dark-brown buzzard with a fork tail – are widespread around towns and fishing villages, where they vie with raucous gangs of house **crows** (*Corvus splendens*) and white-eyed **jackdaws** (*Corvus monedulal*) for scraps. Gigantic pink-headed **king vultures** (*Sarcogyps clavus*) and the **white-backed vulture** (*Gyps bengallensis*), which has a white ruff around its bare neck and head, also show up whenever there are carcasses to pick clean.

Other birds of prey to keep an eye open for, especially around open farmland, are the white-eyed buzzard (*Butastur teesa*), the honey buzzard (*Pernis ptilorhyncus*), the black-winged kite (*Elanus caeruleus*) – famous for its blood red eyes – and shikra (*Accipiter badius*), which closely resembles the European sparrowhawk.

Forest birds

The region's **forests** may have lost many of their larger animals, but they still offer exciting possibilities for bird-watchers. One species every enthusiast hopes to glimpse while in the woods is the magnificent **hornbill**, of which three species have been spotted in the region: the **grey hornbill** (*Tockus birostris*), with its blue-brown plumage and long curved beak, is the most common, although the **Indian pied hornbill** (*Anthracoceros malabaricus*), distinguished by its white wing and tail tips and the pale patch on its face, often flies into villages in search of fruit and lizards. The magnificent **great pied hornbill** (*Buceros bicornis*), however, is more elusive, limited to the forest areas around Molem and Canacona where it may occasionally be spotted flitting through the dense canopy. Growing to 130 centimetres in length, it has a black-and-white striped body and wings, and a huge yellow beak with a long curved casque on top.

Several species of **woodpecker** also inhabit the interior forests, among them two types of golden-backed woodpecker: the lesser **goldenback**, *Dinopium bengalensis*, is the most colourful of the pair, with a crimson crown and bright splashes of yellow across its back. The Cotigao sanctuary in south Goa (see p.213) is also one of the last remaining strongholds of the **Indian great black woodpecker**, which has completely disappeared from the more heavily deforested hill areas further north. In spite of its bright red head and white rump, this shy bird is more often heard than seen, making loud drumming noises on tree trunks between December and March.

Another bird whose call is a regular feature of the Goan forest, particularly in teak areas, is the wild ancestor of the domestic chicken – the **jungle fowl**. The more common variety of the two found in Goa is the secretive but vibrantly coloured red junglefowl (*Gallus gallus*), which sports golden neck feathers and a metallic black tail. Its larger cousin, the grey or sonnerat's jungle fowl (*Galolus sommeratii*), has darker plumage scattered with yellow spots and streaks. Both inhabit clearings, and are most often seen scavenging for food on the verges of forest roads.

Goan music and dance

With reggae and techno blaring out of so many beach bars, you'd be forgiven for thinking Goa's music and dance scene started with the invention of the synthesizer. However, the state boasts a vibrant musical tradition of its own: a typically syncretic blend of east and west that is as spicy and distinctive as the region's cuisine. You won't hear the calypso-like rhythms of Konkani pop or haunting Kunbi folk songs at the full-moon parties, though. Rooted in village and religious life, Goan music is primarily for domestic consumption, played at temple festivals, harvest celebrations, as an accompaniment to popular theatre, and, most noticeably, on the crackly cassette machines of local buses. If you're keen to sample and understand a little more about the state's music and dance, the following account should provide some useful pointers.

Devotional music and dance

Devotional music and dance have played an important part in Hindu temple worship in Goa for at least a thousand years. Traditionally, wealthier temples employed permanent groups of musicians to regale the deity and participate in the annual *Zatra* processions (see p.110). Singers, accompanied by the harmonium, *tabla*, and other percussion instruments, led the performances, which were usually held in the hall in front of the shrine, or in a special musicians' tower erected above the main entrance to the temple precinct. For important festivals, the congregation would also assemble in front of the sanctum to intone devotional songs, known as **kirtans** and **bhajans**.

While music still features in many temple rituals, sacred dance is seldom performed these days. Up until the beginning of the twentieth century, however, most of the larger shrines boasted troupes of specially trained dancers, known as **Devadasis**, literally "wives of the god". Gifted or sold to the temple authorities by their parents at a young age (either as an offering, or in fulfilment of a thanksgiving vow), these women were symbolically married to the deity in a ritual known as *sessa*, after which they effectively became slaves, expected to grant sexual favours to the temple priests and wealthy visitors as well as to fulfil their ritual responsibilities. Formerly an act of worship and regarded as one of the highest classical art forms, this kind of dance degenerated over time into a kind of crude commercial entertainment.

Among the more illustrious descendants of the *Devadasis* caste is the playback singer **Lata Mangeshkar**, who appears in the *Guinness Book of Records* as the world's most recorded artist. With over 30,000 songs and more than 2000 films to her credit, her high vibrato voice has become the hallmark of the Hindi movie soundtrack. Lata was born in Pune, Maharashtra, in 1928, but her father, Dinanath Mangeshkar (also a famous actor and singer) originally came from Mangeshki in Ponda *taluka*. During a visit to her father's village, the star was not allowed to approach the deity in the local temple because of her *Devadasi* roots. As a result of this snub, Lata has refused ever to return to Goa, despite repeated invitations to perform in the state.

The licentious associations of temple dance also account for the rarity with which recitals are given in *devuls* today. You can, however, catch performances of classical Indian dance at secular **venues** around the state, notably the Kala Academy in Panjim (see p.81) and Calangute's Kerkar Art Gallery (see p.139). These two places also host regular recitals of Indian **classical music** by students, teachers, and visiting artistes from elsewhere in India.

Folk music and dance

Wander into almost any Hindu village on the eve of an important *puja*, particularly around harvest time after the monsoons, and you'll experience Goan roots music and dance at its most authentic. The torchbearers of the region's thriving **folk tradition** are the Kunbi class of landless labourers, most often seen bent double in rice paddies, the women with garish coloured cotton saris tied *dhoti*-style around their legs. Agricultural work – planting, threshing and grinding grain, raking salt pans, and fixing fishing nets – provide the essential rhythms for Konkani songs, known as **Kunbi geet**.

More rehearsed performances take place during the Hindu month of Paush (late Feb), when groups of women gather in the village square-cum-dance ground (*mannd*) to sing *dhalos* and *fugdis*. The singing may run over seven or more nights, culminating with outbreaks of spirit possession and trances.

Remo

Ask anyone in Goa to name you a famous Goan and they'll probably say **"Remo"**. The state's most acclaimed musician, singer-songwriter and local hero Remo Fernandes is unknown in the West but enjoys mega-star status among India's young English-speaking middle classes. The secret of his success is his eccentric flair for **fusion**. Dressed in a cotton *dhoti* and twelve-hole Doc Martens, Remo blends Western rock with traditional Indian sounds, spiced up with South American rhythms and overscored by punchy issues-based lyrics. He's also staunchly proud of his Goan heritage, and is as happy crooning *fados* and Konkani folk tunes at local *festas* as performing electric sets in the concert halls of Delhi and Mumbai.

Born in 1953 in the picturesque riverside village of Siolim, near Chapora in north Goa, Remo's earliest musical influence was his father's collection of Portuguese, Latin-American and Goan records. A spell with a college rock band in Mumbai during the 1970s, followed by a couple of years hitching around Europe and North Africa, added new ingredients to this musical melting pot, and in 1980 he founded the ground-breaking fusion band "Indiana", whose extravagant stage costumes and hybrid style would later become hallmarks of the Goan's own career.

Remo's big break, though, came in 1983 with the release of his first solo album, *Goan Crazy*. Recorded and mixed at his family home in Siolim, its multicultural sound and acerbic social commentary showcased Remo's talents as a multi-instrumentalist and lyric writer, finally bringing him to the attention of Mumbai's movie moguls and record companies. A series of hit film scores and a major record deal followed, culminating with his two best-selling albums, *Pack That Smack* and *Bombay City*, which both shot straight to the top of the rock/pop charts.

Then, just at the point when Remo's career looked set to go from strength to strength, tragedy struck. In the monsoons of 2000, three members of his "troupe" – two musicians from the backing band and his personal assistant – were killed in a car accident while on tour in the North Indian city of Kanpur. Since their deaths, Remo has not performed any live concerts, although there were rumours he aimed to complete a solo album recorded by the youngest member of the band shortly before the tragedy, as a tribute to his lost friends.

The most famous Goan folk song and dance form, though, has to be the **mando**. Originally, this slow and expressive dance (whose name derives from the Sanskrit *mandala*, meaning circular pattern) was traditionally performed in circles, but these days tends to be danced by men and women standing opposite each other in parallel lines, waving fans and coloured handkerchiefs. *Mandos* gather pace as they progress and are usually followed by a series of **dulpods**, quick-time tunes whose lyrics are traditionally satirical, exposing village gossip about errant housewives, lapsed priests and so on. *Dulpods*, in turn, merge into the even jauntier rhythms of **deknis**, bringing the set dances to a tumultuous conclusion.

The basic rhythmic cycles, or *ovis*, of Goan folk songs were exploited by early Christian missionaries in their work. Overlaid with lyrics inspired by Bible stories, many were eventually assimilated into the local Catholic tradition: today, the *mando*, for example, is usually danced by Christians on church *festas* and wedding days. It also became the favourite dance of the Goan gentry, who, dressed in ball gowns and dinner suits with fans and flamboyant handkerchiefs, used to perform it during the glittering functions held in the reception rooms of the territory's top houses.

Fados

The most European-influenced of all the Goan folk idioms is the **fado**. Rendered in a turgid mock operatic style, these melancholic songs epitomize the colonial predilection for nostalgia or longing for the home country, known in Portuguese as *saudades*. Ironically, though, few *fadistas* actually laid eyes on the fabled lights of Lisbon or Coimbra they eulogized in their lyrics, and today the

Recommended cassettes

Virtually every music store and street stall in Goa stocks a representative selection of **audio cassettes** by Goan artists. Costing between Rs20 and Rs50, they're usually cheap enough to risk buying on spec, although most retailers (the best are in Panjim and Margao; see p.81 & p.182) will let you listen to them if they are not sealed in plastic. The following are among the safest bets:

Agostinho's Trio *Soul of Music*. Wacky Konkani covers of popular Latin and Western numbers accompanied by accordions, mandolins, violas and conga percussion.

Gavana *Cantando em Goa* (*Viagem Dos Sons*). The only *conjunto* still using exclusively acoustic instruments, Gavana was formed to preserve traditional Goan music and dance, and this CD is their richest offering to date, with an engaging cross-section of *deknis*, *dulpods*, *mandos* and *saudades*-inspired Konkani classics It comes with handsomely illustrated cover notes too, giving lots of background on the songs as well as translations of the lyrics. Sadly, the album is harder to come by than the less exciting *Souvenir* trio of audio cassettes (of which no.3 three is the best).

Lucio *Forwards into the Past* (*Remo Presents*). A string of sombre Portuguese ballads and *bossa novas* by Goa's master *fadista*. Some fine flute-playing by Remo, too.

Oslando *Goa Meu Amor*. One of several soundalike albums by the bespectacled grandfather of Goan folk; this one features a side of Portuguese songs followed by a selection of *Kunbi geets*, *dekhnis* and *dulpods*.

Remo *Goan Gold*. Remo's arrangements of Portuguese and Konkani classics are somewhat marred by incongruous synthesizer sounds, but one track – the hauntingly beautiful *Panch Vorsad* – is outstanding.

fado is a dying art form. However, a couple of renowned folk singers, notably the band leader **Oslando** and singer-guitarist **Lucio Miranda**, invariably include a couple of old *fado* numbers on their albums. Lucio, the greatest living exponent of the form, also gives the odd performance in the five-star hotels around Panjim.

Konkani pop

Rave music aside, most of the sounds you hear around Goa these days are either *filmi* hits from the latest blockbuster Hindi movies or a mish-mash of folk tunes and calypso rhythms known as **Konkani pop**. Backed by groups of women singers and fanfaring mariachi-style brass sections, Konkani lead vocalists croon away with the reverb cranked up against a cacophony of electric guitar and keyboard accompaniment.

Konkani pop is best experienced live (the costumes tend to be as lurid as the music), but if you don't manage to get to a gig, every kerbside cassette-*wallah* stocks a range of popular tapes. No particular artist is worth singling out; nor are many likely to find fans among Western visitors. However, world-music aficionados should definitely check out a couple of cassettes to sample the sometimes surreal blend of musical influences. Underpinning the Portuguese-style melodies are conga-driven African and Caribbean rhythms, Brazilian syncopations, and almost Polynesian-sounding harmonies. The only part of the world Konkani pop sounds like it doesn't come from is India.

Books

There's a surprising dearth of books on Goa, particularly when you consider the reams of printed matter devoted to regions of India formerly colonized by the British. This neglect may well be reversed as the state's tourist
boom gathers momentum, but in the meantime most titles are, with a few
notable exceptions, either specialist tomes on history and architecture, or else
travelogues that feature accounts of short sojourns in the territory.

While many of the titles listed below are stocked by high-street bookshops
in Western countries, those published in India tend only to be available in Goa
itself, usually at a fraction of what they would cost back home. The Other India
Bookstore in Mapusa (above Mapusa Clinic; ☎0832/226 3306, ⓦwww.goa-
com.com/books) is the best-stocked store in the state, and offers an efficient
mail order service via the Internet (ⓦwww.mnet.fr/aiindex/i_oibs). Also
worth a browse for rare out-of-print books, as well as current publications, are
Amazon's Web sites ⓦwww.amazon.co.uk or ⓦwww.amazon.com, through
which you can order several of the more obscure titles listed below. Serious
students of art and architecture should also scour the shelves of academic
libraries, which are a rich source of out-of-print material, including some of
the acknowledged classics on the region. Bona fide Goan literature is in very
short supply, mainly because Konkani was suppressed for centuries by the
Portuguese. If you want to sample the state's contemporary fiction, dip into the
short-story pages of the monthly magazine *Goa Today*, available at most Goan
newsagents.

Wherever a book is in print, the UK publisher is listed first, followed by the
publishers in the US and India, where applicable. If the publisher is located
outside the UK or US, the city is given. Where books are out of print, they are
annotated o/p. Titles marked ▣ are particularly recommended.

History, society and architecture

Teresa Albuquerque *Anjuna: Profile
of a Village in Goa* (Promilla & Co,
New Delhi). A fascinating village
study by one of Goa's most
renowned social historians.
Crammed full of fine-grain detail on
local legends, celebrities, shrines, traditions and other curiosities.

Teresa Albuquerque *Santa Cruz*
(Fernandes Publications, Panjim).
Albuquerque tackles her home
patch, a large village near Panjim
famous throughout the state for its
mafiosi (*goondas*), in the same style as
her previous offering. This one's
equally rich, although too detailed
for a casual read.

Romesh Bhandari *Goa* (Roli
Books, New Delhi). One of the
widest ranging, and quirkiest, general
introductions to Goa published in
recent years. Written by the state's
former governor, it's clearly a labour
of love, filled with asides and historical anecdotes reminiscent of the old
British gazetteers.

Mário Cabral e Sá *Wind of Fire*
(Promilla & Co, New Delhi). A rambling and unfocused, but ultimately
exhaustive account of Goan music
and dance, with essays by different
contributors on subjects ranging
from aboriginal harvest songs to the
influence of Western pop. Among its

strongest chapters is one featuring biographies of some forty or so Goan musicians, great and small, from different traditions and eras.

Mário Cabral e Sá *Legends of Goa* (India Book House, Mumbai). After David Tomory's *Hello Goodnight* (see p.334), the most engaging book to have come out of Goa for years: a compendium of curious historical snippets drawn from across the centuries, handsomely packaged in hardback, and featuring illustrations by the famous Goan cartoonist Mario Miranda.

★ **Helder Carita** *Palaces of Goa* (Cartago, UK). An encyclopedic, richly illustrated overview of civil Indo-Portuguese architecture in Goa, by the world's foremost authority on the subject. The only reason you'd want to buy it, however, are for Nicholas Sapieha's sumptuous photographs; the text is frustratingly incoherent and repetitious and offers little help as a field guide.

Charles Dellon *L'Inquisition de Goa* (Editions Chandeigne, Paris). The only surviving first-hand account of the Goan Inquisition, by a French traveller who experienced it in the seventeenth century. Dellon's chilling narrative, in this French edition illustrated with the original engravings, was the *Papillon* of its day, and remains a shocking indictment of the genocide perpetrated by the colonial clergy – at least, if you can read French (its English translation is out of print and extremely rare).

José Nicolau da Fonseca *Sketch of the City of Goa* (Asian Educational Services, New Delhi). An exhaustive overview of Goan history and society, compiled as part of the British Imperial Gazetteer in 1878. The typically Victorian "Statistical Account of the Territory" has become historical material in its own right, but the

description of Old Goa remains the best of its kind ever published. AES's facsimile edition comes with copies of the original fold-out illustrations.

Richard Hall *Empires of the Monsoon* (HarperCollins, UK). This wide-ranging account of colonial expansion into the Indian Ocean is more erudite and compellingly written than most, tracing the web of trade connections that bound Africa, Europe and India from the fifteenth century onwards. Among its many highlights is a particularly vivid description of Vasco da Gama's voyages (in all their brutality) and Albuquerque's subsequent founding of Goa.

★ **Koshy, Pandit & Mascarenhas** *The Houses of Goa* (Architecture Anonymous, New Delhi). Only its hefty price tag puts this long-awaited layman's guide to Goa's stately homes beyond the reach of casual readers. The prose, though a bit flowery and heavily reliant on sycophantic anecdote, is far more accessible than Helder Carita's, and the photos are top-class. The one real gripe is that the images aren't captioned, so you can't work out where half the places are, which renders the book redundant as a guide.

James Leasor *Boarding Party* (Heinemann, UK, o/p). The definitive story of the sinking of the German spy ship, *Ehrenfels*, in Mormugao harbour by British veterans of the Calcutta Light Horse regiment (see p.177). The melodramatic "faction" style grates after a while, and Leasor somewhat exaggerates the overall importance of the operation to the Asian war effort, but this is a rip-roaring yarn.

Robert Newman *Of Umbrellas, Goddesses & Dreams* (Other India Press). A selection of scholarly essays on Goan culture and society, by an

American anthropologist who's been studying the state since the late 1970s. Most of the pieces focus on religion – notably vision cults, church and temple festivals, and Hindu-Christian cross-overs – with engaging forays into the Konkani issue, fishing controversy and tourism. The writing's packed with insights, but you have to wade through a fair bit of repetitive academic prose to find them.

M.N. Pearson *The Portuguese in India* (CUP, UK). A concise academic history of the Lusitanian empire in the subcontinent, from Vasco da Gama to Salazar. Conceived as a distillation of the most recent historical research in the field, it includes a wealth of amazing statistics relating to trade and military matters, contextualized by sharp insights into Portuguese society across the centuries.

⭐ **José Pereira et al** *India and Portugal: Cultural Interactions* (Marg Publications, India). The cultural legacy of five centuries of Portuguese contact is presented in this copiously illustrated hardback. Subjects covered include the evolution of church architecture to furniture, dance, dress and cuisine, with scores of colour photos and facsimiles of rare sixteenth-century engravings to justify its hefty price tag.

Rowena Robinson *Conversion, Continuity and Change: Lived Christianity in Southern Goa* (Thousand Oaks, UK/Sage Publications, New Delhi). An anthropological monograph drawing on fieldwork in a Salcete village, which the author contextualizes with excerpts from a wide range of historical sources. If you can deal with the academic jargon, this makes a fascinating read, putting paid to any notion that caste disappeared with conversion to Christianity.

Elaine Sanceau *Indies Adventure: the Amazing Career of Alfonso de Albuquerque* (Blackie and Sons, UK). A lengthy but highly readable biography of Goa's first Portuguese governor, who wrested the territory from its former Muslim overlords in 1510.

Sunil Sethi *Indian Interiors* (Taschen). In its 300-page odyssey around India, this sumptuously illustrated coffee-table book pulls back the curtains on five Goan homes, ranging from the eighteenth-century Casa de Braganza in Chandor to a humble beach shack occupied by a couple of foreign expats. You also get to see inside the highly coloured, terrazzo-floored suites of the Nilaya Hermitage at Arpora, diamond tycoon Jimmy Gadzar's monumentally kitsch pad at Fort Aguada, and the Deshprabhus' stately home at Pernem.

Georg Schurhammer *Francis Xavier: His Life and Times* (Loyola, US). A definitive biography of Goa's wandering patron saint, including a graphic rundown of the amputations inflicted on his corpse (see p.98).

Robert Sewell *A Forgotten Empire* (reprinted in facsimile by Asian Educational Services, New Delhi). A concise history of the Vijayanagars, supplemented by the translated chronicles of Domingo Paes and Fernao Nuniz, two Portuguese travellers who visited the royal city at the height of its splendour. Essential reading if you want to get to grips with the history behind Hampi's ruins.

Manohar Shetty (ed) *Ferry Crossing: Short Stories From Around Goa* (Penguin, India). This anthology of Goan fiction, put together by a local poet and widely available in the state, comprises broadly themed short stories woven around the local landscape and people. Translated from Konkani, Marathi and Portuguese, none is what you might call world class, but they offer fresh perspectives on Goan life, particularly the impact of modernization on villages.

Guide books

David Abram, Devdan Sen, Nick Edwards, Mike Ford and Beth Woodridge *The Rough Guide to India* (Rough Guides, UK). Obviously we're biased, but we think this guide, described by *Condé Nast Traveler* as "the Bible for any visitor to India", is the most comprehensive ever published and an indispensable travelling companion if you plan to venture far outside Goa. The fifth edition includes expanded coverage of Kerala, Karnataka, Maharashtra and Mumbai, with nearly 1300 pages of candid accounts and cultural background, backed up by solid practical information. But don't believe us: check it out for yourself on the Rough Guides' Web site, Ⓦ www.roughguides.com.

Mário Cabral e Sá *Goa* (Lustre Press, India). The best of the coffee-table souvenir tomes on sale in the five-star hotels, with excellent colour photos by Jean-Louis Nou.

★ **Maurice Hall** *Window on Goa: A History and Guide* (Quiller Press, UK). Published posthumously

and widely available, this work, completed during the author's retirement after a career as a steel engineer in India, was clearly a labour of love. Covering every conceivable site of historic interest, it offers a concise, highly readable background on all aspects of Goan life, brought to life by dozens of colour photographs.

★ **Anthony Hutt** *Goa: A Traveller's Historical and Architectural Guide* (Scorpion Publishing, UK). A detailed overview of Goa's past and present, with accounts of the main monuments and illustrations and a good index. Ideal if you want to deepen your understanding of the region without getting tangled in nit-picking academic prose.

J.M. Richards *Goa* (Vikas, New Delhi). Now only printed in India, this retired architectural journalist's wide-ranging little book, first published in 1982, touches on most aspects of Goan life, although as an armchair introduction it has been thoroughly eclipsed by David Tomory's *Hello Goodnight*.

Travel writing

R. F. Burton *Goa and the Blue Mountains* (Asian Educational Services, New Delhi). One of the Victorian era's most acclaimed traveller-adventurer-anthropologists, Burton was but a lowly young army officer on sick leave when he wrote this, his first book, in 1847. As an account of Portuguese Goa it's pretty lame, but if you can ignore all the

bigotry and racist asides about "*mestiço* mongrel men", it has its moments (the most infamous being an attempt to abduct a beautiful orphan from a Goan convent, which went wrong when the perpetrators – among them a thinly disguised Burton – carried off the abbess by mistake).

Alexander Frater *Chasing the Monsoon* (Penguin, UK). Frater's wet-season jaunt across the subcontinent took him through a Goa of grey skies and muddy puddles: an evocative account of the region as few visitors see it.

Gita Mehta *Karma Cola* (Mandarin/Fawcett). Satirical look at the psychedelic 1970s freak scene that winds up, appropriately enough, at the Anjuna flea market. Now somewhat dated, but with some hilarious anecdotes and many a telling observation on the excesses of spiritual tourism in India.

Cleo Odzer *Goa Freaks: My Hippie Years in India* (Blue Moon Books, US). A cloyingly self-indulgent account of an American woman's youthful hippy odyssey, revolving around Goa and Mumbai. In more skilled hands, the subject matter might have yielded an entertaining neo-Beat novel, but as it is, the total absence of irony and tone of barely suppressed excitement with which Odzer narrates her brush with destitution ("Sleeping on the street with beggars! Could that happen to me?") is a far cry indeed from Kerouac.

François Pryard *Voyage to the East Indies, the Maldives, the Moluccas and Brazil* (Hakluyt Society, India). Albert Gray's translation of the famous French chronicler's travelogue includes a vivid first-hand description of the Portuguese colony during its decadent heyday. Goa was Pryard's first port of call after he was shipwrecked in the Maldives in 1608.

Frank Simoes *Glad Seasons in Goa* (Viking, India). An affectionate portrait of Goa and its inhabitants by a local author, with a particularly memorable evocation of the joys of *feni* drinking. Widely available in Goa, but harder to find abroad.

★ **David Tomory** *Hello Goodnight* (Lonely Planet, Australia). An upbeat account of Goa through the ages, enlivened with experiences and encounters distilled from over thirty years of visiting and reading about the region. It's all in here: from Albuquerque to Wendell Rodricks and Jungle Barry to the Nine Bar, crammed into 23 chapters of poppy prose that faithfully captures Goa's essential quirkiness. Some will find it short on analysis, but the book's depiction of contemporary tourist culture, in particular, is spot on.

Wildlife and the environment

Salim Ali, Dillon and Ripley *The Handbook of the Birds of India and Pakistan* (OUP, UK). Covers all of South Asia's birds in a single volume, with plates and maps: the definitive work, although hard to come by.

★ **Claude Alvares (ed)** *Fish Curry and Rice: A Citizens' Report on the Goan Environment* (Ecoforum, India). The most thorough overview of Goan green issues ever compiled in a single volume, giving a region-by-region rundown of the state's natural habitats, fol-

lowed by articles outlining the principal threats to the environment from tourism, transport policy, changes in local farming practices, and a host of other eco evils.

P. V. Bole and Yogini Vaghini *Field Guide to the Common Trees of India* (OUP, UK/US). A handy-sized, indispensable tome for serious tree spotters.

Bikram Grewal *Birds of India, Bangladesh, Nepal, Pakistan and Sri Lanka* (The Guide Book Company,

Hong Kong). Five hundred species are detailed in this glossy but practical field guide, most with excellent colour photographs. Based on Salim Ali & Co's authoritative work, and the best of the bunch available in UK and US high-street bookshops.

Insight Guides *Indian Wildlife* (APA Publications, UK). An excellent all-round introduction to India's wildlife, with scores of superb colour photographs, features on different animals and habitats, and a thorough bibliography. Recommended.

P. Killips *A Guide to the Flora and Fauna of Goa* (Orient Longman, Hyderabad). A seventy-page field guide, illustrated with amateur photos but listing all the common species of palms, flowering trees, butterflies, reptiles, mammals, insects and beach creatures.

S. Prater *The Book of Indian Animals* (OUP, UK/Bombay Natural History Society). The most comprehensive single-volume reference book on the subject, although only available in India.

Romulus Whitaker *Common Indian Snakes* (Macmillan, UK). A detailed and illustrated guide to the subcontinent's snakes, with all the Goan species included.

Martin Woodcock *Handguide to the Birds of the Indian Subcontinent* (Collins, UK). For years the market leader, although now superseded by Grewal's guide. Available in lightweight, pocket-sized paperback form, and very user-friendly, with nearly every species illustrated (some in black and white).

Cookery

Madhur Jaffrey *Flavours of India* (BBC Books, UK). Accompanying the popular BBC TV series, the uncrowned *rani* of Indian cookery's latest tome features a couple of dozen Goan dishes, with enlightening background notes and some mouthwatering colour photos.

Language

Language

Language

onkani, an Indo-Aryan offshoot of Sanskrit that took root in the region more than two thousand years ago, is the mother tongue of most Goans, spoken by virtually all of its native inhabitants. Only in 1978, however, was it recognized by Delhi as more than a minor dialect, and another fourteen years elapsed before the Indian government, bowing to popular opinion, named it the state's official language. However, **Maharathi**, the language of Goa's politically and economically powerful neighbour, Maharashtra, remains the principal medium of primary education.

Although the two languages are closely related, the debate over which to use in government has aroused strong feelings over the years – most notably in the run-up to Delhi's decision to rubber-stamp Konkani, which divided the regional press and sparked off violent confrontations between rival groups. The issues at stake, however, have far less to do with which language is more universally understood than with the politics and notions of regional identity. Those Goans who wanted their children taught in Maharathi also tended to favour merger with Maharashtra, whereas the pro-Konkani lobby believed the state would be better off with greater autonomy (See "History", p.297).

An added complication has been the lingering presence of **Portuguese**. Only a tiny number of Goans still speak the former colonial mother tongue, but they tend to be from a well-educated, politically influential elite. The only places you're likely to hear it spoken in the street are the neighbourhood of Fontainhas, Panjim, which remains solidly pro-Portuguese, and in the stately homes of the Velhas Conquistas.

India's official national language, **Hindi**, has a place in Goa, too, largely thanks to the increasing number of settlers from the north of the country and the popularity of "Bollywood" movies. However, the language of higher education, law and the quality press is **English**, which is so prevalent in the resorts that you can easily get by without a word of Konkani or Maharathi. Even fluent English speakers, though, will be flattered if you attempt a few words of their native tongue.

The lists of words and phrases below are intended as an aid to meeting people and travelling independently around more off-the-beaten-track areas of the state, where English is less commonly spoken. Konkani has no official script of its own (Christians tend to use Roman, and Hindus write with Devanagiri), so we've transcribed the expressions phonetically, indicating the correct syllable stress in italics.

Konkani words and phrases

Meeting people

hello/good morning/ good evening	**dio boro *dees* diun**	my name is (David)	**majay nau (David)**
what is your name?	**tu chay nau kit*ay*?**	where do you come from?	**tu koyee-sau yat-ee?**

I come from …	**mau zo gao …**	good	**borem**
how are you (male)?	**kos-o-asaee?**	I am tired	**aoo tsod tok**la
how are you (female)?	**kos-hey-am?**	I am happy	**aoo tsaud koo**shi
thank you	**dio bo**ray kor**unc**	I love Goa	**maka Goeya boray**
Happy Christmas	**Kooshal bhoo**reet		**lak**ta
	Natala	I understand a little	**maka toree Konkani**
Happy Holi	**Holi moo**ba**rak**	Konkani	**sazmata**
may I take your	**au eek fo**to kardum?	I speak a little	**aoo toree Konkani**
photograph?		Konkani	**oolayta**
yes/no	**hoee/na**	goodbye	**miochay**

Getting around and finding accommodation

where can I catch the	**(Calangute) bus**	how much to (Anjuna)?	**kitlay pot-ollay**
bus to (Calangute)?	**ko-ee tam**ta?		**(Anjuna)?**
does this bus go to	**Ee Calangute bus?**	how many kilometres	**(Calangute) kitley**
(Calangute)?		is it to (Calangute)?	**pois asa?**
when does the bus	**bus kitley-anc so**-ta?	turn left/right	**dai-an/ooj-an wot**
leave?		drive more slowly!	**sossegarde sol**ay!
have we arrived in	**(Candolim) poh-lay?**	do you have a room/	**tu jay shee room/**
(Candolim)?		house to rent?	**gora asa?**

Eating and drinking

I am hungry	**maka bhook lag**leah	no sugar	shak**har na**ka
I am thirsty	**maka taan lag**leah	not spicy	mak**ha tikh na**ka
water	**oo**dak	the food is good	**jon boray ha**
no ice	**barf na**ka		

Shopping

how much?	**kitlay?**	I'll take this	**haon hem kha**tan
too expensive!	**ek**dtom ma-araog!	have you got another	**as**lem an**eek assa?**
I don't want it	**maka na**ka tem	one?	

Families

father	**pai (Christian), bapui**	daughter	**dhoo**
	(Hindu)	son	**phoot**
mother	**maee (Christian),**	wife	**bhai**
	avoi (Hindu)	husband	**ghoo**
grandmother	**shamai**	male/female cousin	**primo/prima**
grandfather	**shapai**	older adults (polite)	**tia (female)/tio (male)**

Time and days

now	*at*-ants	afternoon	*don*para	Wednesday	**Boodhw*a*r**
today	**atz**	evening	**sanz**	Thursday	**Virest*a*r**
yesterday	**kal**	night	**rat**	Friday	**Sookar*a*r**
tomorrow	**fal*yam***	Monday	**Som*a*r**	Saturday	**Shenv*a*r**
morning	***sa*kal**	Tuesday	**Mungl*a*r**	Sunday	***Aee-ta*r**

Other useful words

beach	*pray*ia	moon	**tson*drim***	temple	**day-*vool***
cave	**bhuher**	palm tree	**mard**	tender coconut	**adzar**
church	**ig*roz***	river	**wow**	village	**ga**
coconut	**nal**	road	***ros*to**		
doctor	**daktar**	sea	**do*ria***		
hill	***don*goor**	sun	**wot**		

Numbers

1	**ek**	6	**soh**	20	**vees**	150	**dher-chen**
2	**dohn**	7	**saht**	30	**tees**	200	**dho-chen**
3	**teen**	8	**ahrt**	40	**cha-*ees***	1000	**ek-azar**
4	**char**	9	**nou**	50	**po-nas**	2000	**dhon-azar**
5	**pants**	10	**dha**	100	**chem-*bor***		

Note: A hundred thousand is a *lakh* (written 1,00,000); ten million is a *crore* (1,00,00,000). Millions, billions and the like are not in common usage.

Food and drink terms

Goan dishes and cooking terms

ananas	pineapple
apa de camarao	prawn pie with a crisp rice-flour crust
balchao	a preserve of rich red-chilli sauce
bazlele	fried
bharli vaangi	stuffed aubergines (eggplant)
bibo upkari	cashews cooked with spices
cabedala	pungent pork dish
cafreal	spicy fried chicken or fish
caja	cashew nut
caldo verde	Portuguese potato and cabbage
chanyacho ros	dried peas prepared with dry-roasted coconut and whole spices
chourisso	small red pork sausages flavoured with *feni*, *toddi* vinegar and chillies; known as *lingiss* in Konkani
feijoada	butter-bean stew that often comes with chunks of chourisso
gur	coconut sugar

keli	banana	sorpatel	pickled pork seasoned with hot spices; eaten at Christmas and marriage feasts
kishmar	dried and powdered shrimp		
leitao	roast suckling pig; originally a speciality of Coimbra, Portugal	taanoo	rice
		tamari bhaji	a red-spinach dish with onions, chillies and grated coconut
nal	coconut		
neeshtay	fish		
neeshtaychi corri	fish curry water	tel	cooking oil
pilau	Basmati rice stewed in stock and flavoured with whole spices and saffron	toddi	palm sap vinegar or wine
		vindaloo	pork or chicken marinated in an extra-hot and sour curry sauce
rechad	a hot red-chilli paste, mainly used to flavour fish	xacuti	a fiery sauce for meat made with lemon juice, nuts, coconut milk and lots of red chillies
rechado	stuffed with rechad		

Seafood

bangra	mackerel	mandkin	kalamari (squid)
bodorn	tuna	modso	lemon fish
ching-go	lobster	mori	shark
chonok	barramundi	pomflit or pitorshi	pomfret
dzob	mussels		
eison	kingfish	shewter	mullet
gobro	rockfish	sulta	tiger prawns
paloo	bream	tamso	snapper
kooli	crab		

Dishes from other regions

biriyani	rice with saffron or turmeric, whole spices and meat (sometimes vegetables), and often a hard-boiled egg; mild	malai kofta	balls of minced vegetables in a rich spicy sauce
		pilau	rice lightly spiced and pre-fried
cutlet	minced meat or vegetables fried in the form of a flat cake	rogan josh	red lamb curry; a classic Mughlai dish; medium hot
jalfrezi	with tomatoes and green chilli; medium hot	sambar	tangy vegetable and lentil soup with asafoetida and tamarind
jeera	cumin; a *masala* so described will usually be medium hot	subje	white-coconut chutney served with most South Indian dishes
keema	minced lamb	tarka dal	split orange lentils cooked in a *masala* of turmeric, fried garlic and onions
korma	braised in yoghurt sauce with almonds; mild		

Breads and pancakes

batura   soft deep-fried white bread that traditionally accompanies *channa* (chick peas)

chapati   unleavened bread made with mixed white and wholewheat flour, dry-baked on a flat griddle

dosa   crispy rice pancake

idly   steamed rice cake usually served with *sambar*

*kunechi poee   pitta-like unleavened bread, often baked or dry-fried in the shape of a butterfly

nan   white leavened bread baked in a clay oven (*tandoor*)

*pao, or poee   soft and crusty Portuguese-style white bread rolls

papadam   crisp, thin chick-pea-flour cracker, deep-fried or grilled

paratha   wholewheat bread made with butter and griddle-fried; tastes like a chewy pancake and is often stuffed with vegetables or meat

puri   soft white-dough bread that puffs up and crispens when deep-fried in oil

roti   a loosely used term; often just another name for chapati, though it should be thicker, chewier, and baked in a *tandoor*

*sanna   traditional crumpet-like bread rolls made with rice flour, sugar and partially fermented *toddi*

uttapam   griddle-fried, rice-batter pancake, speckled with holes and soft in the middle; often prepared using onions

wada or vada   deep-fried doughnuts made from lentil flour

*Goan terminology; all other bread and pancake terms above refer to North or South Indian cuisine

Cakes and desserts

alebele   pancakes stuffed with grated fresh coconut

batica   coconut cake

bebinca   a ten-layer Christmas cake made with egg yolks, coconut milk and sugar

bolinhas   small, round and syrupy rice-flour cakes

culculs   tiny shell-shaped biscuits

dodol   fudge-like balls of semolina flavoured with roasted coconuts, cashews and raw cane sugar (*jaggery*)

mangada   mango jam

neuros   half-moon-shaped stuffed pastries

Glossary of Hindi and Konkani words

antaralhaya temple vestibule

argashallas pilgrims' hostels in Hindu temples

ashram religious institution built around a spiritual or political leader (guru)

avatar reincarnation of Hindu god on earth, in human or animal form

azulejos white ceramic tile hand-painted in blue and yellow: a traditional Portuguese art form

balcão deep verandah of Goan villas with stone benches where residents relax during siesta and the evenings

bedees tiny Indian cigarettes hand-rolled in brown eucalyptus leaves and tied with cotton thread. The aroma they give off is one of India's quintessential smells.

bhelpuri a quintessentially Mumbai masala mixture of puffed-rice, deep-fried vermicelli, potato, crunchy puri pieces, chilli paste, tamarind water, chopped onions and coriander.

brahmapuri Hindu religious centre

brahmins caste made up of priests and teachers

burqa enveloping black veil worn by Muslim women

cadeirinha traditional Indo-Portuguese sedan chair with two seats facing each other

caravela Portuguese galleon with a triangular sail derived from the Arab dhow

chai Indian tea; usually boiled with lots of milk and sugar

charas cannabis resin (hashish)

chowkidar watchman/caretaker

darshan ritual viewing of a deity or saint; receiving religious teachings

deep stambhas lamp tower positioned outside Hindu temples – a feature introduced to Goa by the Maharathas

deepmal lamp tower (see above)

devta deity

devul temple

dhaba roadside food stall selling local dishes

dharamsala rest house for pilgrims

dhobi man or woman who washes clothes

dhoop thick pliable block of strong incense

dhoti white ankle-length cloth worn by men, tied around the waist, and sometimes hitched up through the legs

dwarpalas guardian deities; in Goa, these feature on the embossed silver doors flanking the temple shrine rooms

feni clear liquor distilled from cashew fruit or coconut sap (*toddi*)

festa Christian feast day connected with a patron saint

filmi popular Hindi movie music

garbhagriha sanctum or shrine room of a Hindu temple

gaur Indian bison

ghat literally "step"; usually refers to the Sahyadri Hills lining the Goan border

ghor house

goenkar (or gaunkar) high-caste landowner

gopura ornamental gateway to a temple enclosure, surmounted by a multi-tiered tower (often decorated with statues)

gram roasted maize, sold on streets all over India

Harijans literally "Children of God" a term introduced by Mahatma Gandhi to designate those outside, or below, the four principal Hindu castes

hidalgos Portuguese nobles

igreja church

kott fort

Kshatriyas the second-highest caste, made up of rulers and warriors

kulfi milk-based, frozen dessert, like ice cream, usually flavoured with pistachio

langur black-faced monkey

lingam phallic symbol in places of worship representing the god Shiva

lunghi male garment; long wraparound cloth, like a *dhoti*, but coloured (usually plaid)

macheela old Portuguese sedan chair, similar to a *cadeirinha*

mandapa assembly hall tacked onto the front of a temple, often with many pillars

mandir temple

mihrab niche in the wall of a mosque indicating the direction of prayer (to Mecca). In India, the *mihrab* is normally in the west wall

mestiço Portuguese name for a person of mixed Indian–European parentage

moksha spiritual release from the cycle of rebirth

mundkar tenants, usually of low caste

nacre rectangles of polished fish scales (often referred to as "oyster shells") traditionally used instead of glass to make windows

naubhat khanna musician's gallery in a Goan temple

Novas Conquistas the "New Conquests" area of Pernem, Satari, Canacona and Sanguem *talukas*, acquired by the Portuguese in the eighteenth century

palacio Indo-Portuguese-style stately home

pariwar devta accessory *devtas*

pradakshena circumambulatory passage around a temple shrine

puja worship

pujari priest

rath processional temple chariot

sala reception room or hall in a *palacio*

sanyasin religious devotee

sati one who sacrifices her life on her husband's funeral pyre in emulation of Shiva's wife. No longer a common practice, and officially illegal

satyagrahas Goan Ghandhi-ites: non-violent protesters against colonial occupation

sesso martel wood

shalwa-camises long shirts and pyjama trousers worn by women and Muslim men

shikhara temple tower or spire

shivalingam see *lingam*

shudras the lowest of the four castes, designating menial workers

sonddios galleries for storing musical instruments in temples

sossegarde a typically Goan phrase, meaning "laid-back"

swami Hindu holy man

taluka administrative district

tiatr (or khel-tiatr) popular Konkani theatre

tilak vermilion paste smeared on the forehead by Hindu worshippers

tirtha literally "crossing place", where the temporal world and divine realms meet, as in a temple bathing pool or sacred river confluence

tulsi vrindavan ornamental pot (*vrindavan*) containing the sacred shrub *tulsi*, a variety of basil, representing a former mistress of Vishnu

vahana the vehicle of a deity: the bull Nandi is Shiva's *vahana*

vaishyas third-highest of the Hindu castes, made up of tradesmen

Velhas Conquistas the Old Conquests area of Bardez, Tiswadi and Salcete

waddo ward, or area of a village

wallah/walli suffix implying occupation or purveyor of something, eg *dhobi-wallah* (laundry man), rickshaw-*wallah* (rickshaw driver), flower-walli (lady flower seller).

Index

and small print

Index

Map entries are in **colour**.

A Rough Guide to Rough Guides

In the summer of 1981, Mark Ellingham, a recent graduate from Bristol University, was travelling round Greece and couldn't find a guidebook that really met his needs. On the one hand there were the student guides, insistent on saving every last cent, and on the other the heavyweight cultural tomes whose authors seemed to have spent more time in a research library than lounging away the afternoon at a taverna or on the beach.

In a bid to avoid getting a job, Mark and a small group of writers set about creating their own guidebook. It was a guide to Greece that aimed to combine a journalistic approach to description with a thoroughly practical approach to travellers' needs – a guide that would incorporate culture, history and contemporary insights with a critical edge, together with up-to-date, value-for-money listings. Back in London, Mark and the team finished their Rough Guide, as they called it, and talked Routledge into publishing the book.

That first *Rough Guide to Greece*, published in 1982, was a student scheme that became a publishing phenomenon. The immediate success of the book – with numerous reprints and a Thomas Cook prize shortlisting – spawned a series that rapidly covered dozens of destinations. Rough Guides had a ready market among low-budget backpackers, but soon also acquired a much broader and older readership that relished Rough Guides' wit and inquisitiveness as much as their enthusiastic, critical approach. Everyone wants value for money, but not at any price.

Rough Guides soon began supplementing the "rougher" information about hostels and low-budget listings with the kind of detail on restaurants and quality hotels that independent-minded visitors on any budget might expect, whether on business in New York or trekking in Thailand.

These days the guides – distributed worldwide by the Penguin Group – offer recommendations from shoestring to luxury and cover more than 200 destinations around the globe, including almost every country in the Americas and Europe, more than half of Africa and most of Asia and Australasia. Our ever-growing team of authors and photographers is spread all over the world, particularly in Europe, the USA and Australia.

In 1994, we published the *Rough Guide to World Music* and *Rough Guide to Classical Music*; and a year later the *Rough Guide to the Internet*. All three books have become benchmark titles in their fields – which encouraged us to expand into other areas of publishing, mainly around popular culture. Rough Guides now publish:

- Travel guides to more than 200 worldwide destinations
- Dictionary phrasebooks to 22 major languages
- History guides ranging from Ireland to Islam
- Maps printed on rip-proof and waterproof Polyart™ paper
- Music guides running the gamut from Opera to Elvis
- Restaurant guides to London, New York and San Francisco
- Reference books on topics as diverse as the Weather and Shakespeare
- Sports guides from Formula 1 to Man Utd
- Pop culture books from Lord of the Rings to Cult TV
- World Music CDs in association with World Music Network.

Visit **www.roughguides.com** to see our latest publications.

Rough Guide Credits

Text editor: Jo Mead
Managing Director: Kevin Fitzgerald
Series editor: Mark Ellingham
Editorial: Martin Dunford, Jonathan Buckley,
Kate Berens, Ann-Marie Shaw, Helena Smith,
Olivia Swift, Ruth Blackmore, Geoff Howard,
Claire Saunders, Gavin Thomas, Alexander
Mark Rogers, Polly Thomas, Joe Staines,
Richard Lim, Duncan Clark, Peter Buckley,
Lucy Ratcliffe, Clifton Wilkinson, Alison
Murchie, Matthew Teller, Andrew Dickson,
Fran Sandham, Sally Schafer, Matthew
Milton, Karoline Densley (UK); Andrew
Rosenberg, Yuki Takagaki, Richard Koss,
Hunter Slaton (US)
Design & Layout: Link Hall, Helen Prior, Julia
Bovis, Katie Pringle, Rachel Holmes, Andy
Turner, Dan May, Tanya Hall, John McKay,
Sophie Hewat (UK); Madhulita Mohapatra,

Umesh Aggarwal, Sunil Sharma (India)
Cartography: Maxine Repath, Ed Wright,
Katie Lloyd-Jones (UK); Manish Chandra,
Rajesh Chhibber, Jai Prakesh Mishra (India)
Cover art direction: Louise Boulton
Picture research: Sharon Martins, Mark
Thomas
Online: Kelly Martinez, Anja Mutic-Blessing,
Jennifer Gold, Suzanne Welles, Cree Lawson
(US); Manik Chauhan, Amarjyoti Dutta,
Narender Kumar (India)
Finance: Gary Singh
Marketing & Publicity: Richard Trillo, Niki
Smith, David Wearn, Chloë Roberts, Demelza
Dallow, Claire Southern (UK); Geoff Colquitt,
David Wechsler, Megan Kennedy (US)
Administration: Julie Sanderson
Manager RG India: Punita Singh

Publishing Information

This fifth edition published Nov 2003 by **Rough
Guides Ltd**,
80 Strand, London WC2R 0RL.
345 Hudson St, 4th Floor,
New York, NY 10014, USA.
Distributed by the Penguin Group
Penguin Books Ltd,
80 Strand, London WC2R 0RL
Penguin Putnam, Inc.
375 Hudson Street, NY 10014, USA
Penguin Books Australia Ltd,
487 Maroondah Highway, PO Box 257,
Ringwood, Victoria 3134, Australia
Penguin Books Canada Ltd,
10 Alcorn Avenue, Toronto, Ontario,
Canada M4V 1E4
Penguin Books (NZ) Ltd,
182–190 Wairau Road, Auckland 10,
New Zealand
Typeset in Bembo and Helvetica to an original
design by Henry Iles.
Printed in Italy by LegoPrint S.p.A

368pp includes index
A catalogue record for this book is available from
the British Library.

ISBN 1-84353-081-3

1   3   5   7   9   8   6   4   2

Help us update

We've gone to a lot of effort to ensure that
the fifth edition of **The Rough Guide to Goa**
is accurate and up-to-date. However, things
change – places get "discovered", opening
hours are notoriously fickle, restaurants and
rooms raise prices or lower standards. If you
feel we've got it wrong or left something out,
we'd like to know, and if you can remember
the address, the price, the time, the phone
number, so much the better.

We'll credit all contributions, and send a
copy of the next edition (or any other Rough

Guide if you prefer) for the best letters.
Everyone who writes to us and isn't already a
subscriber will receive a copy of our full-
colour thrice-yearly newsletter. Please mark
letters: "**Rough Guide Goa Update**" and
send to: Rough Guides, 80 Strand, London
WC2R 0RL, or Rough Guides, 4th Floor, 345
Hudson St, New York, NY 10014. Or send an
email to **mail@roughguides.com**

Have your questions answered and tell
others about your trip at
www.roughguides.atinfopop.com

SMALL PRINT

Acknowledgements

Thanks to Nick Edwards, for two editions' worth of first-class Karnataka updates; text editor Jo Mead and managing editor Claire Saunders, for making this and the other India editions such a smooth ride; Manish Chandra, Rajesh Chhibber and Jai Prakash Mishra for map revisions; Andy Turner, Daniel May and Katie Pringle for typesetting; Mark Thomas and Louise Boulton for picture research; and Ken Bell for proofreading.

In Goa, thank you to the Britto family – Sarah, Francis, Casmiro, Sibyl and Condred – for being such wonderful hosts and making our last few winters in Goa so memorable. For their warm hospitality, thanks also to Ajit Sukhija and "Jack" Ajit Jnr in Panjim; and Shelly, Teresa, Royston and Jenesha in Candolim; Virendra and Akriti Sinh at A Reverie. For Bullshit Info and top Reiki, thank you Axel and Lucie (respectively). For his turtle and other photos, thanks to Denzil Sequeira. And last but not least, thank you Nicholas Maddox from all us beach dogs for being a fearless warrior in the war against mange, and for finding and fixing little Roxy.

Readers' letters

Many thanks to all those readers of the fourth edition who took the trouble to write in with amendments and additions:

Justin Amadeus, E Ashby, Andrew & Pat Batty, Chris Cobb, Clive Collins, Marilyn Docherty, David Gee, Louise Heavens, Bert D'Hooghe, Helen Hotchkiss, Steven Inkersole, Toine Leroi, Jennifer Lewis, Brian Menezes, Val Thomas, Hazel Vincent, Kerry Walker.

Photo Credits

Cover Credits

Main front: Anjuna flea market © Karoki Lewis/Axiom

Small front top picture spices: © David Abram

Small front lower picture: © Helena Smith

Back top picture: Palolem beach © Robert Harding

Back lower picture: fishing boat © Karoki Lewis/Axiom

Introduction

Aswem, North Goa © David Abram

Goan spices © David Abram

Beach shacks, Palolem © David Abram

Boat bow © David Abram

Hindi picture © Liz Barry/Ffotograff

Bus stop © David Abram

Coconut toddy tapper © David Abram

Fishing © David Abram

Things not to miss:

01 Goan breakfast © David Abram

02 Christmas in Goa © Denzil Seqeira

03 Arambol beach © Mike Jones

04 Old Portuguese-era house © David Abram

05 Full-moon party © Vicki Couchman/Axiom

06 Turtles hatching © Denzil Seqeira

07 Mapusa market © David Abram

08 Cashew nuts © David Abram

09 Karmali Ghat © David Abram

10 Traditional fishing boat © Helena Smith

11 Anjuna market © Vicki Couchman/Axiom

12 Colonial architecture © David Abram

13 Panjim Inn © David Abram

14 Usgalimal carvings © David Abram

15 Hampi © David Abram

16 Fontainhas © David Abram

17 Old Goa © David Abram

18 Hindu temple © David Abram

19 Menezes-Braganza house © Helena Smith

20 Palolem beach shacks © David Abram

21 Patnem-Rajbag beach © David Abram

22 Backwater boat rides © David Abram

23 Terekol Fort © David Abram

Black-and-white photos

Taxi in Mumbai © David Abram (p.34)

Old Fontainhas © Helena Smith (p.66)

Church interior, Old Goa © Helena Smith (p.92)

Arambol beach © David Abram (p.120)

Anjuna beach © Barnabas Bosshart/Corbis (p.149)

Margao church scaffolding © Helena Smith (p.170)

Boat at Benaulim with cross on prow © Helena Smith (p.201)

Temple tops and monkeys © Helena Smith (p.218)

Temple at Hampi © Josie Mead (p.229)

Street scene, Mumbai © David Abram (p.240)

Sassoon docks © David Abram (p.254)

Carved angel in Old Goa church © Helena Smith (p.304)

SMALL PRINT

stay in touch

roughnews

Rough Guides' FREE full-colour newsletter

News, travel issues, music reviews, readers' letters and the latest dispatches from authors on the road

If you would like to receive roughnews, please send us your name and address:

Rough Guides, 80 Strand,
London WC2R ORL, UK

Rough Guides, 4th Floor, 345 Hudson St,
New York NY10014, USA

newslettersubs@roughguides.co.uk

Rough Guides travel

key: 🌐 map   ▣ phrasebook   ⊙ cd

Rough Guides publishes new books every month

Rough Guides music & reference

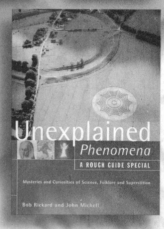

NOTES